# EU *Ordre Public*

**EUROPEAN MONOGRAPHS**

In this series *European Monographs this book. EU order public is the eightieth title. The titles published in this series are listed at the end of this volume.*

# EU *Ordre Public*

Tim Corthaut

Wolters Kluwer
Law & Business

*Published by:*
Kluwer Law International
PO Box 316
2400 AH Alphen aan den Rijn
The Netherlands
Website: www.kluwerlaw.com

*Sold and distributed in North, Central and South America by:*
Aspen Publishers, Inc.
7201 McKinney Circle
Frederick, MD 21704
United States of America
Email: customer.service@aspenpublishers.com

*Sold and distributed in all other countries by:*
Turpin Distribution Services Ltd
Stratton Business Park
Pegasus Drive, Biggleswade
Bedfordshire SG18 8TQ
United Kingdom
Email: kluwerlaw@turpin-distribution.com

*Printed on acid-free paper.*

ISBN 978-90-411-3232-1



Printed and Bound by CPI Group (UK) Ltd, Croydon, CR0 4YY.

# Table of Contents

# Foreword

This book is based on Tim Corthaut's doctoral dissertation which I was responsible for supervising. I was thus a first-hand witness of the enormous amount of work the author put into his research, his ongoing openness towards different ideas and critical comments, and the inexhaustible enthusiasm with which he would examine complex legal issues. As he explains himself, this book invites the reader to accompany him on a journey of discovery whose aim is to explore the conceptual contours of the EU *ordre public*. This is, needless to say, a complex and challenging task requiring the author to embark on a multidimensional and all-embracing analysis of the concept of *ordre public* in the EU legal order.

At the outset, the author explains why it is necessary for every legal order — be it that of the Member States, the EU, or international law — to embrace the concept of *ordre public* in some form. If the purpose of the law is to bring about some degree of order in society and *ordre public* is understood as a set of principles and values which expresses a society's basic political, economic, social and cultural choices, then the concept of *ordre public* would seem to be a condition *sine qua non* for the very existence of any legal order. As that concept is inherently linked to societal choices, it has an autonomous and evolving nature. However, since in all democratic societies the protection of human rights is part and parcel of their *ordre public*, those societies share, to some extent, a common understanding of that concept. For the EU legal order, these findings also hold true. Even if the EU is examined by reference to a reductionist model according to which it is merely an international organization limited to regulating the internal market, its proper functioning would still be subject to some fundamental organizational rules which may require public policy-like protection.

Next, the author moves on to examine a wide range of fields of EU law where the concept of *ordre public* has been applied, either as a matter of national law or as a matter of EU law. The idea behind such comprehensive examination of the case-law is to infer some elements that subsequently serve to define what one must understand by EU *ordre public*. Unfortunately, space constraints prevent me from commenting on each of those fields of EU law. I have nonetheless selected four of them which highlight the fact that the EU *ordre public* applies in very different scenarios, thus illustrating its utility as a versatile and multifaceted concept.

First, the author looks closely at the law on free movement. He argues that considerations grounded in national conceptions of *ordre public* which derogate from the substantive law of the Union are not a '*réserve de souveraineté*'. On the contrary, the national *ordre public* exception must be incorporated into the body of EU law. That process of incorporation does not, in principle, imply that national *ordre public* is replaced by the EU *ordre public*. EU law grants Member States a margin of appreciation within which they may define their own understanding of *ordre public*. In other words, EU law is limited to drawing the external contours of such a margin. The resulting framework which circumscribes the national *ordre public* constitutes the EU *ordre public*. Within the bounds of EU law covered by the EU *ordre public*, a Member State is still free to protect its own societal choices. The case-law thus shows that the EU *ordre public* is, in that sense, the mirror image of the national *ordre public*.

Second, the author examines the application of the concept of '*ordre public*' in relation to private international law which has been largely 'Europeanized'. Indeed, the EU legislator has adopted several Regulations which seek to facilitate judicial cooperation in civil matters, both in terms of solving conflicts of jurisdiction and of determining the applicable law. Notably, EU Regulations provide that a judgment shall not be recognized (or enforced) if such recognition (or enforcement) is contrary to public policy in the State in which recognition (or enforcement) is sought. This shows that the definition of the EU *ordre public* is not always a task for the ECJ to undertake alone. The EU legislator is also empowered to adopt harmonizing measures which provide further guidance as to the way in which Member States may exercise their margin of appreciation when relying on the public policy exception. In this regard, the ECJ has consistently held that, although it is for each Member State to determine what public policy requires, the limits of that concept are a matter of EU statutory interpretation. From cases such as *Krombach*[1] and *Eurofood*,[2] the author draws three main conclusions. First, the public policy exception is reserved for exceptional cases and its limits are determined by the ECJ. The public policy exception must aim to protect an essential rule of law or a right recognized as fundamental. For the author, not every breach of EU law may result in non-recognition, which should be limited to cases involving a 'systemic failure'. Second, the public policy exception applies as *ultima ratio*, i.e. where there are no alternative grounds for refusing recognition or enforcement. Finally, that exception may cover both procedural and substantive issues.

Third, the author explores the cases in which the principle of primacy has served to express and protect the EU *ordre public*. Whilst it is true that EU law tolerates some degree of under-enforcement as a way of honouring the principle of national procedural autonomy, cases such as *San Michele*,[3] *Simmenthal*,[4] and *Lucchini*[5] demonstrate that the principle of primacy applies – as a matter of EU *ordre public* – in order to counter structural and endemic failures in any national legal order which call into

1. Case C-7/98 *Krombach* [2000] ECR I1935.
2. Case C-341/04 *Eurofood IFSC Ltd* [2006] ECR I-3813.
3. Case C-6/65 *San Michele v High Authority* [1965] ECR 27.
4. Case 106/77 *Simmenthal* [1978] ECR 629.
5. Case C119/05 *Lucchini* [2007] ECR I6199.

question the effective application of EU law. The same can be said in relation to the law on remedies. For example, in *Eco Swiss* the ECJ noted that, since arbiters are not entitled to make a preliminary reference to the ECJ, there is a risk of under-enforcement and divergence in the application of EU law. Accordingly, exequatur of an arbitral award rendered in breach of fundamental provisions of the Treaties, such as those on competition law, could not be granted. Moreover, whilst national courts are not, in general, required to raise points of EU law of their own motion, the EU *ordre public* may, under certain circumstances, require them to do so. By virtue of the principle of equivalence, national courts are obliged to 'stretch' the concept of national *ordre public* so as to cover causes of action based on EU law. Similarly, cases such as *Océano Grupo,*[6] *Cofidis*[7] and *Mostaza Claro*[8] show that in order to preserve the *effet utile* of EU legislation adopted in the field of consumer protection, national courts have a duty to raise points of EU law of their own motion.

Fourth, the concept of EU *ordre public* not only applies to test the compatibility of national law with EU law, but also plays an important role where the ECJ and, as the case may be, the European General Court (the 'EGC') are called upon to examine the validity of secondary EU measures. For example, the author looks at the case-law where the ECJ and the EGC have – as a matter of EU *ordre public* – examined of their own motion whether an application is admissible (e.g., the question whether the ECJ (or the EGC) enjoys jurisdiction, whether the contested act is reviewable, whether the application is time-barred, whether the applicants enjoy *locus standi*).

Once the groundwork for a concept of EU *ordre public* has been laid down, the author aims to work out a system to explain and classify the values inherent in that concept. To that effect, he groups those values under four different categories, namely the protection of political power, the protection of the economic order, the protection of the social order and the protection of the cultural order. This part of the book is of great academic interest, given that, to my knowledge, no one had ever before set out, in such a detailed fashion, a catalogue of those values. In this connection, I would like to make a brief comment regarding one of the main theses of the book, according to which EU citizenship lies at the very heart of the concept of EU *ordre public*. In so doing, the author puts forward three convincing arguments that unequivocally show that he is a proud believer in the European idea. First, just like national citizenship, EU citizenship creates a bond of loyalty between the Union and its citizens which is crucial for the functioning of the EU legal order. Indeed, that argument can find some resonance in the case-law of the ECJ pursuant to which 'citizenship of the Union is intended to be the fundamental status of nationals of the Member States'. Second, seen as a catalyst for the exercise of a myriad of rights, notably political rights, EU citizenship deserves the utmost protection under EU law. And third, in light of EU citizenship, free movement is no longer an exclusive right of economically active persons, but simply an expression of human dignity.

---

6. Joined Cases C240/98 to C244/98 *Océano Grupo Editorial and Salvat Editores* [2000] ECR I-4941.
7. Case C473/00 *Cofidis* [2002] ECR I10875.
8. Case C168/05 *Mostaza Claro* [2006] ECR I-10421.

In Part IV of the book, the author looks at the tensions between the objectives which the EU seeks to promote and the protection of national interests based on the maintenance of the national *ordre public*. Whilst not totally discarding a pluralist approach, he posits that those tensions must be resolved so as to release the full potential of the rights which EU law grants to individuals, notably the right to move freely. Taking the mobility of same-sex spouses as a case study, he argues that no EU citizen should suffer from discrimination based on his or her moral convictions. Accordingly, he advocates the legal recognition by the host Member State of same-sex marriages validly concluded in the home Member State. However, value diversity as promoted by the ECJ in *Omega*,[9] is not to be ruled out, but merely subject to stringent conditions. In his view, in order for national societal choices to be compatible with EU law the Member State concerned must comply with four cumulative conditions. First and foremost, the values upon which the contested national measure is based must not be alien to the EU legal order. Second, the national measure at issue must not be in conflict with other fundamental rights recognized by the EU legal order, notably by the Charter. Third, the legitimate interest pursued by the national measure must be protected in a consistent and coherent fashion. Finally, that measure must comply with the principle of proportionality.

The concluding part of the book is more normative than the preceding ones, as it aims to set out a functional model which, according to the author, best apprehends the concept of EU *ordre public*. Inspired by Romain's model,[10] the author draws a distinction between '*ordre public fondamental*' and '*ordre public essentiel*'. Whilst the first category includes the basic constitutional tenets of EU law in terms of both substantive content and institutional structure, the second encompasses secondary EU law and national law implementing EU law which seek to protect the political, economic and social general interest and, as such, are mandatory for private parties. Within this dual categorization of the EU *ordre public*, the author introduces an element of hierarchy which seeks to explain the consequences of applying norms pertaining to the EU *ordre public* to a variety of scenarios. For example, the core of the ECHR would stand at the top of the pyramid of values, whereas secondary EU legislation relating to culture or consumer protection would lie at the bottom.

The book is written in a clear and entertaining style, as the plethora of apposite and original metaphors used by the author demonstrates. Moreover, the author also draws some interesting comparisons with U.S. constitutional law which may shed new light on the way in which one should approach the concept of EU *ordre public*.

On all accounts, the book written by Tim Corthaut is an impressive piece of academic work and I congratulate him.

Prof. Dr Koen Lenaerts
Judge at the Court of Justice of the European Union

9. Case C-36/02 *Omega* [2004] ECR I9609.
10. J.-F. Romain, 'L'ordre public (notion générales) et les droits de l'homme' in *L'ordre public: concept et applications*, ed. J.-F. Romain, M. Grégoire & V. Simonart (Bruxelles: Bruylant, 1995), 59.

# Acknowledgements

A project like this book is not written in isolation. Accordingly, it is only fitting to pay tribute here to the numerous persons and organizations that made this book possible, even though I only have space to acknowledge a few on this page.

Above all I am grateful to Professor Koen Lenaerts, judge at the Court of Justice, and promoter of the doctoral research that is reflected in this book. I had the privilege to work with him for almost a decade, and he continues to inspire me up to this day. The various articles we wrote together honed my skills, and his meticulous revisions of my writings made this undoubtedly a stronger work. I am therefore also very proud that he accepted to write the Foreword to this book.

I also acknowledge the other members of my doctoral jury. Former Advocate General Francis Jacobs, ECJ judge Marko Ilešič, Professor Jules Stuyck and Professor René Foqué all took time from their busy schedules to read my thesis. Their appreciation of my work means a lot to me.

Writing a PhD can be a lonely experience. I was saved from that fate because of the warm support of my colleagues at the Department of International and European Law of the KU Leuven. The Institute for European Law of the KU Leuven is not only a hotbed of talent, but also a place of open discussion and teamwork. It has been an honor to travel the road to a PhD with Dr Nathan Cambien, Dr Marlies Desomer, Dr Kathleen Gutman, Dr Tinne Heremans and Dr Angelina Tchorbadjiyska, and work with Karel Bourgeois, Roel De Meu, Jos De Wachter, Vanessa Galhardo-Galhetas, Dr An Hertogen, Laurent Jadoul, Anne Lamote, Philippe Reyniers and Kristien Vanvoorden. Also my former colleagues at the other institutes deserve my gratitude. I cannot thank them all but I would be remiss if I did not at least thank Dr Kristof Cox, Dr Bart De Meester, Dr Thalia Kruger, Dr Frederik Naert and Dr Sten Verhoeven. Finally, also the current researchers at the Institute for European Law (Professor Geert De Baere, Professor Piet Van Nuffel, Janek Nowak, Timothy Roes, Tina Van den Sanden and Vincent Vercauteren) are always a pleasure to work with, and they were most encouraging of the transformation of my PhD research into this book.

I must also thank all the students I had the privilege of teaching and supervising, with a special word of gratitude to all moot court teams I have been coaching. Part of this book is written in answer to your questions, and because of your struggles with EU law.

This book is very much a book on EU law. However, my thinking has clearly been influenced by my stay in the United States. With the financial and moral support of the Committee on General Scholarships at Harvard University who awarded me a Frank Boas Fellowship for study at Harvard Law School, the Commission for Educational Exchange between the United States of America, Belgium and Luxembourg who granted me a Fulbright Scholarship, and the Belgian American Educational Foundation who made me a honorary B.A.E.F. Fellow, I had the unique opportunity to study at Harvard Law School. It allowed me to further my knowledge of US constitutional law, and test my own insights with leading scholars, and the amazing Harvard LL.M. class of 2005.

The final word of gratitude goes out to my family and friends. They knew this book was important to me, and so they supported me unconditionally. I never took that for granted.Finally, as books are written for posterity's sake, I am pleased to dedicate this one to my nephew and godson, Aaron Corthaut – may he grow old and wise in an ever-closer Union.

T. Corthaut
Leuven, July 2012

# Introduction

**1.** This is a kaleidoscopic book. It must be. In part that is, of course, due to its chaotic author. But I hope that it is largely justified by the peculiar nature of its topic: EU *ordre public*. The European Union, hardly 60 years old, is still a highly dynamic, unsettled legal order, evolving on a daily basis to face up to the changing challenges of twenty-first century politics, economics and social life. Accordingly, it is easy to understand that all research on this ever-evolving legal order, which has developed far beyond the regional economic organization dealing with coal and steel that it once was to become a leading economic and political power, uniting the States and people of 27 countries, and with competences ranging from monetary policy, the environment, education and criminal law to the use of military force, and a matching ambition to lead the way in a globalized world, will inevitably be deeply ingrained by the innumerable facets hiding behind the two letters: EU.

**2.** But if this book really meanders in all directions, it is mainly due to the other element in the title: *ordre public*. How could it be different? The subject has been described as 'a mystery'.[1] Attempts to define it have been likened to adventuring into quicksand, riding a wild horse on a journey into the unknown or walking along a path amidst thorny bushes.[2] So, if we are to survive this perilous adventure into the unknown, we had better expect the unexpected and prepare ourselves for winding roads leading into the far corners of the law.

**3.** If then, one embarks on a study of *EU ordre public*, the perils are bound to multiply, the road to become ever narrower, the horse to become ever feistier – yet the view at the top of the mountain may be ever so spectacular. It sounded easy enough, when I started my research on *EU ordre public*. I tentatively described *ordre public* as the notion, sometimes –albeit inadequately – translated into English as public policy,

1. E. Picard, 'Introduction générale: la fonction de l'*ordre public* dans l'ordre juridique' in *L'ordre public: ordre public ou ordres publics? Ordre public et droits fondamentaux*, ed. M.-J. Redor (Brussel: Bruylant, 2001), 17.
2. J.F. Romain, 'L'*ordre public* (notion générale) et les droits de l'homme' in, *L'ordre public: concept et applications*, ed. J.-F. Romain, M. Grégoire & V. Simonart (Bruxelles: Bruylant, 1995), 8.

which covers the complex of norms at the very heart of a political entity (in this case the European Union) expressing and protecting the basic options taken by that entity regarding its political, economic, social and even cultural order. I still hold on to this definition, broad as it may seem. The opportunity will arise below to provide some more focused views on what is meant by *ordre public*. However, true to the motto 'expect the unexpected' the definition leaves open the possibility to look into a series of related concepts, practices and phenomena, which often are not called *ordre public* but hold a lot in common with it. In the multi-faceted environment of the European Union, where language barriers create additional difficulties – indeed, for our own area of enquiry an adequate English term seems to be lacking – this seems the better option.

**4.** Even if we are to embark on a journey into the unknown, we are not left without guidance. Several authors have, in the past, written on *ordre public*, though rarely in the context of EU law.[3] Where they have done so, the study is usually confined to very specific niches: the limits to the fundamental freedoms,[4] EU procedural law,[5] or the rather peculiar case of the public policy exception in Community private international law and arbitration.[6] Yet at least one author deserves credit for having brilliantly

3. Without the ambition to be exhaustive, see T. Barton, *Der 'Ordre public' als Grenze der Biopatentierung* (Berlin, Erich Schmidt Verlag GmbH & Co, 2004); B. Beignier, A. Bénabent, M.C. Boutard Labarde & T. Revet, *L'ordre public à la fin du XXe siècle* (Paris: Dalloz, 1996); M. Boutelet & J.-C. Fritz, *L'ordre public écologique – Towards an ecological public order* (Brussels: Bruylant, 2005); E. Fohrer, *L'incidence de la Convention européenne des droits de l'homme sur l'ordre public international français* (Bruxelles: Bruylant, 1999); R. POLIN, *L'ordre public* (Paris: PUF, 1996); J.-B. Racine, *L'arbitrage commercial international et l'ordre public* (Paris: LGDJ, 1998); C. Redmann, *Ordre public-Kontrolle von Gerichtsstandsvereinbarungen* (Hamburg: Verlag Dr Kovač, 2005); M.J. Redor, *L'ordre public: ordre public ou ordres publics? Ordre public et droits fondamentaux* (Brussel, Bruylant, 2001); T. Revet (ed.), *L'ordre public à la fin du XXième sciècle* (Paris, Dalloz, 1996); J.-F. Romain, M. Grégoire & V. Simonart (eds.), *L'ordre public: concept et applications* (Bruxelles: Bruylant, 1995); X, *Ordre public et histoire: la naissance d'une mémoire* (Paris: Institut des hautes études de la sécurité interieure, 1994).
4. See for example: F. Chaltiel, 'L'*ordre public* devant la Cour de Justice des Communautés européennes – à propos de l'arrêt *Olazabal* du 26 novembre 2002', *Revue du Marché commun et de l'Union européenne* (2003): 120-123; G. Druesne, 'La réserve d'*ordre public* et l'article 48 du Traité de Rome', *Revue Trimestrielle du Droit européen* (1976/2: 237; G. Lyon-Caen, 'La reserve d'*ordre public* en matière de liberté d'établissement et de libre circulation' *Revue Trimesterielle du Droit Européen* (1966): 693; H. Oosterom-Staples, 'Botsende openbare-ordebegrippen in het Europese Migratierecht', *Nederlands Tijdschrijft voor Europees Recht* (2006): 169-181.
5. See for example: F. Berrod, 'Arrêts « Peterbroeck » et « Van Schijndel »', *Revue du Marché Unique Européen* (1996) 200-204; F. Castillo De La Torre, 'Le relevé d'office par la juridiction communautaire', *Cahiers de droit européen* (2005): 395-463; T. Heukels, 'Ambtshalve plicht om aan direct werkende bepalingen van EG-recht te toetsen?', *Nederlands Tijdschrift voor Europees Recht* (1996): 88-92; C.N. Kakouris, 'Do the Member States Possess judicial procedural autonomy?', *Common Market Law Review* (1997): 1389-1412; A.M. Keessen, 'Ambtshalve toepassing van Europees recht', *Nederlands Tijdschrift voor Europees Recht* (2006): 55-64; M. Struys, 'Le droit communautaire et l'application des règles procédurales nationales', *Journal des Tribunaux-Droit Européen* (2000): 49-54; R. Widdershoven, 'Geploeter bij de ambtshalve toepassing van EG-recht', *Tijdschrift voor Omgevingsrecht* (2003): 178-186.
6. See for example: M. Behar-Touchais, 'Arbitrage et *ordre public* européen', *Revue des Affaires Européennes/Law & European Affairs* (2005): 177-191; L. Bernardeau, 'Cour de justice, 28 mars 2000, Krombach, aff. C-7/98, Rec. p. I-1935', *Revue des Affaires Européennes* (2001-02): 274-283; F. De Ly, 'noot onder Hof van Justitie EG (J.C. Moitinho de Almeida, rapporteur), 1 juni 1999, C-126/97, concl. A-G Saggio (ongepubliceerd)', *Tijdschrift voor Arbitrage* (1999):

completed this perilous journey before: Caroline Picheral.[7] Actually, her ambition was even broader: she ventures into the discovery of a real European public order which encompasses not only the EU but also the European Convention on Human Rights (ECHR) and thus, by clear implication, the legal orders of all parties to that Convention. This is not a foolish idea. After all, the European Court of Human Rights (ECtHR) in Strasbourg has indicated firmly its ambition to develop a European Public Order rooted in the ECHR.[8] But like any good travel guide, Picheral left me curious to embark upon a similar voyage. Much still needs to be discovered, especially in relation to the European Union - which despite the relatively short period that has elapsed since Picheral's book was published - has again gone through a major metamorphosis. Since the publication of Picheral's book, the EU has welcomed a staggering 12 new members, and a real debate about common values is raging with its focus upon the limits of Europe and the 'Europeanness' of its candidate countries, Turkey being the focal point of attention (we must not, of course, forget that the *ordre public* is rooted in the common values of the EU's members). Moreover, the second and third pillars have since been developed far beyond their timid beginnings as witnessed by Picheral. Both the EU and the *ordre public* have a 'variable content'[9] and are in constant need of redefining. So, just as Neil Armstrong did not exhaust opportunities for further discovery and exploration on the moon, leaving us with good reason to seek to return, a new journey across EU law in search of *EU ordre public* makes perfect sense - and a report of this magnitude on it in English will be virtually a first.[10] But as we begin our journey it is, nevertheless, comforting to know that our luggage already contains a sound tradition of scholarship on the EU and on *ordre public*.

**5.** In order to complete a voyage of this magnitude without losing sight of the shore or missing any essential landmarks it seems essential to begin with a good travel itinerary. The starting point will be the premise that any legal order, and thus also the European Union, is founded on certain essential values and principles that are expressed and

100-108; A. Huet, 'Exécution des décisions (Régie nationale des usines Renault SA c/ Maxicar SpA et Orazio Formento)', *Journal du droit international* (2001): 696-701; L. Idot, 'note sous Eco Swiss China Time Ltd. c/ Benetton International NV', *Revue de l'arbitrage* (1999): 639-653; A. Komninos, 'Case C-126/97, *Eco Swiss China Ltd. v. Benetton International NV*, Judgement of 1 June 1999, Full Court', *Common Market Law Review* (2000): 459-478.

7. C. Picheral, L'*ordre public* européen: droit communautaire et droit européen des droits de l'homme (Paris: CERIC - Documentation française, 2001).

8. ECtHR, 23 February 1995, *Loizidou v. Turkey* (preliminary objections), para. 94; G. Cohen-Jonathan, 'L'affaire Loizidou devant la Cour européenne des droits de l'homme. Quelques observations', *Revue générale de droit international public* (1998): 123-144.; see also J. Andriantsimbazovina, 'Splendeurs et misères de l'*ordre public* européen - Les trois dernières années de l'ancienne Cour européenne des droits de l'homme (1996-1997-1998), *Cahiers de droit européen* (2000): 657-718.

9. G. Karydis, 'L'*ordre public* dans l'ordre juridique communautaire: un concept à contenu variable', *Revue Trimestrielle de Droit Européen* (2002) 1-26. On this concept, see also C. Perelman & R. Van Der Elst, (eds.)., *Les notions à contenu variable en droit* (Bruxelles: Bruylants, 1984).

10. This is not to say that the issue has not been addressed in English before, see R. De Lange, 'The European Public Order, Constitutional Principles and Fundamental Rights', *Erasmus Law Review* (2007): 3-24; C. Kessedjian, 'Public Order in European Law', *Erasmus Law Review* (2007): 25-36.

protected by the concept of *ordre public*. This premise will lead us to look more closely at what is traditionally understood by *ordre public*, drawing inspiration from national law and private international law. However, this line of enquiry will inevitably give rise to some major follow-up questions as to the relevance all this has for the EU legal order. Indeed, we will need to dwell on the unique institutional framework of the European Union. This will entail arguments as to the nature of the integration process and the relationship between the European Union, its Member States and its citizens. It will be argued that when it comes to describing the relationship between the national legal orders, each with its own concept of *ordre public*, and an EU concept of *ordre public*, the traditional model of primacy of EU law[11] over national law may need important further fine-tuning. Nonetheless, the basic message of the first Part of this book is that there is such a thing as an autonomous *EU ordre public*, which has a rather intricate co-existence with the concepts of *ordre public* of the EU's Member States.

**6.** If, as will be established, there is an *EU ordre public*, it follows that it must have a particular function and content. However, before embarking on the 'Herculean' task of ascertaining what these are, some further methodological and theoretical choices related to the multinational and multi-level structure of the EU will need to be made. I use the term Herculean not only because of the magnitude of the journey ahead, but also in its Dworkinian sense to highlight one methodological choice from the start. What I purport to do in this research seems best to fit in with the task that awaits the hypothetical Dworkinian super-judge Hercules when faced with a hard case.[12] This whole journey is an attempt to find the rules and principles that best fit the system of the European Union. I will try to reconstruct the legal order of the European Union in a way that best gives meaning to the Treaties, the case law of the Court of Justice of the European Union[13] and the underlying principles of integration, challenged by the stubborn concept of *ordre public* which needs to be given a rightful place within that construct. Consistent with Dworkin's approach, it is argued that, if taken seriously, this undertaking will result in more than a personal version of EU law. The rules and principles that best fit the legal order of the European Union do not come out of thin air. The text of the Treaties, the case law of the Court, the acts of the institutions all exert major influence, almost like competing gravitational forces keeping a galaxy in shape, and any construct must give all such elements a due place. Just as the chain novelist is bound by what has previously been written, anyone interpreting the law is bound by what has come before, so that not just any meaning can be ascribed to the legal texts and not just any construct can be formulated.[14] Like Dworkin, I do not claim to be able to give a final answer – how could I, if the *ordre public* truly is a concept with variable content – but I do not exclude that at any moment in time there is a single

---

11. As to whether the primacy of EC or EU law is in itself a matter of *ordre public*, see *infra*, at II-155 et seq., with a discussion of Case 9/65 *San Michele v. High Authority* [1965] ECR 27.
12. R. Dworkin, 'Hard Cases', *Harvard Law Review* (1975): 1057-1109.
13. The Court of Justice of the European Union is the institution; it encompasses the European Court of Justice (ECJ), the General Court (GC, formerly Court of First Instance, (CFI)) and the specialized courts, in particular the Civil Service Tribunal (CST). See Article 19(1) TEU.
14. R. Dworkin, 'Law as Interpretation', *Texas Law Review*, (1982): 527-550.

reconstruction of the EU legal order that best reflects its underlying rules and principles – so that it is worth striving to define it as best as possible.

**7.** This being said, this piece of research is not an explicit exercise in applied Dworkin in an EU setting. It is indeed not even self-evident that Dworkin's writings can be transposed from their Anglo-American background to the EU context, though I see a sufficient parallel between the EU and US legal systems to consider this a valid option. Both systems are fascinatingly driven by the case law of a Supreme Court, yet are simultaneously constrained by this same case law and a written constitution. Even though the Constitution for Europe is formally buried,[15] I consider the existing set of

15. Treaty establishing a Constitution for Europe (2004) OJ C 310/1. At this stage it seems therefore useful to explain my position as to the value of the Constitution for Europe and the Lisbon Treaty for current legal practice and thus also for this book. When I initiated this project, the Constitution for Europe seemed set to replace the then existing Treaties. The outcome of the French and Dutch referenda, however, effectively meant this never happened. Nevertheless the European Constitution has left a major mark on my conception of the European Union. First, to a large extent the Constitution codified existing law. Second, in its novelties the Constitution offered insight in the marching direction for the integration process, which may also be helpful in deciding cases under the current Treaties. It is in the light of this background that I also read some of the cases of the ECJ in the twilight zone leading to the entry into force of the Lisbon Treaties. The outcome of Case C-176/03 *Commission v. Council* [2005] ECR I-7879, for instance, seemed inspired by Article III-271(2), see in this sense K. Apps, 'Pillars Askew: Criminal Law EC-style', *Columbia Journal of European Law*, 2006, 625-637. This case also demonstrates that this is not a risk-free enterprise. After all by accepting a legal basis for EC criminal law in the environmental sphere under the current Treaties, the Member States are deprived of the corresponding procedural safeguards that are introduced by the Constitution, such as the alarm bell procedure of Article III-271(3). Similarly, the recognition of the constitutional value of the Charter of Fundamental Rights of the European Union in the case law of the ECJ may be seen in this light, see Case C-540/03 *European Parliament v. Council* [2006] ECR I-5769, para. 38. The acceptance of the primacy of third pillar law over national law in Case C-105/03 *Pupino* [2005] ECR I-5285, though again fully defensible on its own terms, may well have been encouraged by Article I-6 of the Constitution and the merger of the pillars; see also K. Lenaerts & T. Corthaut, 'Of birds and hedges: the role of primacy in invoking norms of EU law', *European Law Review* (2006): 288-289. Finally, the requirements put to the national legal orders in terms of effective judicial protection in Case C-432/05 *Unibet* [2007] ECR I-2271, can be first tracked down directly to Article I-29(1), second sentence. Accordingly, while this book has it roots firmly in the actual Treaties, it takes account of the 'gravitational force' of the Constitution on the case law before 2009. This is all the more so, because the Lisbon Treaty (Treaty of Lisbon amending the Treaty on European Union and the Treaty establishing the European Community (2007) OJ C 306/1), which eventually amended the Treaties rather than replace them by a single Constitution, takes up the bulk of the reforms of the Constitution, albeit without the constitutional rhetoric. What the impact is of this change in tone, remains, however, to be seen. For instance, the absence of a reference to the principle of primacy parallel to Article I-6 of the Constitution, does not preclude that primacy continues to be a key constitutional principle of the EU legal order. Accordingly, as the Lisbon Treaty is the latest instalment in an on-going process, reference will be primarily made to its provisions. Reference will be made to the Constitution for Europe, however, whenever there is an issue that is not similarly addressed by the Lisbon Treaty. As the Lisbon Treaty is, moreover, not very readable, reference will in principle be made to the consolidated versions of the Treaty on European Union and the Treaty on the Functioning of the European Union (2008) OJ C 115/1. Moreover, the remarks about the 'gravitational force' of the Constitution for Europe, hold equally true for the corresponding provisions of the Lisbon Treaty in the months before its entry into force. For more on the impact the Constitution and the Treaty of Lisbon may already have on the case law of the EU before its entry into force, see K. Lenaerts, 'De Rome à Lisbonne, la Constitution européenne en marche?', *Cahiers de droit européen* (2008): 229-253.

Treaties and the general principles of law, including fundamental rights, which the ECJ has since ascertained, to amount to a constitution in all but name.[16] The extensive amendments introduced by the Lisbon Treaty, which recycles most innovations contained in the Constitution for Europe, only strengthens that position.[17] Yet, as I purport to write a treatise on *EU ordre public* and not on Dworkin, in the remainder of this book much of this debate will often lie beneath the surface. Nevertheless, the image of the self-conscious Herculean judge seems appropriate for the venture that lies ahead.

**8.** The way I set out to develop this reconstruction of the EU legal order determines the further legs of the voyage. In short, we will approach the *ordre public* from four different angles in order to discover as many aspects of its nature and role in the EU legal order as possible, and along the way we may also discover more about the EU as such. These four Parts will then set the stage for the journey home. In a final Part, the threads are linked and some conclusions drawn. As often happens after an eventful voyage, the conclusion may ultimately seem rather unexceptional. But remember then, where the voyage has started, and where it has brought us along the way.

**9.** In Part II, the journey takes the form of something of a treasure hunt. The aim is to map the multiple ways the concept of *ordre public* appears in EU law. It will lead us to the far-flung reaches of the law in a hunt for references to *ordre public* or similar concepts, even though they may well hide behind different names. First on the itinerary are the instances where public policy seems to appear in the context of the Treaties. This concerns primarily the public policy exceptions to the four freedoms. The application of the principle to the free movement of persons, in particular in light of Directive 2004/38,[18] gives moreover rise to a discussion of the use of *ordre public* in the context of European citizenship and in the context of Schengen. Moreover, a comparison is made with the provisions in respect of competition law where an explicit public policy exception is missing, but the concept not entirely unknown. However, attention is also given to other *ordre public*-related phenomena in the Treaties, in particular the safeguard clause of Article 347 TFEU (old Article 297 TEC) or the limitations to the Court's jurisdiction found in Article 276 TFEU (old Articles 68(2) TEC and 35(5) TEU). The second section is in a sense the mirror image of the first. Whereas the public policy clauses in the Treaties primarily concern national public policy concerns, there is also action taken by the Union to protect these values. Accordingly, an overview is given of the action by the Union to police the internal market and of the gradual development of EU criminal law, enforced through embryonic police (Europol) and judicial services

16. See in this sense already K. Lenaerts, 'Constitutionalism and the Many Faces of Federalism', *American Journal of Comparative Law* (1990): 205-263. See also Case 294/83 *Parti Ecologiste 'Les Verts' v. European Parliament* [1986] ECR 1339, para. 23.
17. T. Corthaut, 'Plus ça change, plus c'est la même chose? A comparison with the Constitutional Treaty', *Maastricht Journal of European and Comparative Law* (2008): 21-35.
18. Directive 2004/38/EC of the European Parliament and of the Council of 29 April 2004 on the right of citizens of the Union and their family members to move and reside freely within the territory of the Member States amending Regulation (EEC) No 1612/68 and repealing Directives 64/221/EEC, 68/360/EEC, 72/194/EEC, 73/148/EEC, 75/34/EEC, 75/35/EEC, 90/364/EEC, 90/365/EEC and 93/96/EEC (2004) OJ L 158/77.

(Eurojust). Third, as the Union is also an actor under international law, there is reason to assume that the Union must also have traces of a concept of *ordre public international.* In this respect, an analysis is made of both the manner in which the EU deals with mandatory norms of international law, and the way the *ordre public* appears in the context of EU legislation in the field of private international law. The final leg collects other important phenomena in the EU legal order that may be linked to the *ordre public.* In light of the judgment in *San Michele,*[19] a first discussion is devoted to the relation between primacy and public policy. Next the focus shifts to the use of *ordre public* in the context of *exequatur* proceedings. Subsequently, we look in depth at the question when national courts are under an obligation to raise issues of EU law of their own motion, which is contrasted with the regime that applies to the ECJ and CFI. Furthermore, the question is tackled as to what limits EU law may pose to the principle of res judicata. Finally, attention is drawn to norms in the EU legal order from which private parties may not deviate by contract.

**10.** The third leg of the journey looks at these areas of law again, but from a different perspective. In light of the foregoing, an attempt is made in Part III to try to map the type of values and interests that are being protected. Underlying this is, of course, the debate about whether the *ordre public* may also protect certain private interests and if not, what the alternative concepts may be. First on the list are certain institutional interests of the EU. After all, we have set out to find content for the EU *ordre public.* However, the concept of *ordre public* is very often used to protect certain Member State interests, especially in the context of free movement within the internal market. Third, certain private interests also seem to warrant extraordinary protection. This of course brings us to the relationship between *ordre public* and fundamental rights. Fourth, a series of particular interests are at times put forward as resulting in specific types of *ordre public* under national law. Accordingly, it may be interesting to see whether they result in similar protection on EU level. In particular, attention will be paid to the *ordre public économique,* the protection of the *lex moneta,* the *ordre public écologique* and the treatment of aliens. Finally, an analysis is necessary of some specific EU wide values. This results in further observations on the status of fundamental rights and the claim that citizenship of the European Union should form part of the EU *ordre public.*

**11.** If the concept of *ordre public* may cover EU interests, national interests and even private interests it seems inevitable that conflicts between these interests will arise. For example, conflicts may arise between EU law and national law, forcing us to further analyse the relationship between the EU legal order and the national legal order. This will lead us in Part IV to arguments on the nature of primacy of EU law, national procedural autonomy, mutual recognition and the development of federal common law. At the same time, there may also be tensions between various norms of EU *ordre public* at the level of the Union. The example of the recognition of same-sex marriages will serve as an example of how these tensions may be dealt with at both the level of the Union and in the relationship between the Union and its Member States. If it

19. Case 9/65 *San Michele v. High Authority* [1965] ECR 27.

appears that the Union is reasonably capable of reconciling such tensions, this may hint at the potential for some deeper constitutional framework to describe the concept of EU *ordre public* and put it into operation.

**12.** This is the perspective for the last stage of the voyage, where we inquire into the constitutional implications of the concept of *ordre public*. The starting point for this leg is the Opinion of Advocate General Jacobs in *Salzgitter*,[20] an Opinion which was my initial inspiration to investigate the concept of *ordre public*. The Advocate General takes issue with the classic distinction between the grounds for annulment of Community acts based on the *légalité externe*, which encompass the rules on competences and the essential procedural requirements and those based on the *légalité interne* which involve the breach of higher Community law and misuse of powers.[21] Only the former can be invoked by the Court of its own motion and can thus be said to be of *ordre public*. Yet, as the Advocate General forcefully argues, this distinction makes little sense. On the one hand, all grounds for annulment ultimately boil down to some violation of higher EU law. On the other hand, and most importantly, the constitutional importance of the rules appears too great to categorize them as either affecting the *légalité interne* or the *légalité externe*. Using this categorization, minor procedural irregularities may be raised by the Court of its own motion, while flagrant human rights violations may be off limits. Rejecting this model, however, creates a whole new set of problems. How do we make an alternative demarcation? How do we determine what is 'constitutionally important'? Moreover, the problem is far from limited to the question of when the ECJ or General Court should raise issues of their own motion. Across this book, numerous phenomena are discussed that all may arguably be related to the EU *ordre public*, but all seem subject to very specific limitations that may result in seemingly conflicting results. Accordingly, may these various strands and processes nonetheless be reconciled in a principled manner? It sounds like an almost impossible task. However, by combining the insights from the preceding Parts, the contours of a defined content for the EU *ordre public* may become apparent. By modifying a functional model first described by Romain[22] to operate at the level of a single State into a model for describing the EU *ordre public* an attempt is made to capture the breadth of the EU *ordre public* and structure the concept so that it may account for the great variety in the way in which the concept operates in the EU legal order. The strength of the model, however, lies not only in its descriptive qualities, but it will also serve as a basis for suggestions *de lege ferenda* that may offer – at least in part – an answer to the criticism of Advocate General Jacobs and support a more principled use of the concept of EU *ordre public* as a tool to help ensure unity in diversity.

---

20. Opinion of AG Jacobs in Case C-210/98 P *Salzgitter v. Commission* [2000] ECR I-5843, paras 125-150.
21. Case C-367/95 P *Commission v. Sytraval and Brink's France* [1998] I-1719, par. 67; K. Lenaerts, D. Arts, D. & I. Maselis; R. Bray, R. (ed.), *Procedural Law of the European Union*, 2nd edition (London: Sweet & Maxwell, 2006), 288-289.
22. M. Ekelmans, 'L'*ordre public* et les lois prohibitives étrangères' in *L'ordre public: concept et applications*, ed. J.-F. Romain, M. Grégoire & V. Simonart (Bruxelles: Bruylant, 1995), 59-61.

**13.** Before embarking on this voyage, it is appropriate to denote one final limitation. The book was initially written as a doctoral dissertation and successfully defended as such in April 2009. Since then the key legal texts upon which the Union was founded have changed dramatically with the entry into force of the Lisbon Treaty. Yet, on a closer look the Lisbon Treaty at best strengthens developments that were already very much there when the book was first conceived. While this book takes into account this change and key evolutions in the case law since, the essence is still quite similar as it was back in 2009. In a sense that should be reassuring, as it suggests that the analysis that will be set out further on has in a sense already stood the test of time. Nevertheless, the consequence of this drafting history is that inevitably the most recent developments may be analysed somewhat less in depth. The most important later case law and legislation are nevertheless taken into account up to 31 May 2012.

# Part I
# Exploring 'Unity in Diversity'

## INTRODUCTION

**I-1.** In this first part we need first to explore the possibility, and even the necessity, for there to be EU *ordre public*. It will be argued first that every legal order is based on fundamental values and principles it needs to protect. Then it will be demonstrated that the EU in this does not differ much from the legal orders of its Member States. This justifies looking briefly into the various roles *ordre public* plays in these legal orders, especially the French and Belgian legal order, the founding Member States of the EU where the concept has best been developed. Subsequently, attention is paid to the role *ordre public* plays in private international law. Again this refers back to national law and practice, but it seems interesting for two reasons. First, it indicates that also in transnational relations there is a place for *ordre public*. Second, as the EU is becoming evermore active in the sphere of private international law, it is inevitable that if nothing else, at least in respect of this part of EU law a doctrine of *ordre public* must exist. A similar reasoning will then lead us to briefly look into the related area of international trade law, in particular, the law of (international) arbitration. With EU law interacting with the law of arbitration, again some clues as to the need for an EU doctrine of *ordre public* may be found. Finally, the existence of *jus cogens* is a clear indication that also the international legal order is based on basic values and principles. Moreover, it is often argued that at the heart of these values are the fundamental rights. Accordingly, an international organization such as the EU, which brings together 27 Member States must at a very minimum share these basic international values and principles.

**I-2.** On the basis of the foregoing, it will thus be argued that a normative concept of *EU ordre public* is therefore not only possible, but also desirable, if not necessary. It will further be argued that this even holds true if, contrary to the model that permeates this thesis, the EU is studied from a more reductionist vision, such as the regulatory model by Lindseth.[1]

**I-3.** However, even if some parallel can be drawn with classic international law and the legal orders of the Member States a series of further theoretical and methodological problems arise. First, it seems important to dig deeper into the relationship between the EU and its Member States. In this way the potential for, but also the difficulties arising from, the introduction of a concept of *ordre public* for the EU, characterized as this international organization established by its Member States in order to realize an 'ever closer union of the peoples of Europe'.[2] It will be argued that there may be as much as four possible relations between the concept of EU *ordre public* and the national legal orders, each corresponding to other aspects of the EU legal order. Accordingly, first, the autonomous character of the legal order will be linked to the existence of an autonomous EU *ordre public.* Second, the likelihood of shared values is linked with some of the core articles of the EU Treaty and the concept of mutual recognition. Finally, the potential for conflict is analysed, but from two perspectives. On the one hand there may be situations where the EU will tolerate certain expressions of the national *ordre public* without claiming it as EU *ordre public.* This is ultimately the expression of the EU motto 'united in diversity'[3] and the principle of subsidiarity. On the other hand, the cases of real conflict will be examined and linked to the principle of primacy.

**I-4.** In the final chapter of this Part, some further methodological issues need to be addressed about how to discern the content of the EU *ordre public.* It will be argued that a good theory about EU *ordre public* will need to reconcile a series of conflicting elements. First, the theory must give sufficient consideration to the unique interests of the EU itself, in light of its mission and its institutional framework. Second, the theory also needs to take into account the role and sovereignty of the Member States. Third, the model must contribute to the development of a coherent legal system. Fourth, the theory must also have sufficient flexibility to deal with a notion, such as *ordre public,* with a variable content. In an attempt to deal with those challenges, some further observations as to the EU system of 'finding the law' and the role of the judge in the EU

1. P. Lindseth, 'Democratic Legitimacy and the Administrative Character of Supranationalism: The Example of the European Community', *Columbia Law Review* (1999): 628-738.
2. Article 1, second alinea TEU.
3. Article I-8 European Constitution. Admittedly, in line with the 2007 IGC Mandate (Council Document 11287/07) which seeks to safeguard the constitutional changes set out in the Treaty establishing a Constitution for Europe but seeks to drop all constitutional rhetoric, the Lisbon Treaty does not incorporate this motto into the existing Treaties. Yet, the content of the Reform Treaty is anything but a rejection of the message the motto embodies. Therefore, like the flag and the anthem, the motto will continue to prosper irrespective of whether it is incorporated in a Treaty or not. See on this also T. Corthaut, 'Plus ça change, plus c'est la même chose? A Comparison with the Constitutional Treaty', *Maastricht Journal of European and Comparative Law* (2008): 21-23.

legal system seem appropriate. In this respect special attention is paid to the role comparative law may have to play.

**I-5.** At the end of this part, the stage will thus be set to effectively examine the various aspects of the EU *ordre public* in the following parts.

# Chapter 1
# The Necessity of an EU Concept of *Ordre Public*

**I-6.** As the starting point for our analysis, we take the observation that any legal order has at its core a set of principles and values that determine the face of that legal order and need to be protected by that legal order.[1] Every legal order indeed has at its base a social, political, economic and cultural stratum. Put in these terms it sounds almost deterministic, if not Marxist,[2] but after all the whole body of the critical legal studies, whether they look at law form a socialist perspective, a gender perspective, a race perspective or some other outside vantage point is entirely premised on the presence of this stratum and aims at the unmasking of it throughout the legal order. However, as this usually results in rather partial views on this stratum, I rather would make the link to what Dworkin calls background rights,[3] the underlying narrative of (embryonic) rights, values and principles that influence and nurture the positive legal order. Some of these background rights, however, grow out to be so important for the legal order that without them that order would irreversibly be altered. As a result, any legal order therefore designates a set of rules and principles at the very heart of a political entity expressing the basic options taken by that entity in respect of its political, economic, social and cultural order and it seeks a way of protecting these. This is where the *ordre public* comes in. Indeed, the *ordre public* is the complex of norms at the very heart of a political entity expressing and protecting the basic options taken by that entity in respect of its political, economic, social and cultural order.

1. See in this sense J. Breillat, '*Ordre public*, ordre social, ordre politique: quelles interactions?' in *L'ordre public: ordre public ou ordres publics? Ordre public et droits fondamentaux*, ed. M.-J. Redor (Brussel: Bruylant, 2001), 247-283.
2. On the role of stratum with Marx, see J. McMurty, *The Structure of Marx's World-View* (Princeton: Princeton University Press, 1978).
3. R. Dworkin, *Taking Rights Seriously* (Cambridge: Harvard University Press, 1977). See also the critical remarks in the review by R.L Brilmayer & J.W. Nickel, *Columbia Law Review* (1977): 819-820.

**I-7.** The existence of an *ordre public* seems inherent in any legal order to the extent that the purpose of law is to organize and protect the functioning of a political entity. One of the functions of law is precisely to bring about some order in society. The opposite of the order brought by the *ordre public* is disorder. In this respect, I agree with Romain that the alternative is a destructive disorder which puts the basic values of society into doubt, not because of a collective societal will to improve the society, but because opposing forces and personal interests have free reign.[4] The *ordre public* fights this negative form of disorder.[5] It is, however, tantalizing to argue that there is also a positive form of disorder, which is said to flow from the fact that society itself evolves and adapts to new situations, resulting in the societal values being redefined.[6] This type of disorder results in a very different tension with the *ordre public*. In this context, what is at stake is not as much antagonism, but the basis for a dynamic concept of *ordre public*, which reflects current societal values and thus evolves with society. *Ordre public* is thus at the heart of the role of the law in ensuring stability in the legal order, but that does not preclude society, and thus the corresponding *ordre public* as well, from evolving.[7]

**I-8.** In the following, subsections I purport to illustrate this premise by looking first at the use of the concept of *ordre public* at the level of national legal orders, in particular those of the (founding) Member States of the European Union. From there we gradually expand our view, with references to private international law, international trade law and ultimately international law. Additionally, the link between *ordre public* and the ECHR is brought to the fore. It will be submitted that as a concept of *ordre public* exists at each of these levels,[8] the EU must necessarily have its own *ordre public*.

## §1.01 NATIONAL LAW: *ORDRE PUBLIC INTERNE*

**I-9.** All founding Member States of the EU have a concept of *ordre public*. The concept has mainly been developed in the context of the validity of contracts concluded by individuals. However, it also has further applications in the context of national procedural law and public law. A very brief overview shows that its limits vary greatly among the national legal orders.[9] However, some lessons can be drawn. Furthermore, apart from a concept of *ordre public interne*, all national legal orders also have a concept of *ordre public externe*, the public policy exception used in their private international law. This, however, will be addressed in section §1.02.

4. J.-F. Romain, 'L'*ordre public* (notion générale) et les droits de l'homme' in *L'ordre public: concept et applications*, ed. J.-F. Romain, M. Grégoire & V. Simonart (Bruxelles: Bruylant, 1995), 10.
5. *Ibid.*
6. *Ibid.*
7. See in this sense also *infra*, I-85 discussing *ordre public* as a notion of variable content.
8. Compare also the description given of *ordre public* by C. Kessedjian, 'Public Order in European Law', *Erasmus Law Review* (2007): 26-27.
9. Prechal and Shelkoplyas speak in this respect of 'the many faces of public policy', see S. Prechal & N. Shelkoplyas, 'National Procedures, Public Policy and EC Law. From Van Schijndel to Eco Swiss and Beyond', *European Review of Private Law* (2004): 600-602.

**I-10.** Three of the founding Members, Belgium, Luxembourg and France still use the napoleonic Code Civil. In its Article 6 the Code directly refers to *ordre public* when it states: '*On ne peut déroger, par des conventions particulières, aux lois qui intéressent l'ordre public et les bonnes moeurs.*', thus prohibiting private parties to conclude contracts contrary to public policy or public morality. Moreover, this is again expressed in Article 1133 which indicates that contracts contrary to public policy or public morality have an illicit cause, and are thus in accordance with Article 1131 null and void. The exact meaning seems to differ slightly among the various legal orders. It is at times submitted that the Belgian definition, derived by the Belgian Court de Cassation from De Page,[10] is somewhat more demanding than the French version as defined by Malaurie,[11] in linking *ordre public* to law and the essential interests of the State, but I agree with Anne Meinertzhagen-Limpens that the differences are in practice rather limited.[12] In essence the *ordre public* aims to protect on the one hand the political and moral order, i.e., the organization of the State, the family and the public morality, and on the other hand the economic and social order, which mainly focuses on the correct functioning of the markets.[13]

**I-11.** The Italian concept of *ordre public* is deemed to be quite close to the French version. Similarly, Article 1343 of the *Codice Civile* finds an illicit cause for a contract if the cause contravenes public policy or public morality or the imperative laws. Key is that the act must be contrary to an imperative law, such as criminal law, or a provision touching on the general foundations of the law.[14]

**I-12.** Remarkably both the *Code Civil* and the *Codice Civile* make a distinction between *ordre public* and public morality. It will be argued below that that distinction is not self-evident, and that often the public morality is seen as a subcategory of the *ordre public*. By contrast, the German *BGB* does not refer to *ordre public*, but seems to combine all aspects under the concept of *guten Sitten*, public morality.[15] The concept of *ordre public* is denounced as not sufficiently defined. Interestingly, the Dutch *NBW* has made the reverse evolution: where traditionally the public morality was far more important than the *ordre public*, both concepts are given the same rank in Article 3:40 NBW.[16] It seems that both concepts refer to contracts that violate unwritten laws. Like in Germany, and Anglo-American law, this contrasts with those instances where the illegality or unenforceability of a contract flows from the violation of a written act.[17] In

10. 'La loi d'*ordre public* est celle qui touche aux intérêts essentiels de l'Etat ou de la collectivité, ou qui fixe dans le droit privé, les bases juridiques fondamentales sur lesquelles repose l'ordre économique ou moral d'une société determinée', see Cass. 9 December 1948, *Pas.*, 1948, I, 699
11. The *ordre public* is defined as 'le bon fonctionnement des institutions indispensables à la collectivité', see P. Malaurie, *L'ordre public et le contrat* (Reims: Matot-Braine, 1953), 69.
12. A. Meinertzhagen-Limpens, 'Quelques aspects de l'*ordre public* en droit in *L'ordre public: concept et applications*, ed. J.-F. Romain, M. Grégoire & V. Simonart (Bruxelles: Bruylant, 1995), 227-228.
13. *Ibid.*, 221-222.
14. See *ibid.*, 222 and the references made therein.
15. *Ibid.*, 224.
16. *Ibid.*, 225.
17. *Ibid.*, 224.

this sense, the German and Dutch concepts are in any event far more restrictive than the *ordre public* of the *Code Civile.*

**I-13.** The concept of *ordre public* or public policy was also not alien to the English and Irish legal systems when those countries joined the Community in 1973. In Anglo-American law, the concept is used in respect of the invalidity (or in the US, under the Restatement 2nd, the unenforceability) of contracts for reasons, developed in the Common Law, beyond the violation of the written law. Again this distinction between violations of written law and acts contrary to other unwritten fundamental rules protecting 'the public welfare'[18] is brought to the fore.

**I-14.** Beyond the validity of contracts, public policy is mainly used in a procedural setting. The continental legal orders usually impose limits on the possibility for private parties to adduce new pleas in law or grounds for review at a late stage in the procedure. Traditionally an exception is made to this rule for violations of rules of *ordre public.* Examples are the Belgian and French procedures before the *Cour de Cassation,*[19] Article 48 of the Dutch Procedural Code. This is often linked to the question whether moreover these arguments can also be raised by the courts of their own motion. Unsurprisingly, in the context of EU procedural law this distinction will return, both in the context of the procedure before the Community Courts and in respect of the demands EU law puts to the national procedural laws. This public policy exception does not seem to be known in the English legal system. Another procedural use of the term is found in Articles 138-139 of the Belgian Code of Civil Procedure creating the possibility for the Ministère Public to intervene in civil cases to protect the *ordre public.* The scope of both procedural exceptions is not undisputed. The first one seems to be quite narrow in the Netherlands,[20] while in Belgium the parties may also use the *ordre public* exception to raise issues in respect of *imperative laws* that protect certain crucial

18. *Ibid.*, 229, nr. 8 and the references made therein.
19. M. Grégroire, 'L'*ordre public* dans la jurisprudence de la cour de cassation' in *L'ordre public: concept et applications*, ed. J.-F. Romain, M. Grégoire & V. Simonart (Bruxelles: Bruylant, 1995), 63-64.
20. For the civil courts see Article 48 Dutch Code of Civil Procedure. For more, see the Opinion of AG Jacobs in Joined Cases C-430/93 and C-431/93 *Van Schijndel and Van Veen* [1995] ECR I-4705, para. 11. For the equivalent rules under Dutch administrative law see A.M. Keessen, 'Ambtshalve toepassing van Europees recht', *Nederlands Tijdschrift voor Europees Recht* (2006): 58-60. See in this respect also Opinion of AG Poiares Maduro in Joined Cases C-222/05, C-223/05, C-224/05 and C-225/05 *Van der Weerd* [2007] ECR I-4233, paras 36-37 where the AG succinctly summarizes the impact of Article 8:69 Awb ('The Court before which proceedings are brought shall give its ruling on the basis of the application, the documents produced, the preliminary investigation and the consideration of the case at the hearing.') as follows: 'Article 8:69 Awb goes on to say that the court has the duty to supplement the legal grounds. Yet, when doing so the court must remain within the ambit of the dispute as defined by the parties. It may only go beyond the ambit of the dispute in order to examine of its own motion grounds of public policy. The notion of public policy, within this context, is defined in the national case-law. It resembles the notion of public policy as it is used, in the analogous context, by the Court of First Instance. Under Dutch administrative law, grounds of public policy mainly concern the jurisdiction of the court, the admissibility of the action, or the competence of the administrative body that issued the contested decision.'

individual interests rather than the collective interests generally associated with *ordre public.*[21] The role of the ministère public, by contrast, is more limited and rather rare.[22]

**I-15.** Finally the notion of *ordre public* is used in public law to denote the powers of the public authorities in maintaining public security.[23] This concept, too, will prove important for EU law, especially in the context of the exceptions to the four freedoms.[24] However, it seems that especially in France this concept has since been inflated ever further. First, it forms the basis for the actions of all kinds of public authorities and the police in maintaining law and order, an *ordre public de police.* In this way the notion of *ordre public* is invoked in relation to criminal law,[25] actions against aliens,[26] sects[27] and terrorism,[28] but also in respect of the public domain,[29] public finances,[30]or even unemployment.[31]

**I-16.** This very brief description of the use of *ordre public* in the Member States does not do justice to all the nuances that come with the use of the concept. However, I do not set out to make a solid comparative study. At this stage all that is needed is to demonstrate the *existence* of the concept and some general indications as to its use. Indeed some general observations can be made that surpass the details of the various legal orders.

21. M. Grégroire, 'L'*ordre public* dans la jurisprudence de la cour de cassation' in *L'ordre public: concept et applications*, ed. J.-F. Romain, M. Grégoire & V. Simonart (Bruxelles: Bruylant, 1995), 63-80.
22. A. Puttemans, 'L'*ordre public* et la loi du 14 juillet 1991 sur les pratiques du commerce sur l'information et la protection du consommateur' in *L'ordre public: concept et applications*, ed. J.-F. Romain, M. Grégoire & V. Simonart (Bruxelles: Bruylant, 1995), 154.
23. J.-F. Romain, 'L'*ordre public* (notion générale) et les droits de l'homme' in *L'ordre public: concept et applications*, ed. J.-F. Romain, M. Grégoire & V. Simonart (Bruxelles: Bruylant, 1995), 28; D. Truchet, 'L'obligation d'agir pour la protection de l'*ordre public*: la question d'un droit à la sécurité' in *L'ordre public: ordre public ou ordres publics? Ordre public et droits fondamentaux*, ed. M.-J. Redor (Brussel: Bruylant, 2001), 299-316.
24. See, *infra*, II-7 et seq.
25. A. Cerf, '*Ordre public*, droit pénal et droits fondamentaux' in *L'ordre public: ordre public ou ordres publics? Ordre public et droits fondamentaux*, ed. M.-J. Redor (Brussel: Bruylant, 2001), 63-83.
26. F. Julien-Laferrière, '*Ordre public* et droit des étrangers' in *L'ordre public: ordre public ou ordres publics? Ordre public et droits fondamentaux*, ed. M.-J. Redor (Brussel: Bruylant, 2001), 285-297.
27. M. Fouquet-Armand, 'Sectes et *ordre public*' in *L'ordre public: ordre public ou ordres publics? Ordre public et droits fondamentaux*, ed. M.-J. Redor (Brussel: Bruylant, 2001), 369-404.
28. F. Epinette, 'Vigipirate' in *L'ordre public: ordre public ou ordres publics? Ordre public et droits fondamentaux*, ed. M.-J. Redor (Brussel: Bruylant, 2001), 337-352.
29. E. Fatôme, '*Ordre public* et domain public' in *L'ordre public: ordre public ou ordres publics? Ordre public et droits fondamentaux*, ed. M.-J. Redor (Brussel: Bruylant, 2001), 187-198.
30. M. Lascombe, & X. Vandendriessche, 'L'*ordre public* et les jurisdictions financières' in *L'ordre public: ordre public ou ordres publics? Ordre public et droits fondamentaux*, ed. M.-J. Redor (Brussel: Bruylant, 2001), 167-186.
31. M. Allais, 'Le chômage et l'*ordre public*' in *L'ordre public*, ed. R. Polin (Paris: PUF, 1996), 53-66.

**I-17.** All legal orders seem to struggle with defining the term *ordre public*. The term is largely undefined in Anglo-American law.[32] In civil law countries, various definitions are being drafted. Some of them have been mentioned above. They sometimes narrowly focus on the interests of the collectivity as described by law. Others refer to far wider concepts. However, none of these definitions seem to fully satisfy the authors - in fact the only thing they seem to agree on is the difficulty of finding an apt definition, hence the colourful metaphors mentioned in the introduction above.

**I-18.** Nonetheless, some elements seem to reappear. First of all, its content is said to be evolving over time. Prime examples in this respect are certain evolutions in respect of the treatment of extra-marital relations.[33] Second, the content seems to vary among States. This seems hardly surprising as there is large agreement that the *ordre public* reflects the fundamental rules of the various legal orders, which implies that each legal order may have its own concept. To the extent that (continental) States do hold a lot in common these differences do not need to be overstated. This will become especially clear when we draw the attention, below, on the link between *ordre public* and fundamental rights. A lot of the confusion seems to flow from the question whether the *ordre public* solely protects collective interests or also covers certain particular interests worth protecting.[34]

**I-19.** This distinction is reflected in a recurring debate as to the difference between *ordre public* and *lois impératives*.[35] Traditionally *ordre public* is said to protect collective interests, in particular the organization of the State, the free market economy and family life. Under the *Code Civil* these are characterized as follows:[36]

- the sanction for their violation is absolute nullity of the contrary act;
- the nullity can be invoked by any interested party, not just the injured party;
- the judge must raise the violation of his/her own motion;
- the invalidated act cannot be confirmed afterwards;
- the prescription period is the maximum term of 30 years.

By contrast, the *lois impératives* are deemed to protect certain individual interests, usually because of some perceived weakness of one of the parties or an imbalance in their relationship. Accordingly, the consequences are traditionally more attenuated:[37]

32. A. Meinertzhagen-Limpens, 'Quelques aspects de l'*ordre public* en droit comparé' in *L'ordre public: concept et applications*, ed. J.-F. Romain, M. Grégoire & V. Simonart (Bruxelles: Bruylant, 1995), 229.
33. For a comparative study, see *ibid.*, 232-240.
34. For an example originating from the French legal order, but with EU-wide implications, see Case C-429/05 *Rampion and Godard* [2007] ECR I-8017, with Opinion of AG Mengozzi.
35. See W. Van Gerven, & S. Covemaeker, *Verbintenissenrecht*, 2nd ed. (Leuven: Acco, 2006), 146 et seq.
36. J. F. Romain, 'L'*ordre public* (notion générale) et les droits de l'homme' in *L'ordre public: concept et applications*, ed. J.-F. Romain, M. Grégoire & V. Simonart (Bruxelles: Bruylant, 1995), 34-35.
37. *Ibid.*, 35.

- the sanction for their violation is relative nullity of the contrary act;
- only the protected party can raise the violation;
- the judge cannot raise the issue of his/her own motion;
- the nullity can be overcome in that the injured party can renounce the protection offered by the rule;
- the prescription period is the standard period for contractual obligations.

**I-20.** However, in practice the distinction does not seem to hold well. It turns out to be rather difficult to discover whether individual or collective rights are being protected. Prime examples are core provisions in respect of company law or consumer protection law.[38] Those seek to protect the rights of investor and shareholders viz. consumers. However, in doing so they may as well have a broader impact on the free exchange of goods and services, which is typically seen as a collective interest. Unsurprisingly, we thus see some convergence between the two. The discussion as to whether the Belgian Cour de Cassation may hear certain arguments relating to the violation of certain *lois impératives* mentioned above is a good example.[39] Moreover, the distinction does not seem to play that much in certain other States, such as Italy. It appears nonetheless possible to draw two lessons. First, an important function of the *ordre public* is to oust certain contrary legal acts. Second, a debate exists as to whether the modalities for this function should not vary according to the nature of the interests protected.[40]

**I-21.** A further recurring theme is the distinction between *ordre public* and *public morality*. In the final analysis, it seems again that the diverging subtleties should not stand in the way of some general conclusions. Often the concepts are mentioned together, and their consequences appear to be largely identical. This already greatly diminishes the import of any clear distinction between them. Furthermore, when distinguished, the focus of *ordre public* lies more with the organization of the State and the markets while *public morality* seems to correspond to an ethical order. This distinction is often made more expressly by distinguishing as to the sources of these two concepts. The organization of the State or the markets requires positive enactment of norms by the competent governmental bodies. Public morality, by contrast, is then rather seen as the unwritten basic ethical rules applicable in a certain society. However, ultimately, those two are clearly influencing each other. Most positive enactments are likely to be concurrent with these societal ethical rules, while these ethics will of course also largely depend on the enacted political and economic

---

38. See in that respect V. Simonart, 'L'*ordre public* et le doit des sociétés' in *L'ordre public: concept et applications*, ed. J.-F. Romain, M. Grégoire & V. Simonart (Bruxelles: Bruylant, 1995), 81-136; A. Puttemans, 'L'*ordre public* et la loi du 14 juillet 1991 sur les pratiques du commerce sur l'information et la protection du consommateur' in *L'ordre public: concept et applications*, ed. J.-F. ROMAIN, M. Grégoire & V. Simonart (Bruxelles: Bruylant, 1995), 137-190. See also Case C-429/05 *Rampion and Godard* [2007] ECR I-8017, with Opinion of AG Mengozzi.
39. See in this respect M. Grégroire, M., 'L'*ordre public* dans la jurisprudence de la cour de cassation' in *L'ordre public: concept et applications*, ed. J.-F. Romain, M. Grégoire & V. Simonart (Bruxelles: Bruylant, 1995), 63-80.
40. See in this sense also A.-C. Van Gysel & J.-F. Romain, 'Conclusions générales: l'*ordre public* entre hétérogénéité en homogénéité' in *L'ordre public: concept et applications*, ed. J.-F. Romain, M. Grégoire & V. Simonart (Bruxelles: Bruylant, 1995), 305-327.

system.[41] Accordingly, it is not surprising to find authors who argue that the *ordre public* encompasses the public morality, while the German legal order mainly functions starting from the *guten Sitten.*[42] Unless stated otherwise, therefore, I will rarely make that distinction.[43]

**I-22.** That does not prevent me from nevertheless recognizing that such a broader concept of *ordre public* thus corresponds to two different realms. In that respect, I am inspired by Raymond Polin who distinguishes between the protection of the *ordre politique* and the *ordre social.*[44] The former is historically the oldest and seems to be the dominant basis for the *ordre public. Ordre public* is thus first in place to ensure the legitimate command power of the government through institutions and laws to ensure stability and security and a basic distribution of wealth. However, this command power is balanced by the protection of the fundamental rights of the subjects of that legal order. Moreover, it entails the distinction between a public sphere and a private sphere the State has to respect. In a second move *ordre public* also corresponds to the *ordre social,* which entails a *just* distribution of wealth, resulting in basic forms of social protection and evolving towards social equality, based on fundamental respect for human dignity.[45]

## §1.02 PRIVATE INTERNATIONAL LAW – *ORDRE PUBLIC EXTERNE*

**I-23.** There is one further form of *ordre public* which can be found in the internal legal order of all Member States, which is the public policy exception used in their private international law, which, despite the misleading terminology, is indeed fundamentally national law. However, given the more universal recognition of the concept in this sphere, it seems appropriate to treat it somewhat separately.

**I-24.** The core problem is universal. As individuals have contacts across the borders of legal orders there are inevitably instances where legal orders are confronted with legal acts stemming from outside their legal order. Sometimes the debate will focus on the recognition or enforcement of certain foreign acts; sometimes the judge will be directed by the applicable choice of law rules to actively apply a certain foreign law;[46]

---

41. In this sense I disagree with Polin who sees this relationship rather as a one way street in which the *ordre social* is entirely dependent on the *ordre politique*, see R. Polin, 'L'*ordre public*' *L'ordre public*, ed. R. Polin (Paris: PUF, 1996), 17-18.
42. A. Meinertzhagen-Limpens, 'Quelques aspects de l'*ordre public* en droit comparé' in *L'ordre public: concept et applications*, ed. J.-F. Romain, M. Grégoire & V. Simonart (Bruxelles: Bruylant, 1995), 225.
43. On the blending of both concepts across the various legal systems, see *ibid.*, 225–227
44. R. Polin, 'L'*ordre public*' *L'ordre public*, ed. R. Polin (Paris: PUF, 1996), 12-25.
45. I find the above-mentioned concepts of *ordre politique* and *ordre social* useful, at least in the way I read them. However, I do not necessarily agree with some of the consequences that are attached to them by Polin, especially in respect of minorities and social strive.
46. On this M. Ekelmans, 'L'*ordre public* et les lois prohibitives étrangères' in *L'ordre public: concept et applications*, ed. J.-F. Romain, M. Grégoire & V. Simonart (Bruxelles: Bruylant, 1995), 257-281.

sometimes even as a matter of national *ordre public*,[47] It seems obvious that the smooth operation of international relations will thus demand some flexibility from all involved.[48] Yet, this does not mean that a State should be compelled to apply foreign laws or implement foreign decisions that may have consequences that are wholly contrary to the established political, economic and moral order of that State. Accordingly, the concept of *ordre public*, which allows for the ousting of certain contrary norms is particularly appealing.

**I-25.** The public policy exception in private international law thus operates in two circumstances.[49] First, it enables the judge, who is directed by the applicable choice of laws rules to apply a particular foreign law, to apply the law of the forum instead, because the application of the foreign law would lead to a result that is contrary to essential political, economic or social norms of the forum. One example may be the refusal to apply the law of a foreign State that may result in the imposition of punitive damages. Accordingly, we are not concerned with the legitimate cause of certain agreements, but with the question what law should govern a certain legal situation. Second, it may result in the refusal to recognize and thus *a fortiori* to enforce certain contrary foreign acts or judgments, for instance the refusal to recognize polygamist marriages.

**I-26.** Given the disruptive impact, which the invocation of the public policy exception may have it, is generally accepted that it is to be applied sparsely.[50] In that respect there seem to be two main techniques. On the one hand the concept of *ordre public* used for the public policy exception in a private international law context seems far more limited than the content of the *ordre public interne*.[51] On the other hand, legal techniques are introduced to attenuate the consequences of the invocation of the public policy exception.[52]

**I-27.** First, as to the content of the *ordre public externe* the basic principle is that, as each legal order has its own conflict rules, each legal order will also freely determine the content of its *ordre public externe*. However, in practice we see that States are often willing to tolerate certain deviations from national practices, even when they would intervene internally against them on grounds of *ordre public*. For instance, at a time when Belgium was still rather conservative in recognizing parentage for children born

47. See in this sense in respect of the Belgian legal order, K. Lenaerts, 'Le statut du droit étranger en droit international privé belge. Vers un nouvel équilibre ?' in *Mélanges offert à Raymond Vander Elst*, vol. II, ed. R. Vander Elst (Bruxelles: Nemesis, 1986), 529-555.
48. See in this sense C. Ryngaert, *Jurisdiction in international law: United States and European perspectives*, diss. KU Leuven, 2006.
49. N. Watté, 'Droit international privé (première partie)', *Revue Critique de la Jurisprudence Belge* (2003): 490.
50. N. Watté, 'Droit international privé (seconde partie)', *Revue Critique de la Jurisprudence Belge* (2005): 274.
51. See on this, J.-F. Romain, 'L'*ordre public* (notion générale) et les droits de l'homme' in *L'ordre public: concept et applications*, ed. J.-F. Romain, M. Grégoire & V. Simonart (Bruxelles: Bruylant, 1995), 25-28.
52. M. Ekelmans, 'L'*ordre public* international et ses effets atténués' in *L'ordre public: concept et applications*, ed. J.-F. Romain, M. Grégoire & V. Simonart (Bruxelles: Bruylant, 1995), 283-303.

from an adulterous relationship, the Belgian Cour de Cassation ruled that while recognition of this relationship would be contrary to Belgian *ordre public interne*, it did not follow that this would justify the invocation of the public policy exception.[53] For this the Cour de Cassation requires the violation of a provision of a Belgian legislative act which the legislator deems essential for the moral, political or economic order and thus requires that it be applied even if the conflict of law rules designate a foreign law. This was not deemed to be the case in respect of the Belgian rules in respect of parentage, which had already started to evolve internally as well.

**I-28.** Unsurprisingly, there is some degree of internationalization of the *ordre public externe*. Not at the least under the influence of fundamental rights treaties, there seems to be some kind of evolution towards focusing on the question whether the foreign law to be applied or foreign act to be recognized respects certain core fundamental rights, both as to substance and as to procedure.[54]

**I-29.** Second, the consequences of the application of the public policy exception are at times further limited.[55] For instance, under the German *Binnenbeziehungstheorie* there is no need for the forum to invoke the public policy exception if the contested act has no consequences in the internal legal order of the forum State, beyond the jurisdictional link with the forum. Furthermore, under the French doctrine of the *effets atténués* the consequences of the invocation of the public policy exception can be further restricted. As the classic example goes, the French judge will refuse to give effect to any claim to marital authority by a polygamist over his troupe of women. However, things may be different if the question arises whether the children born within such a polygamous wedding are deemed to be legitimate children. In this way the public policy may be a barrier to the recognition of some consequences of a foreign act, but not to other instead of ousting the entire controversial act per se.

**I-30.** As the European Union has over time, and especially in recent years, adopted legislation in the field of private international law, these national debates are bound to have an effect on the application of Union rules. Moreover, if there appears to be a shift away from a purely national conception of *ordre public externe*, it does not seem unreasonable to expect that the communautarization of this field of law must also leave its mark in this respect. To what extent this is the case is discussed in Part II, below.

53. J.-F. Romain, 'L'*ordre public* (notion générale) et les droits de l'homme' in *L'ordre public: concept et applications*, ed. J.-F. Romain, M. Grégoire & V. Simonart (Bruxelles: Bruylant, 1995), 25-26.
54. On this, see W.J. Ganshof van der Meersch, 'L'*ordre public* et les droits de l'homme', *Journal des Tribunaux* (1968): 658-663; J.-F. Romain, 'L'*ordre public* (notion générale) et les droits de l'homme' in *L'ordre public: concept et applications*, ed. J.-F. Romain, M. Grégoire & V. Simonart (Bruxelles: Bruylant, 1995), 5-61. See also P. Hammje, 'Droits fondamentaux et *ordre public*', *Revue critique de droit international privé* (1997): 1-31.
55. See on this M. Ekelmans, 'L'*ordre public* international et ses effets atténués' in *L'ordre public: concept et applications*, ed. J.-F. Romain, M. Grégoire & V. Simonart (Bruxelles: Bruylant, 1995), 283-303; E. Fohrer, *L'incidence de la Convention européenne des droits de l'homme sur l'ordre public international français* (Bruxelles: Bruylant, 1999), 84 et seq.

## §1.03 INTERNATIONAL TRADE LAW AND ARBITRATION

**I-31.** A somewhat related application of the public policy exception is the use of the exception in respect of the recognition and enforcement of arbitral awards. Here private parties have initially sought a private solution to their dispute. However, at the end of the procedure the enforcement of the arbitral award usually requires the intervention of courts. Just like foreign legal actors may have reached outcomes that are wholly contrary to the essential aspects of the political, moral and economic order of the forum State, arbitrators may also have reached such outcomes. Again the question arises whether the forum can refuse to give effect to these awards.

**I-32.** In practical terms this results in a mixture of the two previous forms of *ordre public*. On the one hand, arbitrations are based on agreements which are themselves subject to rules as to their validity, including rules as to *ordre public interne* of the law governing the arbitration.[56] This becomes problematic when parties have tried to circumvent certain rules of the forum by subjecting their arbitral procedure to foreign law, as to procedure and, at times, also as to the applicable law. In this respect it is noteworthy that there is a debate, albeit still in its infancy, whether there is also a *transnational public policy*, which would be distinct from any domestic *international public policy*, and reflect concerns that transgress State boundaries.[57] On the other hand, the outcome of an arbitration proceeding may also contravene some of the essential aspects of the political, moral and economic order of the State where enforcement is sought in a way very similar to the questions that arise in respect of the recognition of foreign judgments.[58]

**I-33.** Like any agreement between economic actors, arbitration agreements and the ensuing arbitral awards, may be looked at critically from a competition law perspective. As competition law aims to protect the basic functioning of the markets it is often considered to be part of the *ordre public*. However, EU law has of course had a major impact on the content of competition law. Accordingly, it is not unlikely that EU law, and especially EU competition law, may play a major role when the content of the

56. In the definition of the International Law Association, this type of 'international public policy' 'is to be understood in the sense given to it in the field of private international law; namely, that part of the public policy of a State which, if violated, would prevent a party from invoking a foreign law or foreign judgment or foreign award. It is not to be understood, in these Recommendations, as referring to a public policy which is common to many States (which is better referred to as "transnational public policy") or to public policy which is part of public international law. International public policy is generally considered to be narrower in scope than domestic public policy.', see ILA, *Final Report on Public Policy as a Bar to Enforcement of International Arbitral Awards*, New Delhi Conference (2002).
57. On this, see M. Pryles, 'Reflections on Transnational Public Policy', *Journal of International Arbitration* (2007): 1-8.
58. See on this problem ILA, *Final Report on Public Policy as a Bar to Enforcement of International Arbitral Awards*, New Delhi Conference (2002); ILA, *Interim Report on Public Policy as a Bar to Enforcement of International Arbitral Awards*, London Conference (2000); T. Harris, 'The "Public Policy" Exception to Enforcement of International Arbitral Awards Under the New York Convention', *Journal of International Arbitration* (2007): 9-24.

public policy exception is at issue. To what extent that is the case is discussed in Part II and Part III, below.[59]

## §1.04 PUBLIC INTERNATIONAL LAW

**I-34.** The international community could be described as 'anarchistic', but that does not mean it is without order.[60] Indeed, it can be argued that at the core of international law lays a body of *ordre public international*. The international legal order, too, has some hierarchy of norms built around a set of fundamental norms. Under Article 53 of the Vienna Convention the Law of Treaties (VCLT), and in line with a long history of authors arguing for such approach,[61] a treaty is void if it conflicts with a peremptory norm of general international law. In legal literature the analogy with the national concepts of *ordre public* has not gone unnoticed,[62] even though it has equally been remarked that the transfer of this concept from the internal to the international legal order is not without difficulty.[63] This presupposes a body of peremptory norms, also called *jus cogens*, at the heart of the international legal order.[64] Like in national law it refers to the ground rules of the legal order, rules that are so crucial for the maintaining of the international legal order that they are superimposed on the States.[65] The concept moreover bears resemblance to the concept of obligations *erga omnes* as identified by the International Court of Justice (ICJ) in the *Barcelona Traction Case*[66] and the concept of international crimes.[67] The latter were proposed in Article 19(2) of the 1996 ILC Draft

59. For an extensive analysis on the role of EC law in arbitration proceedings, see N. Shelkoplyas, *The Application of EC law in Arbitration Proceedings* (Nijmegen: WLP, 2003).
60. See in this sense H. Ruiz Fabri, 'L'*ordre public* en droit international' in *L'ordre public: ordre public ou ordres publics? Ordre public et droits fondamentaux*, ed. M.-J. Redor (Brussel: Bruylant, 2001), 85.
61. For an overview, see J.-F. Romain, 'L'*ordre public* (notion générale) et les droits de l'homme' in *L'ordre public: concept et applications*, ed. J.-F. Romain, M. Grégoire & V. Simonart (Bruxelles: Bruylant, 1995), 46-48. See also H. Rollin, 'Vers un *ordre public* réellement international' in *Homage d'une Génération de Juristes au Président Basdevant* (Paris: Pendone, 1960), 451-454.
62. M. Shaw, *International Law*, 4th ed. (Cambridge: Cambridge, University Press, 1997), 97 and the authors referred to therein; J. Verhoeven, 'Droit des traités, réserves et *ordre public* (*jus cogens*)', *Journal des Tribunaux* (1994): 765-767.
63. The main problem is that internal law, explicitly or not, indicates which rules are mandatory, which international law does not, see M. Glennon, 'De l'absurdité du droit impératif (jus cogens), *Revue générale de droit international public* (2006): 534; E. Schwelb, 'Some Aspects of International *Jus Cogens* as Formulated by the International Law Commission', *American Journal of International Law* (1967): 948.
64. For an excellent and accessible overview from an EU perspective, see J. Vanhamme, *Volkenrechtelijke Beginselen in het Europees Recht* (Groningen: Europa Law Publishing, 2001), 29-62.
65. This does, however, not mean that it would be impossible to deviate from them, see in that sense J. Vanhamme, *Volkenrechtelijke Beginselen in het Europees Recht* (Groningen: Europa Law Publishing, 2001), 39-40.
66. *Barcelona Traction, Light and Power Co. Case*, ICJ Reports, 1970, 3, para. 33-34.
67. D.J. Harris, *Cases and Materials on International Law*, 5th ed. (London: Sweet & Maxwell, 1998), 837. See also A.J.J. De Hoogh, 'The Relationship between *Jus Cogens*, Obligations *Erga Omnes* and International Crimes: Peremptory Norms in Perspective', *Austrian Journal of Public International Law* (1991): 183-214.

Articles on State Responsibility[68] which defines an international crime as a 'an internationally wrongful act which results from the breach by a State of an international obligation so essential for the protection of fundamental interests of the international community that its breach is recognized as a crime by that community as a whole'. It has been argued that the three concepts largely refer to the same state actions, so that for instance a treaty authorizing genocide, slavery, acts of armed aggression etc. would be contrary to *jus cogens* and the performance of such treaty an international crime and violate an obligation *erga omnes*.[69] All three elements have therefore been argued to give body to the *ordre public*.[70] It is, however, to be observed that in particular the concept of international crimes is especially controversial, and it has effectively been dropped from the latest version of the Draft Articles.[71]

**I-35.** Moreover, like in national law, it turns out to be quite difficult to determine what elements are part of *jus cogens* or are such *international crimes* and thus part of this international *ordre public*. The VCLT itself hardly offers an answer. From Article 64 VCLT it can be deduced that the content is variable over time in that new peremptory norms may emerge, which then voids and terminates any existing conflicting treaty. From Article 53 VCLT, a two-tier approach may be deduced whereby the norm first rises to the status of general norm of international law and is second recognized by the international community as constituting such a norm.[72] However, this does not offer much more substance. In practice, as is envisaged by Article 66 VCLT it will often depend on the way the concept is being developed by the ICJ and other international tribunals. So far, this has happened with the highest caution.[73] However, at the same time, it is noteworthy that those same courts are often, as Ruiz Fabri calls it following Serge Sur, 'flirting' with the concept of *jus cogens*.[74] Though the status of the norms treated in this way is dubious, they, too, may inform the concept of *ordre public* within the international legal order. Determining the exact content of the concept would in any event greatly surpass the ambit of this research.

**I-36.** As the same Ruiz Fabri points out there is also an international version of the *ordre public de police*. Central to this is the prohibition on the use of force under Article 2(4) of the UN Charter and the concomitant exception of Article 24 of the Charter which

68. Article 19(2) ILC Draft Articles on State Responsibility, *ILC's 1996 Report*, GAOR, 51st Sess., Supp. 10, 125.
69. D.J. Harris, *Cases and Materials on International Law*, 5th ed. (London: Sweet & Maxwell, 1998), 837.
70. H. Ruiz Fabri, 'L'*ordre public* en droit international' in *L'ordre public: ordre public ou ordres publics? Ordre public et droits fondamentaux*, ed. M.-J. Redor (Brussel: Bruylant, 2001), 89-99.
71. See in this respect ILC Draft Articles on State Responsibility with Comments, available at <http://untreaty.un.org/ilc/texts/instruments/english/commentaries/9_6_2001.pdf, 280-281>, May 16, 2012. For the (lack of) consequences of this change in respect of genocide, see *Application of the Convention on the Prevention and Punishment of the Crime of Genocide*, ICJ Reports, 2007, 64, para. 170.
72. M. Shaw, *International Law*, 4th ed. (Cambridge: Cambridge University Press, 1997), 97.
73. See, however, in respect of genocide: *Armed Activities on the Territory of the Congo (New Application 2002) (Democratic Republic of the Congo v. Rwanda)*, ICJ Reports, 2006, 5, para 64.
74. H. Ruiz Fabri, 'L'*ordre public* en droit international' in *L'ordre public: ordre public ou ordres publics? Ordre public et droits fondamentaux*, ed. M.-J. Redor (Brussel: Bruylant, 2001) 97-98.

empowers the UN Security Council to take the necessary measures, including the use of military force under Article 42, to maintain international peace and security.[75] In doing so, the UN Security Council can moreover impose obligations on the UN Member States which take precedence over any contrary treaty.[76] Furthermore, the focus is no longer exclusively on (inter)State conduct. With the development of international humanitarian law and fundamental rights law a clear link starts to grow between international fundamental rights and the international *ordre public*.[77] The emergence of international courts to punish the individual perpetrators of violations of these protective norms, such as the ICTY and the ICC, and to protect these individual fundamental rights, such as the ECtHR, can only strengthen this evolution.[78]

## §1.05 THE ECHR AND THE 'EUROPEAN PUBLIC ORDER'

**I-37.** In the preceding paragraphs reference was regularly made to the linkage between the *ordre public* and human rights, both at the level of the States and in an international, private or public, law context. In particular, at least in respect of European States, which the EU Member States of course all are in light of Article 49 TEU, additional emphasis is laid on the ECHR. As is well-known the ECtHR has described the ECHR as 'a constitutional instrument of European public order (*ordre public*)'.[79] However, what this public order entails has rarely been examined, as has been observed by Frédéric Sudre.[80] Nonetheless, on the basis of the work of authors such as Sudre[81] himself, his promovenda Caroline Picheral[82] and J. Andriantsimbazovina[83] it is

75. *Ibid.*, 99-108.
76. Article 103 UN Charter. For an application, see the *Case Concerning Questions of Interpretation and Application of the Montreal Convention arising out of the Aerial Incident at Lockerbie (Provisional Measures)*, ICJ Reports, 1992, pp 1 and 112. This may of course result in further questions as to what should happen if the UN Security Council itself violates *jus cogens*. Remarkably, the Union Courts have been led into exactly this *terra incognita*, see *infra* at II-130 et seq., the discussion of Case T-306/01 *Yusuf and Al Barakaat International Foundation v. Council and Commission* [2005] ECR II-3533 and Case T-315/01 *Kadi v. Council and Commission* [2005] ECR II-3649. Compare, however, the appeals judgment, Joined Cases C-402/05 P and C-415/05 P *Kadi v. Council* [2008] ECR I-6351, with Opinion of AG Poiares Maduro.
77. On this see S. Marcus-Helmons, 'Droits de l'homme et *jus cogens*' in *Liber Amicorum Frédéric Dumon*, vol. II, ed. M. Chatel, A. Fettweis & M. Storme (Antwerpen: Kluwer, 1983), 1169-1181.
78. In this sense, see H. Ruiz Fabri, 'L'*ordre public* en droit international' in *L'ordre public: ordre public ou ordres publics? Ordre public et droits fondamentaux*, ed. M.-J. Redor (Brussel: Bruylant, 2001), 107-108.
79. ECtHR, 23 February 1995, *Loizidou v. Turkey* (preliminary objections), para. 75.
80. F. Sudre, 'L'*ordre public* européen' in *L'ordre public: ordre public ou ordres publics? Ordre public et droits fondamentaux*, ed. M.-J. Redor (Brussel: Bruylant, 2001), 109-110.
81. *Ibid.*, 109-131; F. Sudre, 'Existe-t-il un *ordre public* européen ?'in *Quelle Europe pour les Droits de l'Homme?*, ed. P. Tavernier (Bruxelles: Bruylant, 1996), 39-80.
82. C. Picheral, *L'ordre public européen: droit communautaire et droit européen des droits de l'homme*, (Paris: CERIC – Documentation française, 2001).
83. J. Andriantsimbazovina, 'Splendeurs et misères de l'*ordre public* européen – Les trois dernières années de l'ancienne Cour européenne des droits de l'homme (1996-1997-1998), *Cahiers de droit européen* (2000): 657-718; J. Andriantsimbazovina, 'L'élaboration progressive d'un *ordre public* européen', *Cahiers de droit européen* (1997): 665.

possible to make some observations, both as to the function and as to the content of this *ordre public européen* flowing from – or better: at the heart of – the ECHR.

**I-38.** As a preliminary point, the concept was, as indicated above, introduced by the ECtHR in *Loizidou.*[84] This in itself may raise some questions as to the role of the judge in finding the law, a point we will address below in respect of the ECJ as well.[85] Interestingly, the argument to be developed there will not differ much from the two arguments that Sudre puts forward to justify the judicial activism in this field of the ECtHR[86] and with which I agree. On the one hand, as the ECHR itself indicated in *Airey*[87] the ECtHR aims to offer effective protection of the rights guaranteed by the Convention, which justifies an autonomous interpretation of certain concepts which is both demanding for the Parties to the Convention and may at times limit the room for manoeuvre they may have under classic international law. On the other hand, the interpretation of the Convention is a balancing act, seeking an interpretation appealing to the prevailing currents of constitutional thought among the Parties to it.[88] With limited power to ensure compliance with its judgment the ECtHR must strive to find a 'common denominator',[89] to make sure its judgments are accepted by the States.

**I-39.** The concept of the European public order has a double function under the ECHR. First, in line with what has been observed above, it serves to strengthen the position of the judge, both at the European and the national level. As to the European judge, the ECtHR foremost invokes the European public order to block certain escape mechanisms, often derived from international law. In this way the ECtHR justifies applying the Convention in cases stemming from situations which have arisen before the defendant State had become a Party to the Convention,[90] or in cases where that State had made certain reservations.[91] Indeed, in *Loizidou* the ECtHR rejected the unilateral restrictions *ratione loci* and *ratione materiae* made by Turkey through which that State had tried to qualify the scope of its engagement under the Convention, in particular in respect of Northern Cyprus.[92] However, the concept of public order also informs the

84. ECtHR, 23 February 1995, *Loizidou v. Turkey* (preliminary objections), para. 75. See, however, also ECtHR, 30 June 2005, *Bosphorus Hava Yolları Turizm ve Ticaret Anonim Şirketi v. Ireland*, paras 155-156; ECtHR, 2 May 2007, *Behrami and Behrami v. France* and *Saramati v. France, Germany and Norway*, para. 145. For more, see also R. De Lange, 'The European Public Order, Constitutional Principles and Fundamental Rights', *Erasmus Law Review* (2007): 11-12.
85. See, *infra*, at I-86 et seq.
86. F. Sudre, 'L'*ordre public* européen' in *L'ordre public: ordre public ou ordres publics? Ordre public et droits fondamentaux*, ed. M.-J. Redor (Brussel: Bruylant, 2001), 115-116.
87. ECtHR, 9 October 1979, *Airey v. Ireland*, para. 24 ('The Convention is intended to guarantee not rights that are theoretical or illusory but rights that are practical and effective').
88. In this sense ECtHR, 6 November 1980, *Guzzardi v. Italy*, para. 95 ('the Convention is to be interpreted in the light of the notions currently prevailing in democratic States').
89. F. Sudre, 'L'*ordre public* européen' in *L'ordre public: ordre public ou ordres publics? Ordre public et droits fondamentaux*, ed. M.-J. Redor (Brussel: Bruylant, 2001), 116.
90. ECtHR, 11 July 1961, *Austria v. Italy*.
91. See for instance the rejection of a Swiss reservation in ECtHR, 29 April 1988, *Belilos v. Switzerland*, paras 50-60.
92. For more, see G. Cohen-Jonathan, 'L'affaire Loizidou devant la Cour européenne des droits de l'homme. Quelques observations', *Revue générale de droit international public* (1998): 123-144.

work of the ECtHR in applying the Convention. The rights in the Convention are subject to a series of limitations as are necessary in a democratic society. Accordingly, the ECtHR is time and again faced with the question whether a certain restriction by a State is indeed justified as it protects that society or whether that restriction rather undermines a democratic society.[93] It is in the latter case that also the empowerment of national judges comes to the fore. Even though the ECtHR does not require national judges to set aside national acts contrary to the Convention, in several Member States that is exactly what the courts are empowered to do, either because of specific legislation[94] or on the basis of court precedent.[95]

**I-40.** This brings us to the second function of the *ordre public*, the exclusion of contrary norms. The ECHR is not only to be used as a framework of reference to assess national legislation, but at times also affects the relations with States that are not Parties to the Convention. First, the ECtHR has indicated that it also puts limits to the application of certain international law instruments. Unsurprisingly, but highly relevant for the position of the EU, the Parties to the Convention cannot transfer sovereignty to an international organ, without ensuring equivalent protection of the rights offered by the Convention.[96] But the Convention may also prevent a Party to the Convention from giving effect to another international agreement, such as an extradition agreement which would result in the extradited person being subject to the inhumane treatment of a long stay on death row.[97]

**I-41.** Second, the European Convention is often used in opposing norms. It is on this point that the ECHR and our discussion of the public policy exception under private international law meet. It can be derived from the case of *Drozd and Janousek*[98] that a State may be prevented from executing a foreign judgment that has been rendered in flagrant violation of the procedural guarantees offered by Article 6 ECHR.[99] Similarly, as argued above, the *ordre public international* is subject to influence from the ECHR

93. For an extensive analysis, see C. Picheral, *L'ordre public européen: droit communautaire et droit européen des droits de l'homme* (Paris: CERIC – Documentation française, 2001), 139-147; see in this respect also J.-F. Romain., 'L'*ordre public* (notion générale) et les droits de l'homme' in *L'ordre public: concept et applications*, ed. J.-F. Romain, M. Grégoire & V. Simonart (Bruxelles: Bruylant, 1995), 49-55.
94. See in this respect Article 4 of the UK Human Rights Act (1998).
95. See in this respect the decision of the Belgian Cour de Cassation in *Franco-Suisse Le Ski*, see Cass. 27 May 1971, *Arr. Cass.* 959.
96. ECtHR, 18 February 1999, *Wait and Kennedy v. Germany*, para. 67 and *Matthews v. UK*, para. 34. That being said the ECtHR in practice adopts a rather deferential approach when it comes to the European Union, see ECtHR, 30 June 2005, *Bosphorus Hava Yollari Turizm ve Ticaret Anonim Şirketi v. Ireland.*
97. ECtHR, 7 July 1989, *Soering v. UK.*
98. ECtHR, 26 June 1992, *Drozd and Janousek v. France and Spain*, para. 110. It is to be noted, however, that this case concerned a criminal case. For examples from French private international law, see E. Fohrer, *L'incidence de la Convention européenne des droits de l'homme sur l'ordre public international français* (Bruxelles: Bruylant, 1999); F. Sudre, 'L'*ordre public* européen' in *L'ordre public: ordre public ou ordres publics? Ordre public et droits fondamentaux*, ed. M.-J. Redor (Brussel: Bruylant, 2001), 125-126.
99. Compare in this respect also ECtHR, 13 February 2001, *Krombach v. France* delivered in a complicated legal saga that also has required the ECJ to deal with this issue, see Case C-7/98 *Krombach* [2000] ECR I-1935. For more, see, *infra*, at II-136 et seq.

and other sources of human rights law and may thus inspire the invocation of the public policy exception to the application of foreign laws.[100]

**I-42.** As a result the concept of *ordre public européen* thus has a double finality: on the one hand it is used to strengthen integration, in closing down certain escape routes for avoiding the application of the Convention; on the other hand aspects of that same public order help to protect an unassailable core or *Wesensgehalt*[101] of the rights protected by the ECHR, even though the Convention allows for certain restrictions as may be necessary in a democratic society.[102] This apparent paradox can be resolved if we turn to the content of the *ordre public européen*. It has been argued that the concept amounts to a 'synthesis' of the ECHR.[103] Indeed, the ECtHR claims the existence at the heart of the Convention of a body of rules which is perceived as fundamental for the European society and which impose themselves on the Parties to the Convention.[104] The Court thus implies the existence of a set of common values, which is developed around the concept of 'the principles characterising a "democratic society"',[105] which accordingly forms the core for the *ordre public européen*.[106]

**I-43.** The concept of a democratic society refers first to a particular political model, 'the only political model contemplated by the Convention and, accordingly, the only one compatible with it'.[107] The ECtHR has stressed that:

> democracy is a fundamental feature of the European public order. That is apparent from the Preamble to the Convention, which establishes a very clear connection between the Convention and democracy by stating that the maintenance and further realization of human rights and fundamental freedoms are best ensured on

100. F. Sudre, 'L'*ordre public* européen' in *L'ordre public: ordre public ou ordres publics? Ordre public et droits fondamentaux*, ed. M.-J. Redor (Brussel: Bruylant, 2001), 129-131. For an in-depth analysis of the (French) praxis in this repsect, see E. FOHRER, *L'incidence de la Convention européenne des droits de l'homme sur l'ordre public international français* (Bruxelles: Bruylant, 1999).
101. E. Von Hippel, *Grenzen und Wesensgehalt der Grundrechte* (Berlin: Duncker und Humblot, 1963).
102. For more on the limitations that are set on the possibility for Contracting Parties to restrict the rights protected by the ECHR, see J. Schokkenbroek, *Toetsing aan de vrijheidsrechten van het Europees Verdrag tot bescherming van de rechten van de mens: een onderzoek naar de toetsing aan de beperkingsclausules bij de Europese vrijheidsrechten in de Europese en in de Nederlandse rechtspraak* (Zwolle: Tjeenk Willink, 1996).
103. J. Andriatsimbazovina, 'L'élaboration progressive d'un *ordre public* européen', *Cahiers de droit européen* (1997): 667.
104. F. Sudre, 'L'*ordre public* européen' in *L'ordre public: ordre public ou ordres publics? Ordre public et droits fondamentaux*, ed. M.-J. Redor (Brussel: Bruylant, 2001), 111.
105. ECtHR, 7 December 1976, *Handyside v. UK*, para. 49.
106. See in this sense: C. Picheral, *L'ordre public européen: droit communautaire et droit européen des droits de l'homme* (Paris: CERIC – Documentation française, 2001), 123-128 and 135-148; F. Sudre, 'L'*ordre public* européen' in *L'ordre public: ordre public ou ordres publics? Ordre public et droits fondamentaux*, ed. M.-J. Redor (Brussel: Bruylant, 2001), 113 et seq.; J.-F. Romain, 'L'*ordre public* (notion générale) et les droits de l'homme' in *L'ordre public: concept et applications*, ed. J.-F. Romain, M. Grégoire & V. Simonart (Bruxelles: Bruylant, 1995), 49-59.
107. ECtHR, 30 January 1998, *United Communist Party of Turkey and others v. Turkey*, para. 45.

> the one hand by an effective political democracy and on the other hand by a common understanding and observance of human rights.[108]

The Court has indeed explained that paragraphs 4 and 5 of the Preamble 'affirm that European countries have a common heritage of political tradition, ideals, freedom and the rule of law'[109] and that 'in that common heritage are to be found the underlying values of the Convention'.[110] The ECtHR has further 'pointed out several times that the Convention was designed to maintain and promote the ideals and values of a democratic society'.[111]

**I-44.** The ECtHR has furthermore explained the relationship between this concept of a democratic society and the rights guaranteed by the Convention. As:

> Articles 8, 9, 10 and 11 of the Convention require that interference with the exercise of the rights they enshrine must be assessed by the yardstick of what is 'necessary in a democratic society', the only type of necessity capable of justifying an interference with any of those rights is, therefore, one which may claim to spring from 'democratic society'[112].

According to the ECtHR[113] from the concept of a democratic society it flows that 'proceedings before the judiciary should be conducted in the presence of the parties and in public and that that fundamental principle was upheld in Article 6 of the Convention'[114]; that 'freedom of expression constitutes one of the essential foundations of a democratic society and one of the basic conditions for its progress and each individual's self-fulfilment'[115] and it 'noted the prime importance of Article 3 of Protocol No. 1, which enshrines a characteristic principle of an effective political democracy'.[116]

**I-45.** In legal literature attempts have been made to put some meat on the bones of this 'skeleton of the European public order'.[117] The first aspect is the respect for human dignity and human life, enshrined in Articles 2 and 3 of the Convention, which the ECtHR has described as 'one of the fundamental values of the democratic societies making up the Council of Europe'.[118]

---

108. ECtHR, 2 September 1998, *Ahmed and Others v. United Kingdom* (merits and just satisfaction), para. 52.
109. ECtHR, 30 January 1998, *United Communist Party of Turkey and others v. Turkey*, para. 45.
110. *Ibid.*; see also ECtHR, 7 July 1989, *Soering v. UK*, para. 88.
111. ECtHR, 30 January 1998, *United Communist Party of Turkey and others v. Turkey*, para. 45; see also ECtHR, 7 December 1976, *Kjeldsen, Busk Madsen and Pedersen v. Denmark*, para. 53; ECtHR, 7 July 1989, *Soering v. UK*, para. 87.
112. ECtHR, 30 January 1998, *United Communist Party of Turkey and others v. Turkey*, para. 45.
113. *Ibid.*
114. ECtHR, 14 November 1960, *Lawless v. Ireland* (*preliminary objections* and *questions of procedure*), 13.
115. ECtHR, 25 September 1995, *Vogt v. Germany*, para. 52.
116. ECtHR, 2 March 1987, *Mathieu-Mohin and Clerfayt v. Belgium*, para. 47.
117. F. Sudre, 'L'*ordre public* européen' in *L'ordre public: ordre public ou ordres publics? Ordre public et droits fondamentaux*, ed. M.-J. Redor (Brussel: Bruylant, 2001), 120.
118. ECtHR, 27 September 1995, *McCann v. Ireland*, para. 147; ECtHR, 7 July 1989, *Soering v. UK*, para. 88.

**I-46.** A second aspect often cited in this respect[119] is the rule of law, which the ECtHR has indeed held to be 'one of the fundamental principles of a democratic society ... , which is expressly referred to in the Preamble to the Convention' and 'from which the whole Convention draws its inspiration'.[120] The rule of law must protect against arbitrariness and therefore implies effective judicial protection, fair procedures and legality of crimes and punishments.[121]

**I-47.** The third core value encompasses pluralism, tolerance and openness.[122] This translates in the freedom of expression and the freedom of the press.[123] It also is evinced by the importance the ECtHR places on political pluralism, with free and fair elections[124] and the special position political parties have in this respect.[125] Finally it lies at the foundation of the protection of religious freedom[126] and educational freedom.[127]

**I-48.** Finally, attention must be drawn to the principle of non-discrimination,[128] which implies avoiding arbitrary distinctions which cannot be justified in a democratic society.[129] Accordingly, there is a high threshold for justifying the unequal treatment of children born out of wedlock[130] or discrimination on the grounds of sex[131] or gender.[132] To this should be added the importance of the protection of minorities.[133] Moreover, in

119. See in this respect F. Sudre, 'L'*ordre public* européen' in *L'ordre public: ordre public ou ordres publics? Ordre public et droits fondamentaux,* ed. M.-J. Redor (Brussel: Bruylant, 2001), 118; J.-F. Romain, 'L'*ordre public* (notion générale) et les droits de l'homme' in *L'ordre public: concept et applications,* ed. J.-F. Romain, M. Grégoire & V. Simonart (Bruxelles: Bruylant, 1995), 49-59.
120. ECtHR, 29 November 1988, *Brogan v. United Kingdom,* para. 58, internal quotations omitted.
121. F. Sudre, 'L'*ordre public* européen' in *L'ordre public: ordre public ou ordres publics? Ordre public et droits fondamentaux,* ed. M.-J. Redor (Brussel: Bruylant, 2001), 118.
122. See in this respect F. Sudre, 'L'*ordre public* européen' in *L'ordre public: ordre public ou ordres publics? Ordre public et droits fondamentaux,* ed. M.-J. Redor (Brussel: Bruylant, 2001), 119; J.-F. Romain, 'L'*ordre public* (notion générale) et les droits de l'homme' in *L'ordre public: concept et applications,* ed. J.-F. Romain, M. Grégoire & V. Simonart (Bruxelles: Bruylant, 1995), 49-59.
123. ECtHR, 25 September 1995, *Vogt v. Germany,* para. 52.
124. ECtHR, 2 March 1987, *Mathieu-Mohin and Clerfayt v. Belgium,* para. 47.
125. ECtHR, 30 January 1998, *United Communist Party of Turkey and others v. Turkey,* para. 46.
126. ECtHR, 26 September 1996, *Manoussakis and others v. Greece,* para 44; ECtHR, 25 May 1993, *Kokkinakis v. Greece,* para. 31.
127. ECtHR, 7 December 1976, *Kjeldsen, Busk Madsen and Pedersen v. Denmark,* para. 50. The religious freedom and the educational freedom often interact, see e.g., ECtHR, 18 December 1996, *Valsamis.*
128. F. Sudre, 'L'*ordre public* européen' in *L'ordre public: ordre public ou ordres publics? Ordre public et droits fondamentaux,* ed. M.-J. Redor (Brussel: Bruylant, 2001), 119-120.
129. EctHR, 23 July 1968, *Case 'relating to certain aspects of the laws on the use of languages in education in Belgium' v. Belgium,* para. 10.
130. ECtHR, 13 June 1979, *Marckx v. Belgium.*
131. ECtHR, 1 February 2000, *Mazurek v. France.*
132. ECtHR, 11 July 2002, *Goodwin v. UK.*
133. J.-F. Romain, 'L'*ordre public* (notion générale) et les droits de l'homme' in *L'ordre public: concept et applications,* ed. J.-F. Romain, M. Grégoire & V. Simonart (Bruxelles: Bruylant, 1995), 49-59. See also ECtHR, 17 February 2004, *Gorzelik v. Poland,* paras 89-93 where the ECtHR also makes the link between minority rights and pluralism.

a democratic welfare State it flows that certain restrictions of rights may be admissible in order to combat certain social inequities.[134]

**I-49.** On the basis of the above, the contours of a substantive *ordre public* built around the core of the ECHR comes to the fore, which puts limits to the room for manoeuvre that is left for the Parties to the Convention, both in respect of the binding force of the Convention itself and as to the margin for appreciation in the application of the Convention. The lesson for the EU seems twofold. On the one hand, it needs to be noted that a community of States having its foundation in a common treaty may indeed develop a body of rules that may properly be described as a public order. On the other hand, not at the least since the EU, though not (yet)[135] a Party to the Convention, is bound to respect the fundamental rights as enshrined in the ECHR by virtue of Article 6(3) TEU, any attempt to define a substantive content to an EU concept of *ordre public* is likely to take the catalogue drawn up in the context of the ECHR into account.

## §1.06 THE NECESSITY OF AN EU CONCEPT OF *ORDRE PUBLIC*

**I-50.** In the preceding chapters it has been argued that all founding Member States know, albeit to varying degrees, a concept of *ordre public* in their own national systems, both for internal use and for ousting certain fundamentally unwarranted external acts. These same Member States have limited some of their sovereign rights[136] upon forming the European Economic Community from which the EC and EU, and ultimately the current Union, have grown. It flows that in the areas where such transfer of sovereignty has taken place the Member States can no longer unilaterally ensure the full protection of these values that are traditionally covered by a national concept of *ordre public*. A few examples can demonstrate the point. The national concept of *ordre public international* may not be entirely accurate to be applied in the context of the Brussels Convention or the subsequent Brussels regulation.[137] Above it was already hinted that in the context of arbitration, there is an important influence of EU competition law. Finally, even as to the internal *ordre public*, new difficulties arise in the context of Union law. For instance, the question may arise whether also certain EU rules may call into question the validity of certain contracts.[138] The *lex moneta*, often seen as a crucial element of the national *ordre public économique*, has of course ceased

134. J.-F. Romain, 'L'*ordre public* (notion générale) et les droits de l'homme' in *L'ordre public: concept et applications*, ed. J.-F. Romain, M. Grégoire & V. Simonart (Bruxelles: Bruylant, 1995), 49-59.
135. As is well-known this was long impossible as it would require an amendment of the treaties, see Opinion 2/94 *ECHR* [1996] ECR I-1759. The required new legal basis was first introduced in Article I-9(2) of the Constitution and is repeated in Article 6(2) TEU in its post-Lisbon version. However, accession requires next that an international agreement be concluded and ratified setting out the conditions for accession, along the lines of the principles laid down in Protocol 8 (2010) OJ C 83/273.
136. Case 26/62 *Van Gend & Loos* [1963] ECR 1.
137. Council Regulation (EC) No 44/2001 of 22 December 2000 on jurisdiction and the recognition and enforcement of judgments in civil and commercial matters (2001) OJ L 12/1.
138. See for instance: Joined Cases C-131/04 and C-257/04 *Robinson-Steele* [2006] ECR I-2531. For more, see *infra*, at II-225 et seq.

to be a national problem in the light of the free movement of capital[139] and the introduction of the euro.[140] Or a tension may arise between national rules of criminal law, deemed to protect the public order, and the rules on free movement.[141] Furthermore, as all Member States are a party to the ECHR, the correct fulfilment of their duties under that Convention requires them to take into account the European public order as developed in the case law of the ECtHR. Accordingly, it seems almost inevitable that there is also an EU concept of *ordre public*, or at the very least an EU doctrine to set out to what extent Member States are precluded from further relying on their own concept of *ordre public*.

**I-51.** This conclusion seems to impose itself even more if we also take some structural elements of the EU construction into account. First, the EU is brought into being through international law instruments, and without having to go into a detailed discussion as to the legal personality of the Union,[142] acts on the international plane. Accordingly, the EU, too, is bound by the fundamental rules governing the international legal order as expressed in the concept of peremptory norms (*jus cogens*). Second, the example of the practice under the ECHR seems highly significant for a related reason. The development of the concept of a 'European public order' comes in the context of the creation, by a treaty expressing common values, of a community of States which guarantee each other and their citizens, the respect of certain fundamental rights under the control of a common Court.[143] The integrative force of this can hardly be underestimated. However, by the same token, the level of integration of the Parties to the Convention pales when compared to the integration process of an ever closer union among the people of Europe in the context of the European Union. Against this background of common values – including, but far from limited to those protected by the ECHR[144] – it seems almost natural to expect to find a legal translation and a legal protection of the basic options taken by the EU in respect of its political, economic,

139. Case 7/78 *Thompson* [1978] ECR I-2247.
140. Case C-359/05 *Estager* [2007] ECR I-581.
141. Case 16/83 *Prantl* [1984] ECR 1299, para. 33; Case C-158/91 *Levy* [1993] ECR I-4827; A. Puttemans, 'L'*ordre public* et la loi du 14 juillet 1991 sur les pratiques du commerce sur l'information et la protection du consommateur' in *L'ordre public: concept et applications*, ed. J.-F. Romain, M. Grégoire & V. Simonart (Bruxelles: Bruylant, 1995), 148; Cerf, A., '*Ordre public*, droit pénal et droits fondamentaux' in *L'ordre public: ordre public ou ordres publics? Ordre public et droits fondamentaux*, ed. M.-J. Redor (Brussel: Bruylant, 2001) 63-83. For more, see *infra*, at II-15.
142. For more see K. Lenaerts & P. Van Nuffel; R. Bray (ed.), *Constitutional Law of the European Union*, 2nd ed. (London: Sweet & Maxwell, 2005), 19-001 to 19-006 and the further references made therein.
143. On the importance in this context of having such a judicial organ, see B. Genevois, 'Remarques sur l'*ordre public*' in *L'ordre public: ordre public ou ordres publics? Ordre public et droits fondamentaux*, ed. M.-J. Redor (Brussel: Bruylant, 2001), 409. See also, more generally, M.L. Volcansek (ed.), *Law above Nations – Supranational Courts and the Legalization of Politics* (Gainesville: University Press of Florida, 1997).
144. In this respect it has been noted that the ECtHR has much to offer to the EU in terms of legitimation of the EU Legal order, the effectiveness of EU law and the enrichment of EU law, see A. Berramdane, 'La Cour européenne des droits de l'homme juge du droit de l'Union européenne', *Revue du Droit de l'Union européenne* (2006): 262-272.

social and even cultural order. That translation is what is commonly called *ordre public.*

**I-52.** Accordingly, at the very least it seems *possible* for the European Union to have a proper concept of *ordre public.* In light of the foregoing I would even argue it is inevitable. With Etienne Picard, reflecting on the possibility of a legal order without a concept of *ordre public* I wonder how the EU legal order could otherwise 'dispense itself from protecting, one way or another, against gaps in the formal rules or against the abuses of freedom'.[145] With Breillat, I envisage the existence of a public order which protects the institutional, political order and guarantees the social order and the exercise of fundamental rights in a democratic society as virtually self-imposing for any legal order.[146] Accordingly, the existence of a concept of *ordre public* for a European Union which, far from aspiring to become a superstate, has the clear ambition to establish a powerful political order and to guarantee the exercise of important rights in a democratic society,[147] not only seems a possibility, but a necessity.

**I-53.** Arguably, the last conclusion rests on a normative idea of what the European Union entails that goes beyond the regulatory models which are sometimes presented to describe the EU.[148] I indeed reject these models as reductionist, in that they do not justice to the fact that the EU entails a project beyond the regulation of the markets, as the ECJ has well understood when it distinguished the EC from other international trade regimes, even as sophisticated as the EEA.[149] Especially since the further development of the three pillars, the European citizenship and a unique bill of rights, the EU cannot be fairly described using the regulatory models. However, even if one were to hold on to such a limited view on the European Union the existence of a concept of *ordre public* seems inevitable. On the one hand, the Member States and the international legal order both function with a concept of *ordre public* in the background, which implies that even the most reductionist vision on the EU must at least have a theory for dealing with the claims these legal orders may pose to the EU on the basis of their concepts of *ordre public.* On the other hand, even a regulatory model has

145. E. Picard, 'Introduction générale: la fonction de l'*ordre public* dans l'ordre juridique' in *L'ordre public: ordre public ou ordres publics? Ordre public et droits fondamentaux*, ed. M.-J. Redor (Brussel: Bruylant, 2001), 21. ('[...] comment un système juridique pourrait-il se dispenser de se protéger, par un moyen ou par un autre, contre l'insuffisance des règles formelles du droit ou contre les abus de la liberté ?'
146. J. Breillat, '*Ordre public*, ordre social, ordre politique: quelles interactions?' in *L'ordre public: ordre public ou ordres publics? Ordre public et droits fondamentaux*, ed. M.-J. Redor (Brussel: Bruylant, 2001), 247-283.
147. On the importance of the principle of democracy for the EU legal order, see K. Lenaerts & T. Corthaut, 'Judicial Review as a Contribution to the Development of European Constitutionalism', in *EU Law for the Twenty-First Century: re-thinking the new legal order*, vol. I, ed. T. Tridimas (Oxford: Hart Publishing, 2004), 53-63. See also, following the entry into force of the Lisbon Treaty, Articles 2 en 10 TEU.
148. See for instance P. Lindseth, 'Democratic Legitimacy and the Administrative Character of Supranationalism: The Example of the European Community', *Columbia Law Review* (1999): 628-738.
149. Opinion 1/91 *Draft agreement relating to the creation of the EEA* [1991] ECR I-6079; see also Case 270/80 *Polydor* [1982] ECR 329, paras 15-16.

at its core, even if no other substantive value were to be acknowledged, certain fundamental organizational rules,[150] which may require public policy-like protection.

**I-54.** In light of the above, we conclude that the European Union, necessarily has a proper concept of *ordre public*. However, transposing to the level of the European Union inevitably provokes further questions ensuing from the relationship between the national legal orders and the EU legal order. In the next part, therefore, that relationship is further analysed and some methodological implications drawn.

150. See for instance F. Bignami, 'Creating European Rights: National Values and Supranational Interests', *Columbia Journal of European Law* (2005): 241-353.

CHAPTER 2

# Developing a Supranational Concept of *Ordre Public*

**I-55.** In the previous section, it was argued that some parallel can be drawn with classic international law and the legal orders of the Member States to justify the existence of an EU concept of *ordre public*. But then a series of further theoretical and methodological problems arise. It thus seems important to dig deeper into the relationship between the EU and its Member States. In this way the potential for, but also the difficulties arising from, the introduction of a concept of *ordre public* for the EU, characterized as this international organization created by its Member States establishing an autonomous legal order for the realization of an ever closer union of the people of Europe.[1] It will be argued that there may be as much as four possible relations between an EU *ordre public* and the national legal orders, each corresponding to other aspects of the EU legal order. Accordingly, first, the autonomous character of the legal order will be linked to the existence of an autonomous *EU ordre public*. Second, the likelihood of shared values is linked with some of the core articles of the EU Treaty and the concept of mutual recognition. Finally, the potential for conflict is analysed, but from two perspectives. On the one hand, there may be situations where the EU will tolerate certain expressions of the national *ordre public* without claiming it as EU *ordre public*. This is ultimately the expression of the EU motto 'united in diversity'[2] and the principle of subsidiarity. On the other hand, the cases of real conflict will be examined and linked to the principle of primacy.

---

1. Article 1 TEU.
2. Article I-8 European Constitution. Admittedly, it is to be noted that this Article is not taken up in the Reform Treaty (see to that effect the 2007 IGC-mandate Council Document 11287/07, but this has more to do with the desire of the Heads of State and Governments to remove all references to anything which may be interpreted as given the EU the character of a sovereign State, rather than a rejection of the actual message it carries. It is not unlikely that the motto, like the anthem and flag, will continue to be used irrespective of its inclusion in the basic Treaties.

## §2.01 AN AUTONOMOUS MULTI-LEVEL LEGAL ORDER

**I-56.** As is well-known the ECJ has early on characterized the European Economic Community as an autonomous legal order. As the Court explained in *Van Gend & Loos*, 'the Community is more than an agreement which merely creates rights and obligations between the contracting states'.[3] Indeed the EC Treaty 'has created its own legal system which, on the entry into force of the Treaty, became an integral part of the legal systems of the Member States and which their courts are bound to apply'.[4] As a result a new international legal order was created where the Member States have 'limited their sovereign rights'[5] and where the institutions can act independently from the Member States[6] and their acts take precedence over the internal norms of the Member States, which are thus not at liberty to deviate from them. This was deemed so important that the ECJ even considered this in itself a matter of '*ordre public communautaire*',[7] though the exact scope of that statement needs to be examined further.[8] Since then the European Community has further evolved into the hybrid structure we currently know as the European Union. This poses a double challenge. On the one hand, the question arises as to what extent what has been said in respect of the EC can be transposed to the EU. On the other hand the question arises what this means for the transposition of a concept of *ordre public* from the Member State level to a supranational body without denying on the one hand the autonomous character of the EU legal order and on the other hand the diversity of the Member States.

**I-57.** As to the position of the EU, I have in a different context already indicated that I have strong preference for a 'unity thesis'[9] in respect of the European Union.[10] With this I mean two things. First, it has as its consequence that the idea of an autonomous legal order with the ensuing concept of primacy of EC law over national law can be transferred to EU law. More fundamentally, it also implies that there is a unity of constitutional values,[11] which will make it possible to speak of a genuine EU *ordre public.*

**I-58.** The best starting point for arguing in favour of the applicability of the principle of primacy among the pillars used to be Article I-6 of the Constitution, and despite the

3. Case 26/62 *Van Gend & Loos* [1963] ECR 1.
4. Case 6/64 *Costa* [1964] ECR 585.
5. Case 26/62 *Van Gend & Loos* [1963] ECR 1.
6. K. Lenaerts, K. & P. Van Nuffel; R. Bray (ed.), *Constitutional Law of the European Union*, 2nd ed., (London: Sweet & Maxwell, 2005), 12, point 1-013.
7. Case 9/65 *San Michele v. High Authority* [1965] ECR 27, at 30.
8. See *infra*, at II-155 et seq.
9. See on this C. Herrmann, 'Much ado about Pluto? The "Unity of the Legal Order of the European Union" Revisited', *EUI Working Papers*, RSCAS 2007/05.
10. T. Corthaut, 'Doorwerking van het tweede pijlerrecht van de EU in de Belgische rechtsorde – de Belgische recher als doe-het-zelver in GBVB aangelegenheden?' in *Doorwerking van internationaal recht in de Belgische rechtsorde*, ed. J. Wouters & D. Van Eeckhoutte (Antwerpen-Oxford: Intersentia, 2006), 380-385. See also, K. Lenaerts & T. Corthaut, 'Of birds and hedges: the role of primacy in invoking norms of EU law', *European Law Review* (2006): 289-290.
11. For a unified approach to the constitutional values of the Union, see A. Von Bogdandy & J. Bast (eds.), *Principles of European Constitutional Law* (Oxford/Portland: Hart, 2007).

rather opaque treatment of the principle in the Reform Treaty, that does not change fundamentally after Lisbon.[12] In Article I-6 the Member States recognized the primacy of all EU law over national law. One could consider this as the long-awaited consummation of *Van Gend & Loos*.[13] But there is more to it. Attached to the Constitution is also a separate declaration[14] explaining that this creates nothing new and is deemed to be reflecting the case law of the ECJ and General Court.[15] This should not come as a surprise. Indeed, the same reasons that have lead the ECJ to establish the primacy of Community law, applied *mutatis mutandis* to the second and third pillar. The EU is likewise established for an indefinite period, and bestowed with own organs, which moreover coincide with the organs of the EC.[16] Similarly, the pre-Lisbon EU had, at least in a functional sense, legal personality.[17] Furthermore, the Union has practical competences, transferred to it by the Member States, which enable the Union to act in such diverse ways as adopting a common definition of terrorism,[18] imposing sanctions against third States,[19] assisting victims of crime[20] and setting up peace-keeping missions far beyond its borders after concluding international treaties solely in the name of the Union.[21] Conversely, it can thus be argued that in those areas the sovereignty of the Member States has been limited. Accordingly, it does not take much imagination to submit that the Member States have thus created a legal order which is binding upon them, even if no enforcement mechanism similar to Articles 226–228 TEC

12. T. Corthaut, 'Plus ça change, plus c'est la même chose? A Comparison with the Constitutional Treaty', *Maastricht Journal of European and Comparative Law* (2008): 22-23.
13. See in that respect T. Schilling, 'The Court of Justice's revolution: its effects and the conditions for its consummation. What Europe can learn from Fiji', *European Law Review* (2002): 445-463. Actually, it could be argued that the principle of primacy was already recognized in Amsterdam, albeit implicitly, in the second consideration of the Protocol No 30 on the application of the principles of subsidiarity and proportionality. See in this sense J.P. Terhechte, 'Temporäre Durchbrechung des Vorrangs des europäischen Gemeinschaftsrecht beim Vorliegen '"inakzeptabler Regelungslücken"?', *Europarecht* (2006): 834-835.
14. Declaration ad Article I-6 (2004) OJ C 310/440.
15. Similarly, the Declaration 17 on the primacy of EU law, attached to the Lisbon Treaty (2007) OJ C 306/256, which seem to compensate for the omission of a provision equivalent to Article I-6 in the Reform Treaty, in effect says nothing else than that the ECJ has long established the principle of primacy and that the case law of the Court will simply continue to apply as long as the ECJ does not change course.
16. Articles 3 and 5 TEU.
17. For more on the legal personality of the EU, see K. Lenaerts & P. Van Nuffel; R. Bray (ed.), *Constitutional Law of the European Union*, 2nd ed. (London: Sweet & Maxwell, 2005), 816-817; see also I. Österdahl, 'The EU and its Member States, Other States and International Organizations – The Common European Security and Defence Policy after Nice', *Nordic Journal of International Law* (2001) 350; r. Wessel , 'De Europese Unie in de internationale rechtsorde', *Mededelingen van de Nederlandse Vereniging voor Internationaal Recht* (2001): 11-37.
18. Council Framework Decision 2002/475/JHA of 13 June 2002 on combating terrorism (2002) OJ L 164/3.
19. See, for instance, Council Common Position 2003/297/CFSP of 28 April 2003 on Burma/ Myanmar (2003) OJ L 106/36.
20. Council Framework Decision 2001/220/JHA of 15 March 2001 on the standing of victims in criminal proceedings (2001) OJ L 82/1.
21. For an example, see Council Decision 2005/680/CFSP of 12 August 2005 concerning the conclusion of the Agreement between the European Union and the Democratic Republic of the Congo on the status and activities of the European Union Police Mission in the Democratic Republic of the Congo (EUPOL Kinshasa) (2005) OJ L 256/57.

was available. Moreover, in light of the duty to abstain laid down in old Article 11(2) TEU and the presence of the preliminary reference procedure in old Article 35 TEU it appears difficult to deny that the drafters of the Treaty shared the concern that the executive force of EU law 'cannot vary from one state to another in deference to subsequent domestic laws, without jeopardizing the attainment of the objectives of the Treaty'.[22] In essence this resonates with the considerations of the ECJ which read into the idea of an ever closer Union laid down in old Article 1 TEU a basis for the concept of *Unionstreue*[23] and accordingly, for the EU holds true as well that:

> it follows from all these observations that the law stemming from the Treaty, an independent source of law, could not, because of its special and original nature, be overridden by domestic legal provisions, however framed, without being deprived of its character as [EU] law and without the legal basis of the [Union] itself being called into question[24].

This reasoning still is important after the Lisbon Treaty. Whereas the pillar structure has formally been dissolved, there still are marked differences between the CFSP and non-CFSP aspects of Union law, and clear remnants of the old pillar structure in the Area of Freedom, Security and Justice. Yet, in light of the foregoing, if the Union had already reached the level of integration I have defended in the past before the entry of the Lisbon Treaty, there is no reason to argue for any lesser level thereafter.

**I-59.** Behind this lies a more fundamental sense of unity. This is strengthened by the structure of the EU Treaty in its post-Lisbon form, which contains apart from the separate rules governing the second pillar, a series of Articles with the clear vocation to apply across the three pillars. Several of these are crucial in ascertaining the underlying values of the political, social, economic and cultural order created by the EU. The Union is thus given a common calling (Article 1 TEU), common values (Article 2 TEU), common aims and objectives (Article 3 TEU) and common institutions (Article 13). Crucial for the argumentation below is the fact that the EU has pursuant to Articles 2 and 6(3) TEU a common foundation on the principles of liberty, democracy, respect for human rights and fundamental freedoms, and the rule of law, principles which are common to the Member States – and respect for these principles is indeed a requirement for membership under Article 49 TEU. They are strengthened by a series of common principles laid down in Title II of the Treaty of the Functioning of the European Union, ensuring that the common values of the Union be ingrained in its policies.

---

22. Compare Case 6/64 *Costa* [1964] ECR 1203. See, nonetheless, the concerns of AG Mengozzi in respect of the inequality in judicial protection between the Member States which results from the fact that not all Member States have enabled their courts to make preliminary rulings to the fullest extent and the ensuing consequences for the *Foto-Frost* case law, see Opinion of AG Mengozzi in Case C-354/04 P *Gestoras Pro Amestía v. Council* and Case C-355/04 P *Segi v. Council* [2007] ECR I-1579, paras 120-130. The ECJ, by contrast, stresses what is nonetheless possible in terms of preliminary references, and thus unity, in this field, see Case C-355/04 P *Segi v. Council* [2007] ECR I-1579, paras 52-55.
23. Case C-105/03 *Pupino* [2005] ECR I-5285, paras 41-43.
24. Again, compare Case 6/64 *Costa* [1964] ECR 1203.

**I-60.** Nonetheless, it is only in the final years before the entry into force of the Lisbon Treaty that the ECJ had been given the opportunity to elaborate on this interconnectedness.[25] Moreover, the Member States have long been struggling to come to terms with the ensuing consequences.[26] The breakthrough was probably the case of *Pupino*[27] in which the ECJ deduced from the common provisions of the TEU a similar concept of the duty to cooperate in good faith as laid down in Article 10 TEC. While Member States are undoubtedly right if they point out that the EU and the EC are distinct legal orders, they can no longer pretend that the two involve entirely independent spheres.[28] As Advocate General Kokott rightly points out we are increasingly confronted with a system of cross-pillarization,[29] which implies that even in making sure that the EC and EU each exercise their separate competences in their own sphere there will be a certain degree of interaction between the two legal orders.[30] The best examples in this respect are presumably the many terrorism-related cases that engulfed the Court in the wake of 9/11, with complicated cross-links in the three pillars. On the one hand, there were the classic sanction cases, aimed at foreign[31] or domestic[32] terror organizations, and thus entraining EU action under the old second viz. third pillar and concomitant action under the then Articles 60, 301 and 308 TEC. On the other hand, the saga of the Passenger Name Records demonstrate which intricate relationship arises if the EC tried to take an effective protection against terrorist threats into account in the implementation of classic EC competences in respect of transport and data management in the internal market.[33] Whether or not one agrees with the answers, these cases gave to these complex legal interactions; above all they serve as evidence of a common set of underlying values, predating the entry into force of the Lisbon Treaty, having its foundation in the rule of law and respect for fundamental rights.[34]

25. For a first overview, see C. Herrmann, 'Much ado about Pluto? The "Unity of the Legal Order of the European Union" Revisited', *EUI Working Papers*, RSCAS 2007/05, 6-11.
26. See in particular the discussion of the arguments put forward by the Member States in Opinion of AG Kokott in Case C-467/05 *Dell'Orto* [2007] ECR I-5557. Unsurprisingly, the countries which feel they have most to lose and are thus most skeptical are the UK and Ireland. The potential for cross-referencing between the pillars may induce these countries to reconsider their limited approach towards the jurisdiction of the ECJ under Article 35.
27. Case C-105/03 *Pupino* [2005] ECR I-5285.
28. Opinion of AG Kokott in Case C-467/05 *Dell'Orto* [2007] ECR I-5557, paras 40-49.
29. See in this respect C. Herrmann, 'Much ado about Pluto? The 'Unity of the Legal Order of the European Union' Revisited', *EUI Working Papers*, RSCAS 2007/05, 6.
30. Opinion of AG Kokott in Case C-467/05 *Dell'Orto* [2007] ECR I-5557, paras 40-49.
31. Joined Cases C-402/05 P and C-415/05 P *Kadi v. Council* [2008] ECR I-6351, at the instigation of the UN Security Council and Case T-228/02 *Organization des Modjahedines du peuple d'Iran v.* Council [2006] ECR II-4665 (see also the follow-up cases Case T-256/07 *People's Mojahedin Organization of Iran v. Council* [2008] ECR II-3019 and Case T-284/08 *People's Mojahedin Organization of Iran v. Council* [2008] ECR II-3457), where the EU was acting of its own motion.
32. Case C-354/04 P *Gestoras Pro Amestía v. Council* [2007] ECR I-1579; Case C-355/04 P *Segi v. Council* [2007] ECR I-1657.
33. Joined Cases C-317/04 and C-318/04 *European Parliament v. Council and Commission* [2006] ECR I-4721.
34. See, for instance, the transparency concerns in Case C-266/05 P *Sison v. Council* [2007] ECR I-1233 and the genuine concern in respect of judicial protection in Case T-253/02 *Ayadi v. Council* [2006] ECR II-2139 and Case C-354/04 P *Gestoras Pro Amestía v. Council* [2007] ECR I-1579; Case C-355/04 P *Segi v. Council* [2007] ECR I-1657. See also, the respect for the administrative rights in Case T-228/02 *Organization des Modjahedines du peuple d'Iran v.*

**I-61.** As a counter-weight to all this unifying pressure, it is important, however, to also recognize the other side of the spectrum. The EU has obviously not replaced the Member States, who remain, albeit usually within certain margins drawn by EU law, competent in some of the most value-driven areas, such as family law,[35] education,[36] health care[37] or taxation.[38] The result is a, deliberately wanted, variance in national approaches and values, as expressed in the Union's motto 'united in diversity'[39] and the principle of subsidiarity. In that respect, I share the view of Sweeney that the relationship between the EU and its Member States 'is not one of conflict, nor does diversity amount to relativism'.[40] The term subsidiarity:

> suggests a degree of loyalty to or (at least) a relationship with a central norm whereas relativism challenges the application of the norm outright. The internalization and normalization of questions about commonality and fragmentation, about 'European' identity and national public policies, becomes a reflection of the EU's nature.[41]

As a result the EU legal order does not merely condone diversity; part of its essence is that it manages to give it a place as part of that legal order. In that respect the Lisbon Treaty, following the outlines of the European Constitution, does an excellent job in expressing this 'normative background, which values diversity, subsidiarity and a dynamic approach to European identity and national public policies'.[42] Of course the post-Lisbon EU treaty sums up 'European values', quite explicitly even in Article 2 TEU. Yet, as important are the constant reminders of the diversity component. The EU motto 'united in diversity' of Article I-8 of the Constitution, though not as such reproduced in the Lisbon Treaty, and the principle of subsidiarity, at least in its competence function, laid down in Article 5 TEU were already mentioned above. But there is also Article 3(3) TEU which *inter alia* requires the EU 'to respect its rich cultural and linguistic diversity, and [to] ensure that Europe's cultural heritage is safeguarded and enhanced' and Article 4(2) which states that 'The Union shall respect the equality of Member States before the Treaties as well as their national identities, inherent in

*Council* [2006] ECR II-4665 and even stronger in Case T-47/03 *Sison v. Council* [2007] ECR II-73* and Case T-327/03 *Stichting Al-Aqsa* [2007] ECR II-79*. The most disappointing case in this series, however, is the pyrrhic victory of the European Parliament, effectively foreclosing effective judicial review of the privacy concerns surrounding the PNR-agreement in Joined Cases C-317/04 and C-318/04 *European Parliament v. Council and Commission* [2006] ECR I-4721.

35. Case C-148/02 *Garcia Avello* [2003] ECR I-11613.
36. Case C-147/03 *Commission v. Austria* [2005] ECR I-5969.
37. Case C-372/04 *Watts* [2006] ECR I-4325.
38. Case C-446/03 *Marks & Spencer* [2005] ECR I-10837.
39. Article I-8 European Constitution. See in this sense also M. Avbelj, '*European Court of Justice and the Question of Value Choices* – Fundamental human rights as an exception to the freedom of movement of goods', Jean Monnet Working Paper 06/04, 10. See, in the context of taxation, K. Lenaerts, '"United in Diversity": also *In Fiscalibus* ?', in *A Vision of Taxes within and outside European Borders' – Festschrift in honor of Prof. Dr Frans Vanistendael*, ed. L. Hinnekens & P. Hinnekens (The Hague: Kluwer Law International, 2008), 617-634.
40. J.A. Sweeney, 'A "Margin of Appreciation" in the Internal Market: Lessons from the European Court of Human Rights', *Legal Issues of Economic Integration* (2007): 41.
41. *Ibid.*
42. *Ibid.*

their fundamental structures, political and constitutional, inclusive of regional and local self-government.'[43] It is, however, submitted that this inherent respect for diversity was already animating the treaties before the entry into force of the Lisbon Treaty as well,[44] whereas the Lisbon Treaty brings these values even more to the fore by incorporating all these elements with the exception of the formal adoption of the motto.

## §2.02 EU *ORDRE PUBLIC* AND NATIONAL *ORDRE PUBLIC*: FOUR SCENARIOS

**I-62.** The inherent tension in the idea of 'united in diversity' brings with it that there are potentially four different possibilities for the relationship between the *ordre public* of the Member States and the EU *ordre public*. First, there is a small category of EU specific *ordre public*, even though often there is some analogy possible with related national concepts. Second, there is an important part of the *ordre public* that is shared between the Member States and the EU. Third, there is a part of the national *ordre public* which is linked to a certain Member State, but which the EU is willing to tolerate, and occasionally even to accommodate. Finally, it cannot be excluded that part of the national *ordre public* is incompatible with the demands of EU membership. Each of these four categories reveals another aspect of the relationship between the EU and its Member States or among the various Member States.

**I-63.** The first category concerns this part of the *ordre public* which is particular to the EU. The idea is that the EU as a separate legal order has certain unique institutions and functions that surpass the legal orders of the Member States. Nonetheless, a certain analogy with national concepts may direct us in identifying some of these aspects. On

43. The Court has picked up on these new values quite quickly, see Case C-208/09 *Sayn Wittgenstein* [2010] ECR I-0000, para. 92, even though the Court is not willing to let it be used to justify any deviation from established Union law, such as equal treatment of part-time workers, even though judges may sometimes be subject to special requirements inherent in their function, see Case C-393/10 *O'Brien* [2012] ECR I-0000, para. 49.

44. In this respect some restraint in the use of the word subsidiarity may be in place. I agree with Florian Sander that currently major difficulties exist in enforcing the subsidiarity principle *sensu stricto, i.e.*, in its function of limiting the extent to which the EU may exercise its competence; moreover, it remains to be seen whether this would change with the introduction of the renewed protocol on subsidiarity and proportionality – see in this respect F. Sander, 'Subsidiarity infringements before the European Court of Justice: futile interference with politics or a substantial step towards EU federalism?', *Columbia Journal of European Law* (2006): 517-571. However, as will be illustrated with many examples below, the case law of the ECJ demonstrates an increasing sensitivity for subsidiarity in the broad sense: the respect for local values and institutions in the face of EU law. Most examples in this respect, such as Case C-36/02 *Omega Spielhallen* [2004] ECR I-9609 deal with moral and cultural issues. However, there are also institutional examples, such as the evolving case law on the standing of regional authorities before the General Court under Article 263(4), see e.g., Joined Cases T-366/03 and T-235/04 *Land Oberösterreich and Austria v. Commission* [2005] ECR II-4005 and the way the ECJ seems willing to reconcile the state aid rules with the policy autonomy of certain constitutionally autonomous regions, see Case C-88/03 *Portugal v. Commission* [2006] ECR I-7115 and Joined Cases C-428/06 to C-434/06 *Unión General de Trabajadores de la Rioja* [2008] ECR I-6747.

the one hand, there are the institutional aspects. One of the functions of the *ordre public* is to protect the political foundations of society. This may translate in certain EU specific rules of *ordre public* character. First, it cannot be excluded that the EU, just like Member States develop the concept of certain 'offences against the State', develop similar measures to protect the EU institutions, for instance making certain attacks on the EU institutions or its Members a separate offence. So far, the EU has, however, not done so. Nonetheless, the development of an own list of terrorist organizations above and beyond the list developed by individual Member States or the UN may be seen in this light.[45] The Union has, moreover, taken measures for the physical protection of public figures[46] and has instructed the Member States to take stock of critical infrastructure.[47] More day to day, however, is the *ordre public* character of the basic rules concerning the functioning of the institutions. The rules on competence and the essential procedural requirements are systematically deemed to be of *ordre public* by the ECJ, with the result that their violation may be raised ex officio by the ECJ.[48]

**I-64.** On the other hand, there are also certain substantive rules which, though a few of those have some equivalent in the national legal order, have a very particular EU position. In this context I have in mind four sets of rules, only for some of which the *ordre public* character has been cleared out. All relate to areas of EU competence where the EU offers an added value beyond the individual Member States and all will be elaborated on below. First, and analogous to national concepts of *ordre public*, there is the protection of the *lex moneta* in respect of the euro. The protection of the euro, as a stable and trustworthy currency, which is an exclusive EC competence, forms a central aspect of the economic *ordre public*, enforced through criminal law,[49] and where the primacy of EC law prevents interference by the Member States.[50] Second, there is the protection of the fundamentals of the intra-Community competition, another aspect of

45. See Council Common Position on the application of specific measures to combat terrorism (2001) OJ L 344/93, as since updated and amended. For the implications of this approach of going alone in terms of judicial protection, see Case C-355/04 P *Segi v. Council* [2007] ECR I-1657, with Opinion of AG Mengozzi and Case T-228/02 *Organization des Modjahedines du peuple d'Iran v. Council* [2006] ECR II-4665.
46. Council Decision 2002/956/JHA of 28 November 2002 setting up a European Network for the Protection of Public Figures (2002) OJ L 333/1.
47. Council Directive 2008/114/EC of 8 December 2008 on the identification and designation of European critical infrastructures and the assessment of the need to improve their protection (2008) OJ L 345/75.
48. On these aspects of the *legalité externe*, see Case C-367/95 P *Commission v. Sytraval and Brink's France* [1998] I-1719; see also K. Lenaerts, D. Arts, & I. Maselis; R. Bray (Ed.), *Procedural Law of the European Union*, 2nd ed. (London: Sweet & Maxwell, 2006), 288-289, point 7-122. For a critique see Opinion of AG Jacobs in Case C-210/98 P *Salzgitter v. Commission and Germany* [2000] ECR I-5843, paras 125 et seq. For more on this, see *infra*, at II-191 et seq. For a model that seeks to take that critique seriously, see, *infra*, part V.
49. Council Decision 2005/511/JHA of 12 July 2005 on protecting the euro against counterfeiting, by designating Europol as the Central Office for combating euro counterfeiting (2005) OJ L 185/35; Council Framework Decision of 29 May 2000 on increasing protection by criminal penalties and other sanctions against counterfeiting in connection with the introduction of the euro (2000) OJ L 140/1.
50. Case C-359/05 *Estager* [2007] ECR I-581. Implicitly the recognition of the *lex moneta* as part of the *ordre public* can also be derived from Case 7/78 *Thompson* [1978] ECR I-2247. For more, see *infra*, at III-75 et seq.

the economic *ordre public*,[51] Indeed, Articles 101 and 102 TFEU have repeatedly been deemed to rank among the rules of *ordre public*.[52] Third, and closely related, in line with Advocate General Geelhoed, the same regime applies in respect of the fundamentals of the rules on state aid.[53] Fourth, I will argue below that the essence of the free movement, at least of persons, deserves similar protection. In that respect, there is one aspect in particular that in my view needs to rank among the EU specific rules of *ordre public*, namely the recognition of EU citizenship,[54] not only because of the idealistic maxim *civis europeus sum*,[55] but also because of the fundamental impact EU citizenship may have on a person's status.[56]

**I-65.** The second category concerns shared aspects of the *ordre public* of the EU and its Member States. In the previous chapter, I argued extensively that the concept of *ordre public* as developed by both the Member States and the ECtHR has a particular place reserved for the protection of fundamental rights. As is well-known, the EU is 'founded on the principles of liberty, democracy, respect for human rights and fundamental freedoms, and the rule of law', values which are said to be common to the Member States[57] and respects in particular the 'fundamental rights as guaranteed by the European Convention for the Protection of Human Rights and Fundamental Freedoms and as they result from the constitutional traditions common to the Member States, as general principles of the Union's law'.[58] The same concern for a common foundation in fundamental rights protection, moreover, lies at the core of Article 7 TEU and the accession criteria of Article 49 TEU. Accordingly, it is not a stretch of the imagination to submit that these basic principles and the respect for fundamental rights are at the core of an *ordre public* that both the Member States and the EU share.

**I-66.** This common foundation is of crucial importance for the effective functioning of the European Union. In a sense, it is the cornerstone upon which the concept of mutual recognition is founded. These observations become particularly important in the

51. Joined Cases C-204/00 P, C-205/00 P, C-211/00 P, C-213/00 P, C-217/00 P en C-219/00 P, *Aalborg Portland A/S et alia v. Commission* [2004] ECR I-123, para. 91
52. Case C-126/97 *Eco Swiss China Time* [1999] ECR I-3055, paras 31-41; Joined Cases C-295/04 to C-298/04 *Manfredi* [2006] ECR I-6619, para.31.
53. Opinion of AG Geelhoed in Case C-119/05 *Lucchini Siderurgica* [2007] ECR I-6199, para. 62. For more, see *infra*, at III-79.
54. Though formally not based on the *ordre public* character of the EU citizenship and free movement rules, see nonetheless the willingness of the ECJ to go beyond the scope of the questions asked in the order for reference if an issue of citizenship or free movement of workers may help the national judge apply EU law, see Case C-392/05 *Alevizos* [2007] ECR 3505, para. 64.
55. Opinion of AG Jacobs in Case C-168/91 *Konstantinidis* [1993] ECR I-1191, para. 46.
56. See in this respect Opinion of AG Jacobs in Case 96/04 *Standesamt Stadt Niebüll* [2006] ECR I-3561; Case C-148/02 *Garcia Avello* [2003] ECR I-11613 and Case C-353/06 *Grunkin and Paul* [2008] ECR I-7639. See, however, *contra*, Afdeling bestuursrechtspraak Raad van State, Nr. 200308607/1, 2 March 2004. For more, see *infra*, at III-54 et seq.
57. Article 2 TEU. Since the Lisbon Treaty, these values, originally laid down in old Article 6(1) TEU, are moreover said to be common to Member States 'in a society in which pluralism, non-discrimination, tolerance, justice, solidarity and equality between women and men prevail'.
58. Article 6(3) TEU. See already old Article 6(2) TEU.

context of the development of the concept of mutual recognition beyond the sphere of the four freedoms.[59] A prelude in this respect was *Krombach* involving the recognition of a civil judgment rendered in other Member States in violation of Article 6 ECHR.[60] However, the rapidly evolving case law in respect of the mutual recognition of judgments in criminal matters makes all this acute. Currently, the case law[61] focuses mainly on the application of the *ne bis in idem* principle laid down in Articles 54–58 of the Convention implementing the Schengen Agreement (CISA).[62] As Advocate General Ruiz-Jarabo Colomer makes clear, the mutual recognition of judgments in criminal matters requires that the whole European Union can be seen as a 'common house' based on fundamental rights,[63] and where the criminal courts have sufficient trust in each other workings that even if the second court would reach other results than the first (foreign) court had, the former will refrain from a substantive reanalysis.[64] The debate, however, does not end with the CISA. A shared foundation based in fundamental rights is also necessary for the new developments of European criminal law, such as the European Arrest Warrant[65] and the European Confiscation Orders.[66] In respect of the former, the ECJ has indeed recognized how it is conceived 'in the light of the high degree of trust and solidarity between the Member States',[67] which seems justified as the ECJ does not fail to observe that both the EU and its Member States are bound in full by the relevant human rights provisions when issuing or implementing a

---

59. For some brief, but interesting observations on the interaction between harmonization, mutual trust and the area for freedom, security and justice (dubbed under reference to Jonathan Faull as 'the new internal market'), see B. Drijbe, 'Interne markt en publieke voorzieningen: een schijntegenstelling', *Sociaal-Economische Wetgeving* (2007): 264.
60. Case C-7/98 *Krombach* [2000] ECR I-1935. See in this sense also M. Fichera & C. Janssens, 'Mutual recognition of judicial decisions in criminal matters and the role of the national judge, *ERA Forum* (2007): 180-181.
61. For a recent overview of the key cases, see B. Van Bockel, 'Case C-436/04, *Criminal Proceedings against Léopold Henri Van Esbroeck*, Judgment of the Court of Justice of 9 March 2006, Second Chamber [2006] ECR I-2333; Case C-150/05, *Jean Leon Van Straaten v. Netherlands and Italy*, Judgment of the Court of Justice of 28 September 2006, First Chamber [2006] ECR I-2333; Case C-467/04, *Criminal Proceedings against G. Francesco Gasparini, José Ma L.A. Gasparini, G. Costa Bozzo, Juan de Lucchi Calcagno, Francesco Mario Gasparini, José A. Hormiga Marrero, Sindicatura Quiebra*, Judgment of the Court of Justice of 28 September 2006, First Chamber [2006] ECR I-9199.', *Common Market Law Review* (2008): 223-244.
62. Convention implementing the Schengen Agreement (CISA) of 14 June 1985 between the Governments of the States of the Benelux Economic Union, the Federal Republic of Germany and the French Republic on the gradual abolition of checks at their common borders (2000) OJ L 239/19 (CISA).
63. Opinion of AG Ruiz-Jarabo Colomer in Case C-150/05 *Van Straaten* [2006] ECR I-9327, para 61.
64. *Ibid.*, para 61. This is even so, when the foreign court had dismissed the issue because of a procedural bar to prosecution, such as a statute of limitation, see Case C-467/04 *Gasparini* [2006] ECR I-9199, with the far more reserved Opinion of AG Sharpston, or when the legal interests protected by the foreign criminal law differ from the legal interests protected by the law of the second state to prosecute, see Case C-288/05 *Kretzinger* [2007] ECR I-6441, paras 31-33.
65. Council Framework Decision 2002/584/JHA of 13 June 2002 on the European arrest warrant and the surrender procedures between the Member States (2002) OJ L 190/1.
66. Council Framework Decision 2006/783/JHA of 6 October 2006 on the application of the principle of mutual recognition to confiscation orders (2006) OJ L 328/59.
67. Case C-303/05 *Advocaten voor de Wereld* [2007] ECR I-3633, para. 57. For a practical application, see Case C-66/08 *Kozłowski* [2008] ECR I-6041.

European Arrest Warrant.[68] With the foregoing, I do not submit, however, that a common human rights background is also a sufficient condition for mutual recognition in criminal matters. Yet, addressing further legitimacy concerns, relevant as they may be, goes beyond the scope of this book.[69]

**I-67.** The third category is reserved for various aspects of the national *ordre public* of individual Member States. As seen in the preceding paragraphs a major part of the substantive *ordre public*, in particular when related to fundamental rights, is shared between the Member States and the Union. However, at times individual Member States put forward certain interests as essential, which the EU may tolerate, or even respect, but which do not carry a similar fundamental weight at EU level. This is a crucial insight. In order to reconcile the national identities of the various Member States with the effectiveness of EU law, at times a compromise is struck, albeit on the terms of the EU. Within limits the various Member States are allowed to develop their own concept of *ordre public*. This national concept of *ordre public* may then be invoked to limit the effect of the application of EU law, especially in the context of free movement law. It has been argued above that a common concept of *ordre public* is a necessary condition for mutual recognition. Yet, this third category of *ordre public*, by setting limits to that principle, serves to demonstrate that it may not be a sufficient condition. However, it is important to note that ultimately, the EU remains in the driver seat. As will be argued below, the ECJ effectively takes on the task of assessing the weight the national concern carries, and it cannot be excluded that some aspects of the national *ordre public* cannot be tolerated. In this sense a 'margin of appreciation' is created for the Member States, even though the EU remains firmly in command, in a way not dissimilar to the way the ECtHR applies that concept.[70]

**I-68.** Two cases serve to illustrate the point. First, the Irish abortion issue. As is well-known, the ECJ dodged the bullet on the restrictive Irish abortion policy by holding that the distribution of leaflets by a student organization informing women of the possibilities for abortions in the UK did not come within the scope of the free movement of services. With no restriction to be justified, an appeal on the *ordre public*

68. Case C-303/05 *Advocaten voor de Wereld* [2007] ECR I-3633, paras 45 and 53. It is, however, to be noted that various constitutional courts seem to disagree. Especially the European Arrest Warrant case of the Bundesverfassungsgericht (judgment of 18 July 2005, 2 BvR 2236/04) contains language that undermines very much this essential mutual trust. The negative results of this approach were rapidly visible, with national courts (e.g., the Spanish *Audencia Nacional* in Madrid) refusing the applicability of the EAW to Germany for want of reciprocity. For more, see the excellent analysis of the judgments of the German, Polish and Czech constitutional courts by J. Komárek, 'European Constitutionalism and the European Arrest Warrant: in Search of the Limits of "Contrapunctual Principles"', *Common Market Law Review* (2007): 9-40. See also M. Fichera, 'The European Arrest Warrant and the Sovereign State: A Marriage of Convenience?', *European Law Journal* (2009): 70-97.

69. For a good assessment, see V. Mitsilegas, 'The constitutional implications of mutual recognition in criminal matters in the EU', *Common Market Law Review* (2006): 1277-1311. See also R. Barents, 'De denationalisering van het strafrecht', *Sociaal-Economische Wetgeving* (2006): 358-374.

70. In this sense, J.A. Sweeney, 'A "Margin of Appreciation" in the Internal Market: Lessons from the European Court of Human Rights', *Legal Issues of Economic Integration* (2007): 27-52.

was superfluous.[71] However, Advocate General Van Gerven, having reached the opposite conclusion as to the applicability of the free movement of services,[72] did need to consider whether a prohibition on distributing this type of information could be justified in light of the special constitutional importance of the right to life of the unborn child.[73] It is important to see that in that respect he does three things. First, he clarified that it is for the ECJ, and thus the EU legal order, to assess whether a certain 'imperative requirement' could be admitted.[74] This goes to my point that cases like this one do not undermine the primacy of EU law, but are well-considered relaxations by the EU of its own rules in order to accommodate the diversity among the Member States. Second, the Advocate General then indeed accepts that the Irish constitutional regime in respect of the life of the unborn amounts to such a mandatory requirement, but even then still a proportionality test must be fulfilled.[75] Third, the restriction is moreover tested in light of the freedom of speech. In this way, the Advocate General ensures that the freedom of speech, which unlike the abortion ban is a common value of both the EU and Ireland,[76] is not overlooked – even though he finds the measure also justified under that heading.[77]

**I-69.** A more recent example of this tolerance for a Member State's very particular *ordre public* is offered by the case of *Omega Spielhallen.*[78] In this case the mayor of Bonn had issued an order prohibiting the applicant from offering at its amusement hall a laser game, imported from the UK, during which players use laser guns to shoot at tags placed on their opponent bodies. The mayor had defended this ban by referring to the public policy, in particular because the German concept[79] of 'human dignity'[80] which

71. Case C-159/90 *Society for the Protection of Unborn Children Ireland* [1991] ECR I-4685.
72. Opinion of AG Van Gerven in Case C-159/90 *Society for the Protection of Unborn Children Ireland* [1991] ECR I-4685, para. 16-21.
73. Article 40.3.3 of the Irish Constitution read at the time 'The State acknowledges the right to life of the unborn and, with due regard to the equal right to life of the mother, guarantees in its laws to respect, and, as far as practicable, by its laws to defend and vindicate that right.'
74. Opinion of AG Van Gerven in Case C-159/90 *Society for the Protection of Unborn Children Ireland* [1991] ECR I-4685, para. 23.
75. *Ibid.*, paras 25-29.
76. See in that respect, more recently, Case C-112/00 *Schmidberger* [2003] ECR I-5659. The Advocate General pioneered in that respect the approach to be taken up by the ECJ in the same year in Case 260/89 *Elliniki Radiophonia Tiléorassi* [1991] ECR I-2925 as to the possibility for the ECJ to assess the compatibility of mandatory requirements raised by the Member States with the fundamental rights, discarding to that effect the more restrictive approach of Joined Cases 60 and 61/84 *Cinéthèque* [1985] ECR 2605.
77. Opinion of AG Van Gerven in Case C-159/90 *Society for the Protection of Unborn Children Ireland* [1991] ECR I-4685, point 38.
78. Case C-36/02 *Omega Spielhallen* [2004] ECR I-9609. For an almost identical case involving the free movement of goods (*in casu* the sale of video media in Germany which have not been examined and classified by the competent authority for the purpose of protecting children and which do not bear a label from that authority indicating the age from which they may be viewed), see Case C-244/06 *Dynamic Medien* [2008] ECR I-505.
79. On the German concept of human dignity, see J. Jones, 'Common Constitutional Traditions: Can the Meaning of Human Dignity under German Law Guide the European Court of Justice?', *Public Law* (2004): 167-187. See also C. Smith & T. Fetzer, 'The uncertain limits of the European Court of Justice's authority: economic freedom versus human dignity', *Columbia Journal of European Law* (2004): 449-454.

is inviolable and thus in principle not allow for any exception or compromise opposes the mock killing of real individuals. The problem was that, though the concept of human dignity is obviously not unknown to EU law, as evidenced by the *biotechnology* case[81] and by Article 1 of the Charter of Fundamental Rights, the concept is not as well-developed and also unlikely to be as demanding as the German concept.[82] Accordingly, the ECJ had to decide whether the local German authorities could rely on their concept of human dignity to justify an obstacle to the free movement of services. The ECJ had previously accepted in *Schmidberger*[83] that protection of fundamental rights recognized and shared by the Community could justify restrictions to intra-Community trade, but Advocate General Jacobs had in that same case rightly warned that 'It cannot...be automatically ruled out that a Member State which invokes the necessity to protect a right recognized by national law as fundamental nevertheless pursues an objective which as a matter of Community law must be regarded as illegitimate'.[84] The ECJ thus had to convince itself that the German constitutional norm is not totally alien to the Union, while staying alert not to canonize the German interpretation of the concept as the EU concept of human dignity. The latter would have been tantamount of suggesting that the UK authorities are in a sense inhumane, and thus technically in breach of old Article 6(1) TEU, by allowing this game on the market, while all those authorities do is acting in accordance with the UK value concept, which hardly seems out of touch with most other Member States that seem to react rather indifferently to this form of entertainment. Moreover, taking over the German position as the EU concept, would also jeopardize the margin left to the EU legislator, if harmonization in this field were to be considered.[85] The solution was again found in allowing for a locally diverse moral reading of the public policy exception of the then Article 46 TEC (now Article 52 TFEU). One the one hand, the ECJ satisfied itself that the concept of human dignity is indeed not alien to the EU legal order.[86] However, it also

80. For a broader analysis of the concept of 'human dignity', see D. Feldman, 'Human Dignity as a Legal Value – Part I', *Public Law* (1999): 683-702 and D. Feldman, 'Human Dignity as a Legal Value – Part II', *Public Law* (2000): 61-76
81. Case C-377/98 *Netherlands v. European Parliament and Council* [2001] ECR I-7079.
82. For comparisons see J. Jones, 'Common Constitutional Traditions: Can the Meaning of Human Dignity under German Law Guide the European Court of Justice?', *Public Law* (2004): 167-187. See also C. Smith & T. Fetzer, 'The uncertain limits of the European Court of Justice's authority: economic freedom versus human dignity', *Columbia Journal of European Law* (2004): 449-459. Smith and Fetzer aptly describe the EC concept as 'hardly less mysterious than a distant star in the night sky; it exists, but few of us know much else about it' (*id.*, at 458).
83. Case C-112/00 *Schmidberger* [2003] ECR I-5659.
84. Opinion of AG Jacobs in Case C-112/00 *Schmidberger* [2003] ECR I-5659, para. 98.
85. In that respect is to be noted that following *Omega Spielhallen*, some in Germany apparently want to go further and impose also a prohibition on violent computer games. See in this respect X, 'Legislative attempts to criminalize violent computer games', *Screen.Shot – the Legal Newsletter for the Games Industry*, February 2007. In those circumstances, the distortion of the internal market may become sufficiently appreciable as to warrant the attention of the EU legislator. On such occasion, the EU legislator should itself be allowed to work out an appropriate level of protection, without being taken hostage by the German concept of human dignity. On harmonization as a tool for policing the internal market, see *infra*, at II-102 et seq.
86. Compare, more recently, Case C-208/09 *Sayn-Wittgenstein* [2010] ECR I-0000, para. 89 where the Court is very explicit in this exercise of linking the national value, with an EU value: 'The European Union legal system undeniably seeks to ensure the observance of the principle of

made it clear that the German concept does not enjoy of this same consensus. Yet, consensus is not required for the application of the public policy exception, so that Germany could lawfully determine for its own territory its own level of protection. The ECJ was moreover quick to add that this also implied that the proportionality test was met, as nothing short of a full ban could assure that this level is effectively attained.

**I-70.** The Court's approach in *Omega Spielhallen* has been the subject of extensive analysis in the legal literature.[87] Though criticism has been levelled at almost every step of the judgment, ranging from its choice for services over goods,[88] over the use of the public policy exception,[89] to its application of the proportionality test,[90] I am of the opinion that the approach by the ECJ was fundamentally sound. It allowed for an important local constitutional norm to be applied, at some cost to the Community, without exporting however the German moral judgment to the entire Community. That being said, I submit nonetheless that the ECJ should have made it clearer that it is indeed still in the driving seat. In particular, the ECJ should in cases like these only defer to the national constitutional norms if the following conditions are satisfied, for

equal treatment as a general principle of law. That principle is also enshrined in Article 20 of the Charter of Fundamental Rights. There can therefore be no doubt that the objective of observing the principle of equal treatment is compatible with European Union law'. The Court, however, must be quite subtle in doing so, because it can of course not imply that the Union shares the Austrian aversion to nobility, without upsetting a number of other Member States.

87. See, *inter alia*, T. Ackerman, 'Case C-36/02, *Omega Spielhallen- und Automatenaufstellungs-GmbH v. Oberbürgermeisterin der Bundesstadt Bonn*, Judgment of the Court of Justice (First Chamber) of 14 October 2004, nyr', *Common Market Law Review* (2005): 1107-1120; A. Alemanno, 'A la recherche d'un juste équilibre entre libertés fondamentales et droits fondamentaux dans le cadre du marché intérieur – Quelques réflexions à propos des arrêts «Schmidberger» et «Omega»', *Revue du Droit de l'Union Européenne* (2004): 709-751; J. Bröhmer, 'Zulässige Untersagung eines Tötungsspiels', *Europäische Zeitschrift für Wirtschaftsrecht* (2004): 753-757; K. Bulterman & H. R. Kranenborg, 'What if rules on free movement and human rights collide? About laser games and human dignity: the Omega case', *European Law Review* (2006): 93-101; G. Chu, ''Playing at Killing' Freedom of Movement', *Legal Issues of Economic Integration* (2006): 85-94; R. De Lange, 'The European Public Order, Constitutional Principles and Fundamental Rights', *Erasmus Law Review* (2007): 3-24; J. Jans, 'Zaak C-36/02, Omega Spielhallen- und Automatenaustellungs-GmbH t. Oberbürgermeisterin der Bundesstadt Bonn', *Sociaal-Economische Wetgeving* (2005): 183-186; J. Morijn, 'Balancing Fundamental Rights and Common Market Freedoms in Union Law: Schmidberger and Omega in the Light of the European Constitution', *European Law Journal* (2006): 15-40; C. Semmelmann, 'Die Menschenwürde als "Spielverderberin"?', *European Law Reporter* (2004): 414-416; D. Simon, '*Ordre public* et «jouer à tuer»', *Europe – Revue Mensuelle du Jurisclasseur*, (December 2004): 19-21; I. Streho, 'Cour de justice, 14 octobre 2004, *Omega*', *Revue des affaires européennes* (2003-2004): 681-685; G. Toggenburg, 'Grundrechte, Grundfreiheiten, Grund zum Nachfragen anlässlich der Rechtssache Omega', *European Law Reporter* (2005): 2-6.

88. C. Semmelmann, 'Die Menschenwürde als "Spielverderberin"?', *European Law Reporter* (2004): 414-415; D. Simon, '*Ordre public* et «jouer à tuer»', *Europe – Revue Mensuelle du Jurisclasseur* (December 2004): 20.

89. For rather critical assessments on this point, see in particular J. Jans, 'Zaak C-36/02, Omega Spielhallen-und Automatenaustellungs-GmbH t. Oberbürgermeisterin der Bundesstadt Bonn', *Sociaal-Economische Wetgeving* (2005): 183-186; see also G. Chu, '"Playing at Killing" Freedom of Movement', *Legal Issues of Economic Integration* (2006): 91-93.

90. G. Chu, '"Playing at Killing" Freedom of Movement', *Legal Issues of Economic Integration* (2006): 93-94.

which I develop on the remarks by Advocate General Jacobs in *Schmidberger,*[91] but also on various concerns raised in the literature.

**I-71.** First, the ECJ should, as it did in *Omega Spielhallen,*[92] assess whether the constitutional norm invoked is not alien to the EU legal order. Cases will be rare where a constitutional norm is completely foreign to the EU, but it should not be wholly inconceivable.[93] In the latter case, the ECJ will have to analyse whether this constitutional norm is not incompatible with the EU legal order. AG Jacobs refers in this respect to the case where a preference is given to the own nationals and thus seems to argue that the ECJ should carry out a non-discrimination test while assessing the legitimacy of the national constitutional norm.[94]

**I-72.** However, even if the norm is not unknown to the EU, the ECJ should secondly check whether the invoked norm is not in tension with other fundamental rights recognized in the EU legal order, most notably in the Charter.[95] An example may clarify the point. Imagine that a Member State imposes a teaching ban on gay persons, arguing that it aims to protect the rights of the child and family life, thus preventing a teacher from another Member State from taking up work in that Member State. Assuming that this would qualify as a restriction to the free movement of workers,[96] the ECJ would have to analyse the justification put forward. The protection of family life and the right of the child are obviously not alien to the EU,[97] and it does not discriminate on the basis of nationality. However, that by itself should not be enough to buttress the acceptability of the local norm. Closer scrutiny should reveal, though, that the Charter of Fundamental Rights of the EU also prohibits discrimination on the ground of sexual orientation.[98] Accordingly, unless the national norm can be balanced with this other

91. Case C-112/00 *Schmidberger* [2003] ECR I-5659, with Opinion of AG Jacobs. See also F. Jacobs, 'Human Rights in the European Union: the role of the Court of Justice', *European Law Review* (2001): 331-341.
92. Case C-36/02 *Omega Spielhallen* [2004] ECR I-9609, paras 33-35.
93. M. Avbelj, '*European Court of Justice and the Question of Value Choices* – Fundamental human rights as an exception to the freedom of movement of goods', Jean Monnet Working Paper 06/04, 66-67.
94. Opinion of AG Jacobs in Case C-112/00 *Schmidberger* [2003] ECR I-5659, para. 97.
95. Compare in this respect the third step in the analysis of AG Van Gerven in Case C-159/90 *Society for the Protection of Unborn Children Ireland* [1991] ECR I-4685, point 38, outlined, *supra*, at I-68, where he assessed whether the ban on distributing flyers for abortion services, would not only serve a legitimate aim, strongly protected by the national legal order, but also whether it would be compatible with the freedom of expression.
96. One could of course object that this ban is fully indistinctly applicable and not more burdensome for foreigners as it is for locals, but in the light of the market access approach displayed in Case C-413/93 *Bosman* [1995] ECR I-4921, it seems not impossible that the ECJ would find a restriction of the free movement.
97. One may think of Articles 7 (respect for private and family life), 9 (right to marry and right to found a family), 14(3) (The freedom to found educational establishments with due respect for democratic principles and the right of parents to ensure the education and teaching of their children in conformity with their religious, philosophical and pedagogical convictions, in accordance with the national laws governing the exercise of such freedom and right) and 24 (rights of the child) of the Charter of Fundamental Rights of the European Union.
98. Article 21 Charter of Fundamental Rights of the European Union. See also, regardless of the Charter, Case C-267/06 *Tadao Maruko* [2008] ECR I-1757.

fundamental value the justification put forward by the Member State, even though not alien to the EU legal order, should be rejected as illegitimate.[99]

**I-73.** Third, the ECJ should also ensure that a 'consistency test'[100] is carried out. If we are to accept that strongly held local values may at times trump the EU legal order, we must be certain that these beliefs are really held that strongly. The ECJ has done so in the past in the context of gambling. The Court had found in *Schindler* that:

> it is not possible to disregard the moral, religious or cultural aspects of lotteries, like other types of gambling, in all the Member States. The general tendency of the Member States is to restrict, or even prohibit, the practice of gambling and to prevent it from being a source of private profit.[101]

Yet, in later cases the ECJ made it clear that if a Member State is in reality not seeking to protect the public from gambling, this justification would fall apart.[102] As this assessment requires factual elements, it is best left to the national court, but the ECJ should not forget to flag it for the national court. In this respect, the dictum in *Omega Spielhallen*, which in this respect notably deviates from the formula used by Advocate General Stix-Hackl, can rightly be criticized as unduly complacent.[103] Indeed, one only

---

99. It could be remarked that if the ECJ had undertaken this exercise explicitly in Case C-36/02 *Omega Spielhallen* [2004] ECR I-9609, also in that case some tension could have been revealed, as the ban on the laser game may well also interact with the freedom of expression and the right of property. However, balancing of these concerns, which I thus explicitly see as a duty for the ECJ, as it is the only way to ensure that in the case of fringe constitutional values the EU legal order is not embarrassed by the local bias, would probably not have resulted in discrediting the human dignity exception.
100. M.K. Bulterman & H.R. Kranenborg, 'What if rules on free movement and human rights collide? About laser games and human dignity: the Omega case', *European Law Review* (2006): 98.
101. Case C-275/92 *Schindler* [1994] ECR I-1039, para. 60.
102. See first, somewhat hesitant, in Case C-67/98 *Zenatti* [1999] ECR I-7289 and Case C-243/01 *Gambelli* [2003] ECR I-13031 and with some impatience in Joined Cases C-338/04, C-359/04 and C-360/04 *Placanica* [2007] ECR I-1891, where AG Ruiz-Jarabo Colomer was even arguing for a full liberalization of the gambling market, see M. Ruttig, 'Das *Placanica*-Urteil des EuGH: Kein 'rien ne va plus' aus Luxemburg', *Zeitschrift für Gemeinschaftsprivatrecht* (2007) 114-117. However, the most recent string of cases in the wake of Case C-42/07 *Liga Portuguesa de Futbol* [2009] ECR I-7633 makes it clear that Member States continue to enjoy a broad margin of appreciation when it comes to how they deal with gambling, see for instance Case C-212/08 *Zeturf* [2011] ECR I-0000 and Case C-347/09 *Dickinger and Ömer* [2011] ECR I-0000, provided the consistency requirement is respected, see e.g., Case C-153/08 *Commission v. Spain* [2009] ECR I-9735.
103. See in this sense G. Toggenburg, 'Grundrechte, Grundfreiheiten, Grund zum Nachfragen anlässlisch der Rechtssache Omega', *European Law Reporter* (2005): 6. That being said, I am not convinced that 'judicial subsidiarity' as Toggenburg calls it should be controlling. It may indeed be that judicial subsidiarity may come at the expense of substantive subsidiarity, i.e., there is a risk that by instructing the national court to again scrutinize the fundamental character of the constitutional value relied upon, the impression is aroused that at the end of the day allowing the national legal order to upheld its constitutional value is something of an anomaly, which the EU is not willing to grant whole-heartedly. See in this sense C. Brown, 'Case C-112/00, *Eugen Schmidberger, Internationale Transporte und Planzüge v. Austria*. Judgment of 12 June 2003, Full Court', *Common Market Law Review* (2003): 1508 ('even if the restriction is ultimately justified, it remains something which is at its heart "wrong", but tolerated'). Yet, in terms of true substantive subsidiarity it should be clear that if a Member State norm or value passes the test outlined above that there is no reason to look down on the national application of that norm to the case at bar.

needs to think of other extreme sports such as paintball or violent computer games to realize that the moral outrage that is about to be allowed to hamper intra-Community trade may well have been far too selective to require deference.[104]

**I-74.** Lastly, and somewhat intertwined[105] with the foregoing, the ECJ should still ensure proportionality. However, as there is no such thing as the principle of proportionality,[106] it is important to see that if we truly want to embrace 'unity in diversity' and thus accept that at times local values may trump EU law, the correct test cannot lie in the least restrictive means test, as this would inevitably result in a new round of bargaining and compromise at the expense of the local value that we are willing to preserve.[107] This does not mean, as is sometimes argued, that in the case of sensitive moral or ethical issues proportionality does not apply.[108] Rather, as the ECJ rightly observes in *Omega Spielhallen* 'the need for, and proportionality of, the provisions adopted are not excluded merely because one Member State has chosen a system of protection different from that adopted by another State',[109] so that if the level of protection the Member State seeks to achieve cannot be compromised nothing short of a total ban may be acceptable. It has been observed[110] in this respect that the discretion left to the Member States is far less limited when the Member State seeks to protect a fundamental right, such as in the *Schmidberger*[111] situation, than when it seeks to restrict such a right, such as in *Carpenter.*[112]

---

104. The ECJ in Case C-36/02 *Omega Spielhallen* [2004] ECR I-9609 did notice this issue of selectivity for it remarks at para. 39, when analysing proportionality, that 'by prohibiting only the variant of the laser game the object of which is to fire on human targets and thus "play at killing" people, the contested order did not go beyond what is necessary in order to attain the objective pursued by the competent national authorities.' However, though proportionality and consistency are not unrelated this goes to prove that they should nonetheless be distinguished. The selectivity indeed means that the effect on intra-Community trade will indeed be marginal, and thus make it likely for the measure to be found proportionate. However, precisely in these cases of selective moral outrage it should first be established whether they carry enough weight to allow them to trump the EU legal order.
105. On this relationship, see J.A. Sweeney, 'A "Margin of Appreciation" in the Internal Market: Lessons from the European Court of Human Rights', *Legal Issues of Economic Integration* (2007): 44.
106. For an overview, see G. De Burca, 'The Principle of Proportionality and its Application in EC Law', *Yearbook of European Law* (1993): 105 et seq.
107. See in this sense M.K. Bulterman & H.R. Kranenborg, 'What if rules on free movement and human rights collide? About laser games and human dignity: the Omega case', *European Law Review* (2006): 100–101
108. See in this sense S. O'Leary & J.M. Fernandez-Martin, 'Judicially Created Exceptions to the Free Provision of Services' in *Services and Free Movement in EU Law*, ed. A. Andenas & W. Roth (Oxford: OUP, 2001), 192.
109. Case C-36/02 *Omega Spielhallen* [2004] ECR I-9609, para. 38. In this respect I disagree with Chu that 'the ECJ essentially renders the whole attempt at applying the "proportionality" principle, in particular the element of "necessity" meaningless', see G. Chu, '"Playing at Killing" Freedom of Movement', *Legal Issues of Economic Integration* (2006): 94.
110. A. Egger, 'EU-Fundamental Rights in the National Legal Order: The Obligations of Member States Revisited', *Yearbook of European Law* (2006): 539.
111. Case C-112/00 *Schmidberger* [2003] ECR I-5659.
112. Case C-60/00 *Carpenter* [2002] ECR I-6279.

**I-75.** With my decisional scheme I thus distance myself from any approach that stresses the universality of fundamental rights or any claim as to the applicability of the 'highest' common standard to the EU.[113] I clearly put forward that, despite the fact that there is a basic commonality in the approach to fundamental rights and other basic societal values at EU level, room for every Member State to draw its own 'fundamental boundaries'[114] must exist. To that extent, I follow the tracks of Weiler[115] Jacobs[116] and Avbelj.[117] However, I do not fully follow them as to the institutional consequences of that approach. I accept that the ECJ may have a role to play in virtually all circumstances where fundamental rights are being invoked together with EU law, including, and that is usually the battle line,[118] in instances where the Member State has derogated from EU law. For me *ERT*[119] is good law. To that extent I gladly take over the definition by Egger as to the scope of EU human rights protection:

> To sum up, Member States must respect fundamental rights in applying primary law, including derogations, and regulations, in transposing directives and framework decisions, [while] adopting national rules which supplement regulations and in applying national law which falls within the scope of Community law[120].

The reason for doing so is in the obvious need to draw a balance. Weiler forcefully argues that every society sets its own 'fundamental boundaries',[121] and it is argued that the ECJ should avoid too much interference with that.[122] I agree, but I would nuance that by joining the EU all Member States added a new set of 'fundamental boundaries', some of which, however, they cannot police themselves. My four-prong test outlined above seeks to make sure that the national fundamental boundary is taken seriously. In that respect there is, in terms of judicial subsidiarity and with a view of engaging in a serious judicial dialogue between the national and EU level, a crucial role for national courts: when referring a case to the ECJ involving a national societal value, the national

113. For such an approach based on a common maximum standard, see L. Besselink, 'Entrapped by the Maximum Standard: On Fundamental Rights, Pluralism and Subsidiarity in the European Union', *Common Market Law Review* (1998): 629-680.
114. The term is coined by J. Weiler, 'Fundamental Rights and Fundamental Boundaries: On Standards and Values in the Protection of Human Rights' in *The European Union and Human Rights*, ed. N. Neuwahl & A. Rosas (Den Haag: Nijhoff, 1995), 51-76
115. *Ibid.*
116. F. Jacobs, 'Human Rights in the European Union: the role of the Court of Justice', *European Law Review* (2001): 331-341.
117. M. Avbelj, '*European Court of Justice and the Question of Value Choices* – Fundamental human rights as an exception to the freedom of movement of goods', Jean Monnet Working Paper 06/04.
118. For an extensive discussion, see A. Egger, 'EU-Fundamental Rights in the National Legal Order: The Obligations of Member States Revisited', *Yearbook of European Law* (2006): 515-553.
119. Case 260/89 *Elliniki Radiophonia Tiléorassi* [1991] ECR I-2925.
120. A. Egger, 'EU-Fundamental Rights in the National Legal Order: The Obligations of Member States Revisited', *Yearbook of European Law* (2006): 522.
121. J. Weiler, 'Fundamental Rights and Fundamental Boundaries: On Standards and Values in the Protection of Human Rights' in *The European Union and Human Rights*, ed. N. Neuwahl & A. Rosas (Den Haag: Nijhoff, 1995), 55.
122. T. Ackermann, 'Case C-36/02, *Omega Spielhallen- und Automatenaufstellungs-GmbH* v. *Oberbürgermeisterin der Bundesstadt Bonn*, Judgment of the Court of Justice (First Chamber) of 14 October 2004, nyr', *Common Market Law Review* (2005): 1117.

court must clearly explain what the real nature of the national 'fundamental boundary' is. But this does not exclude a role for the ECJ. As explained, the ECJ must check whether the value, which it thus should take very seriously, is nonetheless legitimate in the EU legal order by checking whether it does not tread back on the minimum consensus of the Charter (e.g., by 'overlooking' other important rights) or by being wholly incompatible with the EU rights and obligations (e.g., by being openly discriminating on the grounds of nationality or by pursuing purely economic interests). No national court alone can fully ensure any of those two points, so there must be a role for the ECJ in patrolling those common fundamental boundaries the Member States have accepted but are incapable of fully guarding themselves. Yet, in my view, this does not imply a denial of the other, nationally defined 'fundamental boundaries'. To the contrary, as the discussion of the proportionality test makes clear, once the balance struck at the national level is legitimate from an EU perspective, that balance is taken very seriously. Member States will not be asked to compromise any further as to the level of protection they seek. As a consequence a total ban on laser games even for well-informed consenting adults to protect the national fundamental boundary as to human dignity is for instance not out of bounds. One of the reasons[123] which make it attractive to use the 'public policy exception' in free movement cases as the vessel for raising fundamental rights is that the ECJ can clearly indicate to what extent it imposes EU boundaries and to what extent it defers to the national balance.[124] By invoking the public policy exception, which gets a differing national content in every Member State,[125] the ECJ can clearly flag that its final answer is not a definite answer as to the way the balance is to be struck across the EU, but merely indicates what the (wide) margin of appreciation is that is left to the Member State – but only after it has first drawn the red lines of EU constitutional law, in particular the fundamental rights

123. An additional advantage is the fact that it also solves the problem that fundamental rights are not listed as such as mandatory requirements in the Treaty, which can be invoked as a justification for discriminatory restrictions to the four freedoms. Through the public policy exception also, discriminatory restrictions can be justified. Accordingly, it may also not be necessary to decide whether the national measure is discriminatory or not, which also in respect of *Omega Spielhallen* was not self-evident, see J. Jans, 'Zaak C-36/02, Omega Spielhallen- und Automatenaustellungs-GmbH t. Oberbürgermeisterin der Bundesstadt Bonn', *Sociaal-Economische Wetgeving* (2005): 186.

124. In a similar vein, T. Ackermann, 'Case C-36/02, *Omega Spielhallen- und Automatenaufstellungs-GmbH v. Oberbürgermeisterin der Bundesstadt Bonn*, Judgment of the Court of Justice (First Chamber) of 14 October 2004, nyr', *Common Market Law Review* (2005): 1117.

125. In this respect I do not share the criticism by Avbelj, repeated by Morijn, that the concept of public policy is 'conceptually different' from fundamental rights as it is based on 'collectivism' said to be proper to the French *ordre public*. Though there are also some 'collectivist' elements in that concept, the discussion of the national concepts of *ordre public* above offers quite some indications that also fundamental rights can be reconciled with the French concept of *ordre public*. For the criticism, see M. Avbelj, '*European Court of Justice and the Question of Value Choices* – Fundamental human rights as an exception to the freedom of movement of goods', Jean Monnet Working Paper 06/04, 60-62; J. Morijn, 'Balancing Fundamental Rights and Common Market Freedoms in Union Law: Schmidberger and Omega in the Light of the European Constitution', *European Law Journal* (2006): 39.

protection. In some cases, such as *Schmidberger,*[126] a reference to public policy is hardly necessary to the extent that the values asserted are so much in line with the EU core – but even there it could have served a purpose in further bolstering the margin of appreciation left to the Member State. Yet, when a more unusual national value is at stake, the concept of *national* public policy, and the EU limits to that (which I consider in turn to be part, if not the quintessence, of the *EU ordre public*) serves well in at the same time affirming the EU values and allowing the expression of a national value. It truly is taking 'unity in diversity' very seriously.

**I-76.** The foregoing indicates that the EU is capable of accommodating the diverging value concepts any of its Member States may have. However, it should also be clear that the EU does not need to swallow just anything. In light of the strong common background of the Member States it ought to be extremely rare that the value judgments of the EU and the Member States are so much incompatible as causing an inevitable conflict. Yet, this type of conflict cannot be rejected out of hand.

**I-77.** Actually, two different problems may arise. The first one builds further on the foregoing. As argued above, following Advocate General Jacobs, an objective pursued by a Member State may nonetheless be considered illegitimate at EU level.[127] Above an attempt was made at drawing up a checklist for the Court to enable it to assess whether or not a prima facie diverging national value may nonetheless require EU deference. In the two real cases discussed above, *Grogan*[128] and *Omega Spielhallen,*[129] the national value survived scrutiny. However, the fictitious example of a homophobic measure serves to demonstrate that the ECJ may be able to unmask a measure as illegitimate. In those cases, the national rule should fall as a matter of primacy of EU law, irrespective of its constitutional rank.[130] Other examples that have been mooted in legal literature are constitutional preferences for own nationals, e.g., in respect of property and the special protection of animal welfare of animals in the Slovenian Constitution.[131]

126. Case C-112/00 *Schmidberger* [2003] ECR I-5659. However, this was the solution proposed by AG Jacobs in that case. For criticism, see M. Avbelj, '*European Court of Justice and the Question of Value Choices* – Fundamental human rights as an exception to the freedom of movement of goods', Jean Monnet Working Paper 06/04, 60-62; J. Morijn, 'Balancing Fundamental Rights and Common Market Freedoms in Union Law: Schmidberger and Omega in the Light of the European Constitution', *European Law Journal* (2006): 39.
127. Opinion of AG Jacobs in Case C-112/00 *Schmidberger* [2003] ECR I-5659, paras 97-98.
128. Case C-159/90 *Society for the Protection of Unborn Children Ireland* [1991] ECR I-4685 with Opinion of Advocate General Van Gerven.
129. Case C-36/02 *Omega Spielhallen* [2004] ECR I-9609.
130. This does not say anything, however, as to whether all Member States courts will be willing to also uphold the primacy of EU law when a fundamental national value is at stake. For more on the delicate balancing act that may ensue, see for instance J. Komárek, 'European Constitutionalism and the European Arrest Warrrant: in Search of the Limits of "Contrapunctual Principles"', *Common Market Law Review* (2007): 9-40.
131. M. Avbelj, '*European Court of Justice and the Question of Value Choices* – Fundamental human rights as an exception to the freedom of movement of goods', Jean Monnet Working Paper 06/04, 23.

However, I am not convinced that the latter would fail the EU legitimacy test,[132] if its application would also remain within the bounds of what is proportionate.[133]

**I-78.** So far I have described this type of conflict as one between the EU and its Member States. However, it could well be argued that this type of conflict is better analysed as a horizontal conflict between the Member States to be solved using 'deliberative supranationalism' rather than primacy.[134] Indeed, virtually all examples involve issues of free movement and thus instances where the value judgment of one Member State conflicts with that of the Member State where a certain product or service is prohibited. Nonetheless, when 'uncommon national norms'[135] are being put forward by a Member State, the analysis outlined above turns the issue into a conflict between the EU and a Member State, as in my analysis, the ECJ must assess whether the value asserted by the Member State is legitimate *as a matter of EU law*, in particular in light of the Charter of Fundamental Rights.

**I-79.** Moreover, there is also a second scenario, which truly involves a vertical conflict. The most spectacular example of such a conflict may arise when the EU legislator is to impose something which would go against the *ordre public* of some of its Member States. To the extent that the Member States through the Council control the legislator, this should be a rare occurrence. Yet, decision-making is increasingly taken by qualified majority voting, so it cannot be excluded that occasionally a Commission proposal slips through which seeks to impose such a change. Actually, it seems that currently just such a piece of legislation is being envisaged. In its green paper on damages actions for breaches of the EC antitrust rules,[136] the Commission proposes to introduce the award of punitive damages. This, however, is clearly contrary to the *ordre public* of several Member States.[137] Yet, if the Commission plans were to become

132. In this respect attention can be drawn to the introduction by the Lisbon Treaty of the new Article 13 TFEU, a provision on animal welfare, 'since animals are sentient beings'.
133. In that respect attention may be drawn to the diverging outcome of two cases involving the protection of the constitutional language. Admittedly, the ECJ has treated neither of them as a matter of public policy. However, as will be argued *infra*, at III-107 et seq., maybe it should have. One possible explanation of the difference between Case C-379/87 *Groener* [1989] ECR 3967, where it was accepted that an art teacher could be required to know the official constitutional language (Irish), and the total disregard for the special linguistic regime in Belgium in Case C-369/89 *Piageme* [1991] ECR I-2971 and Case C-84/94 *Piageme* [1995] ECR I-2955, may well be because the ECJ did not feel the Belgian linguistic balance truly implicated by the labels on bottles of mineral water.
134. C. Joerges, 'Rethinking European Law's Supremacy with Comments by Damian CHALMERS, Rainer NICKEL, Florian RÖDL, Robert WAI', EUI Working Papers Law No 2005/12. For an application of this model, see also C. Joerges & F. Rödl, 'Informal Politics, Formalized Law and the "Social Deficit" of European Integration: Reflections after the Judgments of the ECJ in *Viking* and *Laval*', *European Law Journal* (2009): 1-19.
135. J. Morijn, 'Balancing Fundamental Rights and Common Market Freedoms in Union Law: Schmidberger and Omega in the Light of the European Constitution', *European Law Journal* (2006): 35.
136. Commission Green Paper, Damages actions for breach of the EC antitrust rules, COM(2005) 672 final.
137. See in that respect J. Gotanda, 'Charting Developments Concerning Punitive Damages: Is the Tide Changing?', *Villanova School of Law Working Papers Series*, 2006/65, 18-20, and the reactions on the green paper by the competition authorities of, *inter alia*, Germany, Finland,

law, these Member States will have to accept this new remedy in their legal order. As a side effect, those Member States will also be precluded from refusing, because of public policy concerns, to recognize any award of such damages in competition cases rendered in another Member States under Regulation 44/2001.[138] In fact, as a further spill-over effect, doubts can be raised as to whether the public policy exception could then still be successfully invoked as a bar to recognition and execution of judgments awarding punitive damages outside competition cases. In any event, in these cases the national constitutional values may hardly be a bar to the application of EU law. At best they may serve to colour the interpretation of the EU act at issue,[139] but to the extent that the EU act applies it takes precedence and displaces any contrary national rule.[140]

## §2.03 CONCLUSION

**I-80.** In this chapter, it has been argued that an autonomous EU concept of *ordre public* can be developed. This concept has undoubtedly its roots in the constitutional traditions of the Member States. Yet, it cannot be deemed to coincide with any one such set of values. First, some of its elements, though often not unknown to the national level, get a unique content at the EU level. Second, the EU has developed its unique set of values, which often allow for the accommodation of diverging constitutional values of the individual Member States, but which in the final analysis may come in direct conflict with contrary national values, a conflict which from the perspective of the EU requires that the national rule will fall.

**I-81.** In the course of the argumentation above the contours of this EU concept of *ordre public* start to appear. In the following Parts, a more thorough analysis will be made of what values are protected and what the consequences are of considering something as part of the EU *ordre public*. However, before taking up this task, it seems useful to pause at some methodological issues, which should help us to define the EU concept of *ordre public* in a more rigorous manner. This will be done in the final chapter of this first Part.

---

Ireland, Lithuania, Norway and Romania, <http://ec.europa.eu/comm/competition/antitrust/actionsdamages/green_paper_comments.html>, 10 May 2012. See also AIPPI – Finnish Group, report Q186, *Punitive damages as a contentious issue of Intellectual Property Rights*, available at <http://www.docstoc.com/docs/52796545/Punitive-damages-as-a-contentious-issue-of-Intellectual-Property>, 10 May 2012.

138. See Article 34(1) of Council Regulation (EC) No 44/2001 of 22 December 2000 on jurisdiction and the recognition and enforcement of judgments in civil and commercial matters (2001) OJ L 12/1.
139. See for instance the stretched interpretation of Article 3(1) of Regulation 1612/68 to accommodate the Irish language policy in Case C-379/87 *Groener* [1989] ECR 3967.
140. Case C-84/94 *Piageme* [1995] ECR I-2955.

CHAPTER 3

# Some Methodological Observations on Determining the Content and Limits of the EU Concept of *Ordre Public*

**I-82.** The first two chapters of Part I have drawn an image of a rather fragmented concept of *ordre public* with its roots in national and international law, and with a content that is in constant tension with the legal orders of the 27 Member States of the Union. It is against this background that we will try to ascertain in the following Parts what the content of the EU *ordre public* is *de lege lata* and what role it has to play in the EU legal order. However, before setting off on this course, it seems useful to have a final look at some of these formal aspects of *ordre public*, as they both affect the methodology of the research, with a strong reliance on the case law of the ECJ, and (thus) qualify the validity of the findings. These issues are the subject of this third and final Chapter.

**I-83.** The first set of formal aspects – and with formal I denote aspects which refer to the nature of the EU *ordre public* and determine its content but do not coincide with that content – is the direct consequence of the foregoing. It has been argued above that the EU *ordre public* does not coincide with any national concept. Accordingly, our analysis will need to have an eye for two competing tendencies. On the one hand, as we set out to analyse the EU *ordre public* strong emphasis should be laid on the demands put by the EU legal order to the concept of EU *ordre public* and the role it has to play in that particular legal order. On the other hand, the concept is bound to be restrained by the need to protect the role and identity of the individual Member States. The former will require us to analyse in detail the specific roles the concept of *ordre public* plays in the EU context (*infra*, Part II) and the nature of the interests that are protected by it (*infra*, Part III). Both are primarily determined by the Treaties, but are only made concrete in the case law of the Court. Accordingly, the best way to determine the content of EU *ordre public* seems to be by identifying the various headings under which *ordre public* may play a role in the EU context, taking into account the lessons from the short overview above of the national and international role of the concept, and then to look at the various manifestations across the case law of the ECJ. The latter basically brings us back to the inherent tensions in any federal construct[1] and will thus require further development on the relationship between the EU and its Member States and the various techniques to overcome such conflict (*infra*, Part IV).

**I-84.** Second, the additional challenge is to find a way to resolve these tensions against the background of a coherent legal system. In that respect I agree with Baquero Cruz that 'the very attempt to study the gaps of a certain branch of the law presupposes the need for a rationally ordered and comprehensive legal system'.[2] Alexy[3] explains that legal research has three components, an empirical component ('what is valid and effective law, including legislation and case law'), an analytical component ('how is the law built, including conceptual, structural and systematic considerations') and a normative component ('how should the law be, looking for the correct solutions to legal problems').[4] All three dimensions are interwoven in this research. Whereas Parts II and III will seek to determine what is linked to the EU *ordre public*, Parts IV and V seek to restructure that information in the light of the larger legal order, the outcome of which is to be tested through a short case study on same-sex marriage. The most important aspect, 'the *opus proprium* of legal science', is nonetheless the analysis.[5] As I indicated in the introduction,[6] I find the most attractive way for obtaining this, a quasi-Dworkinian analysis, a search for the rules and principles that best 'fit' the construct of the European Union and thus best explain and predict the way a balance can be struck in what may often be hard cases involving aspects of the EU *ordre public*. This book is, of course, not meant to be a full treatise on the constitutional order of the European Union. But even without developing a new handbook on EU constitutional law, the constitutional importance and implications of the EU *ordre public* as a European concept of *ordered liberty*[7] need to be made sufficiently explicit. Accordingly,

1. It must be recalled that 'federal' should not be read as referring to any claim to European statehood, but solely in the sense of a legal system in which the exercise of some of the competences of the sub-entities is being exercised at a common level, while others are reserved to them; in the case of 'integrative federalism' such as in the case of the EU, it refers to 'a constitutional order that strives at unity in diversity among previously independent or confederally related component entities' – see K. Lenaerts, 'Constitutionalism and the Many Faces of Federalism, *American Journal of Comparative Law* (1990): 206. Understood in this sense 'federalism, as a means of structuring the relationship between interlinked authorities, can be used either within or without the framework of a nation-state', see K. Lenaerts, 'Federalism: Essential Concepts in Evolution – the Case of the European Union', *Fordham International Law Journal* (1998): 748. See also, E. Young, 'Protecting Member State Autonomy in the European Union: Some Cautionary Tales from American Federalism', *New York University Law Review* (2002): 1641-1642.
2. J. Baquero Cruz, *Between competition and free movement: the economic constitutional law of the European Community* (Oxford: Hart, 2002), 5.
3. R. Alexy, *Theorie der Grundrechte* (Frankfurt am Main: Suhrkamp, 1985), 24-27; R. Alexy, *A Theory of Legal Argumentation* (Oxford: Clarendon, 1989), 250-256.
4. J. Baquero Cruz, *Between competition and free movement: the economic constitutional law of the European Community* (Oxford: Hart, 2002), 4.
5. *Ibiddem*, 4-5, referring to Alexy.
6. *Supra*, at 6-7.
7. Compare: *Palko v. Connecticut*, 302 U.S. 319, 58 S.Ct. 149, 82 L.Ed. 288 (1937).

I attempt to develop a model of EU *ordre public* that takes these various constitutional layers into account (*infra*, Part V).

**I-85.** A third factor to be taken into account is the variability of the notion of *ordre public*. It is indeed argued[8] that the content of the concept of *ordre public* varies over time and place.[9] Above we have already seen how the EU legal order seems nonetheless capable to strike a balance despite value differences among the various Member States or between the Member States and the Union.[10] Nonetheless, this factor causes a major problem for any attempt to determine the content of the EU *ordre public*. The answer to this challenge is three-fold. First, it is appropriate to simply acknowledge this as true. Any statement as to the content of the EU *ordre public* is indeed made within the confines of the current EU borders and reflects the political, social, ethical, economic and cultural opinions of our times. Any attempt to 'list' the content of the EU *ordre public* is thus likely to be somewhat arbitrary and in any event at best a snap shot of current praxis. However, this in itself does not make the effort meaningless. Social change may occur rapidly, but rarely the *basic* political, social, ethical, economic and cultural choices are overrun overnight. At the very least some valuable tendencies for the foreseeable future can be deduced. Moreover, even if such an overview might appear outdated in a few years – or, more likely, decades – time, at least it could still serve as yardstick to assess change. Second, there are counter-indications as to this changing content.[11] The EU by its own constitutive treaty is 'founded on the principles of liberty, democracy, respect for human rights and fundamental freedoms, and the rule of law', principles which are common to the Member States.[12] These are malleable terms, yet all but the strongest relativist, would admit that each of these terms has some kind of core meaning. If anything the EU *ordre public* should at least encompass this immutable core, this *noyau dur*.[13] This does not need to contradict any thesis as to the context-dependency of the content of a concept of *ordre public*. It does, however, again argue strongly in favour of the position that barring a cataclysmic revolutionary change in the EU constitutional fabric, at least some important pointers as to the content of the

8. For an outspoken defence of this thesis, see J. Ghestin, 'L'*ordre public*, notion à contenu variable, en droit privé français' in *Les notions à contenu variable en droit*, ed. C. Perelman & R. Van Der Elst (Bruxelles: Bruylants, 1984), 77 et seq.
9. For a comparative study in support of this argument, see A. Meinertzhagen-Limpens, 'Quelques aspects de l'*ordre public* en droit comparé' in *L'ordre public: concept et applications*, ed. J.-F. ROMAIN, M. Grégoire & V. Simonart (Bruxelles: Bruylant, 1995), 232-249.
10. *Supra*, Part I, Chapter 2.
11. See in this sense, J.-F. Romain, 'L'*ordre public* (notion générale) et les droits de l'homme' in *L'ordre public: concept et applications*, ed. J.-F. Romain, M. Grégoire & V. Simonart (Bruxelles: Bruylant, 1995), 30-31. Romain is of course treating the subject from a national perspective, but the same reasons apply equally at the EU level. See also, E. Picard, 'Introduction générale: la fonction de l'*ordre public* dans l'ordre juridique' *L'ordre public: ordre public ou ordres publics? Ordre public et droits fondamentaux*, ed. M.-J. Redor (Brussel: Bruylant, 2001), 23-28.
12. Article 2 TEU. See also K. Lenaerts, 'Federalism: Essential Concepts in Evolution – the Case of the European Union', *Fordham International Law Journal* (1998): 750.
13. On the idea of a *noyau dur* at the centre of the *ordre public*, and the possibility of defining it, see A.-C. Van Gysel & J.-F. Romain, 'Conclusions générales: l'*ordre public* entre hétérogénéité en homogénéité' in *L'ordre public: concept et applications*, ed. J.-F. Romain, M. Grégoire & V. Simonart (Bruxelles: Bruylant, 1995), 310-312.

EU *ordre public* can safely be formulated. Third, part of the analysis does not concern as much the content, but the process. The argumentation above, as to how the ECJ should deal with an unusual national constitutional value,[14] is not dependent on an immutable EU yardstick. Rather it seeks to describe a method how a balance can be struck between the evolving needs of the EU legal order, and the equally evolving national value-patterns.[15]

**I-86.** This last counter-argument brings us to the role of the judge in finding the law, and thus also in finding these aspects of the law that are so fundamental as to qualify as part of the *ordre public.*[16] In the context of the European Union this leads us in particular back to the role of the European Court of Justice in finding the law. The development of a full theory on finding the law in the EU legal order, covering the details on everything from the relevant interpretative techniques[17] to the development of EU federal common law,[18] of course goes beyond the reach of this research. Nonetheless, it is appropriate to make some remarks on how the ECJ finds the law.[19] This is all the more necessary because I agree with Alexy that the *Richterperspektive* is the primary perspective of the law as *praxis.*[20] This does not exclude other perspectives, but it is in the solution of legal problems from the perspective of the judge that the law shows its primary nature. This in turn seems to validate my choice for a quasi-Dworkinian approach, with its inherent bias in favour of a constantly evolving body of case law.

**I-87.** Three aspects that make the role of the ECJ in finding the law, somewhat different from what classic Member States courts do, deserve special attention. First, the ECJ develops its case law in dialogue with national courts. Second, attention needs to be drawn on the special role of comparative law in finding an acceptable and effective solution. Third, something needs to be said on autonomous law making by the ECJ, the EU variety of *federal common law.*

14. *Supra*, at I-71 to I-86.
15. On the time-sensitiveness of the EU *ordre public*, see also C. Kessedjian, 'Public Order in European Law', *Erasmus Law Review* (2007): 28.
16. On the role of the judge in determining the *ordre public*, see in particular J. Breillat, '*Ordre public*, ordre social, ordre politique: quelles interactions?' in *L'ordre public: ordre public ou ordres publics? Ordre public et droits fondamentaux*, ed. M.-J. Redor (Brussel: Bruylant, 2001), 263 et seq.
17. For a general overview of the ECJ's methods of interpretation, see H.G. Schermers & D. Waelbroeck, *Judicial Protection in the European Union*, 6th ed. (Deventer: Kluwer, 2001), 10-27, §§ 20-52. See also N. Fennelly, 'Legal interpretation at the European Court of Justice', *Fordham International Law Journal* (1997): 656-679. An excellent illustration can be found in the Opinion of AG Ruiz-Jarabo Colomer in Case C-262/06 *Deutsche Telekom* [2007] ECR I-10057, paras 29-46.
18. See on this the impressive article by K. Lenaerts & K. Gutman, '"Federal Common Law" in the European Union: a Comparative Perspective from the United States', *American Journal of Comparative Law* (2006): 1-122.
19. For a more elaborate discussion, see K. Lenaerts & T. Corthaut, 'Rechtsvinding door het Hof van Justitie', *Ars Aequi*, 2006, 581-588, on which the following paragraphs are largely based.
20. R. Alexy, *Theorie der Grundrechte* (Frankfurt am Main: Suhrkamp, 1985), 26-27.

**I-88.** As is well-known, unlike in the US, there are no federal courts with general jurisdiction in the EU. Disputes involving EU law are primarily dealt with by national courts. Yet, these courts have the opportunity to refer preliminary references to the ECJ concerning the interpretation or validity of EU law.[21] Moreover, a system of direct actions ensures that questions as to the validity of EU acts and the liability of the Union can also be brought directly before the ECJ. Against this background an important judicial dialogue takes place.[22] The ECJ, as an appeals court, engages in a judicial dialogue with the General Court, which at times results in interesting developments.[23] Yet, the most important dialogue for our purposes is the dialogue between the ECJ and the national courts.

**I-89.** Virtually all principles of EU law have been developed in the context of preliminary reference procedure at the instigation of national courts. Accordingly, the theory of direct effect was developed at the request of a Dutch court,[24] and it is well-known that the case law on fundamental rights was regularly spurred by the German courts.[25] Yet the dialogue has not ended with the formulation of these core principles. National courts continue to question the ECJ over the practical implications of these principles, especially in the context of their specific national procedural law, for their legal order.[26] As a result the ECJ is increasingly confronted with more detailed questions on reconciling the demands of the EU legal order with the intricacies of the national context where the dispute arose. This has important consequences for the way the ECJ finds the law.

**I-90.** First, there is a risk that the boundary between the task of the national courts and the Community courts is fading. In principle, it is for the national court to set out the

21. The preliminary reference procedure is well-established in respect of EC law in Article 267 TFEU. Since the Lisbon Treaty this is also the only preliminary reference procedure, which has not only replaced Article 234 TEC, but also the less-developed equivalent provided for in old Article 35 TEU in respect of the third pillar.
22. For more on the judicial organization of the EU, see K. Lenaerts, D. Arts & I. Maselis; Bray, R. (Ed.), *Procedural Law of the European Union*, 2nd ed. (London: Sweet & Maxwell, 2006).
23. For an analysis of the interaction between General Court and ECJ, see K. Lenaerts, 'Le Tribunal de première instance des Communautés européennes: regard sur une décennie d'activités et sur l'apport du double degré d'instance au droit communautaire', *Cahiers de droit européen* (2000): 323-411. See for instance the development of the case law on transparency (compare Case T-84/03 *Turco v. Council* [2004] ECR II-4061 with Joined Cases C-39/05 P and C-59/05 P *Sweden and Turco v. Council* [2008] ECR I-0000), terrorism (compare Case T-306/01 *Yusuf and Al Barakaat International Foundation v. Council and Commission* [2005] ECR II-3533 and Case T-315/01 *Kadi v. Council and Commission* [2005] ECR II-3649 with Joined Cases C-402/05 P and C-415/05 P *Kadi v. Council* [2008] ECR I-6351) and Community liability (compare Case T-69/00 *FIAMM and FIAMM Technologies v. Council and Commission* [2005] ECR II-5393 with Joined Cases C-120/06 and C-121/06 *FIAMM and FIAMM Technologies v. Council and Commission* [2008] ECR I-6513). For more examples, see K. Lenaerts & T. Corthaut, 'Rechtsvinding door het Hof van Justitie', *Ars Aequi* (2006): 581-582.
24. Case 26/62 *Van Gend & Loos* [1963] ECR 1, 3.
25. Case 29/69 *Stauder* [1969] ECR 419; Case 11/70 *Internationale Handelsgesellschaft* [1970] ECR 1125; Case 44/79 *Hauer* [1979] ECR 3727. See also F. Jacobs, 'Judicial Dialogue and the Cross-Fertilization of Legal Systems: the European Court of Justice', *Texas International Law Journal* (2003): 548-549.
26. Compare for instance Case 33/76 *Rewe* [1976] ECR 1989 with Case C-62/00 *Marks & Spencer* [2002] ECR I-6325.

relevant facts and for the ECJ to answer the referred issue of EU law. However, as the questions referred to the ECJ become increasingly detailed, it becomes more difficult for the court to give rulings on EU law with a general ring to it. This is not only the case in respect of these fields, such as the Common Customs Tariff, where there always is an important factual element to the legal question,[27] but also cases on classic topics, such as the supremacy of EC law increasingly result in a dictum that is strongly dependent on the national factual context as is evidenced by the *dictum* of the judgment in *Kühne & Heitz.*[28] The result is that other national courts feel compelled to ask follow-up questions as to the impact such a detailed ruling may have for their legal order, where not all of the mentioned elements may be present.[29]

**I-91.** Second, the interaction between the national court and the ECJ also helps to explain the piece-meal development of any doctrine of EU law. The fact that judges may only decide cases as they arise, and are (generally) bound by the issues raised in the course of the dispute, which does also limit the possibility for judges to find the law, is probably one of the most important constitutional limitations flowing from the separation of powers. This implies, however, that the Court may often not be in a position to fully articulate all the consequences of its doctrine. Of course, occasionally there are *obiter dicta* and also opinions of Advocates General which help to better understand the contours of a certain approach. Nonetheless, some degree of uncertainty, if not contradiction, in the legal concepts seems inherent in a case law system such as the EU system.[30] As a result, even coincidence has its role to play in the development of EU concepts.[31]

---

27. For colourful examples see e.g., Case 53/75 *Vandertaelen* [1975] ECR 1647 (involving the definition of ice cream) and Case 155/84 *Onnasch* [1985] ECR 1449 (classification of a sculpture).
28. Case C-453/00 *Kühne & Heitz* [2003] ECR I-837. ('The principle of cooperation arising from Article 10 EC imposes on an administrative body an obligation to review a final administrative decision, where an application for such review is made to it, in order to take account of the interpretation of the relevant provision given in the meantime by the Court where:
    - under national law, it has the power to reopen that decision;
    - the administrative decision in question has become final as a result of a judgment of a national court ruling at final instance;
    - that judgment is, in the light of a decision given by the Court subsequent to it, based on a misinterpretation of Community law which was adopted without a question being referred to the Court for a preliminary ruling under the third paragraph of Article 234 EC; and
    - the person concerned complained to the administrative body immediately after becoming aware of that decision of the Court').
29. See for instance Case C-2/06 *Kempter* [2008] ECR I-411, with Opinion of AG Bot. For more on Case C-453/00 *Kühne & Heitz* [2003] ECR I-837 and Case C-2/06 *Kempter* [2008] ECR I-411, see, *infra*, at II-220 et seq.
30. On the risk of diverging concepts in the case law of the ECJ, and on ways to control them, see also K. Lenaerts & T. Corthaut, 'Towards an internally consistent doctrine on invoking norms of EU law' in *The Coherence of EU Law – The Search for Unity in Divergent Concepts*, S. Prechal & B. Van Roermund (Oxford: OUP, 2008), 496-515.
31. For an elaborate example on the basis of Case C-105/03 *Pupino* [2005] ECR I-5285, see K. Lenaerts & T. Corthaut, 'Rechtsvinding door het Hof van Justitie', *Ars Aequi* (2006): 583-584.

**I-92.** However, the third and probably most important dimension to the dialogue between the national court and the ECJ is precisely the fact that the judgments of the ECJ have, despite their roots in a national factual setting, also a role as binding precedent beyond the original dispute. Other national courts, across the EU, will have to decide cases in accordance with the earlier precedents set by the ECJ. The fact that national courts are generally willing to do so, is far from self-evident, especially since until recently hardly any tool seemed available to force recalcitrant courts into compliance. Recent developments such as the willingness of the Commission to bring infringement actions over failings by the national court[32] and the introduction of state liability for court failures in *Köbler*[33] may perhaps change this to some extent. Yet, so far the most effective way for the Court to make sure its judgments are given due weight is by paying constant attention to the acceptability of a proposed solution for the 27 national legal orders in a manner which, however, does not compromise the effective enforcement of EU law.

**I-93.** The Court is in that respect of course guided by the classic interpretation techniques, which are also known to national courts.[34] However, there are two important further elements, which are typical for the ECJ. A first complication is the requirement to reconcile the meaning of the various language versions, all equally authentic – even though at times the various language versions may actually help to reveal the meaning of a particular term.[35] The crucial element is however the stress on the *effet utile*. The ECJ has set itself the task to interpret the EU legal instruments in such a way that these instruments best attain their objectives. This does not mean that EU law is always interpreted in the immediate interest of the EU. In its teleological approach, a strong emphasis is placed on the objectives of the rule and the legal interests that are protected by it. Recent examples in that respect are the balancing of the interest of the Community with that of bona fide traders caught up in VAT-fraud,[36] but also the interpretation of the possibilities under the EU Treaty to contest certain onerous acts in the context of the fight against terrorism.[37]

32. Case C-129/00 *Commission v. Italy* [2003] ECR I-14637.
33. Case C-224/01 *Köbler* [2003] ECR I-10239. For a further – and perhaps even more salient – example, see Case C-173/03 *Traghetti del Mediterraneo* [2006] ECR I-5177.
34. For a general overview of the ECJ's methods of interpretation, see H.G. Schermers & D. Waelbroeck, *Judicial Protection in the European Union*, 6th ed. (Deventer: Kluwer, 2001), 10-27, §§ 20-52. See also N. Fennelly, 'Legal interpretation at the European Court of Justice', *Fordham International Law Journal* (1997): 656-679. An excellent illustration can be found in the Opinion of AG Ruiz-Jarabo Colomer in Case C-262/06 *Deutsche Telekom* [2007] ECR I-10057, paras 29-46.
35. G. Van Calster, 'The EU's Tower of Babel – The Interpretation by the European Court of Justice of Equally Authentic Texts Drafted in more than one Official Language', *Yearbook of European Law* (1997): 363-393.
36. Compare Case C-255/02 *Halifax* [2006] ECR I-1609 with Joined Cases C-354/03, C-355/03 and C-484/03 *Optigen* [2006] ECR I-483 or Joined Cases C-439/04 and C-440/04 *Kittel* [2006] ECR I-6161.
37. Case C-354/04 P *Gestoras Pro Amestía v. Council* [2007] ECR I-1579 and Case C-355/04 P *Segi v. Council* [2007] ECR I-1657.

**I-94.** Nonetheless, the interest of the Union is demanding for the legal orders of the Member States. Especially the procedural law of the Member States has been transformed, despite the principle of national procedural autonomy, under the demands of effective judicial protection of EU rights and obligations. The most notable examples are presumably the introduction of 'injunctive relief against the Crown' in the UK,[38] which even had a major spill-over effect on cases without an EU element,[39] and above all the development of the doctrine of state liability for breaches of Community law, which is still being refined.[40] Yet, the ECJ can only take such steps if it is assured that the Member States are receptive to these changes, as the Court depends on these national legal orders to enforce EC law.[41]

**I-95.** The ECJ has some special techniques to assess whether a certain outcome may be generally acceptable. Crucial in that respect is the possibility for any Member State to intervene in all case before the Court. These interventions are often inspired by self-interest. Yet, even then these interventions may offer important insights as to the impact and appreciation a certain ruling may have in the various national legal orders, often beyond the confines of the case at bar. This does not mean, however, that Member States always get what they argued for. For instance, the direct effect of certain provisions of the EC Treaty as introduced for the first time in *Van Gend & Loos*[42] was decided over the objections of all Member States participating in the debate before the Court. Similarly, the expansion of the doctrine of state liability was not unequivocally welcomed by the Member States.[43] Member States cannot fight the consequences of the legal order which they themselves designed.[44] This does not render the Member States entirely powerless, as any interpretation can be overridden by amending the Treaties. The *Barber-protocol* shows that this can even be done in respect of core provisions, such as the equal treatment of men and women.[45]

**I-96.** Yet, generally the ECJ has managed to let the above-mentioned Community concepts take root. A major reason is that the ECJ finds support from comparative law, while interpreting EU law. Actually, some articles of the basic Treaties require the

38. Case C-213/89 *Factortame* [1990] ECR I-2433.
39. F. Jacobs, 'Judicial Dialogue and the Cross-Fertilization of Legal Systems: the European Court of Justice', *Texas International Law Journal* (2003): 550.
40. See for instance the above-mentioned development of state responsibility to address failures by national courts, see Case C-224/01 *Köbler* [2003] ECR I-10239; Case C-173/03 *Traghetti del Mediterraneo* [2006] ECR I-5177.
41. K. Lenaerts, 'Interlocking legal orders in the European Union and Comparative Law', *International and Comparative Law Quarterly* (2003): 879-881.
42. Case 26/62 *Van Gend & Loos* [1963] ECR 1.
43. K. Lenaerts & K. Gutman, '"Federal Common Law" in the European Union: a Comparative Perspective from the United States', *American Journal of Comparative Law* (2006): 84-86.
44. See in this respect also the current debate on the enforcement of Community law through criminal sanctions defined by the Community, see Case C-176/03 *Commission v. Council* [2005] ECR I-7879.
45. For more on Case C-262/88 *Barber* [1990] ECR I-1889 and the response to it by the Member States in adopting the *Barber-protocol*, see P. Craig & G. De Búrca, *EU Law: Text, Cases and Materials*, 3rd ed. (Oxford: Oxford University Press, 2003), 869-876.

Court to seek guidance from the Legal orders from the Member States.[46] Earlier we touched already on one of the most important ones. Article 6(3) TEU reads:

> Fundamental rights, as guaranteed by the European Convention for the Protection of Human Rights and Fundamental Freedoms and as they result *from the constitutional traditions common to the Member States*, shall constitute general principles of the Union's law. (emphasis added).

This does not mean that a rough inventory is made of the Constitutions of the Member States to determine whether or not a certain right qualifies as part of the constitutional traditions common to the Member States. The fundamental rights guaranteed by the Union are not the largest common denominator of the national constitutions, nor do they include each and every right protected by one of its Member States.[47] Of course, the Charter of Fundamental Rights, which both the CFI and the ECJ[48] started invoking even before the Lisbon Treaty entered into force, offers an excellent guide in determining the common traditions of the Member States,[49] as all Member States implicitly, but certainly, signed up to it.[50]

**I-97.** The case of *Omega Spielhallen,*[51] which we used above[52] also serves as an example here. It was clear that the prohibition on the contested laser game was an obstacle to the free movement; however, the issue to be determined was whether a *German* concept of human dignity could serve as a justification to a *European* freedom. It is recalled that both the Advocate General and the Court reformulate the question and first examine whether the EU itself knows of a concept of human dignity, and for this they look at the common constitutional traditions of the Member States as they were revealed by a comparative study carried out by the Advocate General,[53] which looked at both national and Community uses of the concept and even international law practice.[54] The Court unsurprisingly agrees that a Community concept of human

46. B. Markesinis & J. Fedtke, 'The judge as comparatist', *Tulane Law Review* (2005): 79.
47. See also, *supra*, at I-75.
48. As to the CFI, see Case T-177/01 *Jégo-Quéré v. Commission* [2002] ECR II-2365, para 42; Case T-54/99 *max.mobil Telekommunikation Service v. Commission* [2002] ECR II-313, para 48. As to the ECJ, see *inter alia* Case C-540/03 *European Parliament v. Council* [2006] ECR I-5769, para 38; Case C-432/05 *Unibet* [2007] ECR I-2271, para 37; Case C-438/05 *International Transport Workers' Federation* [2007] ECR I-10779, para. 43; Case C-341/05 *Laval un Partneri* [2007] ECR I-11767, para. 90.
49. See in this sense B. Markesinis & J. Fedtke, 'The judge as comparatist', *Tulane Law Review* (2005): 77-78.
50. In this respect the replacement of the European Constitution by the Lisbon Treaty hardly had any impact. While the Charter has been given a rather unceremonious place in a protocol, its content is very much alive – so much so that it seems unlikely that even the opt-outs and unilateral declarations will carry much counter-weight.
51. Case C-36/02 *Omega Spielhallen* [2004] ECR I-9609, with Opinion of AG Stix-Hackl.
52. See, *supra*, at I-69 et seq.
53. B. Markesinis & J. Fedtke, 'The judge as comparatist', *Tulane Law Review* (2005): 87-89. For the analysis, see Opinion of AG Stix-Hackl in Case C-36/02 *Omega Spielhallen* [2004] ECR I-9609, paras 74-94.
54. In this sense one could also discern another type of dialogue: the ECJ, despite its supranational character, a domestic court from the perspective of international law, engages in an explicit dialogue with various international courts and tribunals when deciding cases involving international law norms, including human rights, see R. Higgins, 'The ICJ, the ECJ, and the

dignity exists. However, this does not reveal anything as to the scope of its protection. If anything, the study had demonstrated the 'inchoate nature of the concept of human dignity'.[55] As discussed above, the fact that the ECJ ultimately accepted the German prohibition to be a legitimate and proportionate form of protecting human dignity, does not imply however that this also is the level of protection of human dignity required at Union level or to be imposed on other Member States. The Court has at best concluded that a Member State which prohibits this laser game, taking into account the common traditions of the Member States, has given a meaning to the concept of public policy encompassing this demanding standard for human dignity which is acceptable for the Union. The real test for the Union standard, however, can only be ascertained in a case involving the validity of a Union measure, such as a harmonization measure for laser games. The first case in this sense has, however, not revealed a similar hardened stance.[56]

**I-98.** Similarly, the ECJ has found a basis for developing a doctrine of Union liability – and later state liability – in Article 340(2) TFEU.[57] However, even outside these instances where a clear mandate exists, the ECJ will regularly rely on comparative studies, simply because it enables the Court to better assess the impact its ruling may have on the 27 Member States. Both primary and secondary EU law is often inspired by the law of the Member States, with concept and terms that are borrowed from national law.[58] The basic justification for this can be found in old Article 220 TEC, now even more prominently put to the fore in Article 19(1) TEU.[59] In *Brasserie* the ECJ explained that it is its task:

> in pursuance of the task conferred on it by Article [19(1) TEU] of ensuring that in the interpretation and application of the Treaty the law is observed, to rule on such a question in accordance with generally accepted methods of interpretation, in particular by reference to the fundamental principles of the Community legal system and, where necessary, *general principles common to the legal systems of the Member States*[60]

Unfortunately, this comparative work is rarely brought into the spotlight. It is rather rare for the ECJ to indicate that it has examined the laws of the Member States – it is no

integrity of international law', *International and Comparative Law Quarterly* (2003): 1-20; C. Baudenbacher, 'Judicial Globalization: New Developments or Old Wine in New Bottles?', *Texas International Law Journal* (2003): 505-526.

55. Opinion of AG Stix-Hackl in Case C-36/02 *Omega Spielhallen* [2004] ECR I-9609, para. 92.
56. Case C-377/98 *Netherlands v. European Parliament and Council* [2001] ECR I-7079.
57. For a good discussion, see K. Lenaerts, & K. Gutman, '"Federal Common Law" in the European Union: a Comparative Perspective from the United States', *American Journal of Comparative Law* (2006): 84-86. The seminal case on Community liability, *Schöppenstedt*, is in itself a great example of the use of comparative law by the ECJ as it was based on a comparative study ordered by AG Roemer from the Max-Planck Institute, see Case 5/71 *Zuckerfabrik Schöppenstedt v. Council* [1971] ECR 975, with Opinion of AG Roemer.
58. B. Markesinis & J. Fedtke, 'The judge as comparatist', *Tulane Law Review* (2005): 79-80.
59. K. Lenaerts, 'Interlocking legal orders in the European Union and Comparative Law', *International and Comparative Law Quarterly* (2003): 876-877.
60. Joined Cases C-46/93 and C-48/93 *Brasserie du Pêcheur* [1996] ECR I-1026, para 27 (emphasis added).

coincidence that one of the most quoted examples, the *Algera*[61] case, is also one of the eldest. The Opinions of the Advocates General, however, often offer an indication of the comparative work done,[62] which regularly also involves a comparison with non-EU legal systems.[63] Moreover, the ECJ has two discrete advantages. On the one hand, the 27 judges can offer a wealth of insight into each of the legal systems. On the other hand, the ECJ has a highly reputed research department, the works of which are however unseen by the public. Moreover, occasionally the Commission is requested by the Court to produce a comparative study.[64] Nonetheless, some more openness on the use of its comparative material could be welcomed.[65]

**I-99.** Occasionally, comparative research may reveal major differences between the various Member States, which at times may be hard to reconcile. This can be a decisive factor for the Court to choose a Community solution instead.[66] This process requires the ECJ, while interpreting Community law, to give an autonomous definition of concepts, which often have their origin in domains where the Union has hardly any legislative powers, such as family law or the law of property, and which the Community legislator has failed to specify. This process can best be described, using a term taken from US federalism, as the making of *federal common law*.[67] Federal common law is controversial in the US, as it has a major impact, both on the relationship between the courts and the legislator and on the division of competence between the federal level and the Member States.[68] By formulating a rule of federal common law the judge fills a lacuna left by the federal legislator. At the same time, however, a concept or norm is introduced at the federal level at the expense of the default rules of the States. In the European Union, there is little evidence of a similar controversy. Yet, the ECJ is basically doing the same: the Court formulates 'Union and Community concepts, principles and rules of decision...that are not clearly suggested from the face of a provision of primary or secondary law.'[69]

---

61. Joined Cases 7/56 and 3/57 to 7/57 *Algera v. Common Assembly* [1957] ECR 39.
62. P. Herzog, 'United States Supreme Court Cases in the Court of Justice of the European Communities', *Hastings International and Comparative Law Review* (1997-1998): 905.
63. *Ibid.* For a good example see the Opinion of AG Jacobs in Case C-227/04 P *Lindorfer v. Council* [2007] ECR I-6767.
64. K. Lenaerts, 'Interlocking legal orders in the European Union and Comparative Law', *International and Comparative Law Quarterly* (2003): 875. Often comparative studies are also volunteered by the European Commission.
65. B. Markesinis & J. Fedtke, 'The judge as comparatist', *Tulane Law Review* (2005): 89-90. See, however, also K. Schiemann, 'A Response to the judge as comparatist', *Tulane Law Review* (2005): 286-291.
66. K. Lenaerts, 'Interlocking legal orders in the European Union and Comparative Law', *International and Comparative Law Quarterly* (2003): 896-897.
67. K. Lenaerts & K. Gutman, '"Federal Common Law" in the European Union: a Comparative Perspective from the United States', *American Journal of Comparative Law* (2006): 7.
68. *Ibid.*, 4-5.
69. *Ibid.*, 7.

**I-100.** In this way the ECJ has given definitions of a whole range of traditional legal concepts such as 'contract'[70] or 'immovable property'.[71] The possibility for autonomous lawmaking by the ECJ is quite important.[72] Also the above-mentioned doctrine of Union liability has been the result of praetorian rulemaking, and the process is still on-going: recent examples include the (arrested[73]) development of Union liability without fault[74] or the definition of 'force majeure'.[75] It is worth drawing attention to this process of federal common law making in the context of this research. The concept of *ordre public* or public policy is often used by the Union legislator and even appears in the Treaties, but it is never fully defined. Often it is understood to refer to a concept developed in the Member States or even in international practice. Yet, at the same time it never seems to coincide with the concept of a single Member State. Moreover, the concept of federal common law will also appear again further as a technique to deal with this tension of unity and diversity. Replacing 27 national standards by a single EU concept has of course a major unifying force to it. At the same time, when the ECJ defines a concept like 'marriage', as a union between two persons of the opposite sex, its definition may sit uneasy with the *ordre public* of some more permissive Member States, while allowing same-sex marriages may well be upsetting others. Therefore the ECJ has so far displayed quite some sensitivity for the differences between the Member States. In *Reed* the Court already indicated that:

> an interpretation given by the court to a provision of [Regulation 1612/68] has effects in all of the Member States, and that any interpretation of a legal term on the basis of social developments must take into account the situation in the whole Community, not merely in one Member State[76]

and the Court has since continued down this path. Accordingly, the ECJ confirmed in *D and Sweden v. Council* that 'it is not in question that, according to the definition generally accepted by the Member States, the term marriage means a union between two persons of the opposite sex',[77] even though the Court did take note of new developments in the family laws of the Member States. Given the recent introduction of same-sex marriages and partnerships in several EU Member States, it is likely that the ECJ will again have to assess its position.[78]

---

70. For a full discussion of this example, see K. Lenaerts & K. Gutman, '"Federal Common Law" in the European Union: a Comparative Perspective from the United States', *American Journal of Comparative Law* (2006): 102-109.
71. For a full discussion of this example, see, *ibid.*, 59-62.
72. B. Markesinis & J. Fedtke, 'The judge as comparatist', *Tulane Law Review* (2005): 89.
73. Joined Cases C-120/06 P and C-121/06 P *FIAMM and others v. Council and Commission* [2008] ECR I-6513.
74. Case T-279/03 *Galileo International Technology v. Commission* [2006] ECR II-1291. See on this example K. Lenaerts & T. Corthaut, 'Rechtsvinding door het Hof van Justitie', *Ars Aequi* (2006): 587-588.
75. Opinion of AG Kokott in Case C-314/06 *Société Pipeline Méditerranée et Rhône* [2007] ECR I-12273, paras 28-31.
76. Case C-59/85 *Reed* [1986] ECR 1283, para 13.
77. Joined Cases C-122/99 P and C-125/99 P *D and Sweden v. Council* [2001] ECR I-4319, para. 34.
78. For a more extensive analysis of the problems that arise in respect of same-sex marriages, see, *infra*, at IV-62.

**I-101.** In this respect, it is important to stress that the ECJ is not without bounds while finding the law. The ECJ may only create *federal common law* when it has sufficient substantive and adjudicatory powers.[79] This implies on the one hand that the 'system of the Treaties' or certain provisions of primary or secondary law must allow for the creation of *federal common law*. This fits, moreover, neatly with the role of the judge in determining the *ordre public* as seen from a Belgian perspective. The task of the judge is not to create or determine the content of the *ordre public*, but rather has to focus on the core principles of the legal order and the legislation in force of which the judge has to examine their *ordre public* character.[80] Here, too, the old Articles 220 TEC, 288(2) TEC and 6(2) TEU (since Lisbon 19(1) TEU, 340 TFEU and 6(3) TEU) are instrumental.[81] On the other hand, the ECJ can also find the law when it is correctly addressed by the national court under Article 267 TFEU, or on the basis of one of the many courses of action the Treaties provide for.[82] As a matter of content, the ECJ has moreover four possibilities.[83] The Court can explicitly base itself on rules that are common to the Member States as it did in *Algera.*[84] By contrast the Court may also opt for an own autonomous definition detached from any national legal order, as in the case of its definition of 'immovable property'.[85] Between these extremes there are two other solutions. On the one hand, the ECJ may decide to absorb a rule from a particular Member State to serve as the EU standard. A good example in this respect is the principle of proportionality which the ECJ absorbed from the German legal order.[86] On the other hand, the ECJ may opt not to formulate a rule at all and leave the matter up for the Community legislator or the Member States to determine the rule. A good example is the principle of national procedural autonomy, albeit qualified by the principles of equivalence and effectiveness, which applies in the absence of Community harmonization.[87] In this way the ECJ can tailor a solution which both serves the Community interest and the sensitivities of the States. Another good example of such a tailored solution shows the importance of addressing federal common law in the context of this research. It concerns the question whether national courts should raise EC law of their own motion. In principle, Member States are allowed to adhere to a strict system of passivity, yet if they allow for the possibility that certain issues are raised *motu proprio*, national courts in these States must do so in respect of similarly

79. K. Lenaerts & K. Gutman, '"Federal Common Law" in the European Union: a Comparative Perspective from the United States', *American Journal of Comparative Law* (2006): 13.
80. J.-F. Romain, 'L'*ordre public* (notion générale) et les droits de l'homme' in *L'ordre public: concept et applications*, ed. J.-F. Romain, M. Grégoire & V. Simonart (Bruxelles: Bruylant, 1995), 29. That author moreover refers back to the French concept as described in P. Malaurie, *L'ordre public et le contrat* (Reims: Matot-Braine, 1953).
81. K. Lenaerts & K. Gutman, '"Federal Common Law" in the European Union: a Comparative Perspective from the United States', *American Journal of Comparative Law* (2006): 14–15
82. *Ibid.*, 16.
83. *Ibid.*, 16.
84. Joined Cases 7/56 and 3/57 to 7/57 *Algera v. Common Assembly* [1957] ECR 39.
85. Case C-315/00 *Maierhofer* [2003] ECR I-563, paras 33-35. For more on this example, see K. Lenaerts & K. Gutman, '"Federal Common Law" in the European Union: a Comparative Perspective from the United States', *American Journal of Comparative Law* (2006): 61-62.
86. B. Markesinis & J. Fedtke, 'The judge as comparatist', *Tulane Law Review* (2005): 84.
87. Case 33/76 *Rewe* [1976] ECR 1989, para. 5.

important rules of EC law,[88] triggering the question of the existence of an EC *ordre public.*[89]

**I-102.** The bottom line in defining the role of the ECJ in finding the law, however, is acceptability.[90] Like any supranational court, the ECJ develops its case law in a manner which encourages obedience and avoids decisions that it knows are likely to be defied, ignored or evaded.[91] This is evidenced by its tendency for incremental development of legal principles with multiple cases slowly but surely going in a certain direction, and with reactions to them 'softened by the time delay'[92] and decisions rooted as firmly as possible in precedent.[93] It has been argued that the Court has benefited in this respect, in terms of legitimacy, from the absence of a fully-fledged democratic representative body at the EU level, resulting in 'majoritarian judicial activism' which promotes 'the rights and policies of the larger European community (the majority) against the "selfish" or autonomous (depending on the point of view) decisions of national polities (the minority)'.[94] Crucial in this research are, however, precisely those instances where that approach is in tension with stubborn national rules and principles.

**I-103.** This brings us back to the last methodological issues. The discussion of the way the ECJ finds the law holds two important elements which determine the remainder of this research. First, the emphasis on comparative law poses a particular problem. It is hardly feasible within the constraints of a dissertation to conduct a full comparative analysis of the concept of *ordre public* across even a sample of the EU Member States as a prelude to determine an EU concept of *ordre public.* It is even harder to assess in each instance of every value, every principle, every right that may come within the purview of the EU *ordre public* what its status is in the various Member States. The next best thing, then is to draw nonetheless on some comparative and national treatises on *ordre public* and make some 'comparative leaps',[95] without claiming any exhaustiveness. Furthermore, the ECJ, by contrast has the resources to carry out comparative research in controversial cases, and as argued above, effectively does so. Therefore, studying the case law of the ECJ may actually give a rather adequate image as to the

88. See in that respect *inter alia* Joined Cases C-430/93 and C-431/93 *Van Schijndel and Van Veen* [1995] ECR I-4705; Case C-312/93 *Peterbroeck* [1995] ECR I-4599. Recent examples are Case C-168/05 *Mostaza Claro* [2006] ECR I-10421 and Joined Cases C-222/05, C-223/05, C-224/05 and C-225/05 *Van der Weerd* [2007] ECR I-4233.
89. For more on this see *infra,* at II-170 et seq.
90. K. Lenaerts, 'Interlocking legal orders in the European Union and Comparative Law', *International and Comparative Law Quarterly* (2003): 873-896.
91. See on these 'political aspects of judging', M. Volcansek, 'Supranational Courts in a Political Context', in *Law Above Nations – Supranational Courts and the Legalization of Politics,* ed. M. Volcansek (Gainesville: University of Florida Press, 1997), 10. Compare also what has been said in respect of the ECtHR, *supra,* at I-38.
92. M. Poiares Maduro, *We, the Court: the European Court of Justice and the European economic constitution: a critical reading of article 30 of the EC Treaty* (Oxford: Hart, 1998), 10.
93. *Ibid.,* 10.
94. *Ibid.,* 11.
95. On the idea of 'comparative leaps', see P. Foubert, *The legal protection of the pregnant worker in the European Community: sex equality, thoughts of social and economic policy and comparative leaps to the United States of America* (The Hague: Kluwer, 2002).

degree to which a certain concept is acceptable to the Member States.[96] This brings us to the second lesson, namely that the judgments of the Court need to be broadly acceptable. Tracking the case law of the Court as to the instances where *ordre public* comes into play and as to what legal interests are protected may therefore also help to ensure that also the findings of this research are not wholly alien to the relevant actors in the EU legal order. It is just that what will be done in the next parts of this book.

96. This presupposes of course that the research by the ECJ is methodologically sound. On whether this can be ascertained and whether this is the case, see B. Markesinis & J. Fedtke, 'The judge as comparatist', *Tulane Law Review* (2005): 11-167.

# PART II

# The Use of *Ordre Public* and Related Concepts in the EU Legal Order

## INTRODUCTION

**II-1.** In this part, an attempt is made to give an overview of the use of the concept of *ordre public* and some related concepts in the EU legal order. The starting point is found in the Treaties (Chapter 4), which contain a few references to the public order or *ordre public*. However, these references are all used in very specific contexts, most notably the free movement of goods, persons, services and capital, and do not fully exhaust our understanding of the concept of *ordre public sensu lato* as the complex of norms at the very heart of a political entity (in this case the EU) expressing and protecting the basic options taken by that entity in respect of its political, economic, social and cultural order.

**II-2.** Therefore, we also look for other uses of the concept in the EU legal order, often in ways that are analogous to the use of the concept in the national legal order. Accordingly, in Chapter 5 attention is paid to the efforts by the EU to effectively protect the EU *ordre public*. As the EU has taken over legislative competences in numerous fields, the Member States are often no longer fully competent to protect the *ordre public*. Moreover, as indicated above,[1] there is a limited, but not unimportant, body of EU specific rules that may need particular protection. Consequently, the EU takes legislative measures to protect these interests. The most poignant example of this approach is of course the growing role of the EU in the field of criminal law.

**II-3.** In Chapter 6, the consequences are being drawn from the fact that the EU is also an actor under international law. Accordingly, the EU itself has to find a way to deal with the international *ordre public*. In this context, we will first look at how the Court, in particular the General Court, deals with *jus cogens*. Second, attention will be paid to

1. See *supra*, at I-63 to I-64.

the use of the concept in the EU legislation in the field of private international law, which is increasingly pre-empting or replacing the prior national legislations in that domain. As these national legislations all used to provide in some form of protection for the *ordre public international*, a similar protection needs to be ensured by the EU legislation that applies instead. However, at the same time it is likely that – to the extent that these rules seek to establish a true area of freedom, security and justice across the EU – application of this concept between the Member States may have to be limited. This may thus justify, if not an autonomous EU concept of *ordre public*, at least some EU wide limits to its scope and application.

**II-4.** In Chapter 7, before the short intermediate conclusion, it is examined whether certain phenomena and consequences that are often associated with the *ordre public* in the national legal order are also present in the EU legal order. This inquiry yields a mixed bag of instances where the EU *ordre public* may be at work. It will be argued that in order to understand these mechanisms better, it is important to first understand the relationship between the *ordre public* and the primacy of EU law and its effect on the principle of national procedural autonomy with its twin exceptions of equivalence and effectiveness. Second, in line with what has been said in relation to private international law, attention is then paid to the recognition of arbitral awards. Third, the focus is laid on one of the most powerful uses of the *ordre public*: the ex officio application of the law, in our case EU law, by courts both at the national level and at the level of the EU. Fourth, in line with recent observations by AG Geelhoed,[2] the relationship between res judicata and *ordre public* is examined. Finally, the effect of the EU *ordre public* for contractual relationships is examined, revealing EU equivalents of 'imperative' or 'mandatory' laws and some further indications for the existence of EU norms of a truly *ordre public* character.

2. Opinion of AG Geelhoed in Case C-119/05 *Lucchini Siderurgica* [2007] ECR I-6199.

CHAPTER 4

# The Use of *Ordre Public* in the Treaties

**II-5.** The concept of *ordre public* or public policy is used most prominently in the Treaties in the context of the free movement of goods, persons, services and capital (§4.01). It offers a limited protection for the sovereignty of the various Member States, by allowing these States to take certain restrictive measures to protect the very existence of the State, for instance by protecting from terrorism,[1] or, as we have already seen above to protect certain fundamental national values.[2] The concept needs, however, to be seen next to the other justifications laid down in the Treaties for restricting the fundamental freedoms, in particular the related concepts of public security, public health and public morality. The Treaties do not provide for a similar exception in respect of competition law. Yet, recent case law indicates that public policy concerns may also be relevant in this context (§4.02).

**II-6.** The use of the concept of *ordre public* as a means for protecting the stability of the legal order of the Member States also explains other related exceptions in the Treaties. On the one hand, Article 347 TFEU (old Article 297 TEC) provides for a wholly exceptional regime allowing Member States to deal with war and internal disturbances (§4.03). On the other hand, as Member States are thus responsible for the maintenance of internal law and order,[3] Articles 35(5) TEU and 68(2) TEC excluded the jurisdiction of the ECJ to review the proportionality of actions taken for the maintenance of law and order, an oddity that has survived the Lisbon Treaty, and is now found in Article 276 TFEU (§4.04).

1. Case C-100/01 *Olazabal* [2002] ECR I-1098.
2. See, *supra*, at I-65 et seq. with Case C-36/02 *Omega Spielhallen* [2004] ECR I-9609 as most poignant example.
3. This does not affect the fact that Articles 6, 7 and 49 TEU imply that this must be done in full respect for the fundamental rights, most notably those laid down in the ECHR.

## §4.01 THE PUBLIC POLICY EXCEPTIONS TO THE FOUR FREEDOMS

### [A] General Observations

**II-7.** The public policy exceptions in the context of the free movement of goods, persons, services and capital are probably the best-known uses of *ordre public* in EU law. They have been well and widely discussed by a number of authors.[4] Accordingly, I do not seek to repeat their efforts. Nonetheless, a series of observations should be made to explain the function of the public policy exception and its role in the broader context of this book. Instead of making a full analysis of the four freedoms, the discussion of the separate freedoms will be used to bring to the fore various aspects of the relationship between the public policy exception and the fundamental freedoms.

**II-8.** The main aim of the public policy exceptions of Articles 36 TFEU (old Article 30 TEC – goods), 45(3) TFEU (old Article 39(3) TEC – workers), 52(1) TFEU (old Article 46(1) TEC – establishment, and in combination with Article 62 TFEU (old Article 55 TEC) also services) and Article 65(1)(b) TFEU (old Article 58(1)(b) TEC – capital) is to safeguard the application of certain essential rules of national law by excluding the otherwise applicable rules of EU law. This common objective makes it possible to draw some common conclusions in respect of these four exceptions, even though they are worded differently.[5] At first sight, the public policy exceptions differ hardly in this from similar exceptions laid down in numerous other international agreements, including the WTO-agreement.[6] The main concern is thus the protection of *national* public policy, rather than the protection of an EU *ordre public*. However, as Poillot-Peruzzetto[7] rightly remarks, the effect of the public policy exception is notably different from the classic *ordre public* exceptions of national law or private international law. The public policy exception does not result in the exclusion of the will of the parties, but in the exclusion of a part of national legislation.[8] Also, unlike the public policy exception in private international law which results, by way of exception, in the application of the rule of the forum when the foreign law is contrary to the *ordre public* of the forum, the public policy exception in the context of the four freedoms results, by

4. For an excellent overview see H. Schneider, *Die öffentliche Ordnung als Schranke der Grundfreiheiten im EG-Vertrag* (Baden-Baden: Nomos, 1998). See also the parts relating to EU law in C. Picheral, *L'ordre public européen: droit communautaire et droit européen des droits de l'homme* (Paris: CERIC – Documentation française, 2001). See further M. Castillo & R. Chemain, 'La réserve d'*ordre public* en droit communautaire' in *L'ordre public: ordre public ou ordres publics? Ordre public et droits fondamentaux*, ed. M.-J. Redor (Brussel: Bruylant, 2001), 133-166; M.-C. Boutard Labarde., 'L'*ordre public* en droit communautaire' in *L'ordre public à la fin du XXième sciècle*, ed. T. Revet (Paris, Dalloz, 1996), 83-88; C. Kessedjian, 'Public Order in European Law', *Erasmus Law Review* (2007): 25-36.
5. In this sense, M. Castillo & R. Chemain, 'La réserve d'*ordre public* en droit communautaire' in *L'ordre public: ordre public ou ordres publics? Ordre public et droits fondamentaux*, ed. M.-J. Redor (Brussel: Bruylant, 2001), 135.
6. M. Castillo & R. Chemain, 'La réserve d'*ordre public* en droit communautaire' in *L'ordre public: ordre public ou ordres publics? Ordre public et droits fondamentaux*, ed. M.-J. Redor (Brussel: Bruylant, 2001), 133.
7. S. Poillot-Peruzzetto, '*Ordre public* et droit communautaire', *Dalloz Sirey* (1993): 178-179.
8. *Ibid.*, 178.

way of exception, in the integration of the rule of the forum into EU law.[9] What is more, all this happens without there being a conflict between the national public policy and EU law. Rather, EU law takes the national norm into account – not unlike a *loi de police* – because the norm imposes itself[10] as the alternative is often deregulation.[11]

**II-9.** Accordingly, it is fundamental that this national public policy is not without European limits. In this respect I basically agree with the concept of the European *Schranken-Schranken* as put forward by Schneider.[12] The content of the public policy exception is in first instance determined by national law,[13] and may thus differ from one Member State to another;[14] however, it is the ECJ that controls the limits of the concept.[15] In this way the ECJ has a crucial double role to play. On the one hand, the ECJ may set the material and procedural conditions for the invocation of the public policy exception. On the other hand, the ECJ also reserves the possibility to analyse, albeit marginally, whether the national public policy corresponds to a legitimate interest. Under those circumstances it is no longer possible to consider the public policy exceptions as unfettered 'réserves de souveraineté'.[16]

**II-10.** First, as to the material restrictions, it is well known that the restrictions to the four freedoms are all subject to a proportionality requirement. Accordingly, the ECJ may often avoid having to pronounce on the legitimacy of a certain rule put forward as part of the *ordre public*, due to its disproportionate effects.[17] As was demonstrated above, the proportionality test used does take into account, however, the sensitive nature of the protected interests, thus creating something of a margin of appreciation for the Member States.[18] Therefore, while 'such restrictions may be justified only if they are suitable for securing the attainment of the objective pursued and do not go beyond

9. *Ibid.*, 178.
10. *Ibid.*, 178-179.
11. Though some would argue, that no true deregulation takes place, but rather a transformation of two conflicting national norms into a transnational meta-norm, which takes the respective interests sufficiently into account, see C. Joerges, 'Rethinking European Law's Supremacy with Comments by Damian CHALMERS, Rainer NICKEL, Florian RÖDL, Robert WAI', EUI Working Papers Law No 2005/12 (<http://hdl.handle.net/1814/3332>, May 18, 2012),18.
12. H. Schneider, *Die öffentliche Ordnung als Schranke der Grundfreiheiten im EG-Vertrag* (Baden-Baden: Nomos, 1998), 175 et seq.
13. S. Poillot-Peruzzetto, '*Ordre public* et droit communautaire', *Dalloz Sirey* (1993): 178.
14. Case C-36/02 *Omega Spielhallen* [2004] ECR I-9609, paras 37-38, reaffirmed in Case C-244/06 Dynamic Medien [2008] ECR I-505, para. 44.
15. Case 41/74 *van Duyn* [1974] ECR 1337; H. Schneider, *Die öffentliche Ordnung als Schranke der Grundfreiheiten im EG-Vertrag* (Baden-Baden: Nomos, 1998), 73. Schneider also uses the term 'Gemeinschaftsrechtlicher Rahmenbegriff', which indeed neatly captures the idea of a concept the limits of which are determined by EU law, but the content of which flows from the diverse national public policies.
16. For the old concept of public policy as 'la réserve de l'*ordre public*', see G. Lyon-Caen, 'La reserve d'*ordre public* en matière de liberté d'établissement et de libre circulation', *Revue Trimesterielle du Droit Européen* (1966) :693. For a somewhat hesitant switch towards a more nuanced approach, see M. Castillo & R. Chemain, 'La réserve d'*ordre public* en droit communautaire' in *L'ordre public: ordre public ou ordres publics? Ordre public et droits fondamentaux*, ed. M.-J. Redor (Brussel: Bruylant, 2001), 137.
17. Case 352/85 *Bond van Adverteerders* [1988] ECR 2085, para. 36.
18. J.A. Sweeney, 'A "Margin of Appreciation" in the Internal Market: Lessons from the European Court of Human Rights', *Legal Issues of Economic Integration* (2007): 27-52.

what is necessary in order to attain it',[19] the Court will fully take into account the level of protection pursued by the Member States, with the result that even a total ban may still be proportionate.[20]

**II-11.** Second, as to the procedural restrictions, the ECJ has developed in the context of the free movement of persons, a series of requirements as to the procedural guarantees that must be available for those persons whose rights are curtailed because of the public policy. These requirements which affect *inter alia* the duty to state reasons and the possibility for judicial review of the decision,[21] build primarily on the old Council Directive 64/221/EEC,[22] now replaced by Directive 2004/38/EC.[23] However, the ECJ has more recently imposed similar requirements in respect of the free movement of goods. Indeed in *Dynamic Medien*, the Court concluded that:

> Article 28 EC does not preclude national rules, such as those at issue in the main proceedings, which prohibit the sale and transfer by mail order of image storage media which have not been examined and classified by the competent authority for the purposes of protecting young persons and which do not bear a label from that authority indicating the age from which they may be viewed, *unless it appears that the procedure for examination, classification and labelling of image storage media established by those rules is not readily accessible or cannot be completed within a reasonable period, or that a decision of refusal is not open to challenge before the courts*[24]

thus indicating that also in the context of free movement of goods the public policy exception is subject to some procedural restrictions.

**II-12.** Though the various interests that may be protected in the context of the EU *ordre public* are discussed in more detail below (Part III), it is nonetheless appropriate to also address here the issue of the legitimacy review of the national policy that is put forward. Indeed, the ECJ imposes certain 'negative' requirements as to what may qualify as public policy. First, the ECJ has made it clear that economic interests cannot as such qualify as public policy reasons,[25] though certain forms of economic disruption

19. Case C-244/06 *Dynamic Medien* [2008] ECR I-505, para. 42.
20. Case C-36/02 *Omega Spielhallen* [2004] ECR I-9609, para. 39.
21. For examples, see below at II-39 et seq.
22. Council Directive 64/221/EEC of 25 February 1964 on the coordination of special measures concerning the movement and residence of foreign nationals which are justified on grounds of public policy, public security or public health, *English special edition: Series I Chapter 1963-1964*, 117.
23. Directive 2004/38/EC of the European Parliament and of the Council of 29 April 2004 on the right of citizens of the Union and their family members to move and reside freely within the territory of the Member States amending Regulation (EEC) No 1612/68 and repealing Directives 64/221/EEC, 68/360/EEC, 72/194/EEC, 73/148/EEC, 75/34/EEC, 75/35/EEC, 90/364/EEC, 90/365/EEC and 93/96/EEC (2004) OJ L 158/77. This Directive codifies the classic case law of the ECJ in this field, though 'is not an exact replica', see H. Oosterom-Staples, 'Botsende openbare-ordebegrippen in het Europese Migratierecht', *Nederlands Tijdschrift voor Europees Recht* (2006): 170.
24. Case C-244/06 *Dynamic Medien* [2008] ECR I-505, para. 52, emphasis added.
25. Case 352/85 *Bond van Adverteerders* [1988] ECR 2085, para. 34. See also, in the context of the taxation of gambling gains, Case C-153/08 *Commission v. Spain* [2009] ECR I-9735, para. 43.

may bring about similar concerns.[26] Second, since the judgment in *ERT*[27] it is clear that the ECJ will assess whether accepting a particular justification for the restriction of a free movement right does not result in the unjust restriction of a fundamental right.[28] In doing so the ECJ, reverted on its prior *Cinéthèque* judgment.[29] However, this seems fully justified, especially if one accepts the thesis suggested above[30] that the effect of the public policy exception is to integrate the national rule into the body of EU law, to the extent that the Union under Article 2 TEU is based on the rule of law, which respects fundamental rights. Accordingly, to the extent that national law is virtually integrated into Union law because of the public policy exception, this integration must find its limits in the same fundamental rules laid down in Articles 2 and 6 TEU.

**II-13.** In my view, the ECJ has even gone slightly further in its analysis. At least in its more recent case law, it seems to hint at some requirement of communality in the public policy ground put forward. This was particularly strong in *Schindler* where the ECJ observed that:

> it is not possible to disregard the moral, religious or cultural aspects of lotteries, like other types of gambling, in all the Member States. The *general tendency of the Member States* is to restrict, or even prohibit, the practice of gambling and to prevent it from being a source of private profit.[31]

Admittedly, the ECJ has since nuanced that the public policy concern pursued must not be restricted 'to a conception shared by all Member States as regards the level of protection and the detailed rules relating to it'[32] and that as the conception of public policy 'may vary from one Member State to another on the basis of, *inter alia*, moral or cultural views, Member States must be recognized as having a definite margin of discretion'.[33] However, this does not prevent the Court from effectively examining whether or not the interests relied upon, such as the protection of the child[34] or the protection of human dignity,[35] are widely protected and whether this is reflected in

26. Case 72/83 *Campus Oil* [1984] ECR 2727 (disruption in the oil supply may result in a threat to public security). See also in the context of the free movement of capital and the freedom of establishment: Case C-207/07 *Commission v. Spain* [2008] ECR I-111*. See also K.J.M. Mortelmans, 'Botsende algemene belangen en de werking van de interne markt', *SEW* (2004): 246.
27. Case 260/89 *Elliniki Radiophonia Tiléorassi* [1991] ECR I-2925.
28. For an extensive analysis of the limits fundamental rights put to the public policy exception, see H. Schneider, *Die öffentliche Ordnung als Schranke der Grundfreiheiten im EG-Vertrag* (Baden-Baden: Nomos, 1998), 185 et seq.
29. Joined Cases 60 and 61/84 *Cinéthèque* [1985] ECR 2605.
30. *Supra*, at II-9.
31. Case C-275/92 *Schindler* [1994] ECR I-1039 (emphasis added).
32. Case C-244/06 *Dynamic Medien* [2008] ECR I-505, para. 44; see also Case C-36/02 *Omega Spielhallen* [2004] ECR I-9609, para. 37.
33. Case C-244/06 *Dynamic Medien* [2008] ECR I-505, para. 44.
34. Case C-244/06 *Dynamic Medien* [2008] ECR I-505.
35. Case C-36/02 *Omega Spielhallen* [2004] ECR I-9609.

Union law. Accordingly, I submit that behind this apparent deference to national concepts of public policy, a glimpse of a deeper EU *ordre public* is lurking.[36]

**II-14.** The full scope of this EU *ordre public* will be developed below (Part V). However, it may be useful to already signal here that that concept will go beyond elements taken from the common constitutional traditions of the Member States, but also includes the core idea of the four freedoms, even though they are in turn subject to public policy exceptions (but so are, after all, also all fundamental rights[37]). The reason for doing so here is because the ECJ has done all in its power to prevent that the public policy exception may ever consume the rule. This is first evidenced by the classic mantra that as an exception the public policy exception must be construed narrowly.[38] Second, as will be demonstrated below in particular in respect of the free movement of persons (§4.01[B]), the ECJ has always rejected an approach to national public policy which is incongruent with the aims of the internal market. Though public policy exceptions make it possible to discriminate between own nationals and others,[39] the ECJ[40] has fought hard against the bias against aliens which the concept originally had.[41]

**II-15.** As a result, not everything that Member States classify as '*ordre public*' will effectively be accepted by the Court in the context of the four freedoms. A particular example of this is offered by the relationship between national criminal law and public policy. Indeed, Member States often bolster their argument that a certain rule touches on the public policy by pointing out that the rule is sanctioned by criminal penalties.[42] The presence of criminal sanctions may indeed suggest that national authorities consider a particular norm of particular importance, and thus the link from criminal law to *ordre public* is easily made in some Member States.[43] However, the ECJ has made it very clear that there is no such equivalence in the context of EU law as 'legislation does not come within the ambit of the concept of public policy within the meaning of

36. Compare in this respect the interplay between the ECHR and EC law as developed in C. Picheral, *L'ordre public européen: droit communautaire et droit européen des droits de l'homme* (Paris: CERIC – Documentation française, 2001).
37. Case C-292/97 *Karlsson* [2000] ECR I-2737, para. 45; See in this respect the general exceptions clauses in Article 52 in the Charter of Fundamental Rights and the accompanying explanations at (2008) OJ C 303/32.
38. Case 352/85 *Bond van Adverteerders* [1988] ECR 2085, para. 36; Case 36/75 *Rutili* [1975] ECR 1219, para. 27.
39. Case 41/74 *van Duyn* [1974] ECR 1337; Case C-100/01 *Oteiza Olazabal* [2002] ECR I-10981.
40. Case 36/75 *Rutili* [1975] ECR 1219: the mere fact that a worker from another Member State is engaged in the exercise of trade union rights does not make these activities a greater threat to the national *ordre public*.
41. For more on how Member States, especially France had to come to terms with this shift, see D. Simon, '*Ordre public* et libertés publiques dans les communautés européennes', *Revue du Marché Commun* (1976): 201-223; G. Druesne, 'La réserve d'*ordre public* et L'article 48 du Traité de Rome', *Revue Trimestrielle du Droit européen* no. 2 (1976): 228-258
42. Case 16/83 *Prantl* [1984] ECR 1299, para. 33; Joined Cases C-369/96 and C-376/96 *Arblade* [1999] ECR I-8453; Joined Cases C-338/04, C-359/04 and C-360/04 *Placanica* [2007] ECR I-1891.
43. See in this respect A. Cerf, '*Ordre public*, droit pénal et droits fondamentaux' in *L'ordre public: ordre public ou ordres publics? Ordre public et droits fondamentaux*, ed. M.-J. Redor (Brussel: Bruylant, 2001), 63-83.

Article [36 TFEU] merely because it carries penal sanctions'.[44] This is hardly surprising, as Member States would otherwise be able to immunize the most egregious restrictions to the four freedoms by making them the subject of criminal sanctions – as if to add insult to injury. Accordingly, 'although in principle criminal legislation is a matter for which the Member States are responsible, the Court has consistently held that Community law sets certain limits to their power, and such legislation may not restrict the fundamental freedoms guaranteed by Community law'[45] and thus the criminal law of the Member States is not subject to any special deference when it comes to assessing its compatibility with EU law. Similarly, the free movement of persons would unduly be restricted if anyone who ever ran afoul of the criminal law of a Member State could be expelled without more.[46] Accordingly, it has been held that the internal qualification of a norm as of *ordre public* says nothing as to its rank vis-à-vis supranational norms.[47]

**II-16.** However, this does not mean that EU law would not take national criminal law, and the interests protected by it, seriously. First, in the context of the free movement of persons an extensive strand of the case law on public policy deals with the issue of expelling (former) offenders,[48] as was moreover envisaged already early on by the Community legislator in Directive 64/221/EC.[49] Second, if these laws genuinely protect legitimate interests they may well be justified as a mandatory requirement, either because they actually touch on the public policy, or because they protect one of the other listed interests or because they fall under the rule of reason[50] (*infra*, Part III). Third, at least in respect of the free movement of goods, an important number of rules protecting the social and economic order may well escape being caught at all by Article 36 TFEU – and thus do not need any justification at all – as they are selling arrangements in the sense of *Keck and Mithouard*.[51] The latter case involved a criminal prosecution for the crime of selling goods at a loss, of which it could be argued that this

44. Case 16/83 *Prantl* [1984] ECR 1299, para. 33.
45. Joined Cases C-338/04, C-359/04 and C-360/04 *Placanica* [2007] ECR I-1891; Case C-348/96 *Calfa* [1999] ECR I-11, para. 17.
46. Case C-348/96 *Calfa* [1999] ECR I-11.
47. A. Puttemans, 'L'*ordre public* et la loi du 14 juillet 1991 sur les pratiques du commerce sur l'information et la protection du consommateur' in *L'ordre public: concept et applications*, ed. J.-F. Romain, M. Grégoire & V. Simonart (Bruxelles: Bruylant, 1995), 148.
48. See *inter alia*, Case 67/74 *Bonsignore* [1975] 297 with Opinion of AG Mayras; Case 30/77 *Bouchereau* [1977] ECR 1999; Case C-348/96 *Calfa* [1999] I-11.
49. Article 3 Council Directive 64/221/EEC of 25 February 1964 on the coordination of special measures concerning the movement and residence of foreign nationals which are justified on grounds of public policy, public security or public health, *English special edition: Series I Chapter 1963-1964*, 117. See since Article 27 of Directive 2004/38/EC of the European Parliament and of the Council of 29 April 2004 on the right of citizens of the Union and their family members to move and reside freely within the territory of the Member States amending Regulation (EEC) No 1612/68 and repealing Directives 64/221/EEC, 68/360/EEC, 72/194/EEC, 73/148/EEC, 75/34/EEC, 75/35/EEC, 90/364/EEC, 90/365/EEC and 93/96/EEC (2004) OJ L 158/77.
50. For instance in Joined Cases C-369/96 and C-376/96 *Arblade* [1999] ECR I-8453, some, but not all, of the contested measures aimed at offering social protection for (posted) workers, could thus be justified, and thus the violation of these rules could be penalized by the national court. See also, *infra*, at II-72 et seq.
51. Case C-267/91 *Keck and Mithouard* [1993] ECR I-6097.

affects the economic public order. As is well known such limitation of the scope of the free movement rules does not exist in respect of services,[52] establishment[53] and persons.[54] At first sight, this may have as a result that EU law may make serious inroads into rules intended for social protection, even though a Member State could then argue that these rules genuinely aim to protect public policy concerns in order to safeguard them.

**II-17.** To the extent that the public policy exceptions to the free movement are nevertheless primarily aimed at protecting national interests, one final issue needs to be resolved. It has been argued that Article 36 TFEU (and by extension the other exceptions to the free movement) could be abused by a Member State to impose on other Member States their chosen level of protection.[55] Accordingly, Member States should only be allowed to invoke the exceptions for the protection of their own interests, and not that of other Member States.[56] The ECJ seems to agree as far as export to other Member States is concerned.[57] In *Gourmetterie Van den Burg,*[58] the ECJ struck down a Dutch prohibition on the importation of a protected bird, which was not endangered in the Netherlands and lawfully killed in the UK under an exception to Directive 79/409/EEC,[59] which the Advocate General explicitly linked to the fact that the Netherlands should not be allowed to seek to protect birds beyond the terms of the Directive on the territory of another Member State.[60] In *Alpine Investments,* the Dutch prohibition of cold calling could not be extended to protect (potential) customers in France.[61] Oliver and Jarvis[62] justify this approach, under reference to Roth,[63] by pointing to old Article 6(3) TEU, which required respect for the national identities of the Member States, a point made even more forcefully in the current Article 4(2) TEU.[64] I

52. Case C-384 *Alpine Investments* [1995] ECR I-1141; Case C-341/05 *Laval un Partneri* [2007] ECR I-11767.
53. Case C-442/02 *Caixha-Bank France* [2004] ECRI-8961; Case C-438/05 *International Transport Workers' Federation* [2007] ECR I-10779.
54. Case C-413/93 *Bosman* [1995] ECR I-4921.
55. On this P. Oliver & M. Jarvis, *Free Movement of Goods in the European Community*, 4th ed. (London: Thomson/Sweet & Maxwell, 2003), 230-231.
56. Opinion of AG Trabucchi in Case 8/74 *Dassonville* [1974] ECR 837, at 860. See also Opinion of AG Léger in Case C-5/94 *Hedley Lomas* [1996] ECR I-2553 and Case C-1/96 *Compassion in World Farming* [1998] ECR I-1251.
57. For more on export, and the risk of the export of national public policy, see G. Van Calster., 'Export Restrictions – A Watershed for Article 30', *European Law Review* (2000): 335-352.
58. Case C-169/89 *Gourmetterie Van den Burg* [1990] ECR I-2143.
59. Council Directive 79/409/EEC of 2 April 1979 on the conservation of wild birds (1979) OJ L 103/1.
60. Opinion of AG Van Gerven in Case C-169/89 *Gourmetterie Van den Burg* [1990] ECR I-2143, paras 7-10. See also, M. Dougan, 'Minimum harmonization and the internal market', *Common Market Law Review* (2000): 871-873.
61. Case C-384 *Alpine Investments* [1995] ECR I-1141.
62. P. Oliver & M. Jarvis, *Free Movement of Goods in the European Community*, 4th ed. (London: Thomson/Sweet & Maxwell, 2003), 231.
63. W.-H. Roth, 'Altruistische Interessenwahrnemung im Binnenmarkt – eine Skizze' in *Festschrift für Wolfganf Fikentscher*, ed. B. Großfeld, R. Sack, T. Möllers, J. Drexl & A. Heinemann (Tübingen: Mohr Siebeck, 1998), 732.
64. See in this respect also Case C-391/09 *Runevič-Vardyn* [2011] ECR I-0000, a judgment rich on references to Articles 3(3) and 4(2) TEU, and which may perhaps best be understood as

agree, and would point out that this mutual respect, therefore, is effectively only limited to the relationship between Member States. Accordingly, food products not meeting EU standards which are caught during veterinary checks must be destroyed and may not be exported to third countries, even if such products would not be deemed illegal there.[65] Similarly export refunds may be denied if there is evidence that the exported animals were not transported in accordance with EU standards.[66] Admittedly, in both examples there is also a benefit for the Member States concerned. There may be the risk that the meat, if not properly destroyed, is brought onto the Union market illegally; similarly, the animals are after all largely transported throughout the Member States as well. This is unsurprising as the whole reason to adopt EU legislation in the first place is of course the Union interest, as arguably some 'reterritorialisation of authority'[67] takes place when the Union – precisely because the Member States meet the boundaries of the extra-territorial effects of their public policy legislation[68] – legislates instead of the separate Member States for the whole Union. However, this does not take away the fact that the Union will de facto impose its safety standards even vis-à-vis third countries as is evidenced in particular by *Raverco.*[69]

**II-18.** So far I have treated the four freedoms largely indistinctly. As explained, this is justified to the extent that the technique of incorporating certain – but not all – norms intended to protect national policy concerns into the EU legal framework is applicable in respect of all four freedoms.[70] Attentive readers will also have noted that I hardly made any distinction between the various mandatory requirements set forth in Article 36 TFEU or the corresponding articles for persons, services and capital. This, too, can be justified to the extent that the public policy concerns that make Member States want to deviate from the four freedoms cannot be fully caught by the term '*ordre public*' or public policy concern, but rather encompasses also related concerns such as public security, public health, public morality, fundamental rights and other legitimate interests not even listed by the Treaties – all of which will be revisited below in Part III. However, there are also distinctions between the various freedoms when it comes to public policy. Actually, precisely when it comes to the scope of the term public policy

---

accepting that citizens cannot impose the linguistic policy of another Member State onto the administration of another, even though the result is not self-evident in light of earlier case law, in particular Case C-353/06 *Grunkin and Paul* [2008] ECR I-7639.

65. Joined Cases C-129/05 and C-130/05 *Raverco* [2006] ECR I-9297.
66. Case C-96/06 *Viamex Agrar* [2008] ECR I-1413. See also Opinion of AG Bot in Case C-455/06 *Heemskerk and Schaap* [2008] ECR I-8763.
67. D. Chalmers, 'Deliberative Supranationalism and the Reterritorialisation of Authority' in JOERGES, C., 'Rethinking European Law's Supremacy with Comments by Damian CHALMERS, Rainer NICKEL, Florian RÖDL, Robert WAI', EUI Working Papers Law No 2005/12 (<http://hdl.handle.net/1814/3332>, 18 May 2012), 28 et seq.
68. Overcoming the territoriality limits inherent in a classic conflicts of law approach, which Joerges calls 'Deliberative Supranationalism I' is indeed the driving force behind the supranational harmonisation which he describes as 'Deliberative Supranationalism II', see C. Joerges, 'Rethinking European Law's Supremacy with Comments by Damian CHALMERS, Rainer NICKEL, Florian RÖDL, Robert WAI', EUI Working Papers Law No 2005/12 (<http://hdl.handle.net/1814/3332>, 18 May 2012).
69. Joined Cases C-129/05 and C-130/05 *Raverco* [2006] ECR I-9297.
70. Compare C. Kessedjian, 'Public Order in European Law', *Erasmus Law Review* (2007): 27-28.

in Article 36 TFEU and the use of the same term in respect of persons, services and capital there is prima facie an important distinction. Accordingly, it is necessary to briefly look at the various fundamental freedoms separately.

### [B] Free Movement of Goods (Article 36 TFEU)

**II-19.** The free movement of goods and its exceptions have extensively been analysed, so what follows can be rather limited. The main observation to be made is the fact that despite the presence in Article 36 TFEU of an explicit reference to public policy, it is rather difficult to find cases where a restriction to the free movement of goods has effectively been justified on that ground. The reason for this is the fact that Article 36 TFEU refers not only to public policy, but also to a series of related concepts of public morality, public security and public health. These three grounds are all somewhat more concrete so that public policy, as something of a residuary category, has largely been unused. But this should thus not be taken as implying that the underlying national concerns have been ignored. A few selected cases may illustrate the limited role of the public policy exception.

**II-20.** The first case immediately demonstrates the role of the public policy as a residuary category for policy concerns that are closely linked to State interests, but cannot be dealt with as a matter of public security, public morality or public health. In *Thompson* the compatibility with EEC law of a UK norm prohibiting the export of certain silver coins in order to prevent them from being melted abroad was at stake. As the coins were no longer legal tender they could not be considered as capital, but rather had become goods, the export of which was thus banned. The ECJ, in a context of far less sophisticated international monetary policy than we are used to nowadays, accepted that such a:

> ban on exporting such coins with a view to preventing their being melted down or destroyed in another Member State is justified on grounds of *public policy* within the meaning of Article 36 of the Treaty, *because it stems from the need to protect the right to mint coinage which is traditionally regarded as involving the fundamental interests of the State.*[71]

**II-21.** Successful reliance on the public policy exception, however, does not only require a real fundamental interest of the State, but also requires that the proportionality test is met. Accordingly, though France had arguably a case that combating the trade in stolen cars may amount to a public policy concern, this could not justify the national legislation at issue, which made the sale by public auction of second-hand cars from another Member State conditional upon the prior entry of the undertaking which owns the cars offered for sale in the trade register at the place of the sale, as the objective of combating the trade in stolen vehicles could as well be attained through

71. Case 7/78 *Thompson* [1978] ECR 2247, para. 34 (emphasis added).

less restrictive alternatives such as checking of the chassis number.[72] Interestingly, the ECJ did not confirm whether it really considers the prevention of the trafficking of stolen cars a matter of public policy, but rather immediately addressed the issue of proportionality.[73]

**II-22.** In most instances, the public policy concern is however mixed with one of the other compelling interest of Article 36 TFEU. In several cases concerning petroleum reserves, the link was made with public security. In *Cullet,* France argued rather unconvincingly that unrestricted competition in determining the retail prices of petroleum products would result in a threat to public order[74] and public security because it anticipated reactions from retailers.[75] The Court rightly dismissed this as speculative, as it was not made clear why France would not be able to deal with such reactions, in the unlikely event any violence were to occur. Yet, in *Campus Oil,*[76] the ECJ did consider the public security sufficiently implicated to justify an Irish norm requiring importers to cover a certain proportion of their needs by purchases from a refinery situated in Ireland at prices fixed by the competent minister on the basis of the costs incurred in the operation of that refinery, if the production of the refinery cannot be freely disposed of at competitive prices on the market in question in order to guarantee the maintenance of a strategic refinery capacity in Ireland in the face of an international oil crisis, which could otherwise bring all public life to a hold.

**II-23.** Similarly, cases involving certain goods with a sexual connotation are rather dealt with as a matter of public morality. Here, too, one can find examples going both ways. In *Henn and Darby,* the Court accepted that public morality may justify a ban on the importation of certain pornographic materials, even though they could lawfully be marketed elsewhere in the Community and their possession would not necessarily be a criminal offence in the whole of the UK.[77] In *Conegate*, by contrast, the Court was far less impressed with a similar ban on the importation of inflatable dolls, when the possession and even sale of such dolls – presumably from national producers – was not prohibited.[78]

**II-24.** However, attempts were made to also bring non-sexual concerns under the public morality exception. However, at the height of the Sunday trading cases

72. Case C-239/90 *Boscher, Studer & Fromentin* [1991] ECR I-2023, para. 23.
73. Compare Case C-265/06 *Commission v. Portugal* [2008] ECR I-2245, where the ECJ rather generally held that 'the fight against crime and ensuring road safety may constitute overriding reasons in the public interest capable of justifying a hindrance to the free movement of goods', but then rightly concluded that prohibiting the affixing of tinted film to the windows of motor vehicles is disproportionate to these aims.
74. It has indeed been argued that there is a similarity between the public policy of Article 36 TFEU and the 'prevention of disorder' in the limitation clauses of Articles 8 and 10 ECHR, see R. De Lange, 'The European Public Order, Constitutional Principles and Fundamental Rights', *Erasmus Law Review* (2007): 9.
75. Case 231/83 *Cullet* [1985] ECR 305, paras 32-33. Compare also Case C-552/07 *Azelvandre* [2009] ECR I-987.
76. Case 72/83 *Campus Oil* [1984] ECR 2727.
77. Case 34/79 *Henn and Darby* [1979] ECR 3795.
78. Case 121/85 *Conegate* [1986] ECR 1007.

Advocate General Van Gerven rejected an attempt to justify a Sunday trading ban – if any justification would be needed – as a matter of public morality. The Advocate General conceded that the ECJ had accepted in *Henn and Darby* 'that in principle it is for each Member State to determine in accordance with its own scale of values and in the form selected by it the requirements of public morality in its territory'.[79] However, the limits of the term are a matter for Union law, and in his view the prevention of offence to religious convictions does not fall within that concept. Interestingly, he then also rejects that this concern may amount to an issue of public policy as that requires '*the existence ... of a genuine and sufficiently serious threat to the requirements of public policy affecting one of the fundamental interests of society*',[80] which is admittedly not the case in the context of a prohibition of Sunday trading. The source for this definition is the judgment in *Bouchereau,*[81] which deals, however, with the free movement of persons where the public morality exception is not explicitly provided for (see also *infra* §4.01[C]). This narrow reading of public morality and public policy forced the Advocate General, however, to somewhat reluctantly propose an independent mandatory requirement flowing from 'a need to give citizens on one and the same day the opportunity to devote their time to all kinds of (non-working and *inter alia* religious) activities and social contacts'.[82]

**II-25.** The public policy exception, on its own or in combination with public morality, has however recently been given some new breadth, also in the context of the free movement of goods. As already discussed in Part I,[83] it had been suggested by Advocate General Jacobs that in the absence of a listed exception for fundamental rights concerns in Article 36 TFEU, these could be brought under the public policy exception.[84] The ECJ did not need to decide the matter as the measure that needed to be justified – the authorization of a blockade of the Brenner motorway in protest of (European) transport policy – was indistinctly applicable and could thus also be justified irrespective of Article 36 TFEU. However, the suggestion – though the subject of criticism[85] – was taken up in the context of the free movement of services in *Omega*

79. Opinion of AG Van Gerven in Case C-145/88 *Torfaen Borough Council* [1989] ECR 3851, para. 29, referring to Case 34/79 *Henn and Darby* [1979] ECR 3795 and also paras 14-15 of Case 121/85 *Conegate* [1986] ECR 1007.
80. Opinion of AG Van Gerven in Case C-145/88 *Torfaen Borough Council* [1989] ECR 3851, para. 29 (italics added).
81. Case 30/77 *Bouchereau* [1977] ECR 1999, para. 35.
82. Opinion of AG Van Gerven in Case C-145/88 *Torfaen Borough Council* [1989] ECR 3851, para. 30.
83. *Supra,* at I-75 to I-77.
84. Opinion of AG Jacobs in Case C-112/00 *Schmidberger* [2003] ECR I-5659, paras 97-98.
85. On this see *supra,* at I-75 to I-77. In a footnote I noted there, and recall here, that I do not share the criticism by Avbelj, repeated by Morijn, that the concept of public policy is 'conceptually different' from fundamental rights as it is based on 'collectivism' said to be proper to the French *ordre public.* Though there are also some 'collectivist' elements in that concept, the discussion of the national concepts of *ordre public* above offers quite some indications that also fundamental rights can be reconciled with the French concept of *ordre public.* For the criticism, see M. Avbelj, '*European Court of Justice and the Question of Value Choices* – Fundamental human rights as an exception to the freedom of movement of goods', Jean Monnet Working Paper 06/04 (<http://www.jeanmonnetprogram.org/papers/04/040601.pdf>, 18 May

*Spielhallen*,[86] albeit limited to instances where the national protection of fundamental rights went way beyond what is expected in other Member States or – probably – at EU level. Yet, in *Dynamic Medien*[87] the Court got a chance of applying this approach to the free movement of goods. At issue was the requirement that video media had to be labelled with age classifications in accordance with German law, a requirement which was also forced upon a German online seller of video materials bearing – at best – age classifications from other Member States. Several Member States and the Commission all submitted that the protection of young people amounts to issues of public morality and public policy.[88] The ECJ again does not fully decide the matter. After having recognized the position of the rights of the child as fundamental norms enshrined in international agreements and the Charter of Fundamental Rights, the ECJ citing *Schmidberger*[89] merely calls this a 'legitimate interest'[90] which may justify certain proportionate restrictions. Interestingly, as already indicated above,[91] the ECJ then mimics some of its public policy case law in respect of the free movement of persons (without citing it), by imposing certain procedural requirements that must be met for this type of restriction to be proportionate. In particular the Court demands that the procedure for examination, classification and labelling of image storage media established by those rules is readily accessible and can be completed within a reasonable period, or that a decision of refusal is open to challenge before the courts.[92]

**II-26.** Finally, it needs to be observed that Advocate General Mengozzi, in line with what I have argued above[93] the ECJ should have done – but failed to do – in *Omega Spielhallen*[94] (and in *Dynamic Medien*[95] for that matter), engaged in one further check of the public policy concern raised by Germany.[96] It could have been objected that the emphasis on protecting young persons, may have resulted in unjustified inroads into another fundamental right, notably the freedom of expression. The Advocate General notes that the same concerns of public policy and public morality justify, however, under Article 10(2) ECHR also certain restrictions of the freedom of expression. The

2012), 60-62; J. Morijn, 'Balancing Fundamental Rights and Common Market Freedoms in Union Law: Schmidberger and Omega in the Light of the European Constitution', *European Law Journal* (2006): 39.

86. Case C-36/02 *Omega Spielhallen* [2004] ECR I-9609.
87. Case C-244/06 *Dynamic Medien* [2008] ECR I-505.
88. Case C-244/06 *Dynamic Medien* [2008] ECR I-505, paras 36-37.
89. Case C-112/00 *Schmidberger* [2003] ECR I-5659, para. 74.
90. Case C-244/06 *Dynamic Medien* [2008] ECR I-505, 42.
91. *Supra*, at II-11.
92. Case C-244/06 *Dynamic Medien* [2008] ECR I-505, para. 52.
93. *Supra*, at I-77 and I-78.
94. Case C-36/02 *Omega Spielhallen* [2004] ECR I-9609.
95. Case C-244/06 *Dynamic Medien* [2008] ECR I-505.
96. Actually, AG Mengozzi does also not decide whether and how the protection of young persons from explicit video materials falls within one of the categories of Article 36 TFEU, but merely concludes that no-one contests that the protection of young persons is a legitimate interest which may justify certain restrictions of the free movement of goods, see Opinion of AG Mengozzi in Case C-244/06 *Dynamic Medien* [2008] ECR I-505, para. 71.

justifications for restrictions to the four freedoms, though not fully identical, are indeed closely related to the justifications for limitations to certain fundamental rights.[97]

### [C] Free Movement of Persons

**II-27.** The most developed applications of the public policy exception can be found in the context of the free movement of persons. There are three main reasons for this, which up to this day leave their mark on the case law. First, historically, the *ordre public* in the legal order of the Member States has been linked to the treatment of aliens, the *police des étrangers*.[98] Inherent in the migration law of the Member States, and thus in their *ordre public* was indeed some bias against aliens,[99] unpleasantly differentiating between 'us' and 'them'.[100] With the introduction of the free movement of persons and the principle of non-discrimination on the grounds of nationality in the Treaties, this bias of course needed to be nuanced. However, it has not fully disappeared and still results in restrictions on the free movement of persons.[101] Occasionally, the bias reappears in the laws of the Member States in a surprisingly direct manner, as in the case of Austrian legislation that explicitly targeted self-employed persons from the Member States that joined the Union in 2004, with the exception of persons coming from Malta or Cyprus.[102] Moreover, even within EU law the bias still lives on in the relationship with people coming from third countries. On the one hand, the ECJ is still regularly confronted with cases involving the public policy exception in international agreements between the Community and third countries, notably Turkey. Though it is established case law that the rights of Turkey workers which fall within the scope of Decision 1/80[103] must be interpreted *mutatis mutandis* as far as possible in parallel with the Union rules on free movement of persons,[104] the references to the ECJ reveal

97. The Court has explicitly recognized this link in Case 36/75 *Rutili* [1975] ECR 1219, para. 32. For an extensive analysis of this relationship, see C. Picheral, *L'ordre public européen: droit communautaire et droit européen des droits de l'homme* (Paris: CERIC – Documentation française, 2001).
98. On this link, see F. Julien-Laferrière, '*Ordre public* et droit des étrangers' in *L'ordre public: ordre public ou ordres publics? Ordre public et droits fondamentaux*, ed. M.-J. Redor (Brussel: Bruylant, 2001), 285-297.
99. See in this respect also F. Hubeau, 'l'exeption d'*ordre public* et la libre circulation des personnes en droit communautaire', *Cahiers de droit européen* (1981): 207-256.
100. On this 'unpleasant shadow' of different treatment, see Opinion of AG Poiares Maduro in Case C-524/06 *Huber* [2008] ECR I-9705, para. 15.
101. For an overview of what constitutes a restriction on the free movement of persons, see P. Gilliaux, 'Les entraves à la libre circulation des personnes', *Cahiers de droit européen* (2008): 407-459.
102. Case C-161/07 *Commission v. Austria* [2008] ECR I-10671.
103. Decision No 1/80 of the Council of Association of 19 September 1980 on the development of the Association between the European Economic Community and Turkey, notoriously unpublished in the Official Journal.
104. Case C-349/06 *Polat* [2007] ECR I-8167, para. 29; see earlier Case C-434/93 *Bozkurt* [1995] ECR I-1475, paras 14, 19 and 20, and Case C-467/02 *Cetinkaya* [2004] ECR I-10895, para. 42. Recent case law has revealed, however, that there is a limit to this parallelism, as the expulsion of long-term residents from Member States under Article 28(3) of Directive 2004/38/EC can only take place for reasons of public security, which is a more narrow category than the concept of

a strong concern, if not distrust, about the immigration rights that may thus be claimed by Turkish nationals.[105] On the other hand, even the ECJ cannot but admit that in other aspects of the EU migration law this bias is still firmly rooted. Accordingly, in *Commission v. Spain,*[106] the ECJ had to find a way of balancing the rules on the internal free movement of persons with the requirements of maintaining an effective control on third country nationals under the Schengen Information System (SIS).

**II-28.** The second reason for the far more refined approach to public policy in the context of the free movement of persons is the fact that early on the Community legislator has taken the step, probably in order to alleviate some of the concerns mentioned in the first paragraph and stem the potential abuse of the public policy exception, to further elaborate on this in Directive 64/221/EEC.[107] Over time, however, the ECJ has further elaborated on these provisions and developed an even more far-reaching protection. Moreover, as the right of free movement has gradually been expanded to also include persons who are not economically active, this Directive became gradually outdated. Accordingly, the Directive has since been replaced by Directive 2004/38,[108] which does more than merely codify the recent developments.[109]

**II-29.** Third, it needs to be observed that Article 45(3) TFEU, dealing with the exceptions to the free movement of workers, differs in language from Article 36 TFEU. The Article only lists 'public policy, public security or public health'. Notably lacking in this list is a reference to public morality. As a result the notion of public policy – of which I argued above[110] that it functions somewhat as a residuary category, though like any exception it needs to be construed narrowly[111] – has been given somewhat more body in this context, often covering situations one could otherwise consider as raising

---

public policy in Article14(1) of Decision No 1/80, see in particular Case C-371/08 *Ziebell* [2011] ECR I-0000. The consequences may, however, be limited as the Court is now also looking more into the public security component of certain criminal activity, in particular drugs use, see Case C-145/09 *Tsakouridis* [2010] ECR I-0000.

105. Examples include Case C-325/05 *Derin* [2007] ECR I-6495 (where the national court even expressed the fear that Turkish workers may even be treated more favourably than Community workers – contrary to Article 59 of the Additional Protocol to the EU-Turkey Agreement; see in this respect also Case C-325/05 *Derin* [2007] ECR I-6495); Case C-294/06 *Payir* [2008] ECR I-203 (on rights of students and au pairs).
106. Case C-503/03 *Commission v. Spain* [2006] ECR I-1097.
107. Council Directive 64/221/EEC of 25 February 1964 on the coordination of special measures concerning the movement and residence of foreign nationals which are justified on grounds of public policy, public security or public health, *English special edition: Series I Chapter 1963-1964,* 117. See in general, L. Dubouis & C. Blumann, *Droit materiel de l'Union européenne,* 2nd ed. (Paris: Montchrestien, 2001), 57 et seq.
108. Directive 2004/38/EC of the European Parliament and of the Council of 29 April 2004 on the right of citizens of the Union and their family members to move and reside freely within the territory of the Member States amending Regulation (EEC) No 1612/68 and repealing Directives 64/221/EEC, 68/360/EEC, 72/194/EEC, 73/148/EEC, 75/34/EEC, 75/35/EEC, 90/364/EEC, 90/365/EEC and 93/96/EEC (2004) OJ L 158/77
109. H. Oosterom-Staples, 'Botsende openbare-ordebegrippen in het Europese Migratierecht', *Nederlands Tijdschrift voor Europees Recht* (2006): 170. See also N. Nic Shuibhne, 'Derogating from the Free Movement of Persons: When can EU Citizens be Deported?', *Cambridge Yearbook of European Legal Studies* (2005-2006): 187-227.
110. *Supra,* at II-19.
111. See, for instance, Case C-441/02 *Commission v. Germany* [2006] ECR I-3149, para. 34.

issues of public morality.[112] However, as will be made clear below, also other concerns which do not seem to affect the very existence of the State have been brought under the public policy exception.[113] Moreover, also in respect of self-employed persons,[114] and even persons receiving services,[115] a similar evolution has taken place as the exception of Article 52(1) TFEU is similarly restricted to grounds of 'public policy, public security or public health'.

**II-30.** The public policy exception has been elaborated in secondary EU law. Currently, the relevant provisions can be found in Directive 2004/38/EC,[116] which has replaced in this respect the old Directive 64/221/EEC[117] and its extension to self-employed persons, Directive 75/35/EEC.[118] It seems, therefore appropriate to first address these provisions and illustrate them with the relevant case law. Again the reader is reminded that this overview does not seeks to be exhaustive, as the aim of this section is to give an overview of the various appearances of *ordre public* in the EU legal order as building blocks for further analysis in Parts IV and V. As these provisions cover in some instances also non-EU nationals, second, it will be important to address some specific complications that arise because of the combination of the Community regime with the Schengen provisions. Third, though no specific public policy exception exists in the Treaty provisions on European Citizenship, public policy and the Directive also have a role to play in that context. Finally, it needs to be examined to what extent Directive 2004/38/EC fully exhausts the concept of *ordre public*, or whether one could imagine some cases outside its scope.

---

112. Prime examples are a series of cases involving prostitution, see most notably Joined Cases 115/81 and 116/81 *Adoui and Cornuaille* [1982] ECR 1665, but also Case 98/79 *Pecastaing* [1980] ECR 691. See, by analogy, also Case C-268/99 *Jany* [2001] ECR I-8615.
113. See in particular Opinion of AG Jacobs in Case 96/04 *Standesamt Stadt Niebüll* [2006] ECR I-3561 and the follow-up case of Case C-353/06 *Grunkin and Paul* [2008] ECR I-7639, para. 38, but also Case 41/74 *van Duyn* [1974] ECR 1337. Compare also the – unfruitful – invocation of public policy in Case C-379/87 *Groener* [1989] ECR 3967.
114. Most spectacular example are of course prostitutes, see most notably Joined Cases 115/81 and 116/81 *Adoui and Cornuaille* [1982] ECR 1665.
115. Case C-348/96 *Calfa* [1999] ECR I-11.
116. Directive 2004/38/EC of the European Parliament and of the Council of 29 April 2004 on the right of citizens of the Union and their family members to move and reside freely within the territory of the Member States amending Regulation (EEC) No 1612/68 and repealing Directives 64/221/EEC, 68/360/EEC, 72/194/EEC, 73/148/EEC, 75/34/EEC, 75/35/EEC, 90/364/EEC, 90/365/EEC and 93/96/EEC (2004) OJ L 158/77.
117. Council Directive 64/221/EEC of 25 February 1964 on the coordination of special measures concerning the movement and residence of foreign nationals which are justified on grounds of public policy, public security or public health, *English special edition: Series I Chapter 1963-1964*, 117.
118. Council Directive 75/35/EEC of 17 December 1974 extending the scope of Directive No 64/221/EEC on the coordination of special measures concerning the movement and residence of foreign nationals which are justified on grounds of public policy, public security or public health to include nationals of a Member State who exercise the right to remain in the territory of another Member State after having pursued therein an activity in a self-employed capacity (1975) OJ L 14/14.

### *[1] Directive 2004/38/EC*

**II-31.** Article 27(1) of Directive 2004/38 lays down the principle:

> Subject to the provisions of this Chapter, Member States may restrict the freedom of movement and residence of Union citizens and their family members, irrespective of nationality, on grounds of public policy, public security or public health.

In this, it does nothing more than recalling the relevant Treaty provisions, Articles 45(3) and 52(1) TFEU. The Article does, however, further elaborate that 'These grounds shall not be invoked to serve economic ends.' This has so far not resulted in major problems in the context of the free movement of persons. However, as the example above of *Campus Oil*[119] makes clear it cannot be excluded that occasionally certain economic interests may be intertwined with the underlying non-economic concern. This seems a defensible compromise.[120] By contrast, as recent case law demonstrates, if economic self-interest seems to have the upper hand the ECJ still objects to a potentially protectionist use of public policy exceptions, even where some non-economic concerns are arguably also at stake.[121]

**II-32.** Unlike in the case of public health, where the diseases which may result in exclusion are defined under reference to a list of the WHO,[122] understandably no exhaustive list is given of grounds of public policy. Nonetheless, the legislator has attempted to give some content by taking over the definition given by the ECJ in *Bouchereau.*[123] There the Court had recognized:

> that the particular circumstances justifying recourse to the concept of public policy may vary from one country to another and from one period to another and it is therefore necessary in this matter to allow the competent national authorities an area of discretion within the limits imposed by the treaty and the provisions adopted for its implementation[124].

However, the ECJ then went on to provide that as a minimum[125]:

> recourse by a national authority to the concept of public policy presupposes, in any event, the existence, in addition to the perturbation of the social order which any

119. Case 72/83 *Campus Oil* [1984] ECR 2727.
120. H. Schneider, *Die öffentliche Ordnung als Schranke der Grundfreiheiten im EG-Vertrag* (Baden-Baden: Nomos, 1998), 125-126.
121. Case C-341/05 *Laval un Partneri* [2007] ECR I-11767. See also Case C-319/06 *Commission v. Luxemburg* [2008] ECR I-4323, with Opinion of AG Trstenjak.
122. Article 29(1) of Directive 2004/38/EC. See <http://www.who.int/topics/disease_outbreaks/en/> (18 May 2012).
123. Case 30/77 *Bouchereau* [1977] ECR 1999.
124. Case 30/77 *Bouchereau* [1977] ECR 1999, para. 34.
125. As explained in §1, also in respect of the free movement of persons the concept of public policy has EU limits, even though the Member States are giving it content. As the ECJ observes 'The Court, for its part, has always emphasised that the public policy exception is a derogation from the fundamental principle of freedom of movement for persons, which must be interpreted strictly, and that its scope cannot be determined unilaterally by the Member States', see Case C-441/02 *Commission v. Germany* [2006] ECR I-3149, para. 34.

> infringement of the law involves, of a genuine and sufficiently serious threat to the requirements of public policy affecting one of the fundamental interests of society[126].

Accordingly, in Article 27(2), paragraph 2 of Directive 2004/38/EC it is required that the 'personal conduct of the individual concerned must represent a genuine, present and sufficiently serious threat affecting one of the fundamental interests of society'.

**II-33.** This definition offers a series of important elements. First, it promises every person an individual assessment of the personal circumstances surrounding his/her case. Accordingly any legislative measure[127] or administrative practice[128] which would result in the quasi-automatic imposition of certain restrictive measure (usually a prohibition of entry into or residence in the country[129] or expulsion from (part of) the country[130]) is thus prohibited. Member States are thus prevented from taking measures of a 'general preventive nature' as a referring national had phrased it so neatly that the ECJ took over the expression.[131] The classic cases in this respect mostly deal with the consequences of criminal convictions. While Member States, as a matter of international law, cannot expel their own nationals[132] no matter the nature of their conduct, they often envisage that additional sanction in respect of foreign offenders. The ECJ has recognized this competence, despite the fact that, in practice, it may result in a harsher treatment of foreign offenders than offenders holding the nationality of the Member State where the offence is prosecuted. Yet, it has largely curtailed this power by demanding that on an individual basis be examined whether the offender, if he/she falls within the scope of the free movement of persons, still poses a real threat.[133] In this respect, the requirement of a 'genuine, present and sufficiently serious threat' offers further restrictions on the possibility for expelling foreigners. The mere fact of prior convictions - notice the plural - does not in itself constitute a ground for taking restrictive measures.[134] The case law, moreover, offers telling examples of cases where the threat has greatly diminished over time. In *Santillo,*[135] for instance, several years had lapsed between the recommendation of his expulsion and the moment steps were taken to actually expel him. In *Bonsignore,*[136] the national court had even refused to impose a prison sentence on a man who had accidentally killed his brother with a firearm as he had already suffered enough emotionally; accordingly, there was also no reason to assume that the threat - if there ever was one - would be repeated.

---

126. Case 30/77 *Bouchereau* [1977] ECR 1999, para. 35. For a recent affirmation, see Case C-441/02 *Commission v. Germany* [2006] ECR I-3149, para. 35.
127. Case C-348/96 *Calfa* [1999] ECR I-11.
128. Case C-441/02 *Commission v. Germany* [2006] ECR I-3149.
129. Case C-503/03 *Commission v. Spain* [2006] ECR I-1097
130. Case C-100/01 *Oteiza Olazabal* [2002] ECR I-1098.
131. Case 67/74 *Bonsignore* [1975] ECR 297, para. 7.
132. Case 41/74 *van Duyn* [1974] ECR 1337, para. 22. Compare, in respect of the Europe Agreement with the Czech Republic, with Case C-257/99 *Barkoci and Malik* [2001] ECR I-6557, para. 80.
133. Case 30/77 *Bouchereau* [1977] ECR 1999; Case C-348/96 *Calfa* [1999] I-11; Case C-50/06 *Commission v. Netherlands* [2007] ECR I-4383.
134. Article 27(2), paragraph 1 of Directive 2004/38/EC.
135. Case 131/79 *Santillo* [1980] ECR 1585.
136. Case 67/74 *Bonsignore* [1975] ECR 297.

**II-34.** The key question remains, however, what qualifies as 'one of the fundamental interests of society'. Though a detailed analysis of protected interests will be undertaken in part III, a few examples here will already clarify things. As is apparent from the examples above, certain criminal offences may certainly qualify as disturbances, not only of the normal societal order, but also of one of the fundamental interests of society. Under influence of Article 28(3) of the Directive the ECJ, however, increasingly treats criminal behaviour more as a matter of public security, focusing more on the harm to society than on the personal behaviour, in order to make expulsions possible of long-term residents deeply engaged in criminal activity such as drugs trafficking[137] or sex crimes.[138] More problematic, however, are the instances where the Member States is not fully prohibiting a certain activity, or is in any event not in practice imposing criminal sanctions. In *Van Duyn,*[139] the ECJ accepted nonetheless that the UK could refuse the entry of Ms. Van Duyn, who planned to take up a job offer at the Church of Scientology. Though controversial, neither the Church nor its activities were prohibited under UK law and UK nationals could thus freely become a member of the Church, if they so wished. First, one could wonder whether (past) membership of an organization could qualify as personal conduct, as it seems to transfer the sins of the organization on all its individual members. However, the Court found that:

> although a person's past association cannot in general, justify a decision refusing him the right to move freely within the Community, it is nevertheless the case that present association, which reflects participation in the activities of the body or of the organization as well as identification with its aims and its designs, may be considered a voluntary act of the person concerned and, consequently, as part of his personal conduct[140].

With that objection out of the way, the ECJ – recalling that while the public policy exception needs to be interpreted strictly, Member States have nonetheless some margin of discretion[141] – found that:

> where the competent authorities of a Member State have clearly defined their standpoint as regards the activities of a particular organization and where, considering it to be socially harmful, they have taken administrative measures to counteract these activities, the Member State cannot be required, before it can rely

137. The seminal case in this respect is Case C-145/09 *Tsakouridis* [2010] ECR I-0000. As a result there is a limit to this parallelism between the free movement of persons under Directive 2004/38/EC and under Decision No 1/80, as the expulsion of long term residents from Member States under Article 28(3) of Directive 2004/38/EC can only take place for reasons of public security, which is a more narrow category than the concept of public policy in Article14(1) of Decision No 1/80, see in particular Case C-371/08 *Ziebell* [2011] ECR I-0000. See also Case C-303/08 *Bozkurt* [2010] ECR I-0000.
138. Case C-348/09 *P.I.* [2012] ECR I-0000. The fact that the exception used is labelled 'public security' and not 'public policy' does not take away that the reasoning of the Court is largely similar as in the case of public policy in the sense of Article 27. The only difference appears to be the emphasis that is placed on the gravity of the offences, which – at least in the case of sexual exploitation of children or drugs trafficking – are also caught by EU measures in the field of criminal law.
139. Case 41/74 *van Duyn* [1974] ECR 1337.
140. Case 41/74 *van Duyn* [1974] ECR 1337, para. 17.
141. Case 41/74 *van Duyn* [1974] ECR 1337, para. 18.

> on the concept of public policy, to make such activities unlawful, if recourse to such a measure is not thought appropriate in the circumstances[142].

Regrettably, this opens the door for rather arbitrary assessments as to whether national authorities really have spoken out against a certain practice, and creates a grey zone where discrimination on the ground of nationality becomes the rule rather than the exception.

**II-35.** Fortunately, the ECJ has since changed course. Similar to the shift that took place between *Henn and Darby*[143] and *Conegate*[144] mentioned above,[145] the ECJ took a very different stance in *Adoui and Cornuaille.*[146] Actually, chronologically the shift occurred first in the context of the free movement of persons. In any event, the Court eventually expressed the concern that 'the authority empowered to adopt [restrictive] measures must not base the exercise of its powers on assessments of certain conduct which would have the effect of applying an arbitrary distinction to the detriment of nationals of other Member States'.[147] Without acknowledging that it once ruled differently in *Van Duyn,*[148] the Court declares that:

> although Community law does not impose upon the Member States a uniform scale of values as regards the assessment of conduct which may be considered as contrary to public policy, it should nevertheless be stated that conduct may not be considered as being of a sufficiently serious nature to justify restrictions on the admission to or residence within the territory of a Member State of a national of another Member State in a case where the former Member State does not adopt, with respect to the same conduct on the part of its own nationals repressive measures or other genuine and effective measures intended to combat such conduct[149].

Accordingly, to the extent that Belgium effectively condones the activities of prostitutes, it cannot justify expelling other EU nationals who want to take up that same trade. The come-back by Belgium that it is actually seeking to curtail the criminal activities that tend to surround prostitution, had to fail for the same reason, as criminality equally surrounds prostitution irrespective of the nationality of the prostitutes. Moreover, making prostitutes responsible for the crimes of others is incompatible with the requirement of personal conduct.[150]

**II-36.** Completely off the table, then, are restrictions in response to activities that are not only lawful but even protected by EU law or international agreements. The prime example in this respect is *Rutili.*[151] Mr Rutili was an Italian national living and working in France. He got caught up in the post-May 1968 unrest and was quite active in a trade

142. Case 41/74 *van Duyn* [1974] ECR 1337, para. 19.
143. Case 34/79 *Henn and Darby* [1979] ECR 3795.
144. Case 121/85 *Conegate* [1986] ECR 1007.
145. *Supra,* at II-23.
146. Joined Cases 115/81 and 116/81 *Adoui and Cornuaille* [1982] ECR 1665.
147. Joined Cases 115/81 and 116/81 *Adoui and Cornuaille* [1982] ECR 1665, para. 7.
148. Case 41/74 *van Duyn* [1974] ECR 1337, para. 19.
149. Joined Cases 115/81 and 116/81 *Adoui and Cornuaille* [1982] ECR 1665, para. 8.
150. Joined Cases 115/81 and 116/81 *Adoui and Cornuaille* [1982] ECR 1665, paras 10-11.
151. Case 36/75 *Rutili* [1975] ECR 1219.

union distributing pamphlets etc. The French authorities decided to deport him, or at least deny him access to four departments, including the normal place of residence for him and his family. Undoubtedly, industrial action can be disruptive and is not without limits as a matter of Union law.[152] Yet, the right to participate in the activities of a trade union under the same conditions as local workers was at the time explicitly guaranteed by Article 8 of Regulation 1612/68.[153] Accordingly, in the absence of hard proof that the activities of Mr Rutili went well beyond what is a legitimate trade union practice if exercised by French nationals, the restrictive measures taken against him could not be justified.[154]

**II-37.** This case brings us also to the last requirement of Article 27 of Directive 2004/38 which I wish to highlight. As with any exception to the four freedoms, also here the possibilities for Member States are further restricted by the principle of proportionality. Accordingly, in deciding on expulsion, Article 28 requires Member State to 'take account of considerations such as how long the individual concerned has resided on its territory, his/her age, state of health, family and economic situation, social and cultural integration into the host Member State and the extent of his/her links with the country of origin'. The same Article even excludes expulsion on all grounds - including public policy - except public security in the cases of EU citizens who have resided at least 10 years in a Member State, or of minors except if the expulsion is necessary for the best interests of the child, as provided for in the United Nations Convention on the Rights of the Child of 20 November 1989.[155] In general it needs to be observed that the measures taken under the public policy exception, like any exception to the four freedoms, are

152. See recently, Case C-341/05 *Laval un Partneri* [2007] ECR I-11767; Case C-438/05 *International Transport Workers' Federation* [2007] ECR I-10779.
153. Regulation (EEC) No 1612/68 of the Council of 15 October 1968 on freedom of movement for workers within the Community, *Official Journal, English Special Edition 1968 II*, 475. The Regulation has recently been replaced by Regulation (EU) No 492/2011 of the European Parliament and of the Council of 5 April 2011 on freedom of movement for workers within the Union (2011) OJ L 141/1, but Article 8 still exists. Moreover, Community law explicitly protects trade union activities, including industrial action. Moreover, the right to industrial action is also a fundamental right protected in Article 28 of the Charter of Fundamental Rights of the Union, see Case C-341/05 *Laval un Partneri* [2007] ECR I-11767, para. 43; Case C-438/05 *International Transport Workers' Federation* [2007] ECR I-10779, para. 90. Compare also Case C-171/01 *Wählergruppe 'Gemeinsam Zajedno/Birlikte Alternative und Grüne GewerkschafterInnen/UG'* [2003] ECR I-4301.
154. Case 36/75 *Rutili* [1975] ECR 1219, paras 52-53.
155. In this way the Directive offers somewhat greater protection than originally developed by the ECJ, which had found, after examining the impact of Article 8 ECHR, that 'Article [45 TFEU] and Directive 64/221 do not preclude the expulsion of a national of another Member State who has received a particular sentence for specific offences and who, On the one hand, constitutes a present threat to the requirements of public policy and, on the other hand, has resided for many years in the host Member State and can plead family circumstances against that expulsion, provided that the assessment made on a case-by-case basis by the national authorities of where the fair balance lies between the legitimate interests at issue is made in compliance with the general principles of Community law and, in particular, by taking proper account of respect for fundamental rights, such as the protection of family life', see Joined Cases C-482/01 and C-493/01 *Orfanopoulos* [2004] ECR I-5247, para. 100.

limited by fundamental rights, in particular the right to family life[156] under Article 8(2) ECHR[157] as clarified by the ECtHR.[158]

**II-38.** But also less restrictive measures are still subject to this scrutiny. In this respect attention must be drawn to the question whether it is possible to impose a ban on residing in but part of a Member State. In *Rutili,* the ECJ had indeed found this could only be done if a similar restriction could also be imposed on the own nationals of a Member State.[159] This seems too harsh, as it basically forces a Member State into an all-or-nothing approach where a less dramatic measure may suffice. The ECJ has therefore wisely reversed course in *Oteiza Olazabal,*[160] where it was accepted that France could lawfully exclude a person, who had been sentenced in France to 18 months' imprisonment and a four-year ban on residence for conspiracy to disturb public order by intimidation or terror, with links to the Basque separatist movement ETA – a terrorist group, according to the EU[161] – from the areas in the South-West of France neighbouring Spain. The ECJ now explicitly accepts a *qui peut le plus peut le moins* reasoning, even in instances where identical measures are not possible against own nationals,[162] provided that, first, other genuine and effective measures in respect of the own nationals exist[163] and, second, the partial ban otherwise meets the principle of proportionality.[164]

**II-39.** The Directive 2004/38 also puts the public policy exception into effect in a different manner. Like its predecessor, it also provides for a procedural framework in order to ensure that decisions based on public policy (and by extension also on grounds of public security and public health) are indeed taken in accordance with procedures that offer sufficient possibilities for individual examination, and allow for effective judicial review. These procedural guarantees build on extensive case law in this respect developed in the context of Article 64/221. Three elements stand out.

**II-40.** First, persons must be notified *in writing* of the reasons for a decision based on Article 27(1) 'in such a way that they are able to comprehend its content and the implications for them'.[165] This implies, on the one hand, that 'the persons concerned shall be informed, precisely and in full, of the public policy, public security or public

156. Case C-441/02 *Commission v. Germany* [2006] ECR I-3149, para. 109; Joined Cases C-482/01 and C-493/01 *Orfanopoulos* [2004] ECR I-5247, paras 98-99; Case C-60/00 *Carpenter* [2002] ECR I-6279, para. 21.
157. See also Article 7 of the Charter of Fundamental Rights of the EU.
158. See, in particular, ECtHR, 2 August 2001, *Boultif v. Switzerland*, paras 39, 41 and 46.
159. Case 36/75 *Rutili* [1975] ECR 1219, para. 50.
160. Case C-100/01 *Oteiza Olazabal* [2002] ECR I-10981. This time the reversal was very explicit, reducing *Rutili* to its specific facts and rebutting any further argument that may flow from the ordinary territorial scope of residence permits. See also F. Chaltiel, 'L'*ordre public* devant la Cour de Justice des Communautés européennes – à propos de l'arrêt *Olazabal* du 26 novembre 2002', *Revue du Marché commun et de l'Union européenne* (2003): 120-123.
161. See in this respect Annex 2 of Council Common Position 2001/931/CFSP on the application of specific measures to combat terrorism (2001) OJ L 344/93.
162. Case C-100/01 *Oteiza Olazabal* [2002] ECR I-10981, para. 41.
163. Case C-100/01 *Oteiza Olazabal* [2002] ECR I-10981, para. 42.
164. Case C-100/01 *Oteiza Olazabal* [2002] ECR I-10981, paras 43-44.
165. Article 30(1) Directive 2004/38.

health grounds on which the decision taken in their case is based, unless this is contrary to the interests of State security'.[166] On the other hand, the Directive also requires that 'the notification shall specify the court or administrative authority with which the person concerned may lodge an appeal, the time limit for the appeal and, where applicable, the time allowed for the person to leave the territory of the Member State'.[167] The time limit allowed for a person to leave the territory of a Member State is in principle no less than one month.[168] This period may be considerably longer if a person indeed seeks review of the decision. If the application is combined with a request for an interim order, expulsion may – subject to some narrow exceptions – not take place until a decision is taken on the request for interim relief.[169]

**II-41.** This brings us to the second point. The Directive guarantees indeed access to 'judicial and, where appropriate, administrative redress procedures in the host Member State to appeal against or seek review of any decision taken against them on the grounds of public policy, public security or public health'.[170] The aim is to ensure effective judicial protection[171] before an independent body[172] in the face of what should be rather exceptional measures. Accordingly, the review must extend to 'an examination of the legality of the decision, as well as of the facts and circumstances on which the proposed measure is based'.[173] Specifically, the procedure must allow review as to whether the 'decision is not disproportionate, particularly in view of the requirements laid down in Article 28' of the Directive.[174] Though it may happen, for instance because the person complied voluntarily or because a request for interim relief was rejected, that the person concerned has been expelled by the Member State. This is allowed for under the Directive,[175] but cannot preclude that the person concerned appears nevertheless in person to state his/her case, unless 'his/her appearance may cause serious troubles to public policy or public security or when the appeal or judicial review concerns a denial of entry to the territory'.[176] Of course, though not explicitly mentioned by the Directive, the person concerned can also be assisted or represented by a lawyer, and the other procedural rules – including the rules on evidence – may not

166. Article 30(2) Directive 2004/38.
167. Article 30(3), first sentence Directive 2004/38.
168. Article 30(3), second sentence Directive 2004/38.
169. Article 31(2) Directive 2004/38.
170. Article 31(1) Directive 2004/38.
171. Basically, this 'requirement for judicial review of any decision of a national authority reflects a general principle stemming from the constitutional traditions common to the Member States and enshrined in Articles 6 and 13 of the Convention', see Case C-459/99 *MRAX* [2002] ECR I-6591, para. 101.
172. See already under Directive 64/221, the independence requirement put forward by the Court in Joined Cases 115/81 and 116/81 *Adoui and Cornuaille* [1982] ECR 1665, para. 16.
173. Article 31(3), first sentence Directive 2004/38.
174. Article 31(3), second sentence Directive 2004/38.
175. This is sometimes the only way to protect the *ordre public*, as the Court explained in Case 98/79 *Pecastaing* [1980] ECR 691, para 12: 'an interpretation, which would enable the person concerned unilaterally, by lodging an application, to suspend the measure affecting him, is incompatible with the objective of the directive which is to reconcile the requirements of public policy, public security and public health with the guarantees which must be provided for the persons affected by such measures'.
176. Article 31(4) Directive 2004/38.

be less favourable than the conditions applicable to proceedings before other national authorities of the same type.[177]

**II-42.** Third, the impact of any order resulting in the expulsion or denial of entry must by nature be limited in time. Accordingly, after a reasonable time, and in any event after three years, any person subject to such an order must be able to apply to have the order lifted. This is of course the procedural translation of the substantive requirement of the existence of a genuine and present and sufficiently serious risk laid down in Article 27(2) of Directive 2004/38. The same rationale is also behind the requirement that if the expulsion by way of penalty[178] is only to be executed two years or more[179] after its pronunciation that the Member State shall assess whether the conditions justifying the expulsion are still in place.

### *[2] The Free Movement of Persons in Tension with Schengen*

**II-43.** In the foregoing the emphasis has been laid on the personal conduct of the person against whom measures on the basis of public policy are taken and on the need to demonstrate a genuine, present and sufficiently serious risk. The regime of Directive 2004/38/EC is not limited to EU nationals, but also extends to their family members, who may well be of foreign – i.e., non-EU – origin. Third country nationals, however, are also caught by a series of EU measures aimed at controlling (illegal) immigration, which are often far less forgiving. Accordingly, it was only a matter of time before the lenient regime of Article 45(3) TFEU, as elaborated in the Directive, would clash with the Schengen rules.

**II-44.** The Commission brought the issue to the attention of the Court in an infringement action against Spain, taking up the cases of two-third country nationals who were denied visas to join their Spanish spouses in Spain.[180] Their spouses, as Spanish nationals who had been working in Dublin, were in principle entitled to bring their husbands with them upon their return to Spain under *Singh*;[181] however, as it turned

177. See in this respect Joined Cases 115/81 and 116/81 *Adoui and Cornuaille* [1982] ECR 1665, para. 19; Case 98/79 *Pecastaing* [1980] ECR 691, para. 13.
178. This is of course only possible to the extent that at the time of the conviction the material conditions of Article 27 are fulfilled, taken into account all relevant factors laid down in Article 28 – see Article 32(1) Directive 2004/38.
179. In Case 131/79 *Santillo* [1980] ECR 1585, for instance, about eight years had lapsed, resulting in the Court requiring that a new full assessment as to the continued existence of the genuine, present and sufficiently serious threat take place.
180. Case C-503/03 *Commission v. Spain* [2006] ECR I-1097.
181. Case C-370/90 *Singh* [1992] ECR I-4265. This right to return to the EU national's country of origin with a third national spouse is controversial. It is not limited to spouses, see Case C-291/05 *Eind* [2007] ECR I-10719; A. Venekamp, 'Het arrest Eind – Het vrije personenverkeer: een begin zonder einde?', *Nederlands Tijdschrift voor Europees Recht* (2008): 130-136. Moreover this possibility may give rise to abuse of right, see Case C-101/01 *Akrich* [2003] ECR I-9607. For case studies of such evasive techniques, see K. Vanvoorden, 'Stelt het arrest *Jia* een einde aan de België-route?', *Tijdschrift voor Vreemdelingenrecht* (2007): 72-84. However, in Case C-503/03 *Commission v. Spain* [2006] ECR I-1097 no suggestion of such abuse of right was made. Moreover, the ECJ has since explicitly overruled the requirement laid down in Case

out in both instances the husbands were subject to alerts in the SIS entered into by Germany. Such alerts are not necessarily related to anything overly serious, though. In the cases raised, both alerts found their ground in a criminal conviction of several years old. In one case, the criminal conviction was the result of a mundane traffic offence resulting in a fine; in the other case the rejected applicant had been sentenced to five months imprisonment for trying to obtain asylum using a false name.[182] However, these facts were not even known to the Spanish authorities, who had automatically rejected the application once they discovered the alert, without further investigation into the reasons. Spain defended its action by arguing that it was up to the German authorities to make sure that the data in the SIS were accurate and up-to-date, and it explained further that other Schengen States have no option but to reject any visa application made in the face of such an alert.[183]

**II-45.** However, the ECJ has rejected this approach. In a landmark judgment, the ECJ gave clear priority to the guarantees offered to workers *and their spouses* over the restrictions of the Schengen rules. Any other reading would have severally undermined the right of free movement as laid down in the Treaties and developed in the EU legislation and the case law. Accordingly, a refusal of entry of third national spouses of Union workers may only be justified to the extent that this measure is compatible with the restrictive approach taken by the Directive in respect of public policy. Upon proper construction the notification in SIS is to be understood as at best a warning light that there may be ground to assess the application by the person listed in the SIS in the light of public policy or public security. However, this is only the starting point: a Member State that envisages to take a restrictive measure must then actively inquire – and the Member State that made the entry in the SIS is under an obligation to assist the former therein within a reasonable time[184] – into the reason for the entry in SIS and establish whether these reasons still 'represent a genuine, present and sufficiently serious threat affecting one of the fundamental interests of society'. As the Court explains the public policy exception of the Directive is thus far more restrictive than the 'threat to public policy' of Article 96, which arises whenever 'the person concerned has been convicted of an offence carrying a penalty involving deprivation of liberty of at least one year (Article 96(2)(a)), or if he has been subject to a measure based on a failure to comply with national regulations on the entry or residence of aliens (Article 96(3))'.[185] The

C-101/01 *Akrich* [2003] ECR I-9607, paras 50-51 that in order to benefit from the rights provided for in Article 10 of Regulation No 1612/68, the national of a non-member country who is the spouse of a Union citizen must be lawfully resident in a Member State when he moves to another Member State to which the citizen of the Union is migrating or has migrated – see Case C-127/08 *Metock* [2008] ECR I-6241, para. 58.

182. The reason for the alerts is revealed in the Opinion of AG Kokott in Case C-503/03 *Commission v. Spain* [2006] ECR I-1097, para. 21.
183. The first claim is based on Articles 94(1) and 105 CISA, the second claim flows from Articles 5 and 15 CISA – see Case C-503/03 *Commission v. Spain* [2006] ECR I-1097, para. 36.
184. Case C-503/03 *Commission v. Spain* [2006] ECR I-1097, paras 56-58.
185. Case C-503/03 *Commission v. Spain* [2006] ECR I-1097, para. 48. Since the procedures for exchanging information have been amended in order to give – albeit without much enthusiasm, see E. Brouwer, 'Case C-503/03 *Commission v. Spain*, Judgment of the Court (Grand Chamber) of 31 January 2006, [2006] ECR I-1097', *Common Market Law Review* (2008):

Court thus rejects for these categories of aliens[186] the 'automatic effect' of a SIS alert.[187] While the restrictive immigration policies of recent years, and some genuine fear of all things alien – especially, since 9/11, if coming from the Islamic world as with the two persons in the case discussed – may serve to explain, if not justify, such a broad definition of public policy, the same distrust has no place vis-à-vis EU nationals and their family members. Moreover, too much distrust may simply undermine the benefits of Schengen, such as open borders, for all, EU citizens and aliens alike.[188]

**II-46.** As a consequence, while a threat to public policy under Article 96 CISA in principle results in a refusal of visa under Article 5 CISA, this cannot be automatically so for the spouses – or *mutatis mutandis* for other family members entitled to preferential treatment[189] – of Union workers[190] for whom it must first be established that their 'presence constitute[s] a genuine, present and sufficiently serious threat affecting one of the fundamental interests of society'.[191] This seems hardly the case for someone who merely committed a traffic offence. Even in the case of someone who committed immigration fraud there seems an arguable case that since that person is now in principle entitled to a residence permit as the spouse of a Community worker, there is no longer a genuine and present risk that he will have to commit a similar offence again – in that view, paradoxically only the *refusal* of such a permit on the public policy grounds of Article 96 CISA may induce the spouse to again break immigration laws to be together with his wife.[192]

### *[3] European Citizenship*

**II-47.** According to the ECJ, 'Union citizenship is destined to be the fundamental status of nationals of the Member States, enabling those who find themselves in the same

---

1265-1266 – effect to this judgment, see Article 25 of Regulation (EC) No 1987/2006 of the European Parliament and of the Council of 20 December 2006 on the establishment, operation and use of the second-generation Schengen Information System (SIS II) (2006) OJ L 381/4, which lays down 'conditions for entering alerts on third-country nationals who are beneficiaries of the right of free movement within the Community'.

186. For observations as to whether the Schengen regime needs to be nuanced in respect of certain other categories of aliens, such as long-term residents, see E. BROUWER, 'Case C-503/03 *Commission v. Spain*, Judgment of the Court (Grand Chamber) of 31 January 2006, [2006] ECR I-1097', *Common Market Law Review* (2008): 1262-1263.
187. See in this respect E. Brouwer, 'Case C-503/03 *Commission v. Spain*, Judgment of the Court (Grand Chamber) of 31 January 2006, [2006] ECR I-1097', *Common Market Law Review* (2008): 1259-1260.
188. Compare Joined Cases C-188/10 and C-189/10 *Melki* [2010] ECR I-5667.
189. For instance ascendants, see Case C-1/05 *Jia* [2007] ECR I-1.
190. Case C-503/03 *Commission v. Spain* [2006] ECR I-1097, para. 49.
191. Case C-503/03 *Commission v. Spain* [2006] ECR I-1097, para. 55.
192. Immigration fraud, and how to tackle it, continues to spurn difficult questions. On the one hand, the ECJ has accepted that Member States are sometimes too eager to use criminal sanctions whereas non-criminal alternatives exist, see Case C-329/11 *Achughbabian* [2011] ECR I-0000. On the other hand, the Court is not insensitive for the efforts of the Member States to also use their criminal law in the fight against illegal immigration, see Case C-83/12 PPU *Vo* [2012] ECR I-0000.

situation to enjoy the same treatment in law irrespective of their nationality, subject to such exceptions as are expressly provided for.'[193] Citizenship of the Union brings a series of discrete rights enumerated in the Treaties – most notably the right to travel and reside freely in the entire Union[194] – and requires, subject to justified exceptions, equal treatment with the own nationals in accordance with Article 18 TFEU. Whereas there is some kind of quid pro quo in allowing foreigners into the country into the context of the free movement of workers, now Member States must also envisage the desire to travel – and the ensuing costs – of far less attractive persons, such as needy students,[195] homeless persons,[196] drug addicts[197] or pensioners.[198] This right to travel is, however, not unlimited. According to Article 21(1) TFEU 'every citizen of the Union shall have the right to move and reside freely within the territory of the Member States, *subject to the limitations and conditions laid down in the Treaties and by the measures adopted to give them effect*'.[199] For economically active persons, these restrictions largely coincide with the justifiable restrictions under the free movement of workers (or self-employed persons). As discussed above, for them there is an explicit public policy exception in the Treaties, which is elaborated further in Directives. But no such Treaty exception exists for persons who are not economically active.

**II-48.** The exception was however introduced through secondary legislation. The third subparagraph of Article 2(2) of the first residence Directive[200] provided that Member States may not derogate from the right of residence of EU nationals and their family meeting the other criteria of that Directive, save on grounds of public policy, public security or public health. In that event, Directive 64/221 is to apply. Accordingly, in *Orfanopoulos*[201] the ECJ could afford not to inquire too deeply into the status of certain drug addicts with intermittent employment. Irrespective of whether the applicants qualified as workers or not, they could only be expelled if they also met the criteria of Directive 64/221/EEC discussed above.

**II-49.** However, the ECJ went one step further and also found the public policy exception – or rather the restrictions thereto – to be applicable to Union citizens who do not hold lawful residence.[202] Though there is a great deal of common sense in expanding the rules regarding the public policy exception to any EU citizen present on the territory of another Member State as a counterweight to the right to travel, which

193. Case C-184/99 *Grzelczyk* [2001] ECR I-6193, para. 31; Case C-224/02 *Pusa* [2004] ECR I-5763, para. 16.
194. Article 21 TFEU. For applications, see, *inter alia*, Case C-353/06 *Grunkin and Paul* [2008] ECR I-7639; Case C-192/05 *Tas-Hagen* [2006] ECR I-10451. The scope of this right to reside is increasingly expanded, and may even be invoked in certain cases against the own Member State, without prior travel, and give rise to derived rights for third country relatives of (vulnerable) Union citizens, see Case C-34/09 *Ruiz Zambrano* [2011] ECR I-0000.
195. Case C-184/99 *Grzelczyk* [2001] ECR I-6193. See also Case C-209/03 *Bidar* [2005] ECR I-2119.
196. Case C-456/02 *Trojani* [2004] ECR I-7573.
197. Joined Cases C-482/01 and C-493/01 *Orfanopoulos* [2004] ECR I-5247.
198. Case C-224/02 *Pusa* [2004] ECR I-5763.
199. Article 21(1) TFEU (emphasis added).
200. Council Directive 90/364/EEC of 28 June 1990 on the right of residence (1990) OJ L 180/26.
201. Joined Cases C-482/01 and C-493/01 *Orfanopoulos* [2004] ECR I-5247.
202. Case C-50/06 *Commission v. Netherlands* [2007] ECR I-4383.

is inherent in Article 21 TFEU,[203] it is not self-evident that Directive 64/221/EEC applied to this situation. The ECJ was right to point out that it had found in *MRAX*[204] that a national of a non-member State who is a member of the family of a Community national, but who does not fulfil the conditions necessary for lawful residence, must be able to rely on the procedural safeguards provided for by Directive 64/221.[205] Yet, in that case a link existed with the free movement of workers, which could justify application of the Directive. In my view, in the absence of such a link the only way those Union citizens could fall within the scope *ratione personae* of Directive 64/221/EEC as defined in its Article 1(1) is by assuming that they were likely recipient of services.[206] In light of this somewhat tenuous link, it is to be welcomed that Directive 2004/38/EC takes away all doubt as it applies to 'all Union citizens who move to or reside in a Member State other than that of which they are a national, and to their family members'.[207] Accordingly, all what has been said above on the conditions for applying the public policy exception in the context of the free movement of workers applies *mutatis mutandis* to them as well. As a result Member States cannot for instance refuse to provide their citizens with a passport on the sole ground that in the past – before accession of that Member State to the Union – they had breached the immigration laws of another Member State.[208]

### [4] Does Directive 2004/38/EC Exhaust the Concept of Public Policy?

**II-50.** Directive 2004/38/EC offers a balanced tool to Member States for keeping certain persons outside their borders whose personal conduct represents a genuine, present and sufficiently serious threat affecting one of the fundamental interests of society. However, some measures which Member States envisage in order to protect what they perceive as a fundamental interest of society may have little to do with the personal conduct of the person concerned, yet such measures may still result in restrictions on the free movement of persons.

**II-51.** This issue has recently been brought to the fore again in the context of the saga of the name of young Leonard Grunkin-Paul, which has resulted in two references to the ECJ.[209] The facts are neatly set out by Advocate General Sharpston in her Opinion

203. While Article 21(1) TFEU only speaks of the right to move and reside *within* the territories of the Member States, this right can only be fully effective if Member States do not also restrict the travel *to* the territory of the Member States, see Opinion of AG Mazák in Case C-33/07 *Jipa* [2008] ECR I-5157, para. 35, who rightly makes the analogy in footnote 13 to Case C-224/02 *Pusa* [2004] ECR I-5763 and the case law on the four freedoms.
204. Case C-459/99 *MRAX* [2002] ECR I-6591.
205. Case C-50/06 *Commission v. Netherlands* [2007] ECR I-4383, para. 36.
206. This is not made explicit in the judgment, but it is not far-fetched, see Case C-186/87 *Cowan* [1989] ECR 195.
207. Article 3(1) Directive 2004/38/EC.
208. Case C-33/07 *Jipa* [2008] ECR I-5157, para. 27.
209. The first reference, which resulted in Case C-96/04 *Standesamt Stadt Niebüll* [2006] ECR I-3561, was deemed inadmissible as the referring body did not meet the criteria for a 'court' in the sense of Article 267 TFEU. As a result, the judgment did not address the merits of the case.

in the second case.[210] The child Leonhard Matthias was born in Denmark in 1998 to parents Stefan Grunkin and Dorothee Paul. He and his parents have only German nationality (mere birth in Denmark does not automatically confer Danish nationality). For most of his life, he has lived principally in Denmark, where his parents initially lived together. For some months in 2001–2002, he lived with them in Niebüll, in Germany. Since then, he has lived principally with his mother in Tønder, Denmark, but regularly stays with his father in Niebüll, some 20 kilometres distant. Leonhard Matthias's birth was originally registered in Denmark under the surname 'Paul', with 'Grunkin' as a *mellemnavn*. Some months later, at his parents' request, the surname was changed to 'Grunkin-Paul' by virtue of an administrative certificate (*navnebevis*), and a birth certificate indicating that surname was issued. That was possible because he was domiciled in Denmark for purposes of Danish private international law, so that Danish substantive law applied to the determination of his surname. The parents wish to register him with the German authorities in Niebüll, under the surname 'Grunkin-Paul' given to him in Denmark. Pursuant to the German legislation, those authorities refused to recognize that name, insisting that the surname chosen must be either 'Grunkin' or 'Paul'.

**II-52.** The origin of the dispute is the diverging private international law of the Member States in determining the relevant law to govern the name of a child. It becomes, however, a matter of EU law to the extent that as a result of the German refusal to recognize the name given to the child in Denmark, the name of the child becomes unstable, whenever he travels from one Member State to another – which he does frequently. The practical problems, which may have serious consequences in the post 9/11 era as both Advocate Generals rightly point out,[211] definitely amount to a burden on the right to move freely, which Leonard enjoys already and may further enjoy in the future.

**II-53.** The question is then whether this burden could be justified. While Advocate General Sharpston rightfully rejects any such justification in the current case, it is interesting to note that she does not close the door for such a justification in future cases. In the case of Leonard, there is nothing in the name Grunkin-Paul that seems wholly incompatible with the German legal order, which indeed in some instances condones such names. However, the Lithuanian government had put forward a more serious problem, which however did not apply to the case at issue. It argued that:

> no Member State should be required to recognise names given to its nationals in accordance with foreign law if those names are incompatible with the structure of its national language, a fundamental part of its national heritage. Lithuanian

---

However, Advocate General Jacobs had taken position on the merits in an important Opinion. Following this refusal the proceedings between Leonard's parents and the German authorities continued in Germany, eventually resulting in a second ECJ case, Case C-353/06 *Grunkin and Paul* [2008] ECR I-7639 with Opinion of AG Sharpston.

210. Opinion of AG Sharpston in Case C-353/06 *Grunkin and Paul* [2008] ECR I-7639, paras 21-23.

211. Opinion of AG Jacobs in Case C-96/04 *Standesamt Stadt Niebüll* [2006] ECR I-3561, para. 55; Opinion of AG Sharpston in Case C-353/06 *Grunkin and Paul* [2008] ECR I-7639, paras 72-79, particularly at 78.

> surnames take different forms according to whether they are borne by a man or a woman and, if by a woman, according to whether she is married or single. Those differences are inherent in the structure of the language and distorted forms are unacceptable as a matter of national policy.[212]

More in general one could indeed wonder whether the linguistic policy of a Member State may not represent such a fundamental interest of society as to justify certain restrictions in respect of a person's name even when such restrictions result in a burden on the free movement of persons. Indeed, the ECtHR has already found unanimously that the protection of the privacy and family life laid down in Article 8 ECHR, which also encompasses issues relating to the name, is not infringed by the Ukrainian policy of 'Ukrainization' of foreign names - even though this may result in major differences in spelling.[213] The Court does not go into this discussion. Essentially following the Advocate Generals the Court finds, however, that the name rules are a restriction to the free movement right of a European citizen. Crucial for our analysis, the Court adds moreover that '[i]n addition, it must be pointed out that no specific reason was cited before the Court that might possibly preclude recognition of the child Leonhard Matthias's surname, as conferred and registered in Denmark, for instance that that name was *contrary to public policy in Germany*',[214] thus explicitly introducing a public policy exception, akin to the one in private international law, in the context of EU citizenship. In later cases, however, this public policy exception was deemed to weigh strongly enough to justify similar restrictions, when the underlying concerns were - as foretold by the Lithuanian government - related to linguistic policy,[215] or even the abolition of nobility.[216]

**II-54.** It is important to see how far away this situation stands from the cases dealt with under the term public policy in the sense of Directive 2004/38/EC. Persons who insist on using a particular variant of their own name are hardly acutely upsetting the social order in a way that drug users or violent protesters may do. However, they may nonetheless be eroding a fundamental aspect of the national identity. One could argue that this is the natural price for the free flow of persons across the EU. In essence I agree, and often the perceived threat may well be overblown. Yet, to the extent that in extreme cases such immaterial values may also inspire restrictions on the free movement of persons, I submit that the *ordre public* of Article 45(3) TFEU offers also in these cases an apt framework of reference or source of inspiration.[217] In this respect attention must also be drawn to the case of *Groener*.[218] Miss Groener had worked - to general satisfaction - on a temporary basis as an art teacher in an Irish art school where

212. Opinion of AG Sharpston in Case C-353/06 *Grunkin and Paul* [2008] ECR I-7639, para. 84.
213. ECtHR, 11 September 2007, *Bulgakov v. Ukraine.*
214. Case C-353/06 *Grunkin and Paul* [2008] ECR I-7639, para. 38 (emphasis added).
215. Case C-391/09 *Runevič-Vardyn* [2011] ECR I-0000.
216. Case C-209/08 *Sayn Wittgenstein* [2010] ECR I-0000.
217. Admittedly, no such restriction exists in respect of European Citizenship. However, as the ECJ has developed a rule of reason approach towards restrictions on citizenship rights the same concerns can be taken into account in a similar fashion. See in this respect also Y. Borgmann-Prebil, 'The Rule of Reason in European Citizenship', *European Law Review* (2008): 328-350.
218. Case C-379/87 *Groener* [1989] ECR 3967.

the normal working language is English. When after about two years she applied for a permanent appointment with the school this was denied on the grounds that she did not master the Irish language sufficiently – Irish being the first official language of Ireland. Miss Groener contested this requirement, which is obviously quite difficult to fulfil for foreigners, before the High Court in Dublin. The ECJ resolved the case by holding that:

> a permanent full-time post of lecturer in public vocational education institutions is a post of such a nature as to justify the requirement of linguistic knowledge, within the meaning of the last subparagraph of Article 3(1) of Regulation No 1612/68[219] of the Council, provided that the linguistic requirement in question is imposed as part of a policy for the promotion of the national language which is, at the same time, the first official language and provided that that requirement is applied in a proportionate and non-discriminatory manner[220].

It is understandable that the ECJ had some sympathy for the Irish efforts to protect their linguistic heritage, even at the expense of the full effect of the four freedoms. However, by trying to read these concerns into the 'necessity' requirement of Article 3(1) of Regulation No 1612/68 – with the effect that someone who had demonstrated for two years to be fully capable of doing the job is suddenly no longer qualified – the Court made in my view an error. Instead it should have simply admitted that Ireland is imposing a language requirement that goes beyond what is necessary from a functional perspective. However, as the ECJ was convinced of the fundamental interest of society Ireland was thus trying to protect, it should have said so in these terms and thus invoke the public policy exception, as the referring national court in its third question had invited the ECJ to do.[221] Such an approach would have made clear that the outcome of the case is not the result of the functional approach of Article 3(1) of Regulation 1612/68 – and thus the result of a sensible balancing act by the EU legislator – but the direct result of deference of the EU legal order vis-à-vis a fundamental policy of a Member State in a particular position. On the one hand, the concern could thus be addressed without jeopardizing the consistency of the EU legislation. On the other hand, the ECJ would also have made clear that linguistic identity, too, may be a fundamental interest of society.[222] It is no surprise, then, that the ECJ did actually invoke *Groener* when it developed the public policy exception based on linguistic identity in *Runevič-Vardyn.*[223]

**II-55.** The problem is moreover not limited to issues relating to names and language. Any instance where the diverging private international law rules of the Member States

219. Regulation (EEC) No 1612/68 of the Council of 15 October 1968 on freedom of movement for workers within the Community, *Official Journal, English Special Edition 1968 II*, 475.
220. Case C-379/87 *Groener* [1989] ECR 3967, para. 24.
221. Case C-379/87 *Groener* [1989] ECR 3967, para. 10.
222. This could in turn well have changed the outcome of Case C-369/89 *Piageme* [1991] ECR I-2971 and Case C-84/94 *Piageme* [1995] ECR I-2955. In these cases, the ECJ refused to artificially construct EU legislation as to allow a Member State for reasons of linguistic policy to require labelling of bottles of mineral water in the local language. However, the ECJ also failed to envisage justifying this restriction on grounds outside the Directive.
223. Case C-391/09 *Runevič-Vardyn* [2011] ECR I-0000, para. 85.

result in conflicting decisions as to the status of the person there may be a convergence between the private international law concept of public policy and the concept of public policy under the free movement of persons. However, while the underlying value is the same, they continue to work in a different manner and at different stages: the EU exception allows the Member State to continue to apply a national conflicts rule (including a public policy exception) which hinders the free movement of persons; the national exception then results in the non-recognition of the foreign act. In this vein, one could envisage also issues surrounding the recognition of (same-sex) marriages, adoption or divorce where other fundamental interests of society are at play, but where the personal conduct of the person against whom the restrictive measures are taken may not always be relevant.[224] The issue will be revisited below with a case study concerning same-sex marriages.[225]

### [D] Freedom of Establishment and Free Movement of Services

**II-56.** The main function of the *ordre public* exception to the four freedoms is to exclude the full effect of EU law with the effect that a Member State may apply its own law instead, usually in order to keep some foreign danger to one of the fundamental interests of its society at bay. In the context of the free movement of workers the threat comes from the personal background of the person that is seeking employment in the host State. Normally, the activity the person is pursuing should be less of a concern, as Member States are in principle free to regulate lawful employment on their territory. Of course there may be a link between the two, but the personal characteristics are in principle controlling. If a foreign paedophile seeks employment in a kindergarten in the host Member State, the latter may well have every reason to rely on the public policy exception to keep the threat out. However, this is not because there is something wrong with the activity of being a kindergarten teacher, which is a valuable and lawful employment in all Member States, but because the personal characteristics of the person applying for the job make him/her a threat to one of the fundamental interests of society. It is not the activity which is deemed dangerous, but the person. And while own nationals cannot be deported[226] they are treated equally in that they too can be precluded from taking up this job if they are convicted of sexual offences. The anomaly of *van Duyn*[227] is then of course that in that case the ECJ accepted that the UK could allow home-grown Scientology adepts to work for this controversial organization, while a Dutch woman seeking employment as a secretary with Scientology was denied entry on public policy grounds. Furthermore, as the threat generally comes from the disturbing personal conduct of the worker, Member States have generally far less

224. Indeed, as AG Sharpston rightly observes, Leonard can hardly be held responsible for the name change which was carried out years ago by his parents in accordance with Danish law, see Opinion of AG Sharpston in Case C-353/06 *Grunkin and Paul* [2008] ECR I-7639, para. 77.
225. *Infra*, at IV-57 et seq.
226. Case 41/74 *van Duyn* [1974] ECR 1337, para. 22.
227. Case 41/74 *van Duyn* [1974] ECR 1337.

reason to rely on public policy concerns to deny persons to leave the country,[228] though one could think of cases involving the protection of State secrets or persons who seek to elude their lawful incarceration.[229]

**II-57.** By contrast in the case of the freedom of establishment and the free movement of services[230] the threat to the fundamental interests to society may come from both the person and the activity pursued. Just like in the case of the free movement of workers, the exercise of these freedoms may involve persons crossing borders in order to offer[231] or consume[232] certain services. In this respect they are similarly caught by Directive 2004/38/EC.[233] This aspect has sufficiently been discussed above in §4.01[C]. However, due to the gradual shift from a discrimination-based approach to a restriction-based approach in the context of the freedom of establishment,[234] Member States may be confronted with activities on their territories they restrict or prohibit vis-à-vis their own nationals.[235] Against this background justifications, including grounds of public policy, are of the essence for the Member States.

---

228. It is not a coincidence that in *Jipa* even the Romanian government is arguing that its visa restriction cannot be justified, see Case C-33/07 *Jipa* [2008] ECR I-0000 and the accompanying Opinion of AG Mazák. But there are nevertheless cases where the ECJ, reluctantly, did accept the idea of exit restrictions, see Case C-430/10 *Gadyrov* [2011] ECR I-0000 and Case C-434/10 *Aladzov* [2011] ECR I-0000.
229. For this situation, the EU has actually provided a specific tool in the form of the European Arrest Warrant, see Article 1(1) Council Framework Decision 2002/584/JHA of 13 June 2002 on the European arrest warrant and the surrender procedures between the Member States (2002) OJ L 190/1. Interestingly, Article 4(6) of the same Framework Decision provides for an optional ground for refusal, allowing the executing State to refuse rendition 'if the European arrest warrant has been issued for the purposes of execution of a custodial sentence or detention order, where the requested person is staying in, or is a national or a resident of the executing Member State and that State undertakes to execute the sentence or detention order in accordance with its domestic law'. For an application, see Case C-66/08 *Kozłowski* [2008] ECR I-6041.
230. I opt to treat the freedom of establishment and the free movement of services together. While I agree with Jarass that there still is a difference between both freedoms, the difference seems largely one of degree, given the somewhat different underlying objectives of both freedoms, see H. Jarass, 'A Unified Approach to the Fundamental Freedoms' in *Services and Free Movement in EU Law*, ed. M. Andenas & W.-H. Roth (Oxford: OUP, 2002), 141-162.
231. Case C-268/99 *Jany* [2001] ECR I-8615 (prostitution services).
232. Case C-348/96 *Calfa* [1999] ECR I-11(consumers of travel services displaying a drugs habit).
233. Directive 2004/38/EC of the European Parliament and of the Council of 29 April 2004 on the right of citizens of the Union and their family members to move and reside freely within the territory of the Member States amending Regulation (EEC) No 1612/68 and repealing Directives 64/221/EEC, 68/360/EEC, 72/194/EEC, 73/148/EEC, 75/34/EEC, 75/35/EEC, 90/364/EEC, 90/365/EEC and 93/96/EEC (2004) OJ L 158/77.
234. Case C-55/94 *Gebhard* [1995] ECR I-4165; for more on this evolution, see H. Jarass, 'A Unified Approach to the Fundamental Freedoms' in *Services and Free Movement in EU Law*, ed. M. Andenas & W.-H. Roth (Oxford: OUP, 2002), 141-162. See also V. Hatzopoulos & T.U. Do, 'The case law of the ECJ concerning the free provisions of services: 2000-2005', *Common Market Law Review* (2006): 923-991.
235. The opposite, however, also deserves some attention, as in the case of drugs tourism in the Netherlands, whereby both the product itself – though as such lawful in the Netherlands – and the droves of foreign consumers forced the Netherlands to take restrictive measures, effectively reserving the sale of soft drugs to Dutch customers, a restriction to the free movement of services which the ECJ accepted, see Case C-137/09 *Josemans* [2010] ECR I-0000.

**II-58.** In the context of the freedom of establishment one could have expected that this problem is not so acute. Indeed, the older case law focused on a prohibition of discriminatory measures. These measures may then only be justified by the grounds listed in Article 52 TFEU, which must be interpreted strictly. All in all, such discriminatory measures are relatively rare, as the number of lawful activities a Member State has good grounds to reserve to its own nationals is fairly limited. This is of course not to say that Member States have not tried to do so. One good example for our discussion is the case law concerning private security firms, involving diverse national legislations which all sought to limit those services to suppliers of which the allegiance to the Member State is beyond doubt (de facto national security firms), and which the Member States often – in vain – try to justify on grounds of public policy and public security.[236] However, in later case law, undoubtedly inspired by the *Dassonville* criterion[237] in respect of goods, any national measure which is 'liable to hinder or make less attractive the exercise of'[238] the freedom of establishment qualifies as a restriction, which may need to be justified. One such restriction is precisely a general prohibition of a certain activity, which may be lawful in other Member States. For instance in *Caixa Bank*[239] the prohibition imposed on banks in France to offer interest on sight accounts was deemed to be such a restriction vis-à-vis a Spanish bank that tried to enter the French market. While such indistinctly applicable rules may be justified in principle on other imperative grounds as well, the public policy exception could be used here as well to prevent the proliferation on its territory of certain unwanted practices or activities.[240] Classic examples of such practices have often to do with gambling.[241] As already explained above, the ECJ had accepted in *Schindler*[242] that a Member State, if it so wishes, could outlaw gambling on its territory in its entirety on public policy

236. See for instance Case C-465/05 *Commission v. Italy* [2007] ECR I-11091; Case C-114/97 *Commission v. Spain* [1998] ECR I-6717.
237. Case 8/74 *Dassonville* [1974] ECR 837, para. 5.
238. Case C-55/94 *Gebhard* [1995] ECR I-4165, para. 37.
239. Case C-442/02 *Caixa-Bank France* [2004] ECRI-8961.
240. Though in Case C-442/02 *Caixa-Bank France* [2004] ECRI-8961 no such justification could be found, and while the stability of the banking system may touch upon the *ordre public*, that was hardly at issue either.
241. On the issue of gambling, see, *inter alia*, T. Kramer, 'Gambling and Energy in the Internal Market', *ERA Forum* (2007): 313-320; A. Littler, 'The Regulation of Gambling at European Level. The Balance to be Found', *ERA Forum* (2007): 357-371; D. Postel, 'Glücksspiel im europäischen Binnenmarkt nach « Gambelli » und « Placanica » und vor « Winner Wetten »', *Europarecht* (2007): 317-348; M. Ruttig, 'Das *Placanica*-Urteil des EuGH: Kein "rien ne va plus" aus Luxemburg', *Zeitschrift für Gemeinschaftsprivatrecht* (2007): 114-117; S. Sbordoni, S.M. Celest & F. Dionisi, 'Sanctions for Infringements of Gambling Laws in Italy', *ERA Forum* (2007): 405-416; G. Straetmans, 'Case C-6/01, *Anomar v. Estado português*, Judgment of the Court of 11 September 2003 (Third Chamber), nyr; Case C-243/01, *Piergiorgio Gambelli* e.a., Judgment of the Court of 6 November 2003 (Full Court), nyr; and C-42/ 02, *Diana Elisabeth Lindman*, Judgment of the Court of 13 November 2003 (Fifth chamber), nyr.', *Common Market Law Review* (2004): 1409-1428; J.C.M. Van Der Beek & M. De Koning, 'Volgende aflevering Goksaga: Rien ne va plus?', *Nederlands Tijdschrift voor Europees Recht* (2007): 117-123. Compare also with J. Marwell, 'Trade and morality: the WTO public morals exception after *gambling*', *New York University Law Review* (2006): 802-842.
242. Case C-275/92 *Schindler* [1994] ECR I-1039.

grounds and could in any event choose its own level of protection. In *Placanica,*[243] however, the Court took nonetheless issue with a whole series of seemingly indistinctly applicable rules which sought to regulate the betting sector by imposing a series of licensing requirements and police authorizations, which could not be justified by the policy choices made by Italy.

**II-59.** Furthermore, Member States do seem also more concerned with the possibility of exit of their nationals. This is primarily the case in respect of the possibility for companies for changing their corporate structure across the boundaries of several Member States, including the move of their main seat. For Member States, such transfers and corporate restructuring may involve major economic losses, but those do not justify any restriction by themselves. However, the transfer may well be meant to circumvent crucial rules of a Member State legal order. In *Centros,*[244] the ECJ therefore had to strike a balance between the freedom of establishment, which may well be exercised because the financial benefits on offer, and the legitimate interest of Member States to combat fraud and abuse. At stake was the construction set up by Mr and Mrs Bryde, two Danish nationals who first created a company, Centros Ltd., fully in accordance with English company law, with a registered capital of a mere GBP 100, which did not even have to be paid-up. The company was set up at a friend's house in the UK and did not do any business in the UK. Next this 'UK company' sought to set up a branch in Denmark, which was rejected by the Danish authorities who saw in this a ploy to evade the obligation for Danish companies to have a fully paid-up capital of DKK 200,000, as the company would in its ordinary trading activities on the Danish market be virtually indistinguishable from a Danish company. Therefore creditors may well be misled as to the solvability of Centros. It is obvious that such a refusal to register the branch of a company that is lawfully incorporated in another Member State constitutes an obstacle to the freedom of establishment. However, could such restriction be justified? The Court starts by acknowledging that:

> a Member State is entitled to take measures designed to prevent certain of its nationals from attempting, under cover of the rights created by the Treaty, improperly to circumvent their national legislation or to prevent individuals from improperly or fraudulently taking advantage of provisions of Community law[245].

Yet, the Court also finds that 'the fact that a national of a Member State who wishes to set up a company chooses to form it in the Member State whose rules of company law seem to him the least restrictive and to set up branches in other Member States cannot, in itself, constitute an abuse of the right of establishment',[246] and reminds in that respect that it had already ruled in *Segers*[247]:

> that the fact that a company does not conduct any business in the Member State in which it has its registered office and pursues its activities only in the Member State

243. Joined Cases C-338/04, C-359/04 and C-360/04 *Placanica* [2007] ECR I-1891.
244. Case C-212/97 *Centros* [1999] ECR I-1459.
245. Case C-212/97 *Centros* [1999] ECR I-1459, para. 24 and the case law cited therein.
246. Case C-212/97 *Centros* [1999] ECR I-1459, para. 27.
247. Case 79/85 *Segers* [1986] ECR 2375, para. 16.

> where its branch is established is not sufficient to prove the existence of abuse or fraudulent conduct which would entitle the latter Member State to deny that company the benefit of the provisions of Community law relating to the right of establishment.[248]

Under these circumstances, it becomes very hard for a Member State to justify its restriction. The Danish government nonetheless tried to rely on the need to protect creditors, making a further distinction between public creditors and all creditors in general. The ECJ did not agree. First, it is interesting to note that in the opinion of the Court these reasons do not amount to reasons of public policy,[249] probably because the rules at issue concern merely economic losses.[250] As a result, the measures are assessed in light of a classic *Gebhard*[251] rule of reason analysis:

> they must be applied in a non-discriminatory manner; they must be justified by imperative requirements in the general interest; they must be suitable for securing the attainment of the objective which they pursue; and they must not go beyond what is necessary in order to attain it[252].

Second, the measure does not meet these criteria. The ECJ seems to assume that creditors are already largely protected to the extent that they could now that the capital requirements in the UK are different than in Denmark.[253] Moreover, it can think of less restrictive means to protect public creditors.[254] However, this does not mean that the ECJ does not take the concern about defrauding creditors too lightly, and it stresses the right of Member States to actively fight fraud and abuses.[255] Yet, the preventive refusal of any branch of a company not doing business in its place of incorporation is seen as excessively eroding the underlying right of establishment.

**II-60.** In the same vein, the ECJ in *Überseering*[256] rightly found a restriction on the freedom of establishment in German private international law rules which had the effect that a company validly established in the Netherlands, but doing business in Germany, would nonetheless be treated as a company with its principle seat in Germany[257] with the effect that the company would be deprived of its legal personality before German courts, as it had not complied with all relevant incorporation requirements in Germany. While the Court, more clearly than in *Centros*[258] – but still rather reluctantly, acknowledged that 'it is not inconceivable that overriding requirements relating to the general interest, such as the protection of the interests of creditors, minority shareholders, employees and even the taxation authorities, may, in certain

248. Case C-212/97 *Centros* [1999] ECR I-1459, para. 29.
249. Case C-212/97 *Centros* [1999] ECR I-1459, para. 34 ('It should be observed, first, that the reasons put forward do not fall within the ambit of Article 56 of the Treaty').
250. On which interests are protected as a matter of public policy, see *infra*, part III.
251. Case C-55/94 *Gebhard* [1995] ECR I-4165, para. 37.
252. Case C-212/97 *Centros* [1999] ECR I-1459, para. 34.
253. Case C-212/97 *Centros* [1999] ECR I-1459, para. 36.
254. Case C-212/97 *Centros* [1999] ECR I-1459, para. 37.
255. Case C-212/97 *Centros* [1999] ECR I-1459, para. 38.
256. Case C-208/00 *Überseering* [2002] ECR I-9919.
257. The shares in the company had been bought by two Germans residing in Düsseldorf, thus transferring, in the view of the national court, the actual centre of its administration to Germany, therefore making German company law applicable.
258. Case C-212/97 *Centros* [1999] ECR I-1459.

circumstances and subject to certain conditions, justify restrictions on freedom of establishment',[259] it rightly came to the conclusion that depriving a company that has made use of the freedom of establishment of its legal personality does not contribute to any of these concerns.[260] One could, for instance, imagine that if the ECJ goes further down the road suggested by *Cartesio*[261] of also accepting some form of primary right of establishment for companies, that then there may well be instances where the Member States could indeed be justified if they put forward public policy concerns tied to the protection of creditors or employees. Holding otherwise would imply that there may be situations in which a company could unilaterally change its applicable law and escape the obligations it may owe to these actors. Unlike the situation in *Überseering*[262] or *Centros*[263] where these third parties could and should have known in advance they were contracting with a foreign company, the country of origin should be allowed to protect their legitimate expectations in the case of a transfer of seat.

**II-61.** A final example is offered by the *Viking*[264] case. There industrial action had been undertaken by a Finnish trade union, supported by its international overarching federation, against the plans of the shipping company to register the ship under the flag of another Member State. While the workers were exercising a fundamental right as protected by numerous international instruments and Article 28 of the Charter of Fundamental Rights,[265] this did not stop the Court from analysing whether the collective action constituted a restriction of the freedom of establishment.[266] Unsurprisingly,[267] the ECJ found that the strike, especially in combination with the instructions of the international federation barring all other trade unions from negotiating with Viking, qualified as a restriction.[268] The Court then examines whether this restriction may be justified in the light of that same fundamental right. Unlike the

259. Case C-208/00 *Überseering* [2002] ECR I-9919, para. 92.
260. Case C-208/00 *Überseering* [2002] ECR I-9919, para. 93.
261. Case C-2010/06 *Cartesio* [2008] ECR I-9641.
262. Case C-208/00 *Überseering* [2002] ECR I-9919.
263. Case C-212/97 *Centros* [1999] ECR I-1459.
264. Case C-438/05 *International Transport Workers' Federation* [2007] ECR I-10779.
265. Case C-438/05 *International Transport Workers' Federation* [2007] ECR I-10779, para. 43.
266. See Case C-438/05 *International Transport Workers' Federation* [2007] ECR I-10779, paras 46-47. The Court justified this by referring to Case C-36/02 *Omega Spielhallen* [2004] ECR I-9609 and Case C-112/00 *Schmidberger* [2003] ECR I-5659, but these two cases concerned the compatibility of governmental measures inspired by fundamental rights with the free movement. In *Viking*, the exercise of the fundamental right by the trade union was per se the measure. Classically governments have no fundamental rights they can exercise (see in this sense also Case C-470/03 *A.G.M.-COS.MET* [2007] ECR I-2749), so the impugned measure and the exercise of the fundamental right can in principle not coincide. However, by expanding the concept of government for the purposes of Article 43 TEC well into the private sphere, the ECJ now comes to the dubious situation of having to assess the exercise of a fundamental right in the light of the freedom of establishment.
267. Yet, for the ECJ this is less self-evident as it states at Case C-438/05 *International Transport Workers' Federation* [2007] ECR I-10779, para. 53 that 'Contrary to the claims of FSU and ITF, it cannot be considered that it is inherent in the very exercise of trade union rights and the right to take collective action that those fundamental freedoms will be prejudiced to a certain degree'. What soft forms of collective action the Court has in mind is, however, unclear.
268. Case C-438/05 *International Transport Workers' Federation* [2007] ECR I-10779, para. 55.

Court's reasoning in *Omega Spielhallen*[269] and *Dynamic Medien,*[270] the fundamental right is, however, not equated with the *ordre public*. There may be two reasons for this. On the one hand, there may be no need for doing so if the level of protection that is sought does not seem to deviate from the level of protection common at EU level.[271] On the other hand, the Court is reaching the boundaries of its own logic: it seems willing to accept that otherwise private acts may nonetheless be quasi-governmental in nature for the purpose of Article 49 TFEU,[272] but apparently the Court is unwilling to accept that the private bodies involved rely on *public* policy grounds. It has been argued that these grounds are indeed hard to be handled by private parties,[273] though the ECJ itself had earlier explicitly held otherwise in *Bosman.*[274] Actually I agree with this earlier approach, and it will be argued below how public policy concerns may even play a role in the context of EU competition law, which is largely in the private sphere.[275] Admittedly, trade unions could be said to be defending the private interests of workers, but once they do so in the form of collective action and as recognized actors in the national system of collective labour relationships they transcend purely private interests (as is best evidenced by the fact that various individual workers may well disagree with the demands and concessions made during such actions or negotiations, even though they are often de facto – if not legally – bound by the result). Moreover, it could be observed that also sports federations[276] or bar associations[277] may at times have very private interests, though for them this was not seen as a bar to their ability to rely on the public policy. Nonetheless, one week after *Viking,*[278] the Court indeed made this incongruent argument explicit in *Laval* where the Court reserved the public policy exception for the Member State proper and denied its availability to a trade union.[279]

269. Case C-36/02 *Omega Spielhallen* [2004] ECR I-9609.
270. Case C-244/06 *Dynamic Medien* [2008] ECR I-505.
271. Compare in this respect Case C-112/00 *Schmidberger* [2003] ECR I-5659.
272. It would go beyond the scope of this thesis to take a final position as to whether it is appropriate for the court to expand the personal scope of (some of) the four freedoms to private persons. For more on this debate, see *inter alia*, J. Snell, *Goods and Services in EC law – A Study of the Relationship Between the Freedoms* (Oxford: OUP, 2002), 129-167 and J. Baquero Cruz, *Between competition and free movement: the economic constitutional law of the European Community* (Oxford: Hart, 2002). Nonetheless it can be remarked with Snell that the acts of social partners in general and trade unions in particular are not easily caught alternatively through EU competition law, see for instance Case C-67/96 *Albany* [1999] ECR I-5751.
273. J. Snell, *Goods and Services in EC law – A Study of the Relationship Between the Freedoms* (Oxford: OUP, 2002), 147-148.
274. Case C-413/93 *Bosman* [1995] ECR I-4921, para. 86 ('There is nothing to preclude individuals from relying on justifications on grounds of public policy, public security or public health. Neither the scope nor the content of those grounds of justification is in any way affected by the public or private nature of the rules in question').
275. See *infra*, at II-83 et seq., dealing with *inter alia* Case C-519/04 P *Meca-Medina and Majcen v. Commission* [2006] ECR I-6991; Case C-309/99 *Wouters* [2002] ECR I-1577.
276. Case C-49/07 *MOTOE* [2008] ECR I-4863.
277. Case C-309/99 *Wouters* [2002] ECR I-1577.
278. Case C-438/05 *International Transport Workers' Federation* [2007] ECR I-10779.
279. Case C-341/05 *Laval un Partneri* [2007] ECR I-10779, para. 84. One could, perhaps, argue that as the public policy exception was part of a Directive it could not as such be relied upon against a private parte such as Laval. However, to the extent that the Directive is only giving expression to an underlying Treaty right which can apparently be invoked against private parties such reading seems at unease with Case C-114/04 *Mangold* [2005] ECR I-9981.

**II-62.** Yet, one could wonder whether in such a context the private parties at issue have not rather a need for a *private* policy exception: a ground to justify actions which a governmental body cannot, but which a hybrid body – such as trade unions,[280] but also for instance a civil servant exercising his/her right of free speech[281] – must be able to invoke to stress that it also has an outspoken anti-establishment role which cannot be overlooked lest its expressive rights are rendered obsolete.[282] Of course these expressive rights, like all fundamental rights may also be subject to some proportionate limitations, but the standard for assessing whether a private party is abusing his/her free speech rights should not be confused with the test for determining the proportionality of governmental restrictions on the freedom of establishment.[283] Yet, this is exactly what the Court appears to do by invoking in *Viking*[284] the classic *Gebhard*[285] rule of reason analysis. The proportionality standard used is, moreover, not even the *Schindler*[286] proportionality test common in cases where fundamental rights issues are to be balanced with free movement rights, and Member States are allowed to pursue a level of protection of their choice,[287] but the very classic least restrictive means test.[288]

280. Case C-438/05 *International Transport Workers' Federation* [2007] ECR I-10779; Case C-341/05 *Laval un Partneri* [2007] ECR I-11767.
281. Case C-470/03 *A.G.M.-COS.MET* [2007] ECR I-2749. See also the criticism put forward by N. Reich, 'AGM-COS.MET or: who is protected by EC safety regulation?', *European Law Review* (2008): 94. For my reading of that case, see, however, *infra*, at II-82 and accompanying footnotes.
282. See also, *infra*, at II-75.
283. See also S. Prechal & S. De Vries, 'Viking/Laval en de grondslagen van het internemarktecht', *Sociaal-Economische Wetgeving* (2008): 435 suggesting that the proportionality test should be 'coloured' differently if fundamental rights are in tension with the internal market rights.
284. Case C-438/05 *International Transport Workers' Federation* [2007] ECR I-10779, para. 75.
285. Case C-55/94 *Gebhard* [1995] ECR I-4165, para. 37.
286. Case C-275/92 *Schindler* [1994] ECR I-1039.
287. This balancing act is, however, complicated by the somewhat unusual forum that is deciding the dispute. In cases such as Case C-112/00 *Schmidberger* [2003] ECR I-5659 or Case C-36/02 *Omega Spielhallen* [2004] ECR I-9609 the national court hearing the dispute is located in the Member State where the particular choice for putting a particular level of protection of a fundamental right into operation was made that has resulted in the challenged restriction to the free movement. The reference in Case C-438/05 *International Transport Workers' Federation* [2007] ECR I-10779 was, however, made by a UK court. While this is not per se objectionable, as one of the defendants, the International Transport Workers' Federation has it seat there, the result is nonetheless that a UK court is assessing the acceptability of the behaviour of parties to a Finnish labour conflict, which may be rooted in a different model of social action. Interestingly, there are many examples where the ECJ has declined jurisdiction in instances where the compatibility of laws of another Member State was at stake, see Case 104/79 *Foglia* [1980] ECR 745; Case C-153/00 *der Weduwe* [2002] ECR I-11319 or Case C-318/00 *Bacardi-Martini* [2003] ECR I-905. Admittedly, in this case there was no Finnish law that is directly challenged. Yet, the collective action is deemed to fall within the scope precisely because of the role trade unions play in collective labour relations under Finnish law, so that the nature and proportionality of the industrial action cannot fully be detached from that legal context, which does seems impliedly implicated.
288. This plays out in the form of what, as argued by P. Syrpis & T. Novitz, 'Economic and social rights in conflict: Political and judicial approaches to their reconciliation', *European Law Review* (2008): 425, 'seems a curious requirement to apply to a trade union contemplating industrial action, which is usually intended to cause disruption so as to extract concessions from an employer', namely that according to Case C-438/05 *International Transport Workers' Federation* [2007] ECR I-10779, para. 87: 'As regards the question of whether or not the collective action at issue in the main proceedings goes beyond what is necessary to achieve the

In my view, the ECJ should rather instruct the national court to carry out a two-fold test. On the one hand, the national court should assess whether the restriction on the free movement could be justified by one of the classic grounds of justification, including the public policy exception, and – in the case of non-discriminatory measures – also the mandatory requirements. On the other hand, the national court should also, when the expressive rights are at stake of individuals or entities that cannot in full be equated with the government, assess next whether restrictions on the free movement rights that could otherwise not be justified may still be justified in order to give full credit to the non-governmental side of these hybrid actors. In this respect it appears that the ECJ has recognized the right of workers to take action to defend their own wage levels and working conditions; however, the ECJ seems to underrate the role trade unions play in 'regulating the level of wages and employment conditions more generally for all undertakings operating in the same sector or "market"'.[289] As no fundamental right is without limitation, my remarks do not imply that the national court, acting at the Court's instructions, may never find that some restrictions to the free movement caused by the reliance on such expressive rights are at the end of the day disproportionate. However, at least the non-governmental activities of trade unions and the like should no longer solely be assessed by a standard that was designed for governmental action only. On top of the public policy exception, there should thus also be a sort of '*exception de désordre privé*' to protect the anti-establishment role of such actors and their right to create through their opinions and actions some degree of social upheaval, which may at times go at the expense of the four freedoms. The result is admittedly a standard which is less strict for hybrid actors than for the Member States concerned.[290] One could therefore, wonder, whether this may not result in contradictatory results if an applicant such as Viking, assuming that as a result of my alternative reading it would have lost (which is likely, but not a given), would next sue the

objective pursued, it is for the national court to examine, in particular, on the one hand, whether, under the national rules and collective agreement law applicable to that action, FSU did not have other means at its disposal which were less restrictive of freedom of establishment in order to bring to a successful conclusion the collective negotiations entered into with Viking, and, on the other, whether that trade union had exhausted those means before initiating such action'.

289. J. Malmberg & T. Sigeman, 'Industrial action and EU economic freedoms: the autonomous collective bargaining model curtailed by the European Court of Justice', *Common Market Law Review* (2008): 1131; see also, *id.*, at 1140-1141. See also ECtHR, 25 April 1996, *Gustafsson v. Sweden*. This implies that somehow the objective of the industrial action plays a role, maybe even more than the actual hindrance, see A.A.H. Van Hoek & M.S. Houwerzijl, 'Loonconcurrentie als motor van de interne markt? Een tweeluik – Deel 1: De arresten *Viking, Laval en Rüffert*, verdragsaspecten', *Nederlands Tijdschrift voor Europees Recht* (2008): 201-202, who compare in this respect also with the objectives of the protest in Case C-112/00 *Schmidberger* [2003] ECR I-5659.

290. I indeed do not agree with the Opinion of AG Poiares Maduro in Case C-438/05 *International Transport Workers' Federation* [2007] ECR I-10779, para. 40 that if the case had been brought as a challenge to the Finnish legislative framework that this 'would not have affected the substance of the problem: how to reconcile Viking Line's rights to freedom of movement with the rights to associate and to strike of the FSU and the ITF?' The question would be the same, but the defences that could be raised would be markedly different. See in this sense also P. Syrpis & T. Novitz, 'Economic and social rights in conflict: Political and judicial approaches to their reconciliation', *European Law Review* (2008): 421-422.

Member State concerned - *in casu* Finland - for damages flowing from the restrictions to trade that are the result of the failure by Finland to organize its social model in a manner that prevents disruptions of this kind. The solution to that paradox seems to lie, however, in the requirement of a 'sufficiently serious breach', which makes that not just any breach of EU law has to result in state liability[291] so that a Member State does not need to be held liable for any instance where trade unions take some action that a Member State itself could not have taken.

**II-63.** The fear of unwanted activities that may constitute a threat to a fundamental interest of society is even stronger in respect of the free movement of services. The basic position is that goods that are lawfully marketed in one Member State can also be offered in other Member States. This is likely to bring a series of new services on the market, which were previously unknown to the host State. Just like *Cassis de Dijon*[292] lead to increased consumer choice in respect of goods, such a diversification in respect of services is in principle to be welcomed so that consumers can freely choose the services they need.[293] Yet, there are certain risks involved against which the public policy may serve as a shield. The public policy exception is thus not limited as Snell seems to suggest[294] - though he is quick to point out the inconsistency of such an approach with the judgment in *Cullet*[295] in respect of goods - to the personal conduct of the service provider as covered by Directive 2004/38/EC but also to the risk the service itself may pose to the social order. It has already been argued above that Directive 2004/38/EC does not exhaust all relevant aspects of the public policy.

**II-64.** The free movement of services actually covers four situations: the recipient may move towards the provider; the provider may move towards the recipient; the provider and the recipient may both move; or the service itself may move thanks to the modern means of telecommunication.[296] In all these situations, the result may be the distribution of an undesirable service, or at least the distribution of a service under undesirable conditions as selling arrangements are not excluded from the free movement of services in entirely the same way as in the case of goods despite some indications of convergence.[297] It has rightly been argued that 'the morally questionable nature of the

291. Case C-278/05 *Robins* [2007] ECR I-1053, paras 69 et seq.
292. Case 120/78 *Rewe-Zentral* [1979] ECR 749. See for instance also the demise of the German beer purity laws, see Case 176/84 *Commission v. Germany* [1987] ECR 1193.
293. See in this sense W.-H. Roth, 'The European Court of Justice's Case Law on Freedom to Provide Services: Is *Keck* Relevant?' in Freedoms' in *Services and Free Movement in EU Law*, ed. M. Andenas & W.-H. Roth (Oxford: OUP, 2002), 10, on the basis of Case C-76/90 *Säger* [1991] ECR I-4244, para. 14.
294. J. Snell, *Goods and Services in EC law – A Study of the Relationship Between the Freedoms* (Oxford: OUP, 2002), 176.
295. Case 231/83 *Cullet* [1985] ECR 305, discussed, *supra*, at II-22.
296. J. Snell, *Goods and Services in EC law – A Study of the Relationship Between the Freedoms* (Oxford: OUP, 2002), 17.
297. On this *inter alia* J. Snell, *Goods and Services in EC law – A Study of the Relationship Between the Freedoms* (Oxford: OUP, 2002), 70 et seq.; W.-H. Roth, 'The European Court of Justice's Case Law on Freedom to Provide Services: Is *Keck* Relevant?' in Freedoms' in *Services and Free Movement in EU Law*, ed. M. Andenas & W.-H. Roth (Oxford: OUP, 2002), 1-24; J. Da Cruz Vilaça, 'On the Application of *Keck* in the field of Free Provision of Services' in *id.*, 25-40.

service does not remove the activity from the scope of the free movement',[298] but it may trigger a justification for certain restrictions on the service on public policy grounds.

**II-65.** The problem of persons travelling to receive a service contrary to the public policy was at issue in *Grogan*.[299] As discussed above in Part I, at issue was a ban on the distribution of leaflets informing Irish women from the possibility of undergoing an abortion in the UK where such procedure was – contrary to the situation in Ireland at the time – was legal. The ECJ managed to circumvent the issue by holding the ban to be too remote to the provision of the service. However, Advocate General Van Gerven did analyse in full to what extent Ireland's public policy could be relied upon to justify what he – in my view correctly – did see as a restriction on the free movement of services as it discouraged potential Irish recipients of abortion services to travel abroad to receive the service abroad.[300] A special case is the problem of drugs tourism, whereby the attraction of thousands of drugs users from across Europe to a number of border towns in the Netherlands, is in itself the cause of major nuisance and criminal behaviour threatening public security, public health and public order, even though the sale of soft drugs in itself is not illegal. Unsurprisingly the ECJ has accepted that also this situation may justify that the provision of a service – the use of coffee shops – may be restricted by the Dutch authorities by effectively banning the non-resident users.[301]

**II-66.** The case of persons travelling to provide an immoral service is best illustrated by the example of prostitution. Here there is of course a certain overlap with the personal conduct of the service provider. Whether the public policy can truly be relied upon to keep this service out will depend on the attitude taken by the national legal order in respect of prostitution. As is demonstrated by *Jany*[302] the ECJ is not accepting double moral standards in this respect. However, it is also possible that the service is lawful in one Member State, and is offered through a local representative in another Member State, such as in the case of *Läärä*,[303] where a UK company subject to UK control in respect of its activities, with the help of local partners, tried to operate slot machines in Finland. Following *Schindler*,[304] which concerned the sale of lottery tickets under the free movement of goods, the ECJ accepted in that case that the Finnish restrictions, which only allowed one operator carrying a State license to offer these gambling service could be justified on public policy grounds.[305] While one could argue that here, too, there is an element of double moral standards the key difference seems to be that the Court is willing to accept that a State-controlled monopoly on gambling services may help to control some of the negative consequences of gambling, such as crime and

298. J. Snell, *Goods and Services in EC law – A Study of the Relationship Between the Freedoms* (Oxford: OUP, 2002), 7.
299. Case C-159/90 *Society for the Protection of Unborn Children Ireland* [1991] ECR I-4685.
300. Opinion of AG Van Gerven in Case C-159/90 *Society for the Protection of Unborn Children Ireland* [1991] ECR I-4685. For a critical analysis of his reasoning, see, *supra*, part I.
301. Case C-137/09 *Josemans* [2010] ECR I-0000.
302. Case C-268/99 *Jany* [2001] ECR I-8615. The case concerned a Europe Agreement, but the reasoning applies *mutatis mutandis* to the provision of services within the EU.
303. Case C-124/97 *Läärä* [1999] ECR I-6067.
304. Case C-275/92 *Schindler* [1994] ECR I-1039.
305. Case C-124/97 *Läärä* [1999] ECR I-6067, paras 42-43.

fraud, without prohibiting the activity entirely.[306] Later case law indeed demonstrates that the Court is less forgiving if actually double standards are applied.[307]

**II-67.** As to the scenario of both the provider and the recipient travelling one could well imagine a variant of *Grogan,*[308] where a service provider would be offering some kind of travel package involving transport, accommodation and a surgical operation, raising questions as to public health, and – depending on the nature of the medical procedure – also certain ethical issues that can be dealt with under the public policy exception.

**II-68.** Finally, the public policy exception has been relevant in cases where the service has been travelling, rather than the service provider or its recipient. A classic case is the regulation of television services.[309] In several cases[310] the ECJ had to judge on the compatibility of restrictions imposed by Member States on television broadcasts coming from other Member States, usually because of certain forms of advertisements. Originally, the Court did not find such bans incompatible as long as they would also apply to domestic broadcasters.[311] However, in 1991 the ECJ changed its approach, and it considered the application to foreign broadcasters of a series of Dutch rules on the organization of the media in the Netherlands in respect of television advertising to be a restriction on the freedom to provide services.[312] Accordingly, the question arose of their justification. The ECJ accepted in this respect that in principle a cultural policy intended to ensure the plurality of the press could indeed justify certain restrictions. Yet, the measures failed the necessity prong as it is not necessary in order to ensure the plurality of the media in the Netherlands, to also impose rules on the organization of foreign broadcasters.[313] With this judgment, the Court anticipated moreover the entry into force of the first television without frontiers directive,[314] which made it more difficult in later cases to further justify additional restrictions.[315]

---

306. Case C-124/97 *Läärä* [1999] ECR I-6067, paras 37-41.
307. Case C-243/01 *Gambelli* [2003] ECR I-13031, paras 63-69.
308. Case C-159/90 *Society for the Protection of Unborn Children Ireland* [1991] ECR I-4685.
309. One may expect that in future an increasing number of cases may also involve the internet, see already Case C-243/01 *Gambelli* [2003] ECR I-13031; Case C-347/09 *Dickinger and Ömer* [2011] ECR I-0000 and Joined Cases C-447/08 and C-448/07 *Sjöberg* [2010] ECR I-6921 (online gambling) or Case C-323/09 *Interflora* [2011] ECR I-0000; Joined Cases C-236/08 to C-238/08 *Google France and Google* [2010] ECR I-2417 (online advertising).
310. Case 52/79 *Debauve* [1980] ECR 833; Case 62/79 *Coditel* [1980] ECR 881; Case C-288/89 *Stichting Collectieve Antennevoorziening Gouda* [1991] ECR I-4007; Case C-353/89 *Commission v. Netherlands* [1991] ECR I-4069; Case C-56/96 *VT4* [1997] ECR I-3143; Joined Cases C-34/95, C-35/95 and C-36/95 *De Agostini and TV-Shop i Sverige* [1997] ECR I-3843; Case C-6/98 *ARD* [1999] ECR I-7599.
311. Case 52/79 *Debauve* [1980] ECR 833.
312. Case C-288/89 *Stichting Collectieve Antennevoorziening Gouda* [1991] ECR I-4007.
313. Case C-288/89 *Stichting Collectieve Antennevoorziening Gouda* [1991] ECR I-4007, paras 23-25.
314. Council Directive 89/552/EEC of 3 October 1989 on the coordination of certain provisions laid down by law, regulation or administrative action in Member States concerning the pursuit of television broadcasting activities (1989) OJ L 298/23.
315. Joined Cases C-34/95, C-35/95 and C-36/95 *De Agostini and TV-Shop i Sverige* [1997] ECR I-3843; Case C-6/98 *ARD* [1999] ECR I-7599. See also, explicitly dealing with public policy, Joined Cases C-244/10 and C-245/10 *Mesopotamia Broadcast A/S METV* [2011] ECR I-0000.

**II-69.** The broadcaster cases have, however, also revealed a limitation to the freedom to provide services, which is important when addressing the possibility for Member States to block unwanted services. In *Veronica,*[316] the Court recalled it judgment in *Van Binsbergen* where it had held:

> in relation to Article [56 TFEU] that a Member State cannot be denied the right to take measures to prevent the exercise by a person whose activity is entirely or principally directed towards its territory of the freedoms guaranteed by the Treaty for the purpose of avoiding the professional rules of conduct which would be applicable to him if he were established within that State[317].

Accordingly, the Netherlands could prohibit the Dutch broadcaster Veronica from participating in the setting up of a broadcaster in Luxembourg aimed at the Dutch market, as in doing so Veronica was evading 'the obligations deriving from the national legislation concerning the pluralistic and non-commercial content of programmes',[318] which the ECJ confirmed to be cultural policy objectives which 'are objectives relating to the public interest which a Member State may legitimately pursue by formulating the statutes of its own broadcasting organizations in an appropriate manner'.[319] Considered in this sense, these cases seem a complement on the attempts of Member States to prevent the evasion of local rules by making use of the freedom of establishment discussed above,[320] even though an undertaking may freely establish itself in another Member State with the aim of only offering services in another Member State.[321]

**II-70.** Sometimes the service may even be transferred to another Member State without clear communication aides. This is another way of looking at one of the cases central to this book, *Omega Spielhallen.*[322] In that case the service in intra-Community trade was the use of a gaming concept developed by the British company Pulsar and protected in the UK by intellectual copyrights. Franchising of this formula then enabled a German company to offer the contested laser game experience to its customers within Germany. This two-step approach has, however, a further consequence. It results in a German company relying on the freedom of Pulsar to provide services in order to contest in Germany; a German decision on the scope of German public policy restricting the possibility for the German firm to offer its service to German customers. The freedom to provide services of a third party thus becomes a tool for seeking deregulation in what otherwise would be a purely internal situation. Indeed if Omega had invented the game itself, the free movement of services would not have been of any

316. Case C-148/91 *Vereniging Veronica Omroep Organisatie* [1993] ECR I-487, para. 12. See also Case C-23/93 *TV 10* [1994] ECR I-4795.
317. Case 33/74 *Van Binsbergen* [1974] ECR 1299, para. 13.
318. Case C-148/91 *Vereniging Veronica Omroep Organisatie* [1993] ECR I-487, para. 13.
319. Case C-148/91 *Vereniging Veronica Omroep Organisatie* [1993] ECR I-487, para. 10.
320. As Roth observes in *Veronica* the ECJ departed from its earlier case law to deal with such case where no services are given in the home state as a matter of establishment, see W.-H. Roth, 'The European Court of Justice's Case Law on Freedom to Provide Services: Is *Keck* Relevant?' in Freedoms' in *Services and Free Movement in EU Law*, ed. M. Andenas & W.-H. Roth (Oxford: OUP, 2002), 1-24.
321. Case C-56/96 *VT4* [1997] ECR I-3143, para. 22.
322. Case C-36/02 *Omega Spielhallen* [2004] ECR I-9609.

avail. This should, however, not distract us from the fact that *from a Union perspective* there is an actual restriction on the freedom to provide services on the part of Pulsar. From that perspective, it does not really matter whether Pulsar brings itself a suit against the German authorities for not being able to market a service which it lawfully offers in its home State, or whether one of its customers sues because it is prevented from enjoying the service offered to it by Pulsar. Conversely, one may also wonder about the soundness of the public policy concern invoked if in the end the German authorities clash over the scope of the concept of human dignity with its own citizens. However, in a democracy the moral complacency of some of the citizens can hardly be held against the views of the democratically elected authorities.

**II-71.** As a final point, the provision of services from abroad may occasionally also inspire the home State to impose certain restrictions. It has already been indicated above[323] that in principle the public policy concern pursued concerns the *own* public policy, which in the context of the free movement of services means that the host State should not be concerned about the policy choices in the home State and vice versa. As a result in *Alpine Investments,*[324] the Dutch authorities could not lawfully prevent a Dutch company from cold calling potential customers of certain investments in France, though Dutch legislation protected Dutch customers from such practices. This may change, however, if a host State is nonetheless being confronted with the consequences of a different level of protection in the country of the service provider. This occurred in *Koestler*[325] where the ECJ accepted that Germany could prevent the recovery before its courts from the losses incurred by a French bank in making a series of stock market transactions in France. German law considered these losses not as loss from ordinary investment activities but as gambling losses. The ECJ reached the outcome at the time by holding that the rules at issue were not discriminatory.[326] However, under the current test it seems hard to deny that such a measure would qualify as a restriction to the free movement of services,[327] thus raising the issue whether it could be justified on public policy grounds as can be done for other restrictions on gambling.[328] For me this is a hard case as it basically asks whether Germany is entitled to offer protection to one of its nationals for losses the latter incurred abroad, after availing him/her of certain investment opportunities not offered in Germany. These opportunities indeed involved additional risks, but these were probably off-set by the corresponding potential for huge profits. This prospect may well have been the reason for the German investor to seek investment opportunities abroad. Nor could it be said *a priori* that the investor

323. *Supra*, at II-17.
324. Case C-384 *Alpine Investments* [1995] ECR I-1141.
325. Case 15/78 *Société générale alsacienne de banque* [1978] ECR 1971.
326. Case 15/78 *Société générale alsacienne de banque* [1978] ECR 1971, para. 15. See on the Court's approach in this case, J. Snell, *Goods and Services in EC law – A Study of the Relationship Between the Freedoms* (Oxford: OUP, 2002), 56-57.
327. The measure effectively precludes the service provider from obtaining the funds it would otherwise be entitled to under its own law, which surely seems an obstacle to providing this type of service caught under the new approach since Case C-76/90 *Säger* [1991] ECR I-4244.
328. See *inter alia* Case C-275/92 *Schindler* [1994] ECR I-1039; Case C-124/97 *Läärä* [1999] ECR I-6067.

was mislead if he/she deliberately foregoes national investment opportunities for a foreign adventure. Yet, upon balance, denying the public policy exception in such a case would force the Member State – through its courts – to become a part of the very activity it seeks to discourage. Moreover, it may otherwise well have to bear the social cost if one of its nationals is destitute as a result of one of these types of transactions; a social cost which it does not know otherwise internally precisely because of the fact that these contracts are not enforceable.

**II-72.** This exercise of balancing the risk of unforeseen social costs with an effective freedom to provide services is also at the heart of the Directive governing the posting of workers.[329] A strict limitation of the public policy concerns of the host State to its own nationals would imply that the social conditions of workers posted in the host State by a foreign company are fully governed by home State rules. However, such an approach may have a double negative effect. On the one hand, it may result in so-called social dumping[330] in that the influx of the cheaper foreign workers may put pressure on the remuneration and other social rights of the local work forced to which its social security system is tailored. On the other hand, as these foreign workers are likely to stay in the host State for a while, their problems, such as poverty because the foreign wages do not result in adequate spending power in the host State, or medical problems as a result of sub-standard health and safety regulations, may well burden the host State. Accordingly, it is necessary to allow the host State to impose certain minimum requirements. The ECJ therefore accepted in *Arblade*[331] that a Member State may extend its minimum wage to the posted workers, yet it rejected a whole series of other administrative requirements. Directive 96/71/EC elaborates these issues further. Its Article 3 allows Member States to impose on posted workers 'by law, regulation or administrative provision' or, in the construction sector, also 'by collective agreements or arbitration awards which have been declared universally applicable' the host State rules concerning:

(a) maximum work periods and minimum rest periods;
(b) minimum paid annual holidays;
(c) the minimum rates of pay, including overtime rates; this point does not apply to supplementary occupational retirement pension schemes;
(d) the conditions of hiring-out of workers, in particular the supply of workers by temporary employment undertakings;
(e) health, safety and hygiene at work;

329. Directive 96/71/EC of the European Parliament and of the Council of 16 December 1996 concerning the posting of workers in the framework of the provision of services (1997) OJ L 18/1.
330. On the difficulty in defining 'social dumping' and its misuse in the context of the free movement of services, see J. Mulder, 'Aangenomen Dienstenrichtlijn: sociale dumping of het dumpen van socialisme?', *Sociaal-Economische Wetgeving* (2008): 2-9. See also U. Belavusau, 'The case of Laval in the context of post-enlargement EC law development', *German Law Journal* (2008): 2279-2307.
331. Joined Cases C-369/96 and C-376/96 *Arblade* [1999] ECR I-8453.

(f) protective measures with regard to the terms and conditions of employment of pregnant women or women who have recently given birth, of children and of young people;
(g) equality of treatment between men and women and other provisions on non-discrimination.

Moreover Article 3(10) allows the host State to impose 'terms and conditions of employment on matters other than those referred to in the first subparagraph of paragraph 1 in the case of public policy provisions'. However, this cannot mean, of course, that a Member State may impose all its mandatory labour law on the posted workers.[332] The Court has clarified that public policy rather refers to:

> national provisions compliance with which has been deemed to be so crucial for the protection of the political, social or economic order in the Member State concerned as to require compliance therewith by all persons present on the national territory of that Member State and all legal relationships within that State[333].

**II-73.** The widely awaited *Laval*[334] case offered some further insights in the impact of this Directive and its public policy clause. The case arose because some peculiarities of the Swedish model of organizing collective labour relations, but the impressive list of Member States making observations in the case indicates that the case was expected to have implications way beyond Swedish law. The problem arose because Sweden had not made use of its possibility under Article 3(1) to lay down by law a minimum wage that could be imposed on posted workers. Nor had it laid down such a minimum wage in 'collective agreements or arbitration awards which have been declared universally applicable', which in the construction sector is also an option. The reason for this was the practice that in Sweden such a collective agreement is not declared universally applicable, but that it is accepted that the trade unions may launch industrial action against employers who refuse to abide by the agreement. The result is that in practical terms, at least for Swedish workers, these agreements are as binding as if they were declared generally applicable. However, this balance was upset by the refusal by the Latvian company Laval to apply to the Latvian workers it had posted on

332. Opinion of AG Trstenjak in Case C-319/06 *Commission v. Luxembourg* [2008] ECR I-4323, para. 46.
333. Case C-319/06 *Commission v. Luxembourg* [2008] ECR I-4323, para. 29. In my view one could think of certain rules, often enforced through the criminal law of the Member States, relating to the conditions for access to or the exercise of certain professions, such as a prohibition for unqualified or unlicensed persons to perform medical procedures or a requirement for persons working for a private security firm to have a specific government-issued identification – conditions which should logically be extended to posted workers. Similarly, one could think of rules prohibiting certain production techniques, for instance, because of environmental (e.g., unnecessary use of particular chemicals) or ethical concerns (e.g., tests on animals, or certain medical procedures such as (particular forms of) abortion) which posted workers should equally not apply, even though these techniques may be lawful in their country of origin.
334. Case C-341/05 *Laval un Partneri* [2007] ECR I-11767.

a construction site in Sweden, pending actual wage negotiations, a collective agreement the terms of which lay down, as regards some of the matters referred to in Article 3(1), first subparagraph, (a)–(g) of Directive 96/71, more favourable conditions than those stemming from the relevant legislative provisions, while other terms cover matters not referred to in that provision. Laval was not a party to this collective agreement, and the agreement had not been declared generally applicable. The posted workers were moreover not members of the Swedish trade unions, though 65% of them were member of a Latvian trade union that had concluded a collective labour agreement with Laval under Latvian law. In response the trade unions resorted to industrial action involving a blockade of the original construction site and several other sites where Laval was active. Laval then started court proceedings in Sweden to enjoin the Swedish unions from further actions.

**II-74.** The Swedish authorities effectively admitted that there effectively was no minimum wage for the building sector laid down by legislation or collective agreement. Accordingly, the ECJ could but come to the conclusion that Sweden had not made use of its option to impose a minimum wage and thus Laval could also not be required to apply it.[335] As this is in essence a procedural issue, the ECJ is thus not sanctioning social dumping practices – it suffices for Sweden to impose through legislation (or, as in this case, for the construction sector 'by collective agreements or arbitration awards which have been declared universally applicable') a minimum wage to also extend it to posted workers. In this sense, the case should be a relief for most other Member States.

**II-75.** However, sticking to such a literal approach also appears, at first sight, liable to disregard the specific social model introduced by Sweden, to the extent that the trade unions and employers have been given leeway to establish a de facto equilibrium.[336] The ECJ may have missed at least two opportunities to temper the effects of its – otherwise defensible – construction of the Directive. First, as indicated above, the ECJ denies the trade unions the right to rely on the public policy exception laid down in Article 3(10) of the Directive.[337] It could well be argued that this provision could not be used for minimum wages (as the exception is meant for *other* public policy concerns, not listed in Article 3(1)) and the Court is right to point out that the special payments in the collective agreement for certain trade union functions may not be as crucial as to amount to be part of the public policy. However, I find it incongruent to consider the trade unions to be sufficiently governmental for the purposes of invoking then Article 49 TEC against them, but then deny them the right to rely on the public policy exception provided by the Directive (which in this respect arguably further elaborates the public policy exception of the Treaty), in clear contradiction of *Bosman*.[338] Second, having found the actions of the trade unions not covered by the Directive, the ECJ,

335. Case C-341/05 *Laval un Partneri* [2007] ECR I-11767, paras 64-71.

336. See in this respect J. Malmberg & T. Sigeman, 'Industrial action and EU economic freedoms: the autonomous collective bargaining model curtailed by the European Court of Justice', *Common Market Law Review* (2008): 1115-1146.

337. Case C-341/05 *Laval un Partneri* [2007] ECR I-11767, paras 82-84.

338. Case C-413/93 *Bosman* [1995] ECR I-4921, para. 86 ('There is nothing to preclude individuals from relying on justifications on grounds of public policy, public security or public health.

rightly, examined whether the Treaty provision could offer some reprieve. However, just as in the case of the freedom of establishment[339] and the free movement of goods,[340] the Court again fails in my view to duly take the hybrid nature of the defendants into account. I find the Court convincing when it considers trade unions in this context to be sufficiently involved in laying down 'rules which are not public in nature but which are designed to regulate, collectively, the provision of services'[341] as to justify invoking the Treaty provisions against them. The Court should not, however, consider the full scope of their activities solely through that prism. While it may at times well be difficult to draw the line between the two realms of activity, the trade unions also have an anti-establishment role. In that capacity, they are not just laying down the rules as a quasi-legislator; rather they are acting to have the constraints imposed on them while laying down the rules altered. Trade unions would be emasculated if the fact that they participate in a social dialogue would imply that they can only implement a pre-ordained framework (in this case what may and may not be imposed on posted workers pursuant to Directive 96/71) and not use their expressive rights – including the widely recognized right to industrial action[342] – to argue that for the future they want things done differently. It seems questionable that the minimum protection offered by Directive 96/71 should also be the maximum trade unions may strive for, including through industrial action. If it were otherwise, the requirement of Article 3(1) to have an act by the legislator, or at least the intervention of the Member State in universalizing the collective agreement, would not make sense. It is precisely because the social partners may wish to go beyond the boundaries of the Directive that the government should be able to intervene – and carry the final responsibility for not acceding to the wishes of these partners[343] or bear the consequences as a matter of EU

---

Neither the scope nor the content of those grounds of justification is in any way affected by the public or private nature of the rules in question').

339. Case C-438/05 *International Transport Workers' Federation* [2007] ECR I-10779.
340. Case C-470/03 *A.G.M.-COS.MET* [2007] ECR I-2749.
341. Case C-341/05 *Laval un Partneri* [2007] ECR I-117967, para. 96, which indeed builds further on a long line of cases including Case 36/74 *Walrave and Koch* [1974] ECR 1405, paras 17 and 18, Case C-415/93 *Bosman* [1995] ECR I-4921, paras 83 and 84, and Case C-309/99 *Wouters and Others* [2002] ECR I-1577, para. 120.
342. The right is laid down in Article 28 of the Charter. The ECJ itself recognized it in Case C-438/05 *International Transport Workers' Federation* [2007] ECR I-11767, para. 86 as follows: 'it should be borne in mind that it is common ground that collective action, like collective negotiations and collective agreements, may, in the particular circumstances of a case, be one of the main ways in which trade unions protect the interests of their members (European Court of Human Rights, *Syndicat national de la police belge v. Belgium*, of 27 October 1975, Series A, No 19, and *Wilson, National Union of Journalists and Others v. United Kingdom* of 2 July 2002, 2002-V, § 44)'.
343. This is also the case if a Member State makes use – in the absence of a system of 'collective agreements or arbitration awards which have been declared universally applicable' – of alternative forms of collective rule-making under Article 3(8) of the Directive. Whereas the ECJ has in Case C-341/05 *Laval un Partneri* [2007] ECR I-11767, paras 65-71 explicitly recognized that the Directive does not preclude this possibility, it has imposed restrictions that are akin to those imposed on collective agreements which have been declared universally applicable. Above all, it flows from paragraph 66, that the legislator must in this respect make an explicit choice for implementing the legislating in this manner. See in this respect, A.A.H. Van Hoek & M.S. Houwerzijl, 'Loonconcurrentie als motor van de interne markt? Een tweeluik – Deel 2: De

law if they follow them. However, on closer examination, both scenarios assume that the Member State exerts some degree of control over the trade unions and the conduct and outcome of negotiations between management and labour. This was, however, not the case in the Swedish model,[344] where Sweden allowed the trade union to pursue their own strategy, even if that strategy had protectionist consequences. However, if that is the case, the question is whether the trade unions can really be said to be exercising a governmental task as to make them bound by the freedom of services. Rather it seems that Sweden, in providing no control whatsoever on the social partners which may thus try to impose a protectionist *fait accompli* on foreign companies, has defectively implemented Directive 96/71[345] and violated Article 56 TFEU, which may be sanctioned through a *Francovich* action for damages.[346] But it must be one of two things[347]: either the trade unions are actors within the system - and then their actions may be checked against the Directive and the free movement, but then they may also raise the appropriate defences; or they are uncontrolled, self-interested, private parties - but then their behaviour must escape review under the Directive and Article 56 TFEU altogether, though the Member State may perhaps face consequences for not adequately regulating their behaviour.[348] Here the ECJ seems to reproach the Swedish authorities for being too lax in putting Directive 96/71 into operation, and then goes on reproaching the trade unions under Article 49 TEC that they do not spontaneously limit their demands to what is possible under a Directive which is not binding on them.

---

arresten *Laval, Rüffert* en *Commissie/Luxemburg*, interpretatie van de Detacheringsrichtlijn', *Nederlands Tijdschrift voor Europees Recht* (2008): 342-343.

344. On this model, see J. Malmberg & T. Sigeman, 'Industrial action and EU economic freedoms: the autonomous collective bargaining model curtailed by the European Court of Justice', *Common Market Law Review* (2008): 1117-1118.

345. Whether that Member State would have agreed to this Directive if it had realized that it would require it to dramatically reform its system of collective bargaining is, however, another matter; see in this respect C. Joerges & F. Rödl, 'Informal Politics, Formalised Law and the "Social Deficit" of European Integration: Reflections after the Judgments of the ECJ in *Viking* and *Laval*', *European Law Journal* (2009): 17.

346. Compare in this respect Case C-470/03 *A.G.M.-COS.MET* [2007] ECR I-2749 and Case C-112/00 *Schmidberger* [2003] ECR I-5659.

347. Compare also A.A.H. Van Hoek & M.S. Houwerzijl, 'Looncóncurrentie als motor van de interne markt? Een tweeluik - Deel 1: De arresten *Viking, Laval en Rüffert*, verdragsaspecten', *Nederlands Tijdschrift voor Europees Recht* (2008): 197-198, who point at a similar ambiguity underlying Case C-438/05 *International Transport Workers' Federation* [2007] ECR I-10779.

348. Compare in this respect the action, on the basis of Article 4(3) TEU, taken by the Commission in the context of the so-called strawberry wars, see Case C-265/95 *Commission v. France* [1997] ECR I-6959. See in this respect also S. Prechal & S. De Vries, 'Viking/Laval en de grondslagen van het internemarktecht', *Sociaal-Economische Wetgeving* (2008): 431-433, who also observe that actually the Swedish law is being criticized by the Court. While they prefer a 'direct route' whereby the Treaty provisions may be relied upon against trade unions from the perspective of effectiveness, they admit that an 'indirect route' based on Article 4(3) TEU offers a better chance for a seamless fit between national law and EU law, even though it relies more on the opportunities for enforcement national law has to offer. Their las *caveat* appears only partially true, as the existence of a *Francovich* action in the national legal order is in any event mandatory as a matter of EU law, see Joined Cases C-6/90 and C-9/90 *Francovich* [1991] ECR I-5357; Joined Cases C-46/93 and C-48/93 *Brasserie du Pêcheur* [1996] ECR I-1026. The national legal orders must even have tools to review proactively certain restrictive governmental action (or inaction), see Case C-213/89 *Factortame* [1990] ECR I-2433; Case C-432/05 *Unibet* [2007] ECR I-2271.

**II-76.** Barring the full horizontal direct effect of Article 56 TFEU, which the ECJ does not seem to have endorsed explicitly, I would expect that an action for damages against the Member State would be the better alternative then. Above,[349] I have argued in respect of *Viking*[350] that Member States may be able to escape liability on the basis of the 'sufficiently serious breach' prong of the state liability conditions by arguing that the restrictions are the result of the lawful exercise by the trade unions of their expressive rights. However, in a context such as *Laval*[351] such a defence should fail, as regardless of the expressive rights of the trade union, the Member State has itself failed to implement the Directive correctly by not providing any mechanism for ensuring that only the issues enumerated in Article 3(1) are enforced under the procedural conditions put forward by the Directive, so that it cannot claim that the restrictions on the free movement are solely the result of the expressive rights of the trade unions.

### [E] Free Movement of Capital

**II-77.** The free movement of capital is the last of the freedoms to have 'come to age'.[352] The public policy concerns in this context are two-fold. On the one hand, there is the fear that money may be used to fund certain undesirable activities such as terrorism or hatemongering. On the other hand, the money itself may be at the centre of certain activities threatening the social order such as money laundering and fraud. As the free movement of capital also extends to transactions involving third countries, an extra element of sensitivity is added.

**II-78.** The relevant Treaty provisions accordingly provide for a series of specific grounds for justifying restrictive measures in the field of the free movement of capital. Article 65(1)(a) TFEU and the first sentence of Article 65(1)(b) TFEU deal with tax measures. The former takes into account that foreigners may at times need to be treated differently for tax purposes – if only to avoid double taxation – than own nationals. The latter seeks to meet the concerns about tax fraud by justifying rules that are intended 'to prevent infringements of national law and regulations, in particular in the field of taxation and the prudential supervision of financial institutions'. On the basis of *Bordessa*[353] it has been questioned[354] whether the fight against other illegal activities such as money laundering, drug trafficking and terrorism are also caught by this clause, or should rather be treated under the proper exception for public policy and public security. The question is without much practical importance as both grounds lead to the same result. Nevertheless, in my view, the two can be distinguished depending on

349. See, *supra*, at II-62.
350. Case C-438/05 *International Transport Workers' Federation* [2007] ECR I-10779.
351. Case C-341/05 *Laval un Partneri* [2007] ECR I-11767.
352. L. Flynn, 'Coming of age: the free movement of capital case law 1993-2002', *Common Market Law Review* (2002): 773-805.
353. Joined cases C-358/93 and C-416/93 *Bordessa* [1995] I-361, paras 21-22.
354. L. Flynn, 'Coming of age: the free movement of capital case law 1993-2002', *Common Market Law Review* (2002): 795.

whether the money is the purpose, or just the means. Combating fraudulent constructions, including cases of money laundering, would then rather fall under the first part of Article 65(1)(b) TFEU, while measures that are primarily aimed at combating the activities that are likely to be sponsored by the money, such as terrorism, fall within the latter category.[355] However, it is clear that this line is not always clear-cut, especially in the case of money laundering of money related to criminal activities such as drugs trafficking, where depending on a person's perspective the aim of combating either the scourge of drugs addictions[356] or the disruptive money transactions may take precedence.

**II-79.** The actual public policy exception of Article 65(1)(b) TFEU is then mainly concerned with the possible uses of the capital at issue. The landmark case in this respect again[357] involves the controversial Church of Scientology. At issue in *Eglise de Scientology*[358] was a French system of prior authorization for certain sensitive investments, which was challenged by several French and foreign branches of the Church of Scientology who planned to invest in their French branch. The Court closely follows the reasoning it has developed in the context of the free movement of persons. It explains first on the basis of *Rutili*[359] that:

> while Member States are still, in principle, free to determine the requirements of public policy and public security in the light of their national needs, those grounds must, in the Community context and, in particular, as derogations from the fundamental principle of free movement of capital, be interpreted strictly, so that their scope cannot be determined unilaterally by each Member State without any control by the Community institutions[360].

The test for this review of what may constitute public policy is thus similarly the existence of 'a genuine and sufficiently serious threat to a fundamental interest of society'.[361] Furthermore, the ECJ makes clear that 'those derogations must not be misapplied so as, in fact, to serve purely economic ends'[362] and that, finally, 'any person affected by a restrictive measure based on such a derogation must have access

355. On the types of money laundering and the links between money laundering and terrorism, see W. Vlcek, 'Acts to Combat the Financing of Terrorism: Common Foreign and Security Policy at the European Court of Justice', *European Foreign Affairs Review* (2006): 495 and the various reports by the OECD's Financial Action Task Force (FATF, see also <www.fatf-gafi.org>) quoted therein.
356. In the absence of a public health exception in the field of the free movement of capital, the public policy exception seems to be the best alternative for all drugs-related issues – actually as the examples above, such as Case C-348/96 *Calfa* [1999] ECR I-11 demonstrate, this is also the case for the free movement of persons where such specific exceptions does exist, though there a distinction probably needs to be made between the therapeutic and repressive measure in the fight against drugs.
357. See also, *supra*, the discussion regarding Case 41/74 *van Duyn* [1974] ECR 1337.
358. Case C-54/99 *Association Eglise de Scientologie de Paris* [2000] ECR I-1335.
359. Case 36/75 *Rutili* [1975] ECR 1219, paras 26 and 27.
360. Case C-54/99 *Association Eglise de Scientologie de Paris* [2000] ECR I-1335, para. 17.
361. Case 36/75 *Rutili* [1975] ECR 1219, para. 28; Case C-348/96 *Calfa* [1999] ECR I-11, para. 21.
362. Case C-54/99 *Association Eglise de Scientologie de Paris* [2000] ECR I-1335, para. 17.

to legal redress'.[363] Unsurprisingly, the ECJ then also applies again the classic proportionality test:

> measures which restrict the free movement of capital may be justified on public-policy and public-security grounds only if they are necessary for the protection of the interests which they are intended to guarantee and only in so far as those objectives cannot be attained by less restrictive measures[364].

However, the Court clarifies its previous case law[365] to the extent that the Court accepts that a system of prior authorization is not always per se illegal, as the alternative mechanism of declarations of investments, likewise provided for by Article 58(1)(b) TEC, may not always suffice. This is so because 'in the case of direct foreign investments, the difficulty in identifying and blocking capital once it has entered a Member State may make it necessary to prevent, at the outset, transactions which would adversely affect public policy or public security'.[366]

**II-80.** Something of a novelty, however, is the 'twist' in the Court's application of this test. Having thus set the stage for allowing in some instances on public policy grounds the prior authorization of foreign investments – which is moreover a discriminatory measure, as there is no similar control of investments by French nationals in this type of activity and none is required as far as the Court (unlike its Advocate General) is concerned[367] – the Court still strikes down the measure on proportionality grounds. Or rather, it injects in the proportionality test a remarkable legal certainty test. In the Court's view, potential investors are not sufficiently protected from arbitrary decisions as the French legislation merely provides that 'prior authorization is required for every direct foreign investment which is such as to represent a threat to public policy [and] public security, without any more detailed definition'.[368] As has been observed there is something awkward about the French legislation, which almost amounts to an '*Erlaubnispflicht von Revolutionen*', a duty to seek permission to start a revolution[369] as the potential investor must himself/herself decide whether or not his/her investment constitutes a threat to public policy and public security, in which case he/she needs to ask for authorization. However, in no other case the Court has ever asked a Member

363. Case C-54/99 *Association Eglise de Scientologie de Paris* [2000] ECR I-1335, para. 17.
364. Case C-54/99 *Association Eglise de Scientologie de Paris* [2000] ECR I-1335, para. 18; Joined Cases C-163/94, C-165/94 and C-250/94 *Sanz de Lera* [1995] ECR I-4821, para. 23.
365. Joined Cases C-163/94, C-165/94 and C-250/94 *Sanz de Lera* [1995] ECR I-4821; Joined Cases C-358/93 and C-416/93 *Bordessa* [1995] I-361; see also J. Van Der Beek, 'Hoe vrij is het vrije verkeer van diensten en kapitaal?', *Nederlands Tijdschrift voor Europees Recht* (2000): 136.
366. Case C-54/99 *Association Eglise de Scientologie de Paris* [2000] ECR I-1335, para. 20.
367. On the basis of Case 121/85 *Conegate* [1986] ECR 1007, AG Saggio had argued that 'a national measure must not discriminate against foreign capital or capital destined for other countries', which *in concreto*, would imply that 'a preventive measure establishing a prior authorisation procedure for investments from abroad intended to finance high-risk sectors and activities must be accompanied by national measures relating to domestic investments with similar content' – see Opinion of AG Saggio in Case C-54/99 *Association Eglise de Scientologie de Paris* [2000] ECR I-1335, para. 22. However, the Court did not take up the suggestion, focusing instead on the vagueness of the French legislation.
368. Case C-54/99 *Association Eglise de Scientologie de Paris* [2000] ECR I-1335, para. 21.
369. J. Glockner, 'Mitgliedstaatliche Investitionsbeschränkungen gegen die Scientology Church', *European Law Reporter* (2000): 145.

State to further clarify in advance the scope and content of its public policy[370] – but then again in few prior cases individuals were asked to anticipate whether their behaviour would constitute a threat to the public policy. Nevertheless, such clarification in advance can be revealing. Recently, the ECJ has rejected the reliance by Spain on the public security exception in order to justify a prior authorization requirement for investments in the energy sector, when it turned out that the criteria did not only included energy security, but also broader aspects of Spanish energy policy.[371]

**II-81.** Finally, attention must also be drawn to the special safeguard clauses of Articles 66 TFEU (old Article 59 TEC) and 75 TFEU (old Article 60 TEC).[372] The former allows for measures to be taken by the Council in case 'movements of capital to or from third countries cause, or threaten to cause, serious difficulties for the operation of economic and monetary union'. While the *lex moneta* forms part of the public policy, the monetary policy for the Member States whose currency is the euro is an exclusive competence of the Union. Accordingly, only the Council is in a position to effectively take measures in this context. The latter, by contrast, deals with measures regarding third countries, which may be necessary for reasons of (international) security. Two situations are covered. On the one hand, the Union may well have taken measures itself under the CFSP, which are then further implemented through Article 215 TFEU (old Article 301 TEC). On the other hand, whereas Member States used to be able 'for serious political reasons and on grounds of urgency',[373] to take unilateral measures against a third country with regard to capital movements and payments and thus anticipate the adoption of such measures by the Council or fill the void that would arise if the Council were to be deadlocked on the matter, that possibility no longer exists, but is replaced by the possibility for the European Parliament and the Council to adapt a framework in this respect, albeit limited to the fight against terrorism (Article 75 TFEU). If no such a framework is in place, however, it appears that Member States will now rather solely have to rely on Article 347 TFEU to take unilateral measures.

### [F] Conclusion As to the Four Freedoms

**II-82.** The *ordre public* exception allows for the suspension of the full effect of the four freedoms in a Member State, in order to avert a 'genuine and sufficiently serious threat to the requirements of public policy affecting one of the fundamental interests of society'.[374] It is not so that EU law is deemed incompatible with the national *ordre public*. Rather, EU law concedes that the common good may in a particular instance be

370. Very critical of this is C. Kessedjian, 'Public Order in European Law', *Erasmus Law Review* (2007): 34-35 who argues that 'legislators have far less imagination than the marketplace', so that the legislator cannot be faulted for blanket norms when it comes to public policy.
371. Case C-207/07 *Commission v. Spain* [2008] ECR I-111*, para. 55.
372. Since the entry into force of the Lisbon Treaty, this provision is now seen as an element of the Area of Freedom, Security and Justice, rather than an aspect of the free movement of capital.
373. Article 60 TEC.
374. Case 30/77 *Bouchereau* [1977] ECR 1999, para. 35. For a recent affirmation, see Case C-441/02 *Commission v. Germany* [2006] ECR I-3149, para. 35.

better served by a national measure – even one that seems to discriminate on grounds of nationality – which restricts one of the four freedoms. This implies that it is EU law which also determines the boundaries of the exception.[375] First, there is a limited review of the soundness of the policy reason put forward. Second, the invocation of the exception is accompanied by a set of procedural guarantees. Finally, the ECJ and the national court go through some form of review of the proportionality test, taking into account, however, that Member States have quite some discretion as to the level of protection of these fundamental interests of society.[376] Accordingly, sometimes rather drastic measures, such as a total ban on a certain activity may be justified. These EU limitations have been developed in a most elaborate manner in the context of the free movement of persons, where also the legislator has intervened. However, the framework also fits, *mutatis mutandis* and despite small variations, the context of the other freedoms. The classic approach reaches its limits, though, when one of the freedoms is invoked against hybrid entities, persons or organizations that are de facto involved in rule-making but also have an anti-establishment role. It is argued that while these entities should also be allowed to rely on the public policy exception,[377] they should also be granted a further judicially crafted exception – which by analogy I would dub the *exception de désordre privé* – to protect the expressive rights of such hybrid actors in full, even though this may at times go at the expense of the four freedoms. It is submitted that abuses that may ensue may be countered through state liability,[378]

375. Case 41/74 *van Duyn* [1974] ECR 1337; H. Schneider, *Die öffentliche Ordnung als Schranke der Grundfreiheiten im EG-Vertrag* (Baden-Baden: Nomos, 1998), 73 and his concepts of public policy as 'Gemeinschaftsrechtlicher Rahmenbegriff' and 'Schranken-Schranken', both of which neatly capture the idea of a concept the limits of which are determined by EU law, but the content of which flows from the diverse national public policies.
376. Case C-275/92 *Schindler* [1994] ECR I-1039.
377. Case C-413/93 *Bosman* [1995] ECR I-4921, para. 86.
378. Case C-470/03 *A.G.M.-COS.MET* [2007] ECR I-2749. In my reading of that case Finland is upon balance to blame for maintaining an ambiguous position. If it was alerted by the remarks of one of its civil servants it could have easily solved the issue by referring the safety concerns to the Commission, which would have been under an obligation to examine the issue. This would have had the triple advantage that the health and safery issue was taken seriously, the producer would have had a fair opportunity to clear its name if the concern turns out to be unfounded; and the civil servant would be free to continue to speak out – at least until the Commission had examined the issue. The Court has thus not necessarily required a course of action that results in underprotection of the health and safety concerns as suggested by N. Reich, 'AGM-COS.MET or: who is protected by EC safety regulation?', *European Law Review* (2008): 85-100. If, by contrast, Finland was not impressed by the comments made by its civil servant it should have denounced his/her comments far more forcefully, though even then the civil servant may well have been allowed to speak out in his/her private capacity (but Finland should take action if he/she were to make use of his/her office or his/her title). However, by taking neither action, the Member State created an ambiguous situation where the safety issue was not examined properly in accordance with the procedure provided by Directive 98/37/EC of the European Parliament and of the Council of 22 June 1998 on the approximation of the laws of the Member States relating to machinery (1998) OJ L 207/1; the producer was thus also not given a chance to exonerate itself while its sales were plummeting; and it is unclear whether the civil servant is punished for what he/she said or because he/she said it in his/her official capacity. Moreover, in any event Finland may be bound by the injurious actions of its civil servant, even if he/she was not defending an official position, because the civil servant is its agent. Whether that may imply that also the civil servant may be liable in his/her own right, is wisely left to the national legal order to decide. See also H.J. Van Harten, 'Van vrij verkeer, uitingsvrijheid en

provided that Member States are given some margin under the sufficiently serious breach prong to escape liability in cases where the obstacle to trade is merely the result of the exercise of the expressive rights by private or hybrid actors, and no own fault of the Member State can be found.

## §4.02 COMPETITION LAW

**II-83.** In a sense EU competition law is the complement of the four freedoms: restrictions introduced by the Member States on the free flow of goods, persons, services and capital should not be replaced by similar inefficiencies flowing from the structuring of the markets by market forces,[379] even though the respective scope of application of the competition rules and the rules on free movement do not form a 'seamless web'.[380] Accordingly, one could wonder whether there is a role for public policy in this context. At first sight, the answer is no. Public policy does not appear as an exception in Article 101 or 102 TFEU. Moreover, more fundamentally, competition law deals with private parties primarily driven by their own private interests. This could make a public policy exception look somewhat out of place. Yet, on a closer look, this image is not entirely correct.

**II-84.** First, as will be developed further below,[381] competition is fundamental in and of itself. On several occasions, the Court of Justice and its Advocates General have

---

aansprakelijkheid, of: de noodzaak van een gemeenschapstrouwe ambtenaar?', *Nederlands Tijdschrift voor Europees Recht* (2008): 181-188.

379. On this interconnectedness, see in particular J. Baquero Cruz, *Between competition and free movement: the economic constitutional law of the European Community* (Oxford: Hart, 2002); M. Poiares Maduro, *We, the Court: the European Court of Justice and the European economic constitution: a critical reading of Article 30 of the EC Treaty* (Oxford: Hart, 1998).; J. Snell, 'Private Parties and the Free Movement of Goods and Services', in *Services and Free Movement in EU Law*, ed. M. Andenas & W.-H. Roth (Oxford: OUP, 2002), 211-243; T. Heremans, 'Publiek of privaat optreden: een toenemende onverschilligheid in hoofde van het Europese marktrecht? – Enkele beschouwingen naar aanleiding van de zaken Laval en Cipolla' in X, *Recht in beweging – 15 de VRG-alumnidag*, (Antwerpen: Maklu, 2008), 411-428. An extensive discussion on the interconnection between competition law and free movement and the corresponding problems of a differentiated treatment of public and private actions go beyond the scope of this book.

380. See in this respect, S. Prechal & S. De Vries, 'Viking/Laval en de grondslagen van het internemarktecht', *Sociaal-Economische Wetgeving* (2008): 427. See on the limits of the convergence between competition law and free movement law also, K. Mortelmans, 'Towards Convergence in the Application of the Rules on Free Movement and on Competition', *Common Market Law Review* (2001): 613-649. I wonder, however, whether Prechal and De Vries (and see also C. Joerges & F. Rödl, 'Informal Politics, Formalised Law and the "Social Deficit" of European Integration: Reflections after the Judgments of the ECJ in *Viking* and *Laval*', *European Law Journal* (2009): 12) are not making too much out of the comparison between, on the one hand, Case C-438/05 *International Transport Workers' Federation* [2007] ECR I-10779 and Case C-341/05 *Laval un Partneri* [2007] ECR I-11767 and, on the other hand, Case C-67/96 *Albany* [1999] ECR I-5751. In my view it is precisely because the collective labour agreements are not really private acts, and thus in principle not covered by Article 101 TFEU, that they must be assessed in the light of the free movement provisions. However, it would flow from this perspective that the trade unions must then be seen as quasi-governmental actors when collective labour agreements are at issue.

381. *Infra*, at III-77 et seq.

indicated that the nucleus of the unfettered competition is itself an issue of public policy, and should thus be treated as such in the laws of the Member States. Accordingly, the violation of Articles 101 and 102 TFEU,[382] but also of the related provisions on state aid,[383] are among those which Member States should give, as a matter of equivalence,[384] the same treatment as the most fundamental norms of society under national law.[385]

**II-85.** Second, it turns out that at times there is a need to also justify certain restrictions by (quasi-)private parties with a reference to general interest concerns, some of which may be so fundamental that they could fall within the ambit of the public policy or related concepts. One reaction to this situation, as we have seen above, is to make the rules on the free movement applicable to such situations. Under reference to *Bosman*[386] this approach has been defended above, provided that the private party is then actually allowed to rely on the public policy and that nonetheless some further exception is crafted to protect a potential anti-establishment role of the quasi-private body. The alternative solution is to allow quasi-private parties – or even Member States in the rare but not extraordinary cases that EU competition law is applied to them – to justify certain practices that prima facie may be at unease with EU competition law under reference to public policy concerns in the context of an analysis under Articles 101 and 102 TFEU.

**II-86.** The examples may clarify the issue. In *Wouters,*[387] the ECJ accepted that a regulation of the Dutch Bar Association relating to the participation of lawyers in partnerships with private undertakings employing tax consultants and accountants could be examined in the light of Article 101 TFEU, even though it had been argued that the Bar Association was in this respect exercising a function of public authority. In light of that finding, the Court had to decide whether Article 101(1) TFEU effectively prohibits a bar association from imposing a full ban on multi-disciplinary partnerships. The Court could not but acknowledge that the ban had a restrictive effect on intra-Community competition.[388] However, this is not the end of the matter, as:

> not every agreement between undertakings or every decision of an association of undertakings which restricts the freedom of action of the parties or of one of them

382. Case C-126/97 *Eco Swiss China Time* [1999] ECR I-3055, paras 39-40; Joined Cases C-295/04 to C-298/04 *Manfredi* [2006] ECR I-6619, para. 31.
383. Opinion of AG Geelhoed in Case C-119/05 *Lucchini Siderurgica* [2007] ECR I-6199, para. 62.
384. Joined Cases C-222/05, C-223/05, C-224/05 and C-225/05 *Van der Weerd* [2007] ECR I-4233, para. 40.
385. For more on the duty for national courts to raise EU law of their own motion, see *infra*, at II-170 et seq.
386. Case C-413/93 *Bosman* [1995] ECR I-4921, para. 86.
387. Case C-309/99 *Wouters* [2002] ECR I-1577, paras 44-71. For more on this case see R. O'Loughlin, 'EC Competition Rules and Free Movement: An Examination of the Parallels and their Furtherance by the ECJ *Wouters* Decision', *European Competition Law Review* (2003): 62-69; A. Vossestein, 'note under Case C-35/99 *Arduino* and Case C-309/99 *Wouters*', *Common Market Law Review* (2002): 841-863; E. Deards, 'Closed shop versus one stop shop: the battle goes on', *European Law Review* (2002): 619-627. See also E. Loozen, 'Professional ethics and restraints of competition, *European Law Review* (2006): 28-47.
388. Case C-309/99 *Wouters* [2002] ECR I-1577, paras 73-96.

> necessarily falls within the prohibition laid down in Article [101(1)] of the Treaty. For the purposes of application of that provision to a particular case, account must first of all be taken of the overall context in which the decision of the association of undertakings was taken or produces its effects. More particularly, account must be taken of its objectives, which are here connected with the need to make rules relating to organisation, qualifications, professional ethics, supervision and liability, in order to ensure that the ultimate consumers of legal services and the sound administration of justice are provided with the necessary guarantees in relation to integrity and experience[389].

Accordingly, the Court accepts that certain considerations that are closely related to the public policy, could justify - or better: denature - certain restrictions of intra-Community competition. This is of course also subject to a proportionality test, whereby it has 'to be considered whether the consequential effects restrictive of competition are inherent in the pursuit of those objectives'.[390] Interestingly, the proportionality test used is not unlike the test used for the public policy exception to the four freedoms. In answer to the observation that other Member States allowed multi-disciplinary partnerships, the ECJ replied effectively in a manner which is particularly reminiscent of the *Schindler* proportionality discussed above[391]:

> Even if multi-disciplinary partnerships of lawyers and accountants are allowed in some Member States, the Bar of the Netherlands is entitled to consider that the objectives pursued by the 1993 Regulation cannot, having regard in particular to the legal regimes by which members of the Bar and accountants are respectively governed in the Netherlands, be attained by less restrictive means[392].

**II-87.** Likewise, the Court of First Instance (CFI)[393] and, on appeal, the ECJ[394] rejected a challenge by two professional swimmers who had complained to the Commission that the anti-doping rules imposed by the International Olympic Committee and the international swimming federation FINA of which they had run afoul, actually restrict competition within the EU markets in a manner that violates Articles 101 and 102 TFEU. However, whereas the CFI had found that such rules were 'purely sporting rules' which would fall both outside Articles 101 and 102 TFEU and outside Articles 45 and 56 TFEU,[395] the ECJ develops further on its judgment in *Wouters*.[396] While admitting

389. Case C-309/99 *Wouters* [2002] ECR I-1577, para. 97.
390. Case C-309/99 *Wouters* [2002] ECR I-1577, para. 97.
391. Case C-275/92 *Schindler* [1994] ECR I-1039.
392. Case C-309/99 *Wouters* [2002] ECR I-1577, para. 108.
393. Case T-313/02 *Meca-Medina and Majcen v. Commission* [2004] ECR II-3291.
394. Case C-519/04 P *Meca-Medina and Majcen v. Commission* [2006] ECR I-6991. For more, see J. Zylberstein, 'Collision entre idéaux sportifs et contigences économiques dans l'arrêt *Meca-Medina*', *Cahiers de droit européen* (2007): 213-237; J. Sluijs & M. Woerkom, 'Meca-Medina en Majcen (hogere voorziening): Convergentie gepreciseerd, Wouters bevestigd, *Nederlands Tijdschrift voor Europees Recht* (2006): 248-253; S. Weatherill, 'Anti-doping revisited - the demise of the rule of "purely sporting interest"?', *European Competition Law Review* (2006): 645-657.
395. Case T-313/02 *Meca-Medina and Majcen v. Commission* [2004] ECR II-3291, para. 68. On the rejection of the concept of 'purely sporting interest', see S. Weatherill, 'Anti-doping revisited - the demise of the rule of "purely sporting interest"?', *European Competition Law Review* (2006): 645-657.

that as professional sport is an economic activity the rules of these sporting federations can be examined in the light of competition law, the Court again seeks to immunize these rules from an effective challenge on these grounds. The Court accepts that:

> the Commission could rightly take the view that the general objective of the rules was, as none of the parties disputes, to combat doping in order for competitive sport to be conducted fairly and that it included the need to safeguard equal chances for athletes, athletes' health, the integrity and objectivity of competitive sport and ethical values in sport[397]

and it finds next that:

> even if the anti-doping rules at issue are to be regarded as a decision of an association of undertakings limiting the appellants' freedom of action, they do not, for all that, necessarily constitute a restriction of competition incompatible with the common market, within the meaning of Article [101 TFEU], since they are justified by a legitimate objective. Such a limitation is inherent in the organisation and proper conduct of competitive sport and its very purpose is to ensure healthy rivalry between athletes[398].

The ECJ thus seems to accept, on the one hand, that also private parties may at times be called upon to protect public interests, such as athletes' health (which is in the end an expression of the public health); on the other hand, the Court is again cunningly crafting an exception for rules that are 'inherent' in the regulated professional conduct. Interestingly, in this case the ECJ displays far less deference when it comes to proportionality. This seems justified in the particular context of anti-doping rules, which, given the relative short professional careers of most athletes, may have the effect of completely ruining the career of those athletes in a way the professional rules in *Wouters* could not. A total ban on successful lawyers, accountants and tax consultants joining a single multi-disciplinary partnership – where, admittedly, they may be even more successful – is of a different nature than a doping ban prohibiting all relevant professional activity. Accordingly, the Court accepts that:

> the penal nature of the anti-doping rules at issue and the magnitude of the penalties applicable if they are breached are capable of producing adverse effects on competition because they could, if penalties were ultimately to prove unjustified, result in an athlete's unwarranted exclusion from sporting events, and thus in impairment of the conditions under which the activity at issue is engaged in. It follows that, in order not to be covered by the prohibition laid down in Article 101(1) TFEU, the restrictions thus imposed by those rules must be limited to what is necessary to ensure the proper conduct of competitive sport[399].

Nevertheless, the sporting federations seem to have quite some margin in determining the appropriate levels for prohibited substances and the corresponding penalties for those athletes who would exceed these limits. By contrast, a sporting federation which does more than taking administrative decisions as to the rules and conditions under

396. Case C-309/99 *Wouters* [2002] ECR I-1577.
397. Case C-519/04 P *Meca-Medina and Majcen v. Commission* [2006] ECR I-6991, para. 43.
398. Case C-519/04 P *Meca-Medina and Majcen v. Commission* [2006] ECR I-6991, para. 45.
399. Case C-519/04 P *Meca-Medina and Majcen v. Commission* [2006] ECR I-6991, para. 47.

which competitions take place, but also organizes itself certain events for which it concludes deals relating to sponsorships, advertising and insurance not only falls within the scope of Articles 102 and 106 TFEU, but is also not entitled to any particular deference as to these economic activities and may thus not be given the unfettered right to decide whether others may or may not organize similar events.[400]

**II-88.** Years earlier, the Court had also accepted that certain governmental tasks exercised by private parties may escape review under Article 102 TFEU. In *Diego Cali*[401] the applicant challenged before an Italian court the invoice it had received for certain preventive anti-pollution services carries out by the Servizi Ecologici Porto di Genova (SEPG), a company that had exclusively been entrusted with a concession for the prevention c.q. cleaning up of oil pollution in the port of Genova. Following a similar approach in respect of air traffic control services provided by Eurocontrol,[402] the Court accepted that this charge escaped the application of Article 82 TEC because 'the anti-pollution surveillance for which SEPG was responsible in the oil port of Genoa is a task in the public interest which forms part of the essential functions of the State as regards protection of the environment in maritime areas'[403] and thus also the levying of a (State-approved) charge for these services – which moreover were extended to the applicant in the absence of any concrete incident – falls within the scope of the public authority[404] and outside Article 82 TEC,[405] even though it is obvious that such anti-pollution services are definitely an economic activity which in effect was delivered by a private party.

## §4.03 ARTICLE 347 TFEU

**II-89.** Exceptional circumstances may require exceptional measures. That seems to be wisdom behind Article 347 TFEU. Some situations may be so 'wholly exceptional'[406] that the classic public policy and public security exceptions to the fundamental freedoms may not suffice. One can easily understand that if a coordinated attack like the one on 11 September 2001 were to occur in an EU Member State that a similar response by the Member State concerned of shutting down all air traffic may well be a sensible thing to do. Yet, this would also have a major impact on the internal market, affecting the common transport policy and the free movement of goods, persons and services. Under a strict application of Articles 36, 45(3), 52 or 59 TFEU, a Member State would first have to make an individual assessment whether each single passenger

400. Case C-49/07 *MOTOE* [2008] ECR I-4863.
401. Case C-343/95 *Diego Cali & Figli* [1997] ECR I-1547.
402. Case C-364/92 *SAT Fluggesellschaft* [1994] ECR I-43. See, however, also Case T-155/04 *SELEX Sistemi Integrati v. Commissie* [2006] ECR II-4797, where the General Court seemed to assume that Eurcontrol did pursue economic activities. This position was however questioned on appeal, see Opinion of AG Trstenjak in Case C-113/07 P *SELEX Sistemi Integrati* [2009] ECR I-2207, paras 60-69.
403. Case C-343/95 *Diego Cali & Figli* [1997] ECR I-1547, para. 23.
404. Case C-343/95 *Diego Cali & Figli* [1997] ECR I-1547, para. 24.
405. Case C-343/95 *Diego Cali & Figli* [1997] ECR I-1547, para. 25.
406. Case 222/84 *Johnston* [1985] ECR 1651, para. 27.

would constitute a threat to a fundamental interest of society. Of course this is an absurd exercise in the face of an imminent attack with several hijacked passenger planes. Accordingly, there is need for a more general safeguard clause to be used in these extreme circumstances, which - fortunately - are so rare, however, that there is scant case law on the conditions for its application. Yet, even such a safeguard clause does not need to amount to a full 'reserve of sovereignty',[407] beyond the bounds of EU scrutiny[408] as this would be incompatible with the level of judicial protection inherent in an Union based on the rule of law. Moreover the Court has always stressed that the scope of Article 347 TFEU is rather limited: 'it cannot be inferred that the Treaty contains an inherent general exception excluding all measures taken for reasons of public security from the scope of European Union law'.[409]

**II-90.** It flows from the text of the Article that there are three situations where Article 347 TFEU comes into play. The first concerns 'serious internal disturbances affecting the maintenance of law and order', which Advocate General Jacobs rightly describes as 'a breakdown of public order on a scale much vaster than the type of civil unrest which might justify recourse to Article [36 TFEU]'.[410] This also seems to suggest that the correct order for assessing cases is to first assess whether the ordinary exceptions to the free movement may suffice and only when they do not offer an adequate answer consider Article 347 TFEU, even though Advocate General Cosmas proceeded otherwise in *Albore*.[411]

**II-91.** The second situation arises in 'the event of war [or] serious international tension constituting a threat of war'. While it may be relatively easy to assess whether hostilities have broken out of some importance as to speak of 'war', it is less evident when the threshold may be reached in the case of international tension. The crucial, albeit counter-intuitive, insight given by Advocate General Jacobs in this respect is that the threat must be assessed from the subjective perspective of the Member State, which may be at a far better position than any Court to assess the nature of the threat it is facing.[412] Thus in *Commission v. Greece*,[413] the only case so far brought under Article 348 TFEU for alleged breach of Article 347 TFEU and which was removed from the register after the Opinion of the Advocate General but before the judgment, it was argued by the Advocate General that while it may have been unlikely from an outsider point of view that Greece could be dragged into an armed conflict with the Former Yugoslavian Republic of Macedonia, things may well have looked differently to the Greek government taking into account history, nationalistic bidding on both sides and the general instability in the Balkan region at the time where several other former

407. P. Koutrakos, 'Is Article 297 TEC a "reserve of sovereignty?"', *Common Market Law Review* (2000): 1339-1362.
408. Opinion of AG Darmon in Case 222/84 *Johnston* [1985] ECR 1651, at 1656-1657.
409. Case C-38/06 *Commission v. Portugal* [2010] ECR I-1569, para 62.
410. Opinion of AG Jacobs in Case C-120/94 *Commission v. Greece* [1996] ECR I-1513, para. 47.
411. Opinion of AG Cosmas in Case C-423/98 *Albore* [2000] ECR I-5965.
412. Opinion of AG Jacobs in Case C-120/94 *Commission v. Greece* [1996] ECR I-1513, para. 54. Compare in this respect ECtHR, 18 January 1978, *Ireland v. United Kingdom*, paras 78-79.
413. Case C-120/94 *Commission v. Greece* [1996] ECR I-1513.

Yugoslavian states were involved in a civil war. Nevertheless, the general organization of the military,[414] or the planning of the defence of a country during peacetime[415] do not amount to situations envisaged by Article 347 TFEU.

**II-92.** The third situation in which Article 347 TFEU plays a role are situations were a Member State takes measures 'in order to carry out obligations it has accepted for the purpose of maintaining peace and international security'. To a certain extent one could think this option to be overtaken by the existence of the CFSP and the possibility for the Union to implement CFSP measures on the basis of Article 215 TFEU. However, it cannot be excluded that there may be circumstances where a Member State is under special obligations, for instance because of its proximity to the conflict, or where no unanimity could be reached over a CFSP measure necessary for implementing a UN Security Council resolution. In this respect I do not *a priori* exclude the possibility that even a group of Member States may collectively rely on Article 347 TFEU.[416]

**II-93.** The last example suggests at a close relationship between Article 347 TFEU and the CFSP, even though any such link is carefully excluded from the text of the Article. I agree with Koutrakos that there is nonetheless a 'functional link' between the CFSP and Article 347 TFEU.[417] This comes well to the fore if we look at the procedural requirements for Article 347 TFEU. Article 347 TFEU requires that 'Member States shall consult each other with a view to taking together the steps needed to prevent the functioning of the common market being affected' by the measures at issue.' Nothing precludes Member States from fulfilling this obligation in the context of the CFSP, where Article 24(3) TEU provides for an adequate framework. Consultation within the scope of the Council under the CFSP may moreover lead to further action by the EU, which may either make unilateral action by the Member State concerned unnecessary, either because the EU takes a collective measure instead, or because the EU as a whole

414. Case C-273/97 *Sirdar* [1999] ECR I-7403; Case C-285/98 *Kreil* [2000] ECR I-69.
415. Case C-423/98 *Albore* [2000] ECR I-5965. See also Case C-337/05 *Commission v. Italy* [2008] ECR I-2173, where Italy failed to rely on Articles 346 and 347 TFEU to defend its breach of the rules on public procurement for the purchase of helicopters for police and civil protection services, which that Member State argued could also be used in combination with its military in times of war. See also Case T-26/01 *Fiocchi Munizione v. Commission* [2003] ECR II-3961. For more on Article 346 TFEU, which allows Member States some leeway in respect of their essential security interests and their military, see D. Eisenhut, 'The special security exemption of Article 296 EC: Time for a new notion of "essential security interests"?', *European Law Review* (2008): 577-585.
416. *Contra*, P. Koutrakos, 'Is Article 297 TEC a "reserve of sovereignty?"', *Common Market Law Review* (2000): 1345-1346. He argues that otherwise 'the procedure under Article 301 EC would be seriously undermined and the role of a Council Regulation in the sanctions regimes marginalized'. I disagree as there simply can be no Regulation on the basis of Article 301 TEC (or since Lisbon, Article 215 TFEU) if there is not first consensus in the Council as to a common position under the CFSP. While I agree that the CFSP aims at consensus building, and one could imagine that the possibility for some Member States to go alone may thwart that exercise, it cannot be denied that if no consensus is reached, there may nonetheless still be obligations for the purpose of maintaining peace and international security which need to be addressed. If these obligations require derogations from the internal market, Article 347 TFEU seems the only viable alternative.
417. P. Koutrakos, 'Is Article 297 TEC a "reserve of sovereignty?"', *Common Market Law Review* (2000): 1356-1361.

may at times be able to alleviate certain concerns which otherwise may be perceived by a single Member State as amounting 'to serious international tension constituting a threat of war'.[418]

**II-94.** The role of the ECJ – in a procedure under Article 348 TFEU, but also in a preliminary reference procedure[419] – in assessing whether a Member State is making 'improper use of its powers'[420] provided for under Article 347 TFEU is then three-fold. Despite the 'paucity of judicially applicable criteria'[421] the ECJ will first have to review whether a Member State could reasonably have believed to be faced with one of the situations described in Article 347 TFEU. Second, the ECJ will have to assess whether the procedural requirements of Article 347 TFEU have been complied with. In this respect, while I agree that in principle the consultation must take place before the measures are taken,[422] attention should be drawn to the 9/11 scenario set out at the beginning of this section where this may not be possible. Third, as these measures are not taken in a legal vacuum, the ECJ will need to assess whether other fundamental principles of EU law, in particular the principles of equality and proportionality,[423] and the fundamental rights are respected.

**II-95.** In this respect, the Court may in various instances solve the problem from a slightly different angle. The necessity – and thus the proportionality – of a whole series of measures which Member States may envisage could well be lacking if one takes into account that secondary EU law may well already offer a sufficient framework for addressing the concerns of the Member States. Several EU legislative instruments actually take Member State security concerns into account. This is for instance expressly the case with the mandatory ground for refusing access to documents laid down in Article 4(1)(a) of Regulation 1049/2001.[424] In *Centro-Com,*[425] it was accepted that Article 11 of the Export Regulation[426] – which uses a security concept which covers

418. On this, see P. Gilsdorf, 'Les reserves de sécurité du Traité CEE, à la lumière du Traité sur l'Union Européenne', *Revue du Marché Commun* (1994): 19; P. Koutrakos, 'Is Article 297 TEC a "reserve of sovereignty?"', *Common Market Law Review* (2000): 1356-1357. Compare in respect of Article 296 TEC, D. Eisenhut, 'The special security exemption of Article 296 EC: Time for a new notion of "essential security interests"?', *European Law Review* (2008): 577-585.
419. See for instance Case 222/84 *Johnston* [1985] ECR 1651 and in particular the Opinion of AG Darmon, at point 3.
420. Article 348 TFEU.
421. Opinion of AG Jacobs in Case C-120/94 *Commission v. Greece* [1996] ECR I-1513, para. 50.
422. P. Oliver & M. Jarvis, *Free Movement of Goods in the European Community*, 4th ed. (London: Thomson/Sweet & Maxwell, 2003), 406; P. Koutrakos, 'Is Article 297 TEC a "reserve of sovereignty?"', *Common Market Law Review* (2000): 1357-1358.
423. Opinion of AG Jacobs in Case C-120/94 *Commission v. Greece* [1996] ECR I-1513, paras 69-72.
424. Regulation (EC) No 1049/2001 of the European Parliament and of the Council of 30 May 2001 regarding public access to European Parliament, Council and Commission documents (2001) OJ L 145/43. For an application see Joined Cases T-110/03, T-150/03 and T-405/03 *Sison v. Council* [2005] ECR II-1429, para. 51.
425. Case C-124/95 *Centro-Com* [1997] ECR I-87. For a good discussion of the issues at stake, see P. Eeckhout, *External Relations of the European Union – Legal and Constitutional Foundations* (Oxford: OUP, 2004) 431-436.
426. Regulation (EEC) No 2603/69 of 20 December 1969 establishing common rules for exports *Official Journal, English Special Edition* 1969 (II), 590.

both a Member State's internal security and its external security and which, consequently, accepts that the risk of a serious disturbance to foreign relations or to peaceful coexistence of nations may affect the external security of a Member State - could no longer be relied upon by a Member State to take unilateral measures once the Community had adopted its own trade sanctions. Finally, it follows from *Johnston*[427] and *Sirdar*[428] that the equal treatment Directives offer a sufficient framework for taking into account the security concerns of the Member States while preserving the core of the equal treatment provisions, again making it unnecessary for Member States to rely on Article 347 TFEU.

**II-96.** Finally, two remaining issues need to be clarified as to the scope of Article 347 TFEU. On the one hand, the question may arise whether Article 347 TFEU may only be used to deviate from the Treaty or also from secondary legislation. It seems that the latter view is correct, but subject to what has been said above in respect of the fact that several EU instruments drafted in a manner which already takes the security concerns into account, so that reliance on the Article becomes superfluous. On the other hand, the Article seems limited to the functioning of the 'common market' or - after Lisbon - of the 'internal market'. This is particularly remarkable in light of the envisaged merger of the pillars by the Lisbon Treaty. Apparently, Article 347 TFEU will not be available to deviate from the judicial cooperation in criminal matters, for instance. To the extent that the legislation adopted under that chapter often concern fundamental rights this seems a good thing. There may be genuine reason for concern if Member States could rely on Article 347 TFEU to deviate from some essential procedural safeguards because of security concerns, for instance in the context of the fight against terrorism. One has for instance only to think of the extraordinary renditions as promoted by the US following 9/11 to envisage what harm an exception on the basis of Article 347 TFEU to the procedures under the Framework Decision on the European Arrest Warrant[429] in order to justify a similar circumvention of key procedural safeguards for terrorism suspects could do to the rule of law in the Union.

## §4.04 THE EXCEPTIONS TO THE JURISDICTION OF THE ECJ IN THE AREA OF FREEDOM, SECURITY AND JUSTICE PERTAINING TO MEASURES TAKEN FOR THE MAINTENANCE OF LAW AND ORDER AND THE SAFEGUARDING OF INTERNAL SECURITY

**II-97.** The last example is also telling for a further restriction inspired by the *ordre public,* which to a certain extent is the complement of Article 347 TFEU in the jurisdictional sphere. Member States are primarily competent to organize their police and security forces and generally guarantee the maintenance of law and order and the safeguarding of internal security. Unsurprisingly, those same Member States try to

427. Case 222/84 *Johnston* [1985] ECR 1651.
428. Case C-273/97 *Sirdar* [1999] ECR I-7403.
429. Council Framework Decision 2002/584/JHA of 13 June 2002 on the European arrest warrant and the surrender procedures between the Member States (2002) OJ L 190/1.

keep EU interference in those fields as much as possible at bay, even though one could wonder whether the legitimacy of their actions could not be enhanced if they were to be respecting certain EU wide minimum guarantees and be subject to some degree of EU supervision. Accordingly, the level of judicial protection in the Area of Freedom, Security and Justice was deliberately held at a minimum,[430] and even further curtailed in Articles 68(2) TEC and 35(5) TEU in respect of measures taken for the maintenance of law and order and the safeguarding of internal security. While this absence of effective judicial protection has largely been redressed by the Lisbon Treaty, this key exception has been maintained in Article 276 TFEU. The aim of the exception is to exclude all judicial review by the ECJ of the legality and proportionality of measures taken in this respect, barring not only the preliminary reference proceeding, but also all other courses of action.[431]

**II-98.** At first sight the exception could be seen as an unfortunate remnant of the sovereignty of the Member States, explained by the reluctance of the Member States to make EU inroads in their monopoly on the use of force, which is moreover primarily under democratic supervision from national institutions. However, the problem ran deeper. As the Commission has rightly observed, the wording of Article 68(2) TEC also 'appears to exclude any review by the Court of Justice of Community measures adopted by the legislature on the basis of Article 62(1) of the EC Treaty that cover the maintenance of law and order and the safeguarding of internal security'.[432] This is in particular problematic in respect of the EU measures which abolish in principle the controls on the person at the EU internal borders, but also provide for the exceptional possibilities of reintroducing such controls temporarily.[433] The ECJ has, as was argued above,[434] consistently tried to:

> circumscribe the exercise of the powers of the Member States to restrict the freedom of movement of goods, persons or capital in connection with public-policy issues (on the basis of [old] Arts. 30, 39(3) and 46 EC), trying to find the right balance between proportionality and the discretion of the Member States[435].

This balance risks being upset if the ECJ is precluded from at least assessing the validity of EC measures in this field, and from determining the scope of application of any public policy exceptions to the abolishing of internal frontiers. However, it appears that the wording of Article 276 TFEU does not give rise to similar concerns.

---

430. For an overview, see K. Lenaerts, D. Arts & I. Maselis; R. Bray (ed.), *Procedural Law of the European Union*, 2nd ed. (London: Sweet & Maxwell, 2006), chapter 22. For very critical remarks, see X, 'Editiorial Comments – Preliminary rulings and the area of freedom, security and justice', *Common Market Law Review* (2007): 1-7.
431. K. Lenaerts, D. Arts & I. Maselis; R. Bray (ed.), *Procedural Law of the European Union*, 2nd ed. (London: Sweet & Maxwell, 2006), 513 and 515.
432. Communication from the Commission to the European Parliament, the Council, the European Economic and Social Committee, the Committee of the Regions and the Court of Justice of the European Communities, 28 June 2006 COM(2006) 346 final, 6.
433. *Ibid.*; see also X, 'Editiorial Comments – Preliminary rulings and the area of freedom, security and justice', *Common Market Law Review* (2007): 4.
434. *Supra*, at II-7 et seq.
435. X, 'Editiorial Comments – Preliminary rulings and the area of freedom, security and justice', *Common Market Law Review* (2007): 4.

## §4.05 CONCLUSION AS TO THE USE OF THE *ORDRE PUBLIC* IN THE TREATIES

**II-99.** In the first chapter of this Part II, it was demonstrated how public policy concerns are being addressed in the Treaties. It was indicated that these exceptions can hardly be conceived as *réserves de souveraineté*. Quite to the contrary, both the exceptions to the free movement of goods, services persons and capital and even the more ominous safeguard clause of Article 347 TFEU have all been circumscribed in the case law of the ECJ. Only the exception of Article 276 TFEU seems to form a (minor) blot on this blueprint.

**II-100.** The flip side of the coin is that Member States may no longer always be able to take all desired measures for protecting the *ordre public* unilaterally; or at least it seems that some of the difficult balancing between public policy concerns and EU interests could at times better be done at the level of the EU, avoiding the need for an ad hoc assessment on the basis of Articles 36, 45(3) or 52 TFEU. These measures form the object of the next chapter.

CHAPTER 5

# The EU Action to Protect the *Ordre Public*

**II-101.** In the absence of harmonization it is for the Member States to take the necessary measures for the protection of the *ordre public*. However, as the EU is increasingly entrusted with new tasks, it is no surprise that also at the EU level similar concerns may influence decision-making. Accordingly, it is necessary to briefly address the action by the EU to protect the *ordre public*. Within the constraints of this book it is of course impossible to address all areas of competence or to give an overview of all potentially relevant legislation. Rather this chapter seeks to offer some basic insight in the limitations for EU action having an impact on the *ordre public*. Two issues will be focused on. On the one hand, attention will be paid to the action undertaken by the EU to police the internal market (§5.01). On the other hand, the growing body of EU criminal law will be examined (§5.02).

## §5.01 EU ACTION FOR POLICING THE INTERNAL MARKET

**II-102.** Before we turn our attention to the internal market, proper, however, something needs also to be said on other policy fields. First, as the EU has – albeit in limited fields – a series of exclusive competences it is inevitable that to the extent that public policy concerns are raised in those areas that they are addressed at the level of the EU legislator.[1] These areas, listed in Article 3 TFEU, concern key areas of economic life, and in all of them one could see issues of public policy arise. The customs union is at once an expression of the free movement of goods, a tool for the external common commercial policy (itself an exclusive competence) and intertwined with the financial interests of the Union.[2] The establishing of the competition rules necessary for the

1. I use the term legislator in a generic sense, without denoting any particular decision-making procedure, if only because one of these areas of exclusive competence concerns the monetary policy for the Member States whose currency is the euro, which may involve a particular role for the ECB.
2. For an example of the complexities that thus may ensue, see Case T-330/99 *Spedition Wilhelm Rotermund v. Commission* [2001] ECR II-1619; Case T-332/02 *Nordspedizionieri di Danielis*

functioning of the internal market is about writing the 'economic constitutional law'[3] of the European Union and thus about defining the *ordre public économique*. In the same vein, the competence to determine the monetary policy for the Member States whose currency is the euro concerns the *lex moneta*, which likewise falls within the *ordre public*.[4] The common commercial policy is confronted with similar issues of public policy at the international level as addressed above in respect of the internal market.[5] As argued above, in these situations the EU even reserves the right to 'export' its levels of protection.[6] Finally, the conservation of marine biological resources under the common fisheries policy sounds somewhat of a different order. Nevertheless this entails sensitive concerns about balancing economic needs with environmental concerns, often resulting in restrictions enforced through criminal law.[7] The exclusivity implies that Member States can only act in these fields to the extent that they are authorized by the Union. Accordingly, if the EU fails to address certain concerns, there may be the risk of a gap in protection, which the ECJ has occasionally filled in a rather creative manner,[8] for instance by finding that the Member States are to act as 'trustees of the common interest'[9] or by finding authorizations were none are obvious.[10]

**II-103.** Second, the Union has been given shared competences allowing it to pre-empt the action of the Member States in a series of fields touching on public health, public security and public morality, as diverse as environmental protection,[11] blood safety[12] or health and safety at work[13] or on the road.[14] Most of the ensuing legislation has some link with broader transnational problems, but these laws may well apply in situations

---

*Livio v. Commission* [2004] ECR II-4405 – confirmed on appeal, see Case C-62/05 P *Nordspedizionieri di Danielis Livio v. Commission* [2007] ECR I-8647, with Opinion of AG Ruiz-Jarabo Colomer.

3. On this, see J. Baquero Cruz, *Between competition and free movement: the economic constitutional law of the European Community* (Oxford: Hart, 2002).
4. Case 7/78 *Thompson* [1978] ECR 2247; Case C-359/05 *Estager* [2007] ECR I-581; see also *infra*, at III-75 et seq.
5. A good example is international drug trafficking, which has been tackled in the past on the basis of old Article 113 TEEC (now Article 207 TFEU), see Council Regulation (EEC) No 3677/90 of 13 December 1990 laying down measures to be taken to discourage the diversion of certain substances to the illicit manufacture of narcotic drugs and psychotropic substances (1990) OJ L 357/1.
6. *Supra*, at II-17, referring *inter alia* to Joined Cases C-129/05 and C-130/05 *Raverco* [2006] ECR I-9297.
7. An illustration can be found in the facts behind Case T-177/01 *Jégo-Quéré v. Commission* [2002] ECR II-2365. See also Case C-2/88 Imm. *Zwartveld* [1990] ECR I-4405.
8. On authorizations, see K. Lenaerts & P. Van Nuffel; R. Bray (ed.), *Constitutional Law of the European Union*, 2nd ed. (London: Sweet & Maxwell, 2005), 98.
9. Case 804/79 *Commission v. UK* [1981] ECR 1045, para. 30.
10. Case 174/84 *Bulk Oil* [1986] ECR 559.
11. Articles 191-193 TFEU.
12. Article 168(4)(a) TFEU. See for instance Directive 2002/98/EC of the European Parliament and of the Council of 27 January 2003 setting standards of quality and safety for the collection, testing, processing, storage and distribution of human blood and blood components and amending Directive 2001/83/EC (2003) OJ L 33/30; dealing with safety issues, but also with ethical issues such as the voluntary, unpaid and anonymous character of the donations.
13. Article 153(1) TFEU. Moreover, the ECJ has given a wide interpretation of these concepts so that the EU legislator may go to the core of workplace relations, *inter alia* by regulating working time, see Case C-84/94 *UK v. Commission* [1996] ECR I-5755.

that seem purely internal. Once legislation is adopted in those fields, it is EU law that determines the appropriate level of protection, though in most instances the Member States are allowed to go further[15] – subject to respecting the overall limitations of the free movement clauses. Accordingly, the ECJ accepted in *Aher-Waggon,*[16] that while the EU had laid down noise emission standards for airplanes, Germany could still prohibit the importation from Denmark of a plane meeting the EU standard but falling below the German environmental standards. Similarly, Belgium could prohibit, for reasons of animal welfare, health protection and environmental protection, the holding of certain types of mammals, not covered by EU legislation.[17] Yet, the ECJ does not seem to allow this if a Member State tries to apply its higher standard of protection to a situation on the territory of another Member State.[18]

**II-104.** While the match is not perfect,[19] the power of the EU to harmonize for the internal market under Article 114 TFEU serves as a complement for the negative harmonization on the basis of the four freedoms. In doing so, the EU must, in accordance with Article 114(3) TFEU, moreover take into account a high level of protection in respect of health, safety, environmental protection and consumer protection. Accordingly, the EU itself will at times, while taking measures aimed at removing distortions of competition or eliminating obstacles to trade,[20] also take measures that regulate issues of public policy. Sometimes this can be done quite explicitly, and if a uniform regime is introduced it may well be that there is not really an alternative for EU rules regarding these issues. An example is Commission Regulation 874/2004 laying down public policy rules concerning the implementation and functions of the .eu Top Level Domain and the principles governing registration.[21] The .eu Top Level Domain

14. See for instance Council Directive 91/439/EEC of 29 July 1991 on driving licenses (1991) OJ L 237/1. The recent case law stressing the importance of mutual recognition in this context, may, however give rise to some questions as to whether this really contributes to road safety; see for instance Joined Cases C-329/06 and C-343/06 *Wiedemann* [2008] ECR I-4635 and Joined Cases C-334/06 to C-336/06 *Zerche* [2008] ECR I-4691.
15. It has been argued, though that it is not always clear what 'further' means and what limits there may nonetheless be in this respect, especially if fundamental rights may be at stake, see F. De Cecco, 'Room to move? Minimum harmonisation and fundamental rights', *Common Market Law Review* (2006): 10-11.
16. Case C-389/96 *Aher-Waggon* [1998] ECR I-4473.
17. Case C-219/07 *Nationale Raad van Dierenkwekers en Liefhebbers* [2008] ECR I-4475.
18. Case C-169/89 *Gourmetterie Van den Burg* [1990] ECR I-2143. For more on the question when Member States may apply more stringent national provisions in the face of minimum harmonization, see M. Dougan, 'Minimum harmonization and the internal market', *Common Market Law Review* (2000): 853-885, who tries to find middle ground between N. Bernard, 'The future of European economic law in the light of the principle of subsidiarity', *Common Market Law Review* (1996): 633-666 (who excludes any extra-territorial effect of national legislation deviating from the minimum standard) and P. J. Slot, 'Harmonisation', *European Law Review* (1996): 378-397 (who argues that higher standards should be applicable to both internal and intra-Union situations).
19. G. Davies, 'Can selling arrangements be harmonised', *European Law Review* (2005): 370-385.
20. Case C-376/98 *Germany v. European Parliament and Council* [2000] ECR I-8419, para. 95; Case C-210/03 *Swedish Match* [2004] ECR I-11893, paras 26-34.
21. Commission Regulation (EC) No 874/2004 of 28 April 2004 laying down public policy rules concerning the implementation and functions of the .eu Top Level Domain and the principles governing registration (2004) OJ L 162/40.

being introduced by the EU[22] – albeit not on the basis of Article 114 TFEU but on the specific legal basis of Article 156 TEC (now Article 176 TFEU) – only the EU can determine on what domain names may, or may not be registered. This in turn may well involve an additional catch-all public policy clause. Accordingly, Article 18 of Regulation 874/2004 excludes registrations that are deemed 'defamatory, racist or contrary to public policy'. On the one hand, it is the EU who makes the policy choice to exclude certain domain names. On the other hand, the role of the Member States is not entirely excluded, as the Member States (and their courts) determine which names are to be considered 'defamatory, racist or contrary to public policy'.

**II-105.** This seems to be the standard solution for minimizing friction between the EU legal order and the Member States while nonetheless imposing certain common standards: the EU lays down a framework, yet the Member States have some liberty in fine-tuning the standards.[23] The issue comes clearly to the fore in the judgment of the EFTA Court[24] in *TV 1000 Sverige AB*[25] concerning certain restrictions – de facto cutting the transmission – imposed on a Norwegian broadcaster carrying the signal of a Swedish channel offering sexually explicit films, which were deemed by the Norwegian authorities to be pornographic. The referring court in that case had expressly asked whether Article 22 of Directive 89/552[26] sets a common European standard. The provision at issue read in its relevant part:

> Member States shall take appropriate measures to ensure that television broadcasts by broadcasters under their jurisdiction do not include programmes which might seriously impair the physical, mental or moral development of minors, in particular those that involve pornography or gratuitous violence. This provision shall extend to other programmes which are likely to impair the physical, mental or moral development of minors, except where it is ensured, by selecting the time of the broadcast or by any technical measure, that minors in the area of transmission will not normally hear or see such broadcasts.

22. Regulation (EC) No 733/2002 of the European Parliament and of the Council of 22 April 2002 on the implementation of the .eu Top Level Domain (2002) OJ L 113/1.
23. For another example, see Article 3(4) of Directive 2000/31/EC of the European Parliament and of the Council of 8 June 2000 on certain legal aspects of information society services, in particular electronic commerce, in the Internal Market ('Directive on electronic commerce') (2000) OJ L 178/1, where an attempt is made to illustrate the public policy exception with further examples; see on this further C. Kessedjian, 'Public Order in European Law', *Erasmus Law Review* (2007): 31-33.
24. The EFTA Court follows the case law of the ECJ while interpreting EU instruments, so, while not binding the ECJ in any manner, its case law is also directly relevant for the EU – see in this respect K. Lenaerts & P. Van Nuffel; R. Bray (ed.), *Constitutional Law of the European Union*, 2nd ed. (London: Sweet & Maxwell, 2005), 918-919.
25. Case E-8/97 *TV 1000 Sverige AB* [1998] 3 C.M.L.Rep. 318.
26. Council Directive 89/552/EEC of 3 October 1989 on the coordination of certain provisions laid down by law, regulation or administrative action in Member States concerning the pursuit of television broadcasting activities (1989) OJ L 298/23. See now Article 27 of Directive 2010/13/EU of the European Parliament and of the Council of 10 March 2010 on the coordination of certain provisions laid down by law, regulation or administrative action in Member States concerning the provision of audiovisual media services (Audiovisual Media Services Directive) (2010) OJ L 95/1.

The answer of the Court is two-fold. First, relying on *Conegate*[27] and the ECtHR judgment in *Handyside,*[28] the EFTA Court found that all Member States were free to determine what is covered by the terms 'pornography' and 'likely to impair the physical, mental or moral development of minors' 'in accordance with their national legislation and moral standards'.[29] However, on a closer look it turns out that the Directive does have some normative effect in this respect, as the Court finds, second, that 'even if Article 22 mentions "pornography" as content of a programme which might seriously impair the physical, mental or moral development of minors, not all broadcasts of sexually explicit material automatically fall under Article 22, first paragraph, first sentence'.[30] Accordingly, even though the Member States have some discretion in determining the content of their public policy, this margin of appreciation may be curtailed by EU legislation. The ECJ has later also been given the opportunity to elaborate on Article 22a of that Directive which requires that 'Member States shall ensure that broadcasts do not contain any incitement to hatred on grounds of race, sex, religion or nationality', and again the Court gives some leeway to the Member State whilst making sure that EU law determines the margins Member States enjoy. In *Mesopotamia Broadcast,*[31] where a Kurdish TV station established in Danmark was alleged to be stirring up emotions against Turkey, thus jeopardizing international understanding according to the German authorities. The ECJ ultimately accepted:

> that facts such as those at issue in the disputes in the main proceedings, covered by a rule of national law prohibiting infringement of the principles of international understanding, must be regarded as being included in the concept of 'incitement to hatred on grounds of race, sex, religion or nationality'. That article does not preclude a Member State from adopting measures against a broadcaster established in another Member State, pursuant to a general law...on the ground that the activities and objectives of that broadcaster run counter to the prohibition of the infringement of the principles of international understanding, provided that those measures do not prevent retransmission per se on the territory of the receiving Member State of television broadcasts made by that broadcaster from another Member State[32].

**II-106.** While it follows from the above that EU legislation often allows for some leeway for the Member States, fact is that sometimes genuine choices are made at EU level as far as public policy is concerned. Occasionally the link with the public policy is almost inherent in the matter regulated. This is arguably the case with for instance EU legislation in respect of the trade in weapons,[33] drugs[34] or fireworks.[35] Sometimes the legislative choices made may have the effect of allowing certain prohibitions which

27. Case 121/85 *Conegate* [1986] ECR 1007.
28. ECtHR, 7 December 1976, *Handyside v. UK.*
29. Case E-8/97 *TV 1000 Sverige AB* [1998] 3 C.M.L.Rep. 318, para. 24.
30. Case E-8/97 *TV 1000 Sverige AB* [1998] 3 C.M.L.Rep. 318, para. 25.
31. Joined Cases C-244/10 *Mesopotamia Broadast A/S METV* [2011] ECR I-0000.
32. Joined Cases C-244/10 *Mesopotamia Broadast A/S METV* [2011] ECR I-0000, para. 54.
33. Council Directive 91/477 of 18 June 1991 on the control of firearms (1991) OJ L 256/51.
34. Council Directive 2001/83/EC of the European Parliament and of the Council of 6 November 2001 on the Community code relating to medicinal products for human use (2001) OJ L 311/67, in particular Article 71 thereof.

Member States alone apparently cannot take. For instance following the *Piageme*[36] saga, the labelling legislation was adopted to enable Member States to require the use of the language of the region on labels on products for consumers.[37] The reason for this is likely less to be found in a refusal by the court to take the policy concerns at stake seriously, but in the different roles of Articles 30 and 114 TFEU.[38] However, as Article 114 TFEU provides for decision-making through the co-decision procedure, with qualified majority voting in the Council, it may occur that the policy choices of the legislator are not shared by all Member States. In those circumstances, it is up to the ECJ to assess on the basis of the constitutional limits inherent in Article 114 TFEU and the principles of EU law, most notably proportionality, subsidiarity, equal treatment and the fundamental rights, to assess whether the EU legislator could reasonably have adopted the legislation at issue.[39] A good example in this respect is the *biotechnology* case,[40] where the Netherlands raised a series of constitutional and ethical objections against Directive 98/44/EC of the European Parliament and of the Council on the legal protection of biotechnological inventions,[41] forcing the Court to clarify the limits of fundamental principles, such as 'human dignity', in the face of a policy choice by the EU legislator, which enjoys - especially in case of the co-decision procedure - democratic legitimacy. As has been observed,[42] it is this enhanced legitimacy which moreover justifies that the Court is rather skeptical, as in the case of *Piageme*,[43] in respect of restrictions imposed by the Member States, and is rather deferential when it comes to restrictions imposed on the free movement of goods and services in the framework of a harmonizing measure taken for the interest of the internal market.[44] Indeed, it is beyond doubt that the EU legislator may on the basis of Article 114 TFEU take certain restrictive measures, including a total ban on a product, in order to pursue certain non-trade related aims,[45] some of which may well touch on the *ordre public*. Conversely, once the Union has thus explicitly allowed certain products, it is not for Member States to resist the application of that EU legislation on vague moral or

35. Directive 2007/23/EC of the European Parliament and of the Council of 23 May 2007 on the placing on the market of pyrotechnics (2007) OJ L 154/1.
36. Case C-369/89 *Piageme* [1991] ECR I-2971; Case C-85/94 *Piageme* [1995] ECR I-2955.
37. Article 16(2) of Directive 2000/13/EC of the European Parliament and of the Council of 20 March 2000 on the approximation of the laws of the Member States relating to the labelling, presentation and advertising of foodstuffs (2000) OJ L 109/29.
38. See on this difference, G. Davies, 'Can selling arrangements be harmonised', *European Law Review* (2005): 370-385.
39. See in this sense Case C-210/03 *Swedish Match* [2004] ECR I-11893; see also, *infra*, at II-110.
40. Case C-377/98 *Netherlands v. European Parliament and Council* [2001] ECR I-7079.
41. Directive 98/44/EC of the European Parliament and of the Council of 6 July 1998 on the legal protection of biotechnological inventions (1998) OJ L 213/13.
42. G. Davies, 'Can selling arrangements be harmonised', *European Law Review* (2005): 374-375; J. Snell, 'Who's Got the Power? Free Movement and Allocation of Competences in EC law', *Yearbook of European Law* (2003): 337-350.
43. Case C-369/89 *Piageme* [1991] ECR I-2971; Case C-85/94 *Piageme* [1995] ECR I-2955.
44. A classic example is the Directive 69/493/EEC of 15 December 1969 on crystal glass, OJ, *English Special Edition* 1969 (II) 599, which was at issue in Case C-51/93 *Meyhui* [1994] ECR I-3879, see J. Snell, 'Who's Got the Power? Free Movement and Allocation of Competences in EC law', *Yearbook of European Law* (2003): 347.
45. Case C-210/03 *Swedish Match* [2004] ECR I-11893.

religious grounds, as Poland tried to do in respect of certain genetically modified seeds authorized by Directives 2001/18/EC[46] and 2002/53/EC,[47] finding the Court quite unsympathetic as to its objections.[48]

**II-107.** Finally, attention has to be drawn to the rare instances where EU bodies and organs themselves have to decide on the content of the public policy while exercising their competences. The prime example in this respect is the application of the public policy exception laid down in Article 7(f) of Regulation 40/94 on the Community trade mark,[49] later Article 7(1)(f) of Regulation 207/2009.[50] Under supervision of the Union Courts,[51] the Opposition Division and the Appeal Board of the Office for the Harmonization in the Internal Market must refuse registrations of proposed Community 'trade marks which are contrary to public policy or to accepted principles of morality'. The public policy at issue seems not very different from the concerns Member States may raise in the context of the four freedoms. Recent examples concern *inter alia* the registration of the trade mark Dick & Fanny, by a company appropriately called Dick Lexic, the refusal of which was reversed by the Appeal Board on the ground that '[a]ll in all, [...] the mark has, in non-formal English usage, a rather smutty flavour but, since it does not convey any additional message and has a neutral meaning in formal English usage, it falls short of being contrary to public policy or accepted principles of morality';[52] and the registration' of the trade mark 'Bin Laden' (in Latin and Arabic letters) for a clothing line, which was refused in the wake of the 9/11 attacks.[53] Recently, the General Court also upheld the refusal to register a graphic trademark based on the USSR coat of arms, indicating that while the concept of public policy is an autonomous one, the OHIM could, however, take into account the fact that the symbol at issue had been banned by various former communist Member States.[54] It seems, however, that the exception has nonetheless caused some confusion. Accordingly, the

46. Directive 2001/18/EC of the European Parliament and of the Council of 12 March 2001 on the deliberate release into the environment of genetically modified organisms and repealing Council Directive 90/220/EEC (2001) OJ L 106/1.
47. Council Directive 2002/53/EC of 13 June 2002 on the common catalogue of varieties of agricultural plant species (2002) OJ L 193/1.
48. Case C-165/08 *Commission v. Poland* [2009] ECR I-6843.
49. Council Regulation (EC) No 40/94 of 20 December 1993 on the Community trade mark (1994) OJ L 11/1, admittedly adopted on the basis of Article 308 TEC [now 352 TFEU], but nonetheless clearly connected to the internal market.
50. Council Regulation (EC) No 207/2009 of 26 February 2009 on the Community trade mark (2009) OJ L 78/1.
51. For an interesting analysis of the special role of each step in the procedure internally at OHIM and before the General Court and ECJ, see Case C-29/05 P *OHIM v. Kaul* [2007] ECR I-2213.
52. OHIM Board of Appeal, Case R 111/2002-4 *Dick Lexic (DICK & FANNY)*, para. 12.
53. OHIM Board of Appeal, Case R 176/2004-2 *Falcon Sporting Goods (BIN LADIN)*; Case R 177/2004-2 *Falcon Sporting Goods (BIN LADIN)(in Arabic letters)*. The application for registration of the trademark had been made months before the infamous attacks on New York and Washington DC. An appeal against the decision before the CFI has been discontinued, see Order of the CFI in Case T-487/04 *Falcon Sporting Goods v. OHIM* [2006] OJ C 190/21 and Order of the CFI in Case T-488/04 *Falcon Sporting Goods v. OHIM* [2006] OJ C 190/21.
54. Case T-232/10 *Couture Tech v. OHIM* [2011] ECR II-0000, paras 22-43. The Court, moreover, also rejected any invocation of the freedom of expression to rule otherwise, which seems correct. The fact that a particular symbol cannot be registered as a trademark is as such not a

General Court had to clarify that the exception does not cover situations of unfair trade practices where a trader allegedly tried to create the suggestion of a link with another company.[55] Also the General Court dismissed arguments based on the public policy ground for refusal in respect of the registration of the figurative trade mark 'SPORT-INTOPs' for certain activities of online gambling for which the applicant did not hold a license, as it had not been argued that the trademark itself or the service offered under that trademark would be contrary to public policy.[56] One could read this as a marked difference of approach if compared to the rather skeptical approach vis-à-vis gambling taken in *Schindler.*[57] However, on a closer look it seems a correct construction of the public policy exception of Regulation 40/94 which 'refer[s] to the intrinsic qualities of the mark applied for and not to circumstances relating to the conduct of the person applying for the trade mark'.[58] Moreover, it actually is congruent with the deference shown to national policies in respect of gambling: by separating the public policy character of the trademark and the issue of authorization of the service, the General Court maintains the possibility for those Member States which so wish to prohibit certain forms of gambling, while offering protection to the trademark so that it can be used in those Member States where the activity is allowed.

**II-108.** While harmonization may reinforce the 'unity' prong of the Union motto, it seems in tension with the 'diversity' ideal. It even has been argued that in an enlarged Union the limits of harmonization have been reached.[59] While I am not so pessimistic, given the fundamental concerns at stake it seems therefore nevertheless important, if only as a matter of subsidiarity, to also briefly address the limits that are attached to the powers of the EU to impose through Article 114 TFEU certain fundamental policy choices as to the content of the public policy.

**II-109.** Primarily these limits coincide with the constitutional limits the case law has developed on the scope of Article 114 TFEU. It flows from the *passenger name records* case, for instance, that Article 114 TFEU cannot be relied upon to regulate hard core security issues in the fight against internal and external terrorism,[60] while data protection in the context of commercial transactions can otherwise be regulated on that legal basis.[61] Instead the PNR Agreement had to be concluded on the basis of the EU

---

restriction of the freedom of expression, even though the fact that the symbol is deemed to be contrary to public policy may be partially inspired by national legislation that may be in tension with the freedom of expression.

55. Case T-224/01 *Durferrit v. OHIM* [2003] II-1589.
56. Case T-140/02 *Sportwetten v. OHIM* [2005] ECR II-3247.
57. Case C-275/92 *Schindler* [1994] ECR I-1039.
58. Case T-140/02 *Sportwetten v. OHIM* [2005] ECR II-3247, para. 28; Case T-224/01 *Durferrit v. OHIM* [2003] II-1589, para. 76.
59. See in this sense G. Majone, 'Unity in diversity: European integration and the enlargement process', *European Law Review* (2008): 457-481.
60. Joined Cases C-317/04 and C-318/04 *European Parliament v. Council and Commission* [2006] ECR I-4721, with note V. Michel, 'La dimension externe de la protection des données à caractère personnel: acquiescement, perplexité et frustration', *Revue Trimestrielle de Droit Européen* (2006): 549-559.
61. Case C-101/01 *Lindqvist* [2003] ECR I-12971. See also, as to Directive 2006/24/EC of the European Parliament and of the Council of 15 March 2006 on the retention of data generated or

Treaty, thus depriving the European Parliament, who had brought the case, from any effective role in the decision-making process.[62] Furthermore, in the *tobacco advertising* cases[63] the ECJ has laid down specific requirements for the use of Article 114 TFEU. This legal basis may only be used in order to replace national laws by harmonized measures in order to eliminate the obstacles to trade or distortions to competition which may arise as the result of actual or likely divergence between the laws of the Member States.[64] The constitutional limitations on Article 114 TFEU have been widely discussed in legal literature, [65] and it would exceed the scope of this chapter or even this book to repeat this analysis here. Accordingly, I will restrict myself to making four observations that concern directly the issue of EU action affecting the *ordre public*.

**II-110.** The first point that needs attention is the possibility for the EU legislator to take measures on the basis of Article 114 TFEU that may prima facie seem to reduce intra-Union trade. While the ECJ has made clear that Article 114 TFEU does not offer a blanket legal basis to regulate the economy, this does not exclude that the EU is perfectly competent to regulate trade in those circumstances that there indeed is a risk of distortion of competition or obstacles to trade flowing from divergent legislation. In doing so, the EU may well be inspired by other objectives as well, even those that are traditionally in the realm of the Member States, such as public health. Accordingly, in *Swedish Match,*[66] once the ECJ had established that *snus* would be the subject of diverging legislation in the Member States giving rise to obstacles to trade, it conceded that the EU had then a broad policy margin, only capped by the principles of proportionality, subsidiarity and equality, to regulate the trade in that tobacco product as it seemed fit, taking into account a high level of consumer and health protection. Thus the EU legislator has in those circumstances the full scale of options available to regulate a potentially harmful product, including simply authorizing the product ('*snus* for all'), regulating the product ('only safe *snus*') and – as it actually did in the case of *snus* – prohibiting the sale of the product ('no *snus*'). Accordingly, as far as content-based restrictions are concerned the regulatory power of the EU on the basis may go

---

processed in connection with the provision of publicly available electronic communications services or of public communications networks and amending Directive 2002/58/EC (2006) OJ L 105/54, Case C-301/06 *Ireland v. European Parliament and Council* [2009] ECR I-593, with Opinion of AG Bot.

62. This eventually resulted in Council Decision 2007/551/CFSP/JHA of 23 July 2007 on the signing, on behalf of the European Union, of an Agreement between the European Union and the United States of America on the processing and transfer of Passenger Name Record (PNR) data by air carriers to the United States Department of Homeland Security (DHS) (2007 PNR Agreement) (2007) OJ L 204/16. For more on Joined Cases C-317/04 and C-318/04 *European Parliament v. Council and Commission* [2006] ECR I-4721, see also, *infra*, at IV-54.
63. Case C-376/98 *Germany v. European Parliament and Council* [2000] ECR I-8419; Case C-380/03 *Germany v. European Parliament and Council* [2006] ECR I-11573.
64. Case C-376/98 *Germany v. European Parliament and Council* [2000] ECR I-8419, paras 76-86. For a succinct analysis of each of these terms, see K. Gutman 'Case 66/04, Smoke Flavorings; Case C-436/03, SCE; & Case C-217/04, ENISA', *Columbia Journal of European Law* (2007): 147-187.
65. For an overview, see K. Gutman, 'Case 66/04, Smoke Flavorings; Case C-436/03, SCE; & Case C-217/04, ENISA', *Columbia Journal of European Law* (2007): 148-149, footnotes 8, 12 and 13.
66. Case C-210/03 *Swedish Match* [2004] ECR I-11893.

quite far, even in highly sensitive domains. In *Swedish Match*, the fact that the EU was clearly pursuing public health aims, rather than trade aims was thus not an objection, to the extent that the Directive could well be explained in terms of intra-Community trade.[67] However, this means that the EU may thus also take other *public policy* considerations into account. Accordingly, technically there would be nothing to prevent the EU legislator, in response to *Omega Spielhallen*,[68] from adopting legislation imposing certain criteria for electronic games. In doing so, the EU would have the full range of options at its disposal. It could freely allow such games as the UK seems to do, it could impose certain content-based restrictions, or it could heed to certain calls for a total ban on games that are deemed violent or explicit. It probably could even, as in the case of the Television Directive[69] discussed above, defer to the Member States to preclude these games that are deemed contrary to public policy or public morality (with or without implicit guidelines on what is covered by the exception). The only restriction on EU policy making in this field again would be the general principles of EU law and the fundamental rights, including, on the one hand, the human dignity, but, on the other hand, also the freedom of expression.

**II-111.** Second, above[70] it had been argued that the judgment in *Keck*[71] offers some protection for the Member States' discretion in determining their own public policy to the extent that an important group of non-trade rules – the so-called selling arrangements – thus fall, in principle, outside the scope of Article 30 TFEU, which means they are thus free from challenge on free movement grounds. However, the question arises whether this also implies that the EU may thus also not harmonize such measures. From a subsidiarity perspective, this would prima facie make some sense, as it would mean that Member States are – in the absence of an impact on the free movement of goods – free to organize society as they deem fit. However, it has been argued that the relationship between, on the one hand, Article 30 TFEU and *Keck*, which moreover does not exist for the free movement of services, and, on the other hand, the scope of Article 114 TFEU is not one-on-one.[72] This is unsurprising as the legislator taking harmonizing measures 'bridges the gaps' between private actors and competition law and public actors governed by the free movement as 'such measures are generally obligatory to the States and economic actors, and are simultaneously aimed at opening markets, eliminating differences between national regulatory schemes, and ensuring effective competition by creating a level-playing field'.[73] Some national measures

67. Case C-210/03 *Swedish Match* [2004] ECR I-11893, para. 75-77.
68. Case C-36/02 *Omega Spielhallen* [2004] ECR I-9609.
69. Council Directive 89/552/EEC of 3 October 1989 on the coordination of certain provisions laid down by law, regulation or administrative action in Member States concerning the pursuit of television broadcasting activities (1989) OJ L 298/23.
70. *Supra*, II-16.
71. Case C-267/91 *Keck and Mithouard* [1993] ECR I-6097.
72. G. Davies, 'Can selling arrangements be harmonised', *European Law Review* (2005):370-385.
73. J. Baquero Cruz, *Between competition and free movement: the economic constitutional law of the European Community* (Oxford: Hart, 2002), 3.

concerning selling arrangements[74] may indeed not be an obstacle to intra-Community trade, but they may still qualify as causing distortions of competition and thus justify harmonization under Article 114 TFEU. It has been argued that to achieve a balance between these interests and the intrinsic need for regulation, the internal market is a market without frontiers but with values,[75] which may make it necessary to support the free flow of goods with a series of measures - *inter alia* for the protection of consumers[76] - which may well fall within the category of selling arrangements. However, if this is true - and *Swedish Match,*[77] though dealing with a product standard, and the *second tobacco advertising* case[78] may offer some support for such a value-based internal market - then the potential for EU action in likely sensitive areas of national policy accrues accordingly. One may find the legitimacy for such action in the fact that the interference with national public policy is then at least done by the democratically controlled legislator rather than by the unelected courts, but this may only be partially true. The combination of qualified majority voting and deferential treatment of EU legislation by the ECJ may well create the risk of reintroducing the 'majoritarian activism',[79] which is said to run through the ECJ's case law on Article 30 TFEU.

**II-112.** Third,[80] the Court has missed an opportunity to confine the impact of EU action under Article 114 TFEU and avoid needless spill-over in areas that fall wholly outside intra-Union trade. The case in point is *Lindqvist.*[81] Ms. Lindqvist, a church volunteer, was prosecuted under Swedish legislation implementing the data protection Directive.[82] The offence she stood accused of was to have posted - in violation of the

74. One could, for instance, think of certain selling arrangements concerning the sale of medicinal products, which may result in consumers resorting to foreign suppliers, in person or over the internet, thus unduly diverting trade and evading the level of health protection a Member State may validly want to offer.
75. G. Davies, 'Can selling arrangements be harmonised', *European Law Review* (2005): 380.
76. A good example is the Unfair Commercial Practices Directive, which basically concerns the behaviour of the seller, rather than the product (goods or services) at issue and outlaws misleading and aggressive practices that arguably have a public policy dimension as it touches on the contract freedom, the fight against fraud and deceit and even the use of threats and violence, see Directive 2005/29/EC of the European Parliament and of the Council of 11 May 2005 concerning unfair business-to-consumer commercial practices in the internal market and amending Council Directive 84/450/EEC, Directives 97/7/EC, 98/27/EC and 2002/65/EC of the European Parliament and of the Council and Regulation (EC) No 2006/2004 of the European Parliament and of the Council ('Unfair Commercial Practices Directive') (2005) OJ L 149/22. See also T. Wilhelmsson, 'Harmonizing Unfair Commercial Practices Law: The Cultural and Social Dimensions', *Osgoode Hall Law Journal* (2006): 461-500.
77. Case C-210/03 *Swedish Match* [2004] ECR I-11893.
78. Case C-380/03 *Germany v. European Parliament and Council* [2006] ECR I-11573.
79. M. Poiares Maduro, *We, the Court: the European Court of Justice and the European economic constitution: a critical reading of Article 30 of the EC Treaty* (Oxford: Hart, 1998), 61-102.
80. This paragraph retakes an argument made earlier in T. Corthaut, *A Kaleidoscopic Comparative Perspective at the US Commerce Clause and the EU internal market* (Harvard LL.M. long paper), 2005, unpublished manuscript on file with the author and at Harvard University, Langdell Law Library, 75.
81. Case C-101/01 *Lindqvist* [2003] ECR I-12971.
82. Directive 95/46/EC of the European Parliament and of the Council of 24 October 1995 on the protection of individuals with regard to the processing of personal data and on the free movement of such data (1995) OJ L 281/1.

Directive – some gossip about the hobbies and work situations of the members of the congregation of her church on the website of her parrish. None of the actors, not the church, nor Ms. Lindqvist, nor her fellow parishioners whose personal life was disclosed were involved in any relevant form of intra-Community trade. Accordingly, one could well be surprised that such a situation would fall within the scope of a Directive based on Article 114 TFEU. The ECJ indeed recognized that there hardly was a link with intra-Community trade in this case. However, the ECJ then continued by recalling that it had determined in *Österreichischer Rundfunk*[83] 'on the subject of Directive 95/46, which is based on Article 100a of the Treaty, that recourse to that legal basis does not presuppose the existence of an actual link with free movement between Member States in every situation referred to by the measure founded on that basis'.[84] This approach is to be regretted as it needlessly Europeanizes local issues ingrained in local societal values. However, this is not an isolated incidence. Under reference to the foregoing case law, the ECJ for instance also decided that the Brussels I Convention extended to cases where the applicant and defendant were domiciled in the same Member State, provided there was some other 'international' element, such as co-defendants from a third country (who, in turn were protesting – to no avail – that they were dragged into a forum non conveniens).[85] This approach stands in strong contrast with the inter-State commerce clause case of *Jones v. United States*[86] where the United States Supreme Court showed far more sensitivity to the risks of needlessly replacing local policy choices by federal choices. In that case a unanimous Supreme Court interpreted the federal arson statute narrowly to avoid that it would apply to a case of arson in an empty private home, with no obvious links to commerce. The reason for this reluctance is brought to the fore in a powerful manner by Justice Stevens in his short concurring opinion, joined by Justice Thomas, where he observes:

> It also seems appropriate, however, to emphasize the kinship between our well-established presumption against federal pre-emption of state law, and our reluctance to believe Congress intended to authorize federal intervention in local law enforcement in a marginal case such as this. The fact that petitioner received a sentence of 35 years in prison when the maximum penalty for the comparable state offense was only 10 years, illustrates how a criminal law like this may effectively displace a policy choice made by the State.[87]

A similar interpretative presumption against assuming that the EU legislator intended to regulate wholly internal situations without clear nexus with trade, let alone intra-Community trade,[88] while taking measures on the basis of Article 114 TFEU may

83. Joined Cases C-465/00, C-138/01 and C-139/01 *Österreichischer Rundfunk* [2003] ECR I-4989.
84. Case C-101/01 *Lindqvist* [2003] ECR I-12971, para. 40.
85. Case C-281/02 *Owusu* [2005] ECR I-1383, para. 34. For a very critical analysis, see T. Kruger, *Civil Jurisdiction Rules of the EU and their Impact on Third States* (Oxford: OUP, 2008), 34, 115 and 291-297.
86. Jones v. United States, 529 U.S. 848 (2000).
87. Jones v. United States, 529 U.S. 848, 859-860 (2000) (Stevens, J., concurring) (internal citations omitted). For approval of this statement, see D. Kmiec, 'Rediscovering a Principled Commerce Power', *Pepperdine Law Review* (2001): 555.
88. I do not argue that wholly internal situations should never be caught by Article 114 TFEU. I do not object to arguments, analogous to *Wickard v. Filburn*, 317 U.S. 111 (1942) or *Heart of*

do well to restore the balance between unity and diversity. This is not to say that Sweden should not be allowed to outlaw the behaviour of Ms. Lindqvist – the imposition of criminal sanctions was moreover a Swedish choice[89] – but the choice need not to be imposed in the absence of even a remote benefit for the internal market.

**II-113.** Finally, attention must be drawn to Article 114(4) TFEU. On the basis of this provision, it is possible for a Member State to obtain the permission 'to maintain national provisions on grounds of major needs referred to in Article 30, or relating to the protection of the environment or the working environment'. As Schneider[90] observes, this exception needs to be interpreted restrictively and not be seen as an opting-out clause, but rather as an opting-up clause. Member States should not use it to escape the cost of complying with the harmonized standard, but may seek to justify maintaining an even higher level of protection. The aims is thus to allow Member States to exceptionally treat the common standard as a minimum standard.[91] Similarly, on the basis of Article 114(5) TFEU it is possible for Member States to seek to 'introduce national provisions based on new scientific evidence relating to the protection of the environment or the working environment on grounds of a problem specific to that Member State arising after the adoption of the harmonization measure'. However, the threshold for convincing the Commission is extremely high as is evidenced by the recent failed attempt by the Netherlands to obtain approval of a national measure imposing stricter standards in respect of emissions of particulate matter.[92]

**II-114.** From the above, it follows that despite the existence of some constraints on the scope of Article 114 TFEU, the provision can be used to displace the national public policy by a harmonized European approach. The tensions that may ensue are obvious. Moreover as the above-mentioned quote of Justice Stevens shows this issue becomes all the more sensitive if such harmonization also has an effect in the field of criminal law, to which our attention is drawn next.

## §5.02 EU CRIMINAL LAW

**II-115.** It has been argued that Member States cannot hide behind their own criminal law to justify certain restrictive measures as being of *ordre public*. This does not undermine, however, the close link that exists between criminal law and the *ordre*

*Atlanta Motel, Inc., v. United States*, 379 U.S. 241 (1964) that local actions may in the aggregate affect intra-Union trade. From this perspective I have no objection to applying, as it is clearly intended, the Unfair Commercial Practices Directive to a purely local transaction. However, in Case C-101/01 *Lindqvist* [2003] ECR I-12971 there was not even a nexus with any form of trade – with the exception perhaps that by using internet services she is making use of the same channels others may want to use for intra-Union trade.

89. But see, *infra*, at II-116 et seq. as to the possibilities of criminal sanctions imposed by EC law.
90. H. Schneider, *Die öffentliche Ordnung als Schranke der Grundfreiheiten im EG-Vertrag* (Baden-Baden: Nomos, 1998), 42-46.
91. See in this sense, M. Dougan, 'Minimum harmonization and the internal market', *Common Market Law Review* (2000): 880-881.
92. Case T-182/06 *Netherlands v. Commission* [2007] ECR II-1983. See, however, on appeal Case C-405/07 P *Netherlands v. Commission* [2008] ECR I-0000, with Opinion of Kokott.

*public*, as criminalization is one of the techniques to dissuade and sanction breaches of norms that should not be put at jeopardy, such as the fundamental rules of the political, economic, social and cultural order. Accordingly, if the EU seeks to criminalize certain behaviour similar concerns are likely to play in the background. Three issues need to be addressed: the relatively new development of developing criminal law in the Community pillar, the development of criminal law in the third pillar and finally the growing role of the EU in law enforcement through Europol, Eurojust and a possible future European Public Prosecutor. These three points are all the more important in view of the Lisbon Treaty, which integrates criminal law into what used to be the first pillar, thereby enhancing its impact and striking a new institutional balance.[93]

### [A] From Criminal Law in the Old Community Pillar to Article 83(2) TFEU

**II-116.** As has been argued in the preceding section §5.01, the EU takes itself action which affects the establishment of the *ordre public*. It has long been established that the Member States are under an obligation to enforce these measures with 'effective, proportionate and dissuasive sanctions', just like they would sanction the infraction of national laws.[94] These sanctions may well entail criminal sanctions, as is evidenced by the case of *Lindqvist*[95] discussed above. Before the Lisbon Treaty the question arose, however, whether the Community could actually require the Member States to impose criminal sanctions. On the one hand, this may almost seem obvious: if the Community may require that Member States take effective, proportionate and dissuasive sanctions, which may entail criminal sanctions, it may as well specify which sanctions will meet that standard in a specific case. On the other hand, this is anything but obvious, as the criminal law system differs widely among the Member States and is closely linked to the sovereignty of the Member States, who primarily seek to cooperate through the semi-intergovernmental third pillar.

**II-117.** Nevertheless, with two judgments[96] the ECJ put an end to the matter. While the Community did not have a general legislative competence in the sphere of criminal law, the Community could:

> when the application of effective, proportionate and dissuasive criminal penalties by the competent national authorities is an essential measure for combating serious environmental offences, [take] measures which relate to the criminal law of the Member States which it considers necessary in order to ensure that the rules which it lays down on environmental protection are fully effective[97].

93. For more on this evolution, see S. Peers 'EU Criminal Law and the Treaty of Lisbon', *European Law Review* (2008): 507-529.
94. Case 68/88 *Commission v. Hellenic Republic* [1989] ECR 2965, paras 23-25.
95. Case C-101/01 *Lindqvist* [2003] ECR I-12971.
96. Case C-176/03 *Commission v. Council* [2005] ECR I-7879; Case C-440/05 *Commission v. Council* [2007] ECR I-9097.
97. Case C-176/03 *Commission v. Council* [2005] ECR I-7879, para. 48.

Similarly, the Community could also act – also at the exclusion of action under the third pillar – to require the Member States to criminalize on the basis of Article 80(1) TEC certain forms of ship-source pollution.[98] The focus was thus laid on the effectiveness of the EC policy at issue. Criminal law becomes 'a means to an end',[99] namely to ensure the full effectiveness of EC law. While in both cases environmental concerns played a role, this is by no means decisive. The Commission has drawn up a list of EU measures it considers should now be replaced by EC instruments.[100] As Barents[101] observes, one can easily see the possibilities for an EU economic penal law encompassing fields like non-discrimination law, agriculture, financial services, migration, transport, competition, taxation, harmonization for the internal market, counterfeiting of money, and 'specific cases on the basis of Article 308 TEC', though others are less convinced.[102] What was excluded, however, was specifying the type and level of the criminal penalty to be imposed.[103] The latter has, however, become possible since the Lisbon Treaty has introduced the new Article 83(2) TFEU which makes it possible to determine minimum rules in regard of both the definition of criminal offences and the sanctions provided that 'the approximation of criminal laws and regulations of the Member States proves essential to ensure the effective implementation of a Union policy in an area which has been subject to harmonization measures'.

**II-118.** Barents[104] has quite effectively dispelled some objections against this evolution. He has rightly drawn the attention to the fact also other measures which the Community may already adopt may have a punitive character. Moreover, Community measures in respect of criminal law, or – since the Lisbon Treaty – criminal sanctions attached, pursuant to Article 83(2) TFEU, to harmonization measures clearly make it possible to have a more coherent integrated enforcement policy. Furthermore, he is convincing in explaining that the perceived will of the Member States in reserving criminal law to the third pillar, the use of Directives and the principle of subsidiarity did not stand in the way of this approach. It is indeed not self-evident why harmonization of criminal law through the third pillar would have been less threatening for the national legal order. The fact that the Member States eventually agrees to Article 83(2) TFEU only seems to confirm this. Nevertheless, there seems to be some danger in this evolution. If we combine the Court's ruling in the environmental crimes case with its approach in *Swedish Match*[105] and *Lindqvist*[106] the image of a rather slippery slope

98. Case C-440/05 *Commission v. Council* [2007] ECR I-9097.
99. V. Mitsilegas, 'The Transformation of Criminal Law in the "Area of Freedom, Security and Justice"', *Yearbook of European Law* (2007): 5.
100. Communication from the Commission to the European Parliament and the Council on the implications of the Court's judgment of 13 September 2005 (Case C 176/03 *Commission v. Council*) COM (2005) 583 final.
101. R. Barents, 'De denationalisering van het strafrecht', *Sociaal-Economische Wetgeving* (2006): 371.
102. A. Dawes & O. Lynskey, 'The ever-longer arm of EC law: the extension of Community competence into the field of criminal law', *Common Market Law Review* (2008): 140-144.
103. Case C-440/05 *Commission v. Council* [2008] ECR I-9097, para. 70.
104. R. Barents 'De denationalisering van het strafrecht', *Sociaal-Economische Wetgeving* (2006): 370 and 372.
105. Case C-210/03 *Swedish Match* [2004] ECR I-11893.

appears.[107] On the basis of *Swedish Match* it can be argued that once a sufficient link with intra-Union trade has been established, the EU legislator may act in order to set the values for the internal market, and, as the legislative examples cited above[108] demonstrate, also in domains – such as the trade in guns or drugs – that are closely related to national criminal law. From *Lindqvist*[109] it follows that such legislation may also be applied to situations that have no apparent connection to intra-Union trade.[110] Finally, it appears that the EU legislator may actually reinforce the impact of its legislation through criminal law. It is one thing to have the Swedish legislator decide that it would be 'effective, proportionate and dissuasive' to impose criminal sanctions on someone like Ms. Lindqvist, who only has a tenuous link with EU law. It is quite another thing to have the EU legislator impose such sanctions in instances where the legal basis for its action is questionable at best. This is especially so, because there is a fair risk that due to *Lindqvist*[111] the EU legislator may well not have thought through that its legislation may actually apply to persons in her situation, let alone have made an assessment as to the appropriateness of imposing criminal sanctions in such a case. As far as I am concerned, this also answers in the affirmative the 'difficult question' left open by Barents[112] as to whether Member States would be allowed not to prosecute certain EU law crimes on the ground of a national policy of prosecutorial discretion.

**II-119.** These caveats do not seek to reject the possibility of EU criminal law altogether. Actually, while that opinion is heavily contested,[113] I am persuaded by the soundness of a reasoning based on effectiveness as the underlying rationale for EU criminal law. Accordingly, I have no difficulty with EU action to protect its own financial interests.[114] Moreover, the fact that certain areas have become the exclusive competence of the Union makes it virtually inevitable that EU law also determines certain crimes. It would be highly incongruent if some forms of counterfeiting euro bills would be a crime in one

106. Case C-101/01 *Lindqvist* [2003] ECR I-12971.
107. See in this sense, K. Apps, 'Pillars Askew: Criminal Law EC-style', *Columbia Journal of European Law* (2006): 633-634, inspired in part by T. Corthaut, *A Kaleidoscopic Comparative Perspective at the US Commerce Clause and the EU internal market* (Harvard LL.M. long paper), 2005, unpublished manuscript on file with the author and at Harvard University, Langdell Law Library, 74-78.
108. *Supra*, at II-106.
109. Case C-101/01 *Lindqvist* [2003] ECR I-12971.
110. This is not to say that the legislation in Case C-101/01 *Lindqvist* [2003] ECR I-12971 had no link to the internal market, but it is applied in situations where the existence of a link to cross-border trade becomes unpredictable.
111. Case C-101/01 *Lindqvist* [2003] ECR I-12971.
112. R. Barents, 'De denationalisering van het strafrecht', *Sociaal-Economische Wetgeving* (2006): 371.
113. T. Seibert, 'The European Fight against Fraud – The Community's Competence to Enact Criminal Laws and Its Power to Approximate National Criminal Law by Directives', *European Journal of Crime, Criminal Law and Criminal Justice* (2008): 95-98. See also Mitsilegas who somewhat scathingly remarks 'effectiveness trumps sovereignty – and arguably, the express wording of the Treaties', see V. Mitsilegas, 'The Transformation of Criminal Law in the "Area of Freedom, Security and Justice"', *Yearbook of European Law* (2007): 5.
114. For a more cautious approach, see T. Seibert, 'The European Fight against Fraud – The Community's Competence to Enact Criminal Laws and Its Power to Approximate National Criminal Law by Directives', *European Journal of Crime, Criminal Law and Criminal Justice* (2008): 89-124.

Member State, but not in another, due to some difference in the definition.[115] It explains why the Member States have actually acted in this field, albeit in the past through the third pillar.[116] In light of the environmental crimes judgment that seems, however, untenable, and the Lisbon Treaty offers an elegant way out. Finally, the effectiveness of EU law may also require the adoption of criminal law in harmonized areas of shared competence. However, as the exercise of the *jus puniendi* is seen as a crucial attribute of the State and linked to the national identity,[117] it is important that this only happens in those spheres where the Member States have clearly intended to pool the exercise of their competence to such extent that it seems natural that the *jus puniendi* is attributed to the EU in this field. I am, however, not certain that this is always the case when 'harmonization measures' have been adopted, the new threshold in Article 83(2) TFEU. The example of the US[118] is a stark warning in this respect that this should not easily be assumed. It should thus not come as a surprise that recent Commission proposals to introduce criminal sanctions in the fields of intellectual property law[119] and immigration law[120] have not been welcomed unequivocally.[121]

### [B] Third Pillar Law: Area of Freedom, Security and Justice

**II-120.** Article 29(2) TEU provided for autonomous EU action in 'combating crime, organized or otherwise, in particular terrorism, trafficking in persons and offences against children, illicit drug trafficking and illicit arms trafficking, corruption and fraud'. After Lisbon the list of Article 31(1) TFEU is even longer: 'terrorism, trafficking in human beings and sexual exploitation of women and children, illicit drug trafficking, illicit arms trafficking, money laundering, corruption, counterfeiting of means of

115. This is not very far-fetched. Seibert gives the example of how the definition of fraud in Germany covers also acts of omission, while the French definition does not, which may of course also affect the effective enforcement of measures combating fraud against the EU, see T. Seibert, 'The European Fight against Fraud – The Community's Competence to Enact Criminal Laws and Its Power to Approximate National Criminal Law by Directives', *European Journal of Crime, Criminal Law and Criminal Justice* (2008): 105. However, as the law stands, the Community may well have no competence to harmonize the actual penalties to be imposed in respect of such crimes, see S. Peers, 'The European Community's criminal law competence: The plot thickens', *European Law Review* (2008): 408-409.
116. Council Framework Decision 2000/383/JHA of 29 May 2000 on increasing protection by criminal penalties and other sanctions against counterfeiting in connection with the introduction of the euro (2000) OJ L 140/1.
117. R. Barents, 'De denationalisering van het strafrecht', *Sociaal-Economische Wetgeving* (2006): 358.
118. Jones v. United States, 529 U.S. 848 (2000), see *supra*, at II-112.
119. Amended proposal for a Directive of the European Parliament and of the Council on criminal measures aimed at ensuring the enforcement of intellectual property rights COM (2006) 168 final.
120. Proposal for a Directive of the European Parliament and of the Council providing for sanctions against employers of illegally staying third country nationals COM (2007) 249 final.
121. For a critical appraisal, see A. Dawes & O. Lynskey, 'The ever-longer arm of EC law: the extension of Community competence into the field of criminal law', *Common Market Law Review* (2008): 131-158.

payment, computer crime and organized crime', with fraud oddly missing.[122] These serious offences correspond to some of the most poignant examples of justifications raised by the Member States under the public policy exceptions to the free movement.[123] Measures have indeed been taken in respect of *inter alia* drugs,[124] child pornography,[125] people smuggling[126] and terrorism.[127] Yet in reality, EU measures in this field have not been limited to the instances listed. However, as the ECJ explained in upholding the legality of the Framework Decision on the European Arrest Warrant,[128] the offences covered by Article 2 of the Framework Decisions refers to categories of offences 'the seriousness of which in terms of adversely affecting public order and public safety justifies dispensing with the verification of double criminality'.[129] The list of offences may thus also be considered as an authoritative expression of elements of the EU *ordre public*.

**II-121.** Nevertheless, it is precisely this abandonment of the verification of double criminality, which made the European Arrest Warrant so controversial. As Mitsilegas[130] observes one of the key words behind accepting the European Arrest Warrant, but also other third pillar instruments, is mutual trust between the Member States. In the context of offences as serious the ones listed one would expect that this should not pose too much of a problem, but the experience shows that this is far from self-evident.[131] The problem is arguably even more pressing in the context of the application of the *ne bis in idem* principle as laid down in Article 54 of the Convention

---

122. Arguably, criminal measures combating fraud could, however, be taken on the basis of Article 83(2) TFEU when designed to strengthen measures taken on the basis of Article 325 TFEU.
123. See in this respect also Case C-348/09 *P.I.* [2012] ECR I-0000 where the Court accepts that a Member State may rely on the public security exception of Article 28(3) of Directive 2004/38/EC in order to justify the expulsion of a sex offender guilty of offences involving young children and explains how the danger posed by this type of crimes is also reflected in the EU criminal law, in particular Directive 2011/92/EU of the European Parliament and of the Council of 13 December 2011 on combating the sexual abuse and sexual exploitation of children and child pornography, and replacing Council Framework Decision 2004/68/JHA (2011) OJ L335/1.
124. See for instance Council Decision 2003/847/JHA of 27 November 2003 concerning control measures and criminal sanctions in respect of the new synthetic drugs 2C-I, 2C-T-2, 2C-T-7 and TMA-2 (2003) OJ L321/64.
125. Council Framework Decision 2004/68/JHA of 22 December 2003 on combating the sexual exploitation of children and child pornography (2004) OJ L 13/44.
126. Council Framework Decision 2002/629/JHA of 19 July 2002 on combating trafficking in human beings (2002) OJ L 203/1.
127. Council Framework Decision 2002/475/JHA of 13 June 2002 on combating terrorism [2002] OJ L 164/3.
128. Council Framework Decision 2002/584/JHA of 13 June 2002 on the European arrest warrant and the surrender procedures between the Member States (2002) OJ L 190/1.
129. Case C-303/05 *Advocaten voor de Wereld* [2007] ECR I-3633, para. 57.
130. V. Mitsilegas, 'The Transformation of Criminal Law in the "Area of Freedom, Security and Justice"', *Yearbook of European Law* (2007): 14-25.
131. See in particular the Judgment of the Bundesverfassungsgericht on the EAW, 2 BvR 2236/04 (18 July 2005). For more examples, see also J. Komárek, 'European Constitutionalism and the European Arrest Warrant: in Search of the Limits of "Contrapunctual Principles"', *Common Market Law Review* (2007): 9-40; M. Fichera, 'The European Arrest Warrant and the Sovereign State: A Marriage of Convenience?', *European Law Journal* (2009): 70-97.

Implementing the Schengen Agreement.[132] As argued by Barents[133] these concerns, though, may not be as pressing as generally assumed: the concept of mutual recognition, provided it is supported by some minimal degree of harmonization, is sufficiently robust to also apply in respect of the recognition of decisions in criminal matters; moreover, the level of protection of fundamental rights at EU level is such that the risk for enforcing decisions in criminal matters that are wholly contrary to fundamental rights is increasingly unlikely. Nevertheless, there seems to be somewhat more caution on the part of the EU legislator nowadays.[134] A good example in this respect is offered by the preamble of Council Framework Decision 2006/783/JHA on the application of the principle of mutual recognition to confiscation orders,[135] which makes it clear that as the Framework Decision seeks to respect fundamental rights, the confiscation of property may be refused:

> when objective grounds exist for believing that the confiscation order was issued for the purpose of prosecuting or punishing a person on account of his or her sex, race, religion, ethnic origin, nationality, language, political opinion or sexual orientation, or that that person's position may be prejudiced for any of these reasons[136].

However, in the absence thereof, the order should of course be carried through. After all, in light of the requirement for Member States to respect fundamental rights as laid down in Article 6 TEU, the concern lays not so much with systemic deficiencies, but with individual abuses.

**II-122.** The caveat of the preamble of Council Framework Decision 2006/783/JHA[137] is of course also relevant for another reason in the context of this book. Above it was argued that the list of offences laid down in Article 2 of the Framework Decision on the European Arrest Warrant[138] could be considered as an authoritative expression of elements of the EU *ordre public*, to the extent that it denotes these offences which the EU legislator considers to be seriously affecting public order and public security. However, if that is so, then also the limits put forward by the legislator for taking action in this field seem highly revealing of the underlying fundamental values of the EU legal order. The *ordre public* reflects, at least in part, the answer a polity gives to Benjamin

132. See also, *supra*, at I-66.
133. R. Barents, 'De denationalisering van het strafrecht', *Sociaal-Economische Wetgeving* (2006): 365-366.
134. V. Mitsilegas, 'The Transformation of Criminal Law in the "Area of Freedom, Security and Justice"', *Yearbook of European Law* (2007): 19-20.
135. Council Framework Decision 2006/783/JHA of 6 October 2006 on the application of the principle of mutual recognition to confiscation orders (2006) OJ L 328/59.
136. See also, similarly, recital 12 of the Council Framework Decision 2002/584/JHA of 13 June 2002 on the European arrest warrant and the surrender procedures between the Member States (2002) OJ L 190/1.
137. Council Framework Decision 2006/783/JHA of 6 October 2006 on the application of the principle of mutual recognition to confiscation orders (2006) OJ L 328/59.
138. Council Framework Decision 2002/584/JHA of 13 June 2002 on the European arrest warrant and the surrender procedures between the Member States (2002) OJ L 190/1.

Franklin's paradox that any society that is 'willing to give up a little liberty to gain a little more security, deserves neither and will lose both'.[139]

### [C] EU Enforcement of Criminal Law: Europol, Eurojust and the European Public Prosecutor

**II-123.** From the foregoing it is clear that the EU develops its own criminal law, supplementing and at times harmonizing the laws of the Member States. For the enforcement of these laws, however, the EU still largely relies on the Member States. Unlike the US, the EU is not a State equipped with its own police force, courts and prisons. The EU may thus be in the process of developing an EU *ordre public*, it is for the Member States to ensure the public order and security in practice.[140] This implies, however, that the EU has a strong interest in ensuring that these Member State systems function properly and that, given the transnational nature of the crimes the EU is primarily tasked with, these national systems cooperate effectively.

**II-124.** One of the oldest mechanisms for achieving such effective cooperation between the Member States is the European Police Office Europol, established by a Convention under the old Article K.3 TEU.[141] Despite its name, it was not set up as a fully fledged police force, but rather a clearing house for information and a support and coordination service for pan-European criminal investigations[142] and while its tasks have been expanded over time, this is in essence still its main role, as defined in current Article 88 TFEU.[143]

**II-125.** As a complement to the police cooperation through Europol, a second network was set up at the level of the investigating magistrates. Dubbed Eurojust,[144] it is again a body of liaison officers, this time senior members of the judiciary, supporting international investigations, by sharing information, coordinating certain transnational investigations and channelling request for mutual assistance.[145] The final arrests and

---

139. See in this respect also, on the role of the ECJ in striking this balance, V. Hatzopoulos, 'With or without you…judging politically in the field of Area of Freedom, Security and Justice', *European Law Review* (2008): 44-65.
140. See in this sense C. Grewe, 'Europol' in *L'ordre public: ordre public ou ordres publics? Ordre public et droits fondamentaux*, ed. M.-J. Redor (Brussel: Bruylant, 2001), 320.
141. Council Act of 26 July 1995 drawing up the Convention based on Article K.3 of the Treaty on European Union, on the establishment of a European Police Office (Europol Convention) (1995) OJ C 316/1; Convention based on Article K.3 of the Treaty on European Union, on the establishment of a European Police Office (Europol Convention) (1995) OJ C 316/2.
142. For its origin, see F. Boschi Orlandini, 'Europol and the Europol Drugs Unit: A Cooperation Structure in the Making' in *The Third Pillar of the European Union. Cooperation in the fields of justice and home affairs*, ed. J. Monar & R. Morgan (Brussels: European Interuniversity Press, 1994), 209-216.
143. J. Ellermann, 'Vom Sammler zum Jäger – Europol auf dem Weg zu einem ' "europäischen FBI"?', *Zeitschrift für Europarechtliche Studien* (2002): 561-585.
144. Council Decision 2002/187/JHA of 28 February 2002 setting up Eurojust with a view to reinforcing the fight against serious crime (2002) OJ L 63/1.
145. For more, see P. Berthelet & C. Chevallier-Govers, 'Quelle relation entre Europol et eurojust? Rapport d'égalité ou rapport d'autorité?', *Revue du Marché Commun et de l'Union européenne*

prosecutions are, however, still done by magistrates in the various Member States. With the Lisbon Treaty, Eurojust has been given its own explicit legal basis in Article 85 TFEU.[146]

**II-126.** The idea has, however, been launched to take the EU's role one step further. The European Convention, following prior academic suggestions,[147] proposed a European Public Prosecutor, and the suggestion has been taken on board in the Lisbon Treaty, though the conditions for its establishment are such that its coming into being is not self-evident in the current political climate. Accordingly, on the basis of Article 86 TFEU, the Council may by unanimity, and after obtaining the consent of the European Parliament, establish a Public Prosecutor linked to Eurojust in order to combat crimes affecting the financial interests of the Union. This prosecutor will then be allowed to act as a public prosecutor before the courts of the Member States. The protection of the financial interests of the Union is of course a rather narrow task, but it is one that lies at the core of the EU *ordre public*. Moreover, the European Council, again with the consent of the European Parliament, may extend the role of the European Public Prosecutor to include serious crime having a cross-border dimension. If that were to happen, the EU would finally be able to enforce through its own officers EU criminal legislation, albeit still before Member State courts.

(2001): 468-474; F. Dehousse & J. Garcia Martinez, '"Eurojust" et la coopération judiciaire pénale', *Journal des Tribunaux – Droit européen* (2004): 161-174; M. Mangenot, 'Un organe judiciaire pour l'Union européenne: eurojust (1999-2004)', *Eipascope* (2005): 27-31.

146. For more on its current and future role, see A. Suominen, 'The Past, Present and the Future of Eurojust', *Maastricht Journal of European and Comparative Law* (2008): 217-234.

147. W. Van Gerven, 'Constitutional Conditions for a Public Prosecutor's Office at the European Level', *European Journal of Crime, Criminal Law and Criminal Justice* (2000): 296-318.

# CHAPTER 6
# The EU and the International *Public Order*

**II-127.** The EU is itself an actor under international law. Accordingly, it is necessary to briefly assess how the EU complies with those rules of international law which structure international relations and from which the EU therefore cannot deviate (§6.01). In section §6.02 the focus is turned away from public international law to another aspect of the international public order, this time in the context of private international law. As the EU has codified and replaced some of the rules of national private international law, it seems relevant to see whether this has also left its mark on the public policy exception, which is the classic safety valve for national legal orders confronted with unwanted foreign laws or legal decisions.

## §6.01 THE EU AND THE MANDATORY RULES OF INTERNATIONAL LAW

**II-128.** Above it has been recalled briefly how the international legal order has a nucleus of fundamental rules from which no deviation is possible.[1] The EU, as an actor under international, is thus equally bound by *jus cogens*. It has been argued that the EU is also bound by the rules of the *jus dispositivum* from which it has chosen not to deviate.[2] This is, in my view correct, but for our purposes it is unnecessary to take them into account, precisely because the EU *could* decide to deviate from them. This binding force of *jus cogens* on the EU legal order has left its mark on the case law of the ECJ.[3] Above the judgment in *Van Duyn*[4] has been discussed in its consequences for the EU *ordre public*. However, its justification for treating UK nationals different from nationals from other Member States is a direct result from international law: a State may not

1. See *supra*, at I-34 et seq.
2. J. Vanhamme, *Volkenrechtelijke Beginselen in het Europees Recht* (Groningen: Europa Law Publishing, 2001), 121-126.
3. *Ibid.*, 110-113.
4. Case 41/74 *van Duyn* [1974] ECR 1337.

expel its own nationals. Similarly, in *Poulsen,*[5] the ECJ also recognized the precedence of *jus cogens, in casu* core rules of the law of the sea, over secondary EU law.

**II-129.** While the EU is itself not a party to the Charter of the United Nations and thus also not a member of the United Nations, it is submitted that the EU is also de facto bound by those obligations that flow from membership of that organization. Even without having to resort to the substitution theory under which the EU may have implicitly taken over all rights and obligations from its Member States[6] there are two reasons why this is so.[7] On the one hand, all Member States are members of the UN and thus have accepted Article 103 of the UN Charter under which the obligations under the Charter take precedence over all other international agreements. On the other hand, as the UN Charter is an international agreement predating the entry into force of the Treaties, the Member States may under Article 351 TFEU also as a matter of EU law give precedence to these obligations. As the EU should not, as a matter of loyal cooperation,[8] needlessly cause the Member States to violate their obligations under international law– even though in a recent judgment the ECJ seems to have discarded this practice somewhat[9] – the EU is thus also de facto bound by the obligations that flow from the UN membership of the Member States of the EU. Moreover, since the Lisbon Treaty this commitment to 'the principles of the United Nations Charter and international law' is also made express in Article 21 TEU.

**II-130.** The combination of the two foregoing principles may then result in rather intricate legal problems. While Lavranos may be correct to argue that the Community is 'a self-contained legal order that applies *internally* its own hierarchy of norms',[10] it does not follow[11] that it is not bound by a core of binding international obligations. The

5. Case C-286/90 *Poulsen and Diva Navigation* [1992] ECR I-6019.
6. On the substitution theory, see J. Vanhamme, *Volkenrechtelijke Beginselen in het Europees Recht* (Groningen: Europa Law Publishing, 2001): 107-110. While developed in the context of the exclusive competences of the EC in respect of trade (Joined Cases 21-24/72 *International Fruit* [1972] ECR 1219) and the custom union (Case 38/75 *Nederlandse Spoorwegen* [1975] ECR 1439), it seems also invoked by the CFI in Case T-306/01 *Yusuf and Al Barakaat International Foundation v. Council and Commission* [2005] ECR II-3533, paras 243-259 and Case T-315/01 *Kadi v. Council and Commission* [2005] ECR II-3649, paras 193-208.
7. J. Vanhamme, *Volkenrechtelijke Beginselen in het Europees Recht* (Groningen: Europa Law Publishing, 2001), 27-28.
8. See, implicitly in this sense, Case C-377/98 *Netherlands v. European Parliament and Council* [2001] ECR I-7079.
9. Case C-308/06 *International Association of Independent Tanker Owners* [2008] ECR I-4057. It appears that Case C-366/10 *Air Transport Association of America* [2011] ECR I-0000 takes a bit more the middle ground. Whereas the judgment upholds the inclusion of aviation in the EU emission trading scheme as a matter of Union law, it must be observed that the national court failed to ask whether some international norms to which the Union is not subjected, but to which some (or even all) Member States are parties may nevertheless be invoked to block the application of those EU rules on the basis of Article 351 TFEU.
10. N. Lavranos, 'Judicial Review of UN Sanctions by the Court of First Instance', *European Foreign Affairs Review* (2006): 479 (emphasis added). Arguably, the same applies, post-Lisbon to the Union.
11. For a thoroughly argued rejection of the theory that the EC legal order is entirely closed to the application of public international law, see J. Vanhamme, *Volkenrechtelijke Beginselen in het Europees Recht* (Groningen: Europa Law Publishing, 2001), 96-113.

prime examples are the way the *Yusuf* and *Kadi* cases were handled by what then still was the CFI.[12] In these cases, the CFI was asked to review the validity of the listing of certain persons and undertakings in an EC regulation taken pursuant to a Common Position under the CFSP, which in turn sought to implement a resolution of the UN Security Council. The CFI accepted that in light of the foregoing the EU had little margin but to implement the UN Security Council resolutions. However, the question arose whether this primacy of binding UN obligations under Article 103 UN Charter also precluded any form of judicial review, albeit indirectly, of the decisions of the UN Security Council. If so, the EU may be forced – in full disregard of its own fundamental values, as laid down in old Article 6(1) TEU – to implement a UN Security Council resolution even when this resolution would be wholly contrary to *jus cogens*. The solution chosen by the CFI was to accept in principle the primacy of UN obligations, and the ensuing lack of competence to engage in judicial review of resolutions of the UN Security Council, but to make one exception for indirect review in the light of *jus cogens*. As one of the earliest comments[13] on the judgment aptly observed *jus cogens* thus becomes a crucial tool for ensuring the coexistence of the international and Community legal order, as it allows the EU to bow before the primacy of public international law without having to betray the essence of the Community legal order as a legal order based on the rule of law. While one may next have some criticism[14] – and as explained below the ECJ took a wholly different approach on appeal[15] – as to the norms which the CFI considers as included in the concept of *jus cogens* or as to the standard of review, fact is that the CFI thus sought to safeguard the essence of both legal orders.[16]

---

12. Case T-306/01 *Yusuf and Al Barakaat International Foundation v. Council and Commission* [2005] ECR II-3533 and Case T-315/01 *Kadi v. Council and Commission* [2005] ECR II-3649.
13. X, 'Tribunal de Première Instance des Communautés Européennes – Arrêts du 21 Septembre 2005 *T-306/01 YUSUF* et AL *BARAKAAT INTERNATIONAL FOUNDATION et T-315/01 KADI*', *Revue générale de droit international public* (2005): 957.
14. For more on these cases, see X, 'Tribunal de Première Instance des Communautés Européennes – Arrêts du 21 Septembre 2005 *T-306/01 YUSUF* et AL *BARAKAAT INTERNATIONAL FOUNDATION et T-315/01 KADI*', *Revue générale de droit international public* (2005): 957-967; R. Van Ooik & R. Wessel, 'De Yusuf en Kadi-uitspraken in perspectief. Nieuwe verhoudingen in de interne en externe bevoegdheden van de Europese Unie', *Sociaal-economische wetgeving* (2006): 230-241; S. Steinbarth, 'Individualrechtsschutz gegen Maßnahmen der EG zur Bekämpfung des internationalen Terrorismus', *Zeitschrift für Europarechtliche Studien* (2006): 269-285; R. Wessel, 'Editorial: The UN, the EU and Jus Cogens', *International Organizations Law Review* (2006): 1-6; M. Karayigit, 'The Yusuf and Kadi Judgments: The Scope of the EC Competences in Respect of Restrictive Measures', *Legal Issues of Economic Integration* (2006): 379-404; R. Brown, 'Kadi v. Council of the European Union and Commission of the European Communities: Executive Power and Judicial Supervision at European Level', *European Human Rights Law Review* (2006): 456-469; C. Tomuschat, 'case note under Case T-306/01 *Ahmed Ali Yusuf and Al Barakaat International Foundation v. Council* and Case T-315/01 *Yassin Abdullah Kadi v. Council*', *Common Market Law Review* (2006): 537-551; W. Vlcek, 'Acts to Combat the Financing of Terrorism: Common Foreign and Security Policy at the European Court of Justice', *European Foreign Affairs Review* (2006): 491-507.
15. Joined Cases C-402/05 P and C-415/05 P *Kadi v. Council* [2008] ECR I-6351, with Opinion of AG Poiares Maduro.
16. It appears that the General Court is only grudgingly – but nevertheless loyally – accepting the more straightforward approach chosen by the ECJ, see Case T-85/09 *Kadi v. Commission*

**II-131.** Defining the relationship between the EU and *jus cogens* in this manner is not without serious difficulty, however. First, it is clear that the level of judicial protection that can be offered to persons that are subject of an EU regulation implementing a UN Security Council resolution is thus not of the same high level as can be required from the EU when acting autonomously,[17] though the CFI has tried to bridge the gap even further in *Ayadi*[18] by pointing out some additional forms of protection. Second, largely because of this reason, Advocate General Poiares Maduro has on appeal taken a contrary position, which the ECJ has essentially followed. In his view, there is no 'basis in the Treaty from which it could logically follow that measures taken for the implementation of Security Council resolutions have supra-constitutional status and are hence accorded i,mmunity from judicial review'.[19] Under this approach, the implementing regulation must be fully scrutinized in light of EU fundamental rights standards, even if this would imply that the useful effect of Article 103 UN Charter is greatly undermined. In strong language, the ECJ indeed emphasizes that the Regulations at issue are Community acts and that '[i]t is also clear from the case law that respect for human rights is a condition of the lawfulness of Community acts and that measures incompatible with respect for human rights are not acceptable in the Community'.[20] Accordingly:

> the obligations imposed by an international agreement cannot have the effect of prejudicing the constitutional principles of the EC Treaty, which include the principle that all Community acts must respect fundamental rights, that respect constituting a condition of their lawfulness which it is for the Court to review in the framework of the complete system of legal remedies established by the Treaty[21].

This is not to say that the ECJ is a priori not open to the concept of *jus cogens*, but in order to uphold the rule of law within the Union,[22] it is of the opinion that its review of internal acts cannot be restricted to such a deferential review.

**II-132.** Third, there have been instances where the EU has, in turn, decided to fully disregard *jus cogens*. While the EU, also in its external action, is generally rather respectful of international law – as is evidenced also by the many CFSP measures aimed

---

[2010] ECR II-0000, especially para. 121. An appeal against this judgment is pending, see Pending Joined Cases C-584/10 P, C-593/10 P, C-595/10 P *Commission, Council and UK v. Kadi*.

17. Case T-228/02 *Organisation des Modjahedines du peuple d'Iran v. Council* [2006] ECR II-4665; Case T-47/03 *Sison v. Council* [2007] ECR II-73*.
18. Case T-253/02 *Ayadi v. Council* [2006] ECR II-2139.
19. Opinion of AG Poiares Maduro in Joined Cases C-402/05 P and C-415/05 P *Kadi v. Council* [2008] ECR I-6351, para. 28.
20. Joined Cases C-402/05 P and C-415/05 P *Kadi v. Council* [2008] ECR I-6351, para. 284 (internal citations omitted).
21. Joined Cases C-402/05 P and C-415/05 P *Kadi v. Council* [2008] ECR I-6351, para. 285.
22. The ECJ bolsters its argument in Joined Cases C-402/05 P and C-415/05 P *Kadi v. Council* [2008] ECR I-6351, paras 281-285 with multiple references to iconic cases about the rule of law and the task of the Court in enforcing it, including Case 294/83 *Parti Ecologiste 'Les Verts' v. European Parliament* [1986] ECR 1339, para. 23; Opinion 1/91 *Draft agreement relating to the creation of the EEA* [1991] ECR I-6079, paras 35 and 71 and Opinion 2/94 *ECHR* [1996] ECR I-1759, para. 34.

at supporting international courts[23] and international organizations[24] – the Council has in 2006 *scienter* decided to ignore the right of self-determination of the people of the Western Sahara. While the European Parliament had proposed a series of amendments[25] to the Regulation[26] concluding and implementing the EC-Morocco Fisheries Agreement, in order to make certain financial arrangements in the interest of the Western Sahara so that the EU would be able to also honour its *jus cogens* obligations in this respect, the Council took no such action at all. Remarkedly, the European Parliament, after becoming co-legislator in fisheries matters due to the Lisbon Treaty, blocked a renewal of this agreement in 2011 for this reason.[27] Nonetheless, occasionally the Council does take positive action to enforce the mandatory rules of international law. In the fall of 2008, the Union has, for instance, decided to set up a major military operation at sea to combat piracy on the waters near Somalia.[28] Moreover, in its action under the CFSP the EU has nothing to gain from violating the basic rules of the international legal order, in particular in respect of human rights and humanitarian law.[29]

## §6.02 EU HARMONIZATION OF THE INTERNATIONAL *ORDRE PUBLIC* IN EU MEASURES CONCERNING PRIVATE INTERNATIONAL LAW

**II-133.** It has been observed that it is remarkable that the EEC did not from the very start provide in a legal basis to deal with private international law,[30] as it is not difficult

23. Council Common Position 2003/444/CFSP of 16 June 2003 on the International Criminal Court (2004) OJ L 150/67; Council Common Position 2003/280/CFSP of 16 April 2003 in support of the effective implementation of the mandate of the ICTY (2003) OJ 101/22.
24. Council Joint Action 2008/307/CFSP of 14 April 2008 in support of World Health Organisation activities in the area of laboratory bio-safety and bio-security in the framework of the European Union Strategy against the proliferation of Weapons of Mass Destruction (2008) OJ L 106/17; Council Common Position 2005/329/CFSP of 25 April 2005 relating to the 2005 Review Conference of the Parties to the Treaty on the Non-Proliferation of Nuclear Weapons (2005) OJ L 106/32.
25. European Parliament, *Report on the proposal for a Council regulation on the conclusion of the Fisheries Partnership Agreement between the European Community and the Kingdom of Morocco*, A6-0163/2006 final.
26. Council Regulation (EC) No 764/2006 of 22 May 2006 on the conclusion of the Fisheries Partnership Agreement between the European Community and the Kingdom of Morocco (2006) OJ L 141/1.
27. BBC News, 14 December 2011, 'Morocco bans EU fishing vessels amid Western Sahara row' <http://www.bbc.co.uk/news/world-africa-16191266>.
28. Council Joint Action 2008/851/CFSP of 10 November 2008 on a European Union military operation to contribute to the deterrence, prevention and repression of acts of piracy and armed robbery off the Somali coast (2008) OJ L 301/33; Council Decision 2008/918/CFSP of 8 December 2008 on the launch of a European Union military operation to contribute to the deterrence, prevention and repression of acts of piracy and armed robbery off the Somali coast (Atalanta) (2008) OJ L 330/19.
29. On the practice of the EU in complying with international law in general and fundamental rights and humaniatarian law in particular, see F. Naert, *International Law Aspects of the EU's Security and Defence Policy, with a Particular Focus on the Law of Armed Conflict and Human Rights* (Antwerpen: Intersentia, 2010).
30. S. Francq, *L'applicabilité du droit communautaire dérivé au regard des méthodes du droit international privé* (Brussels: Bruylant, 2005), 46.

to understand that the supranational relations that were about to ensue would sooner rather than later also result in a growth in cross-border contacts and contracts, with all the ensuing problems of choice of law, jurisdiction, recognition and enforcement that come with the enforcement of such cross-border relationships. Be that as it may, already in 1968 a Convention was concluded on the basis of Article 293 TEC to address precisely the last three issues. Eventually, the EU was given wide-ranging powers in the field of the harmonization of private international law by the Amsterdam Treaty,[31] and since then the EU has adopted a series of Regulations in this field harmonizing various aspects of private international law.

**II-134.** As has also been indicated above,[32] the classic safety valve of national private international law systems is the international *ordre public*, which enables a State to keep out foreign norms that are wholly incompatible with the foundational values of the national legal order and to prevent the enforcement of foreign judgments decided in accordance with such norms. When the EU displaces these national rules with a single EU framework it must ensure that a similar safety valve is still available, though the communality of values flowing from Article 6 TEU and the increasing mutual trust between the various Member State legal orders may well justify that the *ordre public* is only invoked sparsely. Accordingly, the various EU measures in this field all contain a provision on the *ordre public*, which is, however, subject to certain restrictions imposed by the legislator and the case law of the ECJ. A distinction must be made between the harmonization of the rules on jurisdiction, recognition and enforcement[33] and the harmonization of choice of law rules.[34]

### [A] Jurisdiction, Recognition and Enforcement

**II-135.** The ECJ has indeed had a few instances in which it could clarify the scope of the public policy exception. The first cases concern Article 27(1) of the Brussels I

31. See generally, J. Basedow, 'The Communitarization of the Conflicts of Laws under the Treaty of Amsterdam', *Common Market Law Review* (2000): 687-708.
32. See, *supra*, part I-23 et seq.
33. Council Regulation (EC) No 1346/2000 of 29 May 2000 on insolvency proceedings (2000) OJ L 160/1; Council Regulation (EC) No 44/2001 of 22 December 2000 on jurisdiction and the recognition and enforcement of judgments in civil and commercial matters (2001) OJ L 12/1, which has resulted in case law which will be discussed below. See also Council Regulation (EC) No 2201/2003 of 27 November 2003 concerning jurisdiction and the recognition and enforcement of judgments in matrimonial matters and the matters of parental responsibility, repealing Regulation (EC) No 1347/2000 (2003) OJ L 338/1 (for a dramatic application, see Case C-195/08 PPU *Rinau* [2008] ECR I-5271); Council Regulation (EC) No 4/2009 of 18 December 2008 on jurisdiction, applicable law, recognition and enforcement of decisions and cooperation in matters relating to maintenance obligations (2009) OJ L 7/1.
34. Regulation (EC) No 864/2007 of the European Parliament and of the Council of 11 July 2007 on the law applicable to non-contractual obligations (Rome II) (2007) OJ L 199/40; Regulation (EC) No 593/2008 of the European Parliament and of the Council of 17 June 2008 on the law applicable to contractual obligations (Rome I) (2008) OJ L 177/6.

Convention,[35] which provides that 'a judgment shall not be recognized if such recognition is contrary to public policy in the State in which recognition is sought', a principle which is repeated in Article 34(1) of its successor, the Brussels I Regulation,[36] which however requires that recognition be 'manifestly contrary to public policy'.[37] The key cases in point are *Krombach*[38] and *Renault/Maxicar,*[39] two broadly anticipated[40] and hotly discussed[41] judgments delivered within months from each other, which together offer a good picture of the contours of the public policy exception.

35. Convention of 27 September 1968 on Jurisdiction and the Enforcement of Judgments in Civil and Commercial Matters (1978) OJ L 304/36, as since amended.
36. Council Regulation (EC) No 44/2001 of 22 December 2000 on jurisdiction and the recognition and enforcement of judgments in civil and commercial matters (2001) OJ L 12/1.
37. An addition which, as will be argued below, does not add much, however, as the conditions laid down in the Court's case law make the justified use of the public policy a rarity, see H. Tagaras, 'La revision et communautarisation de la Convention de Bruxelles par le Règlement 44/2001', *Cahiers de Droit européen* (2003): 424-425.
38. Case C-7/98 *Krombach* [2000] ECR I-1935.
39. Case C-38/98 *Régie nationale des usines Renault* [2000] ECR I-2973.
40. A. Piekenbrock, 'Ordre-public-Verstoß durch Inanspruchnahme exorbitanter Zuständigkeit und Verurteilung im strafrechtlichen Abwesenheitsverfahren?', *Praxis des internationalen Privat- und Verfahrensrechts*, 1998, 177-179; see also *Praxis des internationalen Privat- und Verfahrensrechts* (1998): 205-208 and *Europäische Zeitschrift für Wirtschaftsrecht* (1998): 26-29 for the decision of the *Bundesgerichtshof* to refer the case to the ECJ.
41. L. Bernardeau, 'Cour de justice, 28 mars 2000, Krombach, aff. C-7/98, Rec. p. I-1935', *Revue des Affaires Européennes* (2001-02): 274-283; M. Gardeñes Santiago, 'Reconocimiento y ejecución de sentencia extranjera', *Revista española de Derecho Internacional* (2000): 193-197; H. Gaudemet-Tallon, 'note sous Cour de justice des Communautées européennes du 11 mai 2000', *Revue critique de droit international privé* (2000): 504-513; A. Huet, 'Exécution des décisions (Krombach c/ Bamberski)', *Journal du droit international* (2001): 690-696; A. Huet, 'Exécution des décisions (Régie nationale des usines Renault SA c/ Maxicar SpA et Orazio Formento)', *Journal du droit international* (2001): 696-701; L. Idot, 'Exécution', *Europe* (2000): 22; H. Muir Watt, 'note sous Cour de justice des Communautées européennes du 28 mars 2000', *Revue critique de droit international privé* (2000): 489-497; F. Matscher, 'Der Verfahrensrechtliche *ordre public* im Spannungsfeld von EMRK und Gemeinschaftsrecht', *Praxis des internationalen Privat- und Verfahrensrechts* (2001): 428-436; C. Nourissat, 'Interprétation de la notion d' " *ordre public* de l'état requis " visée à L'article 27, point 1, de la Convention de Bruxelles du 27 septembre 1968', *La semaine juridique* (2001): 1894-1901; A. Piekenbrock, 'Kann der Ausschluß des *ordre public* in Art. 28 Abs. 3 EuGVÜ ausnahmlos gelten?', *Praxis des internationalen Privat- und Verfahrensrechts* (2000): 364-366; J.A. Pontier, 'Zaak C-38/98 Régie nationale des usines Renault SA t. Maxicar SpA, O. Formento', *Sociaal-economische wetgeving* (2001): 180-183; M.A. Rodríguez Vázquez, 'Reconocimiento y ejecución de sentencia extranjera', *Revista española de Derecho Internacional* (2000): 197-200; H. Tagaras, 'Chronique de Jurisprudence de la Cour de Justice relative à la Convention de Bruxelles – Années judiciaries 1998-1999, 1999-2000, 2000-2001, 2001-2002', *Cahiers de Droit européen* (2003): 750-762; A.A.H. Van Hoek, 'Case C-7/98 *D. Krombach* v. *A. Bamberski*, Judgment of the Full Court of 28 March 2000 [2000] ECR I-1395', *Common Market Law Review* (2001): 1011-1027; C. Von Bar, 'Anmerkung', *Juristenzeitung* (2000): 725-727; P. Wautelet, 'noot onder H.v.J. 11 mei 2000, *Régie nationale des Usines Renault* / Maxicar SpA, O. Formento', *Tijdschrift voor Belgisch Handelsrecht* (2000): 454-455; X, 'De l'influence de la Convention européenne des droits de l'homme sur l'orde public…international: de l'extra territorialité de la Convention européenne des droits de l'homme (CJCE 28 mars 2000, *Krombach c/ Bamberski*; Civ. 1[re], 16 mars 1999, *Pordéa*), *Revue Trimestrielle de Droit civil* (2000): 944-947; M. Zilinsky, 'Commentaar onder Hof van Justitie EG 28 maart 2000, zaak C-7/98, Weekoverzicht 2000, 11 (D. Krombach t. A. Bamberski)', *Ondernemingsrecht* (2001): 530-532

**II-136.** The saga of *Krombach*[42] is worthy of a novel, and has resulted in litigation in three countries (France, Germany and Austria) and before both the ECJ and ECtHR.[43] Mr Krombach, a German physician, sought to contest in a German court the enforcement of a civil judgment rendered against him by a French court, without hearing his lawyer. The French step daughter of Mr Krombach, the daughter of Mr Bamberski (the man who was seeking to enforce the judgment at issue), had died in suspicious circumstances in Germany while in the care of Mr Krombach, who had given the girl an injection on the day she died. A German criminal investigation was opened, but no prosecution was brought for lack of evidence. However, following a complaint by Mr Bamberski in France, Mr Krombach was eventually summoned to appear before a French *Cour d'Assises*. When Mr Krombach did not appear in personam at the trial, though he did send a lawyer on his behalf, he was held in contempt. As a result, also his lawyer was precluded under French law, as it stood at the time, from presenting a defence. Mr Krombach was found guilty by the jury *in absentia* and sentenced to 15 years in prison for voluntary manslaughter. Moreover, the Cour d'Assises also decided the civil claim brought by the girl's father and awarded EUR 350,000. It is this civil judgment which Mr Bamberski sought to enforce in Germany. The referring court, however, had two major problems with this request. On the one hand, the referring court was concerned about the rather tenuous jurisdictional grounds of the civil judgment, as the Cour d'Assises had assumed jurisdiction on the sole ground of the nationality of the victim. On the other hand, the referring court considered the fact that the judgment of which enforcement was sought was rendered without any possibility for raising a defence a manifest breach of Mr Krombach's fundamental rights as recognized in the German legal order, so that enforcing the judgment would be wholly contrary the German public policy. Accordingly, the *Bundesgerichtshof* asked whether any of these two grounds could justify refusing the enforcement of the French judgment for public policy reasons. Meanwhile Mr Krombach's ordeal was not yet over as he sought to challenge his treatment before the ECtHR and as he got arrested in Austria on an international arrest warrant issued by France, where an appeals court eventually set him free again arguing that the French prosecution was any event barred by the *ne bis in idem* principle laid down in Article 54 SIA discussed above.[44]

**II-137.** For the ECJ, this case offered an opportunity to clarify the scope of the public policy clause of the Brussels Convention. The Court started in a manner which is reminiscent of the approach outlined above in respect of the public policy exception to the four freedoms, but which framed the exception nonetheless in the specific context

42. Case C-7/98 *Krombach* [2000] ECR I-1935.
43. For a very extensive overview of all the relevant circumstances, see ECtHR, 13 February 2001, *Krombach v. France*, paras 9-62.
44. On the basis of Case C-469/03 *Miraglia* [2005] ECR I-2009 and Case C-150/05 *Van Straaten* [2006] ECR I-9327 an arguable case in this respect could indeed be made. This actually raises the question, not before the ECJ, whether also the violation of the *ne bis in idem* principle may taint a civil judgment tied to the criminal conviction in a manner that would justify refusal on grounds of public policy. In light of the prominence that the principle has been given in recent case law, it is very plausible to consider *ne bis in idem* amounts to a 'right recognised as being fundamental' in the sense of Case C-7/98 *Krombach* [2000] ECR I-1935, para. 37.

of the Brussels Convention. This is not surprising as 'the Convention is intended to facilitate, to the greatest possible extent, the free movement of judgments by providing for a simple and rapid enforcement procedure',[45] an aim that can only be achieved through 'a uniform application in all Contracting States of the Convention rules and the relevant case-law of the Court'.[46] Turning to Article 27(1) of the Convention, this implies that 'this provision must be interpreted strictly inasmuch as it constitutes an obstacle to the attainment of one of the fundamental objectives of the Convention'[47] and 'that such recourse is to be had only in exceptional cases'.[48] While the Article speaks of the 'public policy in the State in which recognition is sought' and thus 'the Contracting States in principle remain free [...] to determine, according to their own conceptions, what public policy requires, the limits of that concept are a matter for interpretation of the Convention'.[49] Thus the stage is again set for a role for the ECJ in circumscribing the margin Member States and their courts have in determining public policy.[50] As the Convention – and *a fortiori* Regulation 44/2001, one may add – is adopted within the framework of the EC Treaty, it needs to be interpreted in light of the fundamental rights which form an integral part of the general principles of law whose observance the Court ensures and for which the ECJ draws inspiration from the constitutional traditions common to the Member States and from the guidelines supplied by international treaties for the protection of human rights on which the Member States have collaborated or of which they are signatories, in particular the ECHR.[51] On of these rights that are thus recognized is the right to a fair trial.[52] Against this background, the ECJ had to pronounce whether the two elements put forward, the tenuous jurisdictional basis of the French court or the absence of a proper defence, could be considered to be of *ordre public*.

**II-138.** The first ground for refusal is rejected.[53] Article 28(3) of the Convention precludes *expressis verbis* the use of the public policy clause to call into question the jurisdiction of the court that rendered the judgment of which enforcement is sought. As Advocate General Saggio stresses, this was also the key message of the Jenard Report[54] in this respect.[55] This also is the case for civil judgments delivered by criminal courts, as Article 5(4) of the Convention actually provides for a specific jurisdictional basis for

45. Case C-7/98 *Krombach* [2000] ECR I-1935, para. 19.
46. Case C-7/98 *Krombach* [2000] ECR I-1935, para. 20.
47. Case C-7/98 *Krombach* [2000] ECR I-1935, para. 21.
48. Case C-7/98 *Krombach* [2000] ECR I-1935, para. 21. See also Case 145/86 *Hoffmann* [1988] ECR 645, para. 21 and Case C-78/95 *Hendrikman and Feyen* [1996] ECR I-4943, para. 23.
49. Case C-7/98 *Krombach* [2000] ECR I-1935, para. 21.
50. While this should not come as shock, this possibility had been doubted in the past, see for a discussion of older literature A. Huet, 'Exécution des décisions (Krombach c/ Bamberski)', *Journal du droit international* (2001): 691.
51. Case C-7/98 *Krombach* [2000] ECR I-1935, paras 24-25.
52. Case C-7/98 *Krombach* [2000] ECR I-1935, para. 26.
53. Case C-7/98 *Krombach* [2000] ECR I-1935, paras 29-34.
54. Report on the Convention on jurisdiction and the enforcement of judgments in civil and commercial matters (1979) OJ C 59/1.
55. Opinion of AG Saggio in Case C-7/98 *Krombach* [2000] ECR I-1935, paras 14-15; see also A. Piekenbrock., 'Kann der Ausschluß des *ordre public* in Art. 28 Abs. 3 EuGVÜ ausnahmlos gelten?', *Praxis des internationalen Privat- und Verfahrensrechts* (2000): 364.

this situation – even though, as was the problem in the case at bar, this may mean that a civil claim is heard by a court which is only competent to hear the case because of his criminal jurisdiction based on the passive personality principle. Nevertheless, several authors still question the soundness of some of the 'exorbitant' jurisdiction clauses.[56] Challenging those, however, will have to be done by a preliminary question as to the validity of the Regulation 44/2001 in a case before the court initially exercising jurisdiction, rather than through the public policy exception. In a later case the ECJ would, moreover, make clear that the rules on jurisdiction of Regulation 44/2001 do not amount to rules of public policy which a national court should invoke of its own motion in the absence of a duty to invoke similar competence rules under national law.[57]

**II-139.** In contrast, the breach of the rights of defence does meet the threshold for a breach of public policy. That threshold is very high:

> Recourse to the public-policy clause in Article 27, point 1, of the Convention can be envisaged only where recognition or enforcement of the judgment delivered in another Contracting State would be *at variance to an unacceptable degree* with the legal order of the State in which enforcement is sought inasmuch as it *infringes a fundamental principle*. In order for the prohibition of any review of the foreign judgment as to its substance to be observed, the infringement would have to constitute a *manifest breach of a rule of law regarded as essential* in the legal order of the State in which enforcement is sought *or* of *a right recognised as being fundamental* within that legal order.[58]

The right to a fair trial is such a right which is recognized as being fundamental in the German legal order. Actually, it is 'prominent' in any Member State, as the ECtHR had already found that the 'right of every person charged with an offence to be effectively defended by a lawyer, if need be one appointed by the court, is one of the fundamental elements in a fair trial and an accused person does not forfeit entitlement to such a right simply because he is not present at the hearing'.[59] Actually, the judgments cited by the ECJ in this respect[60] were probably not wholly conclusive in this respect,[61] but that

56. H. Muir Watt, 'note sous Cour de justice des Communautées européennes du 28 mars 2000', *Revue critique de droit international privé*, 2000, 491; A.H.H. Van Hoek, 'Case C-7/98 *D. Krombach* v. *A. Bamberski*, Judgement of the Full Court of 28 March 2000 [2000] ECR I-1395', *Common Market Law Review* (2001): 1023-1026; C. Von Bar, 'Anmerkung', *Juristenzeitung* (2000): 726; M. Zilinsky, 'Commentaar onder Hof van Justitie EG 28 maart 2000, zaak C-7/98, Weekoverzicht 2000, 11 (D. Krombach t. A. Bamberski)', *Ondernemingsrecht* (2001): 531-532.
57. Case C-234/04 *Kapferer* [2006] ECR I-2585.
58. Case C-7/98 *Krombach* [2000] ECR I-1935, para. 37 (emphasis added).
59. Case C-7/98 *Krombach* [2000] ECR I-1935, para. 39.
60. ECtHR, 23 November 1993, *Poitrimol v. France*; EctHR, 22 September 1994, *Pelladoah v. Netherlands*; ECtHR, 21 January 1999 *Van Geyseghem v. Belgium*.
61. X, 'De l'influence de la Convention européenne des droits de l'homme sur l'orde public...international: de l'extra territorialité de la Convention européenne des droits de l'homme (CJCE 28 mars 2000, *Krombach c/ Bamberski*; Civ. 1re, 16 mars 1999, *Pordéa*), *Revue Trimestrielle de Droit civil* (2000): 945. Actually, it was only in ECtHR, 13 February 2001, *Krombach v. France* that the ECtHR would also reject the French rules in the context of jury trials, for more see F. Massias, 'Arrêt Krombach c/ France, 13 février 2001 et Arrêt Van Pelt c/ France, 23 mai 2000', *Revue de science criminelle et de droit pénal compare* (2001): 429-444.

should not detract from the core message: manifest breaches of the fundamental procedural rights as guaranteed by Article 6 ECHR and – one may add – the corresponding the provisions of the Charter of Fundamental Rights may be contrary to public policy in the sense of Article 27(1) and thus justify the refusal of recognition of judgments in civil and commercial matters.[62]

**II-140.** This conclusion is not affected by two further arguments that have been put forward. First, Article 27(2) does not preclude the possibility of an *ordre public procédural*. While it is true that the specific ground of Article 27(2) for situations where the defendant had not been properly summoned may preclude the necessity for invoking the *ordre public*,[63] the ordeal of Mr Krombach demonstrates that a proper summons may not suffice to ensure that the defendant has a fair chance of effectively defending himself/herself, so that recourse to the public policy exception of Article 27(1) is the sole alternative. Second, Article II of the Protocol to the Convention – currently Article 65 of Regulation 44/2001 – provides for a possibility to refuse the recognition of foreign judgments on civil matters delivered by criminal courts in proceedings dealing with involuntary offences, typically road accidents,[64] when a lawyer was precluded from pleading. In *Rinkau*, the ECJ had indicated that this implied *a contrario* that given the gravity of intentional crimes a refusal of the defendant to appear in person could be sanctioned by preventing his lawyer to plead without the risk that the ensuing judgment could not be enforced.[65] This was precisely the case at bar. However, such an interpretation would be wholly incompatible with the fundamental rights jurisprudence put forward by the Court. Accordingly, the ECJ now finds that:

> Article II of the Protocol cannot be construed as precluding the court of the State in which enforcement is sought from being entitled to take account, in relation to public policy, as referred to in Article 27, point 1, of the Convention, of the fact that, in an action for damages based on an offence, the court of the State of origin refused to hear the defence of the accused person, who was being prosecuted for an intentional offence, solely on the ground that that person was not present at the hearing[66].

This reading, whereby the fact that the legislator has made specific arrangements for involuntary crimes should not be read as authorizing restrictions of the fundamental right to a fair trial in cases involving intentional crimes, seems the only one that guarantees the constitutionality of Article 65 of Regulation 44/2001.[67]

62. See in this sense also, more recently, Case C-394/07 *Gambazzi* [2009] ECR I-2563.
63. Case 145/86 *Hoffmann* [1988] ECR 645. See also, for the parallel Article 34(2) of Regulation 44/2001, Case C-283/05 *ASML* [2006] ECR I-12045.
64. Case 157/80 *Rinkau* [1981] ECR 1391, para. 12.
65. Case 157/80 *Rinkau* [1981] ECR 1391, para. 12: 'Another more general guide is the fact that by restricting the right to be defended without appearing in person, which is made available to persons who have committed certain offences, the convention clearly seeks to deny that right to persons being prosecuted for offences which are sufficiently serious to justify its denial'.
66. Case C-7/98 *Krombach* [2000] ECR I-1935, para. 44.
67. As observed, as the difference between involuntary and voluntary crimes does no longer make a difference after Case C-7/98 *Krombach* [2000] ECR I-1935, Article 65 of Regulation 44/2001, seems to have lost most of its meaning in this interpretation, see A.A.H. Van Hoek, 'Case

**II-141.** A few months later the ECJ got a chance of further clarifying its newly devised test for determining what Member States may consider contrary to public policy. This time not a procedural right was at issue, but hard core Community law: the provisions on the free movement of goods and competition law. Renault had obtained in France a judgment condemning the Italian company Maxicar and its Director Mr Formento to pay damages as they were found to be counterfeiting car parts of the Renault brand. Renault sought to enforce that judgment in Italy, but the defendants argued that the judgment was based on an incorrect application of the rules on competition and free movement of goods – two fundamental EC policy areas – and therefore contrary to the *ordre public*. Accordingly, the *Corte d'Appello di Torino* referred questions on the interpretation of the public policy exception and on the substantive issues concerning the relationship between the free movement of goods and competition law on the one hand, and intellectual property on the other. It is clear that the latter set of questions only become relevant, if the public policy exception could indeed be relied on in this case. The Court rightly found this not to be the case.

**II-142.** Basically, the ECJ puts forward the same framework for analysing the issue as in *Krombach*: the exception is of strict interpretation, only to be invoked in exceptional circumstances and while Member States have some discretion its limits are determined by EU law.[68] Accordingly, again the exception may only be relied on:

> where recognition or enforcement of the judgment delivered in another Contracting State would be at variance to an unacceptable degree with the legal order of the State in which enforcement is sought inasmuch as it infringes a fundamental principle. In order for the prohibition of any review of the foreign judgment as to its substance to be observed, the infringement would have to constitute a manifest breach of a rule of law regarded as essential in the legal order of the State in which enforcement is sought or of a right recognised as being fundamental within that legal order[69].

The question is whether the – alleged – incorrect application of substantive Union law may then justify recourse to the public policy exception. The answer is in principle no. The reason is two-fold. The main aim of the Convention is to ensure the circulation of judgments within the EU by ensuring that they are swiftly enforced, so systematic review of their content at the enforcement stage is simply incongruent with that purpose. Any legal order is willing to accept some degree of inaccuracy in the application of the law for the sake of finality, and as will also be argued below[70] the EU legal order is not different at that and EU law thus deserves no special treatment.[71] Furthermore, while the rules on competition law and the free movement of goods may well[72] qualify as 'essential in the legal order of the State in which enforcement is

C-7/98 *D. Krombach* v. *A. Bamberski*, Judgement of the Full Court of 28 March 2000 [2000] ECR I-1395', *Common Market Law Review* (2001): 1015.

68. Case C-38/98 *Régie nationale des usines Renault* [2000] ECR I-2973, paras 24-29.
69. Case C-38/98 *Régie nationale des usines Renault* [2000] ECR I-2973, para. 30.
70. *Infra*, at II-155 et seq.
71. C-38/98 *Régie nationale des usines Renault* [2000] ECR I-2973, para. 32.
72. C. Nourissat, 'Interprétation de la notion d' " *ordre public* de l'État requis " visée à l'article 27, point 1, de la Convention de Bruxelles du 27 septembre 1968', *La semaine juridique* (2001):

sought',[73] as it should be essential to any EU Member State,[74] the remedy for ensuring compliance is not the public policy exception. Rather, mistakes as to the substance are to be rectified by using the remedies that are available against the initial judgment, which if necessary may even lead to preliminary ruling requests if an arguable case under EU law is put forward.[75] Unlike the case of *Krombach*[76] where no defence had been allowed at first instance and where an appeal was likewise precluded as long as he did not surrender himself to the French authorities (and thus go to prison for the time being), Maxicar and Mr Fromento could well have argued their case further before the French courts. Moreover, while the ECJ thus does not need to reach the questions as to the merits of the EU law defence put up by the defendants, the ECJ will undoubtedly be emboldened at that conclusion by the Opinion of Advocate General Alber,[77] who had indicated that the ECJ had already found the arguments of the defendants unconvincing in the *Cicra*[78] case and that the later *Magill*[79] case was also not in their favour. Accordingly, allowing Maxicar and Mr Fromento to raise the public policy exception could only have resulted in further delays. This is not to say, however, that a manifest breach of competition law or the free movement rules could never give rise to public policy concerns. National courts must protect essential rules of EU law in the same manner as they protect essential national rules. However, the procedural context will have to be such that the public policy exception can play its role as *ultimum remedium* to avert unbearable results, and such instances are – fortunately – very rare. I am *not* submitting that the public policy exception will always involve some kind of procedural defect in the sense of the violation of the *ordre public procédural*. However, there will need to be a particular circumstance in which the ordinary remedies for rectifying the error are inadequate, which may be the result of unfair procedural rules,[80] but also because of collusion between the parties[81] or the urgency of the matter, such as in the next example.[82]

---

1901; J.A. Pontier, 'Zaak C-38/98 Régie nationale des usines Renault SA t. Maxicar SpA, O. Formento', *Sociaal-economische wetgeving* (2001): 182. See, however, *contra*, A. Huet, 'Exécution des décisions (Régie nationale des usines Renault SA c/ Maxicar SpA et Orazio Formento)', *Journal du droit international* (2001): 699.

73. Case C-7/98 *Krombach* [2000] ECR I-1935, para. 37.
74. On the public policy nature of the basic rules on competition, see, *infra*, at III-77 et seq.
75. See in this sense also Case C-420/07 *Apostolides* [2009] ECR I-3571, para. 60.
76. Case C-7/98 *Krombach* [2000] ECR I-1935.
77. Opinion of AG Alber in Case C-38/98 *Régie nationale des usines Renault* [2000] ECR I-2973, paras 73-129. AG Alber had answered these questions in the alternative, in case the ECJ would not have shared his opinion that the public policy exception could be relied upon in this case.
78. Case 53/87 *Consorzio italiano della componentistica di ricambio per autoveicoli and Maxicar* [1988] ECR I-6039. Defendant in the case was, moreover, Renault.
79. Joined cases C-241/91 P and C-242/91 P *RTE and ITP v. Commission* [1995] ECR I-743.
80. Case C-7/98 *Krombach* [2000] ECR I-1935.
81. An example, albeit from outside the context of private international law, may be offered by the Opinion of AG Bot in Case C-455/06 *Heemskerk and Schaap* [2008] ECR I-8763, discussed *infra*, at II-182 et seq.
82. See also, *infra*, at II-149.

**II-143.** The third example comes from a completely different context: insolvency proceedings. Council Regulation 1346/2000[83] contains rules about the jurisdiction to open insolvency procedures and about the recognition of the ensuing judgments. In Article 26 it contains a public policy exception which reads:

> Any Member State may refuse to recognise insolvency proceedings opened in another Member State or to enforce a judgment handed down in the context of such proceedings where the effects of such recognition or enforcement would be manifestly contrary to that State's public policy, in particular its fundamental principles or the constitutional rights and liberties of the individual.

The similarity to the two-prong test of *Krombach*[84] (essential rule of law or a right recognised as fundamental) is striking.[85] Its application, however, is tailored to the specific context of international insolvency procedures in which it has to operate, a context characterized by the absence of insolvency procedures with universal scope or harmonized substantive provisions.[86] At issue in *Eurofood*[87] was the insolvency proceeding initiated in Ireland against Eurofood, an Irish company effectively managed from Ireland, but which was part of the large Italian Parmalat concern. The downfall of the latter concern has resulted in a patchwork of proceedings in Italy and abroad. The problem arose because the Irish insolvency procedure had already been opened before the Italian procedure. Moreover, while Eurofood was allowed to join the Italian insolvency procedures, the Italian court-appointed administrator failed, despite numerous requests and an Italian court order, to provide the provisional Irish administrator with the basic details as to the Italian proceedings, thus making it impossible for the Irish administrator to defend the interests of Eurofood and its creditors. Accordingly, one of the questions put to the ECJ by the Supreme Court of Ireland was whether it could refuse the recognition of an Italian judgment relating to the insolvency once it was satisfied that the Italian proceedings were vitiated by clear violation of the right to be heard while it is manifestly contrary to the public policy of Ireland to permit a judicial or administrative decision to have legal effect in relation to persons or bodies whose right to fair procedures and a fair hearing has not been respected in reaching such a decision.

**II-144.** The ECJ has no difficulty in finding that recourse to the public policy exception is indeed appropriate. Rather unceremoniously the Court transposes its approach from *Krombach.*[88] Without particular regard to the wording of the Regulation or other

83. Council Regulation (EC) No 1346/2000 of 29 May 2000 on insolvency proceedings (2000) OJ L 160/1.
84. Case C-7/98 *Krombach* [2000] ECR I-1935.
85. L. Bernardeau, 'Cour de justice, 28 mars 2000, Krombach, aff. C-7/98, Rec. p. I-1935', *Revue des Affaires Européennes* (2001-02): 278-279.
86. Opinion of AG Jacobs in Case C-341/04 *Eurofood IFSC* [2006] ECR I-3813, para. 77 and Recital 11 of Council Regulation (EC) No 1346/2000 of 29 May 2000 on insolvency proceedings (2000) OJ L 160/1.
87. Case C-341/04 *Eurofood IFSC* [2006] ECR I-3813.
88. Case C-7/98 *Krombach* [2000] ECR I-1935.

interpretational aids such as the Virgós-Schmit Report[89] to which the Advocate General referred, the Court uses the same formula: recourse to the public policy clause:

> can be envisaged only where recognition or enforcement of the judgment delivered in another Contracting State would be at variance to an unacceptable degree with the legal order of the State in which enforcement is sought inasmuch as it infringes a fundamental principle. The infringement would have to constitute a manifest breach of a rule of law regarded as essential in the legal order of the State in which enforcement is sought or of a right recognised as being fundamental within that legal order[90].

With the reasoning and outcome of *Krombach* in mind[91] it is then also unsurprising that a breach of the right to be heard, which is so manifest as in this case, may be deemed contrary to public policy.[92] Moreover, as the Advocate General rightly observes, ordinary remedies, such as an appeal against the Italian judgment, could not have offered adequate protection in this case as 'at the early stages of insolvency proceedings time will frequently be of the essence, so that a given procedure must be assessed as it stands'[93] and that failure to observe one [procedural requirement], such as immediate notification of the person concerned, may not necessarily be cured by the existence of another, such as the possibility of challenge'.[94] However, the referring court does receive one warning. It falls upon the referring court to assess whether the conditions are actually fulfilled. In doing so:

> the referring court cannot confine itself to transposing its own conception of the requirement for an oral hearing and of how fundamental that requirement is in its legal order, but must assess, having regard to the whole of the circumstances, whether or not the provisional liquidator appointed by the High Court was given sufficient opportunity to be heard[95].

This may be contrasted with the way the referring court in *Krombach*[96] followed up on the ECJ judgment in that case. The final judgment of the Bundesgerichtshof,[97] while as to its outcome clearly in line with the judgment of the ECJ, has indeed been criticized

89. As AG Jacobs explains, the report is for the insolvency regulation what the Jenard report is for the Brussels Convention. However, the Virgós-Schmit Report, which was the source of many of the recitals in the preamble to the regulation, was never published in the Official Journal, although it exists as a document of the Council of the EU of 8 July 1996 - 6500/1/96. See Opinion of AG Jacobs in Case C-341/04 *Eurofood IFSC* [2006] ECR I-3813, para. 2 and the accompanying footnotes.
90. Case C-341/04 *Eurofood IFSC* [2006] ECR I-3813, para. 63; compare Case C-7/98 *Krombach* [2000] ECR I-1935, paras 23 and 37.
91. The Court has indeed held that the case law under Article 27(1) of the Convention is transposable to the cases under the Insolvency Regulation, see Case C-341/04 *Eurofood IFSC* [2006] ECR I-3813. See also, later, Case C-44/07 *MG Probud Gdynia* [2010] ECR I-417, para 34.
92. Case C-341/04 *Eurofood IFSC* [2006] ECR I-3813, para. 65-67.
93. Opinion of AG Jacobs in Case C-341/04 *Eurofood IFSC* [2006] ECR I-3813, para. 150.
94. Opinion of AG Jacobs in Case C-341/04 *Eurofood IFSC* [2006] ECR I-3813, para. 150.
95. Case C-341/04 *Eurofood IFSC* [2006] ECR I-3813, para. 68.
96. Case C-7/98 *Krombach* [2000] ECR I-1935.
97. BGH, Beschluss vom 29.6.2000 - IX ZB 23/97, *Recht der internationalen Wirtschaft*, 2000, 797-798; *Neue Juristische Wochensschrift*, 2000, 3289-3290; *Juristenzeitung*, 2000, 1067-1068 with note N. Gross, 'Anmerkung - BGH, Beschluß v. 29.6.2000 - IX ZB 23/97 (OLG München)', *Juristenzeitung* (2000): 1068.

for referring solely to the German Constitution as the source for determining the actual standard for the *ordre public.*[98]

**II-145.** While the *ordre public* is so closely tailored to exceptional circumstances that a case-by-case analysis will always be sheer inevitable, it should be possible to draw some lessons from the foregoing overview.

**II-146.** First, there is no place for refined semantic discussions,[99] based on the differing wording of the various public policy clauses[100] or the formulation chosen by the ECJ. The message is plain and simple: public policy is reserved for exceptional cases, and its limits are determined by the ECJ.[101] Recourse to the public policy clause can be envisaged only where 'recognition or enforcement of the judgment delivered in one [Member] State would be at variance to an unacceptable degree with the legal order of the State in which enforcement is sought inasmuch as it infringes a fundamental principle'.[102] Two things may qualify as such a fundamental principle. On the one hand, 'a rule of law regarded as essential in the legal order of the State in which enforcement is sought',[103] which covers the core constitutional rules of a state, but also - arguably - similarly important rules of Community law, such as the principles relating to the free movement of goods or competition law. On the other hand, 'rights recognised as being fundamental within that legal order',[104] which primarily covers the fundamental rights and freedoms as evidenced from the common constitutional traditions of the Member States and reflected in the ECHR and the Charter of Fundamental Rights. As becomes apparent, 'prominent'[105] among these fundamental rights is the right to a fair trial with proper regard for the rights of the defence. Accordingly, the conditions are tailored such that the differing wording of the public policy clauses in EU Regulations in this field, or the addition of the word 'manifestly' to the public policy clause of Regulation 44/2001 are of limited effect.

**II-147.** Second, the public policy exception is a fall-back position. On the one hand, this means that it only comes into play if there is no alternative ground for refusing

98. N. Gross, 'Anmerkung - BGH, Beschluß v. 29.6.2000 - IX ZB 23/97 (OLG München)', *Juristenzeitung* (2000): 1068.
99. See for instance the unhelpful debate on whether *Krombach* has introduced two or three categories of norms that may be of *ordre public*, between H. Gaudemet-Tallon, 'note sous Cour de justice des Communautées européennes du 11 mai 2000', *Revue critique de droit international privé* (2000): 510-511 and H. Tagaras, 'Chronique de Jurisprudence de la Cour de Justice relative à la Convention de Bruxelles - Années judiciaries 1998-1999, 1999-2000, 2000-2001, 2001-2002', *Cahiers de Droit européen* (2003): 759-760.
100. Next to Article 34(1) of Regulation 44/2001 and Article 26 of Regulation 1346/2000, one may also think of Article 22 of Council Regulation (EC) No 2201/2003 of 27 November 2003 concerning jurisdiction and the recognition and enforcement of judgments in matrimonial matters and the matters of parental responsibility, repealing Regulation (EC) No 1347/2000 (2003) OJ L 338/1.
101. See in this sense also Case C-420/07 *Apostolides* [2009] ECR I-3571, paras 55-57.
102. Case C-7/98 *Krombach* [2000] ECR I-1935, para. 37.
103. Case C-341/04 *Eurofood IFSC* [2006] ECR I-3813, para. 63; compare Case C-7/98 *Krombach* [2000] ECR I-1935, paras 23 and 37.
104. Case C-341/04 *Eurofood IFSC* [2006] ECR I-3813, para. 63; compare Case C-7/98 *Krombach* [2000] ECR I-1935, paras 23 and 37.
105. Case C-7/98 *Krombach* [2000] ECR I-1935, para. 38.

recognition, as there often may well be, even though any ground for refusing recognition must interpreted narrowly in order not to defeat the purpose of these Regulations.[106] On the other hand, this also implies that the other, more specific exceptions usually do not exhaust all possible justifications for refusing recognition. Accordingly, it follows from *Krombach*[107] that the exception currently incorporated in Article 34(2) Regulation 44/2001 does not exhaust the procedural guarantees that need to be met to ensure recognition of a judgment, thus leaving room – albeit in exceptional cases – for an *ordre public procédural.*[108]

**II-148.** Third, the public policy exception covers both procedural and substantive issues. The examples so far where the public policy was invoked successfully all concern the *ordre public procédural.* The procedural issues are closely linked to the rights of the defence, as guaranteed by The ECHR and the Charter. While the ECJ limits the use of the public policy exception to 'manifest' breaches, this does not need to lead, in my view, to a situation where the human rights law is 'frozen', as has been argued by van Hoek.[109] Both the ECHR and the Charter of Fundamental Rights seem to be living documents. Actually, as indicated above,[110] the interpretation given to Article 6 ECHR in *Krombach*[111] may well not have been rooted as strongly in the case law of the ECtHR as the judgment seems to suggest. Accordingly, also other breaches of Article 6 ECHR may result in judgments that are contrary to public policy under Regulation 44/2001; one example in this respect are judgments lacking reasons.[112] The *ordre public du fond* cover 'essential' rules of law of both of the Member State legal order. However, as all Member States must give full effect to EU law within their legal order it involves equally essential substantive provisions of EU law. Below an attempt will be made to actually list the rules that seem to qualify for this description.[113] Suffice it to say at this stage that it includes exactly the free movement and competition rules put forward in *Renault/Maxicar.*[114] This seems in line[115] with a judgment of the Court delivered slightly earlier in the context of the recognition of arbitral awards that

106. This means for instance that Article 27(2) of the Convention – now Article 34(2) of Regulation 44/2001 – still has an independent meaning, see H. Muir Watt, 'note sous Cour de justice des Communautées européennes du 28 mars 2000', *Revue critique de droit international privé* (2000): 494
107. Case C-7/98 *Krombach* [2000] ECR I-1935.
108. L. Bernardeau, 'Cour de justice, 28 mars 2000, Krombach, aff. C-7/98, Rec. p. I-1935', *Revue des Affaires Européennes* (2001-02): 279-280. One example of such an instance where national procedural rules had basically resulted in the exclusion of the party opposing recognition from the initial court proceedings (ironically, even though the objective of 'freezing', 'disclosure' and 'unless' orders is to ensure the fair and efficient administration of justice) thus opening up the possibility for refusal of recognition on public policy grounds is Case C-394/07 *Gambazzi* [2009] ECR I-2563.
109. A.A.H. Van Hoek, 'Case C-7/98 *D. Krombach* v. *A. Bamberski*, Judgement of the Full Court of 28 March 2000 [2000] ECR I-1395', *Common Market Law Review* (2001): 1011-1027.
110. *Supra*, at II-139, and accompanying footnotes.
111. Case C-7/98 *Krombach* [2000] ECR I-1935, para. 39.
112. G. Cuniberti, 'The recognition of foreign judgments lacking reasons in Europe: access to justice, foreign court avoidance, and efficiency', *International and Comparative Law Quarterly* (2008): 34.
113. *Infra*, part V.
114. Case C-38/98 *Régie nationale des usines Renault* [2000] ECR I-2973.

'[Article 101 TFEU] constitutes a fundamental provision which is essential for the accomplishment of the tasks entrusted to the Community and, in particular, for the functioning of the internal market',[116] with the result that it should be equated with the public policy as envisaged by the New York Convention. By contrast, and not unimportant in the context of the recognition of judgments, doubts as to the jurisdiction of the initial court to render the judgment at issue - even when based on misapplication of EU rules in this respect - are no ground for reliance on the public policy exception.[117]

**II-149.** If Maxicar and Mr Fromento were thus relying on provisions with an *ordre public* character, the question arises why it is then that they were unsuccessful in their recourse to the public policy exception. This brings us to the fourth point. The *ordre public* clause is an *ultimum remedium* for what I would describe as systemic failures. It can only be invoked to avert wholly unacceptable situations at a time when in fairness no other alternative legal remedy may be available for that legal order to defend itself. Often these situations may arise as a result of, or in combination with, breaches of the right of the defence. Simple mistakes in the application of the law may, however, be remedied through appeals on the substance.[118] In the context of the recognition of orders under Regulation 2201/2003,[119] the Court has taken that even one step further, by holding that while it is fundamental that children be heard in respect of orders in custody cases, the failure to do so can only be remedied by the courts before which the custody dispute has been brought, and cannot lead to non-recognition of the order.[120] It is only when an appeal is made impossible, such as in *Krombach,*[121] or would be ineffective such as in *Eurofood*[122] that there may be need for the public policy exception.[123] In this context it seems appropriate to highlight another particular systemic failure, which in my view may trigger recourse to the public policy exception if essential rules of law are being breached. I submit that it follows from the Court's reliance on the legal remedies of the state of the original judgment to remedy mistakes,[124] that these appeals must be effective. In the context of EU law, this also

115. This holds true, even though the outcomes of both cases is markedly different, see on this, *infra*, at II-149.
116. Case C-126/97 *Eco Swiss China Time* [1999] ECR I-3055. See also, *infra*, at II-163 et seq.
117. Case C-7/98 *Krombach* [2000] ECR I-1935, paras 29-34; see also Case C-341/04 *Eurofood IFSC* [2006] ECR I-3813, paras 38-44. In respect of Council Regulation (EC) No 4/2009 of 18 December 2008 on jurisdiction, applicable law, recognition and enforcement of decisions and cooperation in matters relating to maintenance obligations (2009) OJ L 7/1 this even made explicit in Article 24, *sub* a, *in fine*.
118. Case C-420/07 *Apostolides* [2009] ECR I-3571, para. 60.
119. Council Regulation (EC) No 2201/2003 of 27 November 2003 concerning jurisdiction and the recognition and enforcement of judgments in matrimonial matters and the matters of parental responsibility, repealing Regulation (EC) No 1347/2000 (2003) OJ L 338/1.
120. Case C-491/10 PPU *Andoni Aguirre Zarraga* [2010] ECR I-0000, paras 53-74.
121. Case C-7/98 *Krombach* [2000] ECR I-1935.
122. Case C-341/04 *Eurofood IFSC* [2006] ECR I-3813.
123. Also Case C-126/97 *Eco Swiss China Time* [1999] ECR I-3055 may be seen from this perspective: only at the stage of the recognition of the arbitral award may a controversial issue of EU law be referred to the ECJ.
124. Case C-38/98 *Régie nationale des usines Renault* [2000] ECR I-2973, 33.

implies that courts of last instance must have discharged, subject to the narrow exceptions of *CILFIT*,[125] their obligation to refer questions of EU law to the European Court of Justice.[126] It seems appropriate that if failure to do so results in a judgment that is completely at variance with an essential rule of EU law its recognition can be denied, just like in those circumstances there may be an obligation to reconsider certain administrative acts[127] or ground for damages.[128] I am not suggesting that any failure to refer should result in unenforceability, just like not any breach of that duty gives rise to damages.[129] However, in extreme cases this seems a valid option. One may think for instance of a case where a highest court were to come up with a completely novel reading of Articles 101 and 102 TFEU without referring the matter to the ECJ or instances where a highest court declares itself a norm of EU law invalid - or at least inapplicable - in violation of its duty to refer under *Foto-Frost*[130] or *Gaston Schul.*[131] This also offers an answer to the question whether the primacy of EU law is not itself of *ordre public.*[132] This point will be taken up in more detail below.[133] However, as any failure to apply EU law correctly may in a sense amount to a violation of the principle of primacy, considering the primacy of EU law a matter of *ordre public* for the purposes of the recognition of judgments without qualification would undermine the purpose of these Regulations and seem incompatible with the outcome of *Renault/Maxicar*[134] as it would mean that any mistake in the application of EU law is against public policy.[135] However, an intermediate solution is possible whereby the recognition is only rejected in cases where the refusal to recognize a judgment is limited to instances where the error is the product of a recalcitrant national court or a defective national legal order deliberately ignoring the primacy of EU law. Yet, one may also consider other circumstances that do not invoke instances where the rights of the defence have been trampled. The public policy exception should also be available in those instances where the parties (may) have colluded in the original case, resulting in a judgment that is 'at variance to an unacceptable degree with the legal order of the State in which

125. Case 283/81 *CILFIT* [1982] ECR 3415.
126. For more on the obligation to refer, see K. Lenaerts, D. Arts & I. Maselis; R. Bray (Ed.), *Procedural Law of the European Union*, 2nd ed. (London: Sweet & Maxwell, 2006), 71-82.
127. Case C-453/00 *Kühne & Heitz* [2003] ECR I-837; Case C-2/06 *Kempter* [2008] ECR I-0000. See also Case C-392/04 and C-422/04 *i-21 Germany and ISIS* [2006] ECR I-8559, with note M. Taborowski, 'Joined cases C-392/04 and C-422/04, "i-21 Germany GmbH (C-392/04), Arcor AG and Co. KG (C-422/04), formerly ISIS Multimedia Net GmbH and Co. KG v. Bundesrepublik Deutschland", judgment of the Court (Grand Chamber) of 19 September 2006, not yet reported', *Common Market Law Review* (2007): 1463-1482.
128. Case C-224/01 *Köbler* [2003] ECR I-10239.
129. Case C-224/01 *Köbler* [2003] ECR I-10239; Case C-173/03 *Traghetti del Mediterraneo* [2006] ECR I-5177.
130. Case 314/84 *Foto-Frost* [1987] ECR 4199.
131. Case C-461/03 *Gaston Schul Douane-Expediteur* [2005] ECR I-10513.
132. H. Gaudemet-Tallon, 'note sous Cour de justice des Communautées européennes du 11 mai 2000', *Revue critique de droit international privé* (2000): 512; H. Tagaras, 'Chronique de Jurisprudence de la Cour de Justice relative à la Convention de Bruxelles - Années judiciaries 1998-1999, 1999-2000, 2000-2001, 2001-2002', *Cahiers de Droit européen* (2003): 759-761.
133. See, *infra*, at II-155 et seq.
134. Case C-38/98 *Régie nationale des usines Renault* [2000] ECR I-2973.
135. L. Bernardeau, 'Cour de justice, 28 mars 2000, Krombach, aff. C-7/98, Rec. p. I-1935', *Revue des Affaires Européennes* (2001-02): 280-281.

enforcement is sought inasmuch as it infringes a fundamental principle'.[136] This may also offer another way of looking at *Eco Swiss,*[137] where the parties had appointed arbiters who went on to ignore fundamental rules of EU law. Given the objective risk in arbitration cases that fundamental rules of EU law, such as the rules on competition law, may be kept out of the dispute, it could be argued that once a national court gets involved into the dispute this court may not ignore the EU *ordre public.*

**II-150.** Finally, while the ECJ does not fail to stress that it is up to the Member States to determine what they consider to be a breach of public policy, the limits posed to that discretion are quite firm. The link the ECJ makes with the ECHR fits in neatly with a general process of the Europeanization of the international *ordre public,*[138] which colours the public policy using common European values laid down in the ECHR and the Charter of Fundamental Rights. This process may also have practical consequences. On the one hand, if the concerns are truly shared it is clear that the nationality or domicile of the person who was denied a proper defence is irrelevant.[139] Accordingly, if Mr Krombach had been Dutch, there would have been equal ground for a German court to refuse recognition. More controversial is whether a national court is under an obligation to rely on the public policy exception. This is defended in legal literature[140] on the basis of the (contested[141]) doctrine of ricochet responsibility for human rights violations: by recognizing a foreign judgment which was given in circumstances violating fundamental rights the recognizing court is deemed to be committing a second human rights violation. I find this persuasive as it is fully in line with the idea of developing common standard. However, such an approach runs into seriously difficulties in those instances where a certain procedural defect would also be present in the legal order of the enforcing Member State. For instance, also in Belgium there used to be restrictions on the right of a defendant to be represented by a lawyer without appearing in person. While I am all for effectively enforcing fundamental rights, requiring a national court to refuse recognition on public policy grounds in such

136. Case C-7/98 *Krombach* [2000] ECR I-1935, para. 37.
137. Case C-126/97 *Eco Swiss China Time* [1999] ECR I-3055.
138. For a thorough analysis, albeit focused on France, see E. Fohrer, L'incidence de la Convention européenne des droits de l'homme sur l'*ordre public* international français (Bruxelles: Bruylant, 1999). See also, X, 'De l'influence de la Convention européenne des droits de l'homme sur l'orde public...international: de l'extra territorialité de la Convention européenne des droits de l'homme (CJCE 28 mars 2000, *Krombach c/ Bamberski*; Civ. 1[re], 16 mars 1999, *Pordéa*), *Revue Trimestrielle de Droit civil* (2000): 946-947; C. Nourissat, 'Interprétation de la notion d' «*ordre public* de l'État requis» visée à l'article 27, point 1, de la Convention de Bruxelles du 27 septembre 1968', *La semaine juridique* (2001): 1900-1901.
139. See in this sense A. Huet, 'Exécution des décisions (Krombach c/ Bamberski)', *Journal du droit international* (2001): 692-693; H. Tagaras, 'Chronique de Jurisprudence de la Cour de Justice relative à la Convention de Bruxelles – Années judiciaries 1998-1999, 1999-2000, 2000-2001, 2001-2002', *Cahiers de Droit européen* (2003): 756.
140. F. Matscher, 'Der Verfahrensrechtliche *ordre public* im Spannungsfeld von EMRK und Gemeinschaftsrecht', *Praxis des internationalen Privat- und Verfahrensrechts* (2001): 436; A.A.H. Van Hoek, 'Case C-7/98 *D. Krombach* v. *A. Bamberski*, Judgement of the Full Court of 28 March 2000 [2000] ECR I-1395', *Common Market Law Review* (2001): 1019-1022.
141. H. Tagaras, 'Chronique de Jurisprudence de la Cour de Justice relative à la Convention de Bruxelles – Années judiciaries 1998-1999, 1999-2000, 2000-2001, 2001-2002', *Cahiers de Droit européen* (2003): 755-756.

a scenario seems hard to reconcile with the requirement that 'recognition or enforcement of the judgment delivered in one [Member] State would be at variance to an unacceptable degree *with the legal order of the State in which enforcement is sought* inasmuch as it infringes a fundamental principle'.[142] The ECJ in any event consistently suggest that is a possibility, as it uses the term 'may refuse'[143] or 'can take into account'[144] which should not be attributed solely to the manner in which the question were phrased by the referring national courts.[145]

### [B] Choice of Law

**II-151.** The Community has also undertaken attempts to harmonize the rules on the choice of law. In this respect, two Regulations were eventually adopted: one for non-contractual obligations (Rome II),[146] and one on contractual obligations (Rome I).[147] This is not the place for a full analysis of these complex Regulations. Moreover, there is not yet much case law in point. Nonetheless, two related observations should be made in respect of the use of public policy in this context.

**II-152.** First, the *ordre public* clauses[148] are tailored to the law of the forum. Accordingly, they allow a Member State not to apply a foreign law that would otherwise be applicable, which would be manifestly contrary to its public policy. This begs the question as to how EU law fits in. In my view, the answer is two-fold. On the one hand, to the extent that EU law has become part and parcel of national law, also EU law may result in ousting the foreign law. In this respect, the draft of the Rome I Regulation has been criticized for not making this more explicit, as 'in many areas of Community law basic standards exist and need – as national basic standards – to be protected against the application of foreign law'.[149] On the other hand, it has been argued

142. Case C-7/98 *Krombach* [2000] ECR I-1935, para. 37 (emphasis added).
143. See the dictum in Case C-341/04 *Eurofood IFSC* [2006] ECR I-3813.
144. See the dictum in Case C-7/98 *Krombach* [2000] ECR I-1935.
145. For this suggestion, see A. Huet, 'Exécution des décisions (Krombach c/ Bamberski)', *Journal du droit international* (2001): 696
146. Regulation (EC) No 864/2007 of the European Parliament and of the Council of 11 July 2007 on the law applicable to non-contractual obligations (Rome II) (2007) OJ L 199/40. For more on Rome II, see J.A. Van Der Weide, 'Het verwijzingsrecht voor niet-contractuele verbintenissen Europees geregeld. Een analyse van de Verordening Rome II', *Nederlands Tijdschrift voor Europees Recht* (2008): 214-225.
147. Regulation (EC) No 593/2008 of the European Parliament and of the Council of 17 June 2008 on the law applicable to contractual obligations (Rome I) (2008) OJ L 177/6.
148. Article 26 of Regulation (EC) No 864/2007 of the European Parliament and of the Council of 11 July 2007 on the law applicable to non-contractual obligations (Rome II) (2007) OJ L 199/40; Article 20 of the Proposal for a Regulation of the European Parliament and the Council on the law applicable to contractual obligations (Rome I) COM (2005) 650 final.
149. Max Planck Institute for Comparative and International Private Law, 'Comments on the European Commission's Proposal for a Regulation of the European Parliament and the Council on the law applicable to contractual obligations (Rome I)', *Rabels Zeitschrift* (2007): 337-338.

convincingly,[150] that at least some of EU law may apply regardless of the *ordre public* clause, due to the rules on 'mandatory provisions', the *lois de police.*[151]

**II-153.** This brings us to the second point. Private international law has two techniques for protecting foreign interests. One is the public policy clause, where after analysis of the content of the foreign law, in exceptional circumstances, it is decided not to apply the relevant foreign law to the dispute, and apply to the extent necessary the law of the forum instead. However, if the legislator feels strongly about shielding of certain important interests from the application of foreign law another alternative is available, which short-circuits this analysis. The forum may, subject to certain jurisdictional limitations defined by public international law,[152] decide that its legislation will also apply to certain foreign situations having some effect in its legal order. Irrespective of the content of the foreign law, which may or may not offer similar protection, the forum law applies instead. Accordingly, both Rome I and Rome II contain provisions enabling these 'overriding mandatory requirements'. Again the primary concern is the application of national mandatory requirements. The classic case in point is *Arblade,*[153] discussed above, where the ECJ accepted that Member States could apply their minimum wage legislation (undoubtedly a rule 'regarded as crucial by a country for safeguarding its political, social or economic organization', in the terminology of the Rome I proposal) to posted workers, who are likely to have a labour contract under foreign law. However, it has been argued that directly applicable provisions of EC law – or the national provisions that implement indirectly applicable norms – may also have a similar effect. The case in point is *Ingmar,*[154] where the ECJ held that the regime laid down by the commercial agency Directive,[155] could not be circumvented by concluding an agency contract under the laws of a third country. It has been argued that this not only applies to secondary legislation. Also the rules in respect of competition law have extra-territorial effect,[156] and may thus be enforced in this manner, without need for recourse to the public policy exception proper.[157]

150. S. Francq, *L'applicabilité du droit communautaire dérivé au regard des méthodes du droit international privé* (Brussels: Bruylant, 2005).
151. See in particular Article 9 of Regulation (EC) No 593/2008 of the European Parliament and of the Council of 17 June 2008 on the law applicable to contractual obligations (Rome I) (2008) OJ L 177/6. For more on this provision, see C.G. Van Der Plas, 'Verbintenissen uit overeenkomst: van EVO-verdrag naar Rome I-Verordening', *Nederlands Tijdschrift voor Europees Recht* (2008): 327-328. See on *lois de police* and Joined Cases C-369/96 and C-376/96 *Arblade* [1999] ECR I-8453, which has inspired Article 9, also, *infra,* at II-225 et seq.
152. Extensively on these limitations, see C. Ryngaert, *Jurisdiction in international law: United States and European perspectives,* diss. KU Leuven, 2006.
153. Joined Cases C-369/96 and C-376/96 *Arblade* [1999] ECR I-8453.
154. Case C-381/98 *Ingmar GB* [2000] ECR I-9305.
155. Council Directive 86/653/EEC of 18 December 1986 on the coordination of the laws of the Member States relating to self-employed commercial agents (1986) OJ L 382/17.
156. See for instance Case T-102/96 *Gencor v. Commission* [1999] ECR II-753. See also Joined Cases 89/85, 104/85, 114/85, 116/85, 117/85 and 125 to 129/85 *A. Ahlström Osakeyhtiö v. Commission* [1988] ECR 5193, with Opinion of AG Darmon.
157. See in this respect also the Opinion of AG Léger in Case C-381/98 *Ingmar GB* [2000] ECR I-9305, para. 27.

# CHAPTER 7

# Other Legal Phenomena Linked to the EU *Ordre Public*

**II-154.** In this final chapter of Part II, a series of legal phenomena taken from the EU legal order are analysed that have a bearing on the *ordre public*, without having a firm basis in the treaties or international law. Sometimes the *ordre public* is actually invoked *expressis verbis*, while in other instances the link may be more tenuous and flow from the protected values or the practical effects. In particular, attention will be paid to the non exequatur of arbitral awards (§7.02) contrary to EU law, the ex officio application of EU law by national courts (§7.03[A]) and EU courts (§7.03[B]), limitations on the res judicata (§7.04), the impossibility to deviate by contract from certain EU rules and the corresponding nullity of contrary contracts (§7.05). Behind this rather diffuse list lurks, however, a more fundamental question as to the binding nature of EU law in general and the status of the principle of primacy in particular. This point should therefore be analysed first (§7.01).

## §7.01 *ORDRE PUBLIC* AND PRIMACY

**II-155.** The impact of the principle of primacy has occasionally been compared to the effect of the public policy exception of private international law.[1] The norm of EU law[2] evicts the national norm and replaces it by the norm of the Union. However, as it is the

1. S. Poillot-Peruzzetto, '*Ordre public* et droit communautaire', *Dalloz Sirey* (1993): 181; M.-C. Boutard Labarde, 'L'*ordre public* en droit communautaire' in *L'ordre public à la fin du XXième sciècle*, ed. T. Revet (Paris: Dalloz, 1996), 83-84.
2. As I have indicated elsewhere, I do assume the principle of primacy to apply also in the old third pillar (K. Lenaerts & T. Corthaut, 'Of birds and hedges: the role of primacy in invoking norms of EU law', *European Law Review* (2006): 287-315) and even in the second pillar (T. Corthaut, 'Doorwerking van het tweede pijlerrecht van de EU in de Belgische rechtsorde – de Belgische recher als doe-het-zelver in GBVB aangelegenheden?' in *Doorwerking van internationaal recht in de Belgische rechtsorde*, ed. J. Wouters & D. Van Eeckhoutte (Antwerpen-Oxford: Intersentia, 2006), 377-406).

national law that is ousted, to make the analogy work, one should then consider the national courts as the ordinary judge of EU law, so that national courts are to be equated with EU courts, which may apply their forum law (i.e., EU law) after ousting the 'barbarian' norm (i.e., the national norm that conflicts with EU law, irrespective of whether that norm is a remnant of an era before EU membership, or adopted more recently). The analogy has, moreover, a second flaw as the sheer omnipresence of EU law makes it hard to speak of national law being ousted by way of exception.

**II-156.** A related analogy seems therefore more promising. It has been argued that the effect of EU law is more akin to the effect of a *loi de police.* While Francq has convincingly demonstrated that one cannot consider the whole of EC law as a *loi de police* for the purposes of private international law,[3] she has nonetheless revealed the specific nature of EU norms, which seem to impose themselves,[4] leaving little room for contrary foreign norms, nor for contrary national norms. Again it seems as if directly applicable EU law applies, even though there may also be a competing norm of national law on the horizon. Moreover, even in the case of non-directly applicable norms of EU law, such as in the case of framework decisions and directives, there are sufficient techniques that make sure the impact of EU law counteracts with contrary national law.[5]

**II-157.** If the *ordre public* is supposed to protect the fundamental values of a legal and political order, it is unsurprising that the principle of primacy, which lies at the heart of the legal order, has been dealt with as being of public policy. Above, it was already indicated that some would argue that the 'essential norm' of the *Krombach*[6] test should, therefore, encompass the principle of primacy.[7] In response I argued that the effects of that, however, would necessarily need to be attenuated in order not to undermine the system of the Convention (and thus now of the Brussels I Regulation). In particular, I explained above[8] that not every incompatibility with even fundamental norms of EU law should result in non-recognition; rather this should be reserved for cases involving some kind of systemic failure which made it virtually impossible for the original decision to be taken in circumstances where EU law would be duly taken into account.

**II-158.** However, authors who link primacy to the *ordre public* are supported in their argument by an old order of the ECJ. In *San Michele,*[9] the ECJ was confronted with a request by an Italian company to suspend the proceedings it had brought until the

3. S. Francq, *L'applicabilité du droit communautaire dérivé au regard des méthodes du droit international privé* (Brussels: Bruylant, 2005), 555-576.
4. *Ibid.*, 537-554.
5. On these techniques, see K. Lenaerts & T. Corthaut, 'Towards an internally consistent doctrine on invoking norms of EU law' in *The Coherence of EU Law – The Search for Unity in Divergent Concepts*, ed. S. Prechal & B. Van Roermund (Oxford: OUP, 2008), 496-515.
6. Case C-7/98 *Krombach* [2000] ECR I-1935, paras 23 and 37.
7. H. Gaudemet-Tallon, 'note sous Cour de justice des Communautées européennes du 11 mai 2000', *Revue critique de droit international privé* (2000): 512; H. Tagaras, 'Chronique de Jurisprudence de la Cour de Justice relative à la Convention de Bruxelles – Années judiciaries 1998-1999, 1999-2000, 2000-2001, 2001-2002', *Cahiers de Droit européen* (2003): 759-761.
8. See, *supra*, at II-149.
9. Case 9/65 *San Michele v. High Authority* [1965] ECR 27.

Italian Constitutional Court had been given the chance to rule on the constitutionality of various provisions of the Treaty Establishing the European Coal and Steel Community. Rejecting the request off-hand, the Court argued that suspending the application of the full effect of the Treaties in respect of Italy would result in precisely the type of discrimination *Van Gend & Loos*[10] sought to avoid, and thus it concludes that 'therefore, there must be dismissed as *contrary to Community policy* any application the purpose of which is to establish discrimination of this nature which no law of ratification could introduce into a Treaty prohibiting such discrimination'.[11] Apparently there is thus something like a Community policy – in the working language of the Court, French, an '*ordre public communautaire*', in the language of the case, Italian, an '*ordine pubblico comunitario*' – which is to be distinguished from the national *ordre public*, as it seems unlikely that the Italian legal order would not consider the competences of its constitutional court of paramount importance. This is in and of itself of course important for the thesis developed across this book, as it is one of the most authoritative indications for the existence of such an independent *ordre public*. The question is, however, what implications flow from the elevation of primacy to a norm of EU *ordre public*. While the ECJ has over the years further elaborated on the impact of the primacy of EU law, most notably by affirming the precedence of EU law over all national law, including Member State constitutions,[12] it has never referred explicitly to the *ordre public* status of the principle. Yet, it is argued that this does still play a role in the background.

**II-159.** The case in point is the 'highly exceptional case'[13] *Lucchini*,[14] which concerns one of the most convoluted situations ever to reach the Court. The Italian government had set up a state-aid system. Lucchini considered it was entitled to receiving aid under the scheme and applied for aid, which was provisionally granted in part. Meanwhile the Italian government had notified the Commission of its intention to grant the aid to Lucchini, but apparently in an incomplete manner. Accordingly the Commission initiated a full investigation. At that point, Lucchini grew impatient and sued the government in civil court in order to obtain a judgment condemning the Italian government to pay the remainder of the aid. By June 1990, the Commission had taken a decision declaring the aid incompatible with the common market. However, none of the parties informed the national court of this evolution and a judgment in favour of Lucchini was entered, which was confirmed on appeal. The judgment then became final as a matter of res judicata, and the Italian government eventually adopted a decree ordering the payment of the remainder of the aid. When the Commission next ordered the Italian government to recover the illegal aid, Lucchini went back to court and challenged the decision of the Italian government ordering it to repay the aid by arguing

10. Case 26/62 *Van Gend & Loos* [1963] ECR 1. The ECJ in Case 9/65 *San Michele v. High Authority* [1965] ECR 27 does not mention the case, however.
11. Case 9/65 *San Michele v. High Authority* [1965] ECR 27, at 30; emphasis added.
12. Case 106/77 *Simmenthal* [1978] ECR 629.
13. Opinion of AG Geelhoed in Case C-119/05 *Lucchini Siderurgica* [2007] ECR I-6199, para. 16; M.R. Mok, 'noot onder Hof van Justitie van de Europese Gemeenschappen (Grote Kamer) 18 juli 2007, nr. C-119/05', *Nederlandse Jurisprudentie*, no. 477.
14. Case C-119/05 *Lucchini Siderurgica* [2007] ECR I-6199.

that such action was precluded because of the res judicata effect of the civil judgment. The *Consiglio di Stato* therefore sought the assistance of the ECJ as to whether the res judicata effect could block the recovery of the state aid at issue, given primacy on the one hand, and the fact that recovery is done through national procedural means on the other.

**II-160.** Lucchini and the Czech government pointed at a series of cases – which will be discussed below – as to show that the principle of primacy has in certain instances to yield in favour of the finality of judgments.[15] Accordingly, they pointed out that the ECJ has accepted that competition law claims may be time barred,[16] and that essential issues of EC law, including the rules on the jurisdiction of national courts under Regulation 44/2001, should not be re-examined by an appeals court of its own motion.[17] However, that view is rejected by both the Advocate General and the Court. Advocate General Geelhoed recalls the public policy character of the rules on competition law, which in his view extends to state-aid cases. Moreover, the division of competence in state-aid cases imposes that the Commission is exclusively competent to assess the compatibility of state aid with the common market. According to the Advocate General, it flows from this division of competence that:

> where the national court is required to rule on the granting of aid in accordance with national law, it must always determine whether the obligations arising from Article [108(3) TFEU] or, as in the present case, the equivalent thereof in the corresponding ECSC aid code concerned have been fulfilled and whether there are any Commission decisions which either obstruct the aid disbursement in question or impose restrictions or special conditions on that disbursement[18].

The key is thus the fact that the judgment of the civil court is jeopardizing the fundamental division of competence between the Community and the Member States. Moreover, the intervention of the national courts is also unnecessary in this type of cases, as the recipients of state aid must directly challenge the validity of a decision affecting aid granted to them before the CFI within the period laid down in Article 263(5) TFEU, or stay silent for ever after.[19] The approach of the ECJ is in the same vein. On the one hand, the Commission has exclusive competence to assess the compatibility of state aid with the common market. On the other hand, national courts are not competent to declare EU acts invalid. That power is granted to the EU courts, and Lucchini has not made use of its possibility to challenge the decision before the CFI in a timely manner. Accordingly, the civil court was thus not in a position to implicitly assume the validity of the aid – and thus the invalidity of the Commission decision to the contrary – and if the *Consiglio di Stato* were to defer to that judgment it would implicitly repeat that error. Accordingly, the ECJ concludes that, as 'a national court which is called upon, within the exercise of its jurisdiction, to apply provisions of Community law is under a duty to give full effect to those provisions, if necessary

15. See also, *infra*, Part II, section IV, D.
16. Case C-126/97 *Eco Swiss China Time* [1999] ECR I-3055.
17. Case C-234/04 *Kapferer* [2006] ECR I-2585.
18. Opinion of AG Geelhoed in Case C-119/05 *Lucchini Siderurgica* [2007] ECR I-6199, para. 61.
19. Case C-188/92 *TWD Textilwerke Deggendorf* [1994] ECR I-833.

refusing of its own motion to apply any conflicting provision of national legislation',[20] it flows from the foregoing that:

> Community law precludes the application of a provision of national law, such as Article 2909 of the Italian Civil Code, which seeks to lay down the principle of res judicata in so far as the application of that provision prevents the recovery of State aid granted in breach of Community law which has been found to be incompatible with the common market in a decision of the Commission which has become final[21].

**II-161.** So how does this connect to *San Michele*[22]? In my view, *Lucchini,*[23]*San Michele*[24] and also *Simmenthal*[25] have in common that the principle of primacy itself is put at risk. Lucchini and the Czech government were correct to point out that the EU legal order is willing to accept a degree of error, in return for finality. Accordingly, as will become apparent from the examples below, the EU legal order indeed accepts a degree of under-enforcement of EU law as a result of the ordinary procedural mechanisms which the Member States, as a matter of procedural autonomy, are in principle at liberty to implement, just as they do for cases without an EU law element. However, the principle of national procedural autonomy[26] reaches its limits in the principles of equivalence (the basic principle that procedural rules governing claims of EU law may not be 'less favourable than those governing the same right of action on an internal matter'[27]), and effectiveness (the basic principle that the national procedural rules governing claims of EU law, even when equivalent, may not make it 'impossible in practice to exercise rights which the national courts have a duty to protect'[28]). I submit that the 'effectiveness' may reveal an underlying concern for the stability of the EU legal order. While the EU legal order may accept occasional under-enforcement and even errors in the application of EU law, the EU legal order must protect itself - especially as most of the enforcement is done through the Member State legal systems - against structural, endemic failures to enforce EU law in full.[29] The test should be

20. Case C-119/05 *Lucchini Siderurgica* [2007] ECR I-6199, para. 61, in support of which the ECJ invokes Case 106/77 *Simmenthal* [1978] ECR 629, paras 21 to 24; Case 130/78 *Salumificio di Cornuda* [1979] ECR 867, paras 23 to 27 and Case C-213/89 *Factortame and Others* [1990] ECR I-2433, paras 19 to 21.
21. Case C-119/05 *Lucchini Siderurgica* [2007] ECR I-6199, para. 63.
22. Case 9/65 *San Michele v. High Authority* [1965] ECR 27.
23. Case C-119/05 *Lucchini Siderurgica* [2007] ECR I-6199.
24. Case 9/65 *San Michele v. High Authority* [1965] ECR 27.
25. Case 106/77 *Simmenthal* [1978] ECR 629.
26. For an extensive discussion of the procedural autonomy and its limits, see K. Lenaerts, D. Arts & I. Maselis; R. Bray (Ed.), *Procedural Law of the European Union*, 2nd ed. (London: Sweet & Maxwell, 2006), chapter 3.
27. Case 45/76 *Comet* [1976] ECR 2043, para. 13.
28. Case 45/76 *Comet* [1976] ECR 2043, para. 16.
29. Compare in this respect also the distinction made by Ortlep and Verhoeven between 'direct' and 'indirect' collisions between EU law and national law, whereby they link the former to primacy and the latter to national procedural autonomy - see R. Ortlep & M.J.M. Verhoeven, 'De voorrangsregel versus het beginsel van nationale procedurele autonomie', *Sociaal-Economische Wetgeving* (2008): 471-477. While I have the impression that they may reach very similar results as I do, I disagree with the starting point for their argumentation. I do not see a

whether, if the case could be done over with vigilant[30] parties and in full respect for national procedural law, the under-enforcement or error is likely to be reproduced if no changes are imposed as a matter of effectiveness. Accordingly, in *Kapferer,*[31] a vigilant defendant would already have raised the error in first instance, and the problem would not have arisen. Likewise, most time limits will thus pass constitutional muster, unless there is some other element that makes it impossible to properly raise issues of EU law while meeting the deadline, as was the case in *Peterbroeck.*[32] Against this background, *Lucchini,*[33] *San Michele*[34] and *Simmenthal*[35] are instances where the national legal order is likely to repeat the mistake. In *Lucchini,*[36] if the *Consiglio di Stato* cannot correct the transgression of the exclusive competences of the Commission, it is likely that the self-interest of the parties will result in repeated abuses, as neither the government nor the recipient of the aid may be inclined to raise the illegality of the aid. It has in this respect rightly been observed that in cases concerning the recovery of state aid the issue is not so much to define the procedural conditions under which someone may exercise a right under EU law, but solely concern compliance.[37] In *San Michele*[38] and *Simmenthal,*[39] without reassertion of the principle of primacy, the EU legal order would have systematically been made subject to the views of the Italian constitutional court. Accordingly, the EU *ordre public* status of the principle of primacy must thus be understood: it does not require that any violation of EU law be remedied; however, it imposes itself whenever structural weaknesses of the legal order of the Member State risk denying the very existence of the principle. Whenever such failure - which is at the same a direct challenge to the normal relationship between the EU and national legal orders - occurs the principle of primacy hits back with full force, requiring if necessary, the most dramatic changes to the legal system to restore the constitutional order.[40] These may thus include requiring judges to set aside contrary provisions of national

distinction between 'primacy' and 'national procedural autonomy'. Rather, in cases where the primacy of EU law is in jeopardy the effectiveness limitation on the national procedural autonomy will be transgressed as well, resulting in an obligation on the national court to take all necessary measures, either negatively, by setting aside national procedural norms, or positively, by creating new remedies, in order to reaffirm the primacy of EU law.

30. With 'vigilant' I denote parties that meticulously seek to defend their *own* interests. I do not argue that they are responsible to be mindful of the greater good.
31. Case C-234/04 *Kapferer* [2006] ECR I-2585.
32. Case C-312/93 *Peterbroeck* [1995] ECR I-4599.
33. Case C-119/05 *Lucchini Siderurgica* [2007] ECR I-6199.
34. Case 9/65 *San Michele v. High Authority* [1965] ECR 27.
35. Case 106/77 *Simmenthal* [1978] ECR 629.
36. Case C-119/05 *Lucchini Siderurgica* [2007] ECR I-6199.
37. P. Nebbia, 'Do the rules on State aids have a life of their own? National procedural autonomy and effectiveness in the *Lucchini* case', *European Law Review* (2008): 432.
38. Case 9/65 *San Michele v. High Authority* [1965] ECR 27.
39. Case 106/77 *Simmenthal* [1978] ECR 629.
40. In my view the strong response of the ECJ in Joined Cases C-188/10 and C-189/1 *Melki* [2010] ECR I-5667 can be traced directly to a similar fear - probably not entirely warranted - of a similar challenge to the primacy of EU law within the French judicial system. Likewise the rejection in Case C-173/09 *Elchinov* [2010] ECR I-0000 of the Bulgarian system of binding judgments by the Court of Cassation, even in the face of contrary Union law, must be seen in this light.

constitutional law[41] or to deny the res judicata effect of certain judgments that are taken in blatant defiance of the primacy of EU law.[42] They may also encompass such novelties as enabling the reconsideration of administrative acts,[43] the creation of new remedies[44] or the raising of pleas by judges of their motion.[45] While all these changes may sit uneasy with some national legal orders, they must thus be understood as an answer to a direct challenge to the principle of primacy as a result of a structural inadequacy of a Member State legal order. Actually, as the more recent example of *Unibet*[46] shows, the creation of new remedies may therefore well be limited to precisely those legal orders that offer the inadequate protection. While in the abstract, there is no need for a declaratory relief procedure for challenging, without having to break the law first, the validity of national acts that may be contrary to EU law, such procedure may be required in those Member States that do not have an equivalent alternative.

**II-162.** Against this background, a series of legal phenomena seemingly linked to the EU *ordre public* may now be analysed in further detail. In each instance, it will be important to dissect which part of the outcome can be attributed to the primacy of EU law, channelled through the concept of effectiveness, and which part flows from the particularities of the national legal order where the case arose, channelled through the concept of equivalence. Only the former part, it is submitted, is truly revealing of the EU *ordre public* and may have an impact for all Member State legal order; the latter is indeed limited to those legal orders that have the same, or at least very similar, procedural arrangements in place.

## §7.02 THE EXEQUATUR OF ARBITRAL AWARDS CONTRARY TO PUBLIC POLICY

**II-163.** A first field where the national procedural autonomy with its twin limitations of equivalence and effectiveness meets the public policy is in the very particular context of the enforcement of arbitral awards involving issues of EU law.[47] Over the years this has given rise to two remarkable judgments raising questions as to the interaction between the national and EU concepts of *ordre public*.

**II-164.** The first case is *Eco Swiss*.[48] At issue was the attempt by Benetton to stay the enforcement of an arbitral award ordering it to pay damages to Eco Swiss China Time. One of the central arguments put forward to support this request was that the content

41. Case 106/77 *Simmenthal* [1978] ECR 629.
42. Case C-119/05 *Lucchini Siderurgica* [2007] ECR I-6199. Compare also my remarks, *supra* at II-149, as to the circumstances under which the recognition and enforcement of a judgment could be refused.
43. Case C-453/00 *Kühne & Heitz* [2003] ECR I-837.
44. Case C-224/01 *Köbler* [2003] ECR I-10239; Case C-432/05 *Unibet* [2007] ECR I-2271.
45. Case 106/77 *Simmenthal* [1978] ECR 629, para. 23.
46. Case C-432/05 *Unibet* [2007] ECR I-2271.
47. On the relationship between arbitration and EU law, see N. Shelkoplyas, *The Application of EC law in Arbitration Proceedings* (Nijmegen: WLP, 2003); see also C. Schmitthoff, 'Arbitration and EEC law', *Common Market Law Review* (1987): 143-157.
48. Case C-126/97 *Eco Swiss China Time* [1999] ECR I-3055.

of the award violates Article 101 TFEU. However, Benetton faced two procedural hurdles. On the one hand, national law – *in casu* the relevant provisions of the Dutch Code of Civil Procedure – restricted review of the content of an award to a limited number of grounds, most notably for our purposes, inconsistency with public policy. On the other hand, the time limit for challenging the award was relatively short: a three-month period after the award had been lodged with the court. As a refusal to review the award may lead to under-enforcement of EU law, the national court referred a series of questions as to the consistency of the Dutch procedural rules with the requirements of EU law. Both obstacles eventually boil down to issues relating to the national procedural autonomy and help to illustrate our thesis that a distinction may be made between systemic failures and occasional under-enforcement. However, as so often, the interaction of the requirements of equivalence and effectiveness complicates matters.

**II-165.** The ECJ concludes as to the first issue:

> that a national court to which application is made for annulment of an arbitration award must grant that application if it considers that the award in question is in fact contrary to Article [101] of the Treaty, where its domestic rules of procedure require it to grant an application for annulment founded on failure to observe national rules of public policy[49].

The reason for this is, however, a combination of elements of equivalence and effectiveness. First, the ECJ identifies a structural deficiency. As in principle arbiters may not refer a request for a preliminary ruling to the ECJ, there is a distinct risk of substantial under-enforcement and divergence in the application of EC law, if it would also be impossible to raise issues of EC law on the first occasion that the case comes before a court that is competent to ask for a ruling.[50] That is all the more problematic if we are dealing with fundamental rules of EC law, such as the rules on competition. Indeed, in a since famous quote the Court indicates that:

> according to Article 3(g) of the EC Treaty ([then], after amendment, Article 3(1)(g) EC), [then] Article 85 of the Treaty constitutes a fundamental provision which is essential for the accomplishment of the tasks entrusted to the Community and, in particular, for the functioning of the internal market[51].

Against this background, there seems to be a strong case to argue for mandating review of such awards, at least in the case of such fundamental rules. But as the Dutch legal order seems to offer such a tool, we then make the shift from effectiveness to equivalence as the ECJ finds that '*where its domestic rules of procedure* require a national court to grant an application for annulment of an arbitration award where

49. Case C-126/97 *Eco Swiss China Time* [1999] ECR I-3055, para. 41.
50. Compare, in the specific context of the old Belgian appeals procedure in tax cases, Case C-312/93 *Peterbroeck* [1995] ECR I-4599.
51. Case C-126/97 *Eco Swiss China Time* [1999] ECR I-3055, para. 36. The Court continued by supporting this claim with the observation that '[t]he importance of such a provision led the framers of the Treaty to provide expressly, in Article [101(2) TFEU], that any agreements or decisions prohibited pursuant to that article are to be automatically void'.

such an application is founded on failure to observe national rules of public policy, it must also grant such an application where it is founded on failure to comply with the prohibition laid down in Article [101 TFEU]'.[52] The EU competition rules are to be equated with rules of public policy in the sense of the New York Convention,[53] and thus of Dutch law. Accordingly, we are left with a double message: competition law is fundamental, but the ultimate reason why it can be invoked lies with national law.[54] Nevertheless, the case is rightly understood as also revealing an aspect of the EU *ordre public*.

**II-166.** The ambiguity also permeates the second part of the judgment on the time limit. Having elevated the competition rules to public policy status, the Court does not object, however, to the application of the ordinary Dutch time limit for challenging such an award.[55] At first sight this may come as a surprise, but it should not. In the absence of any evidence to the contrary, the second bar to Benetton's defence, was entirely of its own making. Whereas the impossibility for arbiters to ask for a preliminary ruling may amount to a systemic failure which jeopardizes the uniform application of fundamental rules of EU law, even for the most vigilant and diligent parties, the time limit does not. The potential under-enforcement of EU law that flows from it is accidental (as it is entirely due to the belated response of one of the parties which failed to act in time as it should and could have acted), and outweighed by the systemic interest in finality.

**II-167.** If the reasoning in *Eco Swiss*[56] shifts from effectiveness to equivalence, then *Mostaza Claro*[57] complicates things further as it constantly shifts back and forth

52. Case C-126/97 *Eco Swiss China Time* [1999] ECR I-3055, para. 37, emphasis added.
53. For more on this public policy exception, see T. Harris, 'The "Public Policy" Exception to Enforcement of International Arbitral Awards under the New York Convention', *Journal of International Arbitration* (2007): 9-24.
54. This implies that national procedural law may also put some reasonable restrictions on the scope of the judicial review that will take place, which may moreover differ between the Member States; for a good example of the potential for conflicting outcomes if a same arbitral award is enforced in several Member States, see D. Grisay, 'Règles de concurrence communautaires et *ordre public*: une vieille querelle revisitée par la Cour de cassation française', *Journal de droit européen* (2008): 299-301. The cases discussed there should remind us, moreover, that it does not suffice that – taking into account that one of the key reasons for reviewing the arbitral award is because it is the first time a controversial issue of EU law may be raised and be subject of a preliminary reference procedure – national courts are willing to review arbitral awards as a matter of *ordre public*, but that national courts must then also make sure that they effectively refer cases involving EU law questions to the ECJ if there is doubt as to the exact interpretation of EU law. However, the fact that occasionally a lower national court may make a mistake in the application of EC law during an *exequatur* procedure is unfortunate, but most likely not a systemic failure. Usually an error of such a lower court may easily be rectified on appeal. See nevertheless the rather sceptical position taken by Prechal ans Shelkoplyas, who conclude in S. Prechal &. N. Shelkoplyas, 'National Procedures, Public Policy and EC Law. From Van Schijndel to Eco Swiss and Beyond', *European Review of Private Law* (2004): 607-608 that 'the control of the courts over arbitration on the public policy ground cannot supply a guarantee for the correct and uniform application of EC law in arbitration proceedings. Even assuming that the public policy ground can serve to catch in its nets the misapplication of certain EC rules, these rules will remain few'.
55. Case C-126/97 *Eco Swiss China Time* [1999] ECR I-3055, para. 43-48.
56. Case C-126/97 *Eco Swiss China Time* [1999] ECR I-3055.
57. Case C-168/05 *Mostaza Claro* [2006] ECR I-10421.

between the concepts, and it adds a third dimension by relying on the *effet utile*. At issue in that case was the question whether a national court could refuse to enforce the award from a commercial arbitration between a consumer and a telecom operator, on the basis that the arbitration clause in the contract with the consumer should be considered as an unfair contract term in the sense of Council Directive 93/13/EEC on unfair terms in consumer contracts.[58] Again the only relevant ground for annulling the award would be the inconsistency with public policy. The Court's reasoning has three strands to it. First, there is the *effet utile* of the Directive, which seeks to offer a high level of protection, which, as the ECJ already held in *Oceano* may even require judges to act against certain contract terms of their own motion, if that is the best way of ensuring protection. Seen from this perspective, the best way of protecting a consumer from a – supposedly – unfair arbitration clause is by denying enforcement of the award, even if the consumer did not raise that claim during the arbitration procedures. Second, there is the issue of equivalence: while review of arbitral awards should be limited to exceptional circumstances, it flows from *Eco Swiss*[59] that:

> where its domestic rules of procedure require a national court to grant an application for annulment of an arbitration award where such an application is founded on failure to observe national rules of public policy, it must also grant such an application where it is founded on failure to comply with Community rules of this type[60].

The problem, however, is that the Spanish concept of public policy is not very capacious and may therefore not also include the protection of purely private interests of consumers. So unlike the competition rules in *Eco Swiss*[61] the consumer protection rules in *Mostaza Claro*[62] may simply not be equivalent to the national public policy rules. However, this is where the third strand kicks in. Now that the ECJ has nevertheless spotted a small hole in the wall of national law in the form of the public policy exception, the principle of effectiveness is called in to do the last wrangling to bring the entire wall down. The Court starts to stress the importance of consumer protection, and how it relates – not unlike the rules of competition law at issue in *Eco Swiss* – 'to the accomplishment of the tasks entrusted to the Community and, in particular, to raising the standard of living and the quality of life in its territory',[63] and thus goes beyond purely private interests. At first sight, this is an attempt to mould the Community provision into the national law format, which could be considered as an expression of the principle of equivalence. However, if so then the Court could have sufficed with instructing the national court to refuse the enforcement, if in the light of the foregoing the EC law rules at issue fit the concept of national public policy. Yet, the Court takes it one step further and simply decides that this is the case. On the one hand,

58. Council Directive 93/13/EEC of 5 April 1993 on unfair terms in consumer contracts (1993) OJ L 95/29.
59. Case C-126/97 *Eco Swiss China Time* [1999] ECR I-3055, para. 37.
60. Case C-168/05 *Mostaza Claro* [2006] ECR I-10421, para. 35.
61. Case C-126/97 *Eco Swiss China Time* [1999] ECR I-3055.
62. Case C-168/05 *Mostaza Claro* [2006] ECR I-10421.
63. Case C-168/05 *Mostaza Claro* [2006] ECR I-10421, para. 37.

this requires the Court to engage in interpreting the content of national law, which is wholly outside its province in preliminary reference procedures. On the other hand, to the extent that in doing so the ECJ is effectively rewriting the content of national law, this can only be explained on the basis of the primacy of EC law. Only in this manner can the final conclusion of the ECJ be explained, namely that:

> the Directive must be interpreted as meaning that a national court seized of an action for annulment of an arbitration award must determine whether the arbitration agreement is void and annul that award where that agreement contains an unfair term, even though the consumer has not pleaded that invalidity in the course of the arbitration proceedings, but only in that of the action for annulment[64].

**II-168.** *Mostaza Claro,*[65] as do similar later cases,[66] makes clear that for the EU also consumer protection is of fundamental nature in completing the internal market in order to achieve the objectives of the Community. The fundamental nature of the interests at stake, to which I will come back below,[67] makes the ECJ willing to bend national concepts of public policy. The unconditional dictum, however, also resonates beyond the Spanish legal order.[68] It is tempting to fully explain this on the basis of effectiveness. However, I think there is a further explanation – which is revealed by the 'the Directive must be interpreted' part of the dictum. The principle of national autonomy is not only limited by the twin principles of equivalence and effectiveness. It is also conditioned on the 'absence of harmonization'. It is submitted that certain Directives, such as Directive 93/13/EEC, implicitly harmonize the national procedural rules to the extent necessary for ensuring the level of protection desired by the Directive.[69] In those circumstances the national procedural autonomy, and its exceptions, are largely redundant. It is not the public policy nature of the consumer protection per se, but the will of the Union legislator which is decisive. This being said, however, the fact that the ECJ is so easily persuaded to accept that some Directives, especially in the context of consumer protection, that formally do not claim to be

64. Case C-168/05 *Mostaza Claro* [2006] ECR I-10421, para. 39.
65. Case C-168/05 *Mostaza Claro* [2006] ECR I-10421.
66. Case C-243/08 *Pannon GSM* [2009] ECR I-4713; Case C-40/08 *Asturcom Telecomunicaciones* [2009] ECR I-9579.
67. *Infra*, part III.
68. It may, however, not always be self-evident to transplant the obligation for courts to review *motu proprio* arbitration clauses with Directive 93/13/EEC, see J.J. Van Haersolte-Van Hof & P.J. Kreijger, 'Mostaza Claro/Centro Móvil', *Nederlands Tijdschrift voor Europees Recht* (2007): 23-26. Compare also, *infra*, at II-174 et seq. On the future of such clauses in consumer contracts, see N. Reich, 'More clarity after "*Claro*"?', *European Review of Contract Law* (2007): 41-61.
69. See also S. Prechal &. N. Shelkoplyas, 'National Procedures, Public Policy and EC Law. From Van Schijndel to Eco Swiss and Beyond', *European Review of Private Law* (2004): 594, who also give examples outside consumer protection, such as Joined Cases C-253/96, C-254/96, C-255/96, C-256/96, C-257/96 and C-258/96 *Kampelmann* [1997] ECR I-6907, paras 29-35 where the ECJ held that Council Directive 91/533/EEC of 14 October 1991 on an employer's obligation to inform employees of the conditions applicable to the contract or employment relationship (1991) OJ L 288/32 affected national procedural law as to the burden of proof even though its Article 6 suggested otherwise.

regulating national procedural law may nonetheless have this effect, seems revealing as to the content of the EU *ordre public.*[70]

## §7.03 EX OFFICIO APPLICATION OF EU LAW

**II-169.** The same process also goes a long way in explaining the existence of a duty for national courts to raise, at least in certain circumstances, EU law of their own motion, which is a classic use for the *ordre public* in continental legal systems.[71] At the same time, the model explains the stringent limits to that obligation. This will be contrasted with the corresponding duty of the EU courts to raise certain pleas of EU law of their own motion, which abides by wholly different rules. It is submitted, though, that both help to reveal certain aspects of the content as well as the modes of expression of the EU *ordre public.*

### [A] The Duty of National Courts to Raise EU Law of Their Own Motion

**II-170.** The question whether national courts must raise an issue of EU law[72] is, in the absence of harmonization, subject to national procedural autonomy. Already in *Verholen,*[73] the ECJ accepted the *possibility* that national courts may raise issues of EU law ex officio. However, up to this day, it is unclear under what circumstances national judges may be under an *obligation* to do so, as the ECJ did not take up the suggestion of Advocate General Darmon[74] to create a general duty for courts to apply EC law *motu proprio.* Accordingly, first an overview will be given of the way the ECJ has tempered the national procedural autonomy in this field through the principles of equivalence and effectiveness. Second, some special cases, particularly in the field of consumer protection, will be explained on the basis of the *effet utile* of certain harmonizing measures in that field. Finally, the recent cases of *Van der Weerd*[75] and *Heemskerk and Schaap*[76] will be contrasted to illustrate when EU *ordre public* may require that national procedural rules be set aside.

---

70. See also, *infra,* at III-83 et seq.
71. *Supra,* at I-14.
72. This section is in part based on a presentation and lively discussion at the meeting of the Nederlandse Vereniging voor Europees Recht on June 7, 2007 in Utrecht; for a report on the views expressed at that meeting, see L. Lotens & W.S. Fokkema, 'Verslag van de vergadering van de Nederlandse Vereniging voor Europees Recht op 6 juni 2007', *Sociaal-economische Wetgeving* (2007): 498-504.
73. Joined Cases C-87/90, C-88/90 and C-89/90 *Verholen* [1990] ECR I-3757, para. 15.
74. Opinion of AG Darmon in Joined Cases C-87/90, C-88/90 and C-89/90 *Verholen* [1990] ECR I-3757, para. 19: 'The primacy of Community law cannot be left to the discretion of the national courts, without the risk of its uniform application being seriously compromised. And the national court is under such a duty with regard both to Community rules which have direct effect and to those which do not have such effect'.
75. Joined Cases C-222/05, C-223/05, C-224/05 and C-225/05 *Van der Weerd* [2007] ECR I-4233.
76. Case C-455/06 *Heemskerk and Schaap* [2008] ECR I-8763, with Opinion of AG Bot.

**II-171.** In the absence of harmonization, the question whether national courts must raise issues of their own motion is a matter of national procedural autonomy, subject to the twin exceptions of equivalence and effectiveness. This is crucial, as the traditions of the Member States in this respect seem to be rather divergent.[77] Common law courts traditionally adhere to a strictly passive role, while on the continent there are major differences between the Member States and between the types of proceedings. Accordingly, subject to what will be said below, in principle EU law does not stand in the way of even a total exclusion of the possibility for national courts to raise issues of their own motion in cases involving EU law, if that corresponds to the treatment of similar case involving national law.[78] For this reason, I prefer not to use the term 'procedural rule of reason' proposed by Prechal[79] in the wake of *Van Schijndel and Van Veen.*[80] Whereas in the context of the free movement of goods Member States must always be able to justify any national measure that may be seen as an obstacle to the free movement, the situation is actually reverse in the context of the national procedural autonomy. EU law is willing to put up with even the most serious procedural limitations, without any particular justification[81] (even though there usually is a valid explanation, which the ECJ usually does not fail to notice[82]), provided that the

77. For an overview of the 15 'old' Member States (i.e., before the 2004 enlargement), see F. Castillo De La Torre, 'Le relevé d'office par la juridiction communautaire', *Cahiers de droit européen* (2005): 397-401, who stresses, however, that these differences should not be exaggerated. See also Opinion of AG Jacobs in Joined Cases C-430/93 and C-431/93 *Van Schijndel and Van Veen* [1995] ECR I-4705, paras 32 et seq.
78. Joined Cases C-430/93 and C-431/93 *Van Schijndel and Van Veen* [1995] ECR I-4705.
79. S. Prechal, 'Community law in national courts: the lessons from Van Schijndel', *Common Market Law Review* (1998): 681-706. See also, *infra*, at II-183.
80. Joined Cases C-430/93 and C-431/93 *Van Schijndel and Van Veen* [1995] ECR I-4705. For more on this landmark judgment, often named together with Case C-312/93 *Peterbroeck* [1995] ECR I-4599, decided on the same day but with a different outcomes and accordingly discussed below, see F. Berrod, 'Arrêts « Peterbroeck » et « Van Schijndel »', *Revue du Marché Unique Européen* (1996): 200-204; A. Cahn, 'Anmerkung zum Entscheidungen des Gerichtshofs der Europäischen Gemeinschaften vom 14. Dezember 1995', *Zeitschrift für Europäisches Privatrecht* (1998): 969-980; T. Heukels, 'Joined Cases C-430/93 and C-431/93, *Van Schijndel and Van Veen v. Stichting Pensioenfonds voor Fysiotherapeuten*; and Case C-312/93, *Peterbroeck, Van Campenhout & Cie SCS v. Belgian State*, both judgments of the Court of 14 December 1995 (full Court), not yet reported', *Common Market Law Review* (1996): 337-353; T. Heukels, 'Ambtshalve plicht om aan direct werkende bepalingen van EG-recht te toetsen?', *Nederlands Tijdschrift voor Europees Recht* (1996): 88-92; G. Friden, 'Cour de Justice des Communautés européennes', *Annales de Droit luxembourgeois* (1995): 475-483; M.R. Mok., 'Europees gemeenschapsrecht en nationaal procesrecht', *TVVS: maandblad voor ondernemingsrecht en rechtspersonen* (1996): 25-27; S. Prechal, 'Community law in national courts: the lessons from Van Schijndel', *Common Market Law Review* (1998): 681-706; J. Roldán Barbero, 'Derecho Comuniatario y principios fundamentals del derecho interno (Comentario a las Sentencias del TJCE *van Schijndel* y *Peterbroeck* de 14 de diciembre de 1995)', *Revista de Instituciones Europeas* (1996): 799-815; D. Simon, 'Primauté du droit communautaire – Faculté ou obligation, pour les juridictions nationales, de soulever d'office un moyen tiré de la violation du droit communautaire', *Journal du droit international* (1996): 468-471.
81. This also explains why, as was observed by G. Friden, 'Cour de Justice des Communautés européennes', *Annales de Droit luxembourgeois* (1995): 483, there is no reference to the suitability and proportionality of the justification – there is in principle no need to justify anything.
82. Joined Cases C-430/93 and C-431/93 *Van Schijndel and Van Veen* [1995] ECR I-4705, paras 19-22.

procedural limitation applies equally to national cases and do not 'render virtually impossible or excessively difficult the exercise of rights conferred by Community law'.[83] Thus, in *Van Schijndel and Van Veen*[84] the ECJ accepted that the Hoge Raad should not be required to raise fundamental issues of EU law – again the application of Article 101 TFEU – of its motion in a procedural setting where the parties had been given a chance of raising those issues in two prior instances and the appeal to the Hoge Raad is limited to points of law within the ambit of the dispute as defined by the parties and not requiring new findings of fact. While the ECJ does not fail to note that the 'principle that, in a civil suit, it is for the parties to take the initiative, the court being able to act of its own motion only in exceptional cases where the public interest requires its intervention [...] reflects conceptions prevailing in most of the Member States as to the relations between the State and the individual; it safeguards the rights of the defence; and it ensures proper conduct of proceedings by, in particular, protecting them from the delays inherent in examination of new pleas',[85] even in the absence of this justification the national procedural rule should in principle stand. Accordingly, while in various Member States and the EU legal order, issues of jurisdiction and competence of courts are typical issues which a court should raise of its own motion, the ECJ accepted in *Kapferer*[86] that if Austrian law does not require its appeals courts to do so with national rules of jurisdiction, there is also no obligation to raise the probable violation of the jurisdictional rules laid down in Regulation 44/2001.[87]

**II-172.** However, as the full effect of EU law is better assured if judges do raise issues of their own motion, the principle of loyal cooperation requires that *if* national laws allows for ex officio application by national courts, those courts *must* make full use of that possibility in cases involving an element of EU law. One could say that the Court seeks some kind of 'effective equivalence'. This has two consequences. On the one hand, the national concept of what constitutes public policy may need to be stretched. On the other hand, the possibility offered by national law for judges to raise issues of their own motion becomes an obligation when EU law is involved. The former point can be illustrated, while that case may also be explained on grounds of *effet utile*, by the case of *Mostaza Claro,*[88] where the ECJ – as seen above[89] – made it clear that, whereas under national law rules protecting purely private interests could not be considered as being of *ordre public*, this is arguably different in the case of EU consumer law, which also has a component of market organization going beyond purely private interests. Similarly, in *i-21 Germany,*[90] albeit in the slightly different context of assessing whether an administrative decision should be reassessed after it had become definitive, the ECJ

83. Joined Cases C-430/93 and C-431/93 *Van Schijndel and Van Veen* [1995] ECR I-4705, para. 17.
84. Joined Cases C-430/93 and C-431/93 *Van Schijndel and Van Veen* [1995] ECR I-4705.
85. Joined Cases C-430/93 and C-431/93 *Van Schijndel and Van Veen* [1995] ECR I-4705, para. 21.
86. Case C-234/04 *Kapferer* [2006] ECR I-2585.
87. Council Regulation (EC) No 44/2001 of 22 December 2000 on jurisdiction and the recognition and enforcement of judgments in civil and commercial matters (2001) OJ L 12/1.
88. Case C-168/05 *Mostaza Claro* [2006] ECR I-10421.
89. *Supra*, at II-167.
90. Case C-392/04 and C-422/04 *i-21 Germany and ISIS* [2006] ECR I-8559.

made clear that the German concept of *ordre public* could not be limited to German norms, but should also encompass EU law norms of a similar importance whereby the ECJ strongly suggested - though, as this is ultimately a matter of national law, it rightly did not decide this point[91] - that certain key rules for the organization of the telecommunication markets fit the profile. The second point is illustrated by the case of *Kraaijeveld,*[92] where the referring court had indicated that it had some discretion as to whether it raised certain issues of its own motion. The ECJ responded that:

> [w]here, by virtue of national law, courts or tribunals must, of their own motion, raise points of law based on binding domestic rules which have not been raised by the parties, such an obligation also exists where binding Community rules are concerned... The position is the same if national law confers on courts and tribunals a discretion to apply of their own motion binding rules of law. Indeed, pursuant to the principle of cooperation laid down in Article [4(3) TEU], it is for national courts to ensure the legal protection which persons derive from the direct effect of provisions of Community law[93].

Consequently,[94] if national procedural law *allowed* the referring court to raise *motu proprio* the question whether the administrative authorities stayed within the limits of its authority, it *must* do so in respect of the boundaries imposed by Articles 2(1) and 4(2) of Directive 85/337.[95]

**II-173.** As the national procedural autonomy is not only limited by the principle of equivalence, but also by the principle of effectiveness the question arises whether they may - despite the principled acceptance that national courts are not under a general obligation to raise EU law of their own motion - be instances where the principle of effectiveness may require national courts to invoke EU law *motu proprio*. A case decided on the same day as *Van Schijndel and Van Veen*[96] demonstrates that this is indeed the case. At issue in *Peterbroeck*[97] was the old Belgian procedure for challenging tax assessments. The procedure entailed first an administrative procedure before the

91. As it turned out, the referring court did not take up the suggestion. While this goes to prove the margin of appreciation left to the national court, it is suggested that a more pro-European approach would have been desirable, see M. Taborowski, 'Joined cases C-392/04 and C-422/04, "i-21 Germany GmbH (C-392/04), Arcor AG and Co. KG (C-422/04), formerly ISIS Multimedia Net GmbH and Co. KG v. Bundesrepublik Deutschland", judgment of the Court (Grand Chamber) of 19 September 2006, not yet reported', *Common Market Law Review* (2007): 1463-1482.
92. Case C-72/95 *Kraaijeveld* [1996] ECR I-5403.
93. Case C-72/95 *Kraaijeveld* [1996] ECR I-5403, paras 57-58 (internal quotations omitted).
94. Case C-72/95 *Kraaijeveld* [1996] ECR I-5403, para. 60.
95. Council Directive 85/337/EEC of 27 June 1985 on the assessment of the effects of certain public and private projects on the environment (1985) OJ L 175/40.
96. Joined Cases C-430/93 and C-431/93 *Van Schijndel and Van Veen* [1995] ECR I-4705.
97. Case C-312/93 *Peterbroeck* [1995] ECR I-4599. For specific comments, apart from those listed above in conjunction with Joined Cases C-430/93 and C-431/93 *Van Schijndel and Van Veen* [1995] ECR I-4705, decided on the same day, see M. Dassesse, 'L'arrêt Petercam: Condamnation du délai de soixante jours prévu par le C.I.R. en matière de griefs nouveaux, lorsque le grief concerne le droit communautaire', *Journal du Droit Fiscal* (1996): 169-174; M. Pertegás Sender, 'Peterbroeck', *Columbia Journal of European Law* (1995-96): 179-185; R. Weymüller, 'Nationale Verfahrensvorschriften und Gemeinschaftsrecht: Gerichtliche Prüfungsbefugnis', *Recht der internationalen Wirtschaft* (1996): 346-348. See also, despite the mistaken title, P.

Director of the Tax Administration, and then an appeal before the Court d'Appel, subject only to a further limited review of the legal questions before the Cour de Cassation. The procedural rules governing the procedure before the *Cour d'Appel* were, however, very restrictive as they precluded raising new pleas which had not been invoked before the Director or had not been notified to the registry within a 60 days window after lodging the appeals. The Court of Appeals felt, moreover, that these rules precluded it from raising issues of its motion, but it acknowledged itself that this consequently curtailed its opportunities for raising issues of EU law (*in casu* issues of free movement), and, if necessary, ask for a preliminary ruling. Against this background, the ECJ understood the national court asking primarily:

> whether Community law precludes application of a domestic procedural rule whose effect, in procedural circumstances such as those in question in the main proceedings, is to prevent the national court, seized of a matter falling within its jurisdiction, from considering of its own motion whether a measure of domestic law is compatible with a provision of Community law when the latter provision has not been invoked by the litigant within a certain period[98].

The answer to that question is affirmative. The procedural context made it, if not impossible, at least 'exceedingly difficult'[99] to properly raise issues of EU law. First, the ECJ had long ago ruled that rules that prevent national courts from making preliminary ruling requests should in any event be set aside.[100] Second, as the Cour d'Appel is the first instance hearing the case that is capable of making a reference, and also the only body that will review the case in full, without ex officio application of EU law the 60-day period has the effect of effectively precluding most EU law claims to be raised, thus improperly shielding off the Belgian tax authorities.[101] While such lob-sided procedures are bad enough if applied to arguments derived from national law, they are unacceptable when EU law is involved. Accordingly, if a party in the main proceedings is otherwise deprived of the opportunity to effectively rely, at least in one instance, on the incompatibility of a domestic provision with EU law before a court capable of making a preliminary reference, the national court is under an obligation to compensate for this through ex officio application of the relevant provisions of EU law.

**II-174.** There are, however, more cases where the ECJ has accepted that national courts are under an obligation to raise issues of their own motion. These cases, however, can better be explained on the basis of the *effet utile* of the particular norm that is being enforced. Above it was argued that the duty for the national court to raise the unfairness of an arbitration clause of its own motion could be explained on the basis of

Lambrecht, 'Cour de justice des Communautés européennes – 14 décembre 1990', *Revue Pratique des sociétés* (1996): 113-121.

98. Case C-312/93 *Peterbroeck* [1995] ECR I-4599, para. 11.
99. Case C-312/93 *Peterbroeck* [1995] ECR I-4599, para. 12.
100. Case C-312/93 *Peterbroeck* [1995] ECR I-4599, para. 13; Case 166/73 *Rheinmuehlen* [1974] ECR 33, paras 2-3.
101. Case C-312/93 *Peterbroeck* [1995] ECR I-4599, paras 16-20.

the *effet utile* of the unfair terms Directive.[102] The ECJ has in several other cases recognized other instances where national court must raise issues of consumer protection law of its own motion. These cases are often confusing as they tend to combine a national procedural autonomy analysis with a reasoning based on statutory interpretation. Yet, in my view they can best be understood by assuming that the – often far-reaching – exceptions to national procedural law they advocate are indeed the result of implicit harmonization, thus precluding national procedural autonomy altogether. The best example of how the terms of the debate may become entangled is offered by the case of *Rampion and Godard.*[103] At issue in that case was the application of certain protective rules from the Consumer Credit Directive,[104] or at least their equivalents in the French legal order, which the national court wished to raise of its own motion in order to protect the applicant consumers. In a textbook example of how the preliminary reference procedure may help lower courts from circumventing unattractive national precedents, the national court points out that it is hampered in doing so by the case law of the highest French court, the *Cour de Cassation.* As the referring court explains the *Cour de Cassation* distinguishes between the *ordre public de direction*, which covers rules for the protection of society as a whole, and the *ordre public de protection*, which entails the protection of private interests. Only the former can be invoked by French courts of their own motion, while the *Cour de Cassation* considers the relevant provisions of consumer law to fall within the latter category.[105] Accordingly, the national court seeks to know whether 'Directive 87/102 must be interpreted as allowing the national courts to apply of their own motion the provisions transposing Article 11(2) thereof into national law, particularly in view of the fact that the aim of the Directive is broader than consumer protection alone, extending also to the organization of the market',[106] and thus must be given the status of *ordre public de direction*. The ECJ, following the lead of Advocate General Mengozzi, goes beyond the question referred in answering. First, without much ado the ECJ affirms that it flows from its preamble that 'Directive 87/102 was adopted with the dual aim of ensuring both the creation of a common consumer credit market [...] and the protection of consumers who avail themselves of such credit.'[107] Basically, this should enable the national court to set up an equivalence argumentation – developed in detail by Advocate General Mengozzi[108] – under which the EU rules on consumer credit are henceforth to be treated as rules of *ordre public de direction*. This, however, would also

102. Council Directive 93/13/EEC of 5 April 1993 on unfair terms in consumer contracts (1993) OJ L 95/29.
103. Case C-429/05 *Rampion and Godard* [2007] ECR I-8017.
104. Council Directive 87/102/EEC of 22 December 1986 for the approximation of the laws, regulations and administrative provisions of the Member States concerning consumer credit OJ (1987) L 42/48, as amended by Directive 98/7/EC of the European Parliament and of the Council of 16 February 1998 OJ (1998) L 101/17.
105. Actually, it appears that the same problem also played in the background of Case C-168/05 *Mostaza Claro* [2006] ECR I-10421, though there the national court had not raised the issue so explicitly.
106. Case C-429/05 *Rampion and Godard* [2007] ECR I-8017, paras 16 and 57.
107. Case C-429/05 *Rampion and Godard* [2007] ECR I-8017, para. 59.
108. Opinion of AG Mengozzi in Case C-429/05 *Rampion and Godard* [2007] ECR I-8017, paras 89-90.

imply that through the principle of equivalence the content of French law, as interpreted by the Cour de Cassation, is actually rewritten, which raises major concerns as to the scope of the ECJ's jurisdiction to interpret national law and sets up a potential conflict with the highest court of one of the Member States. Against this background, the ECJ changes gear. It realizes that:

> [all] the same, the referring court asks whether it is possible to transpose to Directive 87/102 the case-law of the Court regarding the possibility for courts to raise of their own motion provisions flowing from Council Directive 93/13/EEC of 5 April 1993 on unfair terms in consumer contracts[109].

If this is so, the ECJ may altogether escape the issue of national procedural autonomy, as qualified by the principles of equivalence and effectiveness. In such circumstances, it is not the overall effectiveness of EU law which requires that courts apply EU law ex officio. Rather, this obligation flows directly from the object and purpose of the provision at issue as such an obligation is the best guarantee to ensure that the level of protection which the EU *legislator* had in mind is attained.[110] Accordingly, based on the analogy to *Océano,*[111] *Cofidis*[112] and *Mostaza Claro,*[113] which all concerned unfair terms in consumer contracts, the ECJ finds that also the consumer credit rules require that the courts raise the relevant rules of their own motion, as the desired level of protection:

> could not be effectively achieved if the consumer were himself obliged to invoke the right to pursue remedies which he enjoys against the grantor of credit in accordance with the provisions of national law transposing Article 11(2) of Directive 87/102, in particular because of the real risk that the consumer may be unaware of his rights or may encounter difficulties in exercising them[114].

**II-175.** The impact of this approach should not be underestimated. Whereas the referring lower court initially asked for an interpretation of Community law which would have enabled it to make use of certain tools within the French legal order to raise the provisions at issue of its own motion, the answer of the Court has a far broader reach. By deriving the obligation for national courts to raise certain issues *motu proprio* from the object and purpose of the Directive, this obligation is no longer limited to the French national legal order. It now becomes an obligation for any national court in the Union, irrespective of the degree of passivity national courts must usually adhere to as a matter of national law. Whereas, one could have been excused for thinking after *Océano*[115] that the obligation to invoke the unfairness of a clause requiring court proceedings to be brought in a court far from the consumer's residence, was linked to the peculiar Spanish procedure, and thus should only apply in similar cases, cases like

109. Case C-429/05 *Rampion and Godard* [2007] ECR I-8017, para. 60.
110. See in this sense also G. Poissonnier, 'La C.J.C.E. donne au juge national le pouvoir d'appliquer d'office le droit communautaire de la consommation', *European Journal of Consumer Law/ Revue européenne de droit de la consommation* (2007-2008): 131-142.
111. Joined Case C-240/98 to C-244/98 *Océano Grupo Editorial* [2000] ECR I-4941.
112. Case C-473/00 *Cofidis* [2002] ECR I-10875.
113. Case C-168/05 *Mostaza Claro* [2006] ECR I-10421.
114. Case C-429/05 *Rampion and Godard* [2007] ECR I-8017, para. 65.
115. Joined Case C-240/98 to C-244/98 *Océano Grupo Editorial* [2000] ECR I-4941.

*Cofidis*[116] and *Rampion and Godard*[117] make it clear that any court in the Union may have to apply these Directives - or at least the corresponding implementing provisions of national law[118] - of their own motion in order to guarantee the desired level of protection. The impact of this lies, moreover, not only on the procedural level. It is clear that the ECJ is also undermining in this manner the classic distinction in continental legal systems between mandatory law and *ordre public*[119] by requiring national courts to connect consequences to rules of the former category that are more generally associated with the latter. The Court even combines the terminology. After first referring to the 'public policy'[120] in the sense of *Eco Swiss,*[121] the ECJ subsequently described the consumer protection rules at issue in *Mostaza Claro* as a 'mandatory provision',[122] 'essential to the accomplishment of the tasks entrusted to the Community'[123] so that 'the nature and importance of the public interest underlying the protection which the Directive confers on consumers justify, moreover, the national court being required to assess of its own motion whether a contractual term is unfair'.[124] Yet, the Court does not fail to stress repeatedly that the core problem is the imbalance between the (private) contract parties.[125] This may at times be confusing, but as the example of *Rampion and Godard*[126] shows the choice is between upsetting the content of national concepts of *ordre public* and ignoring those concepts altogether, using autonomous concepts of EU law instead. Those may of course sound vaguely familiar, but they put everyone on notice that it is the ECJ and the EU legislator who have the final say on their meaning. In order to ensure the uniformity of EU law, the latter may indeed be the better option.

**II-176.** So far these issues have mainly come up in the context of consumer protection. Yet, I see no reason why it should necessarily remain restricted to that area. While I do not advocate a general obligation for national courts to raise issue of 'crystallized' EU law, as was once suggested by former Advocate General Geelhoed,[127] I do think that

116. Case C-473/00 *Cofidis* [2002] ECR I-10875.
117. Case C-429/05 *Rampion and Godard* [2007] ECR I-8017.
118. But see Joined Case C-240/98 to C-244/98 *Océano Grupo Editorial* [2000] ECR I-4941, where the national court seemed to be called on to apply the Directive in order to set aside the conflicting provisions of national law and the consumer contract, for more see T. Corthaut, 'case note under ECJ, 27 June 2000, *Océano Grupo Editorial SA* et al., Joined Cases C-240/98 - C-244/98 and ECJ, 29 January 1998, *Bellone*, Case 215/97 and ECJ, 13 July 2000, *Centrosteel*, Case C-456/98', *Columbia Journal of European Law* (2002): 293-310.
119. On the distinction, see generally, W. Van Gerven & S. Covemaeker, *Verbintenissenrecht*, 2nd ed. (Leuven: Acco, 2006), 78-85, who note, however, that as to the consequences the two concepts are becoming gradually being blurred; see also the extensive discussion of French law in Opinion of AG Mengozzi in Case C-429/05 *Rampion and Godard* [2007] ECR I-8017, paras 76 et seq.
120. Case C-168/05 *Mostaza Claro* [2006] ECR I-10421, para. 35.
121. Case C-126/97 *Eco Swiss China Time* [1999] ECR I-3055.
122. Case C-168/05 *Mostaza Claro* [2006] ECR I-10421, para. 36.
123. Case C-168/05 *Mostaza Claro* [2006] ECR I-10421, para. 37.
124. Case C-168/05 *Mostaza Claro* [2006] ECR I-10421, para. 38.
125. Case C-168/05 *Mostaza Claro* [2006] ECR I-10421, paras 35 and 38.
126. Case C-429/05 *Rampion and Godard* [2007] ECR I-8017.
127. M. Peeters & H.E. Woldendorp, 'Knoppen zonder draden - Interview met prof. mr. L.A. Geelhoed', *Milieu & Recht* (2006): 590-596.

there may be other fields where arguably the level of protection envisaged by the EU legislator may only be assured in full if also national courts contribute sua sponte. This seems primarily so in the context of labour law, where again there may be an imbalance between the parties, and where thus there may be need to protect the worker who may similarly 'be unaware of his rights or may encounter difficulties in exercising them'.[128] Accordingly, I submit that rules relating to for instance holidays[129] and transfer of business[130] – both of which, as will be argued below, are at the very least of mandatory law – fall within this category. However, I can also imagine that the Court would go beyond the equivalence argumentation developed in *Kraaijeveld*[131] and require that also certain complex environmental protection legislation, such as the rules relating to environmental impact assessment, may be invoked *motu proprio*. It can well be argued that the EIA relies on the far greater capabilities of the government to help citizens proactively ensure that the substantive environmental protection offered by national and EU law will not be undermined by a new project.[132] Requiring national courts to raise the failure to carry out an adequate EIA of their own motion would thus compensate for the difficulties individuals with far less funds and expertise may otherwise face in enforcing the substantive environmental norms, which often have an origin in EU law as well, *post factum*.

**II-177.** Actually, one could even wonder whether there should indeed not be a specific regime for 'crystallized'[133] EU law, or for certain hard core rules pertaining to the nucleus of EU law, such as competition law or citizenship. Some interests may be just too important to be ignored completely. Accordingly, there are a few instances in the case law of the Court where this sense of necessity peeks through. The prime example is *Manfredi*.[134] Whereas the ECJ had required the national judge to apply Article 101

128. Case C-429/05 *Rampion and Godard* [2007] ECR I-8017, para. 65.
129. Directive 93/104/EC of 23 November 1993 concerning certain aspects of the organization of working time OJ (1993) L 307/18; see Joined Cases C-131/04 and C-257/04 *Robinson-Steele* [2006] ECR I-2531; Case C-124/05 *Federatie Nederlandse Vakbeweging* [2006] ECR I-3423.
130. Council Directive 77/187/EEC of 14 February 1977 on the approximation of the laws of the Member States relating to the safeguarding of employees' rights in the event of transfers of undertakings, businesses or parts of businesses (1977) OJ L 61/2; see Case 51/00 *Temco Service Industries* [2002] ECR I-969.
131. Case C-72/95 *Kraaijeveld* [1996] ECR I-5403.
132. Compare in this sense also Case C-237/07 *Janecek* [2008] ECR I-6221 in respect of the question whether affected individuals could require authorities to draw up plans to combat air pollution in accordance with Article 7(3) of Council Directive 96/62/EC of 27 September 1996 on ambient air quality assessment and management (1996) OJ L 296/55), as amended by Regulation (EC) No 1882/2003 of the European Parliament and of the Council of 29 September 2003 (2003) OJ L 284/1, where the ECJ decided that 'Article 7(3) of Directive 96/62 must be interpreted as meaning that, where there is a risk that the limit values or alert thresholds may be exceeded, persons directly concerned must be in a position to require the competent national authorities to draw up an action plan, *even though, under national law, those persons may have other courses of action available to them for requiring those authorities to take measures to combat atmospheric pollution*' (emphasis added). Again, prevention through adequate plans devised by the competent authorities is far more efficient than ad hoc enforcement of the air quality norms in case of an incident.
133. M. Peeters & H.E. Woldendorp, 'Knoppen zonder draden – Interview met prof. mr. L.A. Geelhoed', *Milieu & Recht* (2006): 591.
134. Joined Cases C-295/04 to C-298/04 *Manfredi* [2006] ECR I-6619.

TFEU *as a matter of equivalence* in *Eco Swiss*,[135] this qualification is suddenly gone in *Manfredi*.[136] There the ECJ held that 'it should be recalled that Articles [101 and 102 TFEU] are a matter of public policy which must be automatically applied by national courts'[137] and it actually supports that proposition by referring to the two paragraphs in *Eco Swiss* that are most reminiscent of effectiveness,[138] but which do not seem decisive for the outcome of that case. In his Opinion in *Lucchini*,[139] the scope of this statement would even be expanded by Advocate General Geelhoed as in his view also the rules on state aid are rules of public policy. This has the effect that:

> that national courts must always consider, when applying their national law, whether the requirements laid down by the Community legal system have been satisfied and whether the application of national law does not impinge on the Commission's powers in the enforcement of the provisions governing the granting of aid as one of the pillars of the Community legal system[140].

**II-178.** The reference to the public policy in *Manfredi*[141] may well be dismissed as a slip of the pen. The issue is not raised in respect of the merits, but *ex abundantia* to justify the admissibility of the questions referred to the ECJ by an apparently rather zealous national court.[142] The ECJ is probably correct if it had in mind that if the Italian court had a *possibility* under national law to rely on the Articles 101 and 102 TFEU *motu proprio*, it was under an obligation to do so in the light of *Eco Swiss*[143] and *Kraaijeveld*[144] – and of course if the national court then has doubts as to the content of EU law, it may refer the ensuing question to the ECJ. Yet, one has to admit that no such *caveat* is made, and the Court has since then not stopped from stressing the public policy status of the rules of competition law.[145] Moreover, the reference to the public policy in the Opinion of Advocate General Geelhoed in *Lucchini*,[146] seems revealing of a far more fundamental concern about under-enforcement of EU law, beyond the generally acceptable baseline of national procedural autonomy. As argued above,[147] *Lucchini*[148] is of course

---

135. Case C-126/97 *Eco* Swiss China Time [1999] ECR I-3055, para. 41: 'a national court to which application is made for annulment of an arbitration award must grant that application if it considers that the award in question is in fact contrary to Article 85 of the Treaty, *where its domestic rules of procedure require it* to grant an application for annulment founded on failure to observe national rules of public policy' (emphasis added).
136. Joined Cases C-295/04 to C-298/04 *Manfredi* [2006] ECR I-6619.
137. Joined Cases C-295/04 to C-298/04 *Manfredi* [2006] ECR I-6619, para. 31.
138. Case C-126/97 *Eco Swiss* [1999] ECR I-3055, paras 39 and 40.
139. Opinion of AG Geelhoed in Case C-119/05 *Lucchini Siderurgica* [2007] ECR I-6199; see also Opinion of AG Geelhoed in Case C-321/99 P *ARAP and Others v. Commission* [2002] ECR I-4287, para. 189.
140. Opinion of AG Geelhoed in Case C-119/05 *Lucchini Siderurgica* [2007] ECR I-6199, para. 62.
141. Joined Cases C-295/04 to C-298/04 *Manfredi* [2006] ECR I-6619, para. 31.
142. See in this sense N.J.M. De Munnik, 'Geen ambtshalve toepassing van het Europees Recht', *Nederlands Tijdschrift voor Europees Recht* (2007): 249.
143. Case C-126/97 *Eco Swiss* [1999] ECR I-3055.
144. Case C-72/95 *Kraaijeveld* [1996] ECR I-5403.
145. Case C-8/08 *T-Mobile Netherlands* [2009] ECR I-4529, para. 49.
146. Opinion of AG Geelhoed in Case C-119/05 *Lucchini Siderurgica* [2007] ECR I-6199, para. 62.
147. See *supra*, at II-159 et seq.
148. Case C-119/05 *Lucchini Siderurgica* [2007] ECR I-6199, para. 62

symptomatic in this respect, but one may also think of other recent cases such as *Unibet*[149] and *Segi*[150] where the ECJ tried to raise the bar for effective judicial protection – and thus also for the effective enforcement of EU law, which is in the end just the flip side of the coin – in the face of structural deficiencies in the national and EU systems.[151] Just like there may be structural deficiencies that can only be cured by relaxing the principle of res judicata in order to protect fundamental norms of EU law, there may also be a need at times for national courts to compensate for these inadequacies by raising norms of EU law of their own motion.

**II-179.** Above attention was already drawn to one such case, *Peterbroeck,*[152] where this was at stake. The issue can be clarified further by contrasting two recent cases involving the same Dutch rules of procedure.[153] As explained in *Van der Weerd*:

> Article 8:69 of the General Law on administrative judicial procedure provides that the court is to give its ruling solely on the basis of the issues which are put before it. While it is true that paragraph 2 of that Article states that the court is to supplement the pleas in law of its own motion, that provision means, however, that the court is to put the objections made by the applicant against the contested administrative measure into legal form. A distinction falls to be made between that duty to supplement those pleas in law of the court's own motion and the analysis which the court is required to make on its own initiative. Such an analysis is required only in cases involving the application of rules of public policy, that is to say rules relating to the powers of administrative bodies and those of the court itself, and provisions as to admissibility[154].

This is moreover compounded by a second rule, the prohibition on the so-called *reformatio in pejus*, the procedural rule that says that a private applicant should not be worse off after seeking redress against the government before a court. In those circumstances, the margins for ex officio application of EU law by Dutch administrative courts, while not non-existent, may be somewhat limited. The question is when this becomes a problem.

**II-180.** In *Van der Weerd,*[155] the applicants were farmers who had their cattle vaccinated and eventually slaughtered after an outbreak of foot-and-mouth disease on a nearby farm. The tests which had led the government to take this dramatic measure

149. Case C-432/05 *Unibet* [2007] ECR I-2271.
150. Case C-355/04 P *Segi v. Council* [2007] ECR I-1657.
151. For the link between these cases, see T. Corthaut & F. Vanneste, 'Waves between Strasbourg and Luxembourg – The Right of Access to a Court to Contest the Validity of Legislative or Administrative Measures', *Yearbook of European Law* (2006): 475-514, with postscript 671-672, at 671-672.
152. Case C-312/93 *Peterbroeck* [1995] ECR I-4599.
153. For more on the relevant Dutch rules, see J. Jans, *Doorgeschoten? Enkele opmerkingen over de gevolgen van de Europeanisering van het bestuursrecht voor de grondslagen van de bestuursrechtspraak* (Groningen: Europa Law Publishing, 2005), 8-17.
154. Joined Cases C-222/05, C-223/05, C-224/05 and C-225/05 *Van der Weerd* [2007] ECR I-4233, para. 16. See also the comments by Verhoeven as reproduced in L. Lotens & W.S. Fokkema, 'Verslag van de vergadering van de Nederlandse Vereniging voor Europees Recht op 6 juni 2007', *Sociaal-economische Wetgeving* (2007): 499.
155. Joined Cases C-222/05, C-223/05, C-224/05 and C-225/05 *Van der Weerd* [2007] ECR I-4233.

had been carried out by the ID-Lelystad BV laboratory.[156] The applicants wanted to raise – belatedly – the argument that this laboratory was not properly authorized to carry out these tests, as it was not mentioned (properly) in Annex B to Council Directive 85/511.[157] Under the above-mentioned Dutch law, this type of plea could no longer be made, nor would it fall within the public policy exception as traditionally understood in Dutch law so that the referring administrative court could not raise the plea ex officio. The referring court therefore asked whether EU law would require it to do so nonetheless. The ECJ, following the lead of Advocate General Poiares Maduro, albeit in a somewhat more nuanced manner, declined to impose that obligation. After reaffirming the basic framework of national procedural autonomy and its twin exceptions of effectiveness and equivalence,[158] the ECJ analysed both strands. As to equivalence it came to the conclusion that – based on the detailed information provided by the referring court – that the rules at issue would not fit the Dutch concept of public policy, as they do not concern the powers of administrative bodies and those of the court itself, nor have they a bearing on admissibility.[159] Seemingly superfluous at this stage the ECJ also remarks that the rules are being invoked in order to protect purely private interests rather than for reasons of public health.[160] As to the effectiveness the ECJ makes it clear that it is not the importance of the norm that is decisive, as *Van Schijndel and Van Veen*[161] demonstrates that even rules as fundamental as Article 81 TEC, may not always need to be raised by national courts of their own motion.[162] The crucial test, as also hammered home by the Advocate General,[163] is whether the parties were given a genuine opportunity to raise a plea based on Community law before a

156. For background to the dispute, both as to the national procedural setting and the facts, see A.M. Keessen, 'Ambtshalve toepassing van Europees recht', *Nederlands Tijdschrift voor Europees Recht* (2006): 55-64. See also J.H. Jans & T. Marseille, 'Joined Cases C-222/05, C-223/05, C-224/05 and C-225/05 *Van der Weerd and others v. Minister van Landbouw, Natuur en Voedselkwaliteit*, Judgment of the Court (Fourth Chamber) of 7 June 2007, [2007] ECR I-4233', *Common Market Law Review* (2008): 853-862.

157. Council Directive 85/511/EEC of 18 November 1985 introducing Community measures for the control of foot-and-mouth disease (1985) OJ L 315/11, as amended by Council Directive 90/423/EEC of 26 June 1990 (1990) OJ L 224/13.

158. Joined Cases C-222/05, C-223/05, C-224/05 and C-225/05 *Van der Weerd* [2007] ECR I-4233, para. 28.

159. Joined Cases C-222/05, C-223/05, C-224/05 and C-225/05 *Van der Weerd* [2007] ECR I-4233, paras 29-31.

160. Joined Cases C-222/05, C-223/05, C-224/05 and C-225/05 *Van der Weerd* [2007] ECR I-4233, para. 32.

161. Joined Cases C-430/93 and C-431/93 *Van Schijndel and Van Veen* [1995] ECR I-4705.

162. Joined Cases C-222/05, C-223/05, C-224/05 and C-225/05 *Van der Weerd* [2007] ECR I-4233, paras 34-36.

163. Opinion of AG Poaires Maduro in Joined Cases C-222/05, C-223/05, C-224/05 and C-225/05 *Van der Weerd* [2007] ECR I-4233, paras 20-32. The AG provides the following succinct summary, at para. 25: 'Perhaps the case-law can best be summarised as follows: the principle of effectiveness does not impose a duty on national courts to raise pleas based on Community law of their own motion, except in circumstances where this would be necessary in order to ensure that judicial protection is available where Community law confers a right. Therefore, national courts have a duty to intervene when it is necessary to guarantee the protection of rights granted by Community law. Yet, the principle of effectiveness does not entail a general duty for national courts to ensure, under all circumstances, the application of rules arising from the Community legal order.'

national court.[164] If that is so, there is no need for courts to compensate for the failure to do so by raising issues of their own motion, beyond what they are required to do as a matter of equivalence. The Court completes its analysis with a remarkable attempt to also summarize the other key precedents in accordance with this scheme. *Peterbroeck*[165] is distinguished 'by reason of circumstances peculiar to the dispute, which led to the applicant in the main proceedings being deprived of the opportunity to rely effectively on the incompatibility of a domestic provision with Community law'.[166] In line with our argumentation above, *Océano,*[167] *Cofidis*[168] and *Mostaza Claro*[169] are explained by the need to ensure that consumers are given the effective protection promised by EU legislation.[170] Finally, *Eco Swiss*[171] is firmly reduced to a case resting on the principle of equivalence.[172] Accordingly, the ECJ could safely conclude that EU law 'does not require the national court, in an action of the kind which forms the basis of the main proceedings, to raise of its own motion a plea alleging infringement of the provisions of Community legislation, since neither the principle of equivalence nor the principle of effectiveness require it to do so'.[173]

**II-181.** It may, however, be too soon to assume that after *Van der Weerd*[174] the Dutch rules may always be immune to interference from EU law.[175] Close analysis of the judgment and the Opinion of Advocate General Poaires Maduro, seems to suggest that the judgment rests on two assumptions. On the one hand, the ECJ accepts that the parties had a genuine opportunity to raise the issues. On the other hand, the Court also is of the opinion that merely private interests are at stake. However, if a situation were to occur where those premises do not hold true, the logical consequence would seem that EU law may nevertheless require that national courts raise issues of EU law of their own motion. One could wonder whether it suffices that either premise is problematic or whether the conditions are cumulative. In my view, *Peterbroeck*[176] and the consumer law cases[177] seem to argue against the latter option. In

164. Joined Cases C-222/05, C-223/05, C-224/05 and C-225/05 *Van der Weerd* [2007] ECR I-4233, para. 41.
165. Case C-312/93 *Peterbroeck* [1995] ECR I-4599.
166. Joined Cases C-222/05, C-223/05, C-224/05 and C-225/05 *Van der Weerd* [2007] ECR I-4233, para. 40.
167. Joined Case C-240/98 to C-244/98 *Océano Grupo Editorial* [2000] ECR I-4941.
168. Case C-473/00 *Cofidis* [2002] ECR I10875.
169. Case C-168/05 *Mostaza Claro* [2006] ECR I-10421.
170. Joined Cases C-222/05, C-223/05, C-224/05 and C-225/05 *Van der Weerd* [2007] ECR I-4233, para. 40.
171. Case C-126/97 *Eco Swiss* [1999] ECR I-3055.
172. Joined Cases C-222/05, C-223/05, C-224/05 and C-225/05 *Van der Weerd* [2007] ECR I-4233, para. 40.
173. Joined Cases C-222/05, C-223/05, C-224/05 and C-225/05 *Van der Weerd* [2007] ECR I-4233, para. 42.
174. Joined Cases C-222/05, C-223/05, C-224/05 and C-225/05 *Van der Weerd* [2007] ECR I-4233.
175. See, however, in this sense N.J.M. De Munnik, 'Geen ambtshalve toepassing van het Europees Recht', *Nederlands Tijdschrift voor Europees Recht* (2007): 251-252.
176. Case C-312/93 *Peterbroeck* [1995] ECR I-4599.
177. Joined Case C-240/98 to C-244/98 *Océano Grupo Editorial* [2000] ECR I-4941; Case C-473/00 *Cofidis* [2002] ECR I-10875; Case C-168/05 *Mostaza Claro* [2006] ECR I-10421. See also Case C-429/05 *Rampion and Godard* [2007] ECR I-8017.

*Peterbroeck*,[178] though the free movement of persons undoubtedly touches on values beyond the individual, the 'nature and importance of the public interest'[179] at stake were not an issue. In *Rampion and Godard*,[180] the parties undoubtedly had a realistic opportunity of raising the issue of EU consumer law themselves. By contrast, *Mostaza Claro*[181] seems precisely grounded therein. Yet, the lesson of *Van Schijndel and Van Veen*,[182] repeated in *Van der Weerd*[183] seems to be that the importance of the interest is *not* decisive on its own.

**II-182.** Both strands are at issue, however, in *Heemskerk and Schaap*.[184] The applicants had received a subsidy to export cattle to Morocco. However, inspection on board the Irish vessel revealed that the animals were denied sufficient space during the transport. Accordingly, the Dutch authorities ordered that the export restitution be repaid. After the applicants had protested, the relevant authorities had lowered the amount to be repaid. Instead of revoking the export subsidy for all animals, the *Productschap* only sought recovery of the funds paid in respect of the 62 animals that exceeded the capacity of the ship. However, still not satisfied with this outcome, the applicants challenged this decision before the referring court. This court, however, wonders whether, if the sanction for transporting animals in inappropriate conditions is the reduction of the aid, this should not be done in respect of all animals, as the negative consequences of the lack of space will – in the absence of indications to the contrary – have affected all animals, not just the 62 animals transported in excess. However, raising this point creates two related problems of Dutch administrative law. On the one hand, as neither the applicants (for lack of interest, as they seek to overturn any form of recovery), nor the defending administration (who is only asked to defend its second decision against the arguments raised by the applicants, not to put forward other grounds why its decision may nonetheless be illegal) has raised the issue, or indeed has any interest in raising the issue, the point can only be made if the national court could raise it of its own motion, which seems problematic in light of the framework described above. On the other hand, even assuming that the national court would be in a position to invoke the issue ex officio, the result would leave the applicants worse off, as they would have to repay all the subsidies and not just the funds received for the 62 animals transported in excess. This would violate another rule of Dutch law, the prohibition of *reformatio in pejus*.

**II-183.** It is submitted that in the dilemma facing the court sits also the answer. On the one hand, the interests that are at stake are not purely private interests. Animal welfare is a serious public concern per se, recognized by the Treaties.[185] Moreover, the

178. Case C-312/93 *Peterbroeck* [1995] ECR I-4599.
179. Case C-168/05 *Mostaza Claro* [2006] ECR I-10421, para. 38.
180. Case C-429/05 *Rampion and Godard* [2007] ECR I-8017.
181. Case C-168/05 *Mostaza Claro* [2006] ECR I-10421.
182. Joined Cases C-430/93 and C-431/93 *Van Schijndel and Van Veen* [1995] ECR I-4705.
183. Joined Cases C-222/05, C-223/05, C-224/05 and C-225/05 *Van der Weerd* [2007] ECR I-4233, paras 35-38.
184. Case C-455/06 *Heemskerk and Schaap* [2008] ECR I-8763.
185. See in particular Case C-96/06 *Viamex Agrar* [2008] ECR I-1413.

transportation of cattle may have serious consequences for both human and animal health. Furthermore, as the case concerns the distribution of EU funds, also the financial interests of the EU may be at stake. Accordingly, the interests at stake go beyond mere private interests, and may thus justify requiring national courts to raise the issue of their own motion. On the other hand, there seems to be a systemic weakness in the system which prevents the issue of EU law from ever being raised in an effective manner before a competent court. None of the parties have an interest in raising the issue: the government does not want its decision annulled whereas the applicant does not want the decision annulled on a ground that would make things worse. One could argue that the *reformatio in pejus* serves some purpose, in that it is only fair that the government does not get a second bite at the apple, at the expense of the citizen. This may hold true in purely domestic situations, where the rule has the effect of punishing the government for its own failure to enforce its laws properly. Either it had failed to do so by accident, and then this will keep it more alert next time; or it had done so deliberately, but then it has made a choice not to enforce *its own laws*. This may seem a dubious affair, but in a democracy it will only get away with this if not too many other citizens are upset. However, once EU law is involved the picture changes. The government is no longer deciding on the enforcement of its own laws, but of EU law, which it may or may not like (especially since increasingly EU legislation is adopted through the ordinary legislative procedure requiring only a qualified majority). Given the financial burdens involved, it may well be that the government does not mind some degree of under-enforcement, if that benefits its own companies. It can even not be excluded that the democratic process may unjustly reward the government for the way it protects its own citizens, *at the expense of EU law and other Member States.*[186] In those circumstances, it is the duty of national courts to counterbalance this risk of collusion between the parties, by raising EU law of their own motion. Otherwise, it will not even be 'exceedingly difficult' to enforce EU law, it may well be impossible to enforce EU law in a situation like this one. It is in a context like this that my rejection of an approach based on a 'procedural rule of reason'[187] has some practical effect. From a rule of reason perspective there may be convincing reasons as to why the prohibition of *reformatio in pejus* has been introduced, and why extension of it to cases involving EU law does not seem unreasonable, if not fair. However, in my view that is beside the issue: any rule of national procedural law, whether ill-conceived or not,[188] in principle

186. It could be argued, though, that there still is a penalty for the Dutch authorities, as it is undisputed that the Netherlands will have to repay the entire aid to the Commission, irrespective of whether the Dutch authorities manage to reclaim the whole sum from the exporter. Yet, this is only true to the extent that the Commission finds out that such irregularities have occurred, for instance because a preliminary reference draws its attention to it. However, in the absence of such fortunate coincidence, this situation seems generally capable of repetition, yet evading review. In my view, this justifies that national courts intervene *motu proprio*.

187. S. Prechal, 'Community law in national courts: the lessons from Van Schijndel', *Common Market Law Review* (1998): 681-706.

188. Prime example of such an ill-conceived rule, which nonetheless (at least in its naked form, stripped from the additional requirements as to proof in writing) passed constitutional muster is the rule on passing on of tax burdens at issue in Case 199/82 *San Giorgio* [1983] ECR 3595.

is entitled to deference as a matter of national procedural autonomy. However, if its application results in making the application of EU law 'exceedingly difficult or virtually impossible', for instance because there is an inherent risk of collusion, the rule has to go – no matter how defensible it can be in other cases. The focus should thus not be on whether or not the national procedural rule can be defended.[189] Rather the question is whether it can be demonstrated that its application is problematic for the enforcement of EU law, which in my view is indeed so in cases involving a risk of collusion. It accordingly should not come as a surprise that Advocate General Bot develops exactly this argumentation in his Opinion. After extensively reviewing *Van der Weerd*[190] the Advocate General reaches in this case the opposite conclusion, precisely because of the public nature of the interests and the risk that the EU law claim could otherwise never be brought before a competent court.[191] Nevertheless, the ECJ sees things differently. It combines the issues of the possibility for the national court to invoke the relevant rules of EU law *motu proprio* and the prohibition on *reformatio in pejus* and thus simply analyses whether a Dutch court may as a matter of EU law refuse to invoke the rules of EU law at issue. However, its sparely worded reasoning[192] also bypasses any reference to the concept of national procedural autonomy. Underlying its reasoning appears to lie an even deeper concern about respect for national constitutional traditions. Whereas I can appreciate this concern, I am not entirely convinced by the argumentation put forward by the Court. As the issue requires me, however, to go deeper into issues about balancing national constitutional values with EU constitutional values, I will address the Court's approach in more detail in Part IV.[193] Suffice it to say, for now, that I will submit there that in my view the approach of the Advocate General may on closer examination still largely be preserved, even though the outcome may suggest otherwise.

**II-184.** In conclusion, there is no general duty for national courts to raise issues of EU law of their own motion, as the ex officio application of an EU law is in principle governed by the national procedural autonomy. However, as the national procedural autonomy only applies *in the absence of harmonization* and is subject to *equivalence* and *effectiveness*, there are exceptions to that rule. As a matter of equivalence, the national court *must* only raise an issue of EU law, to the extent that a *possibility* exists in the national legal order for raising similarly important norms of national law. As a matter of effectiveness, national courts must compensate for certain inadequacies of the national procedural setting which render it impossible or exceedingly difficult to otherwise raise the issue of EU law before a competent court capable of making a preliminary reference on the matter, by raising issue of EU law *motu proprio*. Some of

189. Actually, it could be pointed out that AG Jacobs considered the national procedural rule at issue in *Peterbroeck* reasonable, though that did not preclude the ECJ from finding the principle of effectiveness breached, see Opinion of AG Jacobs in Case C-312/93 *Peterbroeck* [1995] ECR I-4599, paras 32 et seq.
190. Joined Cases C-222/05, C-223/05, C-224/05 and C-225/05 *Van der Weerd* [2007] ECR I-4233.
191. Opinion of AG Bot in Case C-455/06 *Heemskerk and Schaap* [2008] ECR I-8763, paras 85-146.
192. Case C-455/06 *Heemskerk and Schaap* [2008] ECR I-8763, paras 44-48.
193. See, *infra*, at IV-42 et seq.

these inadequacies may be structural, such as in the case of *Peterbroeck,*[194] where the rules seemed designed for shielding the tax administration. Other rules may in principle be unobjectionable as a matter of EU law, but may become problematic in particular situations where there may be a risk of collusion by the parties, as is illustrated by the different outcomes between *Van der Weerd*[195] and the Opinion of Advocate General Bot in *Heemskerk and Schaap.*[196] However, as demonstrated by *Van Schijndel and Van Veen*[197] or *Kapferer,*[198] there is thus no general duty for national courts to assist those parties that squandered their normal opportunities for raising the issue of EU law, even if fundamental rules of EU law are at issue.[199] The rule of thumb in respect of procedural rights for enforcing EU law still is 'use it or lose it'.[200] Finally, the EU legislator may - explicitly or impliedly - intervene by either formally harmonizing rules of procedural law, or, as is more likely, adopt certain substantive norms that require for their *effet utile* the cooperation of national judges in order to offer effective protection of certain weaker parties.

**II-185.** As a final point on this matter, one may wonder whether there may not also be a final ground for judges to raise issues of their own motion, namely to give full effect to the answer they receive back from the ECJ upon their request for a preliminary ruling. The problem may be illustrated by the judgment in *Mayr.*[201] The national court, confronted with the very peculiar situation of Ms. Mayr who was fired from her job in a *Konditorei* in the week she was supposed to undergo a medical procedure to implant an already fertilized egg into her uterus, wished to know whether a woman in such condition is pregnant in the sense of the relevant Directive.[202] The answer to that question is no. However, the ECJ next decides - ostensibly in a spirit of cooperation with national courts and in the interest of given a complete and effective answer - to

194. Case C-312/93 *Peterbroeck* [1995] ECR I-4599.
195. Joined Cases C-222/05, C-223/05, C-224/05 and C-225/05 *Van der Weerd* [2007] ECR I-4233.
196. Opinion of AG Bot in Case C-455/06 *Heemskerk and Schaap* [2008] ECR I-8763.
197. Joined Cases C-430/93 and C-431/93 *Van Schijndel and Van Veen* [1995] ECR I-4705.
198. Case C-234/04 *Kapferer* [2006] ECR I-2585.
199. The most telling example is probably Case C-126/97 *Eco Swiss China Time* [1999] ECR I-3055, where the ECJ required the national court to raise the issue of competition law of its own motion, but accepted that the national court may nonetheless be precluded from doing so in the case at issue because the interim award was appealed beyond the time limit provided for in national law. The first part of the ruling compensates for the fact that arbitrators may not refer cases to the ECJ; the second part makes it clear that the compensation only serves to ensure that parties have an effective opportunity to make their EC law claims before a court competent to make a reference, but does not dissolve them from due diligence in pursuing these claims.
200. P. Wattel, 'National Procedural Autonomy and Effectiveness of EC Law: Challenge the Charge, File for Restitution, Sue for Damages?', *Legal Issues of Economic Integration* (2008): 111. The author then goes on to nuance that rule in the context of claims for the restitution of taxes, which would lead us, however, beyond the scope of this book.
201. Case C-506/06 *Mayr* [2008] ECR I-1017.
202. Council Directive 92/85/EEC of 19 October 1992 on the introduction of measures to encourage improvements in the safety and health at work of pregnant workers and workers who have recently given birth or are breastfeeding (tenth individual Directive within the meaning of Article 16(1) of Directive 89/391/EEC) (1992) OJ L 348/1. For more on the protection pregnant workers in the EU, see P. Foubert, *The legal protection of the pregnant worker in the European Community: sex equality, thoughts of social and economic policy and comparative leaps to the United States of America* (The Hague: Kluwer, 2002).

clarify further that while Ms. Mayr is not protected by the Pregnancy Directive, she may well fall – if she is fired because of her fertility treatment (of a type which is reserved, if no longer exclusively, then at least still very predominantly for women), which is for the national court to examine – under the basic Directive on equal treatment of men and women.[203] Both points are entirely defensible and together they undoubtedly provide a complete and coherent answer as to the EU law issues surrounding Ms. Mayr's predicament. However, what may the national court do with such an answer? If the answer is sent to a lower court where Ms. Mayr has challenged in broad terms her wrongful dismissal, the national court may not have much difficulty in applying the ruling. However, what if the referring court is a classic last instance court, such as in *Van Schijndel and Veen,*[204] which decides only legal questions within the scope of the appeal? Suppose that Ms. Mayr had appealed a lower court ruling dismissing her case on the ground that she was not pregnant in the sense of the Directive. If she is challenging in broad terms that the lower court has misapplied EU law in not offering full protection to women who undergo a fertility treatment, the clarifications may indeed further her cause. But what if she only challenged the decision on the narrow ground that the lower court had found that she is not pregnant. This approach if taken by the lower court, it now appears from the judgment of the ECJ, is correct. Accordingly, there is prima facie no ground to set aside the lower court judgment. However, there is still the second prong of the ECJ's reasoning which may lead to a different result. Yet, that argumentation is subject to an additional factual assessment, which may not be carried out by such a court, and it raises issues that go beyond the scope of the appeal. Applying the ECJ's ruling in full may thus be incompatible with the customary passivity of courts in the particular national legal order; ignoring it may render the answer given by the ECJ largely hypothetical, which is contrary to vested case law.[205] In my view, there is in such a case no obligation to expand the scope of the case *motu proprio*. The applicant had, in line with *Van der Weerd*[206] and *Van Schijndel and Van Veen*[207] all opportunities to state her claim to the full breadth of EU law, and if she has failed to do so, it is now for her to bear the consequence of this omission. Moreover, on a closer look, the answer given by the ECJ is only partially hypothetical. Admittedly, the result may be that the full answer can no longer be applied to the case at bar, though that is in the end still a matter for the national court to decide. However, as the answers given by the ECJ will also serve as precedent in other cases of the EU, the ECJ cannot be faulted from raising itself other norms of EU law in order to formulate a complete answer that is as much as possible in harmony with all relevant norms. This seems also to be the view of Advocate General Bot who stressed in his Opinion in a recent lotteries case that preliminary rulings are 'necessarily binding where the Court

203. Council Directive 76/207/EEC of 9 February 1976 on the implementation of the principle of equal treatment for men and women as regards access to employment, vocational training and promotion, and working conditions (1976) OJ L 39/40.
204. Joined Cases C-430/93 and C-431/93 *Van Schijndel and Van Veen* [1995] ECR I-4705.
205. For more on hypothetical questions, see K. Lenaerts, D. Arts & I. Maselis; R. Bray (Ed.), *Procedural Law of the European Union*, 2nd ed. (London: Sweet & Maxwell, 2006), 63-69.
206. Joined Cases C-222/05, C-223/05, C-224/05 and C-225/05 *Van der Weerd* [2007] ECR I-4233.
207. Joined Cases C-430/93 and C-431/93 *Van Schijndel and Van Veen* [1995] ECR I-4705.

interprets a provision of Community law to which the national court has not referred'.[208] I agree that the answer is not a mere obiter dictum and will bind the referring court and also all other national courts which are now or in the future confronted with a similar issue in the sense that the judgment constitutes an authoritative interpretation of the relevant rules of EU law. However, for the reasons set out above, I am not convinced that this will necessarily result in the full application of the interpreted provisions before the national court if that would force the national court to go beyond the scope of the conflict before it, as the Advocate General seems to suggest.[209]

### [B] Ex Officio Application by the Court of Justice

**II-186.** The *Mayr*[210] example brings us to the question to what extent the ECJ and the General Court are at liberty to raise issues of their own motion and go beyond the initial scope of the dispute. In general it can be argued that the position of the EU courts seems not dissimilar to the position described above for the Dutch legal order.[211] The position of the ECJ and GC, it has been argued convincingly, is in the middle of the various European traditions 'though one could argue that it leans towards the continental tradition'.[212] At the outset, a distinction must be made between the role of the ECJ in direct actions, in particular the action for annulment, and its role in indirect procedural routes, most notably the preliminary reference procedure. Again the following is not meant to be an all-encompassing analysis of the *relevé d'office*, for which other sources are available,[213] but will serve as another building bloc in the analysis of the EU *ordre public* in general and the various forms in which the EU *ordre public* presents itself in particular.

#### *[1] Direct Actions, Notably the Action for Annulment*

**II-187.** The procedure before the EU courts is governed by two basic principles.[214] On the one hand, the object of the dispute is determined by the initial application, whereas the argumentation in support of the aimed result may somewhat evolve. On the other hand, the Court may not decide *ultra petita*, with the result that the ECJ cannot annul

208. Opinion of AG Bot in Case C-42/07 *Liga Portuguesa de Futebol Profissional and Baw International* [2007] ECR I-7633, para. 211.
209. Opinion of AG Bot in Case C-42/07 *Liga Portuguesa de Futebol Profissional and Baw International* [2007] ECR I-7633, paras 202-209.
210. Case C-506/06 *Mayr* [2008] ECR I-1017.
211. Opinion of AG Poiares Maduro in Joined Cases C-222/05, C-223/05, C-224/05 and C-225/05 *Van der Weerd* [2007] ECR I-4233, para. 37.
212. F. Castillo De La Torre, 'Le relevé d'office par la juridiction communautaire', *Cahiers de droit européen* (2005): 463.
213. Most notably F. Castillo De La Torre, 'Le relevé d'office par la juridiction communautaire', *Cahiers de droit européen* (2005): 395-463. See also W. Rady, *Les moyens d'ordre public dans le contentieux communautaire*, diss. UCL, 2005, 553 p.
214. See in this sense F. Castillo De La Torre, 'Le relevé d'office par la juridiction communautaire', *Cahiers de droit européen* (2005): 402-408.

an act of the institutions in its entirety if only partial annulment was sought. However, within these margins, there is sufficient room for an active role for the EU courts, which may raise certain pleas *motu proprio*. Actually, already in its very first case the ECJ decided to examine a plea of its own motion.[215] In the following paragraphs, it will be discussed first which pleas may qualify for being raised by the Court of its own motion and second whether there is not just a possibility, but also an obligation to raise certain pleas *motu proprio*.

**II-188.** As far as the type of pleas that can be raised *motu proprio* are concerned, I will distinguish from the outset between pleas that relate to the proceedings before the Union Courts and the more substantive pleas that are invoked in support of the form of order sought in the initial application.

**II-189.** On the basis of Article 92(2) of the Rules of Procedure of the ECJ and Articles 111 and 113 of the Rules of Procedure of the General Court, both courts may come to the conclusion of their own motion that an absolute bar to the proceedings exist. The basic conditions for admissibility of a direct action, as they relate to the competence of the ECJ and CFI and thus are at the heart of the institutional balance, are a matter of public policy. Accordingly, the Court will not only examine of its own motion whether it is at all competent,[216] but also whether an action has been brought on time,[217] whether the criteria for *locus standi* have been met[218] or whether the claims brought in an action under Article 258 TFEU correspond to the issues raised in the reasoned opinion.[219] Occasionally, however, the Court manages to circumvent this step by jumping immediately to the merits,[220] a flexible and pragmatic approach[221] which is only useful if the application is (manifestly) unfounded. Furthermore, the Court may also exclude certain pleas, rather than the entire action, of its own motion. For instance

215. Case 1/54 *France v. High Authority* [1954] ECR 1. See also Case 2/54 *Italy v. High Authority* [1954] ECR 37; F. Castillo De La Torre, 'Le relevé d'office par la juridiction communautaire', *Cahiers de droit européen* (2005): 426.
216. For instance, the Court has no jurisdiction to grant an injunction against the institution, see Case T-27/92 *Camera-Lampitelli v. Commission* [1993] ECR II-873, para. 25. For an even stronger case of clear lack of competence, although not raised by the CFI of its own motion, see Case T-338/02 *Segi v. Council* [2004] ECR II-1647.
217. Case T-158/08 *Comune di Ne v. Commission* (unpublished order).
218. For cases under Article 230(4) TEC (now, somewhat modified, Article 263(4) TFEU) involving direct concern, see the order in Case T-341/02 *Regione Siciliana v. Commission* [2004] ECR II-2877, paras 47 et seq.; Case 297/83 *Parti écologiste 'Les Verts' v. Council* [1984] ECR 3339; for a case involving individual concern, see Case T-88/01 *SNIACE v. Commission* [2005] ECR II-1165.
219. Case C-160/08 *Commission v. Germany* [2010] ECR I-3713, paras 40-52.
220. This approach was explicitly endorsed by the ECJ in Case C-23/00 P *Council v. Boehringer* [2002] ECR I-1873 in answer to an appeal against Joined Cases T-125/96 and T-152/96 *Boehringer v. Council and Commission* [1999] ECR II-3427. The ECJ then used the technique to circumvent complex arguments as to the timeliness of an action for annulment brought by a new Member State shortly after its accession to the Union, see Case C-273/04 *Poland v. Council* [2007] ECR I-8925.
221. In this sense F. Castillo De La Torre, 'Le relevé d'office par la juridiction communautaire', *Cahiers de droit européen* (2005): 411-412.

in *Vizcaya Ferries*[222] the Court had to decide of its own motion to what extent the res judicata, which the ECJ expressly deems a matter of public policy, of a prior judgment involving other, but related, parties precluded the applicant from raising certain pleas again.[223]

**II-190.** The second strand of procedural pleas the Court may – or, as will be argued below, must – raise of its own motion concerns the regularity of the procedure before the Court. Accordingly, rejecting arguments put forward to the contrary by Advocate General Sharpston,[224] the ECJ ruled that if an arguable case is made out that there may be doubts as to the impartiality of the lower court, it must raise this matter of public policy of its own motion.[225] While it would follow from *Petrides*[226] that certain procedural safeguards may be waved, the essence of the fundamental right to a fair trial[227] (neatly summed up by the ECJ as 'everyone must be entitled to a fair and public hearing within a reasonable time by an independent and impartial tribunal established by law'[228]), must be considered a matter of public policy. Admittedly, fundamental rights are generally not raised as a matter of public policy in respect of the content of a challengeable act, however here not the *légalité interne* of the challenged act is at stake, but the very essence of the institutional role of the Union Courts. These pleas are more likely to come to the fore during appeals procedures, though also the General Court may in principle note of its own motion certain defects in the procedure before it, such as excessive delays or certain facts that may cast a doubt on its objective or subjective impartiality.

**II-191.** So far the focus was on pleas concerning the admissibility of certain actions or pleas and the regularity of the procedure. The Court may, however, also raise certain substantive issues of its own motion. The classic distinction[229] made in this respect is between pleas concerning the *légalité externe* of the act, encompassing pleas as to the competence of the institutions and the infringement of essential procedural requirements and pleas concerning the *légalité interne*, which encompass pleas alleging infringement of the Treaties or of any rule relating to their application and pleas alleging misuse of powers. Only the former may be raised by the Court of its own

222. Joined Cases C-442/03 P and C-471/03 P *P&O European Ferries (Vizcaya)/Commission* [2006] ECR I-4845, paras 38-52, rejecting the approach of the CFI (Joined Cases T-116/01 and T-118/01 *P&O European Ferries (Vizcaya) and Diputación Foral de Vizcaya v. Commission* [2003] ECR II-2957) and AG Tizzano (Opinion of AG Tizzano in Joined Cases C-442/03 P and C-471/03 P *P&O European Ferries (Vizcaya)/Commission* [2006] ECR I-4845, paras 60-79) on the matter.
223. See also Case C-462/05 *Commission v. Portugal* [2008] ECR I-4183, paras 23-28.
224. Opinion of AG Sharpston in Joined Cases C-341/06 and C-342/06 P *Chronopost v. Ufex* [2008] ECR I-4777, paras 35-46.
225. Joined Cases C-341/06 and C-342/06 P *Chronopost v. Ufex* [2008] ECR I-4777, paras 44-50.
226. Case C-64/98 P *Petrides v. Commission* [1999] ECR I-5187, para. 32.
227. Laid down in Article 6 ECHR and Article 47 of the Charter of Fundamental Rights of the EU.
228. Joined Cases C-341/06 and C-342/06 P *Chronopost v. Ufex* [2008] ECR I-0000, para. 45.
229. K. Lenaerts, D. Arts & I. Maselis; R. Bray (Ed.), *Procedural Law of the European Union*, 2nd ed. (London: Sweet & Maxwell, 2006), 288-289; F. Castillo De La Torre, 'Le relevé d'office par la juridiction communautaire', *Cahiers de droit européen* (2005): 420-421.

motion.[230] This seems prima facie defensible. The rules on competence go to the heart of the political order of the Union. The essential procedural requirements moreover also have a similar value in that they ensure that all relevant actors have been given their rightful chance to provide their input in the decision-making process. However, this division has been criticized by Advocate General Jacobs as this list clearly does not exhaust all fundamental norms of the EU legal order.[231] Notably absent, for instance, are the fundamental rights or the core provisions of the internal market. The test put forward by Advocate General Jacobs to determine whether a norm is of public policy and must be raised by the Court ex officio certainly makes sense, and – as will be argued below – has de facto partially been taken over in the case law. He argues that the norm must serve a fundamental EU objective, be laid down in the interest of third parties or the public in general and not merely in the interest of the persons directly concerned, and that the breach of the rule must be manifest.[232] However, applying this test to norms that are rather concerned with the substantive legality would denature the procedure before the GC and ECJ. In competition cases, it would then virtually suffice to challenge a Commission decision by a timely action reduced to a form of order sought, 'annulment of the act', and one naked argument 'violation of Articles 101 and 102 TFEU', which the GC could then develop of its own motion on the basis of what is 'manifest' in the file, thus reducing the passivity principle to an empty shell. As will be argued more in detail below,[233] a distinction needs to be made between the *ordre public* character of the norm, and the consequences that ensue. In the procedural setting of the procedure before the GC, requiring the GC to raise Articles 101 and 102 TFEU of its own motion would seem irreconcilable with the institutional balance envisaged by the Masters of the Treaties.

**II-192.** The test put forward by Jacobs to determine when a norm must be raised *motu proprio*, is, however, relevant in respect of the *legalité externe*. Indeed, on a closer look at the case law it appears that not all norms that are covered by that label are treated as a matter of *ordre public* which the Court must raise of its own motion. This may mean two things: either the norms are not of *ordre public* or there is no obligation to raise them *motu proprio*. In reality the two issues are related. It will be argued that the first two elements put forward by AG Jacobs go as to the public policy character of the norm, while the second and the third may answer whether or not there is an obligation to raise the issue *motu proprio*.

**II-193.** It has recently been argued again that for a norm to be of public policy it must address a fundamental value and be in the public interest.[234] It is submitted that this

230. Case C-367/95 P *Commission v. Sytraval and Brink's France* [1998] I-1719, para. 62.
231. Opinion of AG Jacobs in Case C-210/98 P *Salzgitter v. Commission* [2000] ECR I-5843, paras 125-150.
232. Opinion of AG Jacobs in Case C-210/98 P *Salzgitter v. Commission* [2000] ECR I-5843, paras 141-143.
233. *Infra*, part V.
234. Opinion of AG Mengozzi in Case C-443/05 P *Common Market Fertilizer* [2007] ECR I-7209, para. 103.

will 'in principle'[235] be the case in respect of the rules on competence, irrespective of whether the competence is limited *ratione temporis*, *ratione materiae* or *ratione personae*. Accordingly, in *Salzgitter*,[236] the ECJ rightly raised the incompetence *ratione temporis* of the Commission to decide on certain state-aid measures of its own motion 'even though none of the parties has asked it do so'. In *Amylum*,[237] the ECJ examined of its own motion a plea raised belatedly disputing whether the Council could create a levy on isoglucose outside the context of the budget proceedings. Finally, in *Kadi*[238] the GC has decided to analyse of its own motion whether the Council was competent to freeze the assets of Taleban figureheads, first on the basis of Articles 61 and 301 TEC, and after the fall of the Taleban regime, on the combined basis of Articles 61, 301 and 308 TEC. In my view, the question of competence also extends to acts that are called into question indirectly. Accordingly, I cannot agree with the argument put forward by the GC in *Common Market Fertilizers*[239] that the Court only needs to investigate of its own motion whether the author of the act had the competence to do so, but that it should not enquire as to whether the secondary legislation invoked as a legal basis by the defending institution could lawfully bestow that competence.[240] However, to the extent that this may call into question the validity of an act adopted by an institution which is not yet a party to the dispute, the Court should invite that institution to make its views on the matter known, which it may do in accordance with Article 24 of the Statute.

**II-194.** In the context of essential procedural requirements the application of these two criteria, however, may occasionally lead to the conclusion that certain essential procedural requirements may still not need to be raised by the Court of its own motion, or rather that not all procedural requirements are essential. The key purpose of these essential procedural requirements is to ensure the full participation of all relevant actors in the decision-making process. In this, these procedural guarantees are linked to more fundamental concerns about democracy and legitimacy of decision-making on the one hand, and, at least in the case of acts with an individual scope of application, with rights of defence and sound administration. Accordingly, it is not difficult to see that they indeed relate to 'a fundamental objective, or in any case a fundamental value,

235. Opinion of AG Mengozzi in Case C-443/05 P *Common Market Fertilizer* [2007] ECR I-7209, para. 103.
236. Case C-210/98 P *Salzgitter v. Commission* [2000] ECR I-5843, para. 57. See also Case 19/58 *Germany v. High Authority* [1960] ECR 225, where the ECJ examined ex officio the plea, which had not formally been raised by the applicant, whether a decision had been taken in time.
237. Case 108/81 *G.R. Amylum v. Council* [1982] ECR 3107, para. 28.
238. Case T-315/01 *Kadi v. Council and Commission* [2005] ECR II-3649, para. 61 et seq.
239. Joined Cases T-134/03 et T-135/03 *Common Market Fertilizers v. Commission* [2005] ECR I-3923, para. 52.
240. See in this sense also Opinion of AG Mengozzi in Case C-443/05 P *Common Market Fertilizer* [2007] ECR I-7209, para. 104: 'I do not believe that, for the purposes of determining whether a plea alleging infringement of the rules on competence is one of public policy, there is any merit in the distinction, made in the judgment under appeal, between the competence of the institution which adopted the contested measure and the competence of the institution which adopted the measure implemented by the contested measure'.

of the [Union] legal order'.[241] To the extent that the aim is to ensure a more legitimate outcome of the decision-making process, it seems arguable that in most instances this is not merely in the interest of the persons directly concerned, but also in the interest of third parties or the public in general. Accordingly, in my view all aspects of the regularity of the legislative process are a matter of public policy which the Court must raise of its own motion. Admittedly, the ECJ has failed to take up this suggestion in the case concerning certain articles of the family reunification Directive.[242] In that case AG Kokott had suggested in her Opinion that the Council had wrongly omitted to resubmit the amended legislative proposal[243] for the family reunification Directive to the European Parliament as is required in the framework of the consultation procedure.[244] The total silence on the part of the ECJ should not necessarily be taken as a rejection of the *ordre public* status of the consultation obligation, but may be explained by the fact that, if well-founded, the plea would likely[245] have led to the annulment of the entire act, which would have required the Court to act *ultra petita*.[246]

**II-195.** However, it may not always be self-evident that certain essential procedural requirements serve more than merely private interests. I agree with Castillo de la Torre that the essential procedural requirements are closely related to those measures that directly affect the formation and expression of the intention of the author of the act.[247] By contrast, certain procedural safeguards may only serve to protect the individual claimants. The point may well be illustrated on the basis of the judgment in the cement cartel cases.[248] The numerous applicants in those cases had all put forward pleas as to certain breaches of their rights of defence. However, as not all pleas were put forward by all the parties, the GC had to assess whether they could be raised by the GC of its own motion in respect of those cases where a particular plea had not been made. Accordingly, the GC decided that the failure by the Commission to request FIC, VNC and Oficemen, during the administrative procedure, to submit their observations on the possible exercise of its power to impose fines under Article 15(2) of Regulation No 17 constituted an infringement of an essential procedural requirement, which, as it

241. Opinion of AG Mengozzi in Case C-443/05 P *Common Market Fertilizer* [2007] ECR I-7209, para. 103; see also Opinion of AG Jacobs in Case C-210/98 P *Salzgitter v. Commission* [2000] ECR I-5843, para. 141.
242. Council Directive 2003/86/EC of 22 September 2003 on the right to family reunification (2003) OJ L 251/12.
243. Opinion of AG Kokott in Case C-540/03 *European Parliament v. Council* [2006] ECR I-5769, paras 55-58.
244. Case C-65/90 *Parliament v. Council* [1992] ECR I-4593, para. 16; Joined Cases C-13/92 to C-16/92 *Driessen* [1993] ECR I-4751, para. 23; and Case C-280/93 *Germany v. Council* [1994] ECR I-4973, para. 38.
245. It has been argued that the violation of an essential procedural requirement, to the extent that its violation risks tainting the volition of the authority adopting the act, usually affects the entire act, see in this sense F. Castillo De La Torre, 'Le relevé d'office par la juridiction communautaire', *Cahiers de droit européen* (2005): 428.
246. See, however, *infra*, at II-202 et seq.
247. F. Castillo De La Torre, 'Le relevé d'office par la juridiction communautaire', *Cahiers de droit européen* (2005): 428.
248. Joined Cases T-25/95, T-26/95, T-30/95 to T-32/95, T-34/95, T-35/95 to T-39/95, T-42/95 to T-46/95, T-48/95, T-50/95 to T-65/95, T-68/95 to T-71/95, T-87/95, T-88/95, T-103/95 and T-104/95 *Cimenteries CBR and Others v. Commission* [2000] ECR II-491.

amounts to a matter of public policy could be extended by the GC to all other applicants that were in the same position.[249] This seems justified as the observations by the companies at risk of being fined may well have influenced the formation and expression of the intention of the Commission. By contrast, the GC only discussed the lack of access to the file in respect of those 39 enterprises that had put forward this claim.[250] This seems defensible as well. While it is undoubtedly true that access to the file may help a party in preparing its defence – and is thus related to a fundamental interest – it will not per se affect the volition of the Commission in adopting the act, as it was still possible for the parties to raise all relevant elements during the procedure. Accordingly, upon balance the right of access to the file seems rather meant to protect the private interests of the various enterprises involved in the cartel investigation, rather than an element that seeks to protect the interests of third parties or the public in general. This seems all the more so, because the GC considers that in order to justify the annulment of the contested act on this basis it must first be assessed whether the applicants' defence was affected by the fact that they were not given proper access to the documents in the investigation file during the administrative procedure,[251] which naturally requires some degree of individualization. Similarly, in the *Turkish televisions* case the GC extended to all parties a plea alleging a breach of the rights of defence which had the result that 'none of the applicants was placed in a position to take a stance and to make known its views on the relevance of the evidence used against it, the procedure leading to the adoption of the contested decisions'.[252] While it has been argued that the Court has been less forthcoming in accepting pleas that have been raised belatedly,[253] it is submitted that these cases may well be explained by the distinction between private and public interests. Accordingly, while the statement by the GC that 'a breach of the rights of the defence, which by its nature is individual, does not fall within the scope of an infringement of essential procedural requirements and, therefore, must not be raised by the Court of its own motion'[254] seems overly broad, closer analysis shows that the alleged infringement, namely the lack of precision in the SO, requires a degree of individualization which makes it less suitable for being raised by the Court of its own motion.[255]

249. Joined Cases T-25/95, T-26/95, T-30/95 to T-32/95, T-34/95, T-35/95 to T-39/95, T-42/95 to T-46/95, T-48/95, T-50/95 to T-65/95, T-68/95 to T-71/95, T-87/95, T-88/95, T-103/95 and T-104/95 *Cimenteries CBR and Others v. Commission* [2000] ECR II-491, para. 487.
250. Joined Cases T-25/95, T-26/95, T-30/95 to T-32/95, T-34/95, T-35/95 to T-39/95, T-42/95 to T-46/95, T-48/95, T-50/95 to T-65/95, T-68/95 to T-71/95, T-87/95, T-88/95, T-103/95 and T-104/95 *Cimenteries CBR and Others v. Commission* [2000] ECR II-491, para. 124 et seq.
251. Joined Cases T-25/95, T-26/95, T-30/95 to T-32/95, T-34/95, T-35/95 to T-39/95, T-42/95 to T-46/95, T-48/95, T-50/95 to T-65/95, T-68/95 to T-71/95, T-87/95, T-88/95, T-103/95 and T-104/95 *Cimenteries CBR and Others v. Commission* [2000] ECR II-491, paras 156-157.
252. Joined Cases T-186/97, T-187/97, T-190/97 to T-192/97, T-210/97, T-211/97, T-216/97 to 218/97, T-279/97, T-280/97, T-293/97 and T-147/99 *Kaufring and Others v. Commission* [2001] ECR II-1337, paras 134-163.
253. F. Castillo De La Torre, 'Le relevé d'office par la juridiction communautaire', *Cahiers de droit européen* (2005): 436-437.
254. Joined Cases T-67/00, T-68/00, T-71/00 and T-78/00 *JFE Engineering Corp. and Others v. Commission* [2004] ECR II-2501, para. 425.
255. This was moreover exactly the way this plea was treated in the Cement Cartel Case, see Joined Cases T-25/95, T-26/95, T-30/95 to T-32/95, T-34/95, T-35/95 to T-39/95, T-42/95 to T-46/95,

**II-196.** It has been submitted that occasionally the ECJ raises pleas of its own motion relating to the *légalité interne,*[256] notwithstanding the *summa divisio* made above. However, closer examination of the examples shows that there may be other explanations. In *Shell*[257] it is not self-evident whether the CFI is addressing the issue of prescription raised belatedly by the applicant because it considers it to be of *ordre public,*[258] or because it is easier to dismiss it as unfounded then to address its admissibility.[259] The argument in *Browet*[260] that the scope of application of the law is of *ordre public* will effectively lead the Court to raising elements of substantive law of its own motion. However, this seems justified for two reasons. On the one hand, the scope of application of the legislation has logically some relationship with the competence of the institutions,[261] either in adopting the contested act or in providing a legal basis for the contested act. On the other hand, it flows from its task to 'ensure that in the interpretation and application of this Treaty the law is observed' laid down in Article 19(1) TEU (old Article 220 TEC) that the Court must in any event correctly construe the legislation – including determining its scope and application – even though the parties may have made no or conflicting submissions in this respect. This translates in appeals procedures into another procedural mechanism, closely related to the raising of pleas ex officio:[262] the substitution of the reasons supporting the decision below, whereby an incorrect legal argumentation is replaced by another argumentation leading, however, to the same outcome. Indeed, when the GC has made an error in law, but the operative part of its judgment continues to stand on other grounds, the appeal is rejected.[263] Far more controversially, however, the GC has at times done the same in direct actions

---

T-48/95, T-50/95 to T-65/95, T-68/95 to T-71/95, T-87/95, T-88/95, T-103/95 and T-104/95 *Cimenteries CBR and Others v. Commission* [2000] ECR II-491, para. 504.

256. F. Castillo De La Torre, 'Le relevé d'office par la juridiction communautaire', *Cahiers de droit européen* (2005): 438-439.
257. Case T-11/89 *Shell v. Commission* [1992] ECR II-757, paras 323-327.
258. I am inclined to argue that it actually is a matter of public policy, at least to the extent it may affect the competence of the institutions to take certain action, see, however, Joined Cases T-305/94 to T-307/94, T-313/94 to T-316/94, T-318/94, T-325/94, T-328/94, T-329/94 and T-335/94 *LVM and Others v. Commission* [1999] ECR II-931, paras 53-54.
259. As the ECJ held in Case C-443/05 P *Common Market Fertilizer* [2007] ECR I-7209, para. 138: 'In fact, the question whether a possible illegality is a matter of public policy is irrelevant where the Court of First Instance correctly holds that the measure at issue is untainted by illegality and consequently does not raise the issue of illegality of its own motion'.
260. Joined Cases T-576/93 to T-582/93 *Browet and Others v. Commission* [1994] ECR II-677; IA-191; II-619.
261. Even though the ECJ sometimes plays fast and loose with that relationship, as criticized above in respect of Case C-101/01 *Lindqvist* [2003] ECR I-12971. Yet, this goes to prove my point that there is a relationship between competence and the scope of application of the act.
262. See on this F. Castillo De La Torre, 'Le relevé d'office par la juridiction communautaire', *Cahiers de droit européen* (2005): 439, based on B. Vesterdorf, 'Le relevé d'office par le juge communautaire' in *Une Communauté de droit: Festschrift für G.C. Rodriguez Iglesias*, ed. N. Colneric (Berlin: Nomos, 2003), 567.
263. K. Lenaerts, D. Arts & I. Maselis; R. Bray (Ed.), *Procedural Law of the European Union*, 2nd ed. (London: Sweet & Maxwell, 2006); F. Castillo De La Torre, 'Le relevé d'office par la juridiction communautaire', *Cahiers de droit européen* (2005): 439. See for instance Case C-30/91 P *Lestelle v. Commission* [1992] ECR I-3755, para. 28 where the CFI had based its judgment on a provision which was long repealed, but whose principles were taken over in later legislation the ECJ invokes instead.

brought against Commission decisions, upholding the Commission's decision after identifying an error in the Commission's reasoning[264] and this even when arguments of *ordre public* where at issue.[265] Often the ex officio substitution is the only manner of rectifying the mistake as the parties may lack the required interest for raising a plea seeking to rectify the reasoning supporting the decision below if it cannot improve their legal position.[266]

**II-197.** Then remains the question whether there are circumstances where the Court is under an obligation to raise pleas of its motion instead of merely having a possibility to do so. The answer again depends on the type of plea raised, and brings us to the second and third criterion put forward by Advocate General Jacobs: the public interest and the manifest breach. As is apparent from the preceding discussion, there may at times be a grey zone as to the public interest involved. I submit that whenever the public interest is undisputed, the Court is under an obligation to raise a norm protecting a fundamental interest of its own motion, provided that the breach is manifest. In those instances where the public interest is debatable, or where the breach is not manifest the Court is not under an obligation to raise the issue *motu proprio*, though it cannot be faulted for doing so. Of course if there is arguably no public interest whatsoever the plea is simply not of an *ordre public* character. The next question is then what qualifies as a 'manifest breach'. In this respect the bottom line should be that the breach must be self-evident from the file as such, even though the Community courts enjoy a large degree of latitude in taking evidence and may thus well be able to make the necessary discoveries *motu proprio*.[267] However, they are not under an obligation to do so. As the ECJ held: '[a]ny such obligation to raise matters of public policy could only exist on the basis of the factual evidence adduced before the Court'.[268]

264. Case T-106/95 *FFSA v. Commission* [1997] ECR II-229, para. 199.
265. Case T-75/95 *Gunzler Aluminium v. Commission* [1996] ECR II-497, para. 55 where the CFI refuses to annul a Commission Decision for violation of the rules on competence – a matter of EU *ordre public* the CFI should raise of its own motion. After finding, at para. 40, that the Commission had relied on the wrong regulation, the CFI concludes nonetheless: 'Even though the Commission should have assessed the applicant' s request under Article 5(2) of Regulation No 1697/79 (see paragraph 40 above), Article 13 of Regulation No 1430/79 and Article 5(2) of Regulation No 1697/79 pursue the same aim, namely to limit the post-clearance payment of import and export duties to cases where such payment is justified and is compatible with a fundamental principle, namely the protection of legitimate expectations. It follows, as noted in paragraph 52 above, that the question whether the error was capable of being detected, within the meaning of Article 5(2) of Regulation No 1697/79, is linked to the existence of obvious negligence or deception within the meaning of Article 13 of Regulation No 1430/79. Although the Commission was wrong in law to examine the case before it under Article 13 of Regulation No 1430/79, that error was of a purely formal nature as it did not, in the specific circumstances of this case, have any decisive influence as to the outcome of the examination. There is accordingly no need to annul the contested decision on the ground that the Commission relied on the wrong legal basis.'
266. For a recent example, see Opinion of AG Trstenjak in Case C-113/07 P *SELEX Sistemi Integrati* [2007] ECR I-2207, paras 60-69.
267. See in this sense also, F. Castillo De La Torre, 'Le relevé d'office par la juridiction communautaire', *Cahiers de droit européen* (2005): 449-457.
268. Case C-234/92 P *Shell v. Commission* [1999] ECR I-4501, paras 68-73.

**II-198.** Returning to the three categories of pleas indicated above which the Court may raise of its own motion, this implies the following. As to the pleas relating to the organization of the Court proceedings, it is undisputed that these are in the public interest. Moreover, as the factual basis for these claims will generally be readily ascertainable from the file, there is in principle an obligation to raise such pleas *motu proprio*. Accordingly, in *Chronopost/Ufex* the ECJ responded to the plea that the composition of the Chamber of the General Court responsible for the judgment under appeal casted doubts as to its impartiality that 'if, in an appeal, a challenge is made in that respect on a ground that is, as in the present case, not manifestly devoid of merit, the [ECJ] is obliged to check the correctness of the composition of the formation of the [GC] which delivered the judgment under appeal'.[269] Requiring a 'manifest breach' may, however, be misleading as it would suggest that the Court is only under an obligation to raise a plea if it is also well-founded. As the outcome of *Chronopost/Ufex* demonstrates, this is not the case. What is required is not so much a glaring breach of EU law, but rather a plea alleging such a breach of which it can easily be ascertained on the basis of the elements of the case readily available to the Court whether the plea is well-founded. In *Chronopost/Ufex*, the composition of the court below was readily available from the file, and the remainder of the matter was fundamentally a legal question as to what is required for a court to be impartial.

**II-199.** When it comes to arguments as to the lack of competence, it has been argued that 'the rules on competence are designed to serve a fundamental objective, or in any case a fundamental value, of the Community legal order - institutional balance - and are normally adopted in the interest of the public in general'. Moreover, as this is primarily a legal question rather than a factual issue, it seems arguable that in respect of these pleas, too, there is in principle an obligation to raise the issue *motu proprio*, as the CFI held in *Laboratoires Servier*[270] and *Common Market Fertilizers*.[271] However, one may of course wonder why, if the breach of the competence rules was so obvious, none of the parties have raised it properly in the first place. As argued above, there is no ground in this respect for a distinction between the competence of the author of the act and the competence of the institution which adopted the act on the basis of which the contested measure was taken.[272] While it is true that the latter may be less self-evident, once the attention of the Court is drawn to it the problem is a legal issue, rather than a factual issue and thus does not require much additional factual information.

**II-200.** Finally, the situation seems different in respect of pleas concerning the essential procedural requirements. As argued above, there is often a thin line between the public

269. Joined Cases C-341/06 and C-342/06 P *Chronopost v. Ufex* [2008] ECR I-4777, para. 47.
270. Case T-147/00 *Laboratoires Servier v. Commission* [2003] ECR II-85, paras 45-46.
271. Joined Cases T-134/03 et T-135/03 *Common Market Fertilizers v. Commission* [2005] ECR I-3923, para. 52, where the CFI made, however a dubious distinction between pleas relating to the competence of the author of the act and pleas relating to the competence of the institution which adopted the act on the basis of which the contested measure was taken.
272. *Supra*, at II-193. Compare in this respect Joined Cases T-134/03 et T-135/03 *Common Market Fertilizers v. Commission* [2005] ECR I-3923, para. 52 with Opinion of AG Mengozzi in Case C-443/05 P *Common Market Fertilizer* [2007] ECR I-7209, para. 104

and private interests protected by the norm. Moreover, in the absence of the adduction of some factual evidence it may be rather difficult for the Court to raise the violation of certain essential procedural requirements *motu proprio*. However, to the extent that the alleged violation may be manifest in that there is no need for much (additional) factual information not readily available in the file, such as in the case of the insufficiency of the statement of reasons, or if – albeit belatedly – a party does put forward the necessary factual elements so that the ground does not appear 'manifestly devoid of merit',[273] the Court must take up the issue *motu proprio*. Accordingly, this is another way of explaining the difference in the Cement Cartel cases[274] between the treatment of the plea as to the possibility to comment on the threat of a fine – which can be easily ascertained and has a direct impact on the development of the intent of the author of the act – and the access to the file, which will have a far more indirect impact and also requires a further individualized assessment whether or not there actually was an impact on the applicants' defence by the fact that they were not given proper access to the documents in the investigation file during the administrative procedure.[275] Similarly, it is also another reason why it would not seem feasible to extend the *relevé d'office* to fundamental norms pertaining to the *légalité interne*, even though they may be protecting interests beyond the parties directly concerned, as in the case of the core rules on competition law.[276] Introducing an obligation for the Court to raise these issues *motu proprio* would only be possible if a concomitant obligation to investigate the relevant facts *motu proprio* were to be introduced, which is in clear contradiction with the concept behind the current rules of procedure of both the GC and ECJ.

**II-201.** There may, however, be further factors that may influence the question whether the Court is under an obligation to raise an issue *motu proprio*, though their impact is far from clear. First, if we accept, as defended above, that a plea concerning an alleged lack of competence may also relate to the competence of the institution which adopted the act on the basis of which the contested measure was taken, there may be a further problem in that the author of that act may not be a party to the dispute, while the Court should not assess the validity of an act of an institution without giving that institution the opportunity to make its position known. In my view, however, this can be solved by inviting that institution to submit its observations to the matter pursuant to Article 24 of the Court's Statute. More in general, however, ensuring that all parties concerned are heard when the Court raises an issue of its own motion is crucial. Accordingly, in *Commission v. Ireland* the ECJ did not fault the General Court for raising the issue of a defective statement of reasons for the challenged Commission competition decision of its own motion, which indeed is a matter of public policy as it

273. Joined Cases C-341/06 and C-342/06 P *Chronopost v. Ufex* [2008] ECR I-4777, para. 47.
274. Joined Cases T-25/95, T-26/95, T-30/95 to T-32/95, T-34/95, T-35/95 to T-39/95, T-42/95 to T-46/95, T-48/95, T-50/95 to T-65/95, T-68/95 to T-71/95, T-87/95, T-88/95, T-103/95 and T-104/95 *Cimenteries CBR and Others v. Commission* [2000] ECR II-491.
275. Joined Cases T-25/95, T-26/95, T-30/95 to T-32/95, T-34/95, T-35/95 to T-39/95, T-42/95 to T-46/95, T-48/95, T-50/95 to T-65/95, T-68/95 to T-71/95, T-87/95, T-88/95, T-103/95 and T-104/95 *Cimenteries CBR and Others v. Commission* [2000] ECR II-491, paras 156-157.
276. Case C-126/97 *Eco Swiss China Time* [1999] ECR I-3055, para. 36; Joined Cases C-295/04 to C-298/04 *Manfredi* [2006] ECR I-6619, para. 31.

is a crucial element for enabling the Union courts to actually review the validity of an act of the institutions.[277] However, it took issue with the fact that it had failed to give the Commission to defend its decision against the criticism that it was not sufficiently reasoned as required by Article 296, second sentence TFEU.[278] Indeed on appeal, the judgment of the General Court was actually reversed on this point.[279] The Court considers this right to be heard in order to be able to contest a plea raised by the Court of its own motion so crucial, that it has even accepted that the decision by the General Court, on appeal from the Civil Service Tribunal, to simply dispose of the case on the basis of a plea raised *motu proprio* jeopardizes the unity of union law, justifying that the ECJ heard the case under the review procedure.[280]

**II-202.** Second, the ECJ cannot, in principle go *ultra petita*, i.e., the pleas invoked *motu proprio* should in principle lead to the outcome requested by the applicant. As argued, this may explain why the ECJ did not raise the failure to consult the European Parliament a second time in the family reunification case, as the European Parliament was only seeking the partial annulment of the act whereas upholding the plea should have resulted in declaring the act void in its entirety. This the Court cannot do: if partial annulment is impossible, the application is dismissed in its entirety as inadmissible.[281] The *ultra petita* argument should, however, not be overstated.

**II-203.** On the one hand, the *ultra petita* must primarily be assessed in respect of the form of order sought. Accordingly, I do not agree with Advocate General Trstenjak that the Court may ignore a plea raised by the intervener on the side of the institution, which would result in the annulment of the act of that institution as requested by the applicant.[282] While it is true that interveners may not alter the scope of the dispute and may in principle only adduce arguments in support of the form of order sought in respect of the party on whose side they are intervening,[283] this limitation becomes irrelevant when pleas concerning the *ordre public* are at issue. The whole point is precisely that, despite the limitations on the parties to (still) put forward certain arguments, the Court raises the issues of its own motion if it gets somehow knowledge of the potential problem. Moreover, in *SELEX Sistemi Integrati*[284] the argument at issue could probably not have been raised in any other manner. This requires, however, some further background to the case. At issue was the decision by the Commission rejecting the complaint by the applicant that Eurocontrol abuses its dominant position in the sense of Article 102 TFEU. The Commission argued that Eurocontrol did not fall

277. Case C-89/08 P *Commission v. Ireland* [2009] ECR I-11245, paras 34-42.
278. Case C-89/08 P *Commission v. Ireland* [2009] ECR I-11245, paras 50-62.
279. Case C-89/08 P *Commission v. Ireland* [2009] ECR I-11245, paras 70-87.
280. Case C-197/09 RX-II *M v. European Medicines Agency* [2009] ECR I-12033.
281. Case 37/71 *Jamet v. Commission* [1972] ECR 483, para. 12; Case C-244/03 *France v. Commission* [2005] ECR I-4021, paras 13-21.
282. Opinion of AG Trstenjak in Case C-113/07 P *SELEX Sistemi Integrati v. Commission and Eurocontrol* [2009] ECR I-2207, paras 25-33.
283. Article 40(4) of the Statute of the Court. For more on the role of interveners, see K. Lenaerts, D. Arts & I. Maselis; R. Bray (Ed.), *Procedural Law of the European Union*, 2nd ed. (London: Sweet & Maxwell, 2006), 566-577.
284. Case C-113/07 P *SELEX Sistemi Integrati v. Commission and Eurocontrol* [2009] ECR I-2207.

within the ambit of that provision since it is not engaged in any economic activity.[285] Accordingly, only the applicant SELEX Sistemi Integrati had an interest in seeking the annulment of this decision. However, the GC[286] found that the Commission was wrong to claim that Eurocontrol did not exercise an economic activity, but then found that the decision could be preserved as there was no abuse of the dominant position (which had been the subsidiary reasoning of the Commission). Having lost at first instance, SELEX Sistemi Integrati appealed to the ECJ. In answering, but without lodging a cross-appeal (as its act had survived the scrutiny in first instance), the Commission indicated that the GC was wrong to find that Eurocontrol was engaged in an economic activity, and suggested – in line with what was argued above – to again substitute the supporting reasoning. By the same token, the argumentation developed by the GC is potentially harmful for Eurocontrol as well. While the Commission decision was not annulled, Eurocontrol will have to be far more careful as to how it operates in the future as it now allegedly falls within the scope of Article 102 TFEU. Confronted with that prospect, Eurocontrol, as a body established by international agreement among a series of European States, some but not all of which are a Member of the EU, argues that it escapes all review as it enjoys 'international immunity'. Whatever the merits of this claim, it seems to question the competence *ratione personae* of the Commission for applying in any form Article 102 TFEU to an international organization such as Eurocontrol. Accordingly, the claim seems a matter of public policy, which – as it is an issue of competence – the Court should raise of its own motion. However, acceding to that plea means that the initial act of the Commission was void *ab initio*. This is a strange position for an intervener on the side of the Commission to take, but it makes perfect sense in the context of the case. Moreover, acceding to that plea should of course lead to the setting aside of the judgment below and the annulment of the act of the Commission. Yet, if it had done so the Court would, in my view, not have gone *ultra petita*, as this is precisely what the applicant/appellant was seeking. The full annulment is already within the scope of the conflict as defined by the parties. Nevertheless, the Court decided to side-step the issue of immunity entirely by accepting that the question whether or not Eurocontrol could fall within the scope of the competition rules is one of substance, and not a jurisdictional matter.[287] The Court continues by explaining that:

> Since the Commission is required under Article 211 EC to ensure that the provisions of the Treaty are applied, it also acted within its powers in examining Selex's complaint and rejecting it by taking the view that Article 82 EC was not applicable to Eurocontrol. Accordingly, there is no need for the Court to examine of its own motion the submissions made by Eurocontrol regarding its immunity[288].

285. See also, *supra*, at II-88.
286. Case T-155/04 *SELEX Sistemi Integrati v. Commission* [2006] ECR II-4797.
287. Case C-113/07 P *SELEX Sistemi Integrati v. Commission and Eurocontrol* [2009] ECR I-2207, para. 62.
288. Case C-113/07 P *SELEX Sistemi Integrati v. Commission and Eurocontrol* [2009] ECR I-2207, paras 63-64. Article 211 TEC has formally been repealed by the Lisbon Treaty, but essentially continues in Article 17(1) TEU.

Nevertheless in the discussion of the merits of the appeal brought by the applicant the Court did reaffirm that at least as a matter of Union law, rather than international law, Eurocontrom is not an undertaking for the purposes of Article 102 TFEU.[289]

**II-204.** On the other hand, in the past it has been argued that the limitation on not stating *ultra petita* does not hold firm in cases where the invalidity concerns the *ordre public*. This seems to follow from an *a contrario* analysis of the statement of the Court on the problem of partial annulment in *Jamet* where the Court held that 'if the Court were to annul the entire measure this would constitute a ruling *ultra petita since the application against the contested decision does not concern public policy*'.[290] Accordingly, it seems fair to argue that an act may *a contrario* be annulled in its entirety notwithstanding the more limited form of order sought if it is tainted by a vice that concerns the *ordre public*. Actually, that would arguably make sense, as the violated norms at issue do not only protect the applicant, but are fundamental norms that also protect the public interest, so that the legal order as whole cannot but benefit from the annulment. It has been argued, however, that the Court should avoid that in doing so, the applicant would be worse off.[291] While I have some sympathy for this argument - above[292] the reasons behind a similar prohibition of the *reformatio in pejus* in Dutch administrative law were put forward - I find that it sits uneasily with the public character of *ordre public*, protecting fundamental interests beyond the applicant.[293] In line with my argument above[294] that the arguments adduced by an intervener, seemingly contrary to its procedural role, may nonetheless be examined ex officio by the Court if they concern a matter of *ordre public*, I submit that any applicant must bear the - fortunately rather exceptional - risk that the challenged act is unmasked as entirely contrary to public policy. A similar course of action has been considered by Advocate General Tesauro in *Deggendorf III*.[295] After having found that a partial annulment of a decision would have 'the effect of permitting the disbursement of aid to an undertaking guilty of non-compliance with an obligation imposed upon it (albeit indirectly) by the Commission to repay other aid',[296] the Advocate General suggested that the Court may examine of its own motion whether the statement of reasons supported the remainder of the act;

289. Case C-113/07 P *SELEX Sistemi Integrati v. Commission and Eurocontrol* [2009] ECR I-2207, para. 82.
290. Case 37/71 *Jamet v. Commission* [1972] ECR 483, para. 12 (emphasis added).
291. F. Castillo De La Torre, 'Le relevé d'office par la juridiction communautaire', *Cahiers de droit européen* (2005):448.
292. *Supra*, at II-183.
293. Compare in this respect the remark made by AG Sharpston, not coincidentally in a case concerning the financial interests of the Union and thus involving a matter of EU *ordre public*, who argues that the recipient of export subsidies may well make itself a mistake if it does not reacts when it receives too much subsidies as the result of a mistake made by the national authorities, see Opinion of AG Sharpston in Case C-281/07 *Bayerische Hypotheken- und Vereinsbank* [2009] ECR I-91, para. 35.
294. *Supra*, at II-203.
295. Case C-355/95 P *Textilwerke Deggendorf v. Commission* [1997] ECR I-2549.
296. Opinion of AG Tesauro in Case C-355/95 P *Textilwerke Deggendorf v. Commission* [1997] ECR I-2549, para. 22.

> and it could reach the conclusion that, in the present case, the requirement to state reasons had not been complied with, for example because, as mentioned, the express declaration of compatibility of the new aid with the common market is not sufficiently proven (or is at any rate contradictory), given the distortion of competition which, according to the Commission itself, arises from the cumulation of the new aid with the previous aid. In that way, the Court would be entitled to annul the decisions in their entirety without this constituting a ruling *ultra petita*[297].

However, it has to be conceded that the Advocate General had himself serious misgivings about this solution, precisely because of the risk of *reformatio in pejus*:

> Although this solution would be legally sound, at least on the basis of a flexible interpretation of the aforesaid case-law of the Court of Justice, it seems to me to ignore the operative procedural principle that the wishes of the applicant with regard to the claim should take precedence. In the present case, the annulment of the decisions in their entirety, when the appellant has (for obvious reasons) expressly sought their annulment only in part, would in the end completely distort the essential outcome of the application which, even if upheld, would entail consequences for the appellant that were ultimately more disadvantageous than if it were dismissed[298].

Accordingly, he ultimately opted for a partial annulment. The Court, however, did not have to take that step, as contrary to its Advocate General it did not uphold any of the pleas put forward by the applicant.

**II-205.** In conclusion, it can thus be argued that the Court is under an obligation to raise in direct actions fundamental norms of Community law which protect interests that go beyond the mere private interests of the parties directly concerned, provided that it can easily be ascertained on the basis of the file – i.e., without further ex officio factual investigation – whether the plea is well-founded. The last requirement justifies that the *relevé d'office* is moreover limited to those norms that either relate to the judicial process or affect the *légalité externe* of the challenged act. However, as a grey zone exists, in particular in respect of pleas relating to essential procedural requirements where the public character may not only always be self-evident or where the need for further factual findings may greatly vary, the Court may arguably raise certain pleas of its own motion in a number of cases where there is not necessarily an obligation to do so. One could wonder, whether, in exceptional cases such as the manifest violation of fundamental rights (one may think of an EU act allowing torture, or an act which is overtly racist) this should not also leave some margin to the ECJ to raise in such cases a plea related to the substantive legality of the act, as in such a case no further factual findings are necessary to ascertain the existence of the breach of a fundamental norm protecting more than the mere private interests of the parties. With this suggestion, we

297. Opinion of AG Tesauro in Case C-355/95 P *Textilwerke Deggendorf v. Commission* [1997] ECR I-2549, para. 23.
298. Opinion of AG Tesauro in Case C-355/95 P *Textilwerke Deggendorf v. Commission* [1997] ECR I-2549, para. 24.

come of course close to the position of AG Jacobs in *Salzgitter,*[299] without, however, having to abandon the *summa divisio* between *légalité externe* and *légalité interne* altogether.[300]

### *[2] Indirect Actions, Notably the Preliminary Reference Procedure*

**II-206.** Certain pleas, notably as to the validity of acts of the EU institutions may also be raised indirectly in the sense that the (validity of the) act was not initially at issue or in any event not on the new ground put forward. At least in one instance the ECJ has raised of its own motion a plea of illegality.[301] In *Société des fonderies de Pont-à-Mousson,*[302] the ECJ raised of its own motion the issue whether the underlying decision 2/57 could serve as a basis for the exemption sought by the applicant - but denied in the contested act - and if not whether that would render the underlying decision invalid. The Court decided to do so because 'it appears to be inappropriate to allow doubt as to the legality of decision no 2/57 to persist, in so far as the answer to this question is relevant to these proceedings',[303] thus suggesting that there is an interest per se in assessing the validity of the acts that are relevant for deciding the dispute. It must moreover be observed that while the plea thus related to the competence of the High Authority to adopt the contested act, which is a matter of *public policy*, the ground for doubting the validity of the underlying act - the principle of equal treatment - is not.[304] Raising a plea of illegality in the course of proceedings may create a problem, as the author of the act may not be present before the Court, which seems to have led the CFI to believe it should be more hesitant in examining a late plea of illegality.[305] However, as argued above,[306] this concern can be alleviated through Article 24 of the Statute. Moreover, it cannot be excluded - as demonstrated by *Common Market Fertilizers*[307] - that the defence put up by the defending institution raises questions as

---

299. Opinion of AG Jacobs in Case C-210/98 P *Salzgitter v. Commission* [2000] ECR I-5843, paras 125-150.
300. Admittedly, this is somewhat ambiguous still. However, on the basis of the model elaborated in Part V, it will be argued that there is a principled basis for including fundamental rights into the group of norms the EU courts may raise *motu proprio*; at the same time it will be argued that the rules on competition law, however, do not qualify in this respect. See, *infra*, Part V and in particular V-32.
301. F. Castillo De La Torre, 'Le relevé d'office par la juridiction communautaire', *Cahiers de droit européen* (2005): 445.
302. Case 14/59 *Société des fonderies de Pont-à-Mousson v. High Authority* [1959] ECR 215.
303. Case 14/59 *Société des fonderies de Pont-à-Mousson v. High Authority* [1959] ECR 215, at 230.
304. See in this respect Case C-279/95 P *Lagnese-Iglo v. Commission* [1998] ECR I-5609, paras 51-55; Joined Cases T-92/00 and T-103/00 *Territorio Histórico de Álava – Diputación Foral de Álava and Others v. Commission* [2002] ECR II-1385, para. 90.
305. Joined Cases T-134/03 et T-135/03 *Common Market Fertilizers v. Commission* [2005] ECR II-3923.
306. *Supra*, at II-192 and II-201.
307. Joined Cases T-134/03 et T-135/03 *Common Market Fertilizers v. Commission* [2005] ECR II-3923; Opinion of AG Mengozzi in Case C-443/05 P *Common Market Fertilizer* [2007] ECR I-7209 (the judgment of the Court on appeal avoided answering the issue).

to the validity of an underlying act, which could not reasonably have been foreseen by the applicant.

**II-207.** The issue of the potential absence of a relevant actor before the Court, is however also an issue in the context of the preliminary reference procedure. Moreover, in that context there is a further concern that is founded in the division of roles between the ECJ and the referring courts, though - as will be demonstrated - there is some margin for flexibility in the name of the effective cooperation between both courts.

**II-208.** The starting point of our analysis[308] is the important degree of deference displayed by the ECJ towards the national court. It is the referring court which alone decides whether or not it refers a case to the ECJ[309] - subject to the limitations flowing from *CILFIT*[310] and *Foto-Frost*[311] - and if so which questions will be submitted to the ECJ.[312] In principle, it is thus the national court which draws the lines for the dispute before the Court, and the ECJ will respect these lines even if certain new issues of law and fact have come up at the hearing following questions from the Court.[313] However, the ECJ is still master of its own competence. Accordingly, it will examine of its own motion whether the conditions for admissibility are fulfilled. Thus the ECJ will examine whether the question has been referred to it by a 'court or tribunal',[314] whether that court is competent to refer preliminary questions,[315] whether the question is not hypothetical[316] or contrived[317] or whether the preliminary reference procedure has been used to circumvent the mandatory time limits for other proceedings.[318]

**II-209.** Moreover, the Court of Justice has given itself quite some latitude to rephrase questions as to render them admissible - as in the classic case where a national court asks the Court to assess the validity of national legislation in the light of EU law, which the Court systematically rephrases as the question of EU law whether EU law precludes national legislation with the effect of the named national legislation[319] - or to better

308. For an excellent overview of the preliminary reference procedure, see K. Lenaerts, D. Arts & I. Maselis; R. Bray (Ed.), *Procedural Law of the European Union*, 2nd ed. (London: Sweet & Maxwell, 2006), Chapters 2, 7 and 10.
309. Joined Cases 31/62 and 33/62 *Milchwerke Heinz Wöhrmann & Sohn and Alfons Lütticke v. Commission* [1962] ECR 501.
310. Case 283/81 *CILFIT* [1982] ECR 3415.
311. Case 314/84 *Foto-Frost* [1987] ECR 4199; see also Case C-461/03 *Gaston Schul Douane-Expediteur* [2005] ECR I-10513.
312. Case 247/86 *Alsatel* [1988] ECR 5987, para. 8; Case C-236/02 *Slob* [2004] ECR I-1861, para. 29. The latter case is particularly interesting as the referring court took up the suggestion that '[i]f, in view of developments in the proceedings, the national court were to consider it necessary to obtain further interpretations of Community law, it would be for that court to make a fresh reference to the Court', resulting in Case C-496/04 *Slob* [2006] ECR I-8257.
313. Case C-226/07 *Flughaven Köln/Bonn* [2008] ECR I-5999, paras 35-38.
314. Case C-96/04 *Standesamt Stadt Niebüll* [2006] ECR I-3561.
315. Case C-404/07 *Katz* [2008] ECR I-7607, paras 27-38 and the accompanying Opinion of AG Kokott, paras 14-21.
316. Case C-343/90 *Lourenço Dias* [1992] ECR I-4673, paras 11-23.
317. Case 104/79 *Foglia* [1980] ECR 745.
318. Case C-188/92 *TWD Textilwerke Deggendorf* [1994] ECR I-833; Case C-239/99 *Nachi Europe* [2001] ECR I-1197.
319. For an example, see Case C-380/05 *Centro Europa 7* [2008] ECR I-349, paras 48-51.

take the legal context into account. As the example of *Mayr*[320] shows, the ECJ does not hesitate to raise of its own motion certain norms of EU law which the national court may have overlooked, if they may nonetheless prove useful for answering the question. This latitude seems completely justified, as the ECJ cannot be expected to explain fully what the law says, if it would be prevented from invoking all relevant norms that may have a bearing on the role of a particular norm within the entire legal order. For instance in *Mayr*,[321] the restrictive interpretation of the concept 'pregnancy' seems far more justified if it is balanced by the presence of a general framework for combating discrimination on grounds of sex. Therefore, it is in the interest of the coherence of the legal order – taking into account the value its judgment has as a precedent for the entire Union, well beyond the case at bar – that the ECJ be allowed to invoke all relevant norms.

**II-210.** The margin for the ECJ to alter the scope of the dispute referred to it by preliminary reference does not end there. The ECJ has even accepted that there may at times be reasons to deviate from the division between reference on the interpretation of certain norms of EU law and references as to the validity of EU law. Examples can be found in both directions.

**II-211.** First, while the preliminary reference procedure does not formally lead to the annulment of the act at issue, a finding as to its invalidity may still have very serious similar consequences, as all legal subjects are put on alert that the act at issue is tainted *ab initio* by a particular defect and should thus not be applied.[322] Accordingly, it may be useful, if possible, to avoid this dramatic outcome by interpreting the act in a manner that avoids the legality problem. Therefore in *Krüger*,[323] the ECJ managed to defuse a challenge to the validity of a regulation based on a perceived unequal treatment as far as export funds were concerned between milk preparations having a basis of coffee and those having a basis of extracts, essences or concentrates of coffee, as on proper interpretation of the regulation there was no such distinction. Similarly, already in *Stauder*[324] the ECJ interpreted a regulation on the distribution of butter surpluses in a manner that avoided a potential conflict with fundamental rights.

**II-212.** Second, occasionally the ECJ has inquired into the validity of certain acts of the institutions whereas the national court had formally only asked a question in respect of the interpretation of such act, even though it will in principle not do so.[325] The main objection against this course of action flows from Article 23 of the Statute of the

320. Case C-506/06 *Mayr* [2008] ECR I-1017. See *supra*, at II-186.
321. Case C-506/06 *Mayr* [2008] ECR I-1017.
322. On the consequences of a finding of invalidity, see K. Lenaerts, D. Arts & I. Maselis; R. Bray (Ed.), *Procedural Law of the European Union*, 2nd ed. (London: Sweet & Maxwell, 2006), 363-368.
323. Case C-334/95 *Krüger* [1997] ECR I-4517, paras 21 and 35.
324. Case 29/69 *Stauder* [1969] ECR 419.
325. Joined Cases 50 to 58/82 *Dorca Marina* [1982] ECR 3949, para. 13.

Court.[326] While the institutions are notified of the decision to refer if the validity or the interpretation of one of their acts is concerned, they may be surprised to find out that a question referred to the Court on the interpretation of the act – for which the European Parliament and the Council rarely intervene, even though it concerns their act – has denatured into a question on the validity of the act, in case the institutions generally prefer to raise a defence. This would be all the more so if the validity of norms that were not referred to in the reference decision could be raised in the course of the preliminary reference procedure.

**II-213.** First, the ECJ has nevertheless held in *Schwarze*[327] that if it flows from the context that it was the intention of the national court to actually ask a question as to the validity, it is not bound by the label suggesting a question as to the interpretation. However, if the question could also be addressed without examining the validity, even though that validity is called into question by the parties by the nature of their answers to the questions on interpretation, the Court will in principle shield behind the fact that the national court has not raised the issue of invalidity.[328]

**II-214.** Second, it has been suggested by Advocate General Kokott in *Pupino* that if the act of which interpretation is sought would be 'tainted by an irregularity whose gravity is so obvious that it cannot be tolerated'[329] as to render the act 'non-existent',[330] that the Court may decide so *motu proprio* in the context of a preliminary ruling on the interpretation. The idea behind this seems to be that any interpretation of such an act would be irrelevant,[331] which in turn touches upon the admissibility of the preliminary ruling request. The threshold for non-existence is quite high, as confirmed by the case she quotes in her support.[332] It is to be noted that the only instance where the

---

326. See in this respect also K. Lenaerts, D. Arts & I. Maselis; R. Bray (Ed.), *Procedural Law of the European Union*, 2nd ed. (London: Sweet & Maxwell, 2006), 50. See also Opinion of AG Poiares Maduro in Case C-127/07 *Arcelor Atlantique et Lorraine* [2008] ECR I-9895, para. 21.
327. Case 16/65 *Schwarze* [1965] ECR 877 at 886.
328. Case C-1/11 *Interseroh Scrap and Metals Trading* [2012] ECR I-0000, para. 46. The case concerns the question whether transporters of certain waste materials are under an obligation to disclose the full details of the company that hired them on certain documents that go to their clients, raising both issues as to the interpretation of the relevant EU legislation, but also questions on the protection of business secrets, which may or may not call into question the validity of the EU legislation at issue.
329. Opinion of AG Kokott in Case C-105/03 *Pupino* [2005] ECR I-5285, para. 48.
330. Opinion of AG Kokott in Case C-105/03 *Pupino* [2005] ECR I-5285, para. 48.
331. Opinion of AG Kokott in Case C-105/03 *Pupino* [2005] ECR I-5285, para. 52: 'Consequently, despite the uncertainties which appear at first sight to exist with regard to the legal basis of the provisions to be interpreted, it must not simply be assumed in this case that those provisions are no longer covered by the Union's legislative powers…Answering the question submitted is therefore not *pointless on the ground that the law to be interpreted is non-existent*.' (emphasis added). See also Case 62/76 *Strehl* [1977] ECR 211, where the ECJ declared of its own motion that, in light of a prior case, the provision of the Regulation which it was supposed to interpret was invalid, with the result that it could conclude at para. 18 that 'the above findings on the validity of the said regulation and decision render superfluous an answer to the questions on their interpretation'.
332. Case C-475/01 *Commission v. Greece* [2004] ECR I-8923, paras 18 et seq.

non-existence has been pleaded with success[333] concerned a combination of elements relating to both the lack of competence and the lack of respect for a series of procedural requirements and formalities and even this finding of non-existence was overturned on appeal, even though the act was still declared invalid.[334] Closer examination of the analysis which the Advocate General carries out, seems to suggest, however, that she is actually rather thinking in terms of some kind of *ordre public* analysis - albeit more deferential than in the case of a direct action. While she does not examine the validity of the Framework Decision at issue in depth, she does investigate with some degree of detail whether there is at least prima facie ground to assume that the Council was competent to adopt the relevant act.[335] It is therefore unclear how much scrutiny she actually favours and which other issues besides competence could be raised in this respect. Be that as it may, such exceptional review, if restricted to flagrant cases - even though not as extreme as in the case of *BASF*[336] - should be welcomed, even though it sits uneasy with Article 23 of the Statute.[337] In such exceptional cases, the role and status of the Court under Article 19(1) TEU to 'ensure that in the interpretation and application of this Treaty the law is observed' would be even more compromised if the Court's willingness to interpret the act at issue in answer to a preliminary reference could be mistaken for the fact the Court is tacitly willing to put up with acts that were taken in flagrant disrespect for the fundamental norms of the legal order. The question is, however, what qualifies as an exceptional case. The Framework Decision at issue in *Pupino*[338] may have been unusual in that it creates rights for the victim and interferes with national criminal procedural law, yet, it does not strike as prima facie wholly outside the ambit of the third pillar. Nevertheless it was the first time the ECJ had to interpret a Framework Decision in what was obviously a high profile case. In my view, the Court should envisage - without being under obligation to do so - to examine the prima facie validity of an act in those cases where a national court asks to interpret the provisions of a controversial piece of legislation, without it having had a prior chance to pronounce on its validity. An example may clarify the point. Imagine that Germany had not challenged[339] the validity of the first Tobacco Advertising Directive[340] and the first question about the Directive to reach the Court was about the interpretation of one of its most controversial provisions. In such a scenario, review of the validity of the Directive *motu proprio* could be appropriate.

---

333. Joined Cases T-79/89, T-84/89, T-85/89, T-86/89, T-89/89, T-91/89, T-92/89, T-94/89, T-96/89, T-98/89, T-102/89 and T-104/89 *BASF AG and Others v. Commission* [1992] ECR II-315.
334. Case C-137/92 *Commission v. BASF and Others* [1994] ECR I-2555, paras 44-54.
335. Opinion of AG Kokott in Case C-105/03 *Pupino* [2005] ECR I-5285, paras 49-51.
336. Case C-137/92 *Commission v. BASF and Others* [1994] ECR I-2555.
337. In this respect it can be observed that the author of the Framework Decision, the Council, did not submit any observation and did not participate in the hearing in Case C-105/03 *Pupino* [2005] ECR I-5285.
338. Council Framework Decision 2001/220/JHA of 15 March 2001 on the standing of victims in criminal proceedings (2001) OJ L 82/1.
339. See, however, Case C-376/98 *Germany v. European Parliament and Council* [2000] ECR I-8419.
340. Directive 98/43/EC of the European Parliament and of the Council of 6 July 1998 on the approximation of the laws, regulations and administrative provisions of the Member States relating to the advertising and sponsorship of tobacco products (1998) OJ L 213/9.

**II-215.** Finally, the ECJ has on one occasion raised of its own motion the validity of an act which was not even referred to in the order for reference. The judgment in *De Haan,*[341] should, however not be overstated, as the fact pattern was rather unique. The national court had inquired under which conditions it was possible for an innocent trader caught up in a case of fraud to obtain a remission of certain custom duties. One of these conditions the Court explains relates to the existence of a special situation. Unbeknownst to the referring national court, the Commission had responded to a request in this respect by the Dutch authorities that no such special situation existed in this case. The custom authorities must base their decision on that opinion. Against this background, the Court decided that for reasons of procedural economy:

> although the national court makes no reference to that decision, the existence and, even more so, the content of which were, because of the date on which it was adopted, probably unknown to it at the time when it made its order for reference, it is appropriate, in order to give that court an answer that will be helpful in resolving the dispute before it, to determine whether that decision was a valid one by examining the question whether the conditions for applying Article 13(1) of Regulation No 1430/79 are in fact satisfied in a case such as that pending before it[342].

Accordingly, this case can hardly be taken as a ground for deducing a broader right of the court to raise issues pertaining to the validity *motu proprio*.

**II-216.** The issue of ex officio validity control also appears in a less extreme variant. As the national court is in principle alone competent to decide which question it refers to the ECJ, the national court may also limit in its order for reference the grounds for invalidity it feels the Court should examine. Accordingly, the ECJ will in principle not allow the parties to the dispute to expand the scope of the debate by adducing new pleas.[343] Nevertheless, here too the ECJ has some margin.[344] First, it may happen that the referring court did not specify the grounds for the invalidity, or only in general terms. In that case, the ECJ will resort to the submissions of the parties[345] and the statement of reasons of the order for reference.[346] Second, the ECJ is not bound by the national concepts in interpreting EU law. Accordingly, whereas it appears that the French concept of equal treatment only requires that like cases are treated alike, the EU concept also requires that unlike cases are treated differently.[347] If a national court then inquires whether a Directive violates the principle of equal treatment, the ECJ is not

341. Case C-61/98 *De Haan Beheer* [1999] ECR I-5003.
342. Case C-61/98 *De Haan Beheer* [1999] ECR I-5003, para. 47.
343. Case C-305/05 *Ordre des barreaux francophones et germanophone* [2007] ECR I-5305, paras 17-19.
344. See in this respect also K. Lenaerts, D. Arts & I. Maselis; R. Bray (Ed.), *Procedural Law of the European Union*, 2nd ed. (London: Sweet & Maxwell, 2006), 361-362.
345. Joined Cases 103 and 145/77 *Royal Scholten Honig* [1978] ECR 2037, paras 16 and 17.
346. Case 41/72 *Getreide-Import* [1973] ECR 1, para. 2.
347. Case C-127/07 *Arcelor Atlantique et Lorraine* [2008] ECR I-9895, with Opinion of AG Poiares Maduro. See for the EU principle Case C-173/07 *Emirates Airlines* [2008] ECR I-5237, para. 39; Case C-344/04 *IATA and ELFAA* [2006] ECR I-403, para. 95; Case C-300/04 *Eman and Sevinger* [2006] ECR I-8055, para. 57; and Case C-227/04 P *Lindorfer v. Council* [2007] ECR I-6767, para. 63.

bound to restrict its analysis to see whether like cases are treated alike, but may also inquire whether unlike cases are treated differently.[348] Finally, it has been argued that there actually exists an exception to the rule in case the defect concerns the *ordre public*.[349] The ECJ has in effect accepted that it may raise of its own motion that the act which it is examining is vitiated by a breach of an essential procedural requirement.[350] Furthermore, and fully in line with the *ordre public* character of the norms at issue, it has been accepted by Advocate General Gand that a similar possibility exists in the case of lack of competence.[351] I share that opinion and would even add that this possibility should likewise be seen as an obligation in those instances where the matter may be easily ascertained on the basis of the file before the Court. However, as the factual findings in a preliminary reference procedure are in principle made by the referring court, this will in practice be limited to elements that are manifest upon simple review of the act at issue, such as a blatant absence of a statement of reasons, an impossible legal basis or the failure to consult the bodies prescribed by the legal basis put forward.

**II-217.** In conclusion, it is submitted that while the ECJ shows great deference to the referring court, which is alone competent to determine whether, and if so, which questions are to be referred to the ECJ. However, the ECJ is alone competent to determine the boundaries of its jurisdiction and assess the admissibility of the requests, if necessary *motu proprio*. Moreover in a spirit of judicial cooperation, the ECJ will reformulate, restructure and if necessary even rewrite the question in order to provide the national court with the most useful answer. I submit that this molding is inherent in its task under Article 19(1) TEU, as it is the only way the ECJ can ensure that all relevant norms are brought into the debate. Similarly, the same role explains why the ECJ may at times switch between interpretation and validity control. Legislation may be valid or invalid, depending on the interpretation given. Conversely, in extreme cases the ECJ should not arouse the impression of giving a tacit seal of approval by interpreting legislation that is at variance with the core norms of the EU legal order.

## §7.04 LIMITATIONS ON THE DEFINITIVE CHARACTER OF DECISIONS, INCLUDING RES JUDICATA

**II-218.** It has been argued above that the EU legal order may well put up with some degree of under-enforcement and even mistakes, provided that the process leading up to that outcome is not vitiated by defects such as to make that outcome pre-ordained, in particular because the parties were denied, discouraged or seduced into not raising the relevant norms of EU law. It has been argued that if such vices occur, the national court may have to compensate ex officio by raising pleas and setting aside national

348. Opinion of AG Poiares Maduro in Case C-127/07 *Arcelor Atlantique et Lorraine* [2008] ECR I-9895, paras 25-27.
349. Opinion of AG Poiares Maduro in Case C-127/07 *Arcelor Atlantique et Lorraine* [2008] ECR I-9895, para. 23.
350. Joined Cases 73/63 and 74/63 *Internationale Crediet en Handelsvereniging 'Rotterdam'* [1964] ECR 1.
351. Opinion of Advocate General Gand in Case 5/67 *Beus* [1968] ECR 83, at 108-109.

procedural rules. The *res iudiciata*, the unassailability of judgments rendered in due course, is one of the most potent procedural bars standing in the way of full enforcement of EU law, yet, as it serves a very good purpose shared by both the national and Union legal orders,[352] namely the finality of the dispute settlement and thus the stability of the legal order it should only be set aside with caution.

**II-219.** The basic assumption therefore is that EU law does not require the res judicata to be ignored. Accordingly, in *Kapferer,*[353] the ECJ accepted that a national appeals court should not reconsider whether it had jurisdiction under Regulation 44/2001[354] in a context where the interested party had failed to appeal the lower court judgment on that ground. However, whenever national law allows for the reconsideration of certain decisions, EU law requires that as a matter of equivalence such treatment is extended to decisions with an EU law component. Thus in *i-21 Germany,*[355] the ECJ accepted that telecom operators who had failed to contest the validity of a decision imposing certain charges in violation of a Directive[356] would suffer the consequences of their failure to make full use of their opportunities to do so, even if their competitor, who was more vigilant in contesting the decision, will alone see its charge set aside. Yet, to the extent that German law allows in exceptional cases for decisions to be set aside at a later time 'if to uphold the act in question would be "downright intolerable" in respect of public policy, good faith, fairness, equal treatment or manifest unlawfulness',[357] such treatment must under similar conditions be extended to decisions involving an element of EU law.

**II-220.** It is only when the national procedural system otherwise renders the enforcement of EU law excessively difficult or virtually impossible that further inroads can be made into the finality of decisions in general and the res judicata in particular as a matter of effectiveness of EU law.[358] There are actually two variants in this respect. The first one is a soft scenario in that it is actually a mixture of elements of equivalence and effectiveness. The cases in point are *Kühne & Heitz*[359] and *Kempter.*[360] The second scenario, where the effectiveness, as an expression of the public policy character of the primacy of EU law plays in full, was already discussed above in section §7.01, as it is illustrated by the case of *Lucchini.*[361]

352. Case C-221/10 P *Artedogan v. Commission* [2012] ECR I-0000, para. 86; Case C-352/09 P *ThyssenKrupp Nirosta v. Commission* [2011] ECR I-0000, para. 123.
353. Case C-234/04 *Kapferer* [2006] ECR I-2585.
354. Council Regulation (EC) No 44/2001 of 22 December 2000 on jurisdiction and the recognition and enforcement of judgments in civil and commercial matters (2001) OJ L 12/1.
355. Case C-392/04 and C-422/04 *i-21 Germany and ISIS* [2006] ECR I-8559.
356. Directive 97/13/EC of the European Parliament and of the Council of 10 April 1997 on a common framework for general authorizations and individual licences in the field of telecommunications services OJ (1997) L 117/15.
357. Case C-392/04 and C-422/04 *i-21 Germany and ISIS* [2006] ECR I-8559, para. 8.
358. Case C-40/08 *Asturcom Telecomunicaciones* [2009] ECR I-9579, paras 36-39.
359. Case C-453/00 *Kühne & Heitz* [2003] ECR I-837.
360. Case C-2/06 *Kempter* [2008] ECR I-411.
361. Case C-119/05 *Lucchini Siderurgica* [2007] ECR I-6199.

**II-221.** In *Kühne & Heitz*[362] the ECJ was confronted with the question by a Dutch court whether EC law requires a court to order the reconsideration of an administrative decision in circumstances where the initial decision had been challenged by the applicant, that challenge had been rejected without a preliminary reference on the EU law issues involved having been made, and where a later judgment of the ECJ in an unrelated case confirms the position of the applicant and thus suggests the invalidity of the initial administrative decision, prompting the applicant to request the reconsideration shortly thereafter. The bottom line is thus that a vigilant applicant had pursued all possible avenues for having the defective administrative decision overturned, but his attempts failed because of the failure of the national courts to give due weight to EU law. It is no coincidence that this situation is also not dissimilar to the circumstances that may trigger state liability for unlawful acts by the judiciary.[363] The ECJ, after considering the specifics of the Dutch legal order, including the fact that in some circumstances – though it is very much debated whether these where relevant for the case at bar[364] – Dutch law allows for such reconsideration, adding nonetheless some flavour of equivalence to the debate eventually came to the answer that a national authority must accede to a request for reconsideration,[365] provided four conditions are fulfilled[366]:

- under national law, [the administrative authority] has the power to reopen that decision;
- the administrative decision in question has become final as a result of a judgment of a national court ruling at final instance;
- that judgment is, in the light of a decision given by the Court subsequent to it, based on a misinterpretation of Community law which was adopted without a question being referred to the Court for a preliminary ruling under the third paragraph of Article 234 EC; and

362. Case C-453/00 *Kühne & Heitz* [2003] ECR I-837.
363. Compare in this respect Case C-224/01 *Köbler* [2003] ECR I-10239; Case C-173/03 *Traghetti del Mediterraneo* [2006] ECR I-5177.
364. There was in any event no obligation to review the act, see M. Taborowski, 'Joined cases C-392/04 and C-422/04, "i-21 Germany GmbH (C-392/04), Arcor AG and Co. KG (C-422/04), formerly ISIS Multimedia Net GmbH and Co. KG v. Bundesrepublik Deutschland", judgment of the Court (Grand Chamber) of 19 September 2006, not yet reported', *Common Market Law Review* (2007): 1472-1473; J. Jans & K.J. De Graaf, 'Bevoegdheid = verplichting? Enkele opmerkingen over de uitspraak van het Hof van Justitie in de zaak Kühne & Heitz"', *Nederlands Tijdschrift voor Europees Recht* (2004): 99-100; T. Barkhuysen & H.M. Griffioen, 'Formele rechtskracht en kracht van gewijsde in het licht van recente EG-jurisprudentie', *Nederlands Juristenblad* (2004): 2133-2134.
365. The 'must accede to' has a double implication. On the one hand, it is the classic approach of the ECJ towards restrictive national procedural rules: if they nonetheless offer some way of reinforcing EU law, the full potential must be used, see in this sense J. Jans & K.J. De Graaf, 'Bevoegdheid = verplichting? Enkele opmerkingen over de uitspraak van het Hof van Justitie in de zaak Kühne & Heitz"', *Nederlands Tijdschrift voor Europees Recht* (2004): 101. On the other hand, following AG Bot in this respect, it also implies that a national administration may not hide behind its discretion to reject the request the second time round, when the review shows that the original decision is in breach of EU law, see Opinion of AG Bot in Case C-2/06 *Kempter* [2008] ECR I-411, paras 51-52.
366. Case C-453/00 *Kühne & Heitz* [2003] ECR I-837, para. 28.

– the person concerned complained to the administrative body immediately after becoming aware of that decision of the Court.

**II-222.** I consider this the soft variant of a duty to reconsider decisions, as the first condition ensures that the possibility for reconsidering administrative decisions is not wholly alien to the national legal order, if not well-rooted. However, the impact of the case does go further than the concrete case of *Kühne & Heitz*[367] or the Dutch legal order.[368] In *Kempter*[369] the ECJ had the opportunity to clarify the criteria, which seemed useful as the criteria may have been overly tailored to the case at bar in *Kühne & Heitz.*[370] The national court in *Kempter* wanted to know whether the third condition means that the claimant must have actually relied on the claim of EU law and whether it follows from the fourth that there is a time limit for requesting the reconsideration. In light of what has been argued above, it would not seem overly harsh to actually require that the applicant should have effectively relied upon the EU law claim before the national law claim. Yet, the Court connects the case law in respect of the duty for national courts to raise certain pleas of EU law *motu proprio* in an interesting manner with the discussion at bar.[371] If we accept that in certain circumstances national courts may be under a duty to compensate for the inertia of the parties by raising pleas of their own motion then it cannot be excluded that even in circumstances where the applicant failed to raise the plea of EU law, the national court should have done so *motu proprio.* In such a case, the failure of the applicant to raise the plea in the initial proceeding will not prevent the third provision of *Kühne & Heitz*[372] from being fulfilled. It is to be noted, however, that the scope of this expansion of the possibilities for seeking reconsideration of an administrative decision, should be concomitant to the restrictions on the duty of national courts to raise pleas of their own motion. As was demonstrated above, this obligation rarely exists in the absence of similar obligations under national law. In this sense it seems that after *Kempter*[373] the impact of *Kühne & Heitz*[374] for the national legal order becomes even more a matter of equivalence. As to the issue of the time limits, the answer of the Court is less surprising, as it leaves the time limit entirely up to national procedural autonomy, subject to the twin exceptions of equivalence and effectiveness. Finally, it has to be observed that while *Kühne & Heitz*[375] concerns a combination of a defective administrative decision and an equally defective court decision by the highest court, the ECJ does not seem inclined to expand its doctrine to the review of judgments

367. Case C-453/00 *Kühne & Heitz* [2003] ECR I-837.
368. The Dutch courts have since been confronted on several occasions with claims based on *Kühne & Heitz*, at least of one which has been upheld. See Hoge Raad 5 October 2007, *JB* 2007/217; *AB* 2008, 1; College van Beroep voor het Bedrijfsleven 28 November 2007, *AB* 2008, 20, where the conditions were deemed not to be fulfilled, contrary to Gerechtshof Amsterdam (Douanekamer) 12 June 2007, *AB* 2008/21.
369. Case C-2/06 *Kempter* [2008] ECR I-411.
370. See in this sense K. Lenaerts & T. Corthaut, 'Rechtsvinding door het Hof van Justitie', *Ars Aequi* (2006): 589-590.
371. Case C-2/06 *Kempter* [2008] ECR I-411, para. 45.
372. Case C-453/00 *Kühne & Heitz* [2003] ECR I-837.
373. Case C-2/06 *Kempter* [2008] ECR I-411.
374. Case C-453/00 *Kühne & Heitz* [2003] ECR I-837.
375. Case C-453/00 *Kühne & Heitz* [2003] ECR I-837.

proper. In *Kapferer* the ECJ unenthusiastically dodged the issue by holding that '[e]ven assuming that the principles laid down in that judgment could be transposed into a context which, like that of the main proceedings, relates to a final judicial decision, it should be recalled that that judgment makes the obligation of the body concerned to review a final decision, which would appear to have been adopted in breach of Community law subject, in accordance with Article [4(3) TEU] to the condition, *inter alia*, that that body should be empowered under national law to reopen that decision',[376] a condition which was not fulfilled.

**II-223.** This does not imply, however, that there is never a case where EU law requires that the res judicata effect of certain national judgments be overridden in full, despite the ECJ emphasizing the importance of res judicata and the finality of judgments for both the national and Community legal order.[377] The case in point is the state-aid case of *Lucchini*[378] and was discussed above in full. For the purpose of our discussion it suffices to recall that two important elements make this case an exceptional one. On the one hand, the norms at issue were of an *ordre public* status as they affected the division of competence between the Member States and the Union in what is moreover a core domain of the economic order the Treaties seek to bring about. However, as *Kapferer*[379] shows, the importance of the norm per se may not be decisive. On the other hand, though, the res judicata of the civil judgment at issue was the key element in a devious scheme, whether purposefully designed or not, to evade the full effect of EU law. It is submitted that national courts will only need to set aside the res judicata effect of judgments, if that is the only way to answer to a direct challenge to the primacy of EU law in a case where a fundamental norm of EU law is at stake.[380] This challenge may, however, not always be as extreme as in the case of *Lucchini*,[381] or at least the incident need not to escalate in the same manner in the ordinary course of events. First, in light of the particular division of competence in the field of competition law, it would follow that the Commission is thus not bound by the res judicata effect of a national court decision, even if given in good faith.[382] Similarly, national appeals courts will have to disregard national judgments if during the procedure a contrary decision is adopted by the Commission.[383] If they doubt the validity of the Commission decision, the national

376. Case C-234/04 *Kapferer* [2006] ECR I-2585, para. 23.
377. See in this respect Case C-234/04 *Kapferer* [2006] ECR I-2585, para. 20; Case C-224/01 *Köbler* [2003] ECR I-10239, para. 38.
378. Case C-119/05 *Lucchini Siderurgica* [2007] ECR I-6199.
379. Case C-234/04 *Kapferer* [2006] ECR I-2585.
380. In this sense I do not entirely agree with P. Nebbia 'Do the rules on State aids have a life of their own? National procedural autonomy and effectiveness in the *Lucchini* case', *European Law Review* (2008): 434-435 that the difference between Case C-119/05 *Lucchini Siderurgica* [2007] ECR I-6199 and Case C-453/00 *Kühne & Heitz* [2003] ECR I-837 is 'a quantitative one, rather than a qualitative one'. There is a qualitative difference: the latter is rather an expression of the principle of equivalence, whereas the former concerns a direct challenge to the primacy of EU law.
381. Case C-119/05 *Lucchini Siderurgica* [2007] ECR I-6199.
382. Opinion of AG Geelhoed in Case C-119/05 *Lucchini Siderurgica* [2007] ECR I-6199, para. 77; C-344/98 *Masterfoods* [2000] ECR I-11369.
383. Case C-344/98 *Masterfoods* [2000] ECR I-11369; Opinion of AG Geelhoed in Case C-119/05 *Lucchini Siderurgica* [2007] ECR I-6199, para. 77.

court should refer a question as to its validity to the ECJ – provided this is not precluded because of *TWD Deggendorf.*[384] In the latter case, however, the interested party has only itself to blame, for not getting its day in court. Nevertheless, if no such direct challenge to primacy is at stake no obligation to set aside the res judicata effect of judgments.[385]

**II-224.** It follows from the above that the EU in principle respects the finality of national administrative decisions and the res judicata of national court decisions, though in instances where these decisions are contrary to EU law all tools available in the national legal order for limiting their impact must be used to the fullest as a matter of equivalence. Moreover, the public policy does have a role to play in this context, too. In extreme cases involving a systemic failure directly threatening a fundamental norm of EU law as a result of a direct challenge to the principle of primacy – itself a norm of EU *ordre public*[386] – national courts are under an obligation to set aside, if necessary of their own motion, any conflicting provision of national law including those precluding a national court from rectifying the breach of EU law for reasons of *res iudiciata.*[387]

## §7.05 NORMS FROM WHICH PRIVATE PARTIES MAY NOT DEVIATE

**II-225.** Above the attention was drawn on two related aspects of the *ordre public* of the Member States. On the one hand, it has been argued that it is increasingly difficult to draw a line between *ordre public* and other mandatory law in line with the French distinction between *ordre public de direction* and *ordre public de protection.*[388] Whereas the former seeks to protect public interests with the result that it can be invoked at all times and if necessary *motu proprio* by the national courts, the latter protects merely private interests with the result that those provisions can only be relied upon by those who are protected by it, who may thus also choose not to do so and voluntarily forego that protection. The case law concerning EU consumer protection makes it clear that EU consumer law sits uneasy with this distinction.[389] While most Member States would normally classify consumer protection rules as mandatory rules, the ECJ makes clear that their effective enforcement requires action by the national courts acting *motu proprio*. On the other hand, it was argued that cases such as *Arblade*[390] indicate that Member States may impose certain protective rules on persons having made use of their free movement rights, even though these persons may have contrary prior labour agreements. In a private international law context, these rules are referred to as *lois de police*, but the same phenomenon may also extend to purely internal situations, in

384. Case C-188/92 *TWD Textilwerke Deggendorf* [1994] ECR I-833. See in this respect Case C-119/05 *Lucchini Siderurgica* [2007] ECR I-6199, paras 53-56.
385. Case C-2/08 *Fallimento Olimpiclub* [2009] ECR I-7501, which explicitly distinguishes that case from Case C-119/05 *Lucchini Siderurgica* [2007] ECR I-6199.
386. Case 9/65 *San Michele v. High Authority* [1965] ECR 27.
387. Case C-119/05 *Lucchini Siderurgica* [2007] ECR I-6199, paras 59-63.
388. See, *supra*, at II-174.
389. See most notably Case C-429/05 *Rampion and Godard* [2007] ECR I-8017, with Opinion of AG Mengozzi; but also Case C-168/05 *Mostaza Claro* [2006] ECR I-10421.
390. Joined Cases C-369/96 and C-376/96 *Arblade* [1999] ECR I-8453.

which case they are referred to as mandatory rules or, at times rules of *ordre public.*[391] Common in all these instances is in any event that the parties may in principle not deviate from the protective norm – in any event not tacitly.

**II-226.** The EU legal order is no stranger to such norms, both in the Treaties and in secondary legislation.[392] What is unclear, however, is the force with which they impose themselves. But for one notable exception (Article 101(2) TFEU), the legal consequences of contrary agreements or behaviour is generally not self-evident from the text of the provision, and thus leaves quite some margin to the ECJ to clarify the matter. It is submitted that this is in any event not a matter for which the Court may defer to the national legal order. This is *in se* not a matter of procedural law, but determines the scope and effect of rights created by EU law. Accordingly, the uniform effective application of EU law requires that the ECJ imposes uniform criteria across the Union, even though this may thus clash with related national concepts. Again the consumer protection cases cited above[393] are cases in point.

**II-227.** The prime example in the Treaties is Article 101(2) TFEU which reads: 'Any agreements or decisions prohibited pursuant to this Article shall be automatically void.' The *ordre public* character of the core provisions of EU law competition law has already been suggested above on several occasions and this provision serves to confirm the view. Article 101(1) TFEU seeks to prohibit all forms of cartels affecting intra-Union trade and Article 101(2) TFEU seems the natural translation of that approach in the sphere of contract law: if no cartels can be formed, contrary agreements should of course not be enforceable either, not between the parties and not vis-à-vis third parties.[394] Article 101(2) TFEU is rather adamant as to its consequences. However, the consequences of most other Treaty provisions are less self-evident. In relatively old case law concerning intellectual property rights the ECJ held rather unwaveringly that:

> it is impossible in any circumstances for agreements between individuals to derogate from the mandatory provisions of the Treaty on the free movement of goods. It follows that an agreement involving a prohibition on the importation into a Member State of goods lawfully marketed in another Member State may not be relied upon or taken into consideration in order to classify the marketing of such goods as an improper or unfair commercial practice[395].

However, it seems that this approach, if at all still good law, is restricted to the particular context of the protection of intellectual property and parallel import.[396] This seems the logical consequences from the principled absence of *Drittwirkung* of the provisions on the free movement of goods. In *Sapod Audic,*[397] the ECJ recalled that

391. See, *supra*, at II-152 et seq.
392. See in this respect also C. Kessedjian, 'Public Order in European Law', *Erasmus Law Review* (2007): 31.
393. See, *supra*, at II-174 et seq.
394. Case 22/71 *Béguelin Import* [1971] ECR 949, para. 29.
395. Case 58/80 *Dansk Supermarked* [1981] ECR 181, para. 17.
396. J. Snell, *Goods and Services in EC law – A Study of the Relationship Between the Freedoms* (Oxford: OUP, 2002), 131-132.
397. Case C-159/00 *Sapod Audic* [2002] ECR I-5031.

certain restrictions to the free movement – such as the packaging requirements at issue in that case – that are the result of freely entered agreements between private parties are not caught by Article 30 TFEU. The matter is, however, increasingly relevant again in the context of the free movement of persons. While the ECJ has failed to take up the suggestion by its Advocates General to unambiguously establish the *Drittwirkung* of the free movement of persons,[398] the Court has nonetheless accepted that certain semi-private labour relations can be challenged on the basis of the provisions of the Treaty.[399] So far these judgments are the result of a clear complaint of one of the partners, usually the worker.[400] The question is whether Court should also refuse to enforce such labour agreements, even if none of the parties contest it, for instance in a dispute concerning the transfer sum for a football player whereby the parties fight over the interpretation of a contract clause on the calculation of the sum, but none of them points to the incompatibility of the contract with the free movement of persons. As the free movement rights raise in prominence – especially in the case of the free movement of persons – this may seem a logical next step. This would of course require additional alertness and sensitivity to such issues on the part of national courts in cases that may, moreover, not always be clear-cut. However, that objection could also be made in respect of the enforcement by national courts of the rules of competition law, where the drafters of the Treaty obviously decided otherwise.

**II-228.** Moreover, private parties are not at liberty when it comes to certain procedural rules laid down in the Treaties. They are precluded from organizing their own preliminary reference procedure outside the normal court structure. Accordingly, as argued above they may not themselves decide to refer questions to the ECJ,[401] nor may they create a fictitious dispute with the sole aim of circumventing the prohibition on hypothetical questions.[402] A further consequence is that arbiters are in principle precluded from asking for a preliminary ruling,[403] as this would be tantamount to allowing private parties to create their own court for these purposes.

**II-229.** The problem of the mandatory nature of EU law also extends to the secondary legislation. Some legislation is adopted with the clear intention to disrupt certain contractual relations. Prime examples are the sanctions regulations taken pursuant to

398. Case C-341/05 *Laval un Partneri* [2007] ECR I-11767, with Opinion of AG Mengozzi; Case C-438/05 *International Transport Workers' Federation* [2007] ECR I-10779, with Opinion of AG Poiares Maduro.
399. Case C-413/93 *Bosman* [1995] ECR I-4921; Case C-281/98 *Angonese* [2000] ECR I-4139. See also J. Bacquero Cruz, 'Free movement and private autonomy', *European Law Review* (1999): 603-620. The ECJ seems even willing to apply the principle of non-discrimination laid down in Article 39 TEC to fully private employers whose role in the collective regulation of the labour and remuneration conditions seems tenuous at best, see Case C-94/07 *Raccanelli* [2008] ECR I-5939, paras 41-48.
400. But see Case C-341/05 *Laval un Partneri* [2007] ECR I-11767.
401. Joined Case 31/62 and 33/62 *Milchwerke Heinz Wöhrmann & Sohn and Alfons Lütticke v. Commission* [1962] ECR 501.
402. Case 104/79 *Foglia* [1980] ECR 745.
403. Case 102/81 *Nordsee* [1982] ECR 1095. For nuances in this respect, see K. Lenaerts, D. Arts & I. Maselis; R. Bray (Ed.), *Procedural Law of the European Union*, 2nd ed. (London: Sweet & Maxwell, 2006), 41-43.

Articles 75 and 215 TFEU,[404] which may even take some ordinary law-abiding citizens off-guard.[405] More important for the current discussion is, however, the growing body of protective EU legislation in the field of consumer law, but also in the field of labour law and the like.

**II-230.** In the field of consumer law, the EU has adopted several instruments to protect consumers. The ECJ has on several occasions made clear that this protection is, however, not just a matter of protection of individual interests, but an integral part of the establishment and functioning of the internal market based on genuine competition. In order to achieve that the EU has adopted a series of mandatory rules aimed at informing the consumer and protecting him/her from imbalanced deals by prohibiting certain unfair commercial practices[406] and prohibiting certain unfair contract terms.[407] The ECJ has, moreover, in general interpreted this protection in a generous manner. Yet, as explained above,[408] its ultimate contribution in ensuring the effective enforcement of these provisions is the marshalling of the national courts which are under an obligation to raise certain of these issues of their own motion, bringing consumer protection close to a matter of public policy.

**II-231.** Slightly less visible is the similar evolution in the field of labour law. The ECJ has, however, on several occasions stressed the mandatory nature of the minimum labour standards imposed by EU law. This is illustrated by the Court's approach in respect of paid annual leave and transfer of undertakings. As to the former, the ECJ has repeatedly emphasized the mandatory nature of the rules at issue. As the Court explains in *FNV* '[h]armonization at Community level in relation to the organization of working time is intended to guarantee better protection of the safety and health of workers by ensuring that they are entitled to minimum rest periods, particularly paid annual leave, and adequate breaks'.[409] It follows that 'entitlement of every worker to paid annual leave must be regarded as a particularly important principle of Community social law *from which there can be no derogations* and the implementation of which by the competent national authorities must be confined within the limits expressly laid down by the directive itself'.[410] Therefore the ECJ rejects contractual agreements

404. See, for instance, Council Regulation (EC) No 194/2008 of 25 February 2008 renewing and strengthening the restrictive measures in respect of Burma/Myanmar and repealing Regulation (EC) No 817/2006 OJ (2008) L 66/1, which contains import and export restrictions, freezes funds and assets and precludes certain investments.
405. Case C-117/06 *Möllendorf* [2007] ECR I-8361.
406. Directive 2005/29/EC of the European Parliament and of the Council of 11 May 2005 concerning unfair business-to-consumer commercial practices in the internal market and amending Council Directive 84/450/EEC, Directives 97/7/EC, 98/27/EC and 2002/65/EC of the European Parliament and of the Council and Regulation (EC) No 2006/2004 of the European Parliament and of the Council ('Unfair Commercial Practices Directive') (2006) OJ L 149/22.
407. Council Directive 93/13/EEC of 5 April 1993 on unfair terms in consumer contracts (1993) OJ L 95/29.
408. See, *supra*, at II-174.
409. Case C-124/05 *Federatie Nederlandse Vakbeweging* [2006] ECR I-3423, para. 26.
410. Case C-124/05 *Federatie Nederlandse Vakbeweging* [2006] ECR I-3423, para. 28 (emphasis added).

whereby a worker is compensated in lieu the next year if he/she has not taken up his/her mandatory leave, as he/she may still need the actual rest for safety and health reasons.[411] It cannot be precluded that this has the effect that in some circumstances the worker may even be 'protected' against his/her will. Similarly in *Robinson-Steele*,[412] the ECJ held that the 'mandatory nature of the entitlement to annual leave'[413] and Article 7 of Directive 93/104/EC[414] preclude a setting off system for specific and general holiday which is not transparent and comprehensible. As to the rules concerning the transfer of undertakings, in *Temco*[415] the ECJ put an end to a series of moves aimed at circumventing the provisions of Directive 77/187/EEC.[416] As a result, the rules will apply to certain former employees of the transferred company notwithstanding the fact that they were laid-off a few days in advance and were thus formally no longer linked to the company by a labour contract.

**II-232.** Furthermore, it is also not a solution to hide behind foreign rules when mandatory EU law is at stake. First, due to the effects doctrine fundamental EU law, such as the rules on competition law, may have some extra-territorial consequences,[417] which may even preclude the application of a fundamental principle such as *ne bis in idem*.[418] Second, as indicated above,[419] certain protective rules cannot be circumvented by concluding an agreement governed by the laws of a third country. For instance the rules concerning the remuneration of commercial agents under the Agency Directive[420] apply even though the chosen alternative may be the law of the country of the principal.[421] Finally, the EU imposes its protection exceptionally also in the context of

411. Case C-124/05 *Federatie Nederlandse Vakbeweging* [2006] ECR I-3423, paras 31-33. This is not to say that there are not instances where such compensation in lieu is necessary, as in the case where the worker has not exercised his right to annual leave because he was on sick leave, see Joined Cases C-350/06 and C-520/06 *Schultz-Hoff* [2009] ECR I-0000, paras 53-62. Similarly, the Court has clarified in Case C-214/10 *KHS* [2011] ECR I-0000, para. 44 that 'Article 7(1) of Directive 2003/88 must be interpreted as not precluding national provisions or practices, such as collective agreements, which limit, by a carry-over period of 15 months on the expiry of which the right to paid annual leave lapses, the accumulation of entitlements to such leave of a worker who is unfit for work for several consecutive reference periods'.
412. Joined Cases C-131/04 and C-257/04 *Robinson-Steele* [2006] ECR I-2531.
413. Joined Cases C-131/04 and C-257/04 *Robinson-Steele* [2006] ECR I-2531, para. 68.
414. Council Directive 93/104/EC of 23 November 1993 concerning certain aspects of the organization of working time (1993) OJ L 307/18.
415. Case 51/00 *Temco Service Industries* [2002] ECR I-969.
416. Council Directive 77/187/EEC of 14 February 1977 on the approximation of the laws of the Member States relating to the safeguarding of employees' rights in the event of transfers of undertakings, businesses or parts of businesses (1977) OJ L 61/26
417. Case T-102/96 *Gencor v. Commission* [1999] ECR II-753. On extraterritoriality of EU law, see also J. Vanhamme, *Volkenrechtelijke Beginselen in het Europees Recht* (Groningen: Europa Law Publishing, 2001); C. Ryngaert, *Jurisdiction in international law: United States and European perspectives*, diss. KU Leuven, 2006.
418. Case C-308/04 P *SGL Carbon v. Commission* [2006] ECR I-5977; Case C-289/04 P *Sowa Denko KK v. Commission* [2006] ECR I-5859.
419. *Supra*, at II-153.
420. Council Directive 86/653/EEC of 18 December 1986 on the coordination of the laws of the Member States relating to self-employed commercial agents (1986) OJ L 382/17.
421. Case C-381/98 *Ingmar GB* [2000] ECR I-9305; for a short, but critical appraisal, see T. Kruger, 'case note under Case C-381/98 *Ingmar GB* [2000] ECR I-9305', *Columbia Journal of European Law* (2002): 85-91. For the wider implications at issue, see V. Van Den Eeckhout, 'Promoting

export. As equally discussed above[422] in *Viamex Agrar*[423] and even more clearly in the case of *Raverco*[424] certain standards as to animal health and public safety are imposed on goods intended for export.

**II-233.** Finally, considering EU law as mandatory laws may at times also help to combat certain distortions of competition that may be the result of imperfect harmonizing measures. A good example of this is offered by the implementation of Directive 2004/113[425] as to insurance contracts. Article 5(1) of the Directive provides that in principle:

> Member States shall ensure that in all new contracts concluded after 21 December 2007 at the latest, the use of sex as a factor in the calculation of premiums and benefits for the purposes of insurance and related financial services shall not result in differences in individuals' premiums and benefits.

However, as a result of Article 5(2) of the Directive, it was possible for Member States under certain conditions to 'decide before 21 December 2007 to permit proportionate differences in individuals' premiums and benefits where the use of sex is a determining factor in the assessment of risk based on relevant and accurate actuarial and statistical data'. In Belgium there seems to have been quite some upheaval over the initial decision of the Belgium government not to make use of this option, whereby it was argued *inter alia* that Belgian insurance contracts would become more expensive and thus less attractive with the result that consumers may turn to insurers from other Member States where the regime is less stringent.[426] However, it was convincingly argued that this fear should be unfounded, as by treating the Belgian legislation as a *loi de police* also foreign contracts will be subject to the Belgian legislation implementing the Directive.[427] The potentially ensuing hindrance for the free movement of services seems justifiable, as it is the result of pursuing the objective of equal treatment between men and women under the conditions laid down in the Directive.[428] The fact that the Directive also envisages that some Member States will still allow other contracts should not be taken as guaranteeing that they may be offered across the Union, as the Directive was taken on the grounds of Article 13(1) TEC which offers a legal basis to adopt legislation enhancing equal treatment, without, however, removing obstacles to trade.

---

Human Rights within the Union: The Role of European Private Law', *European Law Journal* (2008): 105-127, in particular at 114-115.

422. *Supra*, at II-17.
423. Case C-96/06 *Viamex Agrar* [2008] ECR I-1413.
424. Joined Cases C-129/05 and C-130 *Raverco* [2006] ECR I-9297.
425. Council Directive 2004/113/EC of 13 December 2004 implementing the principle of equal treatment between men and women in the access to and supply of goods and services (2004) OJ L 373/37
426. Compare Y. Thiery, 'Verzekering en de (r)evolutie van het geslachtsdiscriminatierecht', *Bulletin des Assurances – De Verzekering* no. 13 (2007): 20-52 with P. Colle, 'Kritische verzekeringsrechtelijke bedenkingen bij de wet ter bestrijding van discriminatie tussen mannen en vrouwen', *Bulletin des Assurances – De Verzekering* no. 13 (2007): 61-67.
427. See on this Y. Thiery, 'Verzekering en de (r)evolutie van het geslachtsdiscriminatierecht', *Bulletin des Assurances – De Verzekering* no. 13 (2007): 35-36.
428. See also Y. Thiery, 'Verzekering en de (r)evolutie van het geslachtsdiscriminatierecht', *Bulletin des Assurances – De Verzekering* no. 13 (2007): 36-38.

Following the landmark judgment of the Court in *Test-Achats*[429] the level-playing field will moreover be restored as the ECJ made it clear that at the end of the transitional period there can no longer be different treatment of men and women on basis of actuarial and statistical data, as preserving Article 5(2):

> which enables the Member States in question to maintain without temporal limitation an exemption from the rule of unisex premiums and benefits, works against the achievement of the objective of equal treatment between men and women, which is the purpose of Directive 2004/113, and is incompatible with Articles 21 and 23 of the Charter[430].

**II-234.** The EU legal order contains a series of mandatory norms which have their origin in the Treaties and secondary legislation. The way their mandatory nature becomes apparent is, however, not uniform. It seems that the EU does not stick to a classic distinction in continental legal systems between merely mandatory norms and rules of *ordre public*. Rather the ECJ simply seeks to ensure that the *effet utile* of the norm is maximized, and it will require such limitations on the autonomy of private parties as necessary to best achieve the object and purpose of the legislation at issue. In doing so, the ECJ nevertheless often seems to stress far more often the public interests involved, and thus seems easily inclined to impose requirements, such as the application ex officio and the protection against the will of the protected, which may traditionally be seen as linked to the *ordre public*.

## §7.06 CONCLUSION

**II-235.** In Part I of this book it was argued that the EU legal order must have its own *ordre public*, distinct from the legal order of the Member States. In this second part it was demonstrated that the EU legal order is familiar with the concept of *ordre public*, which manifests itself, however, in rather diverse forms. The EU concept of *ordre public* indeed is adapted in function of the context and in function of what level of protection needs to be achieved taking into account the underlying objectives of the EU legal order. At times this may result in seemingly conflicting outcomes. For instance, the rules on competition law are generally seen as of *ordre public*,[431] but the consequences of this are not self-evident. In the case of the recognition of arbitral awards it may require ex officio application of EU law by the national court,[432] in some instances it may result in a diminishing of the res judicata effect of national court judgments.[433] Yet, in the context of the recognition of judgments the (alleged) violation of competition rules seems no bar to enforcement,[434] and in the context of the ex officio

429. Case C-236/09 *Association Belge des Consommateurs Test-Achats* [2011] ECR I-0000.
430. Case C-236/09 *Association Belge des Consommateurs Test-Achats* [2011] ECR I-0000, para. 32.
431. Case C-126/97 *Eco Swiss China Time* [1999] ECR I-3055, para. 36; Joined Cases C-295/04 to C-298/04 *Manfredi* [2006] ECR I-6619, para. 31.
432. Case C-126/97 *Eco Swiss China Time* [1999] ECR I-3055. See, *supra*, at II-164 et seq.
433. Case C-344/98 *Masterfoods* [2000] ECR I-11369; Opinion of AG Geelhoed in Case C-119/05 *Lucchini Siderurgica* [2007] ECR I-6199, para. 77. See, *supra*, at II-223.
434. Case C-38/98 *Régie nationale des usines Renault* [2000] ECR I-2973. See, *supra*, at II-141 et seq.

application of EU law much seems to depend on the procedural context.[435] This multitude of ways in which the *ordre public* may come to the fore, may however also be its strength, as it ensures a permanent balance between private and public interest, between legal assertiveness and benevolent passivity, between revolution and finality. In short it ensures that the *ordre public* as primordial tool for protecting the fundamental rules for the protection of the political, economic, social and cultural order is versatile as a Swiss army knife, apt to play a role in the most diverse contexts.

**II-236.** The versatile nature of *ordre public* as a tool, should, however, not distract from the fundamental nature of the values that are protected by it. While, as argued above in Part I, those values may be susceptible to some evolution over time, they are sufficiently stable as to make them ascertainable with some clarity. This will be done in the next Part.

435. See, *supra*, at II-169 et seq.

# PART III
# The Values Protected by the EU *Ordre Public*

## INTRODUCTION

**III-1.** In this Part, the focus is no longer on the techniques for protecting the *ordre public*. Rather we take the analysis one step deeper to ascertain what values are effectively protected by the *ordre public*. Of course, in the previous Part, those values were already hinted at. Yet, having identified in the previous Part, the instances where *ordre public*-related phenomena occur, it is now time to make explicit the underlying fundamental values that are at the core of the EU political, economic, social and cultural order.

**III-2.** This is not self-evident. Actually, it has been argued that the content of the *ordre public* cannot be ascertained.[1] Undoubtedly, the EU *ordre public*, like the *ordre public* in the Member States is subject to evolution. Surely, the exact status of a norm or value is difficult to fathom. But having identified in the previous Part instances where the *ordre public* plays a role, an empirical basis for linking particular values to the EU *ordre public* can be identified. Admittedly, there will be some degree of subjectivity in the weight I give to certain values and the way I analyse the protected interests. However, by focusing solidly on the case law of the ECJ, there will at least be an objective yardstick against which my analysis can be assessed.

1. See in this sense W. Rady, *Les moyens d'ordre public dans le contentieux communautaire*, diss. Université Catholique de Louvain, 2005, 54-65; this scepticism seems due to the fact that this author considers that the substantive (as opposed to procedural) EU *ordre public* is so limited that he describes the notion as '*une apparence plus qu'une réalité*' (*id.*, at 65). By contrast, the first part of this book seeks precisely to rebut this presumption, with the result that in the remainder of this book an attempt is made to define, if not the full content, then at least the contours of this EU *ordre public*.

**III-3.** In order to structure the analysis, I return to the tentative definition of the EU *ordre public* given at the beginning of this book, namely the complex of norms at the very heart of a political entity (in this case the EU) expressing and protecting the basic options taken by that entity regarding its political, economic, social and cultural order. The core values at issue will then translate in four corresponding sections.

**III-4.** In the first chapter of Part III, the focus is on the most 'public' of the protected values, the protection of the political order. In that Part, attention will be given to the constitutional set up of the Union. The emphasis will be laid on how the *ordre public*, in its myriad of appearances discussed in Part II, seeks to ensure, first, that the Union decision-making process functions in the manner provided for in the Treaties, without fear or undue influence and, second, that the outcome of that process is effectively put into operation. Furthermore, attention needs to be paid to the constitutional principles that shape and animate the EU political order. In particular the role is highlighted of those principles that make the EU more than an ordinary international organization, yet far from an all-encompassing super-State. Accordingly, emphasis is laid on both the role of the Member States with their varying national identities and the European citizens, as political actors and bearer of (fundamental) rights.

**III-5.** In the second chapter, the economic order takes centre stage. As the EU was founded as a regional economic integration organization, one may expect that economic integration is at the heart of the EU *ordre public* – and I submit it is. Five fields are brought to the fore. First, the protection of the *lex moneta* of the euro will be addressed. Second, I will address the protection of the core rules of competition on the EU markets. Third, attention turns to the protection of the core of the establishment of the internal market, as 'an area without internal frontiers'.[2] This will lead to a discussion on the fundamental nature of the four freedoms. In this way, the focus increasingly shifts away from public or collective values to the protection of individual, private interests. Yet it will be argued that some of them do fit in the EU *ordre public économique*. This will be demonstrated with fourth, the position of consumer protection law and fifth, the minimum social and labour standards protected by the EU. Only by balancing these elements may the Union truly become a 'highly competitive social market economy', as neatly summarized in the post-Lisbon version of Article 3 TEU.

**III-6.** The third Chapter of Part III focuses on the societal and ethical values that define the EU order. Here there will be room to revisit some of the core values put forward as counterweight to the four freedoms. At the same time, it will reveal some of the complexities in determining what values can truly be said to be part of the EU *ordre public* and which ones are merely national interests that nonetheless seem to be condoned by the EU. In this way, this Chapter will already hint at the intricacies that need to be addressed in Parts IV and V.

**III-7.** The final section of Part III deals with perhaps the most neglected part of the EU *ordre public*, namely the cultural order. If the 'united in diversity' motto is not to remain

2. Article 26(2) TFEU.

dead letter, then cultural and linguistic diversity should not be kept below the radar of the EU *ordre public*.

**III-8.** This classification has of course its limits. Often, there will in any given situation be a mixture of values. A good example is EU citizenship. On the one hand, it protects the citizen-as-political-actor which in and of itself should justify its elevation to public policy status. On the other hand, to the extent that European citizenship is also the culmination of the creation of an area without internal frontiers, there is an economic dimension, too. Similarly, in the context of the free movement it is submitted that both the free movement right itself and some of the exceptions to it are an expression of the EU *ordre public*. It will be submitted below that this apparent paradox, is actually not unique to the EU legal order.

**III-9.** This should also guard us from seeing these protected values as absolutes. As already evident from the examples in Part II, the way these values are given protection and the manner they impose themselves may vary greatly according to the circumstances. For instance, it has been argued above that despite the importance of primacy of EU law for the EU legal order, the EU legal order may well put up with some degree of error and under-enforcement.[3] Similarly, the mere fact that a protected value is relied upon does not result in all other concerns being set aside but rather initiates a further inquiry and balancing act. Again the free movement may serve as an example. Once certain fundamental concerns are put to the fore, a double process kicks off. On the one hand, the genuineness of the concern is probed. For instance, as the Court held in *Placanica* in respect of national restrictive measures on gambling, such measures must 'reflect a concern to bring about a *genuine* diminution of gambling opportunities and to limit activities in that sector in a *consistent and systematic* manner',[4] and there are many other examples where the Court tried to smoke out any protectionist or hypocrite concerns.[5] On the other hand, even when these concerns are genuine, there may still be a further balancing test to ensure that all interests are given appropriate weight. Actually, in Part I[6] the judgment in *Omega Spielhallen*[7] was criticized for not taking this assessment sufficiently serious. By contrast, the case of *Viking*[8] discussed in Part II[9] demonstrates that this balancing may also run the risk of somewhat undermining the value that needed to be protected.

**III-10.** Accordingly, the following overview should be seen for what it is. It is an attempt to give a structured overview of the values that are protected by the EU *ordre*

3. *Supra*, at II-155 et seq.
4. Joined Cases C-338/04, C-359/04 and C-360/04 *Placanica* [2007] ECR I-1891, para. 55 (emphasis added).
5. Case C-268/99 *Jany* [2001] ECR I-8615; Case 121/85 *Conegate* [1986] ECR 1007; Case 124/81 *Commission v. UK* [1983] ECR 203; Case C-243/01 *Gambelli* [2003] ECR I-13031, para. 69; Case C-500/06 *Corporación Dermoestética* [2008] ECR I-5785, para. 39; Case C-347/09 *Dickinger and Ömer* [2011] ECR I-0000.
6. *Supra*, at I-72
7. Case C-36/02 *Omega Spielhallen* [2004] ECR I-9609.
8. Case C-438/05 *International Transport Workers' Federation* [2007] ECR I-10779.
9. *Supra*, at II-61.

*public*. However, this is not the end of the matter. Precisely because of the diverse nature and origin of these protected rights it also serves as another step in the analysis, leading to Part IV where the focus shifts to the ways in which the EU legal order channels the tensions that inevitably will arise as a result of the need to balance these separate values. However, before these tensions are addressed in a more holistic approach to the EU legal order, first the separate building blocks require closer examination, albeit confined to their importance for the EU *ordre public*. This final *caveat* is crucial, as any of the themes that will be addressed, such as competence, fundamental rights, competition or free movement all fill libraries in their own right, largely surpassing the scope of this book.

# CHAPTER 8
# Protection of the Political Order

**III-11.** The *ordre public* protects *inter alia* the core norms and values underlying the political order. In the context of the EU that implies that some rules that are crucial for the functioning of the EU institutions will have a bearing on the EU *ordre public*. The first core concern is to ensure the stability of the political order established by the Treaties and thus to let the institutions exercise their task without improper interference. Moreover, as the EU is founded by its Member States, who are still key players in its institutional set up, also their position needs to be anchored in the *ordre public*. The other aspect is somewhat less tangible, but at least as important. It concerns a set of principles and values that inspire the constitutional order of the EU, bringing the institutional order to life.

**III-12.** The institutional component of the political order will be addressed first (section §8.01). In several points, the various aspects will be discussed further. The starting point is also the bare minimum for proper decision-making: a legal and political order that is secure in that democratic decisions can be taken without fear or undue pressure. This translates in the *ordre public* character of the fight against terrorism and other issues of public security (section §8.01[A]). Second, the core institutional rules which we encountered above in the context of the *relevé d'office*, i.e., the rules on competence and the essential procedural requirements are the legal translation of the proper decision-making and thus at the core of the *ordre public* (section §8.01[B]). Third, the credibility of the EU order does not only depend on its ability to make decisions in a proper fashion, but also in its ability to carry them out in practice. Accordingly, a set of institutional rules in this field, too, may be elevated to the rank of *ordre public* norms. Attention will go primarily to two aspects. On the one hand, the focus is on a series of constitutional principles, such as primacy, direct effect and loyal cooperation that ensure the effective enforcement of EU law in the national legal orders, though other principles, in particular the national procedural autonomy make sure that even then the institutional balance between Member States and Union is not lob-sided (section §8.01[C]). On the other hand, the financial interests of the Union deserve likewise protection as a matter of *ordre public* as this ensures that sufficient means are available for translating policy into action (section §8.01[D]).

**III-13.** The constitutional values are addressed in section §8.02. These values ensure that the Union functions in respect for the international legal order, the rule of law, its Member States and ultimately its citizens. Accordingly, in a first section the *ordre public* status of key international public law is briefly recalled (section §8.02[A]). Second, building on the case law of the Court starting with *Les Verts*[1] and the expression in Article 2 TEU, the core foundations of the EU legal order in the rule of law and democracy are brought to the fore (section §8.02[B]). Third, the quest for 'unity in diversity' throughout this book takes centre stage again with a new discussion of federalism, this time with a focus on those aspects that ensure that the national identities are given their rightful place in the political setup (section §8.02[C]). Finally, attention is paid to the actor that often escapes attention in the EU political framework, but whose role is clearly in the ascendant: the citizen. It is submitted, first, that EU citizenship is per se of an *ordre public* nature, as it encapsulates the role of the citizens of the Member States in the EU political order and serves as the central connecting factor between the individual and the rights and obligations that are bestowed upon him/her by the EU legal order (section §8.02[D]). Second, attention needs then naturally to be paid to those core fundamental rights and freedoms that the EU legal order seeks to protect (section §8.02[E]).

## §8.01 PROTECTING THE INSTITUTIONAL ORDER

**III-14.** The *ordre public* seeks to protect the institutional stability necessary to ensure that the EU decision-making process can take place in due course without fear or improper interference. As already argued above, the key concern is ensuring that the volition of the decision maker is formed in the correct manner and implemented as intended. This starts of course as a bare minimum with the basic physical security of the political actors and the documents they are working with (§8.01[A]). Second this requires that the correct institutional rules in respect of competence and procedure are followed in forming that volition (§8.01[B]). Finally, once a decision is adopted at the EU level, it must also be implemented in an appropriate manner. This requires a set of constitutional principles to ensure effective application of EU law in the Member States (§8.01[C]) and the protection of the financial means to transform the policy into reality (§8.01[D]).

### [A] Security of the Institutions and the Decision-Making Process

**III-15.** As argued above,[2] the fight against terrorism is often linked to the *ordre public*. This is hardly surprising. The *ordre public* is *inter alia* concerned with the protection of

1. Case 294/83 *Parti Ecologiste 'Les Verts' v. European Parliament* [1986] ECR 1339, para. 23.
2. *Supra*, at I-16.

the political order, and terrorism is precisely aimed at influencing the political process in a highly disruptive manner. If that holds true for the Member States, it must also hold true for the EU, which is increasingly at the heart of policy making in Europe. This is reflected in the measures the EU has taken in the wake of the 9/11 attacks on the US. The EU does not only combat terrorist activities in and against its Member States, it is also explicitly concerned with terrorist action taken against international organizations[3] – of which it is of course a prime example. Since the Lisbon Treaty this may, arguably, go as far as involving military action,[4] next to a range of measures within the Area of Freedom, Security and Justice.[5]

**III-16.** Taking into account the supranational nature of the EU, it is likewise unsurprising that the same security concern is also treated as a matter of *ordre public* to the extent that not the EU itself, but its Member States are endangered. Provided that the security concerns are genuine,[6] the Court has on various occasions explicitly made use of techniques linked to the *ordre public* in order to protect both the internal and external security of the Member States. Accordingly, while the ECJ refused to accept that this could justify a limitation of effective judicial protection, the Court accepted that the UK could reserve certain combat police tasks to men in the context of the internal disturbances in Northern Ireland.[7] Similarly, the Court even accepted that the internal security could be threatened by a shortage of oil refinery capacity and could thus justify exceptions to core rules of the EU legal order on free movement of goods.[8] This link between oil security and internal security is arguably even inspiring one of the key novelties of the Lisbon Treaty.[9] But also in the context of the free movement of persons[10] and the free movement of capital[11] telling examples may be found of this protection of the internal security. The discussion above of the safeguard clause of

3. Article 1 of Council Framework Decision 2002/475/JHA of 13 June 2002 on combating terrorism [2002] OJ L 164/3: 'seriously destabilising or destroying the fundamental political, constitutional, economic or social structures of a country *or an international organisation*' (emphasis added).
4. See Article 42(7) TEU, which – if the NATO treaty (which was invoked after 9/11) after which the provision is modelled is any guidance – may well be invoked in the case of an attack by foreign terrorists. See also, even regardless of an actual attack, Article 43(1) TEU, which allows even military operations abroad to support third countries in the fight against terrorism.
5. See Articles 75, 82 and 88 TFEU. See also Article 215 TFEU. The exact delimitation between action under Article 75 TFEU and CFSP-inspired action under Article 215 TFEU is still subject to litigation, see Opinion of AG Bot of 10 January 2012 in pending Case C-130/10 *European Parliament v. Council.*
6. Unlike Case 231/83 *Cullet* [1985] ECR 305, paras 32-33, where France did not explain how (potentially) rising oil prices could result in uncontrollable disturbances of law and order. Compare also Case C-552/07 *Azelvandre* [2009] ECR I-987, where France failed to convince the ECJ that certain data concerning the use of genetically modified crops needs to be kept secret to avoid disturbances at test sites.
7. Case 222/84 *Johnston* [1985] ECR 1651.
8. Case 72/83 *Campus Oil* [1984] ECR 2727.
9. Article 122 TFEU. See also K. Inglis, 'Anticipating New Union Competences in Energy', *Maastricht Journal of European and Comparative Law* (2008): 125-134.
10. Prime example is of course the partial territorial ban on an ETA sympathizer in Case C-100/01 *Oteiza Olazabal* [2002] ECR I-10981.
11. For instance the Court has accepted that certain restrictions on the free movement of capital 'are also permitted in so far as they are designed to prevent illegal activities of comparable

Article 276 TFEU also relates to that concern.[12] As far as the external security of the Member States is concerned, it suffices to point to the special treatment – albeit within limits[13] – that is given in the Treaties to defence matters[14] and the discussion of the safeguard clause of Article 347 TFEU,[15] as demonstrated by the *Commission v. Greece*[16] case. Admittedly, to a large extent these external security concerns are nowadays addressed through the CFSP. For instance, the adoption of EU sanctions[17] and common dual goods lists[18] may render cases such as *Richardt,*[19] where Member States took unilateral export restrictions less frequent. However, this in turn may then justify the treatment of these EU norms with a similar deference.[20]

**III-17.** The security of the decision-making process also comes to the fore in a wholly different manner. Part of the decision-making process and the ensuing documents must be shielded off from the public for security reasons. This is particularly true in foreign policy and defence matters, tasks which the EU increasingly takes on. Therefore, the discussion in the Council on CFSP matters still take place behind closed doors and the general framework for access to documents in the EU provides for the necessary exceptions protecting sensitive documents.[21] The latter are, moreover, topped up by a whole set of security regulations adopted by the Council.[22] This concern for security, while essential for the functioning of the Institutions in certain sensitive domains,

---

seriousness, such as money laundering, drug trafficking or terrorism', see Joined cases C-358/93 and C-416/93 *Bordessa* [1995] I-361, paras 21-22.

12. See, *supra,* at II-97 et seq.
13. Case C-337/05 *Commission v. Italy* [2008] ECR I-2173; Case C-426/98 *Albore* [2000] ECR I-5965.
14. See in particular Article 346 TFEU.
15. See, *supra,* at II-89 et seq.
16. Case C-120/94 *Commission v. Greece* [1996] ECR I-1513.
17. See, *inter alia,* Council Common Position 2007/140/CFSP of 27 February 2007 concerning restrictive measures against Iran (2007) OJ L 61/49; Council Common Position 2004/161/CFSP of 19 February 2004 renewing restrictive measures against Zimbabwe (2004) OJ L 50/66, which are still updated regularly.
18. Though the latter are since the repeal of Council Decision 94/942/CFSP on the joint action concerning the control of exports of dual-use goods (1994) OJ L 367/8 no longer adopted under the CFSP, but directly as a matter of EC law, see Council Regulation (EC) No 1334/2000 of 22 June 2000 setting up a Community regime for the control of exports of dual-use items and technology (2000) OJ L 159/1, as amended since.
19. Case C-367/89 *Richardt* [1991] ECR I-4621, para. 22. See also Case C-83/94 *Leifer* [1995] ECR I-3231.
20. Case C-117/06 *Möllendorf* [2007] ECR I-8361; Case C-124/95 *Centro-Com* [1997] ECR I-87; Case C-84/95 *Bosphorus Hava Yollari Turizm ve Ticaret AS* [1996] ECR I-3956; See in respect of the latter also ECtHR, 30 June 2005, *Bosphorus Hava Yolları Turizm ve Ticaret Anonim Şirketi v. Ireland.* This is, however, not an excuse for ignoring the fundamental rights protection that is inherent in the EU legal order, see Joined Cases C-402/05 P and C-415/05 P *Kadi v. Council* [2008] ECR I-6351.
21. Article 4(1)(a) of Regulation (EC) No 1049/2001 of the European Parliament and of the Council of 30 May 2001 regarding public access to European Parliament, Council and Commission documents (2001) OJ L 145/43.
22. Council Decision 2001/264/EC of 19 March 2001 adopting the Council's security regulations (2001) OJ L101/1.

should however not detract from the basic value of transparency of the decision-making process in the Union.[23] Accordingly, while recognizing the legitimate concerns about sensitive documents,[24] the ECJ has systematically narrowed the scope of the exceptions to Regulation 1049/2001 in order to maximize openness in line with Article 1, second paragraph TEU and Article 15 TFEU.[25] In no event may the desire to protect certain sensitive information lead to unreasoned decisions,[26] or even worse, secret legislation.[27]

### [B] Core Rules on the Institutions and the Decision-Making Process

**III-18.** The next concern addressed through the *ordre public* is the actual functioning of the institutions. At issue is actually a double concern. On the one hand, the institutions must all be limited to their own proper competences. This is the sole way to ensure that decisions are taken by the appropriate body, which in turn offers some guarantees that the relevant actors will thus be involved and that their respective concerns are taken into consideration. This is particularly so in the context of the Union, where the various legal bases correspond to a series of decision-making procedures with varying degrees of input by the Member States and the elected representatives of the people of Europe. On the other hand, the decision-making process must be accompanied by a series of procedural guarantees to ensure in full that the actor(s) taking the final decision has been provided with all relevant input before the decision is made. As already indicated above in the context of the *relevé d'office*, both the rules on competence, vertical (between the EU and its Member States) as well as horizontal (between the EU institutions) (1) and the essential procedural requirements (2) are a matter of *ordre public*.

23. On the importance of transparency in the EU legal order, see F. Weiss & S. Steiner, 'Transparency as an element of good governance in the practice of the EU and the WTO: overview and comparison', *Fordham International Law Journal* (2007): 1544-1586.
24. Case C-266/05 P *Sison v. Council* [2007] ECR I-1233; Joined Cases C-402/05 P and C-415/05 P *Kadi v. Council* [2008] ECR I-6351. The same goes for decisions based on discredited security claims, see Case T-256/07 *People's Mojahedin Organization of Iran v. Council* [2008] ECR II-3019; Case T-284/08 *People's Mojahedin Organization of Iran v. Council* [2008] ECR II-3487, affirmed on appeal in Case C-27/09 P *French Republic v. People's Mojahedin Organization of Iran* [2011] ECR I-0000.
25. For recent examples, see Case C-506/08 P *Sweden v. Commission and MyTravel Group* [2011] ECR I-0000 (legal advice in concentration control); Joined Cases C-39/05 P and C-59/05 P *Sweden and Turco v. Council* [2008] ECR I-4723 (internal legal advice); Case C-64/05 P *Sweden v. Commission* [2007] ECR I-11389 (documents originating from Member State). See also Case T-529/09 *in 't Veld v. Commission* [2012] ECR II-0000 (legal opinion on opening treaty negotiations).
26. Case T-47/03 *Sison v. Council* [2007] ECR II-73*.
27. Case C-345/06 *Heinrich* [2009] ECR I-1659, with principled Opinion of AG Sharpston.

### [1] Competence

**III-19.** The rules on competence of the institutions are considered a matter of *ordre public,*[28] at least when it comes to the question whether the Court should raise the matter of its own motion. This should not come as a surprise. The Union has conferred competences[29] and is said to be based on the rule of law.[30] Accordingly, none of the institutions should upset the ensuing balance by transgressing the boundaries of its competence. This is all the more sensitive in the context of the EU, as any breach of the rules on the division of competence not only upsets the institutional balance, but also has wider ramifications for the relationship between the Member States and the Union.[31] Accordingly, the Court will look closely at the limits of the competence of all actors.

**III-20.** First, the Court will ensure that it does not overstep its own boundaries. As seen above, both in respect of direct actions and in the context of preliminary rulings, the Court will assess whether it is at all competent and whether it can decide the case within the limits of its jurisdiction.[32] Thus, in direct actions, the Court will examine of its own motion whether it is at all competent,[33] whether an action has been brought on time,[34] or whether the criteria for *locus standi* have been met.[35] Similarly, in preliminary reference proceedings, the Court will examine whether the question has been referred to it by a 'court or tribunal',[36] whether that court is competent to refer preliminary questions,[37] whether the question is not hypothetical[38] or contrived[39] or whether the preliminary reference procedure has been used to circumvent the mandatory time limits for other proceedings.[40]

---

28. See, *supra*, Part II, at IV, B and in particular, II-193.
29. Article 5 TEU; see also Article 5(1) TEC.
30. Article 6(1) TEU.
31. On the sensitivities of that relationship, see U. Di Fabio, 'Some Remarks on the Allocation of Competences between the European Union and its Member States', *Common Market Law Review* (2002): 1289-1301.
32. See, *supra*, at II-189 and II-208 et seq. The ECJ has indeed on a regular basis set out the breadth and the limits of its own jurisdiction, see most notably, Case 294/83 *Parti Ecologiste 'Les Verts' v. European Parliament* [1986] ECR 1339.
33. For instance, the Court has no jurisdiction to grant an injunction against the institution, see Case T-27/92 *Camera-Lampitelli v. Commission* [1993] ECR II-873, para. 25. For an even stronger case of clear lack of competence, although not raised by the CFI of its own motion, see Case T-338/02 *Segi v. Council* [2004] ECR II-1647.
34. Case T-158/08 *Comune di Ne v. Commission*, unpublished order.
35. For cases under old Article 230(4) TEC involving direct concern, see the order in Case T-341/02 *Regione Siciliana v. Commission* [2004] ECR II-2877, paras 47 et seq.; Case 297/83 *Parti écologiste 'Les Verts' v. Council* [1984] ECR 3339; for a case involving individual concern, see Case T-88/01 *SNIACE v. Commission* [2005] ECR II-1165.
36. Case C-96/04 *Standesamt Stadt Niebüll* [2006] ECR I-3561.
37. Case C-404/07 *Katz* [2008] ECR I-7607, paras 27-38; see also the Opinion of AG Kokott in that case, paras 14-21.
38. Case C-343/90 *Lourenço Dias* [1992] ECR I-4673, paras 11-23.
39. Case 104/79 *Foglia* [1980] ECR 745.
40. Case C-188/92 *TWD Textilwerke Deggendorf* [1994] ECR I-833; Case C-239/99 *Nachi Europe* [2001] ECR I-1197.

**III-21.** Second, the Court will ensure that the institutions respect the boundaries of their competence. Immediately the major direct actions brought in respect of the division of competence come to mind. Accordingly, cases have been brought in respect of the competences of the institutions, for instance as to the question whether the Council could create a sui generis quasi-legislative procedure outside the normal Treaty rules.[41] Similarly, cases have been lodged in respect of the division of competence between the pillars.[42] Finally, there have been instances where the issue was whether the Union was at all competent to take certain measures.[43] However, in those cases the *ordre public* nature of the issue at stake hardly needs to come to the fore as the actors are themselves highlighting the matter to the fullest. Yet, as seen from the examples above,[44] the Court will, if necessary also raise far more subtle issues of competence of its own motion. Accordingly, examples can be found of the Court raising *motu proprio* issues concerning the competence of the institutions *ratione materiae,*[45] *ratione personae*[46] and *ratione temporis.*[47] Moreover, even in preliminary reference proceedings the Court may intervene in order to protect the division of competence.[48]

**III-22.** Finally, as evidenced by the case of *Lucchini,*[49] the *ordre public* also concerns the division of competence between the Union and its Member States. Accordingly, whenever Member State courts assume tasks that are reserved for the EU institutions, such as assessing the compatibility of state aid with the internal market[50] or the validity of EC measures,[51] the *ordre public* is at stake. The review by the Court does not stop, however, with the Member State courts. Also the political bodies of the Member States are kept in check. Indeed, pre-emption may also prelude Member State legislators from acting, even if they are seemingly doing so to fill a gap in the protection of the public interest left by EU inaction.[52]

---

41. Case C-133/06 *Parliament v. Council* [2008] ECR I-3189.
42. Case C-176/03 *Commission v. Council* [2005] ECR I-7879; Case C-91/05 *Commission v. Council* [2008] ECR I-3651. Even after the Lisbon Treaty this debate has not fully subsided, see e.g., Opinion of AG Bot in Pending Case C-130/10 *European Parliament v. Council.*
43. Case C-376/98 *Germany v. European Parliament and Council* [2000] ECR I-8419; Case C-380/03 *Germany v. European Parliament and Council* [2006] ECR I-11573.
44. *Supra*, at II-193.
45. Case 108/81 *G.R. Amylum v. Council* [1982] ECR 3107, para. 28.
46. Case T-315/01 *Kadi v. Council and Commission* [2005] ECR II-3649, para. 61 et seq.
47. Case C-210/98 P *Salzgitter v. Commission* [2000] ECR I-5843, para. 57. See also Case 19/58 *Germany v. High Authority* [1960] ECR 225, where the ECJ examined ex officio the plea, which had not formally been raised by the applicant, whether a decision had been taken in time.
48. Opinion of AG Kokott in Case C-105/03 *Pupino* [2005] ECR I-5285, paras 48 et seq.; Opinion of Advocate General Gand in Case 5/67 *Beus* [1968] ECR 83, at 108-109.
49. Case C-119/05 *Lucchini Siderurgica* [2007] ECR I-6199.
50. Case C-119/05 *Lucchini Siderurgica* [2007] ECR I-6199.
51. Case 314/84 *Foto-Frost* [1987] ECR 4199; Case C-461/03 *Gaston Schul Douane-Expediteur* [2005] ECR I-10513.
52. Case 124/81 *Commission v. UK* [1983] ECR 203.

### [2] Essential Procedural Requirements

**III-23.** Above it was argued in detail how the essential procedural requirements are likewise considered a matter of *ordre public.*[53] Following Castillo de la Torre[54] at that, I have argued that the core concern is ensuring that the volition of the author of the act is formed in a process that duly takes into account all relevant actors and reasonable factors.[55] Accordingly, the essential procedural requirements primarily ensure full participation of all concerned. In the case of the legislative process, this may entail the need for consultation of the European Parliament[56] or the advisory bodies such as the Economic and Social Committee.[57] It may also involve the participation of a sufficient critical mass of the social partners in concluding agreements in accordance with Article 139 TEC.[58] In administrative procedures, this may take the form of making sure that the person at issue is heard in the allegations raised against him/her and given an opportunity to rebut them.[59] As a result, it should not come as a surprise that also the duty to state reasons is a crucial essential procedural requirement.[60] And the same idea of full participation of course also implies respect for the rights of defence before the Union courts, not in the least when those courts are raising issues of their own motion.[61]

**III-24.** These instances are actually the expression of deeper values underlying the EU legal order. Beneath these essential procedural requirements lay the fundamental values of a political order based on democracy, transparency and accountability.[62] The Lisbon Treaty inserts a new Article 10 TEU which emphasizes that the Union is founded on representative democracy – both within the Member States and on the EU

---

53. *Supra*, at II-194 et seq.
54. F. Castillo De La Torre, 'Le relevé d'office par la juridiction communautaire', *Cahiers de droit européen* (2005): 428.
55. See in this sense also Case 165/87 *Commission v. Council* [1988] ECR 5545, para. 20. The case also demonstrates that if the real concern is to make sure that all relevant opinions are taken on board, it will be difficult to argue the procedural defect of consulting too many bodies.
56. Case C-65/90 *Parliament v. Council* [1992] ECR I-4593, para. 16; Joined Cases C-13/92 to C-16/92 *Driessen* [1993] ECR I-4751, para. 23; and Case C-280/93 *Germany v. Council* [1994] ECR I-4973, para. 38.
57. See in this sense K. Lenaerts, D. Arts & I. Maselis; R. Bray (Ed.), *Procedural Law of the European Union*, 2nd ed. (London: Sweet & Maxwell, 2006), 296.
58. Case T-135/96 *UEAPME v. Council* [1998] ECR II-2335.
59. For more on this duty, see K. Lenaerts, D. Arts & I. Maselis; R. Bray (Ed.), *Procedural Law of the European Union*, 2nd ed. (London: Sweet & Maxwell, 2006), 297-299.
60. On the duty to state reasons, see K. Lenaerts, D. Arts & I. Maselis; R. Bray (Ed.), *Procedural Law of the European Union*, 2nd ed. (London: Sweet & Maxwell, 2006), 301-305; H.G. Schermers & D. Waelbroeck, *Judicial Protection in the European Union*, 6th ed. (Deventer: Kluwer, 2001), 382-395. For examples, see *inter alia*, Case C-350/88 *Delacre v. Commission* [1990] ECR I-395, para. 15; Case 18/57 *Nold v. High Authority* [1959] ECR 41. In the latter case, the matter was raised by the Court *motu proprio*. See on this practice, also, F. Castillo De La Torre, 'Le relevé d'office par la juridiction communautaire', *Cahiers de droit européen* (2005): 429-431. See also recently, Case C-89/08 P *Commission v. Ireland* [2009] ECR I-11245, paras 34-40.
61. Case C-89/08 P *Commission v. Ireland* [2009] ECR I-11245, paras 50-62. See also Case C-197/09 RXII *M v. European Medicines Agency* [2009] ECR I-12033.
62. On these three principles, see also K. Lenaerts & T. Corthaut, 'Judicial Review as a Contribution to the Development of European Constitutionalism', *Yearbook of European Law* (2003): 24-43.

level. Regardless, the ECJ has regularly stressed the value of the democratic representation at the EU level.[63] The principle plays a role in the background in several cases on the division of competence,[64] but also in cases concerning the workings of the European Parliament[65] or the cooperation between the social partners.[66] The transparency part comes of course to the fore in the case law on access to documents,[67] but also in the importance attached to the statement of reasons.[68] The accountability principle requires that the decisions are taken by the appropriate bodies that then can be held accountable afterwards for their actions. Key example is the CFI's finding of primacy of the political process over technocratic decision-making in *Pfizer Animal Health.*[69] In that case, the CFI held that the Council, on proposal from the Commission, was allowed to pay heed to the precautionary principle and refuse the market authorization of an animal antibiotic deemed safe, despite some doubts, by the scientific committee.[70]

### [C] Protection the Effectiveness of EU Law

**III-25.** Once EU law has been adopted in accordance with the appropriate proceedings, a new problem arises. Will it be effectively enforced in the Member States? As the credibility of the legal order depends on its effectiveness in practice, it is submitted that some core principles of EU constitutional law must also be part and parcel of the EU *ordre public*. This is all the more so because the EU legal order has been characterized as one of 'exclusive commandeering'.[71] While this seems somewhat exaggerated, fact is that – unlike the US – the EU needs to rely heavily on its Member States to put its decisions into action. Accordingly, a set of principles ensuring this cooperation needs to be considered as key for the political order. The first, primacy, has already been discussed above in some detail. The second is its right-creating counter-part, direct effect. Third is the principle of loyal cooperation. As a counterweight to too much EU

63. Case 138/79 *Roquettes Frères v. Council* [1980] ECR 3333, para. 33.
64. Case C-300/89 *Commission v. Council* [1991] ECR I-2867, para. 20. See also, more recently, Case C-91/05 *Commission v. Council* [2008] ECR I-3651.
65. Joined Cases T-222/99, T-327/99 and T-329/99 *Martinez v. European Parliament* [2001] ECR II-2823; Case 294/83 *Parti Ecologiste 'Les Verts' v. European Parliament* [1986] ECR 1339.
66. Case T-135/96 *UEAPME v. Council* [1998] ECR II-2335.
67. Joined Cases C-39/05 P and C-59/05 P *Sweden and Turco v. Council* [2008] ECR I-4723; Case C-353/99 P *Council v. Hautala* [2001] ECR I-9565.
68. Case C-266/05 P *Sison v. Council* [2007] ECR I-1233.
69. Case T-13/99 *Pfizer Animal Health v. Council* [2002] ECR II-3305.
70. See in particular Case T-13/99 *Pfizer Animal Health v. Council* [2002] ECR II-3305, para. 201 where the CFI argued: 'That finding can also be justified on grounds of principle relating to the political responsibilities and democratic legitimacy of the Commission. Whilst the Commission's exercise of public authority is rendered legitimate, pursuant to Article 155 of the EEC Treaty, by the European Parliament's political control, the members of SCAN, although they have scientific legitimacy, have neither democratic legitimacy nor political responsibilities. Scientific legitimacy is not a sufficient basis for the exercise of public authority'. See on the relation between science and the political process also more broadly, J. Corkin, 'Science, legitimacy and the law: Regulating risk regulation judiciously in the European Community', *European Law Review* (2008): 359-385.
71. E. Young, 'Protecting Member State Autonomy in the European Union: Some Cautionary Tales from American Federalism', *New York University Law Review* (2002): 1706.

overbearing on the national legal order, the fourth principle is national procedural autonomy. Finally, something needs to be said about evasion of the law.

**III-26.** First, above[72] I have already argued to what extent I consider the principle of primacy to be part and parcel of the EU *ordre public*. Three points deserve to be recalled here. First, there is a basis in the ECJ case law for my claim that primacy is part of the EU *ordre public*, as in *San Michele,*[73] the ECJ actually referred itself to the *ordre public communautaire* when reasserting the primacy of EC law in the face of a challenge by the Italian constitutional court. Second, it has been argued that the principle of primacy is not absolute. The manifold examples discussed in respect of *res iudicata,*[74] time limits,[75] or the duty of national judges to raise issues of EU law *motu proprio*[76] suggest in this respect that the EU may put up with a certain degree of under-enforcement and even error. If national procedural autonomy may limit the impact of the principle of primacy in practice, it is submitted, however, that this suggests that the principle of national procedural autonomy has a similar constitutional rank. If this is true then it seems to follow that if primacy can be elevated to the rank of *ordre public*, the national procedural autonomy may follow suit.[77] Third, whenever the status of EU law is directly challenged, however, the principle of primacy shows its major disruptive force to reassert the hierarchy within the EU legal order without much regard for the recalcitrant Member States legal order. Some of the key examples come from the Italian legal order, with the seminal case of *Costa*[78] where the Court had to respond to a suggestion that Italian courts could ignore the ECJ rulings, the curtailing of the constitutional position of the Italian constitutional court in *San Michele*[79] and *Simmenthal*[80] and the case of *Lucchini,*[81] already discussed *in extenso* above.[82] However, one may also think of cases relating to interim relief, such as *Factortame*[83] and *Unibet*[84] or the triple action against obstinate Member State top courts failing to make preliminary references[85]: state liability,[86] reconsideration of administrative acts that were

72. See, *supra*, at II-155 et seq.
73. Case 9/65 *San Michele v. High Authority* [1965] ECR 27.
74. Case C-234/04 *Kapferer* [2006] ECR I-2585.
75. Case C-126/97 *Eco Swiss China Time* [1999] ECR I-3055.
76. Joined Cases C-222/05, C-223/05, C-224/05 and C-225/05 *Van der Weerd* [2007] ECR I-4233.
77. There are, moreover, further grounds for defending the EU *ordre public* status of the principle of national procedural autonomy, see *infra*, at III-48.
78. Case 6/64 *Costa* [1964] ECR 585.
79. Case 9/65 *San Michele v. High Authority* [1965] ECR 27.
80. Case 106/77 *Simmenthal* [1978] ECR 629. Compare also more recently, in respect of the Constitutional Court in France, Joined Cases C-188/10 and C-189/1 *Melki* [2010] ECR I-5667; or the Bulgarian Supreme Administrative Court, Case C-173/09 *Elchinov* [2010] ECR I-0000.
81. Case C-119/05 *Lucchini Siderurgica* [2007] ECR I-6199.
82. *Supra*, at II-159 et seq.
83. Case C-213/89 *Factortame* [1990] ECR I-2433.
84. Case C-432/05 *Unibet* [2007] ECR I-2271.
85. See in this sense, anticipating Case C-453/00 *Kühne & Heitz* [2003] ECR I-837 and Case C-129/00 *Commission v. Italy* [2003] ECR I-14637, E. Steyger 'De gevolgen van de aansprakelijkheid van de Staat voor rechterlijke schendingen van het EG-recht', *Nederlands Tijdschrift voor Europees Recht* (2004): 21-22.
86. Case C-224/01 *Köbler* [2003] ECR I-10239; Case C-173/03 *Traghetti del Mediterraneo* [2006] ECR I-5177.

previously upheld contrary to EU law[87] and infringement actions.[88] In all these cases, the potential under-enforcement of EU law was due to systemic failures rather than incidental errors that could be rectified by vigilant parties. Put differently, the primacy of EU law was directly challenged by the national legal order and reasserted in full force by the ECJ.

**III-27.** The second constitutional principle that helps to define the constitutional order of the EU, is the related principle of direct effect. In the abstract, this principle, too, is part and parcel of the EU *ordre public* and this for at least two reasons. On the one hand, as the ECJ explained in *Van Gend & Loos*[89] the principle corresponds to an essential feature of the EU legal order, distinguishing it in part from classic international law. As the famous passage goes:

> the conclusion to be drawn from this is that the Community constitutes a new legal order of international law for the benefit of which the States have limited their sovereign rights, albeit within limited fields, and the *subjects* of which comprise not only Member States but *also their nationals*. Independently of the legislation of its Member States, Community law therefore not only imposes obligations on individuals but is also *intended to confer upon them rights which become part of their legal heritage*. These rights arise not only where they are expressly granted by the Treaty, but also by reason of obligations which the Treaty imposes in a clearly defined way upon individuals as well as upon the Member States and upon the institutions of the Community[90].

It is precisely the conferral of rights on individuals, through the direct effect, that characterizes EU law, which per se justifies the elevation of the principle to a matter of public policy. On the other hand, I have argued elsewhere, as a co-author, that direct effect proper is a very specific and refined expression of the primacy of EU law, whereby the national conflicting provision is not only set aside, but whereby the ensuing gap is filled by an EU norm defining a particular obligation to be performed by a particular debtor to the benefit of a particular creditor.[91] As an elaborate derivate of the primacy of EU law, direct effect, therefore, shares the *ordre public* status of the primacy principle.

**III-28.** Precisely because of the fact that the principle of direct effect is interwoven with the principle of primacy of EU law, it is difficult to identify examples *in concreto* where the *ordre public* character of direct effect comes to the fore without being overshadowed by its primacy component. The best example is probably *Van Gend & Loos*[92] itself, where the ECJ had to ascertain for the very first time the possibility of individuals to rely on certain provisions of the Treaty, over the objections of all Member States. In doing so, the ECJ redefined the constitutional order, and thus categorically excluded

87. Case C-453/00 *Kühne & Heitz* [2003] ECR I-837; Case C-2/06 *Kempter* [2008] ECR I-411.
88. Case C-129/00 *Commission v. Italy* [2003] ECR I-14637.
89. Case 26/62 *Van Gend & Loos* [1963] ECR 1.
90. Case 26/62 *Van Gend & Loos* [1963] ECR 1 (emphasis added).
91. See in this sense K. Lenaerts & T. Corthaut, 'Towards an internally consistent doctrine on invoking norms of EU law' in *The Coherence of EU Law – The Search for Unity in Divergent Concepts*, ed. S. Prechal & B. Van Roermund (Oxford: OUP, 2008), 496-515.
92. Case 26/62 *Van Gend & Loos* [1963] ECR 1.

any attempt by the national legal order to undermine those individual rights. The Court made it later also clear that these rights may moreover also flow from the secondary legislation.[93] However, it is clear that any attempt to deny individuals the right to enforce the rights that EU law confers upon them, is impliedly also a direct challenge to the primacy of EU law per se. Yet, occasionally the rights language typical for direct effect comes to the fore in *ordre public* contexts. Most of these examples, such as in the case of consumer protection[94] and certain minimum labour standards,[95] however are also of an *ordre public* character because of the content of the norm rather than that the rights issue per se is in dispute.[96] The same could be said, given the underlying public health concern, in respect of the attempts by the ECJ to carve rights out of seemingly abstract directives aimed at combating pollution.[97] Maybe, the recent case law of the ECJ in respect of triangular relationships could be read as a way of ensuring that the vertical direct effect of directives is not easily circumvented, as it seeks to prevent that governmental bodies may hide behind private third parties.[98]

**III-29.** The third principle may well be considered the work horse of EU law. The principle of loyal, or as Article 4(3) TEU now has it, sincere cooperation is in a sense the jack-of-all-trades of EU law translating the abstract undertakings by the Member States under the Treaties into concrete action or discrete abstention in the interest of the achievement of the objectives of the Union, across the pillars.[99] Accordingly, it is this principle, together with the prohibition of unequal treatment on grounds of nationality laid down in Article 18 TFEU, which is put forward as a Treaty basis for the primacy of EU law.[100] It is through the principle of loyal cooperation that the duty of interpretation in conformity with EU law is put into operation.[101] Moreover, the most far-reaching brake on the national procedural autonomy, the principle of effectiveness, is traditionally linked to the duty of loyal cooperation.[102] In this way the principle also forms the

93. Case 14/68 *Wilhelm* [1969] ECR 1.
94. Case C-168/05 *Mostaza Claro* [2006] ECR I-10421, paras 27-28; Joined Case C-240/98 to C-244/98 *Océano Grupo Editorial* [2000] ECR I-4941, paras 26-28. The problem of the absence of direct effect of directives is of course circumvented if there is implementing legislation in place, but the net result is the same, namely the conferral of rights on the individual, see Case C-429/05 *Rampion and Godard* [2007] ECR I-8017.
95. Case C-124/05 *Federatie Nederlandse Vakbeweging* [2006] ECR I-3423.
96. See, *infra*, at III-83 et seq.
97. Case C-237/07 *Janecek* [2008] ECR I-6221, para. 38 (air quality); Case C-361/88 *Germany v. Commission* [1991] ECR I-2567, para. 16; Case C-59/89 *Commission v. Germany* [1991] ECR I-2607, para. 19; Case C-58/89 *Commission v. Germany* [1991] ECR I-4983, para. 14 (water quality).
98. See Joined Cases C-152/07 to C-154/07 *Arcor* [2008] ECR I-5959; Case C-201/02 *Wells* [2004] ECR I-723. However, these case may of course also be explained purely on the basis of primacy, see K. Lenaerts & T. Corthaut, 'Towards an internally consistent doctrine on invoking norms of EU law' in *The Coherence of EU Law – The Search for Unity in Divergent Concepts*, ed. S. Prechal & B. Van Roermund (Oxford: OUP, 2008), 496-515.
99. Case C-105/03 *Pupino* [2005] ECR I-5285, with Opinion of AG Kokott.
100. Case 6/64 *Costa* [1964] ECR 585.
101. Case C-106/89 *Marleasing* [1990] I-4135, para. 8; Joined Cases C-397/01 to C-403/01 *Pfeiffer* [2004] ECR I-8835, paras 110-113. See also in respect of framework decisions, Case C-105/03 *Pupino* [2005] ECR I-5285.
102. Case 45/76 *Comet* [1976] ECR 2043, para. 12, where the Court moreover links the duty of the national court to provide effective judicial protection to the direct effect of the Treaties.

basis of the effective judicial protection within the Union.[103] Finally, the principle is relied upon to fill the gaps in the constitutional fabric that may threaten its smooth operation, if necessary even by imposing obligations, not only on the Member States but also on the institutions.[104] The ECJ does not rely on some abstract principle of 'federalism' – the word alone would probably ruffle quite some feathers – but through the principle of loyal cooperation at least one very important aspect of the relationship between the EU and its Member States is defined, making it an essential aspect of the EU constitutional legal order and thus worthy of protection as a matter of *ordre public*. However, as will be argued below,[105] loyal cooperation is by no means the only fault line defining that relationship. Yet, the presence of other principles that serve as a counter-balance for the unifying force of the principle of loyal cooperation does not undermine its status as a matter of *ordre public*. Rather it is an argument on the basis of which one can assume that any such counterbalancing principle must also have a similar constitutional rank.

**III-30.** The fourth principle is already one of these counterbalancing principles. While one could well argue that the principle of national procedural autonomy is but an expression of the constitutional background principle of subsidiarity, to which attention will be paid below, there may be something to be said in its favour from an effectiveness perspective as well. As the drafters of the Treaties have chosen a model whereby virtually all EU decisions are directly or indirectly mediated by or combined with elements of national law in order to become fully operational, it seems arguable that national procedural autonomy simply represents the most efficient way to deal with this permanent legal puzzle and ensure effective enforcement of EU law.[106] It may well be that in the grand scheme of things more often than not the most natural and balanced procedural solution is found if Member States are allowed – but at the same time, as a matter of equivalence, in a sense also obligated – to make use of their normal procedural tools to deal with claims of EU law. Seen from this perspective, my argument, elaborated above,[107] that there is no such a thing as a procedural rule of reason actually makes constitutional sense, as there is an implicit assumption in the EU constitutional order that the Member States are likely to have it right.[108] At the same

103. Case C-432/05 *Unibet* [2007] ECR I-2271, para. 38; compare also Case 14/83 *von Colson and Kamann* [1984] ECR 1891, paras 26-28.
104. Case C-2/88 Imm. *Zwartveld* [1990] ECR I-4405.
105. *Infra*, at III-46 et seq.
106. See in this sense, impliedly, Case C-432/05 *Unibet* [2007] ECR I-2271, para 40 ('Although the EC Treaty has made it possible in a number of instances for private persons to bring a direct action, where appropriate, before the Community Court, it was not *intended* to create new remedies in the national courts to ensure the observance of Community law other than those already laid down by national law') (emphasis added), itself based on Case 158/80 *Rewe* [1981] ECR 1805, para. 44.
107. *Supra*, at II-183.
108. In a sense this presumption is also reflected in the Treaties, most notably in Article 4(2) TEU: 'The Union shall respect the equality of Member States before the Treaties as well as their national identities, inherent in their fundamental structures, political and constitutional, inclusive of regional and local self-government. It shall respect their essential State functions, including ensuring the territorial integrity of the State, maintaining law and order and safeguarding national security. In particular, national security remains the sole responsibility of

time, elevating national procedural autonomy to a principle that is part and parcel of the EU *ordre public* also explains why the national procedural autonomy may so often work as a cushion against the blunt force of that other *ordre public* principle, namely primacy. Time limits,[109] rules on recovery,[110] or the competence of the courts,[111] all may result in under-enforcement of EU law, but sustained on grounds of national procedural autonomy. Finally, while I reject a real balancing test in respect of the national procedural autonomy, it also is clear that the clash between primacy and national procedural autonomy cannot always be won by the latter. If it turns out in practice that there is a systemic failure in a Member State that belies the background assumption that Member States are likely to have it right, then it is inevitable that the national procedural rules will have to yield to restore the constitutional order. The cases in point are again *Peterbroeck*[112] and *Eco Swiss.*[113] As demonstrated by the latter the ECJ is more than willing to put up with very short-time limits, in the assumption that they fit in a broader system that also serves national claims and probably fits in with a series of other procedural rules of the legal order. Hence the classic reminder that a procedural rule must be considered against the background of the whole of the national legal order.[114] However, if that analysis demonstrates that there is something systematically wrong then the national procedural rule has to go – no matter how well it is otherwise ingrained in the national legal order. A good example is the *Impact*[115] case where the ECJ indicated that while Member States are in principle at liberty to designate the appropriate court to hear a particular action, there may nonetheless be circumstances under which a Member State cannot set up a specialist labour court to deal with cases under Irish law – including implemented directives – and reserve labour cases involving unimplemented directives for a general court with procedural rules – while undoubtedly fair and adequate, and very much ingrained in the Irish legal system – that are less tailored to deal with industrial relations.

**III-31.** In the previous paragraphs, I have set out a series of constitutional principles that all, in their own ways, ensure the effectiveness of the EU legal order. As a final issue I wish to add, though not really a constitutional principle, a point on combating evasion of the law. The effectiveness and credibility of the EU legal order also requires it to act against attempts to abuse the rights created by that legal order. On the one hand, as argued above, the Member States are sanctioned for inconsistency – at times even hypocrisy – in relying on exceptions relating to the public policy. Accordingly, in

---

each Member State'. This idea is also echoed, or perhaps guaranteed, by the assumption made in Article 2 TEU (and enforced through Article 7 and 49 TEU) of the communality of the fundamental values of the Union to its Member States.

109. Case C-30/02 *Recheio* [2004] ECR I-6051; Case C-126/97 *Eco Swiss China Time* [1999] ECR I-3055.
110. Case 199/82 *San Giorgio* [1983] ECR 3595.
111. Case C-268/06 *Impact* [2008] ECR I-2483; Case C-234/04 *Kapferer* [2006] ECR I-2585.
112. Case C-312/93 *Peterbroeck* [1995] ECR I-4599.
113. Case C-126/97 *Eco Swiss China Time* [1999] ECR I-3055.
114. Joined Cases C-222/05, C-223/05, C-224/05 and C-225/05 *Van der Weerd* [2007] ECR I-4233, para. 33; Case C-312/93 *Peterbroeck* [1995] ECR I-4599, para. 14; Joined Cases C-430/93 and C-431/93 *Van Schijndel and Van Veen* [1995] ECR I-4705, para. 19.
115. Case C-268/06 *Impact* [2008] ECR I-2483.

*Conegate*[116] the UK could not prohibit the import of inflatable dolls, if the sale of these dolls is otherwise lawful. Similarly, the Netherlands[117] and Belgium[118] were precluded from acting against foreign prostitutes as both countries condone prostitution in practice. On the other hand, the credibility of the EU legal order also implies that individuals may be rebuffed for abusing the free movement rights in order to circumvent certain key obligations. As the Court has explained, 'nationals of a Member State cannot attempt, under cover of the rights created by the Treaty, improperly to circumvent their national legislation. They must not improperly or fraudulently take advantage of provisions of Community law'.[119] Accordingly, the ECJ accepts for instance that Member States impose minimum wages on posted workers[120] – a possibility which has since been elaborated on in a Directive,[121] the application of which is not uncontroversial.[122] The ECJ has also acted against so-called U-turns whereby a mother company establishes a daughter company outside its home State but which only offer services in the home State of the mother, thereby circumventing certain mandatory requirements in the home State of the mother company.[123] However, the *Centros*[124] judgment makes clear that the ECJ is rather reluctant to accept such restrictions. Similarly, the ECJ has recently retracted from its judgment in *Akrich*,[125] where it had stated that third-country nationals who want to make use of their secondary free movement rights as a family member of an EU national need prior lawful residence. Inspired by the right to family life as protected by Article 8 ECHR the ECJ no longer accepts this requirement,[126] though this was the main tool for the Member States – who are otherwise still solely competent to decide on the first entry into the Union of a third-country national – to keep unwanted third-country nationals out. The ECJ does still accept that Member States may act against marriages of convenience or other forms of fraud, such as forged papers establishing kinship in the

116. Case 121/85 *Conegate* [1986] ECR 1007. The Court thus returned on Case 34/79 *Henn and Darby* [1979] ECR 3795. See also, *supra*, at II-23 and II-35.
117. Case C-268/99 *Jany* [2001] ECR I-8615.
118. Joined Cases 115/81 and 116/81 *Adoui and Cornuaille* [1982] ECR 1665
119. Case C-196/04 *Cadbury Schweppes* [2006] ECR I-7995, para. 35; see also Case 115/78 *Knoors* [1979] ECR 399, para. 25; Case C-61/89 *Bouchoucha* [1990] ECR I-3551, para. 14; and Case C-212/97 *Centros* [1999] ECR I-1459, para. 24.
120. Joined Cases C-369/96 and C-376/96 *Arblade* [1999] ECR I-8453.
121. Directive 96/71/EC of the European Parliament and of the Council of 16 December 1996 concerning the posting of workers in the framework of the provision of services (1997) OJ L 18/1.
122. Case C-341/05 *Laval un Partneri* [2007] ECR I-11767; Case C-319/06 *Commission v. Luxemburg* [2008] ECR I-4323; Case C-346/06 *Rüffert* [2008] ECR I-0000. See also *supra*, at II-72 et seq.
123. Case C-148/91 *Vereniging Veronica Omroep Organisatie* [1993] ECR I-487. Compare also Case C-311/06 *Consiglio Nazionale degli Ingegneri* [2009] ECR I-1989, where the ECJ denies the homologation under Council Directive 89/48/EEC of 21 December 1988 on a general system for the recognition of higher-education diplomas awarded on completion of professional education and training of at least three years' duration (1989) OJ L 19/16 of a certificate delivered by a Spanish institute on the basis of an Italian education and without requiring any further education in Spain, which the holder invoked to require recognition as engineer in Italy without having to do the Italian state exam.
124. Case C-212/97 *Centros* [1999] ECR I-1459.
125. Case C-109/01 *Akrich* [2003] ECR I-9607, paras 50-51.
126. Case C-127/08 *Metock* [2008] ECR I-6241, para. 57.

form of an individual assessment under Chapter VI of Directive 2004/38.[127] Yet, given the difficulties the Member States may have in proving this abuse, a powerful tool for enforcing their immigration laws is now somewhat dented. In *Petrosian,*[128] by contrast, the ECJ ensured that asylum seekers may not abuse the high level of judicial protection offered by some Member States who suspend the execution of decisions to transfer them to another Member State pending appeals, by creating a *fait accompli* if the length of the appeals proceedings exceeds the six-month time limit laid down in the relevant legislation for organizing their transfer.

### [D] Protection of the Financial Interests of the Union

**III-32.** As Advocate General Bot rightly noticed in *Heemskerk and Schaap*, the protection of the financial interests is a matter of *ordre public.*[129] In my view this, too, is a component of the protection of the political order, as it basically ensures that the legitimate government also has the financial means to put its policies into practice. Actually, in *Heemskerk and Schaap* the matter was not clear-cut, as it was beyond doubt that the Dutch authorities would have had to repay the illegal aid to the Commission, even when they would fail to recover the subsidies from the exporters involved. However, as even in such cases there still is a transaction cost for the Union in monitoring compliance and seeking recovery, it is submitted that even cases where the Member States cover the financial losses, are a matter of EU *ordre public*. Moreover, to the extent that personnel of the Union were to be involved in certain financial irregularities, the political order seems threatened in a second manner as the credibility and legitimacy of the EU authorities are at stake, especially when high-ranking figures are involved.[130]

**III-33.** The European Union thus takes this protection quite seriously. First, it has strict budgetary procedures.[131] Second, there is a budgetary watchdog in the form of the Court of Auditors.[132] Both should ensure transparency and legitimacy to the budget, but do not prevent fraud as such. In order to tackle this risk, Article 325 TFEU envisages the adoption of a series of measures to counter fraud and other illegal activities affecting the Union finances, which has most notably resulted in a general framework for checks and penalties laid down in Regulation No 2988/95.[133] Furthermore, the (criminal) legal system of the Member States is marshalled in, which then should also

127. Case C-127/08 *Metock* [2008] ECR I-6241, para. 74. On these exceptions, see *supra*, at II-31 et seq.
128. Case C-19/08 *Petrosian* [2009] ECR I-495.
129. Opinion of AG Bot in Case C-455/06 *Heemskerk and Schaap* [2008] ECR I-8763, paras 117-119.
130. See, most notably, Case C-432/04 *Commission v. Cresson* [2006] ECR I-6387. The nature of the breach of the legal order, justifies that regardless of any criminal prosecution in the Member States, the Union legal order may itself try its top officials, if only for symbolic reasons, to restore faith in the political order and deter others.
131. Articles 311-325 TFEU.
132. Articles 285-287 TFEU.
133. Council Regulation (EC, Euratom) No 2988/95 of 18 December 1995 on the protection of the European Communities financial interests (1995) OJ L 312/1.

be given full cooperation from the EU institutions.[134] Following the environmental crimes case, speculation is mounting in this respect, as to whether the EU – through the third or even first pillar – could seek to harmonize these Member State criminal laws as to better protect the financial interests of the Union.[135] Yet, eventually also a proper own investigative service, OLAF, was set up within the Commission,[136] with which all EU institutions cooperate.[137] As indicated above, the Lisbon Treaty envisages taking this one step further, as the primary task for a possible future European Public Prosecutor would again be combating fraud against the Union.[138]

**III-34.** As the EU is largely funded by contributions from its Member States, one could wonder whether the EU has not also an interest in protecting the financial interests of the Member States. The answer to this is two-fold, however. On the one hand, the ECJ has made clear that Member States may not rely on purely economic interests to escape their obligations under the Treaties. The fact that a particular EU measure, or the setting aside of a national one, may be expensive is per se not an excuse.[139] At most the ECJ may consider, if and when a Member State puts forward a convincing case of threatening financial hardship in the course of the first Court proceedings where the problem is at issue, to limit the impact of its judgment in respect of past events.[140] But the case law demonstrates great reluctance on the part of the Court to do so.[141] After all, the possibility of state liability is precisely one of the tools to ensure effective enforcement of EU law as it requires that Member States make reparation for loss and damage caused to individuals as a result of breaches of Community law.[142] On the other hand, the ECJ has – particularly in the context of the four freedoms – occasionally accepted that the Member States may take proportionate measures in order to combat tax evasion through 'wholly artificial arrangements',[143] to ensure the coherence of the

134. Case C-2/88 Imm. *Zwartveld* [1990] ECR I-4405.
135. On this, see I. Fromm, ''Ius puniendi:' The Right of the Institutions of the EC to Protect the Financial Interests of the EC from Fraud (Art. 280 paragraph 4 EC Treaty)?', *European Journal of Crime, Criminal Law and Criminal Justice* (2008): 125-142; see also T. Seibert, 'The European Fight against Fraud – The Community's Competence to Enact Criminal Laws and Its Power to Approximate National Criminal Law by Directives', *European Journal of Crime, Criminal Law and Criminal Justice* (2008): 95-98. For more on EU criminal law, see, *supra*, at II-115 et seq.
136. Regulation (EC) No 1073/1999 of the European Parliament and of the Council of 25 May 1999 concerning investigations conducted by the European Anti-Fraud Office (OLAF) (1999) OJ L 136/1.
137. Interinstitutional Agreement of 25 May 1999 between the European Parliament, the Council of the European Union and the Commission of the European Communities concerning internal investigations by the European Anti-fraud Office (OLAF) (1999) OJ L 136/15. The ECB seemed far more reluctant, but had to reconsider after Case C-11/00 *Commission v. ECB* [2003] ECR I-7147.
138. Article 86 TFEU. See also, *supra*, at II-126.
139. Case C-50/99 *Podesta* [2000] ECR I-4039, para. 35.
140. Case C-292/04 *Meilicke* [2007] ECR I-1835; Case C-426/07 *Krawczyński* [2008] ECR I-6021.
141. Case C-292/04 *Meilicke* [2007] ECR I-1835; Case C-426/07 *Krawczyński* [2008] ECR I-6021; Case C-267/06 *Tadao Maruko* [2008] ECR I-1757.
142. For an example linking the issue of state liability with the potentially disruptive effects for the public budget of complying with a prior ECJ ruling, see Joined Cases C-231/06 to C-233/06 *Jonkman* [2007] ECR I-5149.
143. Case C-196/04 *Cadbury Schweppes* [2006] ECR I-7995, para. 72.

tax system[144] and in order to ensure the financial viability of the social security systems.[145] In these cases, the financial interests actually hide deeper concerns about basic solidarity and public health within a Member State, so that the protected interest is more than a merely private interest.[146] By contrast, if the Member State potentially has an alternative route to obtain similar tax income without having to restrict a fundamental freedom in a similar manner, the ECJ will have little difficulty in striking down the measure.[147]

**III-35.** Finally, the *ordre public* nature of the protection of the financial interests of the Union does not mean that the Union needs to be reimbursed at all cost.[148] While customs duties and a portion of the VAT receipts are paid into the EU budget, the ECJ has in respect of both accepted that occasionally the Union must take its losses. Accordingly, while the ECJ takes VAT fraud very seriously,[149] it accepts that occasionally bona fide third parties may get implicated in a VAT carrousel, therefore deserving some leniency.[150] However, as several customs duty cases[151] demonstrate, the *ordre public* nature of the protection of the financial interests of the Union implies that the ECJ is rather restrictive in accepting that a trader could be excused for certain irregularities, though it appears that occasionally the GC is too harsh at that.[152]

## §8.02 CONSTITUTIONAL VALUES AT THE HEART OF THE EU POLITICAL ORDER

**III-36.** In the foregoing part, the focus was laid strongly on the effectiveness of the EU legal order, as a way to ensure that EU policy making is swift and legitimate and its outcome put into operation – often by the Member States – smoothly. However, the EU political order is defined by much more than effectiveness. In the following paragraphs, a series of other values that shape the EU legal and political order are brought to the

144. Case C-204/90 *Bachmann* [1992] ECR I-249, paras 28-33; Case C-300/90 *Commission v. Belgium* [1992] ECR I-305, para. 21.
145. Case C-158/96 *Kohll* [1998] ECR I-1931, para. 41; Case C-372/04 *Watts* [2006] ECR I-4325, para. 103. See also Case C-157/99 *Smits and Peerbooms* [2001] ECR I-5473, para. 72 and Case C-385/99 *Müller-Fauré and van Riet* [2003] ECR I-4509, para. 73.
146. See in this respect J. Snell, 'Economic Aims as Justification for Restrictions on Free Movement' in *Rule of Reason – Rethinking another Classic of European Legal Doctrine*, ed. A. Schrauwen (Groningen: Europa Law Publishing, 2005), 37-56.
147. Case C-292/04 *Meilicke* [2007] ECR I-1835, paras 28-30.
148. It has, however, be argued that in order to enhance the chances of correct reimbursement of the Union, there may also be a special duty of care on the recipient of certain EU funds requiring the recipient to signal itself that a mistake has been made even though it was not itself responsible for the error, see in this sense Opinion of AG Sharpston in Case C-281/07 *Bayerische Hypotheken- und Vereinsbank* [2009] ECR I-91, para. 35.
149. Case C-255/02 *Halifax* [2006] ECR I-1609
150. Joined Cases C-354/03, C-355/03 and C-484/03 *Optigen* [2006] ECR I-483; Joined Cases C-439/04 and C-440/04 *Kittel* [2006] ECR I-6161.
151. Case T-332/02 *Nordspedizionieri di Danielis Livio v. Commission* [2004] ECR II-4405, confirmed on appeal in Case C-62/05 P *Nordspedizionieri di Danielis Livio v. Commission* [2007] ECR I-8647; see also Case C-526/06 *Road Air Logistics* [2007] ECR I-11337.
152. Compare Case C-204/07 P *C.A.S. v. Commission* [2008] ECR I-6135 with the judgment below in Case T-23/03 *C.A.S. v. Commission* [2007] ECR II-289.

attention, and again it is submitted that those values, too, are connected to the EU *ordre public*. First, as an international organization the core values of international law are still part and parcel of the EU legal order (§8.02[A]). Second, according to Article 2 TEU at the heart of the EU values lies the respect for the rule of law. This principle, and the related principles of democracy, transparency, accountability and legal certainty all leave their mark on the EU political order and thus need to be reflected in the EU *ordre public* (§8.02[B]). Third, while in section §8.01 we stressed the top-down aspects of the legal order, with a strong sense of commandeering from the EU to its Member States, the opposite relation, focusing on protecting diversity and national identities exists as well. Accordingly, attention needs to be given to the constitutional background principle of subsidiarity and some of its *ordre public* related manifestations (§8.02[C]). Fourth, next to the EU and its Member States a third actor in the political order must be brought to the fore, namely the citizens. It is submitted that the political component of EU citizenship is the first reason for its *ordre public* status (§8.02[D]). The second reason coincides with the values behind the free movement of persons and will be highlighted below.[153] Finally, in line with the *civis europeus sum* idea put forward by AG Jacobs in *Konstantinidis*[154] it is but a small step from citizenship to the protection of fundamental rights (§8.02[E]). Therefore, far from offering a full treatise on fundamental rights in the EU some aspects raised in the context of the *ordre public*, such as human dignity, procedural rights and equal treatment are to be focused on.

### [A] Protection of the International Legal Order

**III-37.** The values underlying the commitment of the EU to international law are perhaps best reflected by the text of Article 21(1), first sentence TEU, in its post-Lisbon version, which reads:

> The Union's action on the international scene shall be guided by the principles which have inspired its own creation, development and enlargement, and which it seeks to advance in the wider world: democracy, the rule of law, the universality and indivisibility of human rights and fundamental freedoms, respect for human dignity, the principles of equality and solidarity, and respect for the principles of the United Nations Charter and international law.

These concerns are then made more concrete in the various fields of action in Article 21(2) TEU.

**III-38.** Respect for these values is important for the Union, as it is both an international organization itself and an actor under international law.[155] Internally, this respect for the core of international law is reflected in the way the ECJ defines the boundaries of

153. See, *infra*, at III-80 et seq.
154. Opinion of AG Jacobs in Case C-168/91 *Konstantinidis* [1993] ECR I-1191, para. 46.
155. See in this respect R. Uerpmann-Wittzack 'The Constitutional Role of Multilateral Treaty Systems' in *Principles of European Constitutional Law*, ed. A. Von Bogdandy & J. Bast (Oxford/Portland: Hart, 2007), 145-181.

EU law. In *Van Duyn*[156] the ECJ accepted the inevitability of unequal treatment of own nationals and foreigners in cases where a Member State wants to act on *ordre public* grounds, as own nationals may never be expelled. In *Poulsen and Diva Navigation*[157] the ECJ interpreted the territorial scope of EU law in line with international law of the sea. However, a renewed focus on consent also implies that the EU, despite its commitment to multilateralism, does not need to yield for international treaties to which it is not a party, even though the EU Member States are.[158] Furthermore, despite claims as to the autonomous nature of EU law, the basic rules of international law do kick in at times. Accordingly, the ECJ has for instance used the Vienna Convention on Diplomatic Relations in interpreting the Protocol on Privileges and Immunities.[159] Finally, Article 351 TFEU ensures that Member States can still honour the obligations they had undertaken before joining the Union,[160] though Member States must make full use of all possibilities to get out of these obligations[161] and may only hide behind this Article to the extent that there is a real conflict.[162]

**III-39.** On the international plane this commitment is reflected on the one hand in a series of measures adopted by the Union in support of these values, such as CFSP measures aimed at supporting international courts[163] and international organizations,[164] but also measures aimed at explicitly spreading the EU values abroad.[165] On

156. Case 41/74 *van Duyn* [1974] ECR 1337.
157. Case C-286/90 *Poulsen and Diva Navigation* [1992] ECR I-6019.
158. Case C-308/06 *International Association of Independent Tanker Owners* [2008] ECR I-4057.
159. Case C-437/04 *Commission v. Belgium* [2007] ECR I-2513.
160. Moreover, the Union has in turn an obligation not to impede the performance of the obligations of Member States which stem from a prior agreement, see Case C-366/10 *Air Transport Association of America* [2011] ECR I-0000, para. 61.
161. See for example, Case C-170/98 *Commission v. Belgium* [1999] ECR I-5493.
162. An excellent example of this conflict is offered by Case C-158/91 *Levy* [1993] ECR I-4827. At issue was the potential conflict between the IAO Convention 78 which prohibits night work by women, and which France had duly implemented in its internal criminal law (making it a matter of French *ordre public*, moreover), and Council Directive 76/207/EEC of 9 February 1976 on the implementation of the principle of equal treatment for men and women as regards access to employment, vocational training and promotion, and working conditions (1976) OJ L 39/40. See also, for the interaction with a pre-existing investment contract, Case C-264/09 *Commission v. Slovak Republic* [2011] ECR I-0000.
163. Council Common Position 2003/444/CFSP of 16 June 2003 on the International Criminal Court (2004) OJ L 150/67; Council Common Position 2003/280/CFSP of 16 April 2003 in support of the effective implementation of the mandate of the ICTY (2003) OJ 101/22.
164. See *inter alia* Council Joint Action 2008/307/CFSP of 14 April 2008 in support of World Health Organization activities in the area of laboratory bio-safety and bio-security in the framework of the European Union Strategy against the proliferation of Weapons of Mass Destruction (2008) OJ L 106/17; Council Common Position 2005/329/CFSP of 25 April 2005 relating to the 2005 Review Conference of the Parties to the Treaty on the Non-Proliferation of Nuclear Weapons (2005) OJ L 106/32.
165. Often these measures are at the crossroads between the pillars, compare in this respect Council Regulation (EC) No 975/1999 of 29 April 1999 laying down the requirements for the implementation of development cooperation operations which contribute to the general objective of developing and consolidating democracy and the rule of law and to that of respecting human rights and fundamental freedoms (1999) OJ L 120/1 with Council Common Position 2004/85/CFSP of 26 January 2004 concerning conflict prevention, management and resolution in Africa and repealing Common Position 2001/374/CFSP (2004) OJ L 21/25. For more on this, see T. Corthaut, 'An effective remedy for all? Paradoxes and controversies in

the other hand, the international relations of the Union are also subject to scrutiny by the EU courts in light of the principles of EU law that are reflective of international law. The most striking example is perhaps the judgment of the then CFI in *Opel Austria*, where the CFI found in the principle of protection of legitimate expectations a corollary for the international law principle of good faith as codified in Article 18 VCLT.[166] But the ECJ has in the past for instance also assessed whether the EU had lawfully suspended an international agreement with Yugoslavia in the face of atrocities committed on the occasion of the break-up of that country,[167] even though the EU is as such not bound by the Vienna Conventions on the Law of Treaties.[168] Nevertheless, as the Union is adopting ever-stricter economic regulation, often in domains concerning international environmental issues, the Court appears to find it increasingly difficult the balance between respect for international law and ensuring the policy freedom of the democratically empowered EU legislator.[169]

### [B] Protection of the Rule of Law

**III-40.** The Union is based on the rule of law.[170] Reminiscent of the Court's famous finding in *Les Verts* that:

> the European Economic Community is a Community based on the rule of law, inasmuch as neither its Member States nor its institutions can avoid a review of the question whether the measures adopted by them are in conformity with the basic constitutional charter, the Treaty[171]

Article 2 TEU proclaims that the 'Union is founded on the values of respect for human dignity, freedom, democracy, equality, *the rule of law* and respect for human rights, including the rights of persons belonging to minorities.' The Lisbon Treaty expands the list even further than the list in old Article 6(1) TEU by adding that these 'values are common to the Member States in a society in which pluralism, non-discrimination, tolerance, justice, solidarity and equality between women and men prevail'. Arguably, the principles mentioned in Article 2 TEU besides the rule of law can be seen as substantive translations of the abstract principle of the rule of law.

---

respect of judicial protection in the field of the CFSP under the European Constitution', *Tilburg Foreign Law Review* (2005): 119-120.

166. Case T-115/94 *Opel Austria* [1997] ECR II-39, para. 93.
167. Case C-162/96 *Racke* [1998] ECR I-3655.
168. J. Vanhamme, *Volkenrechtelijke Beginselen in het Europees Recht* (Groningen: Europa Law Publishing, 2001), 18-24.
169. See in respect of international aviation Case C-366/10 *Air Transport Association of America* [2011] ECR I-0000; Case C-344/04 *IATA and ELFAA* [2006] ECR I-403; see in respect of international maritime transport, Case C-308/06 *International Association of Independent Tanker Owners* [2008] ECR I-4057.
170. A. Von Bogdandy, 'Constitutional Principles' in *Principles of European Constitutional Law*, ed. A. Von Bogdandy & J. Bast (Oxford/Portland: Hart, 2007), 15-20.
171. Case 294/83 *Parti Ecologiste 'Les Verts' v. European Parliament* [1986] ECR 1339, para. 23.

**III-41.** The first translation of this commitment to the rule of law flows directly from *Les Verts*,[172] where the ECJ concluded the necessity of ensuring sufficient judicial protection through effective judicial review.[173] Accordingly, the ECJ was even willing to slightly bend its restrictive case law as to the *locus standi* of non-privileged applicants in order to ensure that the Green Party could challenge a self-serving financial arrangement dictated by the major fractions in the European Parliament.[174] However, it is well-known that the ECJ has since been highly reluctant to go further down this path. Acknowledging the possibility of imperfect protection against the Community institutions – in the case of the third and *a fortiori* the second pillar the gaps are even blatant – the ECJ made clear that the responsibility for redressing these defects lays squarely with the Member States, who should change the Treaties if need be.[175] However, this is not the end of the story. First, I am on record that I consider the appeals cases in *UPA*[176] and *Jégo-Quéré*[177] unduly restrictive.[178] Second, also the ECJ seems to have come to that insight, though the desired improvement of the level of effective judicial protection is achieved without touching the infamous *Plaumann*[179] test. In *Unibet*[180] the ECJ made clear that all Member States must have in their legal order a way for challenging – directly or indirectly – legislation of the Member States that is contrary to EU law, and this in a manner that does not require the legal subjects to first break the law and thus face the cruel dilemma between risking (at times severe) punishment or enduring potentially unjust legislation. Admittedly, this case primarily concerns the judicial protection against the Member States, where the ECJ has always taken a far stauncher stance.[181] However, its clear finding that if the applicant 'was forced to be subject to administrative or criminal proceedings and to any penalties that may result as the sole form of legal remedy for disputing the compatibility of the

---

172. Case 294/83 *Parti Ecologiste 'Les Verts' v. European Parliament* [1986] ECR 1339.
173. On the importance of judicial review for the rule of law in the EU, see F. Jacobs, 'The State of International Economic Law: Re-thinking Sovereignty in Europe', *Journal of International Economic Law* (2008): 6-14.
174. See in this respect also K. Lenaerts & T. Corthaut, 'Judicial Review as a Contribution to the Development of European Constitutionalism', *Yearbook of European Law* (2003): 2-4.
175. Case C-50/00 P *Unión de Pequeños Agricultores v. Council* [2002] ECR I-6677.
176. Case C-50/00 P *Unión de Pequeños Agricultores v. Council* [2002] ECR I-6677.
177. Case C-263/02 P *Commission v. Jégo-Quéré* [2004] ECR I-3425.
178. T. Corthaut, 'case note under CFI, 3 May 2002, *Jégo-Quéré/Commission*, Case T-177/01 and ECJ, 25 July 2002, *Unión de Pequeños Agricultores/Council*, Case C-50/00 P', *Columbia Journal of European Law* (2003): 141-166; T. Corthaut, 'An effective remedy for all ? Paradoxes and controversies in respect of judicial protection in the field of the CFSP under the European Constitution', *Tilburg Foreign Law Review* (2005): 110-144; T. Corthaut & F. Vanneste, "Waves between Strasbourg and Luxembourg – The Right of Access to a Court to Contest the Validity of Legislative or Administrative Measures', *Yearbook of European Law* (2006): 475-514, with postscript 671-672; K. Lenaerts & T. Corthaut, 'Judicial Review as a Contribution to the Development of European Constitutionalism', *Yearbook of European Law* (2003): 1-41.
179. Case 25/62 *Plaumann v. Commission* [1963] ECR 95.
180. Case C-432/05 *Unibet* [2007] ECR I-2271. For more on this, see K. Lenaerts, 'The rule of law and the coherence of the judicial system in the European Union', *Common Market Law Review* (2007): 1625-1659.
181. Case 222/84 *Johnston* [1986] ECR 1651, para. 18; Case 222/86 *Heylens* [1987] ECR 4097, para. 14; Case C-185/97 *Coote* [1998] ECR I-5199, para. 21; Case C-424/99 *Commission v. Austria* [2001] ECR I-9285, para. 45.

national provision at issue with Community law, that would not be sufficient to secure for it such effective judicial protection',[182] must logically also apply in those cases where the validity of an act of the Union is at stake. Especially since the entry into force of the new Article 19(1), second sentence, TEU - but arguably also even before - Member States are under an obligation to provide for the necessary effective remedies in their legal order to ensure that also EU acts can be reviewed in light of the 'basic constitutional charter'.[183] As this is the only way to ensure - without further Treaty amendments[184] - that the rule of law is indeed upheld as required by Article 2 TEU, it is submitted that Member States are under an obligation of result (and thus no longer a best efforts approach as suggested by *UPA*[185]) as a matter of loyal cooperation to ensure the presence in their legal order of effective remedies. This approach seems, moreover, the only way to justify, notwithstanding the outcome of the case, the relative optimism of the ECJ judgments in *Gestoras Pro Amestia*[186] and *Segi*[187] as to the possibilities for judicial protection in the third (and *a fortiori* second) pillar, especially if compared to the dejected assessment of the applicant's claim at first instance.[188]

**III-42.** The liberty component has been relatively underdeveloped in the case law, but it has been discussed in literature.[189] It could be argued that the deregulating effect of the four freedoms[190] could be seen as an expression of the liberty idea, however, given the Treaty-based exceptions and the rule of reason the Union has never gone through a *Lochner*[191] era of almost unbounded economic freedom. Admittedly, the ECJ has accepted the freedom to conduct a business,[192] as also reflected in Article 16 of the Charter, but this does not seem to have much bite. Nevertheless, occasionally the liberty idea seems to inspire certain decisions. A good example seems the judgment in

182. Case C-432/05 *Unibet* [2007] ECR I-2271, para. 64.
183. Case 294/83 *Parti Ecologiste 'Les Verts' v. European Parliament* [1986] ECR 1339, para. 23.
184. Admittedly the *locus standi* requirements in Article 263(4) TFEU are slightly lowered if compared to Article 230(4) TEC - at least in respect of so-called 'regulatory acts'. However, in respect of legislative acts and in respect of the CFSP acts the problem remains.
185. Case C-50/00 P *Unión de Pequeños Agricultores v. Council* [2002] ECR I-6677, para. 42. The 'as far as possible' language does not return in Case C-432/05 *Unibet* [2007] ECR I-2271, and rightly so.
186. Case C-354/04 P *Gestoras Pro Amestía v. Council* [2007] ECR I-1579.
187. Case C-355/04 P *Segi v. Council* [2007] ECR I-1657.
188. Case T-338/02 *Segi v. Council* [2004] ECR II-1647, para. 38 ('Concerning the absence of an effective remedy invoked by the applicants, it must be noted that *indeed probably no effective judicial remedy is available to them, whether before the Community Courts or national courts,* with regard to the inclusion of Segi on the list of persons, groups or entities involved in terrorist acts.') (emphasis added).
189. A. Von Bogdandy, 'Constitutional Principles' in *Principles of European Constitutional Law*, ed. A. Von Bogdandy & J. Bast (Oxford/Portland: Hart, 2007), 12-14.
190. See in this respect C. Joerges, 'Rethinking European Law's Supremacy with Comments by Damian CHALMERS, Rainer NICKEL, Florian RÖDL, Robert WAI', EUI Working Papers Law No 2005/12 (<http://hdl.handle.net/1814/3332>, 22 May 2012).
191. *Lochner v. New York* 198 U.S. 45 (1905). See nonetheless, I. Eliasoph, 'A "switch in time" for the European Community? Lochner discourse and the recalibration of social rights in Europe', *Columbia Journal of European Law* (2008): 467-508.
192. Case 44/79 *Hauer* [1979] ECR 3727.

*Promusicae*[193] where the ECJ made clear that Member States trying to protect intellectual property rights of the music industry should not do so in a manner that unduly undermines the right of privacy of computer users. It appears that since the entry into force of the Lisbon Treaty, and its binding Charter of Fundamental Rights that the freedom prong may be developed further, with the Court for instance explicitly invoking the freedom to pursue a trade or conduct a business, a fundamental principle of Union law[194] laid down in Article 16 TFEU, in striking a reasonable balance between copyright protection and the legitimate business of internet providers,[195] social network sites[196] and broadcasters.[197]

**III-43.** Democracy, while a rather abstract container concept, is equally at the heart of the EU political order[198] and thus of the EU *ordre public*. The EU conception of democracy has, moreover, been given somewhat more body in the new title II, entitled 'Provisions on democratic principles' in the post-Lisbon version of the TEU, with a clear focus on representative democracy, at the EU level and in the Member States. The concept obviously permeates the case law on essential procedural requirements. As argued the focus of these essential procedural requirements is precisely to ensure that the volition of the legislator is formed in a manner which takes all relevant actors on board. While this does not per se imply full involvement of the European *demos* - if there is one[199] - or its directly elected representatives in the European Parliament,[200] it is clear that ignoring the essential procedural requirements will unacceptably undermine the democratic legitimacy of the Union. On the one hand, in many instances these requirements provide for a role for the European Parliament[201] or for other legitimate

193. Case C-275/06 *Promusicae* [2008] ECR I-271.
194. Case C-1/11 *Interseroh Scrap and Metals Trading* [2012] ECR I-0000, para. 43.
195. Case C-70/10 *Scarlet Extended* [2011] ECR I-0000, para. 46.
196. Case C-360/10 *SABAM* [2012] ECR I-0000, para. 44.
197. Case C-510/10 *DR and TV2 Danmark* [2012] ECR I-0000, para. 57.
198. On the concept of democracy in the EU legal order, see, *inter alia*, C. Closa, 'Constitution and Democracy in the Treaty Establishing a Constitution for Europe', *European Public Law* (2005): 145-164; A. Verhoeven, 'Democratie in het recht van de Europese Unie: een tussenstand na de Europese conventie' in *Recht en democratie – De democratische verbeelding in het recht*, ed. A. Adams & P. Popelier (Antwerpen: Intersentia, 2004), 609-636; A. Peters, 'European Democracy after the 2003 Convention', *Common Market Law Review* (2004): 37-85. See also, E.O. Eriksen & J.H. Fossum (eds.), *Democracy in the European Union. Integration Through Deliberation?* (London: Routledge, 2000); M. Kaufmann, 'Europäische Integration und Demokratieprinzip' (Baden-Baden: Nomos, 1997). See also A. Von Bogdandy, 'Constitutional Principles' in *Principles of European Constitutional Law*, ed. A. Von Bogdandy & J. Bast (Oxford/Portland: Hart, 2007), 20-31; S. Oeter, 'Federalism and Democracy' in *id.*, 53-93.
199. See on this J.H.H. Weiler, 'Does Europe Need a Constitution? Demos, Telos and the German Maastricht Decision', *European Law Journal* (1995): 219-258. See also, rather critical of transplanting a classic concept of democracy to the EU legal order, J. Baquero Cruz, 'The Legacy of the Maastricht-Urteil and the Pluralist Movement', *European Law Journal* (2008): 410-412. See further, arguing that 'Europe does not need a 'constitution' and it does not need a 'people' either', K.-H. Ladeur, ''We, the European People …' – Relâche?' *European Law Journal* (2008): 147-167.
200. Compare Case C-155/91 *Commission v. Council* [1993] ECR I-939 with Case C-300/89 *Commission v. Council* [1991] ECR I-2867.
201. Case C-300/89 *Commission v. Council* [1991] ECR I-2867.

actors, such as the representatives of management and labour,[202] who serve as a proxy for the *demos*. On the other hand, adherence to the essential procedural requirements is maybe even more crucial in those instances where the democratic legitimacy of the decision-making process is dependent on the democratic legitimacy of the organs that supervise or appoint the actors, as in the case of the legislative procedures with consultation of the European Parliament or in the case of the comitology procedures.[203] This also implies that the Union is concerned with the functioning of the democratic bodies of the Union and its Member States. The Court has not failed to stress the importance of the correct organization of the elections for the European Parliament[204] and the Parliament's functioning in practice.[205] Moreover, Article 7 TEU provides for a mechanism[206] under which the EU may act against a Member State that - despite its clear commitments to the values of democracy and the rule of law as crucial conditions for EU membership under Article 49 TEU - would fail to continue functioning fully as a democratic State.

**III-44.** The ECJ has regularly stressed the value of the democratic representation at the EU level.[207] As I have argued elsewhere in more detail as a co-author,[208] the principle plays moreover in the background in several cases on the division of competence,[209] but also in cases concerning the workings of the European Parliament[210] or the cooperation between the social partners.[211] The need for laying sensitive decision firmly in the hand of elected officials that are thus accountable to the public also helps to explain the primacy of the political process over technocratic decision-making in

202. Case T-135/96 *UEAPME v. Council* [1998] ECR II-2335. On the democratic legitimacy of these procedures, see K. Lenaerts & T. Corthaut, 'Judicial Review as a Contribution to the Development of European Constitutionalism', *Yearbook of European Law* (2003): 34-37.
203. To dispel all doubt on this point, I do not reject a priori the democratic legitimacy of decision-making in a manner not involving the European Parliament; however, I do stress the importance of adherence to the procedures in place that serve to compensate for the prima facie absence of a democratically elected body in the decision-making procedure. For more, see A. Verhoeven, *The European Union in Search of a Democratic and Constitutional Theory* (The Hague/London/New York: Kluwer Law International, 2002).
204. Case 294/83 *Parti Ecologiste 'Les Verts' v. European Parliament* [1986] ECR 1339, para. 53. On the composition of the electorate, which does not need to coincide with EU citizenship, see Case C-300/04 *Eman and Sevinger* [2006] ECR I-8055; Case C-145/04 *Spain v. United Kingdom* [2006] ECR I-7917.
205. Joined Cases T-222/99, T-327/99 and T-329/99 *Martinez v. European Parliament* [2001] ECR II-2823; see, also, on appeal Case C-488/01 P *Martinez v. European Parliament* [2003] ECR I-13355.
206. For a critical analysis of this procedure, see A. Williams, 'EU Human Rights Policy and the Convention on the Future of Europe: a Failure of Design', *European Law Review* (2003): 794-813 and A. Williams, 'The Indifferent Gesture: Article 7 TEU, the Fundamental Rights Agency and the UK's invasion of Iraq', *European Law Review* (2003): 3-27.
207. Case 138/79 *Roquettes Frères v. Council* [1980] ECR 3333, para. 33.
208. K. Lenaerts & T. Corthaut, 'Judicial Review as a Contribution to the Development of European Constitutionalism', *Yearbook of European Law* (2003): 24-47.
209. Case C-300/89 *Commission v. Council* [1991] ECR I-2867, para. 20. See also, more recently, Case C-91/05 *Commission v. Council* [2008] ECR I-3651.
210. Joined Cases T-222/99, T-327/99 and T-329/99 *Martinez v. European Parliament* [2001] ECR II-2823; Case 294/83 *Parti Ecologiste 'Les Verts' v. European Parliament* [1986] ECR 1339.
211. Case T-135/96 *UEAPME v. Council* [1998] ECR II-2335.

*Pfizer Animal Health.*[212] In that case the CFI held that the Council, on proposal from the Commission, was allowed to pay heed to the precautionary principle and refuse the market authorization of an animal antibiotic deemed safe, despite some doubts, by the scientific committee.[213]

**III-45.** Finally, Article 2 TEU puts forward one further set of constitutional values related to the rule of law, namely the fundamental rights and freedoms, including equality. I do not intend to ignore them. However, these do not only concern the rule of law in the abstract but also the position of every citizen, indeed of every human being. Given these additional dimensions, and their prominence in legal discourse, I have therefore opted to discuss these fundamental rights and freedoms – and in particular their link to the EU *ordre public* – separately below.[214]

### [C] Federalism: or 'Unity in Diversity'

**III-46.** Two controversial premises to start with, both of which I take from the seminal work of Koen Lenaerts.[215] First, I am willing to use the controversial[216] term federalism in connection to the EU, even though the Union is evidently not a State, provided that the term is given its proper content: 'a system of divided powers … which proceeds from the very essence of constitutionalism which is limited government operating

212. Case T-13/99 *Pfizer Animal Health v. Council* [2002] ECR II-3305.
213. See in particular Case T-13/99 *Pfizer Animal Health v. Council* [2002] ECR II-3305, para. 201 where the CFI argued: 'That finding can also be justified on grounds of principle relating to the political responsibilities and democratic legitimacy of the Commission. Whilst the Commission's exercise of public authority is rendered legitimate, pursuant to Article 155 of the EC Treaty (now Article 211 EC), by the European Parliament's political control, the members of SCAN, although they have scientific legitimacy, have neither democratic legitimacy nor political responsibilities. Scientific legitimacy is not a sufficient basis for the exercise of public authority'.
214. See, *infra*, at I, B, §5 of this Part.
215. K. Lenaerts, 'Constitutionalism and the Many Faces of Federalism, *American Journal of Comparative Law* (1990): 205-263.
216. On the question whether the Union may be appropriately be approached from a federalism perspective, see, *inter alia*, A. Weber, 'Zur föderalen Struktur der Europäischen Union im Entwurf des Europäischen Verfassungsvertrags', *Europarecht* (2004): 841-856; C. Schönberger, 'Die Europäische Union als Bund. Zugleich ein Beitrag zur Verabschiedung des Staatenbund-Bundesstaat-Schemas', *Archiv des öffentlichen Rechts* (2004): 81-120; S. Cassese, 'L'Unione Europea come organizzazione pubblica composita', *Rivista italiano di diritto pubblico comunitario* (2000): 987-992; G.F. Mancini & J.H.H. Weiler, 'Europe – The Case for Statehood. And the Case Against An Exchange', Harvard Jean Monnet Working Paper Series, 1998; C. Hillgruber, 'Das Verhältnis der Europäischen Gemeinschaften un der Europäischen Union zu ihren Mitgliedstaaten – staats- und völkerrechtlich betrachtet', *Archiv des Völkerrechts* (1996): 347-375; T. Risse-Kappen, 'Exploring the Nature of the Beast: International Relations Theory and Comparative Policy Analysis Meet the European Union', *Journal of Common Market Studies* (1996): 53-80. See also A. Von Bogdandy, 'Constitutional Principles' in *Principles of European Constitutional Law*, ed. A. Von Bogdandy & J. Bast (Oxford/Portland: Hart, 2007), 34-51. On the wider consequences for democracy of such an approach, see S. Oeter. 'Federalism and Democracy' in *id.*, 53-93.

under the rule of law'.[217] Immediately, the link with §8.02[B] above comes to the fore – and with it the *ordre public* character of federalism – as federalism concerns are in essence equally about subjecting the exercise of power to the constraints of the law. In this sense, the term has a ring to it that is reminiscent of its use in US constitutional law as a shield of state interests and individual liberty.[218] However, I do not seek to inject the Rehnquist era federalism case law into the EU legal order with the so-called new federalism[219] cases of the US Supreme Court with their awkward stress on 'the dignity of the states as sovereign entities'.[220] To the contrary, the second point I take from Lenaerts is that 'there simply is no nucleus of sovereignty that the Member States can invoke, as such, against the Community',[221] or now the Union. As illustrated by recent ECJ case law on the military,[222] education,[223] taxation[224] and social security[225] there is indeed not a single area of competence where the EU legal order will not permeate the national legal order.[226] Yet, this does not mean that the individual Member States have no significance. If I can be said to have a pro-European bias, it is not only because I am convinced by the Union's achievements in bringing peace, wealth and stability to the old continent. It is also because on a proper construction of the case law, the nationalist fears of an over-arching unifying EU super-State displacing most treasured local values are simply unfounded. Admittedly, in section §8.01 several principles with a unifying effect have been brought to the fore as part and parcel of the EU *ordre public*. However,

217. K. Lenaerts., 'Constitutionalism and the Many Faces of Federalism, *American Journal of Comparative Law* (1990): 205.
218. On US concepts of federalism and its relevance for the EU legal order, see further *inter alia* K. Lenaerts & K. Gutman, '"Federal Common Law" in the European Union: a Comparative Perspective from the United States', *American Journal of Comparative Law* (2006): 1-122; F. Sander, 'Subsidiarity infringements before the European Court of Justice: futile interference with politics or a substantial step towards EU federalism?', *Columbia Journal of European Law* (2006): 517-571; E. Young, 'Protecting Member State Autonomy in the European Union: Some Cautionary Tales from American Federalism', *New York University Law Review* (2002): 1612-1737.
219. M. Killenbeck, 'In(re)dignity: the New Federalism in Perspective', *Arkansas Law Review* (2004): 1-68.
220. F. Sander, 'Subsidiarity infringements before the European Court of Justice: futile interference with politics or a substantial step towards EU federalism?', *Columbia Journal of European Law* (2006): 553; see in particular Seminole Tribe of *Florida v. Florida*, 517 U.S. 44 (1996); *Florida Prepaid Postsecondary Ed. Expense Bd. v. College Savings Bank*, 527 U.S. 627 (1999); *College Savings Bank v. Florida Prepaid Postsecondary Ed.* Expense Bd., 527 U.S. 666 (1999) and *Alden v. Maine*, 527 U.S. 706 (1999).
221. K. Lenaerts, 'Constitutionalism and the Many Faces of Federalism, *American Journal of Comparative Law* (1990): 220.
222. Case C-285/98 *Kreil* [2000] ECR I-69.
223. Joined Cases C-11/06 and C-12/06 *Morgan* [2007] ECR I-9161; Case C-147/03 *Commission v. Austria* [2005] ECR I-5969.
224. Case C-446/03 *Marks & Spencer* [2005] ECR I-10837.
225. Case C-372/04 *Watts* [2006] ECR I-4325.
226. See also the 'unease' of Nic Shuibhne of how the Court deals with the 'competing State/free movement interests', N. Nic Shuibhne, 'Case C-76/05 *Schwarz and Gootjes-Schwarz v. Finanzamt Bergisch Gladbach*, Judgment of the Grand Chamber of 11 September 2007, not yet reported; Case C-318/05, *Commission v. Germany*, Judgment of the Grand Chamber of 11 September 2007, not yet reported; Joined Cases C-11/06 & C-12/06 *Morgan v. Bezirksregierung Köln; Bucher v. Landrat des Kreisen Düren*, Judgment of the Grand Chamber of 23 October 2007, not yet reported', *Common Market Law Review* (2008): 777 et seq.

I submit that in a balanced view of the EU political and legal order, also the counteracting principles – if only to be able to balance out other *ordre public* values – rank as EU *ordre public*.

**III-47.** While there may not be a 'nucleus of sovereignty',[227] the limitations on the reach of the Union are noticeable through the principle of subsidiarity. In this respect, an important terminological issue must be addressed, however. If I speak of subsidiarity in the context of the EU *ordre public,* I primarily mean the constitutional background principle that seeks to regulate the balance between what can be done locally and what should be done by the EU and not the formal additional check on the exercise of EU competence laid down in Article 5 TEU. I agree with Florian Sander that currently major difficulties exist in enforcing the subsidiarity principle *sensu stricto*, *i.e.*, in its function of limiting the extent to which the EU may exercise its competence;[228] moreover, it remains to be seen whether this changes with the introduction of the renewed Protocol on Subsidiarity and Proportionality. However, the case law of the ECJ demonstrates an increasing sensitivity for subsidiarity in the broad sense: the respect for local values and institutions in the face of EU law.

**III-48.** One of the most powerful expressions of this background principle has already been highlighted on several occasions above. It is the national procedural autonomy. As I argued elsewhere 'the ECJ is indeed willing to accept some degree of differentiation among the Member States and employs the requirement of "effectiveness" only as an exception to the rule of national procedural autonomy which falls to be used with moderation'.[229] Accordingly, the Court accepts for instance that judges from Member States that adhere to a strict regime of passivity are generally not under an obligation to raise issues of their own motion.[230] This is more than a choice for the least intrusive means. It may well be argued that there is an underlying constitutional value in relying on the Member State machinery for putting EU law into practice. It is a very plausible assumption that on average the national authorities in shaping national procedures have more likely than not struck a correct balance ensuring effective enforcement of all laws – and thus also EU law – in light of local parameters. For instance, a judicial system with passivity on the side of the bench may be entirely appropriate if off-set by a tradition of vigorous accusatorial debate and a high professional and ethical standard of the barristers appearing in court. It may well be that – while this is not excluded as a matter of vertical division of competence[231] – adopting a harmonized approach to

227. K. Lenaerts, 'Constitutionalism and the Many Faces of Federalism, *American Journal of Comparative Law* (1990): 220.
228. F. Sander, 'Subsidiarity infringements before the European Court of Justice: futile interference with politics or a substantial step towards EU federalism?', *Columbia Journal of European Law* (2006): 517-571. See also G. Davies, 'Subsidiarity: the wrong idea, in the wrong place, at the wrong time', *Common Market Law Review* (2006): 63-84.
229. On the link between subsidiarity and national procedural autonomy, see K. Lenaerts & T. Corthaut, 'Judicial Review as a Contribution to the Development of European Constitutionalism', *Yearbook of European Law* (2003): 18.
230. Joined Cases C-430/93 and C-431/93 *Van Schijndel and Van Veen* [1995] ECR I-4705. For more, see, *supra*, at II-171 et seq.
231. Case 33/76 *Rewe* [1976] ECR 1989, para. 5; Case 45/76 *Comet* [1976] ECR 2043, para. 14.

national procedural law (which moreover covers more than just procedural law *sensu stricto*, as the law governing court proceedings, but also includes for instance certain administrative practices) may well be counter-effective. It is only when this presumption is actually rebutted that the exceptions come into play. On the one hand, the principle of equality can then be explained as the logical consequence of the presumption that the national legal order will generally have it right: if special procedures are created to deal with cases of EU law, it must be examined why the normal proceedings could not suffice, as chances are that an attempt is made to limit the usual efficiency of the national legal order. On the other hand, the principle of effectiveness comes again to the fore as the exception that is needed to address systemic failures. As no system is perfect - and even if it is, the humans that put it into practice are not infallible - deference to the national systems also implies acceptance of the occasional mishap in the enforcement of EU law, just as the occasional error or under-enforcement occurs in the context of national law. However, if it turns out that because of a particular rule of national law EU law hardly stands a chance of being effectively enforced, the national law has to be cast aside. It is only if one accepts that national procedural autonomy ranks on equal footing as the principle of primacy that inspires the effectiveness principle that it can fully be explained why the primacy of EU law does not simply override - or even stronger: does usually not override - national procedural rules that stand in the way of the full enforcement of EU law. It is thus submitted that the national procedural autonomy is equally part of the EU *ordre public*.

**III-49.** The second way that this background principle of subsidiarity becomes concrete is in the increasing respect for national structure and identity. First it was simply proclaimed as such in old Article 6(3) TEU: 'The Union shall respect the national identities of its Member States.' However, the Lisbon Treaty makes it even far more explicit. In new Article 4(2) TEU which reads in relevant part: 'The Union shall respect the equality of Member States before the Treaties as well as their national identities, inherent in their fundamental structures, political and constitutional, inclusive of regional and local self-government.' I submit, however, that this commitment was already deeply rooted in the Union's DNA before the entry into force of the Lisbon Treaty. The previous case law of the ECJ already showed great deference to national identity. Admittedly, there is the classic phrase that Member States cannot hide behind their constitutional system, in particular their federated entities, to elude their obligations under EU law.[232] However, beyond that the Court displays far greater sensitivity to the 'fundamental structures, political and constitutional, inclusive of regional and local self-government' of the Member States. Three examples come to mind. First, while only Member States may act before the EU courts as privileged applicants under Article 263 TFEU, recent case law shows that this may be compensated through a benevolent approach towards *locus standi* of constitutional entities of Member States with autonomous legislative powers under Article 263(4) TFEU.[233] Second, the ECJ has

232. Case C-422/05 *Commission v. Belgium* [2007] ECR I-4749, paras 47-48.
233. Joined Cases T-366/03 and T-235/04 *Land Oberösterreich and Austria v. Commission* [2005] ECR II-4005.

carefully reconsidered the specificity requirement in State-aid cases in order not to upset the ordinary exercise of fiscal powers by constitutionally autonomous entities of the Member States, without however jeopardizing the legitimate EU policy – firmly anchored in the Treaties – of combating illegal state aid.[234] Third, confronted with a question arising from the Belgian constitutional court, which found itself confronted with a conflict over the delimitation of the competences of the Belgian-federated entities in respect of the introduction in Flanders of a special insurance for the non-medical costs related to old age ('Vlaamse zorgverzekering'), the ECJ,[235] unlike Advocate General Sharpston,[236] was careful enough to upset the Belgian constitutional order only to the extent that EU nationals who have made use of their free movement rights were concerned. The difference in treatment between ordinary Flemish and Walloon persons, which flows almost inevitably[237] from the enforcement of the territoriality principle in the Belgian constitutional order, was thus left firmly in the hands of the Belgian constitutional actors. However, it appears that since the Lisbon Treaty introduced Article 4(2) TEU the attention to national identity truly takes centre stage, even when balanced with other fundamental aspects of Union law, such as European citizenship.[238]

**III-50.** Finally, the background principle of subsidiarity comes to the fore in the unofficial motto of the Union: 'unity in diversity', which manifests itself in a series of decisions that carefully take into account national constitutional values. The techniques for doing so may vary greatly, the result is what matters. Accordingly, as explained above[239] in *Groener*,[240] the ECJ stretched the interpretation of the necessity criterion of the last subparagraph of Article 3(1) of Regulation No 1612/68[241] of the Council beyond all plausibility in order to salvage the requirement that all government employees – such as art teacher – know the Irish language. The sole reason for doing so is a clear recognition by the ECJ of the importance for Ireland of maintaining its first constitutional language, and thus a desire to protect the national identity of one of its Member States. In *Grogan*[242] the same result was achieved in a more off-handed manner. By considering the distribution by students of leaflets informing Irish women

234. Case C-88/03 *Portugal v. Commission* [2006] ECR I-7115. See also Joined Cases C-428/06 to C-434/06 *Unión General de Trabajadores de la Rioja* [2008] ECR I-0000, with Opinion of AG Kokott.
235. Case C-212/06 *Government of Communauté française and Gouvernement wallon* [2008] ECR I-1683.
236. Opinion of AG Sharpston in Case C-212/06 *Government of Communauté française and Gouvernement wallon* [2008] ECR I-1683.
237. The Court has made it clear that as divergent legislation within a State with several entities with legislative powers is inherent to the system, it cannot per se constitute discrimination contrary to EU law, see Case C-428/07 *Horvath* [2009] ECR I-6355.
238. Case C-208/09 *Sayn-Wittgenstein* [2010] ECR I-0000, para. 91; Case C-391/09 *Runevič-Vardyn* [2011] ECR I-0000, para. 86.
239. See, *supra*, at II-55.
240. Case C-379/87 *Groener* [1989] ECR 3967.
241. Regulation (EEC) No 1612/68 of the Council of 15 October 1968 on freedom of movement for workers within the Community, *Official Journal, English Special Edition* 1968 II, 475.
242. Case C-159/90 *Society for the Protection of Unborn Children Ireland* [1991] ECR I-4685. See also, *supra*, at I-68.

of the possibilities for going abroad to undergo an abortion too remote from the free movement of services, the ECJ again managed to spare an important national constitutional value. It is important, however, that in doing so, the ECJ also makes sure not to needlessly elevate the national value at issue to an EU value by embracing the national value in the same strong terms as a particular Member State may wish to put forward. Doing so would actually have the opposite effect: diverging national constitutional values may then – at least within the scope and application of EU law – at times have to yield for the elevated national value taken from one of the Member States that has been put forward as the EU standard. Moreover, the EU legislator will then be limited in its discretionary margin, as it will not be allowed to adopt legislation that does not at least offer the same level of protection. That being said, the ECJ has often to walk a narrow line, as at the same time it should not hide that there actually are EU values, which may affect the margins for the Member States. Above,[243] the case of *Omega Spielhallen*[244] was discussed in detail precisely to make this point. While the human dignity ranks prime among EU protected values, as evidenced by the Charter of Fundamental Rights of the EU, the ECJ at the same time had to make clear that the content given to that principle by the German authorities – which the ECJ in practice deferred to – may not necessarily correspond to the scope the Court would give to the principle at EU level.[245] The approach of the Court in *Omega Spielhallen*[246] of safeguarding the German concept of human dignity as a matter of *national* public policy offers an excellent way of striking this difficult balance.[247]

**III-51.** Interestingly, in areas where the value at issue seems firmly entrenched in the ECHR the ECJ finds less need to be so careful, even though it may thus be on a path of upsetting certain national sensitivities. In *Schmidberger*[248] the interpretation given by the ECJ to the freedom of expression was probably sufficiently unexceptional to avoid any major conflict between the national legal orders – especially the Austrian legal order from which the contested measure (an authorization to block the Brenner pass in protest against excessive road traffic) which the ECJ ultimately upheld originated – and the EU legal order. However, it seems unlikely that Member States share in full the approach taken by the ECJ in respect of the scope of protection to be given to the right to family life in *Metock*.[249] Yet, the ECJ seems to hope that Member States will be adopting a similarly broad approach in respect of wholly internal situations, in order to avoid cases of reverse discrimination.[250] In this sense the Court appears to be taking the

243. See, *supra*, at I-69 et seq.
244. Case C-36/02 *Omega Spielhallen* [2004] ECR I-9609.
245. See for instance the far more cautious approach in Case C-377/98 *Netherlands v. European Parliament and Council* [2001] ECR I-7079.
246. Case C-36/02 *Omega Spielhallen* [2004] ECR I-9609. See since then also Case C-208/09 *Sayn-Wittgenstein* [2010] ECR I-0000 and Case C-391/09 *Runevič-Vardyn* [2011] ECR I-0000, where the Court could pick up additional momentum for its approach from Article 4(2) TEU.
247. For more on balancing, see, *infra*, Part IV.
248. Case C-112/00 *Schmidberger* [2003] ECR I-5659.
249. Case C-127/08 *Metock* [2008] ECR I-6241.
250. Case C-127/08 *Metock* [2008] ECR I-6241, para. 79.

view of the Charter and the ECHR as complimentary instruments, offering equivalent protection in their different spheres of application.[251]

**III-52.** In my view the three sets of examples given, the national procedural autonomy, the respect for the national constitutional organization and the deference to national constitutional values, do argue for the recognition of the background principle of subsidiarity as a matter of *ordre public*. The fact that the more visible subsidiarity principle of Article 5 TEU seems more difficult to enforce should not undermine that conclusion. First, the meaning of the subsidiarity principle, namely that the Union shall take action 'only if and in so far as the objectives of the proposed action cannot be sufficiently achieved by the Member States and can therefore, by reason of the scale or effects of the proposed action, be better achieved by the Community', seems generally overestimated. Once a sufficient number of Member States seem convinced of the need of common action in a particular field, especially in the form of harmonizing pre-existing diverging national legislations, the conclusion seems inevitable that the conditions for the principle are fulfilled.[252] Second, that being said, cases like the *first tobacco advertising* case[253] demonstrate some sensitivity on the part of the ECJ to the underlying value of subsidiarity in assessing whether the EU should at all be allowed to take action in a particular field on the basis of Article 114 TFEU. Third, the fact that the national parliaments and the Committee of the Regions have both been given by the Lisbon Treaty of additional enforcement mechanisms in respect of the principle of subsidiarity, which is moreover strengthened through additional requirements as to the type of findings that support the statement of reasons put forward by the institutions,[254] seems to indicate that also this expression of the background principle of subsidiarity will become more visible.

**III-53.** However, it is important to stress that subsidiarity, as a principle at the core of the EU legal order, is there to help ensure the smooth interaction between the national levels and the EU, not as a brake on the effectiveness of the EU. One of the best examples of the confusion surrounding the subsidiarity principle I have ever encountered comes from the Dutch debate on the EU Constitution. Two of the reasons that were put forward to reject the Constitution – though none of them had a direct bearing on the Constitution – were the following. On the one hand, it was said that the Constitution was not doing enough in terms of protecting subsidiarity – and to illustrate that the example was given of the fact that the EU was meddling with local affairs in regulating the safety of playgrounds. On the other hand, the Constitution was criticized for not prohibiting bull fighting. In terms of subsidiarity, this is putting matters upside

251. Case C-256/11*Dereci* [2011] ECR I-0000, paras 70-74.
252. Case C-84/94 *United Kingdom v. Council* [1996] ECR I-5755, para. 47.
253. Case C-376/98 *Germany v. European Parliament and Council* [2000] ECR I-8419.
254. See the new Protocol on the application of the principles of subsidiarity and proportionality (2007) OJ C 306/150. For more see also F. Sander, 'Subsidiarity infringements before the European Court of Justice: futile interference with politics or a substantial step towards EU federalism?', *Columbia Journal of European Law* (2006): 529-532 and P. Kiiver, 'The Treaty of Lisbon, the National Parliaments and the Principle of Subsidiarity', *Maastricht Journal of European and Comparative Law* (2008): 77-83.

down. The safety of rides at playgrounds is no longer a matter of purely local interests when we are talking of slides and swings that are produced in one Member State to be distributed across the Union. By contrast, the fact that the Constitution (or the Lisbon Treaty) does not condemn bull fights – though both contain a ringing endorsement of animal welfare[255] – seems evidentiary of the sensitivity to the national identities of the Member States which the background principle of subsidiarity seeks to ensure. While as a matter of policy a lot may be said both in favour and against bull fighting or the need to ensure playground safety, the principle of subsidiarity is no magical force field that can be turned on and off depending on the political preferences of those invoking it. Rather, in its background form of ensuring 'unity in diversity' it is an immanent constitutional principle and, as the examples discussed above demonstrate, interacts with the EU *ordre public*.

### [D] European Citizenship

**III-54.** I submit without reservation that European citizenship is a matter of public policy and thus that the values European citizenship stands for are at the very heart of the values that deserve protection through EU *ordre public*. There are at least three reasons why this is so. First, in analogy to national citizenship, European citizenship creates a bond between the individual and the EU political order appealing to a sense of loyalty that is crucial for the functioning of that legal order. Second, the status of citizen of the Union is the catalyst for a myriad of rights for the individual. Foremost among them are a set of political rights converting the citizens of the Member States into political actors at the EU stage. This alone should suffice to conclude to the *ordre public* status of European citizenship, as there is no reason why these political actors deserve any less protection than the institutions or Member States in an 'ever closer'[256] 'Union of Citizens and States'.[257] Furthermore, European citizenship may also hold the promise of a legal order subject to the rule of law where fundamental rights are protected in full. Finally, European citizenship, in combination with the principle of equal treatment laid down in Article 18 TFEU, also induces a multiplication effect for a series of crucial social rights. Third, European citizenship expands the right of free movement to persons who are not or no longer fully economically active. It will be argued below how free movement is in essence an expression of human dignity. This, too, justifies elevating European citizenship, to the rank of EU *ordre public*.

**III-55.** First, citizenship is the formal inclusion of the individual into the polity.[258] Above it was indicated how the *ordre public* is sometimes used to stress the difference

255. See Article III-121 European Constitution and Article 13 TFEU.
256. Preamble TEU, 13th recital.
257. J.A. Hoeksma, 'De EU als Unie van Burgers en Lidstaten', *Nederlands Juristenblad* (2008): 330-334.
258. See in this respect also A. Schrauwen, 'Naar een waarlijk 'fundamentele status'? Democratie en Europees Burgerschap na het Verdrag van Lissabon', *Sociaal-Economische Wetgeving* (2008): 290.

between '"us" and "them"',[259] between aliens and members of the polity. If the treatment of aliens is a matter of public policy precisely because of concerns in respect of the levels of integration and loyalty outsiders have vis-à-vis the polity, it seems only obvious that the confirmation of this loyalty in the form of the bestowing of citizenship is also a matter of public policy. Admittedly, the way one becomes a European citizen is somewhat atypical. European citizenship does not replace any form of national citizenship, but rather complements a pre-existing citizenship of one of the Member States. A lot has been said since its introduction as to whether the European citizenship is sufficiently rooted and has sufficient to offer in order to ensure a similar allegiance as traditionally connected with citizenship of a State.[260] However, this misses the point, as the intention of the drafters, as evidenced by the use of the citizenship terminology, is indeed to arouse this 'sense of belonging'.[261] The ECJ, moreover, plays into that feeling by indeed maximizing the communality aspects of EU citizenship. Accordingly, there is no second-guessing as to how one became an EU citizen: once someone has the nationality of a Member State, all others must accept that person as an EU citizen.[262] Furthermore, in interplay with the Union legislator, the ECJ is shaping the citizenship of the Union as 'the fundamental status of nationals of the Member States',[263] offering access to new rights,[264] both at the EU level and at the level of the Member States, redefining the scope and application of EU law[265] and above all including the citizen in a unique form of solidarity.[266]

**III-56.** Second, the status of citizen of the Union is the catalyst for a myriad of rights for the individual.[267] On the one hand, the Treaties provide for a series of enumerated

259. *Supra*, at II-27.
260. See, *inter alia*, H. Manciaux, 'L'introuvable citoyenneté de l'Union dans le projet de Constitution pour l'Europe', *JurisClasseur Europe* (2004): 3-6; E. Delaney & L. Barani, 'The promotion of 'symmetrical' European Citizenship: a federal perspective', *European Integration* (2003): 95-114; L.M. Diez-Picazo, 'Citoyenneté et identité européennes', *European Review of Private Law* (2003): 771-786; K. Kostakopoulou, 'Nested "old" and "new" citizenships in the European Union: Bringing out the Complexity', *Columbia Journal of European Law* (1999): 389-413; J. Shaw, 'The Interpretation of European Union Citizenship', *Modern Law Review* (1998): 293-317; C. Closa, 'The Concept of Citizenship in the Treaty on European Union', *Common Market Law Review* (1992): 1137-1169. See also S. Kadelbach, 'Union Citizenship' in *Principles of European Constitutional Law*, ed. A. Von Bogdandy & J. Bast (Oxford/Portland: Hart, 2007), 453-499.
261. A. Schrauwen, 'European Union Citizenship in the Treaty of Lisbon: Any Change at All?', *Maastricht Journal of European and Comparative* Law (2008): 63.
262. Case C-200/02 *Zhu and Chen* [2004] ECR I-9925, para. 37. See already in respect of the free movement of persons Case C-369/90 *Micheletti* [1992] ECR I-4239, para. 10.
263. Case C-403/03 *Schempp* [2005] ECR I-6421, para. 15.
264. See, *infra*, at III-56.
265. Case C-66/08 *Kozłowski* [2008] ECR I-6041.
266. Case C-209/03 *Bidar* [2005] ECR I-2119, para. 56; Case C-184/99 *Grzelczyk* [2001] ECR I-6193, para. 44. The concept of solidarity in EU law has already been picked up in literature as having a broader constitutional meaning, also outside the case of citizenship, see M. Ross, 'Promoting solidarity: from public services to a European model of competition?', *Common Market Law Review* (2007): 1057-1080. See also A. Von Bogdandy, 'Constitutional Principles' in *Principles of European Constitutional Law*, ed. A. Von Bogdandy & J. Bast (Oxford/Portland: Hart, 2007), 32-34.
267. See also A. Schrauwen, 'Naar een waarlijk 'fundamentele status'? Democratie en Europees Burgerschap na het Verdrag van Lissabon', *Sociaal-Economische Wetgeving* (2008): 290-291.

rights: the right to move and reside freely within the territory of the Member States (Article 21(1) TFEU), active and passive voting rights in municipal elections (Article 22(1) TFEU) and elections for the European Parliament (Article 21(2) TFEU), diplomatic protection by other Member States (Article 23 TFEU), the right to petition the European Parliament (Article 24, paragraph 2 TFEU), the right to address the European Ombudsman (Article 24, paragraph 3 TFEU) and the right to receive answer back from any of the institutions in the same official language as the request was made in (Article 24, paragraph 4 TFEU). These rights may not sound very impressive, but appearances can be defective. The right to travel and take up residency has reshaped the polities of all the Member States in a manner that is so profound that I will return to it below in more detail.[268] The other rights are expressions of the attempt to create a bond between the Union and the nationals of the Member States. The right to stand as a candidate and vote in EU elections is obviously a major political right. Admittedly, at first sight this only concerns the right to vote and stand in *another* Member State, the other aspects of elections for the European Parliament being governed by a separate act of primary law, but this has been widened by the Court in recent case law to also become relevant in cases where citizens are enforcing their voting rights in elections for the European Parliament against their own government.[269] The political rights attached to European citizenship turn the nationals of the Member States into political actors in the EU legal order.[270] Just like the other political actors, the Member States and the institutions, the role of the citizens is thus key to the political order and thus worthy of protection as a matter of EU *ordre public*. While undoubtedly less weighty, the same can be said of the right to petition the European Parliament, address the European Ombudsman and communicate with the institutions in the official language of one's choice - as these rights are all instrumental in allowing citizens to have their voice heard in the decision-making process, which is precisely what the *ordre public* also protects in respect of Member States and institutions.

**III-57.** On the other hand, the ECJ has turned EU citizenship also into a focal point for a myriad of rights that are conferred upon the own nationals by the legal order of the Member States. The mechanism for doing so is simple in its ingenuity. Casting aside its unconvincing approach taken in *Martinez Sala,*[271] the ECJ since *Trojani*[272] adopts a

---

268. See, *infra*, at III-60 et seq.
269. Case C-300/04 *Eman and Sevinger* [2006] ECR I-8055. For the background to this case, see L. Besselink, 'Nederlands postkoloniaal kiesrecht: het Europees Parlement en de Tweede Kamer', *Nederlands Tijdschrift voor Europees Recht* (2007): 64-71.
270. See in this respect also J. Shaw, 'The Political Representation of Europe's Citizens: Developments - Court of Justice of the European Communities - Decisions of 12 September 2006, Case C-145/04, *Spain v. United Kingdom*, and Case C-300/04, *Eman and Sevinger v. College van Burgemeester en Wethouders van Den Haag*', *European Constitutional Law Review* (2008): 162-168; L.F.M. Besselink, 'Case C-145/04, *Spain v. United Kingdom*, judgment of the Grand Chamber of 12 September 2006; Case C-300/04, *Eman and Sevinger v. College van Burgemeester en Wethouders van Den Haag*, judgment of the Grand Chamber of 12 September 2006; ECtHR (Third Section), 6 September 2007, Applications Nos. 17173/07 and 17180/07, *Oslin Benito Sevinger and Michael Godfried Eman v. the Netherlands (Sevinger and Eman)*', *Common Market Law Review* (2008): 787-813.
271. Case C-85/96 *Martínez Sala* [1998] ECR I-2691.
272. Case C-456/02 *Trojani* [2004] ECR I-7573.

two-prong argumentation.[273] First, it finds that a citizen of the Union trying to make use of his/her citizenship rights, most notably the right to travel, is clearly exercising a right conferred by the Treaties. Accordingly, such a person clearly falls within the scope of application of the TEC, which as it happens is the trigger for making Article 18 TFEU applicable. So, second, any such person is entitled not to be discriminated against on the grounds of his/her nationality and thus receive the same treatment as a person holding the nationality of the Member State concerned, unless there is an objective reason why the two should be treated differently. In this way, EU citizens of the various Member States can become deeply rooted in the social fabric of the Member State where they reside, and depending on the level of their integration the need for equal treatment becomes evermore pressing. Accordingly, a passing tourist on holiday or truck driver may be entitled to the same language regime in court cases as the locals.[274] A foreign student may – as is also stipulated by legislation[275] – in principle not rely on the host State for financial aid for his/her studies.[276] However, the ECJ accepts that the position may evolve over time for those who are increasingly integrated but struck by a series of unfortunate events.[277] In the case of someone who ended up in another Member State for a wholly unrelated reason – for instance because they went to live with a relative as a minor – there may be even no reason whatsoever to deny the same support as for the locals once that person goes to university.[278] The only limit is the establishment of a 'genuine link with the society'[279] of the host Member State, the intensity of which varies depending on the societal role played by the right at issue. The emancipating effect of EU citizenship should thus not be underestimated. As it shapes a society where nationals from other Member States are no longer treated as suspicious aliens but as equal participants in the social and political order of the Member States, the citizenship of the Union seems also for this reason a matter of EU *ordre public*. This is all the more so if the Court, moreover, develops its case law further to target not only include discriminations, but also non-discriminatory restrictions that unduly hinder persons from exercising their right to travel to and reside in another Member State.[280]

273. For an extensive overview of the case law and its broader constitutional implications, see E. Spaventa, 'Seeing the wood despite the trees? On the scope of Union citizenship and its constitutional effects', *Common Market Law Review* (2008): 13-45.
274. Case C-274/96 *Bickel and Franz* [1998] ECR I-7637.
275. See Article 24(2) of Directive 2004/38/EC of the European Parliament and of the Council of 29 April 2004 on the right of citizens of the Union and their family members to move and reside freely within the territory of the Member States amending Regulation (EEC) No 1612/68 and repealing Directives 64/221/EEC, 68/360/EEC, 72/194/EEC, 73/148/EEC, 75/34/EEC, 75/35/EEC, 90/364/EEC, 90/365/EEC and 93/96/EEC (2004) OJ L 158/77.
276. On the impact of this legislation, compare Case C-158/07 *Förster* [2008] ECR I-8507, with the contrary Opinion of AG Mazák who argued in favour of granting the student maintenance grant despite the legislative framework.
277. Case C-184/99 *Grzelczyk* [2001] ECR I-6193.
278. Case C-209/03 *Bidar* [2005] ECR I-2119.
279. Case C-209/03 *Bidar* [2005] ECR I-2119, para. 62.
280. See, for instance, Case C-353/06 *Grunkin and Paul* [2008] ECR I-7639; Case C-192/05 *Tas-Hagen* [2006] ECR I-10451. See already earlier Opinion of AG Jacobs in Case C-224/02 *Pusa* [2004] ECR I-5763. For more on this evolution, see X., 'Editorial Comments – Two-speed European Citizenship? Can the Lisbon Treaty help close the gap?', *Common Market Law Review*

**III-58.** This role of EU citizenship as an anchor point for rights conferred by both the national and the EU legal orders has since inspired many to take the analogy with national citizenship one step further. It has been argued that citizenship has three major components: the civil, the political and the social.[281] Arguably, the political component is mainly covered by the explicit rights provided for by the Treaties, and the social component is fleshed out through the case law of the ECJ. The civil component, however, concerns the classic civil rights, 'the rights necessary for individual freedom – liberty of the person, freedom of speech, thought and faith, the right to own property and to conclude valid contracts and the right to justice'.[282] The link between EU citizenship and civil rights was already famously brought to the fore even before the formal EU citizenship was established in the catch phrase '*civis europeus sum*' in the eloquent argument by Advocate General Jacobs for ensuring that citizens wherever they go in the Union would always be certain to enjoy these basic civil rights, including *in casu* the right to one's name.[283] While the ECJ could address the issue in *Konstantinidis*[284] by reframing the matter in its classic freedom of establishment case law, the exact same issue of the recognition of a foreign name has since returned at least twice in the context of EU citizenship.[285] Whereas these cases may all be solved as an application of the non-discrimination principle, as if the name were some kind of social advantage that is being denied, the Opinion of Advocate General Jacobs in *Standesamt Stadt Niebüll*[286] makes clear that really more is at stake. As he explains 'a person's name is a fundamental part of his or her identity and private life, the protection of which is widely recognized in national constitutions and international instruments'[287] and he thus rightly concludes that:

> [i]t thus seems to me totally incompatible with the status and rights of a citizen of the European Union – which, in the Court's phrase, is 'destined to be the fundamental status of nationals of the Member States' – to be required to bear different names under the laws of different Member States[288].

---

(2008): 1-11; E. Spaventa, 'Seeing the wood despite the trees? On the scope of Union citizenship and its constitutional effects', *Common Market Law Review* (2008): 13-45.

281. In this sense M. Feintuck, *'The Public Interest' in Regulation* (Oxford: OUP, 2004), 45, based on T.H. Marshall, *Citizenship and Social Class* (Cambridge: Cambridge University Press, 1950) and *id.., Sociology at the Crossroads and Other Essays* (London: Heinemann, 1969).
282. T.H. Marshall, *Citizenship and Social Class* (Cambridge: Cambridge University Press, 1950), 10-11; see further M. Feintuck, *'The Public Interest' in Regulation* (Oxford: OUP, 2004), 45.
283. Opinion of AG Jacobs in Case C-168/91 *Konstantinidis* [1993] ECR I-1191.
284. Case C-168/91 *Konstantinidis* [1993] ECR I-1191.
285. Case C-148/02 *Garcia Avello* [2003] ECR I-11613; Opinion of AG Sharpston in Case C-353/06 *Grunkin and Paul* [2008] ECR I-7639 (see in this respect also the Opinion of AG Jacobs in Case C-96/04 *Standesamt Stadt Niebüll* [2006] ECR I-3561).
286. Opinion of AG Jacobs in Case C-96/04 *Standesamt Stadt Niebüll* [2006] ECR I-3561.
287. Opinion of AG Jacobs in Case C-96/04 *Standesamt Stadt Niebüll* [2006] ECR I-3561, para. 55.
288. Opinion of AG Jacobs in Case C-96/04 *Standesamt Stadt Niebüll* [2006] ECR I-3561, para 56 (internal citations omitted). See, nevertheless, the outcome of some later cases, where that concern was balanced with other public policy interests, see Case C-208/09 Sayn-Wittgenstein [2010] ECR I-0000; Case C-391/09 *Runevič-Vardyn* [2011] ECR I-0000.

It really becomes an issue of the EU citizen as bearer of civil rights. The ECJ, therefore, unsurprisingly followed that line, though without stressing the underlying fundamental rights, when it agreed in the follow-up case of *Grunkin and Paul* that:

> Article [21 TFEU] precludes the authorities of a Member State, in applying national law, from refusing to recognise a child's surname, as determined and registered in a second Member State in which the child – who, like his parents, has only the nationality of the first Member State – was born and has been resident since birth[289].

**III-59.** This trend is moreover reinforced by two recent developments. On the one hand, the integration of the Charter of Fundamental Rights of the EU[290] into the Treaties (albeit by reference),[291] since the Lisbon Treaty entered into force has provided the EU with its own human rights catalogue. Admittedly, the Charter can only be invoked against the Member States when they are acting within the scope of Union law,[292] a point which the Court clarified neatly in *Dereci.*[293] Yet, if one accepts that at

289. Case C-353/06 *Grunkin and Paul* [2008] ECR I-3561, para. 19.

290. Charter of Fundamental Rights of the European Union (2008) OJ C 303/1. See on the relationship between citizenship and the Charter also A. Schrauwen., 'Naar een waarlijk 'fundamentele status'? Democratie en Europees Burgerschap na het Verdrag van Lissabon', *Sociaal-Economische Wetgeving* (2008): 291-292.

291. Article 6 TEU in its post-Lisbon version. See also – somewhat sceptical – J. Baquero Cruz, 'What's Left of the Charter? Reflections on Law and Political Mythology', *Maastricht Journal of European and Comparative Law* (2008): 65-75.

292. See Article 51 of the Charter, as authoritatively clarified by the 'Explanations relating to the Charter of Fundamental Rights in view of Case 260/89 *Elliniki Radiophonia Tiléorassi* [1991] ECR I-2925. The ECJ has, moreover, argued this point – albeit in answering whether general principles of EC law could be invoked, such as the prohibition on grounds of age, which is after all also included in the Charter – in Case C-427/06 *Bartsch* [2008] ECR I-7245, paras 14-25, carefully weighing the limits of the Court's finding in Case C-144/04 *Mangold* [2005] ECR I-998, para. 75 that 'where national rules fall within the scope of Community law...and reference is made to the Court for a preliminary ruling, the Court must provide all the criteria of interpretation needed by the national court to determine whether those rules are compatible with the general principles of Community law'.

293. Case C-256/11*Dereci* [2011] ECR I-0000, paras 70-74 where the Court had to explain whether the right to family life could be invoked by EU citizens and their third-country national family members against their own Member State, in situation where the EU citizen had never moved to another Member State in the sense of Article 21 TFEU before. The Court started its reasoning invoking Case C-400/10 PPU *McB.* [2010] ECR I-0000, para. 53 to explain that 'in so far as Article 7 of the Charter of Fundamental Rights of the European Union ('the Charter'), concerning respect for private and family life, contains rights which correspond to rights guaranteed by Article 8(1) of the ECHR, the meaning and scope of Article 7 of the Charter are to be the same as those laid down by Article 8(1) of the ECHR, as interpreted by the case law of the European Court of Human Rights'. It then continued, however – again invoking *McB*, para. 51 and Joined Cases C-483/09 and C-1/10 *Gueye and Salmerón Sánchez* [2011] ECR I-0000, para. 69 – to stress that 'it must be borne in mind that the provisions of the Charter are, according to Article 51(1) thereof, addressed to the Member States only when they are implementing European Union law. Under Article 51(2), the Charter does not extend the field of application of European Union law beyond the powers of the Union, and it does not establish any new power or task for the Union, or modify powers and tasks as defined in the Treaties. Accordingly, the Court is called upon to interpret, in the light of the Charter, the law of the European Union within the limits of the powers conferred on it'. The Court then lies out the practical consequence of that: 'Thus, in the present case, if the referring court considers, in the light of the circumstances of the disputes in the main proceedings, that the situation of the

least[294] citizens who have made use of their free movement right fall within the scope of the Treaty for the purpose of relying on Article 18 TFEU, then surely any action of a Member State vis-à-vis this person may come within the scope of the Charter as well. On the other hand, the ECJ continues to be confronted with claims by citizens in contexts that are at the core of classic human rights protection. Accordingly, the ECJ accepts that the optional exception to the European Arrest Warrant enabling Member States to refuse the extradition of their own nationals to undergo punishment abroad if they are incarcerated in their home country[295] – promoting family life, and addressing concerns, real or perceived, of treatment of prisoners abroad – should also extend to EU citizens who do not hold the nationality of the executing State, but have an equally genuine link with that society.[296] Admittedly, one could also see the existence of this exception, as in part inspired by distrust in the level of human rights protection in other Member State, and thus as evidence that we have not yet reached the stage of *civis europeus sum*. After all, if we had, there would be no ground for distrust, for the civil rights component of EU citizenship would offer sufficient protection against abuse wherever an EU citizen goes. Essentially, the same fundamental rights protection would apply regardless of where in the EU the citizen finds himself/herself. However, I prefer to read the judgment as a sign of the growing sensitivity to the civil aspect of EU citizenship,[297] as it allows EU citizens from other Member States to effectively enjoy the same high level of fundamental rights protection as the locals.

**III-60.** Third, EU citizenship is a matter of *ordre public*, as far as I am concerned, because of its effect of universalizing the free movement of persons beyond the sphere of economic migration.[298] I will submit below, when addressing the protection by the EU *ordre public* of the economic order that I consider the four freedoms to be part and parcel of the EU *ordre public économique*. However, even apart from this economic aspect, the free movement of persons, and by extension the other of the four freedoms, is so fundamental because it is an expression of the very first right of the Charter of

applicants in the main proceedings is covered by European Union law, it must examine whether the refusal of their right of residence undermines the right to respect for private and family life provided for in Article 7 of the Charter. On the other hand, if it takes the view that that situation is not covered by European Union law, it must undertake that examination in the light of Article 8(1) of the ECHR.'

294. And in exceptional cases also others, see Case C-34/09 *Ruiz Zambrano* [2011] ECR I-0000, but only when the 'genuine enjoyment of the substance of the rights conferred by virtue of that status' as citizen of the Union is at risk, see and compare Case C-434/09 *McCarthy* [2011] ECR I-0000; Case C-256/11*Dereci* [2011] ECR I-0000.

295. Article 4(6) of Council Framework Decision 2002/584/JHA of 13 June 2002 on the European arrest warrant and the surrender procedures between the Member States (2002) OJ L 190/1.

296. Case C-66/08 *Kozłowski* [2008] ECR I-6041. See also Case C-123/08 *Wolzenburg* [2009] ECR I-9621.

297. It has been argued that there even is a duty to protect the fundamental rights of EU citizens, see J. Suerbaum, 'Die Schutzpflichtdimension der Gemeinschaftsgrundrechte', *Europarecht* (2003): 390-416; see also L. Jaeckel, 'The duty to protect fundamental rights in the European Community', *European Law Review* (2003): 508-527.

298. This expansion has also left it mark on the free movement of workers, see M. Cousins; 'Free movement of workers, EU citizenship and access to social advantages', *Maastricht Journal of European and Comparative Law* (2007): 343-359.

Fundamental Rights of the EU, human dignity.[299] I submit that the true revolutionary force of the free movement lies in its emancipating capability, enabling all EU citizens to realize their full potential, beyond the boundaries of the State where they were born and thus become more complete human beings.[300] As a result of the free movement, a Dutch aspiring painter who has a calling to go and paint sunflowers in the Provence may do so, in the same way as four Belgian ladies may move to Winterberg in order to pursue their dream of creating a Belgian Olympic bobsleigh team. Seen from this perspective, the free movement of persons is then about being all you can be, about offering opportunities for self-realization beyond the normal boundaries of the home state. The case law of the ECJ actually bears witness to this. Why else should Germany separately fund a student to study abroad while it is offering excellent education at home at virtually no cost, if not because it turns out that the particular curriculum is simply not on offer in Germany so that Germany would otherwise be standing in the way of the realization of the full potential of one of its citizens.[301] The other freedoms - goods, capital and services - may then be considered as derivative rights that ensure, on the one hand, the material conditions for this self-realization (one cannot travel without clothes; one cannot live in Winterberg to start a bobsleigh team if one could not enjoy the local hospitality or bring the necessary funds to buy equipment) and, at least as important, guarantee, on the other hand, that the whole Union in turn may also enjoy the fruits of allowing its citizens to realize their full potential in the form of new products, services and financial profits. Accordingly, even if one does not travel abroad one's good business ideas or clever inventions may cross the boundaries of the Member States. Services can be enjoyed locally or abroad, goods may circulate freely and as money makes the world go round, the capital to make it all economically viable should flow freely accordingly. I submit that here may lay the deeper rationale for cases such as *Cowan*[302] or *Carpenter*[303] which may otherwise[304] seem to overstate the real impact on intra-Union trade. They ensure that Mr Cowan can enjoy in full his role as a

299. One could also make a similar argument on the basis of the constitutional principle of liberty, which 'has been a core element of integration theory from its early stages. W Hallstein understood *European integration*, with its tendency to a continental scope, *as a significant expansion of the individual's space of autonomous action*', see in this respect A. Von Bogdandy, 'Constitutional Principles' in *Principles of European Constitutional Law*, ed. A. Von Bogdandy & J. Bast (Oxford/Portland: Hart, 2007), 13 (emphasis added).
300. Without seeking to engage in a full analysis of the concept, it is submitted that this approach fits in neatly with an approach to EU law as 'cosmopolitan law', which 'increasingly speaks to individuals and not to nation-states' as McGlynn puts it. See in this respect, P. Eleftheriadis, 'Cosmopolitan Law', *European Law Journal* (2003): 241-263; I. Ward, 'Kant and the Transnational Order: Towards a European Community Jurisprudence', *Ratio Juris* (1995): 315-329. For a defence of this approach, see C. McGlynn, *Families and the European Union: law, politics and pluralism* (Cambridge: Cambridge University Press, 2006), 2-5.
301. Joined Cases C-11/06 and C-12/06 *Morgan* [2007] ECR I-9161. See also Case C-56/09 *Zanotti* [2010] ECR I-4517, where it is nuanced that the expense should not be made above and beyond the maximum set for corresponding national tuition compensation.
302. Case C-186/87 *Cowan* [1989] ECR 195.
303. Case C-60/00 *Carpenter* [2002] ECR I-6279.
304. See in this sense L. Jadoul & F. Vanneste, 'Case C-60/00. Mary Carpenter v. Secretary of State for the Home Department (E.C.J. July 11, 2002)', *Columbia Journal of European Law* (2003): 447-455.

consumer of services in a foreign city, or that Mr Carpenter can add just this little extra to his business by also maintaining his overseas contacts. Even marginal increases in the opportunities to go abroad for people like Mr Carpenter or Mr Cowan, may have nonetheless major effects – in the individual case and, in any event, in the aggregate – not only on the level of economic exchange across the Union, but also in respect of the exchange of ideas, ambitions and experiences among the peoples of Europe, which in turn has at the very least the potential to invigorate both personal development and EU-wide integration. This emancipating force is also visible in a number of cases concerning children who, once they have started school in another Member State on the basis of what is now Article 10 Regulation 492/2011[305] as children of Union workers, gain an independent right to continue that education, even if that means that their primary carers will need to be given social assistance and residence permits long after they ceased to be a Union worker.[306] At the same time this approach of free movement explains also some of its limits. First the limits imposed by the Treaties and the case law of the Court in the form of mandatory requirements, are the limits that should ensure that one person's self-realization does not become another person's doom. As an expression of human dignity, the free movement finds its limits in the dignity of others. Free movement as self-realization is obviously not an excuse to be all the paedophile[307] or drugs dealer one can be,[308] for instance, and the same caution extends *mutatis mutandis* to the instruments and fruits in the form of goods, services and capital as outlined above.[309] Second, if free movement really is an expression of human dignity one could object that there is no sound reason to limit it to EU nationals. The answer to that is two-fold. First of all, despite deep-held believes about fundamental rights being universal, they do not exist in the absence of a legal order. Moreover, this legal order may not solely be concerned with the dignity of human beings, but there may also be an aspect of the dignity of States and international organizations.[310] The limitation of the free movement right to EU nationals arises because of the inherent limitations of a legal order that also recognizes States. However, and this is the second part of the answer, this only goes as far as this really is an issue. There is an important strand of the ECJ case law that actually seeks to expand the reach of these rights to third-country nationals, either because there are international agreements in play – so instances where these other subjects, the States or international organizations have had their role to play – or because the fate of a Union citizen may also be at stake. The prime example of the former is the rather inclusive interpretation of the various

305. Regulation (EU) No 492/2011 of the European Parliament and of the Council of 5 April 2011 on freedom of movement for workers within the Union OJ (2011) L 141/1. See also old Article 12 Regulation (EEC) No 1612/68 of the Council of 15 October 1968 on freedom of movement for workers within the Community, *Official Journal, English Special Edition 1968 II*, 475.
306. Case C-310/08 *Ibrahim* [2010] ECR I-1065; Case C-480/08 *Texeira* [2010] ECR I-1107.
307. Case C-348/09 *P.I.* [2012] ECR I-0000.
308. Case C-145/09 *Tsakouridis* [2010] ECR I-0000.
309. *Supra*, at II-7 to II-82.
310. See on the concept of dignity of states, L. Oppenheim, *International Law: A Treatise*, Vol. I (London: The Law Book Exchange, 2006), 203-206. Even within federal entities this may still play a major role, see *Alden v. Maine*, 527 U.S. 706 (1999); for more see M. Killenbeck, 'In(re)dignity: the New Federalism in Perspective', *Arkansas Law Review* (2004): 1-68.

association agreements and their derived instruments.[311] The other scenario is demonstrated by such diverse cases as those concerning the posting of third-country nationals by EU companies in other Member States,[312] the restrictive reading of the Schengen agreement in respect of third-national spouses in *Commission v. Spain*[313] or the right of residence of third-country relatives as established in *Chen*,[314] *Jia*[315] and most decisively *Metock*[316] and *Ruiz Zambrano*.[317] Moreover, also in the case of family reunification, which by definition involves at least one third-country national who has built up some ties with a Member State before the family reunification takes place, the Court will not allow Member States to throw up too many barriers.[318] Similarly, in the case of long-term residents, the Court will not easily accept unequal treatment in the access to certain core social benefits.[319] Third, conversely this also explains to a certain extent what the boundaries are in relying on this free movement right against one's own Member State. As the ECJ stresses in *Metock* there is a risk of reverse discrimination, but its effect is surely limited if all Member States are a party to the ECHR,[320] as the core of this right of self-realization may also be covered by classic fundamental rights including the freedom of expression, assembly and religion, the right to family life and the right to property applicable outside the scope of Union law.[321] Moreover, the Member States may not preclude an EU citizen from going abroad to realize his/her full potential.[322] So while one cannot force the Belgian

311. See *inter alia*, Case C-294/06 *Payir* [2008] ECR I-203; Case C-97/05 *Gattousi* [2006] ECR I-11917; Case C-265/03 *Simutenkov* [2005] ECR I-2579.
312. Case C-244/04 *Commission v. Germany* [2006] ECR I-885; Case C-43/93 *Vander Elst* [1994] ECR I-3803.
313. Case C-503/03 *Commission v. Spain* [2006] ECR I-1097.
314. Case C-200/02 *Zhu and Chen* [2004] ECR I-9925.
315. Case C-1/05 *Jia* [2007] ECR I-1.
316. Case C-127/08 *Metock* [2008] ECR I-6241.
317. Case C-34/09 *Ruiz Zambrano* [2011] ECR I-0000.
318. Case C-578/08 *Chakroun* [2010] ECR I-1839.
319. Case C-571/10 *Kamberaj* [2012] ECR I-0000.
320. Case C-127/08 *Metock* [2008] ECR I-6241, para. 79.
321. Case C-256/11*Dereci* [2011] ECR I-0000, paras 70-74.
322. As confirmed by Case C-499/06 *Nerkowska* [2008] ECR I-3993, the citizenship rules also preclude legislation that would discourage people from leaving their home country. One could object that the ECJ has nonetheless allowed Belgium to withhold certain unemployment benefits in Case C-406/04 *De Cuyper* [2006] ECR I-6947, but that does not seem to contradict my argument. Precisely because he was claiming unemployment benefits– at least in the Court's view (the only point of criticism I have on the judgment, is on this qualification which is legally correct but fails to take into account the realities of the Belgium labour market) – Mr De Cuyper seemed still interested in participating in the Belgium labour market, as he claims benefits reserved for persons who want to realize something in Belgium. If he then contradicts himself by going abroad, and taking into account the non-exportability of certain benefits, it is understandable that he has to forego this benefit. However, he is still free to go abroad using other financial means or in order to participate in the labour market of another Member State. Accordingly, real pensioners, who by contrast are not seeking benefits connected to their continuing participation in the labour market they left behind, may effectively challenge certain rules that deter them from or (financially) punish them for leaving, see Case C-224/02 *Pusa* [2004] ECR I-5763. See also Case C-520/04 *Turpeinen* [2006] ECR I-10685. See also Case C-353/06 *Grunkin and Paul* [2008] ECR I-7639; Case C-192/05 *Tas-Hagen* [2006] ECR I-10451. See already earlier Opinion of AG Jacobs in Case C-224/02 *Pusa* [2004] ECR I-5763. For more on this evolution, see X., 'Editorial Comments – Two-speed European Citizenship? Can the

government to build a bobsleigh track, the Belgian government cannot stop Belgian women who want to move to the Alps to learn this challenging sport. Moreover, as demonstrated by *Morgan,*[323] under certain circumstances the government may even have to fund this foreign adventure.

**III-61.** Finally, there is also a political component to this right of free movement. The free movement has strengthened the potential of *exit* as a serious alternative over *voice.* Persons, and not only merely those engaged in intra-Community trade, whether they belong to a minority or not, who for whatever reason no longer feel at home in their Member State – oppressed may be too strong, taking into account that Member States are supposed to respect the rule of law and fundamental rights – may now also consider moving to a more welcoming Member State and thus vote with their feet. While again this may only apply to a small minority of persons, its potential – for instance in case of major regime switches, such as the coming into power, after democratic elections, of an extreme right government – should not be dismissed a priori. Only in exceptional cases, may Member States try to restrict this right to leave the country.[324]

### [E] Fundamental Rights

**III-62.** The link between fundamental rights and the *ordre public* is not surprising. As the French writer Émile-Auguste Chartier – better known as Alain – wrote: 'la liberté ne va pas sans l'ordre, l'ordre ne vaut rien sans la liberté'. Above[325] it was described how the ECtHR has construed a genuine 'European Public Order'[326] on the basis of the ECHR. It is precisely the combination of the basic rules of the political and legal order – as outlined in the foregoing paragraphs – and the fundamental liberties that is seen to be at the heart of the *ordre public,* indeed it has been dubbed *'l'ordre public fondamental'.*[327] Within the EU legal order this linkage becomes manifest in the special position human dignity, fundamental rights – including the rights of the child but also procedural rights – and the principle of equal treatment take in the EU constitutional order.[328]

**III-63.** First, attention should be paid to human dignity. It is laid down in Article 1 of the Charter of Fundamental Rights and as the explanations to the Charter explain 'none of the rights laid down in this Charter may be used to harm the dignity of another

---

Lisbon Treaty help close the gap?', *Common Market Law Review* (2008): 1-11; E. Spaventa, 'Seeing the wood despite the trees? On the scope of Union citizenship and its constitutional effects', *Common Market Law Review* (2008): 13-45.

323. Joined Cases C-11/06 and C-12/06 *Morgan* [2007] ECR I-9161.
324. Case C-434/10 *Aladzov* [2011] ECR I-0000; Case C-430/10 *Gadyrov* [2011] ECR I-0000.
325. See, *supra*, at I-37 et seq.
326. ECtHR, 23 February 1995, *Loizidou v. Turkey* (preliminary objections), para. 75.
327. J.-F. Romain, 'L'*ordre public* (notion générale) et les droits de l'homme' in *L'ordre public: concept et applications,* ed. J.-F. Romain, M. Grégoire & V. Simonart (Bruxelles: Bruylant, 1995), 32-33.
328. For an overview, see Ph. Alston. (ed.), *The EU and Human Rights* (Oxford: Oxford University Press, 1999); see also J. Kühling, 'Fundamental Rights' in *Principles of European Constitutional Law,* ed. A. Von Bogdandy & J. Bast (Oxford/Portland: Hart, 2007), 501-547.

person, and that the dignity of the human person is part of the substance of the rights laid down in this Charter. It must therefore be respected, even where a right is restricted'.[329] The ECJ first recognized its existence in the EU legal order in the *biotechnology* case,[330] however, without clarifying its exact scope and impact. The link between the *ordre public* and human dignity was made very explicit, though, in *Omega Spielhallen.*[331] As explained extensively above,[332] the ECJ had to rely on the public order exception to the free movement of services in order to give proper weight to the *German* concept of human dignity in the face of a ban on a laser game. While I have argued that this German concept does not need to coincide with the EU concept of human dignity, which may mainly be defined only in the face of cases like the *biotechnology* case[333] where the policy margin of the EU legislator is at stake, this should not detract from the fact that *Omega Spielhallen*[334] is a clear confirmation of the importance the EU legal order attaches to human dignity. As the Court explained:

> the Community legal order undeniably strives to ensure respect for human dignity as a general principle of law. There can therefore be no doubt that the objective of protecting human dignity is compatible with Community law, it being immaterial in that respect that, in Germany, the principle of respect for human dignity has a particular status as an independent fundamental right[335].

**III-64.** The ECJ is moreover increasingly adamant about the place fundamental rights have in the EU legal order. In furtherance of Article 6 TEU, the fundamental rights are used as a limitation on both the Union and the Member States. As far as the Union is concerned this is evidenced in two ways, though 'limitation' may not be the most fortunate term. After all, if fundamental rights are at the core of the EU legal order, cases where fundamental rights take precedence over EU policies are in a sense not limiting the Union, but rather allowing it to live up to its own values as laid down in Article 6 TEU. Nevertheless, on the one hand, the *Schmidberger*[336] case offers a great example how respect for fundamental rights – *in casu* the freedom of expression – serves as a justification for restricting the free movement of goods,[337] a justification which Advocate General Jacobs, moreover, linked explicitly to the *ordre public.*[338] On the other hand, the recent appeals judgment in *Kadi*[339] makes a dramatic case for

329. Explanations relating to the Charter of Fundamental Rights (2007) OJ C303/17.
330. Case C-377/98 *Netherlands v. European Parliament and Council* [2001] ECR I-7079, para. 70.
331. Case C-36/02 *Omega Spielhallen* [2004] ECR I-9609.
332. See, *supra*, at I-69 et seq.
333. Case C-377/98 *Netherlands v. European Parliament and Council* [2001] ECR I-7079.
334. Case C-36/02 *Omega Spielhallen* [2004] ECR I-9609.
335. Case C-36/02 *Omega Spielhallen* [2004] ECR I-9609, para. 34.
336. Case C-112/00 *Schmidberger* [2003] ECR I-5659
337. Actually, if one accepts as I submitted *supra*, at III-60, that the free movement of persons – and as derivative the free movement of goods – are an expression of human dignity because of their emancipating effect, Case C-112/00 *Schmidberger* [2003] ECR I-5659, could be read as a case about balancing the expressive rights of the protesters with the expressive value in free movement. With alternative channels for the free movement of goods available, it then seems correct that the additional message of the protesters was given preference.
338. Opinion of AG Jacobs in Case C-112/00 *Schmidberger* [2003] ECR I-5659, para. 95
339. Joined Cases C-402/05 P and C-415/05 P *Kadi v. Council* [2008] ECR I-6351.

enforcing fundamental rights within the EU legal order vis-à-vis the EU institutions, even – or maybe precisely – in the most sensitive areas, such as the imposition of sanctions on individuals suspected of links with terrorist organizations in execution of an UNSC resolution. In no uncertain terms the ECJ, after recalling the importance of fundamental rights,[340] concluded:

> that the obligations imposed by an international agreement cannot have the effect of prejudicing the constitutional principles of the EC Treaty, which include the principle that all Community acts must respect fundamental rights, that respect constituting a condition of their lawfulness which it is for the Court to review in the framework of the complete system of legal remedies established by the Treaty[341].

A clearer expression of how fundamental rights are at the heart of the EU constitutional order – and are thus a matter of EU *ordre public* is hardly imaginable. Since the Lisbon Treaty brought a binding Charter it appears that the gloves are now fully off, with the result that the Court is now finally striking down pieces of EU legislation on the ground that they breach fundamental rights,[342] fully living up to its role as a constitutional court for the Union. The fundamental rights also serve as a limitation on the Member States, at least when they are acting within the scope of EU law.[343] This, too, was confirmed again in dramatic fashion recently, when the ECJ reversed its prior *Akrich*[344] ruling because of the right to family life and held that spouses of EU nationals who made use of their free movement rights should be given a residence permit to allow them to stay with their partner, even though they had no prior lawful residence in the country.[345]

**III-65.** The fundamental rights protected go beyond the classic civil and political rights and freedoms as set out in the ECHR. Accordingly, while I have been somewhat sceptical as to the approach taken by the ECJ in *Viking*[346] and *Laval,*[347] fact is that in these cases the Court makes it clear that also core social rights, such as the right to take industrial action, are well-rooted in the EU legal order.[348] Similarly, the ECJ seems willing to even accept limitations to the free movement of goods – in particular DVDs, which are moreover also protected as a matter of freedom of expression – in order to give additional protection to minors in accordance with the Convention on the Rights of the Child.[349] Crucial in this development is again the drawing up of the Charter of

340. Joined Cases C-402/05 P and C-415/05 P *Kadi v. Council* [2008] ECR I-6351, paras 283-284.
341. Joined Cases C-402/05 P and C-415/05 P *Kadi v. Council* [2008] ECR I-6351, para. 285.
342. Joined Cases C-92/09 and C-93/09 *Schecke and Eifert* [2010] ECR I-0000; Case C-236/09 *Association Belge des Consommateurs Test-Achats* [2011] ECR I-0000.
343. Case 260/89 *Elliniki Radiophonia Tiléorassi* [1991] ECR I-2925.
344. Case C-109/01 *Akrich* [2003] ECR I-9607.
345. Case C-127/08 *Metock* [2008] ECR I-6241.
346. Case C-438/05 *International Transport Workers' Federation* [2007] ECR I-10779, para. 43.
347. Case C-341/05 *Laval un Partneri* [2007] ECR I-11767, para. 90.
348. However, it is unclear whether the ECJ has realized the full breadth of the rights of trade unions in the case law of the ECtHR, see in this respect J. Malmberg & T. Sigeman, 'Industrial action and EU economic freedoms: the autonomous collective bargaining model curtailed by the European Court of Justice', *Common Market Law Review* (2008): 1131-1132.
349. Case C-244/06 *Dynamic Medien* [2008] ECR I-505, para 40-41.

Fundamental Rights, which indeed also incorporates these more recent evolutions in human rights law.[350]

**III-66.** As the Union does not have its own police or military forces – and to the extent that it has through its Member States, the jurisdiction of the ECJ is particularly limited – the main way for the EU institutions to interact with the EU citizen is through legal decisions. It is therefore unsurprising that a substantial part of the fundamental rights case law of the ECJ focuses on procedural aspects. As the examples on essential procedural requirements demonstrate, the EU courts must regularly rule on issues concerning the right to be heard,[351] the rights of the defence,[352] the impartiality of judges[353] or the reasonable duration.[354] However, as the case law on *ne bis in idem* in competition cases demonstrates, the ECJ never overlooks the specificity of the EU legal order.[355] Moreover, although the national procedural autonomy is one of the bedrocks of the EU legal order, the case law of the ECJ also contains several examples where rules of national procedural law are challenged, as the ECJ seeks to ensure that national courts offer effective judicial protection in cases involving an element of EU law.[356] Accordingly, the ECJ requires foremost that individuals effectively have access to a national court to enforce EU law[357] – without having to break the law first[358] – but also ensures that remedies are available to block the enforcement of judicial decisions that were taken in proceedings that are contrary to fundamental rights.[359]

**III-67.** Finally, something must be said on the principle of equality, which one could arguably also treat separately as a constitutional principle in its own right, but which I choose to discuss here in the fundamental rights section,[360] because of its link with the

350. See *in casu* Article 28 (right to collective bargaining and action) and Article 24 (rights of the child) of the Charter of Fundamental Rights of the European Union (2010) OJ C 83/389.
351. Joined Cases C-402/05 P and C-415/05 P *Kadi v. Council* [2008] ECR I-6351.
352. Joined Cases T-25/95, T-26/95, T-30/95 to T-32/95, T-34/95, T-35/95 to T-39/95, T-42/95 to T-46/95, T-48/95, T-50/95 to T-65/95, T-68/95 to T-71/95, T-87/95, T-88/95, T-103/95 and T-104/95 *Cimenteries CBR and Others v. Commission* [2000] ECR II-491, paras 475-487; Joined Cases T-186/97, T-187/97, T-190/97 to T-192/97, T-210/97, T-211/97, T-216/97 to 218/97, T-279/97, T-280/97, T-293/97 and T-147/99 *Kaufring and Others v. Commission* [2001] ECR II-1337, paras 134-163.
353. Joined Cases C-341/06 and C-342/06 P *Chronopost v. Ufex* [2008] ECR I-4777, para. 47.
354. Case C-185/95 P *Baustahlgewebe v. Commission* [1998] ECR I-8417. See also Joined Cases C-120/06 P and C-121/06 P *FIAMM v. Council and Commission* [2008] ECR I-6513, paras 191-214.
355. See, *inter alia*, Case C-289/04 P *Sowa Denko KK v. Commission* [2006] ECR I-5859, paras 50-63; Case C-308/04 P *SGL Carbon v. Commission* [2006] ECR I-5977, paras 26-39. Contrast with the case law in criminal matters, see, *inter alia*, Joined Cases C-187/01 and C-385/01 *Gözütok and Brügge* [2003] ECR I-1345; Case C-288/05 *Kretzinger* [2007] ECR I-6441; Case C-367/05 *Kraaijenbrink* [2007] ECR I-6619.
356. Arguably, the justification for these standards imposed in respect of national law is Article 6 ECHR, see S. Prechal & N. Shelkoplyas, 'National Procedures, Public Policy and EC Law. From Van Schijndel to Eco Swiss and Beyond', *European Review of Private Law* (2004): 593.
357. Case 222/84 *Johnston* [1985] ECR 1651.
358. Case C-432/05 *Unibet* [2007] ECR I-2271.
359. Case C-7/98 *Krombach* [2000] ECR I-1935; Case C-341/04 *Eurofood IFSC* [2006] ECR I-3813. See also, *supra*, at II-136 et seq.
360. Admittedly, I tend to use the terms 'right' and 'principle' almost interchangeably; it appears indeed that it is very difficult in the EU legal order to make much of distinction between the

Charter of Fundamental Rights of the EU.[361] Equal treatment of course goes to the heart of the EU legal order.[362] From the very start Article 18 TFEU laid down a clear prohibition on any form of discrimination based on nationality[363] within the scope of the Treaties,[364] as a complement on the even more specified expressions of that same principle in respect of the four freedoms[365] or taxation.[366] Furthermore, the ECJ has been particularly adamant in ensuring the equal treatment between men and women, at least in respect of equal pay, laid down in Article 157 TFEU (old Article 141 TEC).[367] The message has really come across, up to the point that Article 2 TEU in its post-Lisbon version now lists it expressly as one of the values the EU shares with the Member States. I have, therefore, no difficulty in submitting that the EU *ordre public* seeks to protect against both forms of discrimination.

**III-68.** Article 21(1) of the Charter of Fundamental Rights of the EU prohibits, however, also discrimination on any ground such as sex, race, colour, ethnic or social origin, genetic features, language, religion or belief, political or any other opinion, membership of a national minority, property, birth, disability, age or sexual orientation. Largely, these grounds correspond to the grounds for Union action combating discrimination set out in Article 19 TFEU (old Article 13 TEC). The question is, however, whether these grounds carry the same weight as the two grounds, nationality and equal treatment of men and women, which the Treaty protects separately with directly applicable provisions. The question has come to the fore in the wake of the case of *Mangold*,[368] where the ECJ – in order to overcome the fact that Germany had not yet fully implemented a Directive combating age discrimination at work – rather controversially found that also the non-discrimination on grounds of age are a general

two, see C. Hilson, 'Rights and Principles in EU law: a Distinction without Foundation?', *Maastricht Journal of European and Comparative Law* (2008): 193-215.

361. Charter of Fundamental Rights of the European Union (2010) OJ C 83/389.
362. For extensive discussions of EU equal treatment law, see, *inter alia*, D. Martin, *Egalité et non-discrimination dans la jurisprudence communautaire* (Bruxelles: Bruylant, 2006) ; E. Ellis, *EU Anti-Discrimination Law* (Oxford: OUP, 2005); A. Dashwood & S. O'Leary (eds.), *The Principle of Equal Treatment in E.C. Law. A Collection of Papers by the Centre for European Legal Studies (Cambridge)* (London: Sweet & Maxwell, 1997).
363. Specifically on the discrimination on grounds of nationality, see E. Bribosia, E. Dardenne, P. Magnette & A. Weyembergh, *Union Européenne et Nationalités – Le principe de non-discrimination et ses limites* (Bruxelles: Bruylant, 1999).
364. For more on the qualifier 'within the scope of the Treaties', see Case C-427/06 *Bartsch* [2008] ECR I-7245. While I submit that the non-discrimination on grounds of nationality is a bedrock principle of the EU legal order and therefore arguably part of the EU *ordre public*, I do not argue in any way that this would mean that the principle applies beyond the boundaries laid down in Article 18 TFEU.
365. Articles 30 *juncto* 36 TFEU; 45(2) TFEU; 52 TFEU; 56 *juncto* 62 TFEU; 63 *juncto* 65(3) TFEU.
366. Articles 110 and 111 TFEU.
367. For an overview, see T.K. Hervey & D. O'Keeffe (eds.), *Sex Equality Law in the European Union* (Chichester: Wiley, 1996); E. Ellis, 'The Recent Jurisprudence of the Court of Justice in the Field of Sex Equality', *Common Market Law Review* (2000): 1403-1426. For a critical appraisal of the new directives in this field, see K. Athela, 'The Revised Provisions on Sex Discrimination in European Law: A Critical Assessment', *European Law Journal* (2005): 57-78. See also S. Pager, 'Strictness v. Discretion: The European Court of Justice's Variable Vision to Gender Equality', *American Journal of Comparative Law* (2003): 553-609.
368. Case C-114/04 *Mangold* [2005] ECR I-998.

principle of EU law, which could be relied on directly before the national court in a labour dispute between two private parties. This approach was heavily criticized by Advocate General Mazák,[369] who saw in this a manoeuvre to circumvent the constitutional limitations the drafters of the Treaties had put in place when they only provided for a legal basis – to be implemented through Directives, which do not enjoy horizontal direct effect – for further EU action rather than a directly applicable principle as in the case of Articles 18 and 157 TFEU.

**III-69.** There may be another way of looking at this issue, which in my view may nonetheless justify the Court's insistence on protecting against discrimination on ground of old age. Without seeking to open a full comparative analysis[370] at this point, it is suggested that comparison with the so-called suspect classes in US equality analysis[371] or the case law of the ECtHR[372] may be revealing. It is therefore also not surprising to find references to US case law in point in several recent Advocate General Opinions dealing with various forms of discrimination.[373] Article 21 of the Charter prohibits discrimination 'on any ground' and then goes on to list an impressive list of classic grounds for discrimination. However, this does not preclude on the one hand that there may be other forms of discrimination – after all there is a general principle of EU law of non-discrimination – and second, that the weight of the various forms of discrimination may differ. It is here that the comparison with the US constitutional doctrine or the case law of the ECtHR has had some effect, in identifying different levels of scrutiny, depending on the ground on which discrimination takes place. It is submitted that a similar way of thinking is also inspiring the Court's case law on this point, though the end result is more something of a sliding scale,[374] rather than the three (more or less) well-defined different categories of review provided for in US constitutional law.

369. Opinion of AG Mazák in Case C-411/05 *Palacios de la Villa* [2007] ECR I-8531, paras 137-138. For a somewhat more nuanced approach, see Opinion of AG Sharpston in Case C-427/06 *Bartsch* [2008] ECR I-7245.
370. For the most compelling study in this respect, see D. Martin, *Egalité et non-discrimination dans la jurisprudence communautaire* (Bruxelles: Bruylant, 2006).
371. For more, see J. Choper, R. Fallon, Y. Kamisar & S. Shiffrin, *Constitutional Law*, 9th ed. (St. Paul (Minn.): West, 2001), 1137 et seq. See also the famous footnote 4 of *United States v. Carolene Products Co.*, 304 US 144 (1938) where the US Supreme Court indicated the potential need for more exacting scrutiny of legislation that either seeks to curtail the democratic political process or is directed against particular religions or racial minorities.
372. See in this respect E. Howard, 'The Case for a Considered Hierarchy of Discrimination Grounds in EU Law', *Maastricht Journal* (2006): 445-470.
373. Opinion of AG Jacobs in Case C-227/04 P *Lindorfer v. Council* [2007] ECR I-6767, 57 et seq.; Opinion of AG Sharpston in Case C-427/06 *Bartsch* [2008] ECR I-7245, para. 45. See also the US literature quoted by AG Poiares Maduro in his Opinions in Case C-303/06 *Coleman* [2008] ECR I-5603 and Case C-54/07 *Feryn* [2008] ECR I-5187.
374. In legal literature this sliding scale is often (mis)taken for an overly casuistic approach by the ECJ, see in this sense D. Martin, *Egalité et non-discrimination dans la jurisprudence communautaire* (Bruxelles: Bruylant, 2006), 611.

**III-70.** On the one extreme we find discrimination on the ground of racial or ethnic origin, for which a specific, strict and far-reaching Directive[375] has been adopted on the basis of Article 13 TEC and which is even combated with EU criminal law measures.[376] Discrimination on this ground[377] is in virtually all circumstances indefensible, and the *Feryn*[378] case demonstrates that the Court – fired up by an inspiring Advocate General Poiares Maduro[379] – is hardly forgiving for any detrimental behaviour that is inspired by racial considerations. Given their particular role in the EU legal order, the equal treatment between men and women, at least in labour relations, and the non-discrimination on the grounds of nationality are also close to this extreme, though the ECJ is not entirely insensitive to the innate differences between men and women.[380] In US case law, the equality between men and women is said to enjoy slightly less protection than in the case of racial equality – but the gap seems limited.[381] Recent case law shows that the principle has in any event still serious bite, both against the Member States[382] and vis-à-vis the EU institutions.[383] Other cases traditionally put forward for special scrutiny involve alienage, illegitimacy, mental retardation and sexual orientation.[384] Recent case law shows how discrimination on the ground of gender – such as in the case of transsexuals – is increasingly given almost the same weight as discrimination on the grounds of sex.[385] Discrimination on the grounds of sexual orientation, though treated somewhat more casually, also provokes an increasingly heightened form of scrutiny,[386] even though the ECJ is wrestling with provisions and

375. Council Directive 2000/43/EC of 29 June 2000 implementing the principle of equal treatment between persons irrespective of racial or ethnic origin (2000) OJ L 180/22. For an analysis, see M. Mahlmann, 'Gleichheitsschutz und Privatautonomie Probleme und Perspektiven der Umsetzung der Richtlinie 2000/43/EG gegen Diskriminierungen aufgrund von Rasse und ethnischer Herkunft', *Zeitschrift für europarechtliche Studien* (2002): 407-425; see also E. Howard., 'Anti Race Discrimination Measures in Europe: An Attack on Two Fronts', *European Law Journal* (2005): 468-486.
376. Framework Decision 2008/913/JHA of 28 November 2008 on combating certain forms and expressions of racism and xenophobia by means of criminal law (2008) OJ L 328/55.
377. But not every case involving unequal treatment of third-country nationals can be cast as a case involving racism or xenophobia, see Case C-571/10 *Kamberaj* [2012] ECR I-0000, paras 47-50.
378. Case C-54/07 *Feryn* [2008] ECR I-5187.
379. Opinion of AG Poiares Maduro in Case C-54/07 *Feryn* [2008] ECR I-5187; see also his vigorous opinion – albeit in the context of discrimination on the grounds of disability – in Case C-303/06 *Coleman* [2008] ECR I-5603.
380. See on this, in particular in the context of pregnancy and equally in a comparative perspective, P. Foubert, *The legal protection of the pregnant worker in the European Community: sex equality, thoughts of social and economic policy and comparative leaps to the United States of America* (The Hague: Kluwer, 2002). For criticism of the rigor with which the ECJ assess cases involving gender equality, see S. Pager, 'Strictness v. Discretion: The European Court of Justice's Variable Vision to Gender Equality', *American Journal of Comparative Law* (2003): 553-609.
381. *United States v. Virginia*, 518 U.S. 116 (1996).
382. The seminal Case 43/75 *Defrenne* [1976] ECR 455 is still regularly an issue, see *inter alia*, Case C-300/06 *Voß* [2007] ECR I-10573 or Joined Cases C-231/06 to C-233/06 *Jonkman* [2007] ECR I-5149.
383. Case C-227/04 P *Lindorfer v. Council* [2007] ECR I-6767.
384. J. Choper, R. Fallon, Y. Kamisar & S. Shiffrin, *Constitutional Law*, 9th ed. (St. Paul (Minn.): West, 2001), 1292 et seq.
385. Case C-423/04 *Richards* [2006] ECR I-3585; Case C-117/01 *K.B.* [2004] ECR I-541.
386. Case C-267/06 *Tadao Maruko* [2008] ECR I-1757; Case C-147/08 *Römer* [2011] ECR I-0000.

considerations aimed at blocking same-sex marriages.[387] On the other extreme there is the case of *Chacón Navas*,[388] where the ECJ refused to inflate the concept of non-discrimination on grounds of disability, to also include temporary illness. While 'any ground' may of course also include illness, the EU legislator has so far not acted to protect against discrimination on this ground, which is moreover not as such listed in Article 19 TFEU, and the temporary nature and varying intensity of illnesses also make this a particular difficult ground to work with. The other grounds that are listed in Article 21 of the Charter tend to hover between the two extremes. This seems in particular the case for discrimination on the grounds of disability and age, both of which have been argued not deserve special scrutiny as both 'can affect both the ability and the availability to do a job or use a good or service'.[389] However, it has been argued also that disability occupies an intermediate position given the status also of Member States law in the field,[390] and the ECJ has condemned quite strongly even the far more subtle discrimination on ground of disability in a case where someone was targeted because of her kinship to a disabled family member.[391] On age discrimination the jury is still out. After a strong, but criticized,[392] start,[393] the Court seems to accede to calls for a more moderate stance.[394] However, the fact that the principle of age discrimination allows for more exceptions than for most other grounds in Directive 2000/78[395]:

> should, however, not be interpreted as putting age discrimination at the bottom of a perceived 'hierarchy' of discrimination grounds under the Directive. Rather, it constitutes an expression of the material differences between those grounds and in the way they function as legal criteria. It is not a matter of value or importance, but a matter of how to entrench the scope of the prohibition of discrimination adequately.[396]

387. See in particular recital 22 Council Directive 2000/78/EC of 27 November 2000 establishing a general framework for equal treatment in employment and occupation (2000) OJ L 303/16 – which the ECJ swiftly casts aside in Case C-267/06 *Tadao Maruko* [2008] ECR I-1757, paras 58-60. See further Article 9 Charter of Fundamental Rights of the European Union (2010) OJ C 83/389. See also Case C-147/08 *Römer* [2011] ECR I-0000.
388. Case C-13/05 *Chacón Navas* [2006] ECR I-6467.
389. See E. Howard 'The Case for a Considered Hierarchy of Discrimination Grounds in EU Law', *Maastricht Journal* (2006): 465 (disability) and 467 (age).
390. M. Bell & L. Waddington, 'Reflecting on inequalities in European equality law', *European Law Review* (2003): 366.
391. Case C-303/06 *Coleman* [2008] ECR I-5603.
392. See Opinion of AG Mazák in Case C-411/05 *Palacios de la Villa* [2007] ECR I-853. See also K. Riesenhuber, 'Case: ECJ – Mangold', *European Review of Contract Law* (2007): 62-71.
393. Case C-114/04 *Mangold* [2005] ECR I-998.
394. Case C-411/05 *Palacios de la Villa* [2007] ECR I-853, with Opinion of AG Mazák. See also Opinion of AG Sharpston in Case C-427/06 *Bartsch* [2008] ECR I-7245 and Opinion of AG Mazák in Case C-388/07 *The Incorporated Trustees of the National Council on Ageing (Age Concern England)* [2009] ECR I-1569. Pension cases remain very difficult, the pension age itself is off-limits, but the conditions for exercising pension rights are covered by Directive 2000/78/EC, compare Joined Cases C-250/09 and C-268/09 *Georgiev* [2010] ECR I-0000 with Case C-499/08 *Ingeniørforeningen i Danmark* [2010] ECR I-0000.
395. Council Directive 2000/78/EC of 27 November 2000 establishing a general framework for equal treatment in employment and occupation (2000) OJ L 303/16.
396. Opinion of AG Mazák in Case C-388/07 *The Incorporated Trustees of the National Council on Ageing (Age Concern England)*, nyr, para. 76.

In any event, the suggestion that the prohibition of age discrimination is no longer a general principle of EU law,[397] is contradicted by the Court's more recent case law.[398]

**III-71.** It is submitted that equal treatment is one of the bedrock principles of the EU legal order as it protects 'a society in which pluralism, non-discrimination, tolerance, justice, solidarity and equality between women and men prevail'.[399] In this sense, I submit that the ECJ was correct in *Mangold*[400] to generalize the prohibition of age discrimination laid down into a general principle of EU law, provided its scope of application is limited to situations that have also otherwise a link to EU law.[401] Accordingly, this principle, too, should be reflected in a substantive EU *ordre public*, but it will obviously only have bite in situations that have a link with EU law.[402] However, the impact the principle has in a particular case will vary according to the situation and to the ground on which discrimination takes place. Discrimination on the grounds of racial or ethnic origin is solidly anchored, also from an international perspective,[403] as evidently prohibited by a Directive with a broad material scope, very limited exceptions and simple enforcement mechanisms.[404] Given their particular role within the scope of the Treaties, the same applies almost evenly strong in the EU context to the equal treatment on grounds of nationality and sex. Other grounds are treated on something of a sliding scale, but when the threshold for scrutiny is reached the EU legal order will offer protection against unjustifiable unequal treatment.[405]

397. See in this sense, C. Canazza, 'Arrêt *Palacios*: la Cour tempère l'interdiction des discriminations fondées sur l'âge', *Journal de droit européen* (2008): 81. For a more nuanced comment on Case C-411/05 *Palacios de la Villa* [2007] ECR I-853, see L. Waddington, 'Case C-411/05 *Palacios de la Villa* v. *Cortefiel Servicios SA*, Judgment of the Court (Grand Chamber) of 16 October 2007', *Common Market Law Review* (2008): 895-905.
398. Case C-447/09 *Prigge* [2011] ECR I-0000, para. 38; Case C-555/07 *Kücükdeveci* [2010] ECR I-365, para. 21.
399. Article 2 TEU in the post-Lisbon version.
400. Case C-114/04 *Mangold* [2005] ECR I-998.
401. See in this respect Case C-427/06 *Bartsch* [2008] ECR I-7245.
402. See in this respect Case C-427/06 *Bartsch* [2008] ECR I-7245, dispelling any doubts in this respect that may have arisen as a result of a warped reading of Case C-114/04 *Mangold* [2005] ECR I-998.
403. E. Howard., 'The Case for a Considered Hierarchy of Discrimination Grounds in EU Law', *Maastricht Journal* (2006): 453.
404. On these three elements, see *ibid.*, 446-447.
405. Actually, the discussion on the retirement age is a good example of this balance. On the one hand, the ECJ has not hesitated, despite its recital 14 of Directive 2000/78 which indicates that the Directive is to be without prejudice to national provisions laying down retirement ages, to accept that Directive 2000/78 actually applies to national measures governing the conditions for termination of employment contracts where the retirement age, established by the Member States has been reached. On the other hand, the ECJ is willing to grant the Member States nonetheless a wide policy margin as to the appropriate measures flowing from their policy choices as to social policy. See in this respect Case C-411/05 *Palacios de la Villa* [2007] ECR I-853. See also Opinion of AG Mazák in Case C-388/07 *The Incorporated Trustees of the National Council on Ageing (Age Concern England)* [2009] ECR I-1569.

## §8.03 CONCLUSION AS TO THE PROTECTION OF THE POLITICAL ORDER THROUGH THE EU *ORDRE PUBLIC*

**III-72.** The foregoing discussion has demonstrated that the EU has a hard core of institutional provisions and constitutional values. The EU *ordre public* must correspond to these provisions and values and offer adequate protection for Member States, institutions and citizens alike. However, the EU *ordre public*, defined as the complex of norms at the very heart of a political entity (in this case the EU) expressing and protecting the basic options taken by that entity regarding its political, economic, social and cultural order, protects more than just the political order. Actually, as the example of European citizenship and the discussion of the principle of equal treatment reveal, the constitutional values behind these concepts also hint at a broader social and economic order. Accordingly, in the following sub-parts attention will be paid to the fundamental underlying policies of the EU legal order the EU *ordre public* seeks to protect. First up is the economic order.

# CHAPTER 9
# Protection of the Economic Public Order

**III-73.** The recent turmoil on the financial markets following the so-called sub-prime mortgage crisis is a stark reminder about the enormous impact economic instability may have for the whole of society. Accordingly, the *ordre public* does not merely seek to ensure political stability, but also protects the basic choices taken by a society as to the organization of the markets. As Baquero Cruz rightly stresses there is a 'reciprocal interaction between the constitution and the socio-economic framework in which it operates'.[1] As the EU was initially set up as an organization for economic integration, it is therefore to be expected that the EU *ordre public* also encompasses an important *ordre public économique*.

**III-74.** Taking into account on the one hand what is generally considered to be part and parcel of the *ordre public économique* in the national legal orders[2] and on the other hand the specific role of the European Union in economic life, at least five areas can be identified where the EU *ordre public* offers protection. First, as the monetary policy of the countries that have adopted the euro has become an exclusive competence of the Union, the protection of the *lex moneta* in respect of the euro must be a matter of EU *ordre public* (§9.01). Second, as the ECJ has indicated itself in *Eco Swiss*[3] and *Manfredi*,[4] competition law is a matter of EU *ordre public* (§9.02). Third, in the context of the discussion of EU citizenship it was argued above that the free movement of persons is a matter of EU *ordre public* because of its inherent link with human dignity.

1. J. Baquero Cruz, *Between competition and free movement: the economic constitutional law of the European Community* (Oxford: Hart, 2002), 26. Some authors indeed use the term 'economic constitution', see M. Poiares Maduro, *We, the Court: the European Court of Justice and the European economic constitution: a critical reading of Article 30 of the EC Treaty* (Oxford: Hart, 1998); A. Hatje, 'The Economic Constitution' in *Principles of European Constitutional Law*, ed. A. Von Bogdandy & J. Bast (Oxford/Portland: Hart, 2007), 587-632.
2. See A. Meinertzhagen-Limpens, 'Quelques aspects de l'*ordre public* en droit comparé' in *L'ordre public: concept et applications*, ed. J.-F. Romain, M. Grégoire & V. Simonart (Bruxelles: Bruylant, 1995), 221-256.
3. Case C-126/97 *Eco Swiss China Time* [1999] ECR I-3055.
4. Joined Cases C-295/04 to C-298/04 *Manfredi* [2006] ECR I-6619.

It was, moreover, argued that as a derivative also the other freedoms should enjoy a similar status. As the free movement of goods, services and capital is in a sense the complement of the undistorted competition within the internal market, it will be submitted that all four freedoms can be considered as an expression of the EU *ordre public économique* (§9.03). Fourth, within the internal market special protection is given to consumers. The way the ECJ ensures this protection seems to imply that also consumer protection is a matter of EU *ordre public* (§9.04). Finally, it is submitted that the EU *ordre public* also seeks to guarantee a minimum level of protection of the European workforce (§9.05).

## §9.01 PROTECTION OF THE *LEX MONETA*

**III-75.** Even before the introduction of the euro, it was accepted by the ECJ that Member States could deviate from the rules on the free movement of goods in order to protect the *lex moneta*. In *Thompson,* the ECJ thus allowed the UK to impose a ban on exporting silver coins with a view of preventing their being melted down 'because it stems from the need to protect the right to mint coinage which is traditionally regarded as involving the fundamental interests of the state'.[5] Similarly, the ECJ accepted that a Member State could require the exporter of a large amount of bank notes to declare such exports, though this hinders the free movement of capital.[6] As Oliver observes, the justification for this is not a purely economic interest, but 'would be subsumed within one of the recognized categories of justification, particularly public policy, public security and the prevention of tax fraud'.[7] Justifiable restrictions to the free movement of capital seek indeed primarily to ensure the trust in and stability of the financial system of the Member States.[8] The recent banking crisis, however, has made it clear that there may also be need for a pan-European approach in regulating the financial sectors.

**III-76.** This is all the more so, as the introduction of the euro entails a shift of the responsibility for ensuring monetary stability to the EU. As the Lisbon Treaty confirms,[9] the monetary policy of the countries whose currency is the euro is a matter of exclusive competence of the Union.[10] Accordingly, the Treaties do not only provide rules for the day to day management of the euro, but also for cases of major monetary instability.[11] The ECB has, moreover, demonstrated its robust power to intervene in support of financial markets, even though the financial crisis is testing this to its limits.

5. Case 7/78 *Thompson* [1978] ECR I-2247, para. 34.
6. Joined Cases C-358/93 and C-416/93 *Bordessa* [1995] I-361.
7. P. Oliver & M. Jarvis, *Free Movement of Goods in the European Community*, 4th ed. (London: Thomson/Sweet & Maxwell, 2003), 236.
8. See also, *supra*, at II-77 et seq.
9. See in this sense K. Lenaerts & P. Van Nuffel; R. Bray (ed.), *Constitutional Law of the European Union*, 2nd ed. (London, Sweet & Maxwell, 2005), 97-98 who accepted this exclusivity already as *de lege lata* before the entry into force of the Lisbon Treaty.
10. Article 3(1)(c) TFEU.
11. See Articles 143-144 TFEU.

Moreover, the euro is protected through a series of public law measures,[12] including EU criminal law.[13] However, the ECJ has also protected the trust in the euro in a very different manner. In *Estager,*[14] the Court rejected French rules that resulted in certain fines previously expressed in French francs being converted into euro in a manner that did not fully reflect the official exchange rate. While France is of course entitled to raise the amount for certain fines, the principles of transparency, legal certainty and continuity at the basis of Regulation 1103/97[15] required that this was not done in a manner that put the conversion process itself in doubt, undermining public trust in what was at the time a fledgling currency. Finally, while respect for proper proceedings is in itself a matter of public policy, the fact that the ECJ rebuked efforts by the Council to develop alternative procedures and instruments to combat excessive deficits also serves to shore up the credibility and stability of the euro.[16] It is thus submitted that the protection of the integrity and stability of the euro, as protected by the *lex moneta,* requires the type of governmental intervention to protect an essential aspect of our economical order that may only be explained by its status as EU *ordre public.* The measures taken in support of the eurozone as a result of the financial crisis can only further bolster this status, especially since they now also provide in sanctions against the Member States in case of non-compliance.[17] At the level of the Member States

12. Council Regulation (EC) No 1338/2001 of 28 June 2001 laying down measures necessary for the protection of the euro against counterfeiting (2001) OJ L 181/6, as since amended by Council Regulation (EC) No 44/2009 of 18 December 2008 amending Regulation (EC) No 1338/2001 laying down measures necessary for the protection of the euro against counterfeiting (2009) OJ L 17/1. Also Member States that have not yet introduced the euro are under an obligation to offer sufficient protection, see Council Regulation (EC) No 1339/2001 of 28 June 2001 extending the effects of Regulation (EC) No 1338/2001 laying down measures necessary for the protection of the euro against counterfeiting to those Member States which have not adopted the euro as their single currency (2001) OJ L 181/11, as amended by Council Regulation (EC) No 45/2009 of 18 December 2008 amending Regulation (EC) No 1339/2001 extending the effects of Regulation (EC) No 1338/2001 laying down measures necessary for the protection of the euro against counterfeiting to those Member States which have not adopted the euro as their single currency (2009) OJ L 17/4.
13. Council Framework Decision 2000/383/JHA of 29 May 2000 on increasing protection by criminal penalties and other sanctions against counterfeiting in connection with the introduction of the euro (2000) OJ L 140/1; Council Decision 2005/511/JHA of 12 July 2005 on protecting the euro against counterfeiting, by designating Europol as the Central Office for combating euro counterfeiting (2005) OJ L 185/35.
14. Case C-359/05 *Estager* [2007] ECR I-581.
15. Council Regulation (EC) No 1103/97 of 17 June 1997 on certain provisions relating to the introduction of the euro (1997) OJ L 162/1. See also Council Regulation (EC) No 974/98 of 3 May 1998 on the introduction of the euro (1998) OJ L 139/1.
16. Case C-27/04 *Commission v. Council* [2004] ECR I-6649. Note in this respect also the atypical speed with which this case was treated by the Court, reflective of the need for swift reassurance of financial markets.
17. See in this respect in particular the so-called six-pack, of five legislative and one non-legislative measures, to strengthen the macroeconomic framework of the eurozone: Regulation (EU) No 1173/2011 of the European Parliament and of the Council of 16 November 2011 on the effective enforcement of budgetary surveillance in the euro area (2011) OJ L 306/1; Regulation (EU) No 1174/2011 of the European Parliament and of the Council of 16 November 2011 on enforcement measures to correct excessive macroeconomic imbalances in the euro area (2011) OJ L 306/8; Regulation (EU) No 1175/2011 of the European Parliament and of the Council of 16 November 2011 amending Council Regulation (EC) No 1466/97 on the strengthening of the surveillance of budgetary positions and the surveillance and coordination of economic policies

attention must be drawn to the Treaty on Stability, Coordination and Governance in the EMU,[18] which should result in tighter control over the budget discipline of the participating Member States, with even a role for the Court of Justice.[19] For private parties, it may be worth drawing the attention to Article 12(3) of the Treaty establishing the European Stability Mechanism,[20] which imposes the inclusion of collective action clauses in all new euro government securities, which creates the possibility of by-passing hold-outs in the case of a hair-cut. As argued above, this type of interference with contractual rights is strongly tied to the *ordre public*.

## §9.02 PROTECTION OF THE ECONOMIC COMPETITION

**III-77.** The European Union was established with the explicit task to ensure that competition is undistorted. In order to achieve this aim, the EU institutions have been given far-reaching powers, unprecedented for any supranational organization and even atypical for some of its own Member States, to act directly against both Member States and individual undertakings. While the reformulation of these objectives in the Lisbon Treaty may give rise to some raised eyebrows, fact is that a separate Protocol[21] reaffirms the commitment of the EU to undistorted competition and, more importantly, the tools for enforcing this policy are unaffected. I thus agree with Baquero Cruz that the – as he calls it – 'Community economic constitutional law' cannot be considered neutral as it imposes clear limitations to the policy margin left for the Union and the Member States as to how the balance between market forces and government intervention must be struck.[22] However, this should in my opinion not lead to the conclusion that the EU economy cannot be shaped into 'a highly competitive social market economy', as the Lisbon Treaty proclaims. The ECJ has indeed stressed that the old Treaties already had a 'social purpose' as it flew from Article 2 TEC that 'the Community is to have as its task, *inter alia*, the promotion of "a harmonious, balanced and sustainable development of economic activities" and "a high level of employment

(2001) OJ L 306/12; Regulation (EU) No 1176/2011 of the European Parliament and of the Council of 16 November 2011 on the prevention and correction of macroeconomic imbalances (2011) OJ L 306/25; Council Regulation (EU) No 1177/2011 of 8 November 2011 amending Regulation (EC) No 1467/97 on speeding up and clarifying the implementation of the excessive deficit procedure (2011) OJ L 306/33; Council Directive 2011/85/EU of 8 November 2011 on requirements for budgetary frameworks of the Member States (2011) OJ L 306/43.

18. For the text, see <http://european-council.europa.eu/media/639235/st00tscg26_en12.pdf> (21 May 2012).
19. Article 8 Treaty on Stability, Coordination and Governance in the EMU.
20. The treaty implements Article 136 (3) TFEU. For the text, see <http://www.european-council.europa.eu/media/582311/05-tesm2.en12.pdf> (21 May 2012).
21. Protocol (No 27) on the Internal Market and Competition (2008) OJ C 115/309.
22. J. Baquero Cruz, *Between competition and free movement: the economic constitutional law of the European Community* (Oxford: Hart, 2002), 76-80. it has, therefore, been argued that competition law indeed has a constitutional dimension in the EU legal order, see J. Drexl, 'Competition Law as Part of the European Constitution' in *Principles of European Constitutional Law*, ed. A. Von Bogdandy & J. Bast (Oxford/Portland: Hart, 2007), 633-674.

and of social protection"'.[23] Precisely for this reason, as will be developed further below,[24] some of these corrective measures in the field of consumer protection and social law should equally be seen as protective of core values of the economic order and thus a matter of EU *ordre public*.

**III-78.** The ECJ has not failed to note the importance of this objective in language that explicitly refers to the role competition law plays for the EU *ordre public*. In *Eco Swiss* the Court called Article 3(1)(g) TEC 'a fundamental provision which is essential for the accomplishment of the tasks entrusted to the Community and, in particular, for the functioning of the internal market'[25] and it went on to explicitly link Article 101 TFEU to the public policy, at least in the sense of the New York Convention.[26] The latter qualifier is even completely absent in *Manfredi* where the ECJ plainly concluded that 'Articles [101 and 102 TFEU] *are a matter of public policy* which must be automatically applied by national courts.'[27] Likewise, in *Aalborg Portland*, the ECJ clarified the criteria to be taken into account for the setting of fines in competition matter by observing that '[o]bjective factors such as the content and duration of the anti-competitive conduct, the number of incidents and their intensity, the extent of the market affected *and the damage to the economic public order* must be taken into account'.[28] Moreover, as the aim to protect undistorted competition, the public policy status should equally be extended to the rules on state aid, as was rightly observed by Advocate General Geelhoed.[29]

23. Case C-438/05 *International Transport Workers' Federation* [2007] ECR I-10779, paras 78-79; Case C-341/05 *Laval un Partneri* [2007] ECR I-11767, paras 104-105. See also S. Prechal & S. De Vries, 'Viking/Laval en de grondslagen van het internemarktecht', *Sociaal-Economische Wetgeving* (2008): 433-435.
24. *Infra*, at III-83 et seq.
25. Case C-126/97 *Eco Swiss China Time* [1999] ECR I-3055, para. 36.
26. Case C-126/97 *Eco Swiss China Time* [1999] ECR I-3055, para. 38.
27. Joined Cases C-295/04 to C-298/04 *Manfredi* [2006] ECR I-6619, para. 31. It is, however, unclear whether this implies that all competition law is of public policy. In particular discussion has arisen as to the status of the individual and block exemptions under Article 101(3) TFEU, though some of these concerns may have been alleviated since Article 101(3) TFEU can be applied by the national court following the entry into force of Council Regulation (EC) No 1/2003 of 16 December 2002 on the implementation of the rules on competition laid down in Articles 81 and 82 of the Treaty (2003) OJ L 1/1. See, nevertheless, C. Liebscher, 'European Public Policy after Eco Swiss', *American Review of International Arbitration* (1999): 89-93; see also S. Prechal & N. Shelkoplyas, 'National Procedures, Public Policy and EC Law. From Van Schijndel to Eco Swiss and Beyond', *European Review of Private Law* (2004): 605.
28. Joined Cases C-204/00 P, C-205/00 P, C-211/00 P, C-213/00 P, C-217/00 P en C-219/00 P, *Aalborg Portland A/S et alia v. Commission* [2004] ECR I-123, para. 91 (emphasis added). See also Case C-386/10 P *Chalkor AE Epexergasias Metallon v. Commission* [2011] ECR I-0000, para. 57; Case C-389/10 P *KME Germany v. Commission* [2011] ECR I-0000, para. 124.
29. Opinion of AG Geelhoed in Case C-119/05 *Lucchini Siderurgica* [2007] ECR I-6199, para. 62. The ECJ also speaks of the 'mandatory nature of the supervision of State aid by the Commission', see Case C-5/89 *Commission v. Germany* [1990] ECR I-3437, para. 14. For the consequences of this, including its effect on the legitimate expectations recipients of state aid may have, see P. Nebbia, 'Do the rules on State aids have a life of their own? National procedural autonomy and effectiveness in the *Lucchini* case', *European Law Review* (2008): 431-434.

**III-79.** The public policy status of the rules seeking to protect the undistorted competition is also reflected in the impact these rules have.[30] As the ECJ stresses '[t]he importance of [Article 3(1)(g) TEC] led the framers of the Treaty to provide expressly, in Article [101(2)] of the Treaty, that any agreements or decisions prohibited pursuant to that article are to be automatically void'.[31] It is also evident from the existence of a strong EU-wide network of competition authorities[32] that may even take punitive action in the form of fines reflective of the impact on the economic public order.[33] Likewise, its importance also explains why Member States must maximize the opportunities for raising issues of competition law, which may also take the form of judges raising the issue of their own motion.[34] As argued above, this is not contradicted by the outcome of *Renault/Maxicar,*[35] as in that case the Member State where the judgment, the enforcement of which was sought, originated from offered ample opportunity to raise the issue so that there was no need to upset the advantages of swift enforcement under the Brussels Convention. By contrast, the fervour with which the ECJ intervened in the Italian legal order in *Lucchini*[36] may well in part be explained because the disrespect for the division of competence between the Commission and the national authorities - itself a matter of public policy - also undermined the effective enforcement of these fundamental rules of the economic *ordre public* of the Union.

## §9.03 THE FREE MOVEMENT ASPECTS OF THE INTERNAL MARKET

**III-80.** There are two main reasons why, upon balance, the four freedoms all reflect core values that deserve protection as a matter of EU *ordre public.* On the one hand, I have argued above, in respect of the free movement aspect of the citizenship of the EU that this could ultimately be considered as an expression of human dignity, in that it gives persons the chance to develop themselves in ways that they may not do so in their own Member State and in that it conversely allows - even for those persons who do not travel themselves - to have the fruits of their creativity in the forms of goods or services or financial instruments distributed across the Union.[37] Stressing the expressive value of the four freedoms also helps to explain why the four freedoms go beyond profit-oriented transactions, as evidenced by the broad concept of 'worker'[38] or the extension

30. See also, *supra*, at II-83 et seq.
31. Case C-126/97 *Eco Swiss China Time* [1999] ECR I-3055, para. 36.
32. On the division of labour between the Commission and the national competition authorities within this European Competition Network, see Council Regulation (EC) No 1/2003 of 16 December 2002 on the implementation of the rules on competition laid down in Articles 81 and 82 of the Treaty (2003) OJ L 1/1.
33. Joined Cases C-204/00 P, C-205/00 P, C-211/00 P, C-213/00 P, C-217/00 P en C-219/00 P, *Aalborg Portland A/S et alia v. Commission* [2004] ECR I-123.
34. Case C-126/97 *Eco Swiss China Time* [1999] ECR I-3055; Joined Cases C-295/04 to C-298/04 *Manfredi* [2006] ECR I-6619, para. 31.
35. Case C-38/98 *Régie nationale des usines Renault* [2000] ECR I-2973.
36. C-119/05 *Lucchini Siderurgica* [2007] ECR I-6199.
37. See, *supra*, at III-60.
38. Case 66/85 *Lawrie-Blum* [1986] ECR 2121; Case 196/87 *Steymann* [1988] ECR I-6159.

of the free movement of capital to charitable societies[39] and even gifts *in natura*.[40] It also offers a strong foundation for the Court's finding in *Heylens* that 'free access to employment is a fundamental right which the Treaty confers individually on each worker in the Community'.[41] On the other hand, competition law and the four 'fundamental freedoms'[42] are in a sense two sides of the same coin - after all the aim in both cases is to avoid that new barriers to intra-Community trade are being erected, in the latter case (primarily) by Member States and in the former case (primarily) by undertakings.[43] As the ECJ seems to consider the protection of undistorted competition within the internal market a matter of public policy,[44] it seems almost inevitable that the same should apply to the free movement of goods, services and capital. In order to avoid any form of distortion of competition within the internal market, also the rules protecting the customs union, in particular the absolute prohibition on customs duties or measures having equivalent effect of Article 30 TFEU,[45] and on discriminatory taxation should be included in the economic *ordre public* of the Union.

**III-81.** Treating the fundamental freedoms as a matter of public policy may sound somewhat confusing. After all, above I explained in detail the existence of public policy exceptions to these freedoms. So does this mean that there are public policy exceptions to the public policy? Or even more unsettling, are there in light of *Cassis de Dijon*[46] even other exceptions to my public policy? The answer is nuanced. First, throughout this book I develop my arguments starting from a broad definition of *ordre public* as the complex of norms at the very heart of a political entity (in this case the EU) expressing and protecting the basic options taken by that entity regarding its political, economic, social and cultural order. While the public policy exceptions to the free movement tap into that vast reservoir they do not exhaust the concept, as is evidenced by the many other *ordre public*-related instances discussed so far. Second, there is a link between the core right and the exceptions. This is best brought to the fore in Article 36 TFEU where the public policy exception is followed by the important disclaimer that 'such prohibitions or restrictions shall not, however, constitute a means of arbitrary discrimination or a disguised restriction on trade between Member States'. Even the use of the public policy exception may not result in the full erosion of the principle of free movement of goods. This leads almost seamlessly into the third point: the relationship between the public policy exception and the other exceptions. It is conventional wisdom that in

39. Case C-386/04 *Centro di Musicologia Walter Stauffer* [2006] ECR I-8203.
40. Case C-318/07 *Persche* [2009] ECR I-0000, with Opinion of AG Mengozzi.
41. Case 222/86 *Heylens* [1987] ECR 4097, para. 14.
42. T. Kingreen, 'Fundamental Freedoms' in *Principles of European Constitutional Law*, ed. A. Von Bogdandy & J. Bast (Oxford/Portland: Hart, 2007), 549-584.
43. On this relationship, see in detail J. Baquero Cruz, *Between competition and free movement: the economic constitutional law of the European Community* (Oxford: Hart, 2002).
44. See, *supra*, at III-77 et seq.
45. See in this sense S.A. De Vries, *Tensions within the Internal Market – The Functioning of the Internal Market and the Development of Horizontal and Flanking Policies* (Groningen: Europa Law Publishing, 2006), 46 who supports his view under reference to Case 46/76 *Bauhuis* [1977] ECR 5.
46. Case 120/78 *Rewe-Zentral* [1979] ECR 749.

principle[47] the mandatory requirements not listed in the Treaties cannot be used to justify measures that openly discriminate on the basis of the origin of the goods or services or the nationality of the person involved. Put differently, while all these exceptions seek to protect some societal interest, it is argued that the listed exceptions somehow protect a societal value that is so fundamental as to justify a discriminatory measure, even though the lists of the various freedoms tend to differ and the most extensive one, Article 36 TFEU, may appear somewhat haphazard in what is included (e.g., archaeological finds) and what is left out (e.g., environmental protection). If, like I do is this book, one reasons from a perspective where the free movement is seen as a direct expression of the human dignity, as a way of ensuring self-realization, this distinction is quite far-reaching as it implies that there are instances where a Member State can hold the self-realization of the own nationals dearer than the self-realization of other EU citizens, which seems hard to reconcile with the universality of the underlying concept of human dignity. The solution to the conundrum is two-fold. On the one hand, the core message of the last sentence of Article 36 TFEU is precisely that pure discrimination on the grounds of origin, i.e., abuse of the public policy exception in masquerading a measure that can only be explained in terms of protectionism or fear of all things alien, is simply not allowed, exactly because it would mean that one is arbitrarily restricting the EU-wide emancipating function of the free movement. On the other hand, as also argued above in the context of citizenship,[48] human dignity is of course not the only value driving the EU legal order. The concept is at least limited by the human dignity of others and the dignity of states. From this perspective some of the key cases can easily be explained. First, while Member States may act against harmful goods and services, as the case law stands now,[49] there are no instances where a product or a service[50] may be prohibited without similar national measures in place.[51] In the context of the free movement of persons, the only case that comes close to the

47. The classic exception is the treatment of waste in Case C-2/90 *Commission v. Belgium* [1992] ECR I-4431.

48. See, *supra*, at III-60.

49. Older case law may show a slightly different picture, see Case 34/79 *Henn and Darby* [1979] ECR 3795, but this case was overruled by Case 121/85 *Conegate* [1986] ECR 1007.

50. For instance in Case C-36/02 *Omega Spielhallen* [2004] ECR I-9609 the actual service of offering the game to consumers was done by a German company that was thus called back by the German authorities. Admittedly, what was not analysed in detail was the question whether the service that was in intra-Community trade, namely the license to offer this type of game, would be the subject to similar restrictions, that is whether a German firm that would have developed a similar game concept, while being precluded from offering it on the German market, would be precluded from licensing it out to companies in other Member States where the game would otherwise be legal.

51. One could argue that as some lotteries cases (see e.g., Case C-124/97 *Läärä* [1999] ECR I-6067, or more recently, Opinion of AG Bot in Case C-42/07 *Liga Portuguesa de Futebol Profissional and Baw International* [2009] ECR I-7633) seem to protect a national monopoly this does not seem entirely true. However, the monopoly in these cases is precisely a manner to keep control over the domestic activity; moreover, to the extent that the Member State measure cannot be explained in terms of the desired level of protection the ECJ is far less forgiving, see Case C-243/01 *Gambelli* [2003] ECR I-13031, paras 63-69 and Joined Cases C-338/04, C-359/04 and C-360/04 *Placanica* [2007] ECR I-1891. See also Case C-347/09 *Dickinger and Ömer* [2011] ECR I-0000.

contrary is *Van Duyn*,[52] which I do not consider good law for the reasons set out above[53] and which is probably overruled by *Adoui and Cornuaille*.[54] Second, most other cases can be explained as a form of recognition of the dignity of the state, in that while *per* Article 26 TFEU within the internal market the frontiers are being abolished the Member States still continue to exist with internationally defined borders. Accordingly, expulsions are as a matter of international law only possible in respect of persons other than own nationals. While expulsions are thus a discriminatory obstacle to the free movement of persons in the sense that they only affect aliens, they can only be taken in a context where a Member State is taking other far-reaching measures against its own nationals.[55] Also the preventive measures Member States may take to control certain capital transfers - especially if they still have a separate currency in place - can be seen from this perspective. Finally, also *Campus Oil*[56] may be seen from this perspective. While the self-sufficiency measure was a truly discriminatory measure, it may be seen in the context of the case as aimed at avoiding the total collapse of the oil supply and from there the very existence of the state. While that assessment may in retrospect have been exaggerated - and the ECJ has been quick to dismiss attempts to resurrect it[57] - taking it seriously as a premise may explain why this measure could pass muster.

**III-82.** There is a second, related, question to this distinction between the types of exceptions to the free movement, namely whether the public policy exception (and the related grounds of justification) may also be invoked by private parties. For the reasons set out above,[58] I consider the Court's approach in *Bosman* the most accurate one. There the ECJ held that 'neither the scope nor the content of those grounds of justification is in any way affected by the private nature of the rules in question'.[59] Admittedly, one could be concerned that private parties may be driven by self-interest[60] and the *Wouters*[61] case, albeit taken from the context of competition law, shows that some checks in that respect are necessary. However, when private parties are entrusted with a regulatory role they should not be punished for genuinely seeking to also uphold essential non-economic values in the wider public interest.

## §9.04 THE EU *ORDRE PUBLIC* AND CONSUMER PROTECTION

**III-83.** In the foregoing paragraphs, it was argued that there is a sound basis for distinguishing between the listed exceptions to the free movement and the other

52. Case 41/74 *van Duyn* [1974] ECR 1337.
53. See, *supra*, at II-34.
54. Joined Cases 115/81 and 116/81 *Adoui and Cornuaille* [1982] ECR 1665.
55. Case 41/74 *van Duyn* [1974] ECR 1337, para. 22; for more in this respect see, *supra*, at II-33.
56. Case 72/83 *Campus Oil* [1984] ECR 2727.
57. Case 231/83 *Cullet* [1985] ECR 305.
58. See, *supra*, at II-61.
59. Case C-415/93 *Bosman* [1995] ECR I-4921, para. 82.
60. On this concern, see J. Baquero Cruz, *Between competition and free movement: the economic constitutional law of the European Community* (Oxford: Hart, 2002), 111.
61. Case C-309/99 *Wouters* [2002] ECR I-1577.

mandatory requirements which the ECJ has accepted over time. In *Kohl,*[62] the Court has made clear that this distinction also holds true when it comes to consumer protection: as consumer protection is not listed in Article 36 TFEU, national measures seeking to protect consumers should not be equated with the public policy. However, this is not the end of the matter. As the reasoning of *Cassis de Dijon*[63] only holds true in the absence of harmonization, nothing has been said on the public policy status of Union measures seeking to protect consumers. It should be noted that consumer protection, while not explicitly mentioned in Article 36 TFEU, does feature prominently in Article 114(3) TFEU as one of the concerns the Union legislator must take into account when adopting harmonizing measures – and thus a concern which should also be protected to the fullest in enforcing such legislation. The case law discussed above[64] on the question whether national courts should invoke these provisions *motu proprio* seems to suggest that there nonetheless is a link with the EU *ordre public.*

**III-84.** The key message of these cases[65] is that national courts indeed should apply these provisions of their own motion, even if their national procedural law would otherwise counsel against such approach. What is important at this point of our discussion is why the ECJ is taking this stance. The Court clearly does not consider EC consumer protection law as merely aimed at private interests. Indeed in trying to justify why the *effet utile* of the relevant rules require national courts to act of their own motion, the ECJ does not only rely on the inequality between the parties, but in *Mostaza Claro* it also stresses that:

> as the aim of the Directive is to strengthen consumer protection, it constitutes, according to Article 3(1)(t) EC, a measure which is essential to the accomplishment of the tasks entrusted to the Community and, in particular, to raising the standard of living and the quality of life in its territory.[66]

The Court moreover explicitly sees the analogy to the role competition law plays in this respect as it had earlier stressed in *Eco Swiss.*[67] This should hardly be surprising as one of the objectives of EU competition policy, as evidenced by the explicit reference to consumers in Article 101(3) TFEU, is precisely the protection of consumers.

**III-85.** While the national rules on protecting consumers should thus not be seen as a matter of *ordre public* in the sense of Article 36 TFEU, it seems safe to consider that EU consumer protection rules may nevertheless be a matter of EU *ordre public.* On the one

62. Case 177/83 *Kohl* [1984] ECR 3651, para. 19.
63. Case 120/78 *Rewe-Zentral* [1979] ECR 749.
64. See, *supra*, at II-174 et seq.
65. Case C-243/08 *Pannon GSM* [2009] ECR I-4713; Case C-40/08 *Asturcom Telecomunicaciones* [2009] ECR I-9579; Case C-429/05 *Rampion and Godard* [2007] ECR I-8017; Case C-168/05 *Mostaza Claro* [2006] ECR I-10421; Case C-473/00 *Cofidis* [2002] ECR I-10875; Joined Cases C-240/98 to C-244/98 *Océano Grupo Editorial* [2000] ECR I-4941.
66. Case C-168/05 *Mostaza Claro* [2006] ECR I-10421, para 37.
67. Case C-168/05 *Mostaza Claro* [2006] ECR I-10421, para 37, referring back to Case C-126/97 *Eco Swiss China Time* [1999] ECR I-3055, para. 36.

hand, they are in close connection to the rules relating to competition policy[68] and – to the extent that a level-playing field in respect of consumer protection may enhance consumer trust in intra-Union trade and thus remove both obstacles to trade and distortions to competition – also the groundwork of the internal market. On the other hand, I submit that the reason the ECJ seems to go further than the Member States, who at best consider consumer protection a matter of *ordre public de protection* with less protection, may also have to do with a concern about output legitimacy of the Union. While the EU – and the Lisbon Treaty makes that very explicit – promises a market system with social corrections, truth be told the EU actually has fairly little tools to make a real difference in terms of offering social protection in the lives of its citizens. Unlike the Member States, which can as a last resort, at least to a certain extent, compensate for certain market failures through their vast system of social security no such fall-back position exists for the EU. To illustrate my point, consider the problem in *Rampion and Godard.*[69] If the investment the pair has made goes sour, the first line of defence is consumer protection law, but if worse came to worse and they would lose it all, they may still be taken care of in their basic needs by the French welfare system. While that may be a meagre form of consolation, it is one the EU cannot offer. In the absence of a plan B, the only way to make the EU policies in this field credible is by making them sufficiently robust, for instance by requiring national courts to make sure these Directives (or at least their implementing national legislation) are complied with even if a consumer would fail to invoke them in a timely manner. The EU simply does not have many opportunities to directly protect its citizens, and even less alternatives, so that it can ill afford that people feel betrayed by the promise of EU protection when push comes to shove. Admittedly, the policies of the Union in this field do not apply in a legal vacuum, but apply against the background of the Member States systems, so that one could argue that if Member States may offer a second line of care through their social security system in case their *ordre public de protection* does not suffice, they may do the same in case EU consumer protection law is not fully protective. Yet, the point is that a more effective EU consumer protection policy that is also identifiable as such precisely offers an opportunity for the EU to act on its own for the protection of individuals. That being said, the weight of these justifications clearly is far less than the arguments put forward, for instance, in defence of the EU *ordre public* status of fundamental rights or EU citizenship, which, as argued below, may have an impact on where consumer protection fits in a broader model as to the EU *ordre public.*[70]

68. That is not to say that consumer welfare and economic freedom may not at times be in conflict, see L. Lovdahl Gormsen, 'The conflict between economic freedom and consumer welfare in the modernisation of Article 82 TEC', *European Competition Journal* (2007): 329-343.
69. Case C-429/05 *Rampion and Godard* [2007] ECR I-8017.
70. See, *infra*, Part V, in particular at V-36 et seq.

## §9.05 PROTECTION OF SOCIAL AND LABOUR STANDARDS THROUGH THE EU *ORDRE PUBLIC*

**III-86.** The same rationale may also explain why the ECJ is quite adamant in ensuring effective enforcement of what little EU regulation there is in respect of labour standards and labour relations. Again, the credibility of the Union as a social Union depends on the Union making the most of the relatively few instruments that are at its disposal, in offering effective protection to workers. Moreover, here, too, as a side effect a level playing field is created across the Union, which in turn should stimulate workers to make the most of their free movement rights without fear that if their adventures are hampered by illness, accident or unemployment they will lose out. Perhaps the most effective protection is indeed offered within the context of the free movement of persons, where the Treaties, EU legislation[71] and the Court's extensive reading thereof[72] greatly extend the social rights EU nationals enjoy in another Member State. However, also the limited EU legislation directly seeking to regulate labour relations are treated as if they protect values that are part of the EU *ordre public*.

**III-87.** First, the ECJ has given effective bite to the equal treatment of men and women in labour relations, by shoring it up with the guarantee of an effective remedy to address unequal treatment. While this was already at the heart of *Johnston,*[73] the language used in *Coote*[74] in my view points directly to a public policy concern. At issue in the case was the question whether Ms. Coote could challenge the refusal of her former employer - which had dismissed her earlier illegally due to her pregnancy, a dismissal which Ms. Coote had challenged before a court, but was eventually settled outside court - to provide her with a reference that would make it easier for her to find a new job. The ECJ finds she could, and stresses both the fundamental nature of the equality between and men and women and the need for effective judicial protection, stating:

> Article 6 of [Directive 76/207/EEC][75] is an essential factor for attaining the fundamental objective of equal treatment for men and women, which, as the Court

71. See in particular Regulation (EU) No 492/2011 of the European Parliament and of the Council of 5 April 2011 on freedom of movement for workers within the Union (2011) OJ L141/1; Regulation (EC) No 883/2004 of the European Parliament and of the Council of 29 April 2004 on the coordination of social security systems (2004) OJ L 166/1, which has replaced Regulation (EEC) No 1408/71 of the Council of 14 June 1971 on the application of social security schemes to employed persons and their families moving within the (1971) OJ L 149/2, as since amended.
72. For extensive reading of Regulation 1612/68, see for instance Case 152/73 *Sotgiu* [1974] 153; Case 59/85 *Reed* [1986] ECR 1283; for cases involving Regulation 1408/71, see *inter alia*, Case C-287/05 *Hendrix* [2007] ECR I-6909; Case C-396/05 *Habelt* [2007] ECR I-11895.
73. Case 222/84 *Johnston* [1985] ECR 1651.
74. Case C-185/97 *Coote* [1998] ECR I-5199.
75. Council Directive 76/207/EEC of 9 February 1976 on the implementation of the principle of equal treatment for men and women as regards access to employment, vocational training and promotion, and working conditions (1976) OJ L 39/40. Article 6 of this Directive requires Member States to provide for effective remedies.

has repeatedly held, is one of the fundamental human rights whose observance the Court has a duty to ensure[76].

This fits of course in seamlessly with what has been said above in respect of equal treatment and fundamental rights.[77]

**III-88.** Second, as was discussed above,[78] the ECJ has strengthened the protection of workers right to paid holidays, up to the point that it limits the contractual freedom of the employer and employees.[79] The reason for doing so can be found in the underlying health and safety concerns[80] that form the bedrock for the working time directive,[81] but also – as Advocate General Tizzano rightly stressed[82] – in the elevation of the right to a paid holiday to a fundamental social right in the Charter of Fundamental Rights of the Union.[83] Even without this additional justification the Court has curtailed the possibilities for tampering with working conditions when business units and their workers are transferred to another company.[84] While this type of transfers may be another way of helping to establish the internal market, the Court does well in trying to combat abuses.[85]

**III-89.** Third, while I have expressed my doubts as to the necessity for deciding the *Viking*[86] and *Laval*[87] cases the way they came out, it has to be admitted that the ECJ is generally sensitive to this risk of social dumping. Actually, even before Community legislation was in place to protect posted workers, the Court already made it clear that Member States were entitled to require compliance with the minimum wages of the host State.[88] Even *Laval*[89] was not so much about denying the Swedish authorities to offer sufficient protection to the labour standards of posted workers – by relying on the provisions of the Directive,[90] including if necessary and appropriate its public policy exception – as it was about the requirement that this be done properly by the

76. Case C-185/97 *Coote* [1998] ECR I-5199, para. 23, internal citations omitted.
77. See, *supra*, at III-62 et seq.
78. See, *supra*, at II-231.
79. Case C-124/04 *Federatie Nederlandse Vakbeweging* [2006] ECR I-3423; Joined Cases C-131/04 and C-257/04 *Robinson-Steele* [2006] ECR I-2531.
80. See also, *infra*, at III-97 et seq.
81. Council Directive 93/104/EC of 23 November 1993 concerning certain aspects of the organization of working time (1993) OJ L 307/18. For the defence of its legal basis, see Case C-84/94 *United Kingdom v. Council* [1996] ECR I-5755.
82. Opinion of AG Tizzano in Case C-173/99 *BECTU* [2001] ECR I-4881, para. 26.
83. Article 31 (2) Charter of Fundamental Rights of the European Union (2010) OJ C 83/389.
84. Case C-51/00 *Temco Service Industries* [2002] ECR I-969.
85. See also, in respect of Council Directive 2001/23/EC of 12 March 2001 on the approximation of the laws of the Member States relating to the safeguarding of employees' rights in the event of transfers of undertakings, businesses or parts of undertakings or businesses (2001) OJ L 82/16, Case C-396/07 *Juuri* [2008] ECR I-8883.
86. Case C-438/05 *International Transport Workers' Federation* [2007] ECR I-10779.
87. Case C-341/05 *Laval un Partneri* [2007] ECR I-11767.
88. Joined Cases C-369/96 and C-376/96 *Arblade* [1999] ECR I-8453.
89. Case C-341/05 *Laval un Partneri* [2007] ECR I-11767.
90. Directive 96/71/EC of the European Parliament and of the Council of 16 December 1996 concerning the posting of workers in the framework of the provision of services (1997) OJ L 18/1.

competent Swedish State authorities, rather than implied in the behaviour of trade unions.

**III-90.** Taken together, these examples signal that while the competence of the Union in respect of labour law and labour relations is not particularly extensive, the Court has construed the laws that were nonetheless adopted in a manner that is reflective of the importance of the underlying values that need to be protected. While by and of itself that may not be sufficient to elevate these norms to be reflective of the EU *ordre public*, I submit that this threshold is nonetheless met for two mutually reinforcing reasons. On the one hand, because the values at issue are intrinsically linked with other values – equality, fundamental rights, public health and safety – that are arguably part and parcel of the EU *ordre public*. On the other hand, the same concern for output legitimacy that may also explain why the ECJ does not deal with consumer law as a matter of *ordre public de protection* affecting solely private interests may also be lurking here. Just like the Union can only offer effective legislation when it comes to preventing dubious trade practices or dangerous products, it can also only promise safe working conditions. Unlike the Member States, who can also help out afterwards through their worker's compensation scheme and sickness pay if people fall the victim of dangerous products or a dangerous or unhealthy working environment, the Union has no such alternative and must thus ensure that its protective legislation is particularly effective in avoiding and immediately redressing incidents before long-term damage is done. Of course, the same *caveat* as expressed in respect of consumer protection[91] applies here as well. The EU legislation in this field does not operate in isolation from national laws, which may thus offer a fall-back position. However, there is in my view some intrinsic value in effective social protection by the Union in its own right, if it seeks to shed the image of being largely a liberal, free trade project. Nevertheless, also in respect of the place of EU social and labour legislation in a broader model of the EU *ordre public*, some further nuances may be necessary.[92]

91. See, *supra*, at III-85.
92. See, *infra*, Part V, in particular, at V-36 et seq.

# CHAPTER 10
# Protection of the Social Order

**III-91.** According to our tentative definition, the EU *ordre public* also relates back to the core values and principles for the organization of the social order in the EU. In the first place, this is manifested in the protection of public morality, whereby the question again becomes what moral standards are being upheld: national standards or EU standards. Second, this heading also offers me a framework to bring some other concerns to the fore in the penumbra of the *ordre public*, in particular the protection of public health, the protection against aliens and the potential of an *ordre public écologique*. Finally, as the most serious disturbances of the social order are often translated into criminal offences, some observation should be made in that respect as well.

## §10.01 PUBLIC MORALITY

**III-92.** As some of the most telling examples[1] discussed in Part II demonstrate, the public policy is often relied upon to uphold certain moral standards. The fact that this occurs is hardly surprising, as in the context of the free movement of goods there is a specific justification aimed at protecting public morality, and it was argued above[2] that the public policy exception takes on that role in the context of the other freedoms. The real problem is, however, to determine what counts as a common EU standard to which all Member States can be expected to live up, and what constitutes a more peculiar standard of a particular Member State, to which nonetheless some deference is shown in line with the idea of 'unity in diversity'. There are basically three instances where the ECJ will refer to common standards.

1. Case 34/79 *Henn and Darby* [1979] ECR 3795; Case E-8/97 *TV 1000 Sverige AB* [1998] 3 C.M.L.Rev. 318; Case C-36/02 *Omega Spielhallen* [2004] ECR I-9609; Case C-244/06 *Dynamic Medien* [2008] ECR I-505; Case C-159/90 *Society for the Protection of Unborn Children Ireland* [1991] ECR I-4685, with Opinion of AG Van Gerven.
2. See, *supra*, at II-18.

**III-93.** First, in Article 2 TEU, the Treaty itself refers to a set of values the Member States have in common. We have primarily discussed those values above[3] from a constitutional perspective, as inspiring constitutional limits to the EU legal order. However, to the extent that human rights also figure prominently among them, there is also a dimension to these values that may interact with the public morality. Accordingly, in *Dynamic Medien*[4] the ECJ could safely refer to the rights of the child as incorporated in the EU legal order in determining the margin left to the German authorities to require distributors of DVDs to use the German age classification system.

**III-94.** Second, the common standard may be the result of legislation adopted by the Union. As indicated above in various pieces of EU legislation open-ended references to public policy or public morality are included. Usually, the open-ended nature of these norms is based on two premises, each with two limbs. First, there is a willingness to allow the Member States some leeway in the determination of specific cases. On the one hand, this is necessary because it is often hard to predict the cases that will fall under the exception in detail in advance. For instance it is hard to predict in advance the ingenious – but potentially offensive – trademarks copywriters may come up with.[5] On the other hand, this also allows for some local sensitivities to be taken into account, as is well demonstrated by the observations of the EFTA Court in *TV 1000 Sverige AB*[6] on the question what broadcast should be considered pornographic. Second, there is nonetheless also an assumption that there will be some degree of communality. On the one hand, this implies that it may be expected that all Member States will find at least some behaviour contrary to the public morality so that none of them will be too shocked by the attempts by another Member State to clamp down on a particular activity. This in turn counsels for some alertness on the side of the actors in the decision-making process to make some standards sufficiently clear in advance. For instance, some Western Member States may well be surprised by the sensitivity some Eastern European States display as to the use of old communist symbols.[7] If an outright ban on particular symbols would be proposed at EU level, the conflicting concerns of the Member States may of course already be factored in during the negotiations in the Council, though it would depend on the legal basis whether a minority view could be marginalized or not.[8] However, precisely when container terms as 'public policy' or 'public morality' are used the far-reaching reading some Member States may have of such terms may not always be self-evident from the start. On the other hand, and in answer to the latter problem, it is also necessary that the ECJ in interpreting these

3. See, *supra*, at III-36 et seq.
4. Case C-244/06 *Dynamic Medien* [2008] ECR I-505.
5. For examples in this respect, see, *supra*, at II-107.
6. Case E-8/97 *TV 1000 Sverige AB* [1998] 3 C.M.L.Rev. 318.
7. See, in this respect the order in Case C-328/04 *Vajnai* [2005] ECR I-8577, where the ECJ dodged the issue on jurisdictional grounds.
8. The flip side of this argument is of course that if Member States find a strong degree of communality, they may be willing to adopt specific, far-reaching legislation. A good example seems Council Framework Decision 2004/68/JHA of 22 December 2003 on combating the sexual exploitation of children and child pornography (2004) OJ L 13/44. See also Framework Decision 2008/913/JHA of 28 November 2008 on combating certain forms and expressions of racism and xenophobia by means of criminal law (2008) OJ L 328/55.

container terms lays down some minimum content and some outer limits to what the concept may mean in the context of a particular piece of legislation. Here, too, the judgment of the EFTA Court in *TV 1000 Sverige AB* could be recalled: despite leaving the Member States some leeway in interpreting the term 'pornography' it warns that 'not all broadcasts of sexually explicit material automatically fall under'[9] the exception at issue. Conversely, while there is as such no pan-European ban on the use of communist symbols, the General Court did accept that the OHIM took into account the fact that such a prohibition exists in some Member States and therefore refused the registration of the coat of arms of the USSR as a Union trademark on public policy grounds.[10]

**III-95.** Third, even in the absence of EU legislation the ECJ sometimes makes assumptions as to the communality of certain values. Accordingly, in *Schindler* the ECJ explicitly recognizes 'the moral, religious or cultural aspects of lotteries, like other types of gambling, in all the Member States',[11] which may even justify a ban on lottery activities. However, the core problem – in particular in the context of the free movement – is precisely that this degree of communality is usually rather limited. It is precisely because of different moral sensitivities about gambling – but also in respect of sexually explicit materials,[12] or even laser games[13] – that these cases arise. However, this is not to say that even then communality may not be brought in through the backdoor. The persuasive strength of the Court's approach in *Omega Spielhallen*[14] is in the way it tries to frame the invocation of 'human dignity' as a justification for prohibiting the laser game at issue in a broader EU context. By explaining that the Union itself is attached to the principle of human dignity and that – as it is moreover reflected in the ECHR and the Charter of Fundamental Rights[15] – this also applies to the Member States the ECJ creates the groundwork for its verdict, in that it makes it clear that the outcome ought to feel entirely alien to non-Germans. At the same time, though, the ECJ also makes sure not to overstate this communality: it rightly suggests nowhere that the EU concept of human dignity would equally *require* (rather than allow) that such laser games should be banned, and it also makes no effort to require other Member States to frown upon this laser game.[16] However, the Court does create some understanding why it is not completely outrageous that the German authorities seek to prohibit a German company from offering this particular game in Germany. A similar technique is used in *Sayn-Wittgenstein*: while the abolition of all references to nobility may be typical for the Austrian form of republicanism, which the Court of course

9. Case E-8/97 *TV 1000 Sverige AB* [1998] 3 C.M.L.Rev. 318, para. 25.
10. Case T-232/10 *Couture Tech v. OHIM* [2011] ECR II-0000.
11. Case C-275/92 *Schindler* [1994] ECR I-1039.
12. Case 34/79 *Henn and Darby* [1979] ECR 3795; Case 121/85 *Conegate* [1986] ECR 1007.
13. Case C-36/02 *Omega Spielhallen* [2004] ECR I-9609.
14. Case C-36/02 *Omega Spielhallen* [2004] ECR I-9609.
15. Admittedly, the Court does not refer explicitly to the ECHR and the Charter of Fundamental rights, but it defers in Case C-36/02 *Omega Spielhallen* [2004] ECR I-9609, para. 34 to paragraphs 82-91 of the Opinion of AG Stix-Hackl, which in turn relies on a whole series of sources in this respect, including the Charter of Fundamental Rights.
16. See in this respect also, *supra*, at I-69.

cannot extend to all other Member States, several of which are constitutional monarchies, the ECJ nevertheless embedded this Austrian approach into the broader idea of equality before the law as embedded in the Charter, and thus deemed common to the Member States.[17]

**III-96.** As a result, the public policy exception may thus at times *not* be reflective of the EU *ordre public*. However, even to the extent that the Court has made it clear that the exception is being invoked to justify a particular national approach, there may be some lesson in it about the content of the EU *ordre public*. On the one hand, if the exception is correctly framed in a broader EU perspective, such as in the case of the human dignity in *Omega Spielhallen*,[18] the protection of the moral integrity of children in *Dynamic Medien*,[19] or – less controversial – the freedom of speech in *Schmidberger*,[20] at least some indication on the EU (moral) standards may nonetheless become apparent. On the other hand, I have stressed above the necessity for some scrutiny about the compatibility of national fringe standards. Cases where the public policy exception is invoked to protect pure national moral sensitivities nonetheless tell us also something about the limits of the tolerance the Union is willing to give to national values that are outside the mainstream. For instance, it may be that a particular national constitutional value illegally discriminates on the grounds of nationality,[21] or excessively undercuts another fundamental right.[22] The readiness of the Court to denounce such a constitutional value, or to let it pass,[23] is equally revealing as to the moral values at the heart of the EU *ordre public*. Moreover, also if the Member State concerned seems hardly capable of fully explaining the exact nature of its concern, as in the case of the Polish objections over the use of genetically modified organisms in line with Union legislation, where the Polish authorities were considered to be mixing up religious and moral arguments with public health concerns,[24] the Court may decide to brush the objections aside.

## §10.02 PUBLIC HEALTH

**III-97.** It has been argued that a close link exists between public health and the *ordre public*, as the former concept encompasses in practice two strands: on the one hand

17. Compare paras 88 and 89 of Case C-208/09 *Sayn-Wittgenstein* [2010] ECR I-0000.
18. Case C-36/02 *Omega Spielhallen* [2004] ECR I-9609.
19. Case C-244/06 *Dynamic Medien* [2008] ECR I-505.
20. Case C-112/00 *Schmidberger* [2003] ECR I-5659.
21. See in this sense the hypothetical put forward in the Opinion of AG Jacobs in Case C-112/00 *Schmidberger* [2003] ECR I-5659, paras 97-98.
22. See in this respect the third step in the analysis of AG Van Gerven in Case C-159/90 *Society for the Protection of Unborn Children Ireland* [1991] ECR I-4685, para. 38, outlined, *supra*, at I-68, where he assesses not only whether the ban on distributing flyers for abortion services serves a legitimate aim, strongly protected by the national legal order, but also whether the ban is compatible with the freedom of expression.
23. Compare the analysis of AG Van Gerven in his Opinion in Case C-159/90 *Society for the Protection of Unborn Children Ireland* [1991] ECR I-4685 with the contrary assessment in ECtHR, 29 October 1992, *Open Door and Dublin Well Woman v. Ireland*.
24. Case C-165/08 *Commission v. Poland* [2009] ECR I-6843.

there is a concern about maintaining public sanitary public protection levels; on the other hand there is also an element of a personal fundamental right to physical, psychological and social well-being.[25] Also in the context of the EU, these two strands come together. The ECJ has actually injected the same definition of health, which it has taken from the World Health Organization,[26] into the Treaties in *UK v. Council* on the Working Time Directive, a case that actually lays at the crossroads of these two strands as it combines the concern about the personal well-being of the worker with broader concerns about safety, not only of the individual worker but also of third parties.[27] The case law of the Court, often based on the explicit grounds for justification in this respect included in the provisions on the free movement, reflects indeed both strands and offers some telling examples supporting the argument that the EU *ordre public* also seeks to protect the physical, psychological and social well-being of the persons in its jurisdiction, despite the limited competence of the Union in the field of public health.[28]

**III-98.** First, the protection of public health is reflected in the possibility for Member States to impose – in the absence of harmonization – certain sanitary provisions to protect both human and animal health even though they may be restrictive of intra-Union trade. However, like other restrictions they only apply to the extent that the Union has not itself exercised its police power[29] by taking the necessary protective measures;[30] they should not be protectionist[31] and they are subject to a proportionality test.[32] The case law shows that Member States regularly run afoul of these requirements, often in high-profile cases, *inter alia* on UHT milk,[33] BSE,[34] and Christmas turkeys.[35] Nevertheless, the case law does grant quite some margin to both the Member States[36] and the Union[37] to take measures to protect the health of humans and animals in the face of scientific uncertainty as to the health risks involved. The introduction of

25. M.-L. Moquet-Anger, '*Ordre public* et santé publique' in *L'ordre public: ordre public ou ordres publics? Ordre public et droits fondamentaux*, ed. M.-J. Redor (Bruxelles: Bruylant, 2001), 201.
26. The definition is taken from the preamble to the Constitution of the World Health Organization to which all Member States belong, for the full text see <http://www.who.int/governance/eb/who_constitution_en.pdf> (22 May 2012).
27. Case C-84/94 *United Kingdom v. Council* [1996] ECR I-5755, paras 25-49.
28. On the scope of the EU health competences, see V. Michel, 'La compétence de la Communauté en matière de santé publique', *R.A.E-L.E.A* (2003-2004): 157-184.
29. Several pieces of EU legislation in effect give the Commission wide-ranging powers to take the necessary emergency measures, see for an application, *inter alia*, Case C-157/96 *National Farmers' Union* [1998] ECR I-2211.
30. Case C-241/01 *National Farmers' Union* [2002] ECR I-9079.
31. Case 40/82 *Commission v. UK* [1982] ECR 2793, para. 37; Case C-219/07 *Nationale Raad van Dierenkwekers en Liefhebbers* [2008] ECR I-0000, para. 39.
32. Case 124/81 *Commission v. UK* [1983] ECR 203.
33. Case 124/81 *Commission v. UK* [1983] ECR 203.
34. Case C-241/01 *National Farmer's Union* [2002] ECR I-9079.
35. Case 40/82 *Commission v. UK* [1982] ECR 2793.
36. Case 174/82 *Sandoz* [1983] ECR 2445. See also the very broad deference shown in Joined cases C-171/07 and C-172/07 *Apothekerkammer des Saarlandes* [2009] ECR I-4171; whereas the referring national court was inquiring whether public authorities should have set aside German federal legislation hindering the establishment of pharmacies of their own motion, the ECJ never got to that question finding that there actually was no unjustified restriction of the free movement in the first place.
37. Case T-13/99 *Pfizer Animal Health v. Council* [2002] ECR II-3305.

the precautionary principle in the EU legal order[38] is likely to strengthen this tendency.[39] Perhaps the best way the public policy nature of these measures is demonstrated is the way they are taken without much consideration of the specificities of individual cases. In the face of a more or less acute risk the prime concern is to contain the risk and to restore consumer confidence, even if this goes at the expense of potentially innocent or in any event unaffected farmers[40] or traders.[41] Moreover, as the case of *Raverco*[42] demonstrates once a health risk has been detected no risk is taken and a product may have to be destroyed, even though it could lawfully be brought onto a foreign market.

**III-99.** The case law shows, however, also an increasing sensitivity to the other strand of public health protection, namely the gradual formulation of a fundamental right to physical, psychological and social well-being. The case most in point is *Watts,*[43] concerning a British woman who had grown impatient with British waiting lists for medical procedures and thus sought a hip transplant in France at the expense of the NHS. On the one hand, this case offers another example of the emancipating force of the free movement provisions which justifies, in my view, treating those as of *ordre public,*[44] as *in casu* they quite literally give Ms. Watts her mobility and thus her life back. On the other hand, in this case there is a clear tension between two competing views on public health evidenced by 'an inherent tension between, on the one hand, the inevitable existence of waiting lists and their role as instruments for managing and allocating limited resources and, on the other hand, the interests of patients in receiving adequate and timely treatment'.[45] The 'public' character of the public health exception, which as such may justify some restrictions to the free movement of services, in order to set up a universal health insurance system,[46] is confronted with the individual right of patients to get effective treatment. The Court rightly draws the line in defending restrictive national health care systems at the point where their restrictions do no longer translate into the attainment of a high level of health protection,[47] for

38. Under the current Treaties, the principle can be found in Article 174(2) TEC on environmental protection, but it has a broader vocation. For a thorough analysis of the principle, see A. Trouche, 'Le principe de précaution, entre unité et diversité: étude comparative des systèmes communautaire et OMC', *Cahiers de droit européen* (2008): 279-338.
39. Case C-504/04 *Agrarproduktion Staebelow* [2006] ECR I-679, para.39; Case C-157/96 *National Farmers' Union* [1998] ECR I-2211, paras 63-64.
40. Case C-189/01 *Jippes* [2001] ECR I-5689, where the ECJ upheld the EU's policy of preferring sanitary slaughter and use vaccination as a last resort in the face of an outbreak of foot and mouth disease, *in casu* at the expense of someone keeping sheep as a hobby.
41. Case C-183/95 *Affish* [1997] ECR I-4315 upholding a total prohibition on the import of Japanese fish, regardless of whether the fish is actually contaminated.
42. Joined Cases C-129/05 and C-130 *Raverco* [2006] ECR I-9297.
43. Case C-372/04 *Watts* [2006] ECR I-4325.
44. See, *supra*, at III-80 et seq.
45. Opinion of AG Geelhoed in Case C-372/04 *Watts* [2006] ECR I-4325, para. 86.
46. Case C-372/04 *Watts* [2006] ECR I-4325, para. 103. See also Case C-158/96 *Kohll* [1998] ECR I-1931, para. 41; Case C-157/99 *Smits and Peerbooms* [2001] ECR I-5473, para. 72; and Case C-385/99 *Müller-Fauré and van Riet* [2003] ECR I-4509, para. 73.
47. Case C-372/04 *Watts* [2006] ECR I-4325, para. 104.

instance because they prevent patients from obtaining adequate treatment within a reasonable time.

## §10.03 PROTECTION FROM AND AGAINST ALIENS

**III-100.** Historically, one of the most fruitful areas for the application of the *ordre public* concerned the treatment of aliens.[48] As argued above, one of the main contributions of the EU legal order is precisely that it has to a certain extent taken away this fundamental distrust of aliens, as a necessary corollary of the free movement of persons.[49] However, this distinction between 'us' and 'them' has not disappeared entirely from the EU legal order. Whereas internally we may have done away with 'this unpleasant shadow'[50] of different treatment, the rules in respect of third-country nationals – at least to the extent that they are unrelated to EU nationals[51] – still are based on a paradigm that allows for selection and control of the influx of aliens into the EU. The *ordre public* exceptions in this field reflect this reality. In particular the concept of 'a threat to public policy' of Article 96 of the Convention Implementing the Schengen Agreement, has a scope that goes well beyond what is acceptable internally, as is demonstrated by the case of *Commission v. Spain,*[52] discussed above.[53] Accordingly, the EU *ordre public* also has this element of *Realpolitik* in the values it protects and the persons that may be benefit from it. In admitting this, I do not renege on my assessment as to the status of the principle of equal treatment or the free movement as elements of the EU *ordre public*. Rather, it is a reminder of the fact that the various elements of the EU *ordre public* at times need to be balanced against each other.[54] Similarly, the Court has accepted that the fact that a person has been a member of an organization which, because of its involvement in terrorist acts, is on the EU watch list and that person has actively supported the armed struggle waged by that organization does not automatically constitute a serious reason for considering that that person has committed 'a serious non-political crime'[55] or 'acts contrary to the purposes and principles of the United Nations'[56] on the basis of which his/her asylum application can be denied; however, if a case-by-case analysis reveals that the person has actually committed certain specific acts, it is not necessary for his/her exclusion that he/she actually is a

48. F. Julien-Laferrière, '*Ordre public* et droit des étrangers' in *L'ordre public: ordre public ou ordres publics? Ordre public et droits fondamentaux*, ed. M.-J. Redor (Bruxelles: Bruylant, 2001), 285-297.
49. See, *supra*, at II-27. For recent examples of cases where the ECJ nevertheless had to combat this form of distrust or prejudice, see Case C-524/06 *Huber* [2008] ECR I-9705 and Case C-161/07 *Commission v. Austria* [2008] ECR I-10671.
50. Opinion of AG Poiares Maduro in Case C-524/06 *Huber* [2008] ECR I-9705, para. 15.
51. Case C-127/08 *Metock* [2008] ECR I-6241; Case C-503/03 *Commission v. Spain* [2006] ECR I-1097.
52. Case C-503/03 *Commission v. Spain* [2006] ECR I-1097.
53. See, *supra*, at II-43 et seq.
54. *Infra*, Part IV.
55. Article 1 F(b) of the The Convention Relating to the Status of Refugees, signed in Geneva on 28 July 1951 (*United Nations Treaty Series*, vol. 189, p. 150, No. 2545 (1954)).
56. Article 1 F(c) of the The Convention Relating to the Status of Refugees, signed in Geneva on 28 July 1951 (*United Nations Treaty Series*, vol. 189, p. 150, No. 2545 (1954)).

threat to the host country.[57] Without negating the principle of equal treatment or other fundamental rights, it seems inevitable that the stability of the socio-economic order and fundamental concerns about public security in a post-9/11 world will always require some degree of immigration control.[58] The latter part is again somewhat in contrast with the treatment of even the worst offenders under Directive 2004/38, who are entitled to an individualized assessment and can only be expelled if he/she is currently a genuine threat to the host State.[59] However, the way the Member States implement the Union immigration and asylum policy raises in turn major issues of fundamental rights, which require sufficient communality between the Member States for the system to work.[60]

## §10.04 EU *ORDRE PUBLIC ÉCOLOGIQUE*

**III-101.** The concern for the environment and all living beings on our planet has not always been at the forefront of the concerns of the European Union. Notably absent from the Rome Treaty was indeed any reference to an EEC competence in respect of the environment, or any explicit recognition of the protection of the environment as a justification for limitations to the fundamental freedoms, though already before the changes brought by the Single European Act the Court had already recognized the constitutional importance of environmental protection as 'one of the Community's essential objectives'.[61] However, the current state of the law reveals a different picture. The current Treaties reflect the shift of European society as a whole towards more environmentally conscious ways of living and thinking that also give rise in the Member States to the idea of an *ordre public écologique*.[62] Accordingly, the Treaties now contain an explicit set of EU competences for the protection of the environment. They even instruct the Union to exercise those competences by taking into account the precautionary principle[63] and instruct the Union to take into account a high level of environmental protection when taking measures for the harmonization of the internal market.[64] Since Amsterdam, the Union even explicitly recognizes that all animals are

57. Joined Cases C-57/09 and C-101/09 *B and D* [2010] ECR I-0000.
58. Joined Cases C-188/10 and C-189/1 *Melki* [2010] ECR I-5667; Case C-83/12 PPU *Vo* [2012] ECR I-0000.
59. Case C-348/09 *P.I.* [2012] ECR I-0000, para. 31.
60. Joined Cases C-411/10 an C-493/10 *N.S.* [2011] ECR I-0000. Here the Court had to qualify, following the judgment of the ECtHR of 21 January 2011 *M.S.S. v. Belgium and Greece* the obligation of Member States under the Dublin II Regulation to refer an asylum applicant back to the country where they first entered the Union, if it appears that that Member State cannot guarantee effective judicial protection of the alien.
61. Case 240/83 *Association de défense des brûleurs d'huiles usagées* [1985] ECR 531. On this case and the gradual development of environmental protection as a constitutional value, see also F. Jacobs, 'The Role of the European Court of Justice in the Protection of the Environment', *Journal of Environmental Law* (2006): 185-206.
62. See in general, M. Boutelet & J.-C. Fritz, *L'ordre public écologique – Towards an ecological public order* (Brussels, Bruylant, 2005).
63. Article 191(2) TFEU
64. Article 114(3) TFEU.

'sentient beings',[65] a point that is put even more centrally in the post-Lisbon version of the Treaties.[66]

**III-102.** The Court's case law also reflects this growing concern and has early on recognized that the environment is 'one of the Community's essential objectives'.[67] First, the ECJ has recognized the special nature of environmental concerns in the context of the free movement, recognizing the special position of waste[68] and upholding measures that were close of being discriminatory.[69] Second, the Court has in recent years taken the opportunity to interpret the EU legislation – especially in respect of the Common Agricultural Policy – in a manner that hammers home the clear desire to also protect animal welfare. Accordingly, the ECJ has upheld serious reductions in export subsidies in cases where the animals were transported in violation of the relevant legislation.[70] Third, the ECJ has accepted that the Community may marshal in criminal law in order to effectively protect the environment, even at a time when that was not as such provided for in the Treaties.[71]

## §10.05 EU *ORDRE PUBLIC* AND EU CRIMINAL LAW

**III-103.** This final example brings us seamlessly to the final point in respect of the protection of societal values. Another way of looking at what values are protected by the EU *ordre public* may indeed be to check what values are protected by the criminal laws adopted by the Union. Crime is indeed the ultimate disturbance of the social order. Whereas for the reasons explained above,[72] the relationship between the national criminal law and the *ordre public* cannot offer a complete match, it seems likely that the EU criminal law does reflect some of the core sensitivities of the EU legal order, even though it cannot exhaust the values covered by the EU *ordre public*, if only because of the limited competences of the Union in this respect.

**III-104.** Analysing what is protected through the criminal law of the Union then mainly seems to strengthen the assessments made above. A short survey of the Framework Decisions adopted – rightly or wrongly[73] – by the Union reveals indeed a close match

65. Protocol (No 33) on the Protection and Welfare of Animals (2006) OJ C 321 E/314.
66. Article 13 TFEU.
67. Case 240/83 *Association de défense des brûleurs d' huiles usagées* [1985] ECR 531.
68. Case C-2/90 *Commission v. Belgium* [1992] ECR I-4431.
69. Case 302/86 *Commission v. Denmark* [1988] ECR 4607.
70. Case C-96/06 *Viamex Agrar* [2008] ECR I-1413; Case C-207/06 *Schwaninger Martin* [2008] ECR I-5561. See also Case C-455/06 *Heemskerk and Schaap* [2008] ECR I-8763, with Opinion of AG Bot.
71. Case C-176/03 *Commission v. Council* [2005] ECR I-7879. See also – though technically a matter of transportation policy, but clearly inspired by environmental concerns – Case C-440/05 *Commission v. Council* [2007] ECR I-9097.
72. See, *supra*, at II-15.
73. On the limits set by the division of competence before the Lisbon Treaty introduced Article 83(2) TFEU, see the discussion, *supra*, at II-115 et seq. of Case C-176/03 *Commission v. Council* [2005] ECR I-7879; Case C-440/05 *Commission v. Council* [2007] ECR I-9097. However, what is more in point here is that either way, the EU as a whole was and is indeed competent to adopt criminal law measures in order to protect a series of values linked to the EU *ordre public*.

with the values identified so far. First, there is a set of rules at protecting the stability of the State by maintaining public security.[74] Second, specific crimes correspond to specific public policy concerns identified, such as the protection of public morality through the fight against child pornography or sexual exploitation,[75] human trafficking[76] or racism and xenophobia;[77] the protection of the environment by creating environmental offences;[78] the protection of public health (and the reduction of crime) by fighting drugs trafficking;[79] the fight against illegal immigration;[80] or the protection of the euro and the monetary system by combating counterfeiting.[81] Finally, there is a set of procedural rules[82] that try to reconcile the need for effective enforcement with the need – also identified as an issue of EU *ordre public* – to uphold fundamental rights. As argued above,[83] the *ordre public* reflects in this respect, the answer the EU gives to Benjamin Franklin's paradox that any society that is 'willing to give up a little liberty to gain a little more security, deserves neither and will lose both'.

---

74. Council Framework Decision 2002/475/JHA of 13 June 2002 on combating terrorism (2002) OJ L 164/3.
75. Directive 2011/92/EU of the European Parliament and of the Council of 13 December 2011 on combating the sexual abuse and sexual exploitation of children and child pornography, and replacing Council Framework Decision 2004/68/JHA (2011) OJ L335/1.
76. Directive 2011/36/EU of the European Parliament and of the Council of 5 April 2011 on preventing and combating trafficking in human beings and protecting its victims, and replacing Council Framework Decision 2002/629/JHA (2011) L 101/1.
77. Framework Decision 2008/913/JHA of 28 November 2008 on combating certain forms and expressions of racism and xenophobia by means of criminal law (2008) OJ L 328/55.
78. Council Framework Decision 2005/667/JHA of 12 July 2005 to strengthen the criminal law framework for the enforcement of the law against ship-source pollution (2005) OJ L 255/164; Council Framework Decision 2003/80/JHA of 27 January 2003 on the protection of the environment through criminal law (2003) OJ L 29/55.
79. Council Framework Decision 2004/757/JHA of 25 October 2004 laying down minimum provisions on the constituent elements of criminal acts and penalties in the field of illicit drug trafficking (2004) OJ L 335.
80. Council framework Decision 2002/946/JHA of 28 November 2002 on the strengthening of the penal framework to prevent the facilitation of unauthorized entry, transit and residence (2002) OJ L 328/1.
81. Council Framework Decision 2000/383/JHA of 29 May 2000 on increasing protection by criminal penalties and other sanctions against counterfeiting in connection with the introduction of the euro (2000) OJ L 140/1 as amended by Council Framework Decision 2001/888/JHA of 6 December 2001 amending Framework Decision 2000/383/JHA on increasing protection by criminal penalties and other sanctions against counterfeiting in connection with the introduction of the euro (2001) OJ L 321/3.
82. See, *inter alia*, Council Framework Decision 2002/584/JHA of 13 June 2002 on the European arrest warrant and the surrender procedures between the Member States (2002) OJ L 190/1; Council Framework Decision 2006/783/JHA of 6 October 2006 on the application of the principle of mutual recognition to confiscation orders (2006) OJ L 328/59; Council Framework Decision 2003/577/JHA of 22 July 2003 on the execution in the European Union of orders freezing property or evidence (2003) OJ L 196/45.
83. See, *supra*, at II-122.

CHAPTER 11

# The Protection of the Cultural Order

**III-105.** In my definition, I included the protection of the cultural order as a separate subset of EU *ordre public*. That choice seems defensible in the light of the judgment of the Court in *Groener*,[1] where the ECJ gave special deference to the protection of the first constitutional language of Ireland. It is submitted that if the Union takes its motto 'unity in diversity' seriously, certain cultural elements that help to build the cultural identity of the Member States, and thus indirectly also the cultural diversity of the Union, may require additional protection as a matter of public policy. Article 22 of the Charter of Fundamental Rights therefore explicitly proclaims that '[t]he Union shall respect cultural, religious and linguistic diversity'. Admittedly, there are thus links with the protection of social cohesion and also of the political system, but it is submitted that the cultural order cannot be identified entirely with either of them.

**III-106.** The original Treaties were largely silent on culture. However, there was one remarkable exception. Among the explicit justifications or restrictions to the free movement of goods of Article 36 TFEU[2] features the 'protection of national treasures possessing artistic, historic or archaeological value'. The provision thus allows the Member States to take action to avoid that key elements of their cultural heritage are not taken from the country and sold to the highest bidder. Long-lasting disputes between Member States over ancient art treasures, such as the Elgin Marbles,[3] demonstrate that these treasures indeed arouse strong (national) sentiments, which would probably not subside - likely rather the opposite - if EU law were to contradict the claims of the country of origin. Recognizing this right thus serves a dual purpose. On the one hand, it allows Member States to assert their cultural identity to the fullest extent. On the other hand, it also avoids that the EU has to antagonize Member States

1. Case C-379/87 *Groener* [1989] ECR 3967.
2. On the desirability to amend Article 30 36 TFEU in order to take culture better into account, see N. Nic Shuibhne, 'Labels, Locals, and the Free Movement of Goods' in *Culture and European Union Law*, ed. R. Craufurd Smith (Oxford: OUP, 2004), 99-112.
3. On the Elgin Marbles and the ensuing debate, see <http://en.wikipedia.org/wiki/Elgin_Marbles> (22 May 2012).

sentiments in this respect, which creates a far stronger basis for the Union to then stimulate cultural interaction between the culturally diverse and self-confident Member States in line with Article 167 TFEU.[4] It has been argued, moreover, that also a series of derogations – often temporary – in the Accession Treaties or Treaty Protocols which often operate in a similar manner as Article 36 TFEU, may be considered as 'identity markers'.[5]

**III-107.** The most pressing manner for the Union to be confronted with the cultural diversity of its Member States, however, is the issue of language.[6] This is not a trivial point. Literally the first legislative act adopted by the Council under the EC Treaty was to lay down the language regime for the institutions,[7] as the Treaties – while drafted in the official languages of all Member States, all versions being equally authentic[8] – had stayed silent on the matter. The absence of such a Treaty basis for linguistic equality in the Union has since had dire consequences, as the Court has effectively accepted that the Council may decide to limit the use by certain bodies, most notably the Office of Harmonization for the Internal Market, of some languages to the benefit of a few languages that are more widely spoken.[9] Despite this, the Court has in the past shown that it can be sensitive to national concerns about language.

**III-108.** The prime example is *Groener*[10] where the ECJ accepted that Ireland could impose a requirement to master Irish, the first constitutional language of Ireland – but hardly spoken in practice, on a Dutch art teacher seeking permanent employment who had already worked satisfactorily as an art teacher in Ireland without using Irish on a temporary basis. Remarkably, the ECJ was thus willing to inject the legitimate 'policy for the protection and promotion of a language of a Member State which is both the

---

4. For an overview, see R. Craufurd Smith, 'From heritage conservation to European identity: Article 151 EC and the multi-faceted nature of Community cultural policy', *European Law Review* (2007): 48-69.
5. C. Hilson, 'The Unpatriotism of the Economic Constitution? Rights to Free Movement and their Impact on National and European Identity', *European Law Journal* (2008): 186-202. The author deals with derogations and declarations concerning, *inter alia*, abortion, property acquisition, football and alcohol; he indicates, somewhat unsurprisingly, that if the Court is perceived as a genuine threat, there will likely be a derogation, otherwise a declaration may suffice. The interesting consequence of this analysis is, however, that a same concern – such as abortion – may thus be the subject of a Protocol in respect of one Member State (e.g., Malta, and already earlier, Ireland) and of a Declaration vis-à-vis another (e.g., Poland).
6. For an overview of EU language law, see B. De Witte., 'Language Law of the European Union: Protecting or Eroding Linguistic Diversity?' in *Culture and European Union Law*, ed. R. Craufurd Smith (Oxford: OUP, 2004), 205-241. See also N. Nic Shuibhne, *EC law and minority language policy: culture, citizenship and fundamental rights* (The Hague: Kluwer, 2002).
7. Regulation No 1 of the Council of 15 April 1958 determining the languages to be used by the European Economic Community, *Official Journal, English Special Edition (I)* (1952-1958), 59.
8. For more the consequences of multiple equally authentic language versions, see G. Van Calster, 'The EU's Tower of Babel – The Interpretation by the European Court of Justice of Equally Authentic Texts Drafted in more than one Official Language', *Yearbook of European Law* (1997): 363-393. For recent examples, see, *inter alia*, Case C-187/07 *Endendijk* [2008] ECR I-2115; Case C-239/07 *Sabatauskas* [2008] ECR I-7523.
9. Case C-361/01 P *Kik v. OHIM* [2003] ECR I-8283.
10. Case C-379/87 *Groener* [1989] ECR 3967.

national language and the first official language'[11] into the interpretation of the functional language criterion of old[12] Article 3(1) of Regulation 1612/68[13] which was precisely adopted to avoid that legitimate demands in respect of linguistic knowledge - making sure that one can safely and effectively carry out a job, such as communicating with patients or follow up safety instructions - could become an insurmountable barrier shielding off the national labour market. As argued, above, I think the ECJ reached the right outcome, but in an inappropriate manner. On a correct construction of Article 3(1) there is no room for such considerations to play a role in the imposition of a linguistic standard on a foreign worker. However, the ECJ could well have taken up the explicit suggestion by the national court[14] in this respect to decide that Article 3(1) does not exhaust the language regime for workers and that this policy for the protection and promotion of a language of a Member State which is both the national language and the first official language may therefore be enforced as a matter of public policy, under the conditions, in particular proportionality, otherwise linked to the exercise of that exception. It appears that this is also the approach which the Court eventually took in *Runevič-Vardyn* where the Court did recognize that the linguistic policy of a host State may weigh enough as to allow them not to recognize the alien features of a foreign alphabet, and thus spell the name of the applicants somewhat differently.[15]

**III-109.** Apart from the fundamental nature language can have for the constitutional identity of the Member States and their citizens,[16] which the ECJ moreover seems to accept in *Groener,*[17] there are at least three practical reasons to translate this fundamental societal value into a matter of public policy. First, as demonstrated by *Groener,*[18] the net result - and to a certain extent even the intention - of imposing a language criterion, while prima facie indistinctly applicable, is to keep non-nationals

11. Case C-379/87 *Groener* [1989] ECR 3967, para. 19.
12. Since replaced by Article 3(1) of Regulation (EU) No 492/2011 of the European Parliament and of the Council of 5 April 2011 on freedom of movement for workers within the Union (2011) OJ L141/1.
13. Regulation (EEC) No 1612/68 of the Council of 15 October 1968 on freedom of movement for workers within the Community, *Official Journal, English Special Edition 1968 II*, 475.
14. Case C-379/87 *Groener* [1989] ECR 3967, para. 10.
15. Case C-391/09 *Runevič-Vardyn* [2011] ECR I-0000.
16. That is not to say that the flip side of this, namely that language may be used by a Member State to oppress a linguistic minority, should not also be a matter of concern for the EU; on this see, for instance, G. Guliyeva, 'Lost in transition: Russian-speaking, non-citizens in Latvia and the protection of minority rights in the European Union', *European Law Review* (2008): 843-869. See also, A. Van Bossuyt, 'Is there an effective European legal framework for the protection of minority languages? The European Union and the Council of Europe screened', *European Law Review* (2007): 860-877.
17. Case C-379/87 *Groener* [1989] ECR 3967, para. 19. See also Case C-391/09 *Runevič-Vardyn* [2011] ECR I-0000, paras 85-86, where this is further embedded with references to Article 4(2) TEU and Article 22 of the Charter of Fundamental Rights.
18. Case C-379/87 *Groener* [1989] ECR 3967.

out.[19] Such a discriminatory practice, if at all allowed, should be based on a Treaty-based exception. Second, as demonstrated by *Piageme,*[20] if the ECJ correctly construes the applicable legislation, without taking into account the linguistic sensitivity, then its own credibility may be saved, but only at the expense of the constitutional value that needed protection. In offering no alternative for taking the Belgian linguistic situation into account the ECJ was also deeply interfering with the precarious constitutional balance in that country – despite the commitment, under the Lisbon Treaty ingrained in Article 4(2) TEU to 'respect the equality of Member States before the Treaties as well as their national identities, inherent in their fundamental structures, political and constitutional, inclusive of regional and local self-government'. Perhaps a case such as *Runevič-Vardyn*[21] may herald a more nuanced approach in this respect, under which cases such as *Piageme* could in the future be decided differently. Third, the problem will continue to resurface, also in situations that do not involve prior EU legislation that could be interpreted in a manner that is conscious of the sensitivity of linguistic policy. A first example in this respect surfaced in the margin of *Grunkin and Paul.*[22] The Lithuanian government has rightfully warned that there may be ground not to recognize unconditionally a foreign name, or the spelling thereof, if that would conflict with 'the structure of its national language, a fundamental part of its national heritage'.[23] While the Court has not taken up the opportunity to address this issue – if it had, it would in any event only have been *obiter* – it is significant that the ECJ did accept that there is a public policy exception in citizenship cases that could have justified for instance the non-recognition of family names.[24] To the extent that – as is submitted here – protection of the linguistic identity of a country could be a matter of public policy, the Court now has a more appropriate alternative. That is exactly what happened in the case of *Runevič-Vardyn.*[25]

**III-110.** Finally, there is another – highly sensitive – reason why language may become a matter of public policy. Language is an important tool to integrate foreigners into a society. In that respect, it touches upon various other aspects of the public policy. It is only by mastering the language of the society where one lives that one can fully participate in the *polis*, and thus the fact that the government speaks the language of its citizens – but also conversely that the citizens may master the language they are governed in – may be crucial for the political order. Also, it is an important tool for integrating individuals into the broader social fabric. An important number of societal tensions may be the result of a breakdown in communication. A lot of these occur regardless of the language and affect natives as well as non-natives, as they may be the result of neglect of neighbourhoods, or an insufficient level of education etc. However,

19. See in the context of the recognition of qualifications of lawyers, Case C-506/04 *Wilson* [2006] ECR I-8613, paras 63-77; see also Case C-193/05 *Commission v. Luxemburg* [2006] ECR I-8673.
20. Case C-369/89 *Piageme* [1991] ECR I-2971; Case C-85/94 *Piageme* [1995] ECR I-2955.
21. Case C-391/09 *Runevič-Vardyn* [2011] ECR I-0000.
22. Case C-353/06 *Grunkin and Paul* [2008] ECR I-7639. For more on the example, see, *supra*, II-51 et seq., in particular at II-54.
23. Opinion of AG Sharpston in Case C-353/06 *Grunkin and Paul* [2008] ECR I-7639, para. 84.
24. Case C-353/06 *Grunkin and Paul* [2008] ECR I-7639, para. 38.
25. Case C-391/09 *Runevič-Vardyn* [2011] ECR I-0000.

at the very least it cannot be denied that these problems can be greatly compounded by a language problem. Accordingly, with the risk of injecting myself head-on into a very sensitive political debate – in particular in Belgium – I do submit that the public policy exception – precisely because its role as societal safety valve – may in some circumstances justify certain linguistic requirements public authorities may want to impose, for instance in the context of social housing. However, my argument should not be overstated. The Member States cannot do away with fundamental rights to housing or education altogether.[26] However, there may be instances where a language condition – especially if coupled with an active policy to encourage people to learn that language – may be justified when long-term commitments are involved. For instance, a local authority should not be allowed to refuse shelter to a family whose private home was destroyed by fire on the basis of limited knowledge of a particular language. However, a government may want to ensure that if it creates a new social housing estate by renting out – and *a fortiori* selling – new housing units that the social fabric may not become dysfunctional because of a language barrier. Similarly, a city council cannot refuse children to participate in certain after-school activities on the basis that they are non-natives. However, it should perhaps be allowed to refuse children to participate in particular activities – just like under Article 3(1) of Regulation 492/2011[27] adults may be refused access to a particular job – if the functional language level is not sufficient to understand and follow-up essential safety instructions, provided that the council at the same time also actively stimulates non-natives to rapidly attain the functional language level required so that they may soon participate fully and safely. Probably, the language requirements for allowing children to participate in a football game may be close to none – and allowing children to participate may actually create an environment in which they start to pick up the language rudimentarily. However, things may be different if the city council also offers children the change of taking part in diving initiations for which some prior theory lessons may be essential, or – less high-risk, but equally challenging for the organizers, especially if there are gaps in the communication – tries to offer certain forms of entertainment for special needs children. Admittedly, one could object that the ECJ has in the past rejected a similar concern – expressed as a matter of public policy – put forward by Germany in justification of that country's policy of making the grant of a residence permit to the family members of a Community worker subject to the worker having sufficiently comfortable living quarters to house also his next of kin.[28] However, it is submitted that while it is true that 'measures adopted on grounds of public policy and for the maintenance of public security against the nationals of Member States of the Community cannot be justified on grounds extraneous to the individual case' or be based 'on reasons of a "general preventive nature"',[29] the case of language requirement is

26. See in this Case C-571/10 *Kamberaj* [2012] ECR I-0000 where long term resident third-country nationals were discriminated against in their access to social housing.
27. Regulation (EU) No 492/2011 of the European Parliament and of the Council of 5 April 2011 on freedom of movement for workers within the Union (2011) OJ L141/1.
28. Case 249/86 *Commission v. Germany* [1989] ECR 1263.
29. Case 249/86 *Commission v. Germany* [1989] ECR 1263, para. 18. See also Case 67/74 *Bonsignore* [1975] ECR 297.

different. Indeed, what is at issue is not so much the extraneous question what wealth one has – or even more remote, what wealth the Union worker to whom one is related possesses – but rather a question of ones own personal skills and characteristics. What I propose is an assessment whether the individual citizen has sufficient relevant knowledge of the local language to perform a particular task – for instance to safely participate in certain activities or to integrate in a housing development – without risk for the perturbation of the social order.[30]

**III-111.** It is obvious that the language requirements that may thus be imposed will often be quite minimal. It may well be that often the linguistic knowledge required maybe at the level of knowing the difference between left and right, between red and green, or the days of the week. Moreover, I have not forgotten about my own criticism of the judgment in *Omega Spielhallen*[31] that the analysis should not stop at finding a seemingly legitimate constitutional value, but should also include a review whether the invoked constitutional value – in this case the protection of a constitutional language of a Member State, in light of its social and political consequences – is not used in a manner that unduly reduces other fundamental values.[32] Accordingly, precisely because I recognize the sensitivity of the language issue, I do not object to an analysis which seeks to weigh the *ordre public* value of language with other norms of the same status, such as fundamental rights (in the examples *inter alia* the right to adequate housing or the rights of the child) and the principle of equal treatment. Undoubtedly, the latter principle looms large in this context, and I agree that any intent of malice or assertion of superiority must be smoked out. The point is, however, that – despite these

30. The ECJ will have an opportunity to address this problem, as the Belgian Constitional Court has referred to it *inter alia* the question: 'Should Articles 21, 45, 49, 56 and 63 of the Treaty on the Functioning of the European Union and Articles 22 and 24 of Directive 2004/38/EC of the European Parliament and of the Council of 29 April 2004 on the right of citizens of the Union and their family members to move and reside freely within the territory of the Member States amending Regulation (EEC) No 1612/68 and repealing Directives 64/221/EEC, 68/360/EEC, 72/194/EEC, 73/148/EEC, 75/34/EEC, 75/35/EEC, 90/364/EEC, 90/365/EEC and 93/96/EEC, be interpreted as precluding the scheme introduced by Book 5 of the Decreet van het Vlaamse Gewest van 27 maart 2009 betreffende het grond- en pandenbeleid, entitled 'Wonen in eigen streek' ('Living in one's own area'), namely the scheme whereby in certain so-called target municipalities the transfer of land and any constructions erected thereon is made subject to the buyer or the tenant being able to demonstrate a sufficient tie with the municipality within the meaning of Article 5.2.1(2) of that decree?', see Pending Case C-203/11 *All Projects & Developments* (2011) OJ C 219/05. A similar question was also referred in Pending Case C-197/11 *Libert.* (2011) OJ C 211/25: 'Are Articles 21, 45, 49, 56 and 63 TFEU and Articles 22 and 24 of Directive 2004/38/EC of the European Parliament and of the Council of 29 April 2004 on the right of citizens of the Union and their family members to move and reside freely within the territory of the Member States amending Regulation (EEC) No 1612/68 and repealing Directives 64/221/EEC, 68/360/EEC, 72/194/EEC, 73/148/EEC, 75/34/EEC, 75/35/EEC, 90/364/EEC, 90/365/EEC and 93/96/EEC to be interpreted as precluding the scheme established by Book 5 of the Decree of the Flemish Region of 27 March 2009 on land and real estate policy, entitled 'Living in your own region', which, in certain communes referred to as 'target communes', makes the transfer of land and buildings thereon conditional upon the purchaser or the lessee demonstrating a sufficient connection with those communes for the purposes of Article 5.2.1., §2 of the Decree?'
31. Case C-36/02 *Omega Spielhallen* [2004] ECR I-9609.
32. See in this sense, *supra*, at I-72.

*caveats* – imposing a language requirement for certain services cannot a priori deemed to be contrary of EU law and may be reflective of the EU *ordre public*. After all, even the EU legislator has allowed certain language requirements,[33] over the initial hesitation of the Court in *Piageme*.[34] It appears, moreover, that also the ECJ may again be willing to accept certain obstacles flowing from linguistic requirements,[35] as it has already rejected a challenge by the Commission against German legislation which required that certain documents concerning posted workers be available at the work place for the benefit of the German authorities in German.[36] It is submitted that the Courts willingness to accept some major inconvenience for the persons at issue in *Runevič-Vardyn*[37] who may now find themselves confronted with two very different spelling variants of their names, is further indication that linguistic concerns may at times be invoked even when the fundamental freedoms and fundamental rights (e.g., to the name) are at stake.

## §11.01 CONCLUSION

**III-112.** In this Part, an attempt was made to charter the values that lurk behind our short-hand definition of the EU *ordre public* as the complex of norms at the very heart of a political entity (in this case the EU) expressing and protecting the basic options taken by that entity regarding its political, economic, social and cultural order. It has been argued that indeed for each of these four categories a number of values may be identified which could rightly claim a place in a substantive concept of the EU *ordre public*. Accordingly, I tried to effectively bring these values underlying the EU legal order in general, and the case law of the ECJ shaping that order in particular, to the fore – without, however, any claim that thus an exhaustive list was drawn up. At the very least, however, the contours of a clearer picture are emerging.

**III-113.** At the same time, the last example discussed, on the status of language, reveals that the work is not over, yet. Drawing the contours of a substantive EU *ordre public* is one thing. However, as the examples demonstrate, still tensions may exist. On the one hand, there is no guarantee – quite to the contrary – that the EU *ordre public* is fully reflective of the various national *ordres publics*, and even if certain values are shared – such as, in my opinion, sensitivity to the protection of the linguistic identity and diversity of the Union and its Member States – there is no reason to assume that there is any agreement as to the intensity with which certain values need protection. On the other hand, the example of language requirements for social housing is also revealing in another sense. Assuming for the sake of argument that I am correct as to the

33. Directive 2000/13/EC of the European Parliament and of the Council of 20 March 2000 on the approximation of the laws of the Member States relating to the labelling, presentation and advertising of foodstuffs (2000) OJ L 109/29.
34. Case C-369/89 *Piageme* [1991] ECR I-2971; Case C-85/94 *Piageme* [1995] ECR I-2955.
35. See in this sense also J. Vanhamme, 'De l'équivalence des langues dans le marché intérieur: l'apport de la Cour de Justice', *Cahiers de droit européen* (2007): 359-380.
36. Case C-490/04 *Commission v. Germany* [2007] ECR I-6095.
37. Case C-391/09 *Runevič-Vardyn* [2011] ECR I-0000.

possibility for Member States to rely on the *ordre public* to justify certain restrictions to free movement rights, there may still be the need to also balance between the various values the EU itself seems to put forward as part of the public policy. Therefore, an attempt to describe how the EU *ordre public* may be reconciled with the national legal orders, but also how the various values protected by the EU *ordre public* may be reconciled internally, will be undertaken in Part IV.

# PART IV
# The EU *Ordre Public* as Source of Conflict and Reconciliation between Legal Orders

## INTRODUCTION

**IV-1.** In the previous parts, first, the case for the existence of an EU *ordre public* was made (Part I) and, subsequently, an attempt was made to put some meat on the bones of the EU *ordre public*, by tracking the various forms of its manifestation in the EU legal order (Part II) and the values that are arguably protected by it (Part III). During that analysis, I hinted on several occasions at the autonomy of the EU *ordre public* and the potential for conflict with the Member States. It has been argued throughout that the EU *ordre public* is distinct from the *ordre public* of any of its Member States. Similarly, it has been argued that on various occasions the EU legal order puts certain limits on the Member States, for instance by rejecting too casual invocations of the public policy exceptions.[1] In some cases, the conflict may even go deeper and reveal a clear division of minds between the EU and (some of) its Member States.[2] At the same time, on many occasions it was stressed that the conflict may often be circumvented[3] or the blow, if any, lessened. Accordingly, the autonomous EU *ordre public* may at the same time be cause of conflict and, as it nonetheless also has roots in the legal order of the Member States, a tool to overcome divergence.

**IV-2.** The classic features of EU law – primacy, direct effect – may easily set the stage for grand conflicts between the national legal order and the EU legal order. Add some sensitive moral issues, as is arguably the case for part of the EU *ordre public*, and one may have the recipe for a rather explosive mix whereby 'Brussels' appears to dictate

1. See, *inter alia*, Case 231/83 *Cullet* [1985] ECR 305; Case 249/86 *Commission v. Germany* [1989] ECR 1263.
2. See, e.g., Case C-369/89 *Piageme* [1991] ECR I-2971; Case C-85/94 *Piageme* [1995] ECR I-2955.
3. See, *inter alia*, Case C-36/02 *Omega Spielhallen* [2004] ECR I-9609; Case C-379/87 *Groener* [1989] ECR 3967.

the moral choices of ordinary citizens.[4] Admittedly, as argued above, primacy and direct effect are a matter of EU public policy, and there are thus also cases were the EU legal order is asserting its position quite confidently. However, on closer examination the situation is far more nuanced. As one of its underlying premises, this book takes the Union's motto 'united in diversity' seriously – and it is submitted that the EU legal order in practice often does, too. Therefore, at least as important as the classic gloomy scenarios of clashes between the EU legal order and the national legal orders are the myriads of instances where a modus vivendi between the two was found.

**IV-3.** Therefore, this Part will first address both sides of the coin. On the one hand, the autonomous nature of the EU legal order, and thus also of its *ordre public*, requires that the Union may act at times independently from its Member States and implies that the Union may at times even collide with them. Accordingly, there may be a need to further develop the concept of supremacy briefly in the following paragraphs and pay some attention to potential fault lines. On the other hand, the bulk of this Part will nevertheless be devoted to the various techniques that in practice limit or avoid some of these damaging conflicts, without therefore denying the EU *ordre public* its specific status.

**IV-4.** At the end of the previous Part also another potential conflict was flagged. The potential for conflict as to the impact of the values protected by the EU *ordre public* is not limited to the relationship between the EU and its Member States, but also permeates the decision-making process at the EU level. It is almost trivial to observe that in any given case several public policy values may be at issue, which may advocate for seemingly different outcomes. What is less trivial, however, is the way the ECJ should be dealing with such conflicts. Without there being need – and indeed space – for a full analysis of the processes of constitutional balancing in the context of this book, it may be useful to bring together a few pieces of the puzzle in this respect that were revealed in the course of our analysis in the preceding parts.

**IV-5.** Finally, an attempt is made to bring together these two lines of conflict – and the potential for reconciliation that comes with them – in a brief analysis of the status of same-sex marriages in EU law.

4. This appears to be the underlying concern of the Polish government in Case C-165/08 *Commission v. Poland* [2009] ECR I-6843.

CHAPTER 12

# EU *Ordre Public* and National Legal Orders: 'Can Two Walk Together, Except They Be Agreed?'

**IV-6.** The inspiration for the chapter heading is a great article by Iris Canor on the relationship between EU law and international law,[1] and ultimately goes back to the Old Testament,[2] but the quote also goes to the heart of the matter: if the EU *ordre public*, despite drawing heavily on the common constitutional traditions of the Member States, is autonomous and distinguishable from the *ordres publics* of its Member States, is conflict not inevitable, and are there, nonetheless, ways to reconcile both?

**IV-7.** In order to answer these questions – which are intimately intertwined – it seems useful to analyse more deeply how far the reach of the EU legal order over the Member States stretches. It is only to the extent that the EU is really in a position to make binding demands vis-à-vis the national legal orders that all-out open conflicts may arise. At the same time, the intricacies of the various constitutional doctrines in play, such as primacy and pre-emption, leave room for something of a constitutional grey zone. It is this grey zone, however, that also offers the breathing space necessary to avoid or defuse conflicts – or at least to postpone them for another day.

## §12.01 ASSERTING THE AUTONOMY AND SUPREMACY OF THE EU LEGAL ORDER

**IV-8.** There is a clear centralist strand in the EU legal order, which is, however, manifested in various ways. First, there is the concept of pre-emption, which affects the

1. I. Canor, 'Can two walk together, except they be agreed?' The relationship between international law and European law: The incorporation of United Nations sanctions against Yugoslavia into European Community law through the perspective of the European Court of Justice, *Common Market Law Review* (1998): 137-187.
2. Amos 3:3.

Member States right to take a particular course of action that may undermine the action of the Union. Second, there is the primacy of EU law, in a sense the remedy for the enforcement of pre-emption, ensuring that conflicting provisions of national law may be cast aside. Third, there is the concept of effectiveness, of *effet utile*, linked to the duty of sincere cooperation laid down in Article 4(3) TEU, requiring Member States to take the necessary positive action to ensure the full effect of EU law. Before these three points are addressed, it is important to remind that the primacy of the EU legal order is itself of *ordre public*.

**IV-9.** Karen Alter[3] has convincingly demonstrated that the twin doctrines of supremacy and direct effect have a direct bearing on the rule of law, as together they form an answer to what she describes as 'the vicious circle of international law: weak legal mechanisms with poor compliance'[4] in that the effective enforcement of EU law is greatly enhanced by allowing Member State courts to enforce EU law, which becomes evermore ingrained in the various national legal orders, against the Member State authorities, who in turn are far less inclined to disregard national courts than they may be willing to disrespect international organizations.[5] Yet, at the same time, the Court has made it clear early on that it is crucial – a matter of *ordre public* – that those national courts are in fact giving full effect to EU law and are not undermining the effectiveness of EU law because of national constitutional requirements.[6] Similarly, the judicial Kompetenz-Kompetenz[7] is placed squarely within the ECJ, which is alone competent – at least within the scope of the old Community pillar and after the Lisbon Treaty in any case also in respect of the Area of Freedom, Security and Justice and in more limited fashion also in respect of the CFSP[8] – to decide on the validity of secondary legal

---

3. K. Alter, *Establishing the Supremacy of European Law* (Oxford: Oxford University Press, 2001), 207 et seq.
4. *Ibid.*, 211.
5. See in a similar vein also E. Szyszczak, 'Making Europe more relevant to its citizens: effective judicial process', *European Law Review* (1996): 351-364.
6. Case 9/65 *San Michele v. High Authority* [1965] ECR 27; see also Case 106/77 *Simmenthal* [1978] ECR 629 or, more recent, Joined Cases C-188/10 and C-189/10 *Melki* [2010] ECR I-5667.
7. The Member States, of course, still have a final say as Masters of the Treaty, see U. Di Fabio, 'Some Remarks on the Allocation of Competences between the European Union and its Member States', *Common Market Law Review* (2002): 1289-1301. For the impact of this on how EU *ordre public* may be shaped, see, *infra*, Part V.
8. In the old second and third pillar, the situation is more nuanced. I submit that in the old third pillar Case 314/84 *Foto-Frost* [1987] ECR 4199 applied to the extent that a Member State has allowed its courts to refer cases to the ECJ – but with the additional caveat that even then the courts in other Member States may be bound by the judgments of the ECJ in that field. The Irish experience teaches, nevertheless, that effective judicial protection in the absence of access to the ECJ through the national courts is not self-evident, see E. Fahey, 'How to be a Third Pillar guardian of fundamental rights? The Irish Supreme Court and the European arrest warrant', *European Law Review* (2008): 563-577. In the second pillar, Member States courts must – anticipating the post-Lisbon Article 19(1), second sentence TEU – offer equivalent protection; see in this sense also T. Corthaut, 'Plus ça change, plus c'est la même chose ?', *Maastricht Journal of European and Comparative Law* (2008): 25. Since the Lisbon Treaty the third pillar has been formally integrated in the TFEU and is without doubt subject to the principle of primacy. As for the CFSP the role of the ECJ is more limited, but there are nevertheless options for judicial review by the ECJ when individuals are targeted (Article 275 TFEU). Outside that I

instruments.[9] While this blunt assertion of supremacy may not always have gone down well with the Member States – it has even been compared to a coup d'Etat[10] and the principle of primacy was one of the few elements of the Constitution for Europe[11] not to make it into the Lisbon Treaty[12] – largely because the principle has too often been seen as creating a form of 'hierarchical superiority',[13] it is important to recognize that there is such an EU-strengthening current in the EU legal order.

### [A] Pre-emption

**IV-10.** This is not the place to develop a full theory of pre-emption, but some observations may nonetheless be helpful. I agree with Schütze[14] that the pre-emption doctrine in the EU is still largely underdeveloped, but that some lessons can be learned, *inter alia*, on the basis of the experience of the US legal order, even though the US pre-emption doctrine 'may lack theoretical elegance'.[15] Important for my argumentation is the link the pre-emption doctrine has with the static viz. dynamic division of competence. With the static division of competence I refer to the division of competence as anticipated in broad terms by the Treaties, and made explicit in Title I of Part One of the TFEU. With the dynamic division of competence, I try to catch the actual division of competence at a given moment in time, which depends on the totality of legal acts that have entered into force by that point in time, and which is dynamic as it fluctuates with the adoption and abolition of EU legal acts.

**IV-11.** On the one hand, the existence of pre-ordained categories of exclusive, shared and supporting competences has also consequence for the possibilities for pre-emption and indirectly also for the EU *ordre public*. First, the exclusive competence corresponds with field pre-emption in that it basically excludes any activity of the Member States – at least in the absence of any explicit or implicit authorization by the Union[16] – from a certain policy field, irrespective of whether Member State action is in any way

stand by my argument that Article 19(1), second sentence TEU now requires Member State courts to offer adequate judicial protection, if need be by not applying CFSP measures contrary to higher norms of EU law.

9. Case 314/84 *Foto-Frost* [1987] ECR 4199; Joined Cases C-188/10 and C-189/10 *Melki* [2010] ECR I-5667, para. 54.
10. T. Schilling, 'The Court of Justice's revolution: its effects and the conditions for its consummation. What Europe can learn from Fiji', *European Law Review* (2002): 445-463.
11. Article I-6.
12. Not that this makes much difference in practice, see T. Corthaut, 'Plus ça change, plus c'est la même chose ?', *Maastricht Journal of European and Comparative Law* (2008): 18-19; see also M. Kumm, 'The Jurisprudence of Constitutional Conflict: Constitutional Supremacy in Europe before and after the Constitutional Treaty', *European Law Journal* (2005): 285.
13. A. Verhoeven, *The European Union in Search of a Democratic and Constitutional Theory* (The Hague/London/New York: Kluwer Law International, 2002), 309.
14. R. Schütze, 'Supremacy without pre-emption? The very slowly emergent doctrine of Community pre-emption', *Common Market Law Review* (2006): 1023-1048.
15. *Altria Group v. Good*, 55 U.S. 70 (2008).
16. Article 2(1) TFEU; Case 804/79 *Commission v. UK* [1981] ECR 1045.

negatively affecting the Union policy in that field. This is important for our argumentation because the attentive reader may have noticed that a series of elements identified so far as having a place in a substantive concept of EU *ordre public* actually correspond with those exclusive competences.[17] The *lex moneta* flows from the exclusive competence in respect of the monetary policy for the Member States whose currency is the euro, the customs union is an exclusive competence and a matter of *ordre public*, and also the establishing of the competition rules necessary for the functioning of the internal market has a corollary in the EU *ordre public* status of these rules.

**IV-12.** Second, the two further categories of competence are being defined in function of the possibility for field pre-emption. According to the definition of shared competence laid down in Article 2(2) TFEU:

> When the Treaties confer on the Union a competence shared with the Member States in a specific area, the Union and the Member States may legislate and adopt legally binding acts in that area. The Member States shall exercise their competence to the extent that the Union has not exercised its competence. The Member States shall again exercise their competence to the extent that the Union has decided to cease exercising its competence.

This stands in contrast with the areas where the Union only has supporting competences, as defined in Article 2(5) TFEU:

> In certain areas and under the conditions laid down in the Treaties, the Union shall have competence to carry out actions to support, coordinate or supplement the actions of the Member States, without thereby superseding their competence in these areas.

The distinction between these two categories is not without consequence for the questions that are confronted in this book. A telling example may be taken from one of those areas that the Treaty is ambiguous about, namely research and technology. While formally listed under the heading of shared competence, Article 4(3) TFEU adds that 'in the areas of research, technological development and space, the Union shall have competence to carry out activities, in particular to define and implement programmes; however, the exercise of that competence shall not result in Member States being prevented from exercising theirs', which almost sounds as if the Union has rather a supporting role in these fields. The question is, however, not merely a matter of labels. Above several examples have been discussed that illustrate the difficulties that are posed by EU standards in respect of ethical questions.[18] It is not difficult to imagine the sensitivities that would be in play if the EU were to legislate in respect of stem cell research or in respect of the use of human embryos in the framework of

17. For more on exclusive competences, and the rationale behind the list in Article 2(1) TFEU, see R. Schütze, 'Dual federalism constitutionalised: the emergence of exclusive competences in the EC legal order', *European Law Review* (2007): 3-28.
18. Case C-244/06 *Dynamic Medien* [2008] ECR I-505; Case C-377/98 *Netherlands v. European Parliament and Council* [2001] ECR I-7079; Case C-159/90 *Society for the Protection of Unborn Children Ireland* [1991] ECR I-4685.

scientific research.[19] The question of the qualification of scientific research as a shared competence or not has, however, deeper consequences, which are acerbated because of the ethical questions attached to research and development.[20] It is clear that the first concern of Article 2(5) TFEU is to ensure that both the EU and the Member States may set up programmes and spend money on scientific research. The fact that the EU sets up a programme should not pre-empt the Member States from also funding research in the same domain. However, if the EU were to allow stem cell research and set up a programme for funding it, are Member States then nevertheless entitled to prohibit that type of research within their borders, even though that implies that research labs in some Member States will lose out on money and the overall effectiveness of the EU research policy may be weakened? Or conversely, if the EU were to decide to prohibit research on human embryos is the EU then merely prohibiting EU funded research in that field, or are the Member States pre-empted from setting up their own programmes to engage in research on human embryos? The detailed description of the role of the Union in developing a policy in respect of research, technological development and space in Articles 179–190 TFEU suggests that the Union has a supporting role, 'complementing the activities carried out by the Member States',[21] whereby it appears unlikely that the Member States could be required or prohibited to carry out a particular form of research. Nevertheless, there may well be a strong normative force - despite the questionable democratic legitimacy of Commission decision-making in this field - of the 'initiatives aiming at the establishment of guidelines and indicators, the organization of exchange of best practice, and the preparation of the necessary elements for periodic monitoring and evaluation', which the Commission may take in 'close cooperation' with the Member States under Article 181 TFEU. Upon balance, this policy domain would have been better categorized as a supporting competence.[22]

**IV-13.** On the other hand, the link with the dynamic division of competence also helps to nuance the impact. Pre-emption only plays a role to the extent that the Union has effectively adopted legislation and to the extent that Union law is applicable. Accordingly, while it is true - as demonstrated by the *biotechnology* case,[23] or *National*

19. See on this problem C. Starck, 'Ist die finanzielle Förderung an embryonalen Stammzellen durch die Europäische Gemeinschaft rechtlich zulässig?', *Europarecht* (2006): 1-25. Compare also European Parliament, *European Parliament resolution on the trade in human egg cells*, P6_TA (2005) 0074.
20. For an overview of the rather non-transparent manner the EU tackles some of these ethical issues through the European Group on Ethics in Science and New Technologies, see H. Busby, T. Hervey & A. Mohr, 'Ethical EU law? The influence of the European Group on Ethics in Science and New Technologies', *European Law Review* (2008): 803-842.
21. Article 180 TFEU.
22. Nevertheless, also outside the competences in respect of research and development very similar issues may come up, and the (conservative) balance struck in those cases involving shared competences involving VAT, such as Case C-86/09 *Future Health Technologies* [2010] ECR I-5215 and Case C-262/08 *CopyGene* [2010] ECR I-5053, both involving umbilical cord preservation for stem cell recovery, or regarding the protection of intellectual property in the case of biotechnological inventions as in Case C-34/10 *Brüstle* [2011] ECR I-0000, do have consequences for the entire Union as a result of the pre-emptive effect of Union law.
23. Case C-377/98 *Netherlands v. European Parliament and Council* [2001] ECR I-7079. See also Case C-165/08 *Commission v. Poland* [2009] ECR I-6843.

*Farmers' Union*[24] – that Member States are precluded from adopting their own rules on matters they may well consider of national public policy in the face of EU legislation,[25] there are still many instances where no such legislation exists. This is the flip side of the remarks made about the approach by the ECJ in *Omega Spielhallen*:[26] it is precisely in the absence of EU standards on laser games that the ECJ could authorize the German authorities to invoke their own concept of human dignity as a matter of public policy, without implying that henceforth the Union or the other Member States must adhere to similar standards. Similarly, national law only has to yield to EU law to the extent of the conflict, as pre-emption does not per se invalidate the legislation.[27] As Schütze rightly remarks national legislation is only set aside to the extent of the conflict as a matter of primacy.[28] Accordingly, national rules which may be incompatible with the free movement may well still be invoked against persons or goods from third countries.[29]

### [B] Primacy

**IV-14.** This brings us almost naturally to primacy as another technique to assert the autonomy of EU law. The principle is simple and was restated eloquently in *Nimz*:

> that a national court which is called upon, within the limits of its jurisdiction, to apply provisions of Community law is under a duty to give full effect to those provisions, if necessary by refusing of its own motion to apply any conflicting provision of national legislation, and it is not necessary for the court to request or await the prior setting aside of such provision by legislative or other constitutional means[30].

The only situation where a conflict between national law and EU law is not decided in this manner is when another constitutional principle, such as the principle of legality and the related principle of the retroactivity of the milder penal law, stands in the way of the result otherwise envisaged by EU law or when the constitutional limits of the legal instrument would be transgressed, for instance by imposing of itself obligations on an individual when the instrument does not allow for this.[31] However, primacy is

---

24. Case C-241/01 *National Farmers' Union* [2002] ECR I-9079.
25. Nevertheless the combination of the rules on free movement and the harmonising measures result in a cycle of 'deregulation' and 're-regulation'; see in this respect S. Weatherill, 'Pre-emption, Harmonisation and the Distribution of Competence to Regulate the Internal Market' in *The Law of the Single European Market – Unpacking the Premises*, ed. C. Barnard & J. Scott (Oxford/Portland: Hart, 2002), 41-73.
26. Case C-36/02 *Omega Spielhallen* [2004] ECR I-9609.
27. B. De Witte, 'Direct effect, supremacy and the nature of the legal order' in *The Evolution of EU Law*, ed. P. Craig & G. De Búrca (Oxford: OUP, 1999), 189.
28. R. Schütze, 'Supremacy without pre-emption? The very slowly emergent doctrine of Community pre-emption', *Common Market Law Review* (2006): 1023-1048.
29. See in this sense also A. Verhoeven, *The European Union in Search of a Democratic and Constitutional Theory* (The Hague/London/New York: Kluwer Law International, 2002), 310-311.
30. Case C-184/89 *Nimz* [1991] ECR I-297, para. 19.
31. Joined Cases C-387/02, C-391/02 and C-403/02 *Berlusconi* [2005] ECR I-3565, para. 72 et seq. Compare also Case C-80/06 *Carp* [2007] ECR-4473.

merely the conflict rule aimed at solving the inconsistency between the national law and the EU rule; the actual invalidation of the national rule is something that is uniquely the province of national constitutional law. As a result while national courts are under an obligation not to apply the inconsistent norm, the norm may still be part and parcel of the national legal order.[32] This approach is not dissimilar to the position taken by the Spanish Constitutional Court, which distinguishes, even though it admits that both terms are often – as indeed in the preceding paragraphs – used interchangeably, between primacy, which may result in a national norm not being applied, and supremacy, which affects the validity of the national norm and which is seen as still a matter of national law.[33]

**IV-15.** The relationship with the public policy plays out in a double manner. First, the national court is under a duty to set aside any conflicting provision of national legislation *of its own motion.*[34] Let this obligation, however, not be misunderstood: this is not a general empowerment of national courts to raise all EU law of their own motion. However, to the extent that a national court's attention is drawn to a conflict between national and EU law it must attach to that conflict the natural consequence of refusing to apply the contrary national provision to the extent of the conflict, regardless of whether the parties have asked explicitly to do so or whether national law would otherwise allow it to set aside legislation.[35]

**IV-16.** Second, the exclusionary effect may thus also have an effect on domains that may be linked to the national public policy, as the following three examples demonstrate. The first is the case of *Marleasing*, which is well-known for its restatement of the duty for national courts to interpret their national law as far as possible in the light of EU law.[36] However, the interpretation advocated by the Court – in case that the list laid

32. See in this sense A. Verhoeven, *The European Union in Search of a Democratic and Constitutional Theory* (The Hague/London/New York: Kluwer Law International, 2002), 310-311.
33. Tribunal Constitucional, Opinion 1/2004 of 13 December 2008 on the Treaty establishing a Constitution for Europe. For an excellent annotation focusing *inter alia* on the concept of primacy, see F. Castillo De La Torre, 'Tribunal Constitucional (Spanish Constitutional Court), Opinion 1/2004 of 13 December 2008 on the Treaty establishing a Constitution for Europe', *Common Market Law Review* (2005): 1169-1202.
34. Case 106/77 *Simmenthal* [1978] ECR 629, para. 24.
35. Admittedly, the judgment in Joined Cases C-397/01 to C-403/01 *Pfeiffer* [2004] ECR I-8835 seems to suggest that this does not extend to non-implemented Directives, though this appears to be contradicted by the later statement of principle in Joined Cases C-387/02, C-391/02 and C-403/02 *Berlusconi* [2005] ECR I-3565, para. 72 that 'according to the Court's well-established case-law, ... the national courts which made the references would be required to set aside, under their own authority, those new articles without having to request or await the prior repeal of those articles by way of legislation or any other constitutional procedure', even though the ECJ then needs to temper the impact of this statement because 'a directive cannot of itself impose obligations on an individual and cannot therefore be relied on as such against that individual' and because of the principle of retroactivity of the milder penal law. See in this respect also K. Lenaerts & T. Corthaut, 'Towards an internally consistent doctrine on invoking norms of EU law' in *The Coherence of EU Law – The Search for Unity in Divergent Concepts*, ed. S. Prechal & B. Van Roermund (Oxford: OUP, 2008), 496-515.
36. Case C-106/89 *Marleasing* [1990] I-4135, para. 8.

down in Article 11 of Directive 68/151/EEC[37] is exhaustive as to the potential grounds of nullity of a company – had also the effect of excluding the crucial provision of ordinary Spanish civil law according to which contracts without cause or whose cause is unlawful have no legal effect, as was allegedly the case with the founder's contract establishing the defendant company. The Directive 68/151/EEC thus clearly had the effect of limiting a rule of Spanish public policy to instances not covered by the Directive.[38] The second example is the case of *Michaniki.*[39] While it is argued below[40] that the Court is actually quite forthcoming in taking the Greek concerns about pluralism in the media and the fight against fraud and corruption in the context of public procurement procedures on board, the result of the case is nonetheless the finding that EU law precludes 'a national provision which, whilst pursuing the legitimate objectives of equal treatment of tenderers and of transparency in procedures for the award of public contracts, establishes an irrefutable presumption that the status of owner, partner, main shareholder or management executive of an undertaking active in the media sector is incompatible with that of owner, partner, main shareholder or management executive of an undertaking which contracts with the State or a legal person in the public sector in the broad sense to perform a works, supply or services contract',[41] even though that national provision is mandated by Article 14(9) of the Greek Constitution. The final example has also been used above: in extreme cases the primacy of EU law may result in the setting aside of some of the most sacred rules of national procedural law, such as the finality of judgments, as was the case in *Lucchini.*[42]

### [C] Effectiveness

**IV-17.** The third way to establish the autonomy of the EU legal order that needs to be brought to the attention is found in the various techniques to ensure the *effet utile* of EU law. There are areas where EU law mandates special levels of protection that go beyond what Member States would ordinarily treat as matters of public policy. As argued above, this is in particular so in respect of consumer protection and labour law. This special status translates into specific remedies. Accordingly, on the ground of the effet utile of the directive national courts are under an obligation to invoke certain consumer protection directives of their own motion, regardless of whether consumer protection

37. First Council Directive 68/151/EEC of 9 March 1968 on coordination of safeguards which, for the protection of the interests of members and others, are required by Member States of companies within the meaning of the second paragraph of Article 58 of the Treaty, with a view to making such safeguards equivalent throughout the Community, *Official Journal, English Special Edition 1968 I*, 41.
38. For more on the impact of this example, see V. Simonart, 'L'*ordre public* et le doit des sociétés' in *L'ordre public: concept et applications*, ed. J.-F. Romain, M. Grégoire & V. Simonart (Bruxelles: Bruylant, 1995), 102-103.
39. Case C-213/07 *Michaniki* [2008] ECR I-9999.
40. See, *infra*, at IV-25.
41. Case C-213/07 *Michaniki* [2008] ECR I-9999, para. 69.
42. Case C-119/05 *Lucchini Siderurgica* [2007] ECR I-6199.

is otherwise a matter of public policy in the Member State concerned and even regardless of whether it is otherwise at all acceptable for national courts in that Member State to raise issues *motu proprio.*[43] Likewise, the ECJ has considerably strengthened the status of the working time directive, with the effect that contractual agreements may usually not suffice to opt-out of its protection.[44]

**IV-18.** The effectiveness of EU law also results in an arsenal of alternative remedies for ensuring effective application of EU law. Despite the principle of national procedural autonomy, Member States have not only had to set aside a series of inadequate provisions of national procedural law. In many instances, also new procedures had to be created. Accordingly, we now have state liability for breaches of EU law by any organ of a Member State, including the courts.[45] Member States have to provide for sufficient forms of interim relief.[46] They must also make sure that no person is put in a position where the only way he/she can challenge the incompatibility of national law with EU law is by breaking the law.[47] Moreover, starting from a controversial interpretation of Dutch law the Court has crafted a new remedy for re-assessing administrative decisions that would otherwise have become final and unassailable, which is also relevant outside the Dutch context.[48]

## §12.02 WHILE LEAVING ROOM FOR RECONCILIATION

**IV-19.** In the preceding section a picture of the EU legal order was painted as one that strongly weighs on the national legal orders. I see also no reason to deny that it does so or to minimize that impact. It suffices to recall the various remedies listed in the last paragraph to see how demanding the EU legal order can be for the Member State legal orders. Yet, the story does not end there. The European legal order, for all its heavy-lifting principles, does not form a superstate displacing its Member States. Accordingly, it is inevitable that we also focus on the various techniques that have been developed to counterbalance these overarching tendencies of the Union and reassert the important role played by the 27 Member States united in diversity. In this section, this is done in two ways. First, the attention is drawn to some theoretical answers to the apparent conundrum how the supremacy of the EU legal order can be reconciled with the continued existence of 27 sovereign Member States. While this book is largely construed in an inductive manner, it appears useful to have a brief analysis of some of the more reflective literature as a soundboard for our findings. Second, in a far more pragmatic fashion an overview is given of various techniques in the case law of the

43. See in this respect, *supra*, at II-174 et seq.
44. Case C-124/04 *Federatie Nederlandse Vakbeweging* [2006] ECR I-3423; Joined Cases C-131/04 and C-257/04 *Robinson-Steele* [2006] ECR I-2531; Joined Cases C-350/06 and C-520/06 *Schultz-Hoff* [2009] ECR I-179. See *supra*, at II-231.
45. Case C-224/01 *Köbler* [2003] ECR I-10239; Case C-173/03 *Traghetti del Mediterraneo* [2006] ECR I-5177.
46. Case C-213/89 *Factortame* [1990] ECR I-2433; Case C-432/05 *Unibet* [2007] ECR I-2271, para. 67.
47. Case C-432/05 *Unibet* [2007] ECR I-2271, para. 64.
48. Case C-453/00 *Kühne & Heitz* [2003] ECR I-837; Case C-2/06 *Kempter* [2008] ECR I-837.

Court to get around this problem, particularly when it comes to issues that are related to public policy, as it is often there that national sensitivities and EU demands may collide.

### [A] The Theory

**IV-20.** Most authors who have tried to deal with the conundrum of reconciling the position of the Member States and the Union - often in response to the *Maastricht Urteil*[49] of the German constitutional court[50] - return to Neil MacCormick's famous essay, in fact an amended speech, 'Beyond the Sovereign State'.[51] In it the author actually does three things. He signals that empirically Member States have in fact lost quite a lot of attributes that are traditionally linked to sovereignty, *inter alia* to the European Union.[52] Yet, at the same time, Member States still exist next to the European Union and thus could theoretically still unilaterally revoke that transfer to the Union. The solution to the conundrum then lies in a system where that power is ultimately not used so that 'different systems can overlap and interact, without necessarily requiring that one be subordinate or hierarchically inferior to the other or to some third system',[53] an idea that is equally expressed by the Spanish Constitutional Court.[54] Now, this last point evokes the image of a 'pluralist legal order', which seems attractive at first but needs to be nuanced seriously to function in practice.[55]

**IV-21.** On the one hand, the idea of a pluralist legal order has been picked up by authors such as Poiares Maduro[56] and Komárek.[57] Poiares Maduro has indeed introduced a tantalizing metaphor for the relationship between the Union and the Member States in general and the ECJ and the highest Member States courts in particular with his concept of 'contrapunctual law'. The idea is that the Union and the Member States

---

49. Bundesverfassungsgericht, 12 October 1993, BVerfG, 89, 155, available in English translation in [1993] 2 C.M.L.R., 57.
50. For an overview, see J. Baquero Cruz, 'The Legacy of the Maastricht-Urteil and the Pluralist Movement', *European Law Journal* (2008): 389-422.
51. N. Maccormick, 'Beyond the Sovereign State', *Modern Law Review* (1993): 1-18.
52. See in this respect also K. Schiemann, 'Europe and the loss of sovereignty', *International and Comparative Law Quarterly* (2007): 475-490.
53. N. Maccormick, 'Beyond the Sovereign State', *Modern Law Review* (1993): 8.
54. Tribunal Constitucional, Opinion 1/2004 of 13 December 2008 on the Treaty establishing a Constitution for Europe; see also F. Castillo De La Torre, 'Tribunal Constitucional (Spanish Constitutional Court), Opinion 1/2004 of 13 December 2008 on the Treaty establishing a Constitution for Europe', *Common Market Law Review* (2005): 1169-1202.
55. Actually, as was pointed out, the model the Spanish Supreme Court has in mind is far less oriented to such a pluralist model than its pragmatic end result may suggest, but primarily concerned about reconciling its classic ideas about the supreme position of the Spanish constitution with the exigencies of the Union, see F. Castillo De La Torre, 'Tribunal Constitucional (Spanish Constitutional Court), Opinion 1/2004 of 13 December 2008 on the Treaty establishing a Constitution for Europe', *Common Market Law Review* (2005): 1182.
56. M. Poiares Maduro, 'Der Kontrapunkt im Dienste eines europäischen Verfassungspluralismus', *Europarecht* (2007): 3-31; M. Poiares Maduro, 'Contrapunctual law: Europe's constitutional pluralism in action', in *Sovereignty in Transition*, ed. N. Walker (Oxford: Hart, 2003), 501-537.
57. J. Komárek, 'European Constitutionalism and the European Arrest Warrant: in Search of the Limits of "Contrapunctual Principles"', *Common Market Law Review* (2007): 9-40.

have different roles to play, as they are also accountable to different audiences. The Union institutions, including its Court, are accountable to the Member States and Peoples of Europe, twice plural; the Member State institutions, including the national courts, are accountable to the people(s) of their Member State. Moreover, the ECJ and national courts appear to be starting from different scripts (or sheet music to further the metaphor): the Treaties viz. the national constitutions. However, in music various musicians do not always have to play in unison; there can be added value if each plays its own part, its own tune, but nevertheless takes into account some basic principles of counterpoint and it is submitted that courts, both at the national and the EU level, should proceed in a similar manner. The result is that 'any legal order (national or European) must respect the identity of the other legal orders; its identity must not be affirmed in a manner that either challenges the identity of the other legal orders or the pluralist conception of the European legal order itself'.[58] This has in particular the effect that 'no court should assume supremacy of its legal order, be it the constitutional courts on one hand or the ECJ on the other. Pluralism means that no formal hierarchy exists among the applicable legal orders'.[59] However, this pluralism is in dire need of checks. Poiares Maduro proposes a holistic approach. First, 'courts should seek consistency and vertical and horizontal coherence in the whole of the European legal order',[60] implying that the national courts deciding cases involving EU law must take full account of the decisions of the ECJ and of other national courts and as Komárek observes the same is conversely true for the ECJ.[61] Second, 'courts should reason in universal terms, thus taking into account the European context'.[62] As Komárek's own analysis of how the various constitutional courts dealt with the European Arrest Warrant,[63] this is often not what plays out in practice.[64]

**IV-22.** It seems therefore, on the other hand, that giving up entirely on supremacy, or at least primacy, may not be commendable. Actually, several authors seem to have come to that same conclusion, albeit often along different routes. I agree with Baquero Cruz that in a federal structure there must ultimately be a conflict rule,[65] and he points out that even MacCormick seems to have come to accept the doctrine of primacy and

58. M. Poiares Maduro, 'Contrapunctual law: Europe's constitutional pluralism in action', in *Sovereignty in Transition*, ed. N. Walker (Oxford: Hart, 2003), 526.
59. J. Komárek, 'European Constitutionalism and the European Arrest Warrant: in Search of the Limits of "Contrapunctual Principles"', *Common Market Law Review* (2007): 30.
60. M. Poiares Maduro, 'Contrapunctual law: Europe's constitutional pluralism in action', in *Sovereignty in Transition*, ed. N. Walker (Oxford: Hart, 2003), 528.
61. J. Komárek, 'European Constitutionalism and the European Arrest Warrant: in Search of the Limits of "Contrapunctual Principles"', *Common Market Law Review* (2007): 31; J. Komárek, 'Federal elements in the Community judicial system: Building coherence in the Community legal order', *Common Market Law Review* (2005): 27-30
62. J. Komárek, 'European Constitutionalism and the European Arrest Warrant: in Search of the Limits of "Contrapunctual Principles"', *Common Market Law Review* (2007): 31.
63. Council Framework Decision 2002/584/JHA of 13 June 2002 on the European arrest warrant and the surrender procedures between the Member States (2002) OJ L 190/1.
64. J. Komárek, 'European Constitutionalism and the European Arrest Warrant: in Search of the Limits of "Contrapunctual Principles"', *Common Market Law Review* (2007): 31-33.
65. J. Baquero Cruz, *Between competition and free movement: the economic constitutional law of the European Community* (Oxford: Hart, 2002), 22.

direct effect.[66] However, the existence of a conflict rule does not exclude that the constitutional set up may be centred on conflict prevention. It is in this sense that I interpret the excellent analysis of Verhoeven, who suggests loyalty as the alternative to hierarchy.[67] Actually, she, too, has to bring primacy back to the fore, but then as an expression of loyalty.[68] The advantage of such an approach is that it is both ingrained in the Treaties, in particular Article 4(3) TEU and in line with the actual scope and effect of primacy, signalling an inconsistency between national law and EU law, but not invalidating the national law as that is reserved for the national legal order.[69] In broader terms, focusing on loyalty implies that national courts should in principle give precedence to EU law, unless a constitutional value is at stake for which no equivalent protection exists, whereas the ECJ must try to accommodate these various national constitutional values as far as possible by incorporating those values into the EU legal order or allowing for differentiation.[70] In a similar vein Kumm has proposed the principle of best fit, proposing that the:

> task of national courts is to construct an adequate relationship between the national and the European legal order on the basis of the best interpretation of the principles underlying them both. The right conflict rule or set of conflict rules for a national judge to adopt is the one that is best calculated to produce the best solutions to realise the ideals underlying legal practice in the European Union and its Member States[71].

Judges must thus seek 'the interpretation of the relationship between national constitutions and the EU constitution that best fits and justifies legal practices in the European Union, seen as a whole'.[72] While we thus see a similar holistic approach as set forward by Poiares Maduro reappear, there is, however, a difference in that Kumm explicitly 'expects from national constitutional judges […] to give up the supremacy of the national constitutions if this is required by the principle of best fit, which guides the interpretation of the national and European constitutions in case of their conflict'.[73]

**IV-23.** Ironically, but inevitably, it appears that even the literature that seeks to reconcile the underlying tensions between the legal orders of the Member States and

66. N. Maccormick, *Questioning sovereignty: law, state, and nation in the European Commonwealth* (Oxford: OUP, 2001), 107. However, upon closer reading of that cite and the following paragraphs it seems that MacCormick still is not fully convinced that the EU could not have functioned if based on mediation through national law, as in the case of the ECHR.
67. A. Verhoeven, *The European Union in Search of a Democratic and Constitutional Theory* (The Hague/London/New York: Kluwer Law International, 2002), 304 et seq.
68. *Ibid.*, 309-317.
69. *Ibid.*, 310. See also, *supra*, at IV-14.
70. *Ibid.*, 317-319.
71. M. Kumm, 'The Jurisprudence of Constitutional Conflict: Constitutional Supremacy in Europe before and after the Constitutional Treaty', *European Law Journal* (2005): 286.
72. *Ibid.*, 286.
73. J. Komárek, 'European Constitutionalism and the European Arrest Warrant: in Search of the Limits of "Contrapunctual Principles"', *Common Market Law Review* (2007): 34. See M. Kumm, 'The Jurisprudence of Constitutional Conflict: Constitutional Supremacy in Europe before and after the Constitutional Treaty', *European Law Journal* (2005): 269-274.

the Union is itself subject to serious tensions,[74] so what lessons may be drawn from all this for the purpose of this book? I see at least three points.

**IV-24.** First, I do not want to give up too easily on MacCormick's insight that the national legal orders still have the intrinsic power to unilaterally revoke their federal obligations. Actually, in light of the introduction in the Lisbon Treaty of an exit clause in Article 50 TEU – which provides for negotiations on the terms of a Member State's departure from the Union, but essentially allows for unilateral withdrawal – this implicit possibility is even made very concrete. However, somewhat paradoxically the presence of an explicit withdrawal clause may also have a disciplining effect on national constitutional courts: as a formal procedure is provided for withdrawal from the Union, one could wonder whether it then falls upon a constitutional court to refuse to apply Union law if the Member State has not initiated that procedure.[75]

**IV-25.** Second, I can largely agree with the idea of Verhoeven to analyse the relationship between the Union and its Member States in terms of loyal cooperation. This has as primary effect that national courts should in principle give precedence to EU law, unless a constitutional value is at stake for which no equivalent protection exists.[76] Incidentally, this same deference is displayed by the ECtHR vis-à-vis the

74. So much so, that the ultimate viability of the 'pluralist view' is being called into question, see J. Baquero Cruz, 'The Legacy of the Maastricht-Urteil and the Pluralist Movement', *European Law Journal* (2008): 414, who submits that 'a third workable way between the national constitutional position and the European position may not exist: *tertium non datur*'. I largely share the concerns put forward by Baquero Cruz; however, I submit that also underlying the case law of the ECJ there is, nonetheless, a genuine strand that genuinely seeks to reconcile the two positions. Whether that approach is tenable in the long run remains to be seen, but for now the pluralist literature does offer a framework of reference for these attempts (see in this respect also L. Azoulai, 'Le rôle constitutionnel de la Cour de justice des Communautés européennes tel qu'il se degage de sa jurisprudence', *Revue Trimesterielle du Droit Européen* (2008): 39-45), which are very much real as the various techniques taken from the case law and discussed, *infra*, at IV-27 et seq. demonstrate – though they could, admittedly, largely be qualified as far less objectionable 'discursive pluralism'. I note, for instance that Baquero Cruz, like me, appears to welcome by and large the judgment of the Court in Case C-36/02 *Omega Spielhallen* [2004] ECR I-9609 (see, *ibid.*, 416-417).

75. Actually, the Spanish Constitutional Court seems to have come to the same conclusion, indentifying the exit clause as the ultimate guarantor of the supremacy of the Spanish Constitution, see Tribunal Constitucional, Opinion 1/2004 of 13 December 2008 on the Treaty establishing a Constitution for Europe; see also F. Castillo De La Torre, 'Tribunal Constitucional (Spanish Constitutional Court), Opinion 1/2004 of 13 December 2008 on the Treaty establishing a Constitution for Europe', *Common Market Law Review* (2005): 1187.

76. A. Verhoeven, *The European Union in Search of a Democratic and Constitutional Theory* (The Hague/London/New York: Kluwer Law International, 2002), 318. Often the attention is then drawn to equivalent human rights protection, but since Case 11/70 *Internationale Handelsgesellschaft* [1970] ECR 1125 it seems fair to say that usually such equivalent protection actually exists – at least in respect of the Community pillars, which is why I actually advocate for a role for the national courts in reviewing some acts of the EU in spite of Case 314/84 *Foto-Frost* [1987] ECR 4199 (see, *supra*, fn. 11). However, perhaps a far better is example is the respect for national constitutional norms on competence and legislative procedure. The EU is not concerned with whether the central state or a regional authority must implement a directive; nor will the correct implementation from an EU perspective depend on whether all relevant national advisory bodies were consulted. However, from a national perspective these are essential constitutional norms, for which indeed no equivalent protection exists. A national constitutional court has thus every reason to strike down national legislation implementing a

European Union,[77] and – at least in the original approach taken by the General Court[78] – by the European Union vis-à-vis the UN Security Council.[79] I would, moreover, add that account must be taken of the various tools that are at the disposal of Member States to make sure their special sensitivities are taken into account. First, already several Member States have tried to include special derogations at the level of the Treaties, and as the opt-outs in respect of the Charter of Fundamental Rights of the EU in the Lisbon

directive or framework decision on the grounds that the national constitutional division of competence was not respected, even though that will of course undermine the effectiveness of Union law. Yet, while undermining to a certain extent the effectiveness Union law in its day to day operation it is not denying the principled applicability of Union law. For instance, even after a national constitutional court has struck down the national implementing legislation, the underlying directive or framework decision may still have serious consequences in the form of vertical direct effect or *Francovich* liability. Moreover, internal constitutional difficulties are not a defence in an infringement procedure under Article 226 TEC, see e.g., Case C-236/99 *Commission v. Belgium* [2000] ECR I-5657, para. 23; Case C-358/03 *Commission v. Austria* [2004] ECR I-12055, paras 12-13. That being said, EU law may, however, be relevant to the interpretation of national constitutional law, as also national constitutions must as far as possible be interpreted in a manner that is consistent with EU law, see, for instance, the adjustment of the Belgian rules on the division of competence in the recent judgment of the Belgian Constitutional Court, judgment 11/2009 of 21 January 2009, <http://www.const-court.be/public/f/2009/2009-011f.pdf> (23 May 2012) in light of the judgment of the ECJ in Case C-212/06 *Government of Communauté française and Gouvernement wallon* [2008] ECR I-0000. See also, in respect of possible similar developments in Italy, G. Della Cananea, 'The Italian Constitutional Court and the European Court of Justice: From Seperation to Interaction? – Comment on Constitutional Court, Order n. 103 of 16 April 2008 – *Presidente del Consiglio dei ministri v. Regione Sardana*', *European Public Law* (2008): 523-531. For more thought-provoking examples, see also W. Phelan, 'Can Ireland legislate contrary to European Community law?', *European Law Review* (2008): 531-549.

77. ECtHR, 18 February 1999, *Matthews v. UK*; ECtHR, 30 June 2005, *Bosphorus Hava Yollari Turizm ve Ticaret Anonim Şirketi v. Ireland*.
78. Case T-306/01 *Yusuf and Al Barakaat International Foundation v. Council and Commission* [2005] ECR II-3533; Case T-315/01 *Kadi v. Council and Commission* [2005] ECR II-3649.
79. One could wonder whether this is still the case after the appeals judgment Joined Cases C-402/05 P and C-415/05 P *Kadi v. Council* [2008] ECR I-6351. Actually, I think it still does – though the Court has been criticized for this in the past, see I. Canor, 'Can two walk together, except they be agreed?' The relationship between international law and European law: The incorporation of United Nations sanctions against Yugoslavia into European Community law through the perspective of the European Court of Justice, *Common Market Law Review* (1998): 137-187. Upon closer examination of the judgment the ECJ is fully deferential vis-à-vis the UNSC: it does not seek to review the UNSC resolution at all. Rather, the Court is actually examining the internal validity of measures taken by the Union to implement the UNSC resolution. In this respect it is not doing anything else than what national constitutional courts may also validly do when dealing with measures of EU law: even if a particular result may be mandated by superior EU law, the way of getting to that result must still also comply with national constitutional law. After all, *Kadi* is only a hard case if the Council would fail to meet the burden of proof in the reparation act it is entitled to adopt; by contrast if the Council manages to state clearly the reasons why the applicants are still on the list, there simply will be no conflict between the EU legal order and the UNSC resolution. Nevertheless, the former scenario cannot entirely be excluded; compare in this respect the response of the Council to Case T-284/08 *People's Mojahedin Organization of Iran v. Council* [2008] ECR II-3487 in Council Decision of 26 January 2009 implementing Article 2(3) of Regulation (EC) No 2580/2001 on specific restrictive measures directed against certain persons and entities with a view to combating terrorism and repealing Decision 2008/583/EC (2009) OJ L 23/25.

Treaty[80] demonstrate this may concern basic constitutional values.[81] Second, regardless of the formal use of enhanced cooperation – which seems politically undesirable – it turns out that numerous pieces of EU legislation actually provide for all kinds of exceptions, derogations, transitional measures or – as in the case of the Savings Directive[82] – even downright alternative regimes. One could wonder whether the ECJ must be particularly forthcoming in trying to help out Member States that have failed to seek a legislative solution that allows them to take a particular constitutional value into account. Third, no legislation, and not even the Treaties, is set in stone. In this respect Karen Alter interestingly draws the attention to the possibility that Member States may want to provoke an unfavourable ruling from the ECJ in order to muster sufficient political support to make the necessary amendments.[83] Furthermore, it often remains to be seen whether there really is a conflict between national constitutional values and EU law.[84] For instance in *Michaniki*,[85] even when confronted with an exhaustive list[86] of grounds for excluding participation in a contract, the ECJ appears willing to grant the Member States some margin of discretion in the way they seek to safeguard the 'principles of equal treatment of tenderers and of transparency which

80. See in particular the Protocol on the Application of the Charter of Fundamental Rights of the European Union to Poland and the United Kingdom (2007) OJ C 306/156; Declaration 61 by Poland on the Charter of Fundamental Rights of the European Union (2007) OJ 306/270. See also the willingness displayed by the European Council to reassure Ireland on its fundamental values in a bid to sway the Irish electorate to endorse the Lisbon Treaty in a second referendum, see European Council, Brussels, 11 and 12 December 2008, *Presidency Conclusions*, at point 3.
81. On the negative impact this may have on the perception – even though legally the impact of these opt-outs seems rather limited – of the communality of certain fundamental values in the EU, see X, 'Éditorial – L'Union, une communauté de valeurs?', *Revue Trimesterielle du Droit Européen* (2008): 1-3.
82. Council Directive 2003/48/EC of 3 June 2003 on taxation of savings income in the form of interest payments (2003) OJ L 157/38, which grants Austria, Belgium and Luxembourg the right to maintain for a very significant period a complete alternative system for the taxation of savings income.
83. K. Alter, *Establishing the Supremacy of European Law* (Oxford: Oxford University Press, 2001), 228. She does not indicate how successful they are at this. The difficulty of Austria in convincing other Member States to adjust the rules for student mobility in the wake of Case C-147/03 *Commission v. Austria* [2005] ECR I-5969 seems to suggest they hardly are.
84. This also implies, however, that national courts must, whenever, there is a fear that the national level of protection may be incompatible with the exigencies of EU law, refer the matter to the ECJ, which may interpret EU legislation in a way that solves the matter, or, in extreme cases, may find the EU legislation at issue invalid also as a matter of the EU fundamental rights standard. This may well offer a solution to most of the problematic cases signalled in A. Albi, 'Ironies in Human Rights Protection in the EU: Pre-Accession Conditionality and Post-Accession Conundrums', *European Law Journal* (2009): 51-57. These matters, unlike what the Estonian court decisions she quotes seem to imply, are never a matter of *acte clair*; moreover, to the extent that the interpretation of EU law manifestly suggests that a crucial norm of national constitutional law must be breached, arguably the validity of that EU instrument is at issue, requiring a preliminary reference to the ECJ under Case 314/84 *Foto-Frost* [1987] ECR 4199. On the dangers of disrespect for the obligation – in particular in respect of courts of last instance – to refer cases to the ECJ, see J. Baquero Cruz, 'The Legacy of the Maastricht-Urteil and the Pluralist Movement', *European Law Journal* (2008): 418-419.
85. Case C-213/07 *Michaniki* [2008] ECR I-9999.
86. Article 24 of Council Directive 93/37/EEC of 14 June 1993 concerning the coordination of procedures for the award of public works contracts (1993) OJ L 199/54 is indeed found to be exhaustive, see Case C-213/07 *Michaniki* [2008] ECR I-9999, paras 37-49.

[...] constitute the basis of the Community directives on the award of public contracts',[87] whereby it was accepted that 'each Member State is best placed to identify, in the light of historical, legal, economic or social considerations specific to it, situations propitious to conduct liable to bring about breaches of those principles'.[88] Accordingly, if in Greece there may be particular concerns about the influence of media concerns on the way public procurement proceedings are carried out it is imaginable that in Greece specific safeguards 'with the public interest objective of maintaining the pluralism and the independence of the media'[89] or 'fighting against fraud and corruption'[90] - not coincidentally values that the ECJ has also recognized in other contexts as legitimate objectives[91] - are put in place by the Greek authorities. However, the loyalty must be displayed on both sides. While EU law may thus accommodate the Greek concerns, the Greek legal order must still respect the principle of proportionality in the way it seeks to give due weight to its specific concerns in the broader context of the EU principles of equal treatment of tenderers and of transparency. An almost blanket ban on the involvement in public procurement procedures of companies with a link to media organizations as at issue in *Michaniki* is accordingly incompatible with the principle of proportionality.[92] This should, however, not distract from the fact that EU law is not inherently incompatible with the interests the Greek authorities seek to protect, which implies that an alternative Greek law may well be compatible with EU law thus making it possible to safeguard both the Greek constitutional value and the integrity of EU law.

**IV-26.** Third, the flip side is that, conversely, also the ECJ will have to take national constitutional values into account. Basically, if a constitutional court were really to detect a major inconsistency between the national legal order and the EU legal order, this should be the cue for the Court of Justice to reassess whether there is not also something wrong at EU level.[93] The prime example still is the ECJ's reaction to the first *Solange* decision of the *Bundesverfassungsgericht.*[94] On second thought, the Court's initial reluctance to accept judicial review of ECSC acts in the light of fundamental rights as spelled out in cases such as *Stork*[95] and *Geitling*[96] appeared unattractive if seen

87. Case C-213/07 *Michaniki* [2008] ECR I-9999, para. 55.
88. Case C-213/07 *Michaniki* [2008] ECR I-9999, para. 56 (internal citations omitted).
89. Case C-213/07 *Michaniki* [2008] ECR I-9999, para. 59.
90. Case C-213/07 *Michaniki* [2008] ECR I-9999, para. 59.
91. See in respect of pluralism of the media, Case C-368/95 *Vereinigte Familiapress Zeitungsverlags- und vertriebs* [1997] ECR I-3689, para. 18; Case C-250/06 *United Pan-Europe Communications Belgium* [2007] ECR I-11135, paras 41-42. In respect of fighting fraud and corruption, see Case C-275/92 *Schindler* [1994] ECR I-1039, paras 57-60; Joined Cases C-338/04, C-359/04 and C-360/04 *Placanica* [2007] ECR I-1891, para. 46.
92. Case C-213/07 *Michaniki* [2008] ECR I-9999, paras 61 et seq.
93. That is not to say that the Court should always give in to the national pressure, especially if the national objections are ill-formulated, if not il-conceived, see Case C-165/08 *Commission v. Poland* [2009] ECR I-6843.
94. Bundesverfassungsgericht, 29 May 1974, BVerfGE 37, available in English translation in [1974] 2 C.M.L.R. 540.
95. Case 1/58 *Stork v. High Authority* [1959] ECR 17.
96. Joined Cases 36, 37, 38 and 40/59 *Geitling v. High Authority* [1960] ECR 423.

from the long-term interest of an ever-closer union. In changing course in *Internationale Handelsgesellschaft,*[97] the Court actually did two things. On the one hand, it avoided a direct clash with the German legal order, and basically avoided that the MacCormick's power-that-should-not be used had to be invoked by the German constitutional court. On the other hand, the ECJ also transformed the EU legal order into a legal order that offered better protection, is rooted in the rule of law, and thus also becomes far more appealing for both the Member States and the People of Europe. That being said, the large majority of conflicts between the national legal orders and the Union are not on this epic scale. But even so, the Court is under a constitutional duty flowing from Article 4(2) TEU to take the national identities of the Member States into account. For dealing with these small level conflicts - even when they concern constitutional norms - grand theories about supremacy and legal pluralism may, however, be unnecessary. In fact, the ECJ has indeed an extensive toolkit at its disposal to accommodate both the Union and the national legal orders. In choosing a particular solution, the ECJ, too is basically seeking *the best fit*. In this sense the solution has a definite Dworkinian feel to it, which has not gone unnoticed.[98] While this seems to give quite some latitude to the ECJ, it is to be observed that as both the effectiveness of EU law and the protection of national identity are deeply rooted in the EU constitutional order, the idea of best fit has actually a disciplining effect on the political choices the Court may make.

### [B] Techniques

**IV-27.** Accordingly, it seems appropriate at this point of the analysis to focus on the various instruments in the Court's toolkit to give a place to the national constitutional values and the national identities while still maintaining the overall coherence of the EU legal order. The examples chosen to illustrate these techniques will, moreover, also bring us immediately back to the EU *ordre public* and its relationship with the national legal orders.

#### *[1] Inclusion*

**IV-28.** The first technique is the integration of the national norm into the EU legal order. This was notably done in *Internationale Handellsgesellschaft*[99] with the protection of fundamental rights, for which the ECJ relies on the constitutional traditions of the Member States[100] and key international agreements to which (virtually) all Member

97. Case 11/70 *Internationale Handelsgesellschaft* [1970] ECR 1125.
98. M. Kumm, 'The Jurisprudence of Constitutional Conflict: Constitutional Supremacy in Europe before and after the Constitutional Treaty', *European Law Journal* (2005): 286, fn. 84.
99. Case 11/70 *Internationale Handelsgesellschaft* [1970] ECR 1125.
100. Case C-112/00 *Schmidberger* [2003] ECR I-5659, para. 71.

States are party to.[101] As already argued above,[102] this is not to say that the ECJ must elevate any fundamental right to EU status and offer the highest level of protection nor the lowest common denominator. Perhaps one of the most nuanced restatements of the Court's approach comes from the testimony of the ECJ President Skouris before the working group of the Convention preparing the Constitution for Europe:

> [it] should be borne in mind that common constitutional traditions do not form a direct source of Community law and the Court of Justice is not bound by them as such; they constitute a source of inspiration for it in discerning and defining the scope of the general principles of law that apply in the Community legal order. It follows that it is not the Court's duty to discern, and, as it were, mechanically transpose into the Community legal order, the lowest common denominator of constitutional traditions common to the Member States. The Court draws inspiration from those traditions in order to determine the level of protection appropriate within the Community legal order and for that very reason appreciates them more freely.[103]

**IV-29.** By integrating an equivalent fundamental rights standard in the EU legal order, the Court has indeed avoided major constitutional conflicts. Accordingly, the decision of the Austrian authorities to allow a demonstration to take place on the Brenner motorway, with major consequences for international transport and thus also for the free movement of goods across the Union, could easily be reconciled with the EU legal order.[104] As EU law allows for justifiable exceptions to the free movement and the Union, too, recognizes the freedom of speech, it was not too difficult to accept that the Austrian measure, while formally an obstacle to trade, was not a breach of Community law. Similarly, the Court has recently integrated also the Convention on the Rights of the Child into the EU legal order, with the effect that a German labelling requirement for DVDs and the like could pass constitutional muster.[105]

**IV-30.** The Charter of Fundamental Rights of the Union[106] has, moreover, taken this level of integration several steps further. First, the Union henceforth has its own 'bill of rights', inspired by those same national constitutional traditions and international agreements. The has become legally binding upon entry into force of the Lisbon Treaty, but even before it already worked as a major source of inspiration, which is hardly surprising as it probably is the most comprehensive restatement of those common constitutional traditions available and it enjoys the support of the Commission, the European Parliament and the Council (and thus the Member States) who have all

101. In the first place the ECHR, see e.g., Case C-60/00 *Carpenter* [2002] ECR I-6279, but also other international agreements are a source of inspiration, *inter alia*, European Social Charter of 18 November 1961 and Convention of the International Labour Organization of 25 June 1958 (see Case 149/77 *Defrenne* [1978] ECR 1365) or the International Covenant on Civil and Political Rights and the Convention of the Rights of the Child (see Case C-244/06 *Dynamic Medien* [2008] ECR I-505, para. 39).
102. See, *supra*, at I-75.
103. Hearing of Judge Skouris, 17 September 2002, Working Group II, Document 19.
104. Case C-112/00 *Schmidberger* [2003] ECR I-5659.
105. Case C-244/06 *Dynamic Medien* [2008] ECR I-505.
106. Charter of Fundamental Rights of the European Union (2000) OJ C 364/1; Charter of Fundamental Rights of the European Union (2008) OJ C 303/1.

allowed their respective Presidents to proclaim it solemnly - twice.[107] Second, the Charter is, however, far from perfect. On the one hand, it seems to take the level of integration of national constitutional norms even further. Not only is the level of protection offered by the ECHR integrated through Article 52(3) of the Charter as a minimum level of protection for the Union,[108] but in Article 53 of the Charter, entitled 'level of protection' a further avenue is opened up as it stated that:

> [n]othing in this Charter shall be interpreted as restricting or adversely affecting human rights and fundamental freedoms as recognised, in their respective fields of application, by Union law and international law and by international agreements to which the Union or all the Member States are party, including the European Convention for the Protection of Human Rights and Fundamental Freedoms, and by the Member States' constitutions.

This provision has been criticized for potentially undermining the supremacy of EU law[109] as it seems to open up the door for the introduction of national constitutional provisions offering protection beyond the level recognized in the Charter. To a certain extent I can understand that critique, and below I will draw the attention to some cases that could be read in that light.[110] However, for me a partial solution lies in the 'their respective fields of application' clause. In my view that may have the effect of allowing those national norms to play a role in assessing the validity of national implementing measures and national measures derogating from EU law, but they cannot be invoked to challenge the validity of Union measures.[111] On the other hand, criticism has also

107. The Charter was first proclaimed on 7 December 2000 in Nice and again on 12 December 2007 in Strasbourg. Moreover, the Charter was moreover also accepted by the 2004 IGC as part of the Treaty establishing a Constitution for Europe.
108. In this manner, any risk that a national court may find itself trapped between conflicting interpretations of the fundamental rights standards between the ECJ and ECtHR, as feared by C. Van De Heyning, 'De nationale gerechtshoven tussen het Hof Mensenrechten en het Hof van Justitie: de onmogelijke keuze?', *Rechtskundig Weekblad* (2008): 1058-1070, should be close to non-existent. The ECJ also in practice picks up the evolutions in the ECtHR case law, see for instance Joined Cases C-411/10 an C-493/10 *N.S* [2011] ECR I-0000, immediately conforming to ECtHR of 21 January 2011 *M.S.S. v. Belgium and Greece*.
109. J.B. Liisberg, 'Does the EU Charter of Fundamental Rights Threaten the Supremacy of Community Law? Article 53 of the Charter: a fountain of law or just an inkblot?', Jean Monnet Working Paper 4/01.
110. See, *infra*, at IV-38 et seq. (discussing Case C-36/02 *Omega Spielhallen* [2004] ECR I-9609 and Opinion of AG Van Gerven in Case C-159/90 *Society for the Protection of Unborn Children Ireland* [1991] ECR I-4685) and at IV-42 et seq. (discussing Case C-455/06 *Heemskerk and Schaap* [2008] ECR I-8763). See also Case C-19/08 *Petrosian* [2009] ECR I-495, where the ECJ endorsed a differentiated approach as to the starting point for the period for expulsion of rejected asylum seekers to another Member State under Article 20 of Council Regulation (EC) No 343/2003 of 18 February 2003 establishing the criteria and mechanisms for determining the Member State responsible for examining an asylum application lodged in one of the Member States by a third-country national (2003) L 50/1, so that Member States who offer a high level of judicial protection by suspending the execution of certain asylum decisions pending appeals are not put in an impossible position of being unable to transfer the asylum seekers if their appeal fails.
111. This seems largely to correspond with the approach defended by A. Verhoeven, *The European Union in Search of a Democratic and Constitutional Theory* (The Hague/London/New York: Kluwer Law International, 2002), 341-342, with one important difference in that we disagree on the scope of Article 51 of the Charter. For an example, where the Court partially dodged the

been levelled against Article 51 of the Charter, or at least against the expansive reading of that provision in the explanations.[112] As already indicated above,[113] I essentially agree with the position taken in *ERT*[114] that human rights protection by the ECJ also extends to the validity of national measures derogating from norms of EU law, as otherwise the ECJ would be seen as legitimizing certain exceptions to Union law, which are contrary to its own human rights conception.[115] Admittedly, the potential for clashes between the EU fundamental rights standard and the national fundamental rights standards would be more limited if the scope of the Charter was limited to cases of mere implementation of EU law and not encompass cases involving derogation. However, the alternative[116] is hardly a harmonious interlacing of the EU standard and the national standards, either, as it basically relies solely on the national system of human rights protection despite the fact that the case still has a major EU component.[117] My point is not that EU law cannot be compromised in order to protect some other societal value, including the protection of fundamental rights, as clearly that is possible.[118] The point is, however, that this should only happen if the social benefits make it worthwhile. Sacrificing the effectiveness of EU law in a manner that results additionally in a violation of fundamental rights does not seem to meet that standard, and even reflects badly on the EU. Accordingly, the ECJ has a legitimate role in assessing the compatibility with fundamental rights of national measures that deviate from EU law. That is what the Court has been doing since the entry into force of the Lisbon Treaty, and this has hardly been to the detriment of the national legal orders.[119]

---

bullet by hiding after the fact that the referring court only inquired into the interpretation and not the validity of the EU norm at issue, see Case C-1/11 *Interseroh Scrap and Metals Trading* [2012] ECR I-0000.

112. A. Verhoeven, *The European Union in Search of a Democratic and Constitutional Theory* (The Hague/London/New York: Kluwer Law International, 2002), 354-358
113. See, *supra*, at I-70.
114. Case 260/89 *Elliniki Radiophonia Tiléorassi* [1991] ECR I-2925.
115. For an extensive analysis in this sense, see A. Egger, 'EU-Fundamental Rights in the National Legal Order: The Obligations of Member States Revisited', *Yearbook of European Law* (2006): 515-553.
116. As in the Court's original approach, see e.g., Joined Cases 60 and 61/84 *Cinéthèque* [1985] ECR 2605.
117. It is important to note that as the Union now has a comprehensive human rights catalogue – in most instances surpassing if not the depth then at least the size of the bills of rights of the Member States – the issue may well no longer be whether the Union is offering equivalent protection, but whether or not the Member States are inclined to advance a particular national policy at the expense of both the free movement and the EU human rights standard. The observations of the Member States in Case C-127/08 *Metock* [2008] ECR I-6241 demonstrate that unlike the early seventies the ECJ may now be ahead of the Member States in terms of fundamental rights protection. Interestingly, it has been noted that if the EU were to become too protective of fundamental rights the supremacy of EU law may be jeopardized as well, because Member States courts may seek to apply national standards instead, see A. Young, 'The Charter, Constitution and Human Rights: is this the Beginning or the End for Human Rights Protections by Community Law?', *European Public Law* (2005): 236-237.
118. Case C-112/00 *Schmidberger* [2003] ECR I-5659; Case C-368/95 *Vereinigte Familiapress Zeitungsverlags-und vertriebs* [1997] ECR I-3689.
119. Perhaps the most prominent examples in this respect are Case C-208/09 *Sayn-Wittgenstein* [2010] ECR I-0000 and Case C-391/09 *Runevič-Vardyn* [2011] ECR I-0000.

Cases like *Familiapress*[120] demonstrate, moreover, that the Court may do so in a manner that allows the national court to tailor the solution to the very particular national situation. Therefore, I also accept a moderate role for Article 53 of the Charter so that such national measures, whether they are implementations or derogations, may be tested against both the EU standard and a more protective national standard. In the case of derogations this can, moreover, only lead to the same or better degree of application of EU law as a breach of the national standard results in a barrier to the enforcement of EU law (which the ECJ was even willing to condone) being set aside. Only the additional application of a more restrictive national fundamental right standard to a national implementing measure that has cleared the EU standard may lead to (temporary) under-enforcement of EU law, as the national authorities will have to seek an alternative way of giving full effect to EU law that is also respectful of national law. Yet, I also draw the attention to other instruments in the Court's toolkit to achieve a similar result.

**IV-31.** The inclusion of the national fundamental rights standard, moreover, does not solely depend on the Court of Justice. Also the EU legislator may explicitly envisage that outcome. A telling example is Framework Decision 2008/913/JHA on combating certain forms and expressions of racism and xenophobia by means of criminal law,[121] which – quite controversially – turns behaviour that may well otherwise be covered by the freedom of expression into criminal offences.[122] While the freedom of expression in

120. Case C-368/95 *Vereinigte Familiapress Zeitungsverlags- und vertriebs* [1997] ECR I-3689, para. 34: '[...] Article 30 of the EC Treaty is to be interpreted as not precluding application of legislation of a Member State the effect of which is to prohibit the distribution on its territory by an undertaking established in another Member State of a periodical produced in that latter State containing prize puzzles or competitions which are lawfully organized in that State, provided that that prohibition is proportionate to maintenance of press diversity and that that objective cannot be achieved by less restrictive means. This assumes, *inter alia*, that the newspapers offering the chance of winning a prize in games, puzzles or competitions are in competition with small newspaper publishers who are deemed to be unable to offer comparable prizes and the prospect of winning is liable to bring about a shift in demand. Furthermore, the national prohibition must not constitute an obstacle to the marketing of newspapers which, albeit containing prize games, puzzles or competitions, do not give readers residing in the Member State concerned the opportunity to win a prize. It is for the national court to determine whether those conditions are satisfied on the basis of a study of the national press market concerned'.

121. Framework Decision 2008/913/JHA of 28 November 2008 on combating certain forms and expressions of racism and xenophobia by means of criminal law (2008) OJ L 328/55.

122. Article 6(1) of Framework Decision 2008/913/JHA of 28 November 2008 on combating certain forms and expressions of racism and xenophobia by means of criminal law (2008) OJ L 328/55 requires Member States to make the following 'intentional conduct' a criminal offence:
(a)publicly inciting to violence or hatred directed against a group of persons or a member of such a group defined by reference to race, colour, religion, descent or national or ethnic origin;
(b)the commission of an act referred to in point (a) by public dissemination or distribution of tracts, pictures or other material;
(c)publicly condoning, denying or grossly trivializing crimes of genocide, crimes against humanity and war crimes as defined in Articles 6, 7 and 8 of the Statute of the International Criminal Court, directed against a group of persons or a member of such a group defined by reference to race, colour, religion, descent or national or ethnic origin when the conduct is carried out in a manner likely to incite to violence or hatred against such a group or a member of such a group;

the ECHR and in the case law of the ECJ is not without boundaries,[123] it cannot be excluded that some Member States are traditionally more tolerant in the utterances they condone. To meet the concern of these Member States, apart from allowing Member States some further margin in the intensity the conduct must have before it becomes a crime,[124] Article 7 of the Framework Decision was included. Article 7(1) of the Framework Decision reminds – in a sense superfluously stating what should be obvious – that '[t]his Framework Decision shall not have the effect of modifying the obligation to respect fundamental rights and fundamental legal principles, including freedom of expression and association, as enshrined in Article 6 of the Treaty on European Union'. The real novelty is, however, Article 7(2) which states:

> This Framework Decision shall not have the effect of requiring Member States to take measures in contradiction to fundamental principles relating to freedom of association and freedom of expression, in particular freedom of the press and the freedom of expression in other media as they result from constitutional traditions or rules governing the rights and responsibilities of, and the procedural guarantees for, the press or other media where these rules relate to the determination or limitation of liability.

This effectively integrates the national human rights standard into the Framework Decision. This provision should be welcomed as an attempt to reconcile different constitutional traditions regarding the freedom of speech,[125] while ensuring that in any event the worst cases of racist or xenophobe abuse are being punished in all Member States. Yet, it is clear that this may also create a grey zone whereby some publications – in print, but for instance also on the internet – may be condoned in one Member State and still fall foul of the criminal laws of another Member State, despite the attempts to streamline the rules on jurisdiction for these offences.[126] It seems however fair to assume that the limitations on the free movement of goods and services that may ensue out of such divergent legislations may be justified as a matter of public policy.

**IV-32.** It is moreover, not just national fundamental rights standards that are being integrated into EU law. As the examples discussed above demonstrate, EU legislation may also accommodate – within certain limits – for national considerations of public

---

(d)publicly condoning, denying or grossly trivializing the crimes defined in Article 6 of the Charter of the International Military Tribunal appended to the London Agreement of 8 August 1945, directed against a group of persons or a member of such a group defined by reference to race, colour, religion, descent or national or ethnic origin when the conduct is carried out in a manner likely to incite to violence or hatred against such a group or a member of such a group.

123. When it comes to hate speech, the ECtHR is even increasingly leaving the States a wide margin of appreciation, see for instance ECtHR 16 July 2009, *Féret v. Belgium*.

124. See Articles 6(2) to 6(4) of Framework Decision 2008/913/JHA of 28 November 2008 on combating certain forms and expressions of racism and xenophobia by means of criminal law (2008) OJ L 328/55.

125. See also consideration 6 of Framework Decision 2008/913/JHA of 28 November 2008 on combating certain forms and expressions of racism and xenophobia by means of criminal law (2008) OJ L 328/55, where it is recognized that 'Since the Member States' cultural and legal traditions are, to some extent, different, particularly in this field, full harmonization of criminal laws is currently not possible'.

126. Article 9 of Framework Decision 2008/913/JHA of 28 November 2008 on combating certain forms and expressions of racism and xenophobia by means of criminal law (2008) OJ L 328/55.

morality[127] or public policy.[128] This works reasonably well if the legislation is indeed drafted in a manner to invite such national value considerations to be taken into account. However, I have above criticized the Court for the way it has tried in *Groener*[129] to inject an important national constitutional value – the protection of the first constitutional language of Ireland – into the functional language requirement of then Article 3(1) of Regulation 1612/68.[130] I do not object against the fact that this important constitutional value was taken into account as I have even strongly defended that sensitivity to linguistic identity and diversity is part and parcel of the EU public policy. However, injecting this concern into the provision at issue was not the right way to do so, as the Court's own credibility is on the line when it warps the meaning of the functional language requirement in a manner that undermines the object and purpose of the Regulation that seeks to promote the free movement of workers. The case of *Runevič-Vardyn* demonstrates, moreover, that this concern can also be taken into account without twisting the limits of statutory interpretation.[131] There are after all other techniques to reach the same result that nonetheless leave the legislation intact. For this reason I welcome, by contrast, the approach taken by the General Court in respect of the interpretation of the public policy exception of Regulation 40/94,[132] which has restricted the latter's application to the offensiveness of the registered trademark and not of the activities of the applicant or the goods of services for which a trademark is registered.[133] The latter aspects may then still be examined in a different context, in particular in the form of a public policy exception to the free movement of goods or services, but thus without there being need to sacrifice the integrity and consistency of Regulation 40/94. That being said the General Court has also made it clear that the public policy exception in this context is capacious enough to take on board sensitivities – such as the use of former communist symbols – that may be far more troubling for some Member States than for most others, thus allowing the OHIM as an EU institution to pay heed to a national sensitivity.[134]

---

127. Council Directive 89/552/EEC of 3 October 1989 on the coordination of certain provisions laid down by law, regulation or administrative action in Member States concerning the pursuit of television broadcasting activities (1989) OJ L 298/23. For an application, see Case E-8/97 *TV 1000 Sverige AB* [1998] 3 C.M.L.Rep. 318, discusses, *supra*, at II-105.
128. Regulation (EC) No 733/2002 of the European Parliament and of the Council of 22 April 2002 on the implementation of the .eu Top Level Domain (2002) OJ L 113/1, as discussed, *supra*, at II-102.
129. Case C-379/87 *Groener* [1989] ECR 3967.
130. Regulation (EEC) No 1612/68 of the Council of 15 October 1968 on freedom of movement for workers within the Community, *Official Journal, English Special Edition 1968 II*, 475. See currently, Article 3 of Regulation (EU) No 492/2011 of the European Parliament and of the Council of 5 April 2011 on freedom of movement for workers within the Union (2011) OJ L141/1.
131. Case C-391/09 *Runevič-Vardyn* [2011] ECR I-0000.
132. Council Regulation (EC) No 40/94 of 20 December 1993 on the Community trade mark (1994) OJ L 11/1, now replaced by Council Regulation (EC) No 207/2009 of 26 February 2009 on the Community trade mark (2009) OJ L 78/1.
133. Case T-140/02 *Sportwetten v. OHIM* [2005] ECR II-3247, para. 28; Case T-224/01 *Durferrit v. OHIM* [2003] II-1589, as discussed, *supra*, at II-105.
134. Case T-232/10 *Couture Tech v. OHIM* [2011] ECR II-0000.

### [2] Circumventing the Problem

**IV-33.** On several occasions, the ECJ has dodged the bullet by circumventing the source of potential conflict.[135] There may be sound constitutional reasons to do so. Some applicants indeed try to convert what is essentially an internal conflict about ethical standards or fundamental rights protection into a matter of EU law.[136] As EU standards should only apply in cases where the Member States are implementing EU law, or at most seek to derogate from it,[137] the ECJ is correct in declining to answer the question if no EU law element is present. Accordingly, the Court's refusal to get involved into a debate on Austrian criminal procedure in *Kremzow,*[138] where a convicted murderer was seeking damages in a *Francovich* action on the basis that by being locked up illegally because his trial was held in breach of the procedural guarantees of the ECHR – at least that was his claim – his potential right of free movement had quite literally been unjustifiably curtailed, seems entirely justified. Similarly, the Court seems fully justified, in light of Article 4(2) TEU requiring respect for the national identity, including the constitutional set up of the Member States, to limit the scope of application of Union law in such a way that the inherent policy differences between the various entities with constitutional autonomy within a federal state are not deemed to violate per se Union law, even though the price may be some degree of fragmentation of the internal market, beyond what would have been accepted at the level between the Member States. Accordingly, the ECJ has accepted that the mere existence of differences in the way entities with constitutional autonomy choose to implement the EU agricultural policy does not as such amount to a breach of the principle of equal treatment.[139] Similarly, the ECJ has taken into account the limited territorial competences of those entities so that their state-aid measures, which by definition will only cover part of the territory of the Member States, will not for that reason alone be deemed in breach of the non-selectivity requirement.[140] Finally, the Court has accepted that any discrimination between the nationals of a Member State, at least to the extent that they have not made prior use of their right to move, that

---

135. See also K.J.M. Mortelmans, 'Botsende algemene belangen en de werking van de interne markt', *Sociaal-Economische Wetgeving* (2004): 243-245.
136. See, however, on the vague line on what constitutes a purely internal situation, N. Nic Suibhne, 'Free movement of persons and the wholly internal rule: time to move on?', *Common Market Law Review* (2002): 731-771.
137. See on the division between the instance when the Charter can apply and the instances when the applicants will have to rely on the ECHR, as they are not in a situation covered by EU law, see Case C-256/11*Dereci* [2011] ECR I-0000, paras 70-74.
138. Case C-299/95 *Kremzow* [1997] ECR I-2629.
139. Case C-428/07 *Horvath* [2009] ECR I-6355.
140. Case C-88/03 *Commission v. Portugal* [2006] ECR I-7115; Joined Cases C-428/06 to C-434/06 *Unión General de Trabajadores de La Rioja (UGT-Rioja)* [2008] ECR I-6747. That is not to say that such taxes cannot be problematic from a different angle. Accordingly in Case C-169/08 *Presidente del Consiglio dei Ministri* [2009] ECR I-10821, the ECJ clarified that Article 107 TFEU 'must be interpreted as meaning that tax legislation, adopted by a regional authority, which establishes a tax on stopovers, such as that at issue in the main proceedings, to be imposed only on natural and legal persons whose tax domicile is outside the territory of the region, constitutes a State aid measure in favour of undertakings established in that territory'.

results from the application of different social security regimes by the various entities with constitutional autonomy is to be considered to form a purely internal situation, beyond the reach of Union law.[141]

**IV-34.** However, the Court may at times be inclined to play fast and loose with the existence of such connecting factors, allowing it on occasion to circumvent the problem of potentially conflicting standards. The most notable example is the *Grogan* case[142] where the ECJ was asked to assess the compatibility of Irish law, effectively prohibiting students from informing women about the possibility of undergoing an abortion in the UK, with the rules on the free movement of services. Advocate General Van Gerven found that the Irish law indeed formed an obstacle to the free movement of services. He then had to engage in an arduous attempt to explain why the measure could nonetheless be justified because of an imperative requirement given the special sensitivity in the Irish constitutional order vis-à-vis abortion and was not disproportionate, despite the chilling aspect it also has on the freedom of speech. On the latter point, the Advocate General would later be contradicted by the ECtHR, which ruled in its *Open Door*[143] judgment that the measure constituted a breach of that fundamental freedom. All this demonstrates that the ECJ risked being dragged into a very sensitive debate. The Court avoided that outcome, however, by deciding that the:

> link between the activity of the students associations of which Mr Grogan and the other defendants are officers and medical terminations of pregnancies carried out in clinics in another Member State is too tenuous for the prohibition on the distribution of information to be capable of being regarded as a restriction within the meaning of [then] Article 59 of the Treaty[144].

While this approach had undoubtedly the desired effect of defusing a potential clash between the EU legal order and the Irish legal order, it is not without criticism. First, the analysis of the Advocate General in the case and other case law of the Court, including the preceding *Cowan*[145] case and the more recent *Carpenter*[146] and *Metock*[147] cases, make the claim as to the tenuous link rather doubtful. Second, assuming for a moment that the Court is correct in arguing that – as the student associations could not be seen

141. Case C-212/06 *Government of the French Community and Walloon Government* [2008] ECR I-1683, para. 39. This does not mean that the Court is blind to the ensuing reverse discrimination, but it is for the national courts to take the national measures necessary to address this using equivalent tools of national constitutional law, *ibid.*, para. 40. The Belgian Constitutional Court, did not take up the suggestion though, see Belgian Constitutional Court no. 11/2009 of 21 January 2009.
142. Case C-159/90 *Society for the Protection of Unborn Children Ireland* [1991] ECR I-4685 with contrary Opinion of Advocate General Van Gerven. For a broader discussion, see, *supra*, at I-68.
143. ECtHR, 29 October 1992, *Open Door and Dublin Well Woman v. Ireland.*
144. Case C-159/90 *Society for the Protection of Unborn Children Ireland* [1991] ECR I-4685, para. 24.
145. Case C-186/87 *Cowan* [1989] ECR 195.
146. Case C-60/00 *Carpenter* [2002] ECR I-6279. Admittedly, though I personally agree with the judgment, this case has been challenged for overstepping the boundary between what falls within the scope of EU law and what should be outside of it, see, *inter alia*, L. Jadoul & F. Vanneste, 'Case C-60/00. Mary Carpenter v. Secretary of State for the Home Department (E.C.J. July 11, 2002)', *Columbia Journal of European Law* (2003): 447-455.
147. Case C-127/08 *Metock* [2008] ECR I-6241.

as agents for the abortion clinics – there was no sufficient link, I object to the manner in which the ECJ goes on to answer the question. By concluding that '*[i]t is not contrary to Community law* for a Member State in which medical termination of pregnancy is forbidden to prohibit students associations from distributing information about the identity and location of clinics in another Member State where voluntary termination of pregnancy is lawfully carried out and the means of communicating with those clinics, where the clinics in question have no involvement in the distribution of the said information',[148] the ECJ gives the false impression that it has somehow ruled on the Irish measure and found it compatible with Article 56 TFEU – suggesting quite some openness at the EU level to a highly restrictive abortion policy – whereas the whole aim of the evasive action on jurisdictional grounds was precisely not to have to take a stand on the matter. Therefore, I prefer the approach taken by the ECJ in its order in the *Vajnai*[149] case. There the ECJ dodged the issue of whether 'Article 269/B, first paragraph, of the Hungarian Criminal Code, which provides that a person who uses or displays in public the symbol consisting of a five-point red star commits – where the conduct does not amount to a more serious criminal offence – a minor offence' is compatible with EU law, by again explaining that there was in its view too tenuous a link with EU law. However, it did not give an apparent seal of approval to the Hungarian law. Instead the Court simply decided that as:

> Mr Vajnai's situation is not connected in any way with any of the situations contemplated by the provisions of the treaties and the Hungarian provisions applied in the main proceedings are outside the scope of Community law [...] the Court clearly has no jurisdiction to answer the question referred by the Fövárosi Bíróság[150].

**IV-35.** The *Vajnai*[151] case may also serve to demonstrate that the Court may not just be dodging a thorny issue of national law. While admittedly the factual setting – involving a home-made cardboard red star – and the way the national court phrased the questions were not very appealing, underlying the case lies also a potentially difficult issue of EU law, which the Court could even have taken up as part of its analysis as to its jurisdiction in the matter, but which it thus skilfully dodged, namely whether 'use restrictions' come within the scope of the free movement of goods. That controversial issue has only subsequently been addressed by the ECJ.[152] The compatibility of the Hungarian law has, however, also come back before the General Court in a case

148. Case C-159/90 *Society for the Protection of Unborn Children Ireland* [1991] ECR I-4685, para. 32 (emphasis added).
149. Case C-328/04 *Vajnai* [2005] ECR I-8577.
150. Case C-328/04 *Vajnai* [2005] ECR I-8577, paras 14-15.
151. Case C-328/04 *Vajnai* [2005] ECR I-8577.
152. See Case C-110/05 *Commission v. Italy* [2009] ECR I-519, with Opinions of AG Bot and AG Léger; see also the Case C-142/05 *Mickelsson and Roos* [2009] ECR I-4273, with Opinion of AG Kokott, The length it took the Court before deciding the issues, may give an idea about the contentiousness of the issue at the time. See further, L. Prete, 'Of Motorcycle Trailers and Personal Watercrafts: the Battle over *Keck*', *Legal Issues of Economic Integration* (2008): 133-155. See also L. Gormley, 'Silver threads among the gold...50 years of the free movement of goods', *Fordham International Law Journal* (2008): 1666-1672.

concerning a trademark based on the coat of arms of the USSR, where the General Court did bite the bullet by deciding that there was no problem of fundamental rights law.[153]

**IV-36.** The opposite situation may nevertheless also occur. The Court may actually display some eagerness to answer the human rights issue, despite the tenuous link with EU law. In the preceding paragraph, the attention was already drawn to *Carpenter*[154] and *Metock*.[155] However, while perhaps controversial, these cases are at least consistent if one accepts the Court's premise that they indeed have a link with EU law, a view which I indeed am willing to subscribe to.[156] However, at least in one case that eagerness seems to have gotten the better of the Court. In *Karner*,[157] after having found that the case did not raise a matter of free movement of goods – as the Austrian rule at issue, a prohibition to advertise that the goods on offer come from an insolvency procedure, falls within the scope of the *Keck*[158] exception – nor that it came within the scope of the free movement of services, nevertheless felt compelled to tackle head-on whether the measure could be reconciled with the freedom of speech under Article 10 ECHR.[159] While the Court's analysis in this respect seems fairly unobjectionable as to the merits, the Court should have left this matter exclusively for the national court to decide.

### *[3] Tolerance*

**IV-37.** A third manner for the Court to show sufficient deference to national constitutional values is what I would describe as tolerance without endorsement. There is a thin line between the situation described above where the ECJ tries to incorporate the national constitutional values into the EU legal order and the scenario that is before us now.[160] In both instances, the ECJ ultimately allows for the national value to be taken

153. Case T-232/10 *Couture Tech v. OHIM* [2011] ECR II-0000, paras 67-73. I agree with the outcome of that case, but I would, however, point out that there is a difference between refusing to register a trademark, the chilling effect on speech is almost negligible, and the prohibition on the use of a particular sign across the board.
154. Case C-60/00 *Carpenter* [2002] ECR I-6279.
155. Case C-127/08 *Metock* [2008] ECR I-6241.
156. See in this respect also Case C-34/09 *Ruiz Zambrano* [2011] ECR I-0000; and contrast with the follow-up judgment in Case C-256/11*Dereci* [2011] ECR I-0000, where the ECJ outlined the limits for relying on the Charter of Fundamental Rights and the protection of Union law quite adequately.
157. Case C-71/02 *Karner* [2004] ECR I-3025.
158. Case C-267/91 *Keck and Mithouard* [1993] ECR I-6097.
159. It has been argued that the ECJ may have felt – contrary to AG Alber – that it could not be excluded that there was nonetheless some kind of link to Council Directive 84/450/EEC of 10 September 1984 concerning misleading and comparative advertising (1984) OJ L 250/17, but that link seems tenuous at best; see F. De Cecco, 'Room to move? Minimum harmonization and fundamental rights', *Common Market Law Review* (2006): 15-16.
160. To illustrate this thin line, compare Case C-244/06 *Dynamic Medien* [2008] ECR I-505 with Case C-36/02 *Omega Spielhallen* [2004] ECR I-9609. While the Court in *Dynamic Medien* is extensively quoting from the latter case, it appears that the German standards in respect of the protection of the child are actually quite close to what the ECJ would itself see as an appropriate

into account in the case before it. However, whereas the case of inclusion of the national norm results in the affirmation of constitutional values which the Union and the Member States largely have in common, this may not be so in the case of tolerance. At issue are rather fringe constitutional values: national constitutional values that are either very specific for a particular Member State, or – while rooted in a common tradition – are elevated in a manner that goes beyond what the ECJ would see as the ordinary level of protection based on the common constitutional traditions of the Member States.

**IV-38.** The case in point is *Omega Spielhallen,*[161] which has been discussed in detail above,[162] so that here only the insight need to be recalled that through the use of the public policy exception the ECJ was capable to allow the German authorities sufficient leeway to uphold the German concept of human dignity in what was essentially a conflict between a German service provider and the German authorities over the types of games he could offer to his largely German customers, without however having to endorse that German concept of human dignity as the Union concept of human dignity, even though the concept is not as such alien to the EU legal order.

**IV-39.** One could see in this a way of putting Article 53 of the Charter of Fundamental Rights into operation, in deferring to the national constitutional norm offering higher protection. However, some caution is warranted. The reason why I have treated Article 53 of the Charter rather as a form of inclusion is the following. In the scenario envisaged the idea is that a national measure implementing EU law is first reviewed in the light of the ordinary EU standard, and – if it survives that scrutiny – may also be reviewed against whatever higher standard of national constitutional law. One could, for instance, imagine that a national measure prohibiting certain forms of advertising is first analysed as a restriction on the free movement of services,[163] which is then deemed justified, despite its impact on commercial free speech as the EU standard seems rather tolerant in respect of such restrictions.[164] Under Article 53 of the Charter, the national court would, however, be correct in analysing this restriction – which thus passes constitutional muster as far as EU law is concerned – in the light of its own national constitutional provisions on free speech and find that the measure is nevertheless incompatible with the national constitution. The effect is thus that the freedom of the citizen is additionally protected in that its government is precluded from restricting his/her rights further in cases involving an element of EU law than in cases

level of protection; it appears that this cannot be said of the German interpretation of human dignity advanced in *Omega Spielhallen*.

161. Case C-36/02 *Omega Spielhallen* [2004] ECR I-9609.
162. See, *supra*, at I-69 et seq.
163. One could think of a variation on Case C-134/03 *Viacom Outdoor* [2005] ECR I-1167.
164. Case C-71/02 *Karner* [2004] ECR I-3025, para. 51; Case C-251/01 *RTL Television* [2003] ECR I-12489, para. 73. The ECJ seeks to follow the case law of the ECtHR in this respect, see ECtHR, 20 November 1989, *Markt intern Verlag and Beermann v. Germany*, para. 33; and ECtHR, 28 June 2001, *VGT Verein gegen Tierfabriken v. Switzerland*, paras 69-70. See also Opinion of AG Ruiz Jarabo-Colomer in Case C-421/07 *Damgaard*, nyr, paras 67 et seq. where the borderline between advertising and journalism is at issue.

without such link. In cases such as *Omega Spielhallen*,[165] the opposite takes place. Instead of analysing the governmental action twice, first in the light of the EU standard and a second time in the light of the national standard, the freedom of the citizen ends up being more restricted than it would if only the EU standard would apply.

**IV-40.** In a sense this tolerance resembles the margin of appreciation left by the ECtHR to the Parties to the ECHR[166]: within a certain band Member States are free to aim for a particular level of protection, even though that may not correspond to the level set forth by other Member States or with the level the ECJ or ECtHR judges would themselves impose if given free reign and despite the extra limitations that ensue for EU law.[167] Accordingly, it is clear that such 'tolerance' of deviating national constitutional standards must be subject to some conditions as set out above,[168] as it may otherwise result in undermining both the full effect of EU law and – even though tolerance is not to be equated with EU endorsement of the national constitutional standard – confusion as to what the position of the Union on such matters is. In particular, the actions of Member States – formally taken with the intention to better protect fundamental constitutional values – may well result in a one-dimensional approach that unduly overstates the importance of particular constitutional values, such as human dignity, the protection of children, the sanctity of marriage, to the detriment of both EU law and other fundamental freedoms that are also recognized by the EU legal order, such as the freedom of expression (as in the Opinion of Advocate General Van Gerven in *Grogan*[169]), or also the freedom of assembly, and the protection of property rights (as in the case of *Omega Spielhallen*[170]). It is precisely to counter these concerns that I have set out in the course of the discussion of those case in Part I, a four-pronged test before unusual national constitutional standards are allowed to result in obstacles to the free movement.[171]

### *[4] Beyond National Procedural Autonomy?*

**IV-41.** Both the integration of national constitutional values into substantive Union law and the tolerance displayed by the ECJ in regard of certain especially demanding national substantive constitutional norms have their mirror image in the way the Union deals with national procedural norms. The basic rule has been explained in detail above and thus only needs to be recalled briefly at this stage: in the absence of harmonization the principle of national procedural autonomy provides that Member

165. Case C-36/02 *Omega Spielhallen* [2004] ECR I-9609.
166. On this, J.A. Sweeney, 'A 'Margin of Appreciation' in the Internal Market: Lessons from the European Court of Human Rights', *Legal Issues of Economic Integration* (2007): 27-52.
167. See in this sense Case C-275/92 *Schindler* [1994] ECR I-1039.
168. See, *supra*, at I-71et seq.
169. Opinion of AG Van Gerven in Case C-159/90 *Society for the Protection of Unborn Children Ireland* [1991] ECR I-4685, in particular if contrasted with ECtHR, 29 October 1992, *Open Door and Dublin Well Woman v. Ireland.*
170. Case C-36/02 *Omega Spielhallen* [2004] ECR I-9609.
171. See, *supra*, at I-71 et seq.

States may – and in a sense must – apply their own procedural laws in cases involving EU law, provided that such rules are not less favourable than those governing similar domestic actions (principle of equivalence) and are not framed in such a way as to render virtually impossible or excessively difficult in practice the exercise of rights conferred by Community law (principle of effectiveness).[172] One could argue that unless the effectiveness of EU law requires otherwise the EU legal order is content with borrowing the national procedural rules. This may even have the effect that also crucial norms of EU law – which may be considered a matter of EU *ordre public* – will not be enforced, precisely because similar rules of national law are not enforced either.[173]

**IV-42.** However, in the judgment in *Heemskerk and Schaap*[174] the ECJ appears to have taken a wholly different path, which seems more akin to a retreat of the EU legal order in the face of an essential national constitutional value than a form of national procedural autonomy, though its surprisingly short reasoning makes it difficult to gauge the true intentions of the Court from the judgment. Above, I have defended the solution to this case proposed by Advocate General Bot, who was of the opinion that the EU rules at issue, which had impact both on animal welfare and the EU financial interests, could be considered as weighty enough to be treated as norms with *ordre public* status, with the effect that the referring court had to raise these provisions of its own motion, even when this would result in *reformatio in pejus*, putting the applicant in a worse position than if he/she had not challenged his/her reduced sanction.[175] The ECJ, which effectively treats the ex officio application and the *reformatio in pejus* as one,[176] clearly does not agree that EU law needs to be enforced in such a draconic manner. Its argumentation is, however, extraordinary. No reference whatsoever is made to the concept of national procedural autonomy or its exceptions. Actually, for the reasons set out in the Opinion of the Advocate General it appears quite defensible that the effectiveness of EU law requires that the national court invokes the provisions at issue of its own motion. Indeed, in spite of the judgment, I still consider *Heemskerk and Schaap* an example of a systemic failure. Instead, the ECJ answers literally in two sentences:

> In that regard it should be pointed out that Community law cannot oblige a national court to apply Community legislation of its own motion where this would have the effect of denying the principle, enshrined in its national procedural law, of the prohibition of *reformatio in pejus*.
>
> Such an obligation would be contrary not only to the principles of respect for the rights of the defence, legal certainty and protection of legitimate expectations,

172. Case C-234/04 *Kapferer* [2006] ECR I-2585, para. 22; Case C-78/98 *Preston* [2000] ECR I-3201, para. 31.
173. For a good example, see Case C-234/04 *Kapferer* [2006] ECR I-2585. See also, *supra*, at II-219 et seq.
174. Case C-455/06 *Heemskerk and Schaap* [2008] ECR I-8763.
175. Opinion of AG Bot in Case C-455/06 *Heemskerk and Schaap* [2008] ECR I-8763. For the full discussion of the case, see, *supra*, at II-182 et seq.
176. Case C-455/06 *Heemskerk and Schaap* [2008] ECR I-8763, para. 44. This makes it very difficult to argue definitively as to whether the ECJ would also reject the concept of a substantive EU *ordre public* or the possibility that – provided there is no problem in terms of *reformatio in pejus* – national courts may have to raise the norms at issue of their own motion.

> which underlie the prohibition, but would expose an individual who brought an action against an act adversely affecting him to the risk that such an action would place him in a less favourable position than he would have been in, had he not brought that action[177].

**IV-43.** This answer strikes as troublesome in more than one way. First, the ECJ does not explain why this case should not be analysed under the normal framework of national procedural autonomy and its twin exceptions of equivalence and effectiveness. Second, the Court appears to accept as a fact that the prohibition on *reformatio in pejus* is deeply ingrained in the Dutch legal order and seems to have - arguably - a basis in a set of constitutional values that are also shared (though the Court does not stress this) by the EU legal order. This then must per se justify that the EU legal order does not press any further, even though the effective enforcement of EU law provisions protecting fundamental values - animal welfare and the financial interests of the Union - that are arguably a matter of EU *ordre public* is clearly in jeopardy, and despite that in the case at bar collusion between the government and the applicants cannot a priori be excluded.[178] Third, the cited constitutional values underlying the cherished Dutch constitutional rule prohibiting *reformatio in pejus* - of which it is thus unclear whether they must solely be seen from the perspective of Dutch law, or whether the ECJ has switched to a more general analysis inspired by, for instance, Article 47 of the Charter of Fundamental Rights - are upon balance threatening to almost all forms of ex officio application. This may be problematic, as we have seen above that ex officio application of EU law is common practice before the EU courts,[179] and that this is also an obligation for national courts - in particular in consumer protection cases.[180] After all, any case where a court invokes a norm of its own motion has the effect of somewhat upsetting the parties, who may now have to answer unexpected points of law and face the prospect of losing a case that would otherwise have been won. Provided that the parties have been given the opportunity to argue on the novel argument,[181] and within the constraints of the *petitum*, there does not appear a major problem in terms of rights of the defence, legal certainty and protection of legitimate expectations. Why is it that the rights of defence of this applicant are more endangered than the rights of the defence of Cofidis[182] or Francefinance,[183] other professionals against whom EU law could be invoked *motu proprio*, despite the fact that national law would ordinarily not allow for this? One could, admittedly, argue that in those cases the *petitum* is somewhat different in that the consumer will probably have implied that the national court must offer

177. Case C-455/06 *Heemskerk and Schaap* [2008] ECR I-8763, paras 46-47.
178. Admittedly, one could wonder, though, why, if there really was collusion, the applicant is not simply sticking to the deal but in stead brings a case against the government. However, there are two forms of collusion. One form is where there actually was a deliberate deal, and then one may even come close to cases of corruption. The other form is where the governments de facto allow their enterprises to bend the rules by sub-par enforcement.
179. See, *supra*, at II-186 et seq.
180. See, *supra*, at II-170 et seq.
181. Case C-89/08 P *Commission v. Ireland* [2009] ECR I-11245; Case C197/09 RX-II *M/European Medicines Agency* [2009] ECR I-12033.
182. Case C-473/00 *Cofidis* [2002] ECR I-10875.
183. Case C-429/05 *Rampion and Godard* [2007] ECR I-8017

him/her maximum protection, even though his/her action may have been clumsily formulated (as it fails to invoke the relevant provisions of EU law, or at least the national rules that implement those provisions), while Heemskerk and Schaap only want to have the decision set aside to the extent that they still have to repay certain export subsidies; it appears indeed from the order for reference[184] that the applicants are only seeking the annulment of the decision to revoke the restitution for 62 animals so that it is not before the national court whether the applicants have received more than is rightfully theirs in respect of all the other animals. The result would have been different if the annulment of the entire administrative decision was sought. In such a scenario, if the national court applies the EU rules at issue *motu proprio*, there may still be room for the national authorities to take a new decision in line with the reasoning of the national court. The only thing that changes is that this follow-up decision may be less attractive then originally anticipated by the applicant.[185] Such a situation resembles that of SELEX Sistemi Integrati discussed above, a company that was seeking the annulment of a Commission decision, but may have been very unhappy about the side-effects of the additional ammunition – in the form of arguments of EU *ordre public* relating to the competence of the Commission to take a decision vis-à-vis Eurocontrol – that have been raised in the course of proceedings, as they could indeed have resulted in the annulment of the Decision, but jeopardize the chances of the applicant to obtain a more favourable decision when the Commission reassesses the matter.[186] Furthermore, even the fact that on appeal a sanction is raised is not uncommon in the criminal systems of the Member States. Actually, raising fines in administrative procedures cannot even be excluded altogether in proceedings before the Union courts as a result of Article 261 TFEU.[187] Arguably, that possibility is explicitly provided for in the legislation, whereas it seems excluded in the Dutch legislation. However, even then the issue remains how far the constitutional values put forward by the ECJ carry outside the case before it.

184. College van Beroep voor het bedrijfsleven, 9 November 2006, LJN: AZ2235, AWB 05/686 and 05/687, point 5.4.
185. Actually, in first answering the substantive questions raised by the national court (see in particular Case C-455/06 *Heemskerk and Schaap* [2008] ECR I-8763, para. 39), the ECJ seems to envisage implicitly that some sort of follow-up decision may still be taken by the Dutch administration; otherwise, the answers given seem largely hypothetical, as the national court is given the reassurance that it may follow national procedural law so that it seems inevitable that it will not raise the issue of its own motion. However, as the result is that the national court should now simply dismiss the action, any new decision would not be the result of the procedure before the national court, but should depend on whatever powers the Dutch administration may have or not have to reconsider administrative decisions at this stage.
186. Nevertheless, see Opinion of AG Trstenjak in Case C-113/07 P *SELEX Sistemi Integrati v. Commission and Eurocontrol* [2009] ECR I-2207, paras 25-33, who seems similarly confused. The Court eventually side-stepped the issue. For more, see, *supra*, at II-203.
187. Admittedly, the General Court has in the past struggled with this unlimited jurisdiction to decide on fines, to the extent that raising a fine may be difficult to reconcile with the prohibition to decide *ultra petita*. See in this respect Joined Cases T-67/00, T-68/00, T-71/00 and T-78/00 *JFE Engineering Corp. and Others v. Commission* [2004] ECR II-2501, paras 576 and 579. It seems, that if the Commission had asked in its defence brief that the fines be increased the CFI would indeed have done so, which implies that appealing a Commission decision in the EU legal order is not per se risk free. For more, see K. Lenaerts, D. Arts & I. Maselis; R. Bray (ed.), *Procedural Law of the European Union*, 2nd ed. (London: Sweet & Maxwell, 2006), 447-451.

**IV-44.** The national court's observations about just how narrow the *petitum* before it is may go a long way in explaining why the Court felt that it had to defer in some way to what is still, despite the troublesome effects described above, a legitimate rule of Dutch administrative law. Nevertheless, I think the Court, if it felt so compelled, could have reached the same result with far less collateral damage if it had argued its judgment in somewhat more detail. In my view, the Court should, first, have applied the classic test in respect of national procedural autonomy, with its twin exceptions of equivalence and effectiveness, in line with the argumentation set forth by the Advocate General. At this point, the argumentation would thus be heading for the contrary solution, effectively urging the national court to raise the norms at issue of its own motion, even if this makes the applicant worse off. Second, if only to safeguard those instances of EU law (procedures in direct actions before the GC and ECJ, consumer law cases, the jurisdiction under Article 261 TFEU, other instances involving systemic failures) and national law (*inter alia* in criminal matters) where EU law may or even must be raised by courts of their own motion or where *reformatio in pejus* is not precluded a priori, the Court should have added – unlike what it seems to suggest, possibly inadvertently, in its actual judgment[188] – that this solution is not as such contrary to the right to an effective remedy and a fair trial, as guaranteed by Articles 6 and 13 ECHR and Article 47 of the Charter of Fundamental Rights. Third, the ECJ could then nonetheless have made a U-turn in a manner that takes into account the specific situation of the Dutch legal order without putting the procedures before the EU courts or in other Member States at risk, by arguing along the following lines. First, the ECJ could have stressed that while, as argued, demanding the national court to apply of its own motion the provisions at issue with the effect of putting the applicant in a worse position than if he/she had not initiated proceeding is not contrary to the right to an effective remedy and a fair trial, as guaranteed by Articles 6 and 13 ECHR and Article 47 of the Charter of Fundamental Rights; the national court has nevertheless indicated that, in accordance with a deeply rooted constitutional tradition, Dutch administrative courts are precluded from raising certain norms of their own motion in situations where this would result in *reformatio in pejus*. This approach has been defended as seeking to protect the legitimate expectations of legal subjects in their interaction with the national administrative authorities and aims to strengthen the right of access to a court, as it ensures that no one is discouraged from challenging governmental acts out of fear of being worse off afterwards. Accordingly, the Dutch legal order essentially seeks to strengthen rights as recognized by Articles 41 and 47 of the Charter of Fundamental Rights.[189] Second, the Court could then have pointed out that in line with

188. Case C-455/06 *Heemskerk and Schaap* [2008] ECR I-8763, para. 47.

189. The Court could, if it considers the risk of judgments *ultra petita* really problematic, make also this point more explicit. However, the manner in which it does is, in line with what has been argued, not without consequence. If it condemns this in a general manner, it would have the effect of elevating this to the Union standard. The ECJ may indeed validly put forward an autonomous EU standard in this respect, but it is unclear what the Union would gain from doing so and whether the ECJ would be able to make the scope of its concern sufficiently clear. A prohibition on deciding cases *ultra petita* may not be too problematic for the procedures before the ECJ, if one follows the line taken by Opinion of AG Tesauro in Case C-355/95 P *Textilwerke Deggendorf v. Commission* [1997] ECR I-2549, para. 24 (see also, *supra*, at II-204).

the rule laid down in Article 53 of the Charter,[190] legal subjects should be entitled, when challenging before a national administrative court national measures taken in the implementation of Union law, to rely on national procedural rules that aim to offer a higher level of protection of the rights guaranteed by the Charter. Third, against that background, the ECJ could more safely conclude that Union law 'does not require national courts to apply, of their own motion, a provision of [Union] law where such application would lead them to deny the principle, enshrined in the relevant national law, of the prohibition of *reformatio in pejus*'.[191]

**IV-45.** Accordingly, the same result may be reached, but in a manner that appears more respectful of both the EU legal order and the legal orders of the Member States as it makes the underlying interests of both more explicit. In my view, there may be at least four advantages of this approach. First, it explains the link between the traditional reasoning in terms of national procedural autonomy and the alternative outcome put forward here. This outcome is thus no longer an unreasoned retreat of Union law in the face of a particularly challenging national constitutional requirement, but fits in a broader constitutional framework. It makes it clear that it will not suffice for Member States to submit that something is a deeply rooted rule of national procedural law to get away with whatever EU law defeating rule they may cherish. Second, somewhat paradoxically, the enforcement of EU law would be given a serious boost as the signal would be given to the national legal orders that national courts should in principle invoke such norms of EU *ordre public* of their own motion, even in situations where that is to the detriment of the applicant in order to effectively protect these essential EU values and counterbalance a systemic failure. Third, the reasoning safeguards a whole series of existing procedural rules applicable both in the Member States and at EU level. Fourth, the essential constitutional value cherished by the Dutch legal order is effectively safeguarded as well. Accordingly, there thus is a principled manner to deal with similar rules in other Member States if such rules exist, without upsetting, however, the national legal orders that have no difficulty with *reformatio in pejus*.

**IV-46.** All in all, while I consider the Court's reasoning in *Heemskerk and Schaap*[192] somewhat deficient, I submit that beneath its approach there may actual lie an interesting additional tool for reconciling the EU legal order and the national legal

---

However, the ECJ may have a hard time explaining the impact this may have on national procedural law in those Member States where this was so far not an issue: are national courts in such Member States henceforth to stop raising issues ex officio if that leads to judgments *ultra petita*? and if so, does this apply for all national proceedings involving an issue of EU law, or only for national administrative proceedings of the type at issue in Case C-455/06 *Heemskerk and Schaap* [2008] ECR I-8763 (thus leaving for instance criminal proceedings unaffected)?

190. I deliberately use 'in line with the rule laid down in Article 53 of the Charter', to circumvent the problem that the Charter of Fundamental Rights was formally not yet fully part and parcel of EU primary law when Case C-455/06 *Heemskerk and Schaap* [2008] ECR I-8763 was decided, even though the ECJ had already made several references to it, without further reservations – see in particular, Case C-432/05 *Unibet* [2007] ECR I-2271 and Case C-303/05 *Advocaten voor de Wereld* [2007] ECR I-363 where the ECJ has dropped any reference to *Selbstbindung*, as initially put forward in Case C-540/03 *European Parliament v. Council* [2006] ECR I-5769.

191. Case C-455/06 *Heemskerk and Schaap* [2008] ECR I-8763, para. 48.

192. Case C-455/06 *Heemskerk and Schaap* [2008] ECR I-8763.

orders. Usually national procedural autonomy, and its twin exceptions of equivalence and effectiveness, should suffice to strike the appropriate balance between the demands of the EU legal order and the required intrusion into the domain of national procedural law. However, just like there are certain safety valves that allow the Court - provided that the impact on the EU legal order is not disproportionate - to accommodate certain hard-felt, legitimate national substantive values, *inter alia* through the public policy exceptions in the context of the free movement or Article 53 of the Charter of Fundamental Rights, it seems possible to create the possibility for the Court to show a similar deference to national law in procedural issues when deeply rooted fundamental national rules that are genuinely aimed at offering a higher level of protection are at stake. To avoid abuses, it is however, crucial that the Court makes it clear what the ordinary demands of the EU legal order are, what the ordinary limits of the national procedural autonomy in the case at bar are and why it is nonetheless appropriate to display some additional deference.

#### *[5] Mutual Recognition*

**IV-47.** Mutual recognition is essentially a quasi-solution, an interim outcome for the tension between the diversity in national laws and Union law. So far we have mainly focused on the vertical dimension of the potential conflict between the national law of a Member State and the demands posed by the EU legal order. However, there is also a horizontal dimension to the debate. In reality there are not two colliding monoliths of national law and EU law; the relationship seems more akin to an asteroid belt where the 27 legal orders and the Union legal order are interwoven in an intricate play of attraction and repulsion. The diversity of the Member States legal orders combined with the intended cross-border effects of EU law, which are most visible but far from restricted to the free movement rights, implies that the differences between the legal orders of the Member States create mutual tensions under the aegis of the EU. Mutual recognition in essence is prima facie the easy way out of the conflict: by introducing a default rule that Member States should recognize each others decisions and assessments the Union ensures that the divergence between the Member States does not spill-over onto the Union level. On the one hand, the objective of the Union in encouraging cross-border relationships is safeguarded; on the other hand, the Union is not primarily taking sides as mutuality implies that each Member State should recognize the acts of the other Member States. This has as its upshot that no Member State must change its own traditions, as long as it is willing to accept that some foreign decisions, assessments and values may trickle down, just as their decisions, assessments and values will find their way abroad.

**IV-48.** However, this is the naïve version of mutual recognition. The reality is that mutual recognition is as much part of the solution as it is part of the problem. First, it is in essence only a temporary solution: it applies only 'in the absence of common rules',[193] encouraging a political solution to overcome the divergence that will then be endowed with the additional legitimacy needed to impose it as a matter of supremacy, albeit subject to the further nuances made in that respect above. Second, while the EU is not taking sides vis-à-vis the underlying conflict is but partially true: the net result is that the EU sides by default with the foreign norm. This is defensible from an EU perspective, as it best ensures the cross-border realizations of the Union. Yet, if unchecked, this has the paradoxical result that Member States may see their most exotic rules and value judgments recognized abroad, while they have to scale them back at home in order to accommodate the foreign values. Third, mutual recognition is, however, not unchecked. As a natural corollary to mutual recognition, there are public policy exceptions that may justify disregarding the foreign rule or act. These exceptions may well be envisaged from the start, as in the case of the free movement, but if they are not they will be introduced, as in the case of European citizenship,[194] or expanded, as in the long line of cases since *Cassis de Dijon*,[195] in the case law of the Court. If upheld, these exceptions also result in an implied choice by the Union, this time in favour of the rule of the receiving state. In a sense, mutual recognition does not put an end to any substantive divergence as to policy. Mutual recognition works great in removing redundancy in that if particular values have already been sufficiently taking into account, if certain tests have already been carried out, there is no need to allow a Member State to redo these checks in a marginally different (perhaps, but not necessarily, marginally better) way. Similarly, if a Member State sends out the signal – as Belgium did in *Garcia Avello*[196] when the exasperated Belgian authorities in a bizarre move suggested naming the children Garcia, a solution that would have been contrary to both Belgian and Spanish legal tradition – that it is not seriously concerned by alternative solutions, there is no good reason to undermine the effectiveness of the free movement. But if there is a genuine policy conflict underlying the divergent legislation the conflict will not be solved through mutual recognition,[197] but by some form of balancing of interests. Fourth, as cases like *Omega Spielhallen*[198] demonstrate, the borderline between internal and supranational conflicts is a thin one. Those fortunate enough to adduce sufficient transnational links may have a chance of challenging internal rules which others may not have. The outcome of that case demonstrates that this challenge does not need to be successful, and that the EU legal order is sufficiently refined to take legitimate national values seriously, but the fact remains – and,

193. Case 120/78 *Rewe-Zentral* [1979] ECR 749, para 8.
194. For a good example, see Case C-353/06 *Grunkin and Paul* [2008] ECR I-7639 with Opinion of AG Sharpston. See also the Opinion of AG Jacobs in Case C-96/04 *Standesamt Stadt Niebüll* [2006] ECR I-3561.
195. Case 120/78 *Rewe-Zentral* [1979] ECR 749.
196. Case C-148/02 *Garcia Avello* [2003] ECR I-11613.
197. See in this sense, A. Verhoeven, *The European Union in Search of a Democratic and Constitutional Theory* (The Hague/London/New York: Kluwer Law International, 2002), 308-309. See also J. Weiler, 'The constitution of the common market place: text and context in the free movement of goods', in, *The Evolution of EU Law*, ed. P. Craig & G. De Búrca (Oxford: OUP, 1999), 365 who speaks of ensuring 'functional parallelism', rather than conflict resolution.
198. Case C-36/02 *Omega Spielhallen* [2004] ECR I-9609. On this point see also, *supra*, at II-70.

admittedly, even more so if the constraints I have proposed above[199] are given due weight – that the Member States may be on the defensive over its own rules with its own citizens.[200] Taken together, a far more nuanced picture appears. As Verhoeven succinctly observes:

> [t]hus, the mutual recognition principle operates a delicate balance. It allows the Member States to preserve their national identity when enacting legislation while leaving sufficient room for the realisation of the internal market. To that end, Member States can only uphold national rules if they successfully demonstrate that these rules further interests that are worth pursuing and are insufficiently protected by the laws of another Member State.[201]

This is particularly important as the Tampere European Council has dubbed mutual recognition 'the cornerstone of judicial cooperation in both civil and criminal matters within the Union',[202] thus expanding its use far beyond its original confines.[203] As the case of *N.S.* demonstrates mutually recognition, or full deference to the procedures in other Member States, in the Area of Freedom, Security and Justice reaches its limits, if the other Member States fail to guarantee at least a basic level of protection common to all Member States.[204] It is submitted that the Union, barring the atomic option of using Article 7 TEU, has fairly little tools to enforce the required level of communality to make mutual recognition workable in the Area of Freedom, Security and Justice.[205]

---

199. See, *supra*, at I-71 et seq.
200. On this, see C. Herrmann, 'Much ado about Pluto? The 'Unity of the Legal Order of the European Union' Revisited', *EUI Working Papers*, RSCAS 2007/05 (<http://www.iue.it/RSCAS/WP-Texts/07_05.pdf>, 23 May 2012).
201. A. Verhoeven, *The European Union in Search of a Democratic and Constitutional Theory* (The Hague/London/New York: Kluwer Law International, 2002), 309.
202. European Council, Tampere, 15 and 16 October 1999, *Presidency Conclusions*,33. See in this respect also J. Meeusen, 'Instrumentalisation of Private International Law in the European Union: Towards a European Conflicts Revolution ?', *European Journal of Migration and Law* (2007): 301
203. For an effect on conflicts of law, see Case C-353/06 *Grunkin and Paul* [2008] ECR I-7639; see also J. Meeusen, 'Instrumentalisation of Private International Law in the European Union: Towards a European Conflicts Revolution ?', *European Journal of Migration and Law* (2007): 287-305; D. Coester-Waltjen, 'Annerkennung im Internationalen Personen- Familien- und Erbrecht und das Europäische Kollisionsrecht', *IPrax* (2006): 392-401; H.-P. Mansel, 'Anerkennung als Grundprinzip des Europäischen Rechtsraum', *Rabels Zeitschrift* (2006): 651-731. For examples in criminal matters, see e.g., Case C-150/05 *Van Straaten* [2006] ECR I-9327; Case C-467/04 *Gasparini* [2006] ECR I-9199; M. Fichera & C. Janssens, 'Mutual recognition of judicial decisions in criminal matters and the role of the national judge, *ERA Forum* (2007): 177-202; V. Mitsilegas, 'The constitutional implications of mutual recognition in criminal matters in the EU', *Common Market Law Review* (2006): 1277-1311. For more on the preconditions for the legitimacy of mutual recognition in these areas, see also, *supra*, at I-66.
204. Joined Cases C-411/10 an C-493/10 *N.S* [2011] ECR I-0000, following the painful condemnation of not only the real culprit, Greece, but also the state sending the asylum seeker back in accordance with the EU rules, Belgium in ECtHR of 21 January 2011 *M.S.S. v. Belgium and Greece*.
205. I wonder whether it would not be possible to enforce Article 67(1) TFEU against the Member State, on the basis that it is the *conditio sine qua non* for mutual recognition as meant in Article 67(4) TFEU, but also 82 TFEU, so that a lack of fundamental rights protection undercuts the effectiveness of EU legislation in the AFSJ. Of course it is not self-evident for the Commission to enforce what at first appears to be a broadly worded principled statement addressed to the Union against the Member States. But the Union cannot achieve that level of protection without

### [6] *Link with the Role of the Court in Finding the Law*

**IV-49.** Already at the end of Part I, some observations were made as to the role of the ECJ in finding the law.[206] Those observations should briefly be recalled here. So far we have argued that the ECJ must look for the 'best fit' solution in striking a balance between national and EU interests and indicated a series of techniques for giving sufficient weight to fundamental Member State values whilst protecting the integrity of EU law. Underlying these techniques are, however, deeper considerations as to how the ECJ should decide cases. The use of comparative law[207] and the conscious development of EU federal common law[208] described above serve as guarantees that in striking this balance the Court may strive for a maximal degree of acceptability of its solution in the eyes of national legal orders in general and national courts in particular.

---

the help of its Member States, and the provision is at least within the jurisdiction of the Court and thus theoretically enforceable through infringement procedures on the basis of Articles 258-260 TFEU, avoiding the highly politicized route of Article 7 TEU.

206. See, *supra*, at I-87 et seq.

207. On the use of comparative law by the ECJ, see B. Markesinis & J. Fedtke, 'The judge as comparatist', 80 *Tulane Law Review* (2005): 11-167; K. Schiemann, 'A Response to the judge as comparatist', *Tulane Law Review* (2005): 281-296; K. Lenaerts, 'Interlocking legal orders in the European Union and Comparative Law', *International and Comparative Law Quarterly* (2003): 873-906. On the importance of comparative law research in the context of the EU *ordre public*, see R. De Lange, 'The European Public Order, Constitutional Principles and Fundamental Rights', *Erasmus Law Review* (2007): 22-23.

208. On federal common law, see K. Lenaerts & K. Gutman, '"Federal Common Law" in the European Union: a Comparative Perspective from the United States', *American Journal of Comparative Law* (2006): 1-122.

## Chapter 13
# Balancing the Interests of the Union

**IV-50.** In some aspects, the Union legal order is confronted with the same challenges as national legal orders, and the solutions put forward by the ECJ are often not much dissimilar to what other courts would do. One such issue is the question as to how the ECJ tries to balance the various interests of the Union. As most of this should sound familiar, it can be dealt with in a somewhat more limited fashion. Nevertheless, there are some analogies to what has been described above vis-à-vis the relationship with the Member States that deserve some closer attention.

**IV-51.** First, the ECJ, like any other constitutional court has to try to balance the various interests underlying the EU legislation. As the ECJ is hereby interpreting legislation adopted by the EU institutions, which despite whatever may be said about a democratic deficit in the Union, enjoy some democratic legitimacy, it is unsurprising that in doing so the ECJ displays quite some deference vis-à-vis the outcome of the legislative process and probably more than vis-à-vis the acts of national legislators who could more easily be expected not to be acting fully in the Union interest. Importantly, this deference even applies in cases where the European Parliament may not be fully involved. Good examples of the foregoing are offered by two cases taken from the context of visa, asylum and immigration, *Metock*[1] and *European Parliament v. Council.*[2] In the former case the ECJ, over the objections of the Member States – and in the absence of EU legislation – explicitly overruled its prior *Akrich*[3] judgment and decided that also the third-country national spouses who had never before stayed legally in a Member State, *in casu* Ireland, should be given a right of residence to stay with their EU national husbands or wives who have made use of their right to move to that Member State. The picture appears of a Union which seeks to maximize both the mobility of its citizens and the protection of the right to family life. In a sense, there is not much need to balance anything in this case at the EU level, as those two core values of the EU legal

1. Case C-127/08 *Metock* [2008] ECR I-6241.
2. Case C-540/03 *European Parliament v. Council* [2006] ECR I-5769.
3. Case C-109/01 *Akrich* [2003] ECR I-9607.

order coincide to strengthen each other. One may wonder whether the outcome would be the same if the EU legislator had adopted rules under which some of the applicants would be denied a right of residence. The *family reunification* case indeed demonstrates that the ECJ is far less inclined to upset a political compromise balancing the interests of the Union in controlling migration and protecting family life, even though the role of the European Parliament had been quite limited in reaching that balance.[4] The same message seems to flow from the rare cases where Member States – after having been outvoted in the Council – have tried to challenge the validity of an act of the Union on fundamental rights grounds. As argued above, while the ECJ is quite willing to accept the existence of a fundamental right to human dignity, this does not result in major limitations on the ability of the EU legislator to protect certain controversial biotechnological inventions.[5]

**IV-52.** The need to balance certain interests may, however, also reach the Court through preliminary references. Here, too, the deference to the acts of the EU legislator, especially in areas of economic regulation is striking, as may be demonstrated by the ease with which the Court seems to accept the expropriating effect of the EU market organization in wine on Ms. Hauer.[6] Nevertheless, in recent years the Court has demonstrated that it will ultimately not shrink from the responsibility to strike down Union legislation as contrary higher EU law including the fundamental rights protected by the Charter, if the situation so warrants.[7] However, the need for implementation of EU law by the national authorities does create an additional complexity for the Court. Often the ECJ does not only need to assess whether the EU has itself created an acceptable balance between competing interests, on top of that the ECJ must also consider how much margin the balance thus achieved leaves open for national implementing measures that may propose a slightly different mix. A key example of this is offered by the case of *Promusicae*.[8] Starting point was a series of otherwise unexceptionable Directives dealing with e-commerce,[9] copyright protection in the information society[10] and intellectual property,[11] which taken together outlaw certain

4. Actually, as the Opinion of AG Kokott demonstrates, the role of the European Parliament had even be further curtailed – though the European Parliament had failed to notice it and the ECJ seems unwilling to raise it of its own motion – to the extent that it had not even been properly re-consulted over the amended proposal, see Opinion of AG Kokott in Case C-540/03 *European Parliament v. Council* [2006] ECR I-5769, paras 52-58. See also, *supra*, at II-194.
5. Case C-377/98 *Netherlands v. European Parliament and Council* [2001] ECR I-7079.
6. Case 44/79 *Hauer* [1979] ECR 3727.
7. Case C-236/09 *Association Belge des Consommateurs Test-Achats* [2011] ECR I-0000; Joined Cases C-92/09 and C-93/09 *Schecke and Eifert* [2010] ECR I-0000.
8. Case C-275/06 *Promusicae* [2008] ECR I-271.
9. Directive 2000/31/EC of the European Parliament and of the Council of 8 June 2000 on certain legal aspects of information society services, in particular electronic commerce, in the Internal Market (2000) OJ L 178/1.
10. Directive 2001/29/EC of the European Parliament and of the Council of 22 May 2001 on the harmonization of certain aspects of copyright and related rights in the information society (2001) OJ L 167/10.
11. Directive 2004/48/EC of the European Parliament and of the Council of 29 April 2004 on the enforcement of intellectual property rights (2004) OJ L 157/45, and corrigendum, (2004) OJ L 195/16.

forms of file-sharing of copyrighted materials over the internet. The Directives thus seek to protect certain intellectual property rights, probably limiting in a way the freedom of information and the freedom of expression, but that seems inevitable when protecting copyrighted materials. What is not, inevitable, however, is the manner in which these Directives - or at least the national implementing legislation - should be enforced. In order to identify individual users of software that can be used in illegal file-sharing, the rights owners are particularly interested in certain data held by internet providers. The applicants in the case therefore argue that the Directives should also be seen as requiring the Member States to allow such organizations access to that information in both civil and criminal cases. It is clear that this would greatly enhance the effectiveness of the enforcement of EU law, by increasing the possibilities for (successfully) bringing cases to court, as protected by Article 47 of the Charter, and efficiently protect intellectual property rights as provided for in Article 17(2) of the Charter. Yet, under Spanish law that possibility seems to have been limited to criminal prosecutions only. There is good reason to be reluctant in distributing the data sought, as it concerns sensitive private information protected as a matter of privacy. Accordingly, the ECJ had to analyse whether Union law, in particular Directives 2000/31, 2001/29 and 2004/48, read also in the light of Articles 17 and 47 of the Charter, must be interpreted as requiring Member States to lay down, in order to ensure effective protection of copyright, an obligation to communicate personal data in the context of civil proceedings. Actually, that question hides two questions. First, the Court determines that the provisions at issue do not preclude such an obligation, as this would indeed greatly enhance the enforcement and is not precluded by any explicit exception to the contrary. Second, the Court needs to determine whether this obligation to communicate personal data in the context of civil proceedings is also mandatory for the Member States. On this point something special happens, because in answering this question the Court becomes acutely aware of the aspect that the national court has been silent on in its question, namely the protection of personal data. The Court, therefore, decides to balance the effective protection of intellectual property and the right to an effective remedy, both protected by the Charter of Fundamental Rights, with the further fundamental rights guaranteeing the protection of personal data and hence of private life. Against this background, it becomes clear that the interests underlying the Directives at issue ought not to become so dominant as to require Member States to impose the release of personal information in civil trials. Moreover, there may even be good reasons to doubt whether the correct balance of interests underlying the entire EU legal order does not call into question the ECJ's prior finding that the Directives per se do not preclude Member States from imposing such an obligation. The answer to the national court is therefore quite nuanced:

> Directives 2000/31, 2001/29, 2004/48 and 2002/58 do not require the Member States to lay down, in a situation such as that in the main proceedings, an obligation to communicate personal data in order to ensure effective protection of copyright in the context of civil proceedings. However, Community law requires that, when transposing those directives, the Member States take care to rely on an interpretation of them which allows a fair balance to be struck between the various fundamental rights protected by the Community legal order. Further, when

> implementing the measures transposing those directives, the authorities and courts of the Member States must not only interpret their national law in a manner consistent with those directives but also make sure that they do not rely on an interpretation of them which would be in conflict with those fundamental rights or with the other general principles of Community law, such as the principle of proportionality[12].

A similar reasoning has since been applied to quite a number of cases involving the balancing between intellectual property rights and the development of all kinds of services in the information society.[13] In a similar vein, the ECJ has also had the task of balancing the interests of privacy and freedom of expression in the context of Article 9 of Directive 95/46,[14] which allows for certain exception to the limits on data protection 'solely for journalistic purposes'. Again the national court is given instructions which should enable it to assess whether the balance was unduly upset in the case at issue, which concerned the publication of the tax details of 1.2 million tax payers in a local newspaper.[15]

**IV-53.** The difficulties surrounding the Court's deference are best demonstrated when it comes to fundamental rights protection in the context of the EU external action. Some authors have been scathing in their criticism and speak of double standards.[16] Even setting aside extreme cases such as the war in Iraq, there is indeed a current in the EU legal order that results in different approaches when external relations are at issue. What is interesting in that respect is that some parallels may be drawn with the way the ECJ deals with national constitutional values that are somewhat out of the mainstream. Yet, as the appeals case in *Kadi*[17] demonstrates this should not be overstated.

**IV-54.** In the absence of a political questions doctrine, both the ECJ and the GC have in the past managed to display remarkable deference towards the way the EU deals with foreign affairs, even when fundamental rights are at stake. Both courts have indeed found some quasi-jurisdictional ways out of disputes with a sensitive external relations aspect that are not entirely dissimilar to the way the ECJ has dodged the bullet on for instance the Irish abortion issue.[18] In the *PNR* case[19] the ECJ thus awarded the European Parliament a Pyrrhic victory. The European Parliament had challenged both the legal basis and the compatibility with the protection of personal data of the decision

12. Case C-275/06 *Promusicae* [2008] ECR I-271, para. 70.
13. Case C-70/10 *Scarlet Extended* [2011] ECR I-0000; Case C-360/10 *SABAM* [2012] ECR I-0000; Case C-510/10 *DR and TV2 Danmark* [2012] ECR I-0000.
14. Directive 95/46/EC of the European Parliament and of the Council of 24 October 1995 on the protection of individuals with regard to the processing of personal data and on the free movement of such data (1995) OJ L 281/1.
15. Case C-73/07 *Satakunnan Markkinapörssi* [2008] ECR I-9831, paras 50-62.
16. A. Williams, 'The Indifferent Gesture: Article 7 TEU, the Fundamental Rights Agency and the UK's invasion of Iraq', *European Law Review* (2003): 3-27.
17. Joined Cases C-402/05 P and C-415/05 P *Kadi v. Council* [2008] ECR I-6351.
18. Case C-159/90 *Society for the Protection of Unborn Children Ireland* [1991] ECR I-4685. See also, *supra*, at IV-34.
19. Joined Cases C-317/04 and C-318/04 *European Parliament v. Council and Commission* [2006] ECR I-4721.

to conclude the controversial PNR Agreement[20] with the US, which enables the US authorities to access selected private details of airline passengers. The European Parliament argued that Article 95 TEC could not serve as a legal basis, though it did not really put forward an alternative. To the extent that the Council would be correct to rely on the same legal basis as the Directive 95/46, the European Parliament argued that this would imply that the international agreement was thus affecting a directive decided by co-decision so that under Article 300(3) TEC the European Parliament should have had the right of assent, which means that it could have blocked the agreement. It had plenty of reason to do so, because the European Parliament was also highly concerned about the protection of the right of privacy, although the Opinion of the Advocate General[21] makes it clear that the case is far from a slam dunk in that respect. However, crucially for our argument, the ECJ indeed finds fault with the legal basis, but not in the manner the European Parliament had envisaged it. Instead, the ECJ finds that the agreement is aimed primarily at combating international terrorism and should thus fall under Article 24 TEU. This has as its immediate effect that the act of the Council should indeed be annulled, but without there being need for assessing the Council decision under the heading of fundamental rights.[22] However, the upshot is that given the limited jurisdiction of the Court in the second and third pillar, the European Parliament is also robbed of raising the issue again when the Council will have concluded a new agreement on the correct legal basis. In light of the dubious wording of that new agreement, which has since been adopted,[23] it is even unclear whether there will ever be a private party that may have standing to challenge the decision[24] to conclude the new agreement, even through the national courts. The Court has thus not only dodged the sensitive issue in the case before it, but has effectively precluded from it being raised again in later litigation. The Member States are of course quite pleased with this deference to the external action, which they, too seem to be treasuring. For instance, they ensured that the issue may also not be taken up in the

20. Council Decision 2004/496/EC of 17 May 2004 on the conclusion of an Agreement between the European Community and the United States of America on the processing and transfer of PNR data by Air Carriers to the United States Department of Homeland Security, Bureau of Customs and Border Protection (2004) OJ L 183/83, and corrigendum at (2005) OJ L 255/168.
21. Opinion of AG Léger in Joined Cases C-317/04 and C-318/04 *European Parliament v. Council and Commission* [2006] ECR I-4721, paras 207-262.
22. Joined Cases C-317/04 and C-318/04 *European Parliament v. Council and Commission* [2006] ECR I-4721, para. 61.
23. Agreement between the European Union and the United States of America on the processing and transfer of Passenger Name Record (PNR) data by air carriers to the United States Department of Homeland Security (DHS) (2007 PNR Agreement) (2007) OJ L 204/18 which according to its own terms 'is not intended to derogate from or amend the laws of the United States of America or the European Union or its Member States' and 'does not create or confer any right or benefit on any other person or entity, private or public'.
24. Council Decision 2007/551/CFSP/JHA of 23 July 2007 on the signing, on behalf of the European Union, of an Agreement between the European Union and the United States of America on the processing and transfer of Passenger Name Record (PNR) data by air carriers to the United States Department of Homeland Security (DHS) (2007 PNR Agreement) (2007) OJ L 204/16.

context of the EU Agency for Fundamental Rights,[25] as contrary to its name the Agency solely operates in respect of the TEC.[26]

**IV-55.** Also the way the General Court has dealt with the *Yusuf*[27] and *Kadi*[28] cases may be seen from this perspective. While I have quite some sympathy for the attempt of the General Court to reconcile maximum respect for the international legal order and the fundamental rights that are at the heart of the legal order by using the vehicle of *ius cogens* to come to a balancing act, fact is that also that solution was not free from criticism,[29] as at the end of the day neither the EU fundamental rights standard was met, nor was a fully credible interpretation given to the concept of *ius cogens.*[30] Against this background the appeals judgment[31] is distinctly refreshing, as it tackles the fundamental rights issue head-on: the sanctions are the result of a legislative act of the Union and are thus subject to the EU standard for fundamental rights protection, even though this may be at the expense of the manner the Member States are discharging their obligations under international law in general and the UN Charter in particular. Moreover, in cases that do not involve UN Security Council resolutions targeting particular groups or individuals[32] also the General Court has since taken a far stronger stance,[33] and it has eventually also accepted the ECJ's approach in *Kadi.*[34] This heightened sensitivity to fundamental rights in respect of matters relating to external relations is to be welcomed. However, one important *caveat* should be made. It is important to ensure that the pendulum does not swing entirely to the other side, with the effect that the respect for international law, in particular by the Member States may be jeopardized. While the appeals case in *Kadi*[35] has thus resulted in more protection for individuals, the same reasoning has already had the opposite effect in *Intertanko.*[36]

25. Council Regulation (EC) No 168/2007 of 15 February 2007 establishing a European Union Agency for Fundamental Rights (2007) OJ L 53/1.
26. The Regulation was adopted on the basis of Article 308 TEC. According to Article 3, its scope is limited to the 'competencies of the Community as laid down in the Treaty establishing the European Community' so that the Agency 'shall deal with fundamental-rights issues in the European Union and in its Member States when implementing *Community* law' (emphasis added). One cannot but wonder whether the entry into force of the Lisbon Treaty should not result in a revision of this mandate.
27. Case T-306/01 *Yusuf and Al Barakaat International Foundation v. Council and Commission* [2005] ECR II-3533.
28. Case T-315/01 *Kadi v. Council and Commission* [2005] ECR II-3649.
29. See, for instance, Ecke, C., 'Judicial Review of European Anti-Terrorism Measures – The *Yusuf* and *Kadi* Judgments of the Court of First Instance', *European Law Journal*, 2008, 74-92, who scathingly speaks of a 'combination of various errors of law'.
30. For more, see, *supra*, at II-130 et seq.
31. Joined Cases C-402/05 P and C-415/05 P *Kadi v. Council* [2008] ECR I-6351.
32. Though, in all those cases the generic UNSC resolution 1373 (2001) still sits in the background.
33. Case T-228/02 *Organisation des Modjahedines du peuple d'Iran v. Council* [2006] ECR II-4665; Case T-327/03 *Stichting Al-Aqsa* [2007] ECR II-79*; Case T-256/07 *People's Mojahedin Organization of Iran v. Council* [2008] ECR II-3019. See also the third annulment, delivered a record-breaking one day after oral argument, Case T-284/08 *People's Mojahedin Organization of Iran v. Council* [2008] ECR II-3487.
34. Case T-85/09 *Kadi v. Commission* [2010] ECR II-0000.
35. Joined Cases C-402/05 P and C-415/05 P *Kadi v. Council* [2008] ECR I-6351.
36. Case C-308/06 *International Association of Independent Tanker Owners* [2008] ECR I-4057.

There the Court refused to follow its Advocate General[37] in interpreting Union legislation imposing (criminal) liability in a more modest way that would have brought the EU approach more in line with the obligations of its Member States under Marpol.[38]

**IV-56.** All this demonstrates that the ECJ – like any other national constitutional court – tries to reconcile various conflicting interests, both when it is assessing the validity of acts of the institutions – and the *Kadi*[39] appeals demonstrate that it is no longer true that the ECJ never strikes down EU legislation for breach of fundamental rights – and when it is interpreting EU law, often at the request of national courts. As the discussion of *Promusicae*[40] demonstrates, those national courts may inject into the balancing of the EU interests again a series of national interests as well. Therefore, it may be appropriate to look at a somewhat more elaborate case study where all these levels are fully interwoven.

37. Opinion of AG Kokott in Case C-308/06 *International Association of Independent Tanker Owners* [2008] ECR I-4057.
38. Compare also the outcome of another recent environmental case, Case C-188/07 *Commune de Mesquer* [2008] ECR I-4501. See, moreover, also the artful dodging of complex issues in respect of the Chicago Convention in Case C-366/10 *Air Transport Association of America* [2011] ECR I-0000.
39. Joined Cases C-402/05 P and C-415/05 P *Kadi v. Council* [2008] ECR I-6351.
40. Case C-275/06 *Promusicae* [2008] ECR I-271.

# CHAPTER 14
# Case Study: Same-Sex Marriages

**IV-57.** The European Union does not have any explicit competence at all to regulate sensitive issues of family law such as marriage.[1] Actually, the issue is so sensitive that in Article 9 of the Charter of Fundamental Rights of the EU the right to marry and the right to found a family are explicitly linked to national law: 'The right to marry and the right to found a family shall be guaranteed in accordance with the national laws governing the exercise of these rights.' Yet, as marriage is in most legal orders, including the EU legal order, often used as a key connecting factor for the application of legislation and the conferral of rights, it is inevitable that also in the EU legal order the concept is in need of a definition. Accordingly, as the traditional concepts about family and marriage are increasingly under pressure and with three Member States effectively opening up marriage to same-sex couples, the question how the EU should deal with same-sex marriages becomes acute.

**IV-58.** At the same time, precisely because of the sensitivity of the matter and the divergence of national approaches, the question how to deal with same-sex marriages in EU law allows for a limited practical test for some of our insights on how the ECJ should deal with divergence between the various Member States while maintaining the effectiveness of Union law. The debate plays out at two levels. First, the question will be addressed how the EU deals internally with the divergent concepts of marriages. In particular, the focus will be placed on the case of *D and Sweden v. Council*[2] and its legislative follow-up. Second, the focus is shifted to the question whether Member States may refuse to recognize the marriages validly concluded in another Member State on the sole ground that the partners are not of the opposite sex. To answer that

1. Case C-267/06 *Tadao Maruko* [2008] ECR I-1757, para. 59.
2. Joined Cases C-122/99 P and C-125/99 P *D and Sweden v. Council* [2001] ECR I-4319. I will focus on the appeals case, which confirmed the original finding of the CFI in Case T-264/97 *D v. Council* [1999] ECR II-1 and [1999] ECR IA-1. For a critical analysis of that decision, see G. Scapucci, 'Court of First Instance Refuses to Recognize Swedish 'Registered Partnership' Rights and Duties', *European Public Law* (2000): 355-366.

question, attention is first paid to the impact of EU legislation in respect of non-discrimination – as this could prima facie form a basis for changing the national definitions of marriage, even though it will be argued that the impact is fairly limited. Next, the question is answered whether the principle of mutual recognition should not also be extended to marriages concluded in another Member State, or whether non-recognition may nonetheless be justified on grounds of (national) public policy.

## §14.01 THE HORIZONTAL CONFLICT: SAME-SEX MARRIAGE AT EU LEVEL

**IV-59.** The most direct way the European Union was itself confronted with the concept of marriage was when the issue was raised in the context of the interpretation of its own Staff Regulations. Mr D, a Swedish civil servant of the Council claimed the right to certain benefits related to his spouse, on the grounds of his Swedish registered partnership, which, while not equated with marriage as such, extends all the material benefits of marriage to the partners of such a partnership. The claim – supported by Sweden – was for that Member State in a sense the continuation of the political battle it had lost when the relevant version of the Staff Regulations was passed. Sweden had indeed argued that arrangements should be made to put such registered partnerships on equal footing with marriage, but the Council had only agreed to ask the Commission to investigate the impact of such a move without embracing it at the time.

**IV-60.** As the ECJ noticed, this was the first time it was invited to define the concept of marriage for the purpose of the Staff Regulations, which became essential as benefits could only be extended to Mr D if the Staff Regulations concept of 'marriage' and 'spouse' were capacious enough to encompass 'registered partnerships' and 'same-sex partners'. As argued above,[3] a situation where the legislator uses a term it has failed to determine and relates to an area where the EU has as such no material competence, as with marriage and family law, may give rise to the creation of EU federal common law. Indeed, the ECJ both had the required adjudicatory power (an appeal had properly been lodged in an admissible direct action against a decision of the Council) and substantive power (as the issue concerned the interpretation of an otherwise valid instrument of EU law) to decide the matter itself.[4] However, what is not set in stone is which rule the ECJ should adopt as the EU rule. In theory, the Court could have crafted an autonomous definition of marriage or taken over one from one of the Member States, arguing that it best fits the needs of the Union. However, the ECJ is not blind for the situation in its Member States. Accordingly, it finds that 'according to the definition generally accepted by the Member States, the term marriage means a union between two persons of the opposite sex'.[5] Furthermore, the Court is not unaware of the evolution in various Member States towards new forms of partnerships, and it takes

3. See, *supra*, at I-99 et seq.
4. For more on this example, and its link with the creation of EU federal common law, see K. Lenaerts & K. Gutman, '"Federal Common Law" in the European Union: a Comparative Perspective from the United States', *American Journal of Comparative Law* (2006): 52 et seq.
5. Joined Cases C-122/99 P and C-125/99 P *D and Sweden v. Council* [2001] ECR I-4319, para. 34.

note of comparative studies in this respect,[6] yet it finds that 'apart from their great diversity, such arrangements for registering relationships between couples not previously recognised in law are regarded in the Member States concerned as being distinct from marriage'.[7] The Court, moreover, takes account of the refusal of the EU legislator to put such partnerships on equal footing with marriage. Accordingly, the ECJ basically decides not to adopt a novel EU definition, but it defers the matter entirely to the EU legislator. For the time being, this implies, however, that:

> the fact that, in a limited number of Member States, a registered partnership is assimilated, although incompletely, to marriage cannot have the consequence that, by mere interpretation, persons whose legal status is distinct from that of marriage can be covered by the term married official as used in the Staff Regulations[8].

**IV-61.** This reasoning reveals two related points. First, the ECJ seems very cautious to upset the traditional concept of marriage, as it feels that the large majority of the Member States was not yet ready to change. However, it leaves open the possibility that its views may thus also evolve if the position of the Member States were to change dramatically. Second, the best way for the Court to be certain whether such shift has taken place is a change in the legislation. By deferring the matter to the EU legislator, the Member States are indeed given the opportunity to put their cards on the table. This shift has taken place remarkably fast. Already in 2004, the Council amended its Staff Regulations to extend the benefits given to married persons to '[o]fficials in a nonmarital relationship recognised by a Member State as a stable partnership'.[9] Accordingly, the EU courts may now take a different approach. Indeed, the Civil Service Tribunal has already accepted, in a case that concerned a Dutch 'samenlevingsovereenkomst' between a man and a woman that henceforth non-marital relationships that meet three criteria will be treated for the purpose of awarding certain benefits to EU civil servants as a marriage. First, 'the partners must form a "couple", in other words a union of two persons',[10] which sounds self-evident, but Dutch law apparently also allows for cohabitation agreements that involve more than two persons. Second, the 'partners' relationship must have public and formal aspects[11], i.e., it must have been officialized in a legal document subject to specific formal requirements as national law may require. Third, '"non-marital partners" must be understood as referring to a situation where the partners' cohabitation is characterized by a certain stability and they are linked, during that cohabitation, by reciprocal rights and obligations, relating to their cohabitation'.[12] On appeal, the General Court largely

6. Joined Cases C-122/99 P and C-125/99 P *D and Sweden v. Council* [2001] ECR I-4319, para. 35.
7. Joined Cases C-122/99 P and C-125/99 P *D and Sweden v. Council* [2001] ECR I-4319, para. 36.
8. Joined Cases C-122/99 P and C-125/99 P *D and Sweden v. Council* [2001] ECR I-4319, para. 39.
9. Recital 8 of Council Regulation (EC, Euratom) No 723/2004 of 22 March 2004 amending the Staff Regulations of Officials of the European Communities and the Conditions of Employment of Other Servants of the European Communities (2004) OJ L 124/1.
10. Case F-122/06 *Roodhuijzen v. Commission* [2007] ECR 0000, para. 38.
11. Case F-122/06 *Roodhuijzen v. Commission* [2007] ECR 0000, para. 39.
12. Case F-122/06 *Roodhuijzen v. Commission* [2007] ECR 0000, para. 40.

agreed with the approach taken by the Civil Service Tribunal, only faulting the General Court for being too inquisitive still in verifying in detail, on the basis of an examination both of the 'samenlevingsovereenkomst' between the applicant at first instance and Ms H and of the provisions of the Netherlands legislation, the reciprocal rights and obligations relating to the cohabitation of Mr Roodhuijzen and his companion, as in its view the Staff Regulations do not require verification of whether the consequences stemming from the partnership entered into by the official concerned are 'similar in numerous respects' to those stemming from a marriage, or indeed a 'geregistreerd partnerschap'.[13] As a result of this approach, same-sex marriages, but also a host of other stable non-marital relationships, whether between same-sex partners or otherwise, will now be treated like marriage. In this respect the Civil Service Tribunal also clarified that even in instances where the applicant could have married, as in the case of a same-sex pair when one person holds the Belgian nationality, it is possible to claim the rights on the basis of a registered partnership instead if marriage is not option for specific reasons related to the situation of the applicant.[14] It may well be that it is precisely the fact that the Regulation affects such a diverse set of stable relationships, rather than purely same-sex marriages, that may have created broad enough a basis for the Member States to endorse this extension. However, it seems to flow from this that the Member States are no longer fundamentally opposed to the possibility of awarding stable same-sex couples the same benefits as married couples.[15] However, as the General Court makes clear the interpretation of the Staff Regulations leaves the competence of the Member States in determining their marriage policy intact.[16]

13. Case T-58/08 P *Commission v. Roodhuijzen* [2009] ECR II-3797, para. 98.
14. Case F-96/08 *W. v. Commission* [2010] ECR I-0000. The Tribunal observes how Article 46 of the Belgian Code on International Private Law rejects any prohibition of marriage between persons of the same sex contained in the national legislation of either member of the couple, thus making it clear that such a prohibition is contrary to the prevailing social and legal perceptions in Belgium. However, the Tribunal also notes that there may nevertheless be good reasons not to marry, as in the case of the applicant who – while holding Belgian nationality – also holds Moroccan nationality and has still ties to Morocco, a country where homosexuality is still crime. Accordingly, the applicant's access to marriage in Belgium cannot be regarded as practical and effective within the meaning of the case law.
15. Council Regulation (EC, Euratom) No 723/2004 of 22 March 2004 amending the Staff Regulations of Officials of the European Communities and the Conditions of Employment of Other Servants of the European Communities (2004) OJ L 124/1 was adopted shortly before the accession of 10 new Member States to the Union. As some of them may be markedly more reserved as to alternatives to the traditional family, one could object that my argument needs to be nuanced. I am not convinced, however, that this is necessary. After all, the new Member States are supposed to sign up to the entire acquis. If this would have been unacceptable for them, they could have negotiated a specific arrangement or – *à la limite* – stayed out of the Union. This is not to say that this arrangement is now set in stone. However, until the Council deems it necessary to undo these changes because of a new shift in Member States' sentiment, whether the result of enlargement or otherwise, this regime seems to suggest that, for now, Member States display far more openness towards alternative partnerships.
16. Case T-58/08 P *Commission v. Roodhuijzen* [2009] ECR II-3797, para. 87.

## §14.02 VERTICAL CONFLICTS: DOES EU LAW REQUIRE MEMBER STATES TO RECOGNIZE SAME-SEX MARRIAGES?

**IV-62.** We now shift our attention to the treatment of same-sex marriages in a transnational context: are Member States under an obligation to recognize a same-sex marriage duly concluded in one Member State when the couple invokes the benefits for spouses that flow from the free movement of persons. It is one thing to require – as flows from the recent changes to the Staff Regulations – the Union, as a supranational body to adjust, as far as possible, to the diverse forms of partnerships Member States have created alongside classic marriages. It is a wholly different thing to require the same from the Member States, namely that they, too, adjust their family law when acting in the context of EU law. Below, I deliberately set out to focus my argumentation on the situation of same-sex marriages, even though only three Member States (Belgium, the Netherlands and Spain) have so far created such institution. Many more Member States have meanwhile created certain forms of registered partnerships that are open to same-sex couples, and are for those couples often the only alternative to marriage. However, the question whether such same-sex partnerships should be treated equally with heterosexual marriage requires a double burden, as there is not only the same-sex problem, but also the question whether such a partnership is to be equated with marriage, especially if the legislator has deliberately decided not to use the term marriage to denote the alternative registered partnership or – as is often the case – has withheld certain rights associated with marriage. Nevertheless, some of the arguments in support of the recognition of same-sex marriages may also help to shore up an argumentation in favour of such partnerships. Moreover, as the ECJ has, so far, not had to tackle the problem of same-sex marriages directly, some of the key cases go back to those types of partnerships.

**IV-63.** The starting point for the analysis concerns indeed a partnership, and it immediately reveals the additional difficulties. In *Reed,*[17] the ECJ was confronted with a heterosexual unmarried British couple living in the Netherlands, where one of them was employed. Under Dutch law, an alien having a stable relationship and forming a household with a Dutch national could receive a residence permit. However, when Ms. Reed asked for a similar residence permit on the grounds of her relationship with the English worker, this was denied. The referring court hearing the challenge to this refusal and asked the ECJ three questions corresponding to two possible solutions. On the one hand, the question was asked whether the term 'spouse' in Article 10 of the now defunct Regulation 1612/68[18] could also be used to denote the heterosexual partner in this stable relationship. On the other hand, regardless of that analysis, there may still be a form of unequal treatment on the basis of nationality to the extent that partners of Dutch nationals in such a partnership were entitled to a residence permit,

17. Case 59/85 *Reed* [1986] ECR 1283.
18. Regulation (EEC) No 1612/68 of the Council of 15 October 1968 on freedom of movement for workers within the Community, *Official Journal, English Special Edition 1968 II*, 475.

while partners of other EU nationals were not. Despite the fact pattern relating to a heterosexual partnership, the Court's answer has broader implications.

**IV-64.** First, the ECJ finds that as this Regulation had to apply equally in all Member States there is need for one single definition of the term 'spouse',[19] and it decides that:

> in the absence of any indication of a general social development which would justify a broad construction, and in the absence of any indication to the contrary in the regulation, it must be held that the term 'spouse' in article 10 of the regulation refers to a marital relationship only[20].

This finding is significant for three reasons. First, the Court refuses to equate marriage and other forms of partnerships, significantly upping the burden for further argumentation to the contrary. Second, such further argumentation to the contrary is, however, not entirely precluded as the interpretation is given 'in the absence of any indication of a general social development which would justify a broad construction',[21] which opens the door that the Court may one day have to revise its position. This is particularly justified, as its decision to go for one definition of 'spouse' must mean that if that concept would receive a different meaning over time in the Member States, the interpretation of the Regulation may have to be adjusted to deal with this new social reality. Third, the concept of 'spouse' is linked to 'a marital relationship only',[22] but if we are discussing the possibility of the recognition of same-sex marriages, there arguably is a marital relationship, so that *Reed* does not need to be a bar for recognition.[23]

**IV-65.** Second, the ECJ takes up the second avenue, setting out an approach that will be dominating all further legislative and judicial developments in this field. It accepts that to the extent that the Netherlands recognizes this type of partnerships and is willing to grant a residence permit when one of the partners is Dutch, the Dutch authorities must grant this same 'social advantage' in the sense of Article 7(2) of Regulation 1612/68 on a non-discriminatory basis to the partner of all EU nationals working in the Netherlands.[24] The recognition is thus fully based on the willingness of the host State to give such couples internally certain advantages, and turns that willingness into a broader obligation vis-à-vis all EU workers. The focus is thus on consistency of the treatment of such relationships whether they involve foreign nationals or own nationals. This approach seems useful in the case of these undefined partnerships, whereby the rights may vary greatly between the Member States. It even appears that the couple had more rights as a partnership under the laws of the host State than they had in their own country. However, this route may not be ideal if we

19. Case 59/85 *Reed* [1986] ECR 1283, paras 12-13.
20. Case 59/85 *Reed* [1986] ECR 1283, para. 15.
21. Case 59/85 *Reed* [1986] ECR 1283, para. 15.
22. Case 59/85 *Reed* [1986] ECR 1283, para. 15.
23. Arguably, there the later finding in Joined Cases C-122/99 P and C-125/99 P *D and Sweden v. Council* [2001] ECR I-4319, para. 34 that the 'term marriage means a union between two persons of the opposite sex' is far more damaging. However, as argued above, that case seems already taken over by events, see Case F-122/06 *Roodhuijzen v. Commission* [2007] ECR 0000.
24. Case 59/85 *Reed* [1986] ECR 1283, paras 17-30.

deal with far more formalized relationships, such as registered partnerships or *a fortiori* full-blown marriages. If the host Member States has introduced the concept of same-sex marriage in its own legislation the equal treatment argument seems to require that the host State extends the benefits of such marriage to foreign married same-sex couples. However, in all other cases it will not help for the foreign couple to obtain rights related to marriage in the absence of an equivalent institution in the host State. Nevertheless, to the extent that the host Member State may have an alternative partnership, it is submitted that this Member State should at least extend whatever benefits it grants under that partnership to same-sex couples that are legally married according to the laws of another Member State.

**IV-66.** However, the *Reed* formula has greatly influenced legal developments since. First, one could have thought that the general non-discrimination Directive[25] may have some impact on this issue, as it seeks *inter alia* to combat discrimination on the grounds of sexual orientation, albeit limited to employment and occupation. Yet, the impact of this Directive is quite limited in practice. In *Tadao Maruko*[26] the ECJ did accept that Directive 2000/78 may affect the question whether a same-sex couple should be granted the same benefits as a married couple, despite the fact that recital 22 thereof states that 'This Directive is without prejudice to national laws on marital status and the benefits dependent thereon.' This is quite delicate, as this Directive operates irrespective of the existence of a cross-border element, and thus has the potential for upsetting also purely national arrangements. Nonetheless, the Court's approach is fully respectful of national approaches to such relationships. In line with *Reed*[27] it solely requires that Member States are consistent in the way they treat such partnerships without requiring any particular level of protection as such. The Court holds simply:

> that the combined provisions of Articles 1 and 2 of Directive 2000/78 preclude legislation such as that at issue in the main proceedings under which, after the death of his life partner, the surviving partner does not receive a survivor's benefit equivalent to that granted to a surviving spouse, even though, under *national law*, life partnership *places persons of the same sex in a situation comparable to that of spouses* so far as concerns that survivor's benefit[28].

The Directive accordingly does not say anything about whether Member States must one way or another recognize long-term same-sex relationships and give them similar advantages to married couples. However, to the extent that a Member State does recognize same-sex partnerships and to the extent that it is willing to equate such partnerships in some aspects with marriage, it would be a direct discrimination on the grounds of sexual orientation to deny such partners certain benefits that married couples would receive in a comparable situation. The Court has since confirmed that approach in respect of the German long-term registered partnership in a case where the

25. Council Directive 2000/78/EC of 27 November 2000 establishing a general framework for equal treatment in employment and occupation (2000) OJ L 303/16.
26. Case C-267/06 *Tadao Maruko* [2008] ECR I-1757.
27. Case 59/85 *Reed* [1986] ECR 1283.
28. Case C-267/06 *Tadao Maruko* [2008] ECR I-1757, para. 73 (emphasis added).

benefit at issue was a supplementary pension, which enables the pensioner to support his/her partner.[29]

**IV-67.** The impact of the *Reed* approach is even clearer when compared to the recent legislative evolutions in this field.[30] In Directive 2004/38,[31] which basically replaces Regulation 1612/68 in this respect, with the result that the rights of spouses do not reappear in the recast version of Regulation 492/2011,[32] a small overture was made towards the recognition of stable non-marital relationships but again all depends on the approach taken by the host State. Article 2(b) extends the status of 'family member' beyond 'spouses',[33] to:

> the partner with whom the Union citizen has contracted a registered partnership, on the basis of the legislation of a Member State, if the legislation of the host Member State treats registered partnerships as equivalent to marriage and in accordance with the conditions laid down in the relevant legislation of the host Member State.

A registered partnership concluded in one Member State will only sort effect to the extent that the host Member State is willing to treat it as similar to a marriage. The first notable application of this provision does not bode well. Albeit strictly speaking *in obiter*, the *Verwaltungsgericht* Karlsruhe[34] has indicated that it would be of no avail to treat a same-sex marriage concluded in the Netherlands between a person from Taiwan and a Dutch national working in Germany, which – as will be discussed below[35] – the German court had refused to recognize as such, akin to a German registered partnership for deciding whether the spouse could receive a resident permit for relatives of EU

29. Case C-147/08 *Römer* [2011] ECR I-0000.
30. For an overview, see C. McGlynn, *Families and the European Union: law, politics and pluralism* (Cambridge: Cambridge University Press, 2006), 127-138.
31. Directive 2004/38/EC of the European Parliament and of the Council of 29 April 2004 on the right of citizens of the Union and their family members to move and reside freely within the territory of the Member States amending Regulation (EEC) No 1612/68 and repealing Directives 64/221/EEC, 68/360/EEC, 72/194/EEC, 73/148/EEC, 75/34/EEC, 75/35/EEC, 90/364/EEC, 90/365/EEC and 93/96/EEC (2004) OJ L 158/77.
32. Regulation (EU) No 492/2011 of the European Parliament and of the Council of 5 April 2011 on freedom of movement for workers within the Union (2011) OJ L141/1.
33. Still, and important for our argumentation, the legislator has not defined the term 'spouse', thus keeping open the possibility that partners in same-sex marriages are spouses. However, the legislative drafts demonstrate the great reluctance of the Council and the Commission to consider same-sex spouses, even though the European Parliament had argued differently, see M. Bell, 'Holding Back the Tide? Cross-Border Recognition of Same-Sex Partnerships within the European Union', *European Review of Private Law* (2004): 620-621.
34. VG Karlsruhe, 9 September 2004, 2K 1420/03, *IPRax*, 2006, 284-287. For comments, see A. Röthel, 'Annerkennung gleichgeschlectiger Ehen nach deutschem und europäischem Recht', *IPRax* (2006): 250-253; R. Koolhoven, 'Het Nederlandse opengestelde huwelijk in het Duitse IPR – de eerste rechterlijke uitspraal is daar!', *NIPR* (2005): 138-142. See also J. Meeusen, 'Instrumentalisation of Private International Law in the European Union: Towards a European Conflicts Revolution ?', *European Journal of Migration and Law* (2007): 297-298; D. Coester-Waltjen, 'Annerkennung im Internationalen Personen- Familien- und Erbrecht und das Europäische Kollisionsrecht', *IPrax* (2006): 395-396.
35. See, *infra*, at IV–71

workers, as under German law the rights of such a *Lebenspartnerschaft* are not to be equated fully with marriage.

**IV-68.** However, prima facie, at least when it comes to the right of residence – but thus not for other advantages – there may be a second avenue in Article 3(2) of Directive 2004/38. That provision states that:

> Without prejudice to any right to free movement and residence the persons concerned may have in their own right, the host Member State shall, in accordance with its national legislation, facilitate entry and residence for the following persons: [...](b) the partner with whom the Union citizen has a durable relationship, duly attested.

Yet, a debate has erupted over the scope of this provision. The same *Verwaltungsgericht* for instance seems of the opinion that the right of such persons again fully depends on the legislation of the host State.[36] Also McGlynn seems to think that this provision merely gives a 'legislative basis for *Netherlands v. Reed*',[37] but considers that the:

> decision regarding entry and residence remains at the discretion of Member States, albeit that the exercise of that discretion is to be justified after 'extensive examination' and the Directive [...] is to be implemented without discrimination on a wide variety of grounds, including sexual orientation[38].

Also Bell accepts that this provision 'is obviously not a *right* to move to another state, but a right to have your request for entry and residence seriously considered'[39] and puts his hopes on the duty to implement the Directive in a non-discriminatory manner as required by recital 31 of the Directive. This restrictive approach seems, moreover, to a certain extent supported by recital 6 which states that:

> [i]n order to maintain the unity of the family in a broader sense and without prejudice to the prohibition of discrimination on grounds of nationality, the situation of those persons who are not included in the definition of family members under this Directive, and who therefore do not enjoy an automatic right of entry and residence in the host Member State, *should be examined by the host Member State on the basis of its own national legislation*, in order to decide whether entry and residence could be granted to such persons, taking into consideration their relationship with the Union citizen or any other circumstances, such as their financial or physical dependence on the Union citizen.

---

36. VG Karlsruhe, 9 September 2004, 2K 1420/03, *IPRax* (2006): 284-287. On this point, see D. Coester-Waltjen, 'Annerkennung im Internationalen Personen- Familien- und Erbrecht und das Europäische Kollisionsrecht', *IPrax* (2006): 395-396.
37. C. McGlynn, *Families and the European Union: law, politics and pluralism* (Cambridge: Cambridge University Press, 2006), 130.
38. *Ibid.*, 130. The reference to the 'extensive examination' comes from the final sentence of Article 3(2) of Directive 2004/38 which reads: 'The host Member State shall undertake an extensive examination of the personal circumstances and shall justify any denial of entry or residence to these people'.
39. M. Bell, 'Holding Back the Tide? Cross-Border Recognition of Same-Sex Partnerships within the European Union', *European Review of Private Law* (2004): 625.

However, if the rights of entry and residence under Article 3(2)(b) may become subject to the same restrictions as imposed by the Member States are at issue in Article 2(b) then the added value of the former provision becomes highly doubtful. Therefore, in line with arguments put forward in the literature,[40] I argue that all partners in a duly attested durable relationship, so *a fortiori* persons in a registered partnership or same-sex marriage, have a right of entry and residence under Article 3(2)(b), though they will not be able to rely on Directive 2004/38 for other benefits.[41] The reference to national law should then be read in the sense that every Member State shall grant the right of residence, however, the conditions it attaches to that right of residence may vary – for instance in respect of administrative formalities and duration – and the Member States may apply their own procedural and substantive requirements for carrying out the 'extensive examination of the personal circumstances' in line with the margins left to the Member States in Chapter VI of the Directive in respect of public health, public security and public policy.[42] Such outcome seems, moreover, far more respective of the protection of the right to family life[43] – and the Court has already recognized in *Eyüp*[44] that also in the absence of marriage people may live together as a family[45] – and the free movement of persons as guaranteed by the Treaty, which the Directive as an instrument of secondary law may not restrict.

40. D. Coester-Waltjen, 'Annerkennung im Internationalen Personen- Familien- und Erbrecht und das Europäische Kollisionsrecht', *IPrax* (2006): 395-396; E. Jayme, 'Das internationale Privatrecht im System des Gemeinschaftsrechts – Tagung in Macerata', *IPRax* (2006): 68.
41. However, they may then next perhaps still be entitled to certain benefits on the basis of Council Directive 2000/78/EC of 27 November 2000 establishing a general framework for equal treatment in employment and occupation (2000) OJ L 303/16. Yet, the effect thereof should not be overstated. Cases such as Case C-267/06 *Tadao Maruko* [2008] ECR I-1757 and Case C-147/08 *Römer* [2011] ECR I-0000 indicate that the Court's case law until now presupposes the existence of some form of fleshed-out same-sex partnership next to marriage. However, Member States that do not have this, are left largely unaffected. But it is precisely in respect of those Member States that one may need to invoke Article 3(2)(b) of Directive 2004/38/EC rather than Article 2(b), so that the fact that one may eventually receive a residence permit on the ground of Article 3(2)(b) should not necessarily be seen as extending any rights in the sense of Directive 2000/78/EC.
42. On these conditions, see, *supra*, at II-30 et seq.
43. On the importance of the right to family life in the context of the free movement of persons, see Case C-60/00 *Carpenter* [2002] ECR I-6279; Case C-127/08 *Metock* [2008] ECR I-6241. In this respect I would share the 'surprise' of Waaldijk if the Court would refuse to recognize same-sex partners – *a fortiori* if they are married in accordance with the laws of one of its Member States – as family members worthy of protection of their family life, see K. Waaldijk, 'Free Movement of Same-Sex Partners', *Maastricht Journal of European and Comparative Law* (1996): 280. See also A. Clapham, & J.H.H. Weiler, 'Lesbians and Gay Men in the European Community legal Order', in *Homosexuality: A European Community Issue – Essays on Lesbian and Gay Rights in European Law and Policy*, ed. K. Waaldijk & A. Clapham (Dordrecht: Martinus Nijhoff/Kluwer, 1993), 43-46. McGlynn points nevertheless out that the ECtHR still has to find that homosexual relationships are covered by the right to family life, see C. McGlynn, *Families and the European Union: law, politics and pluralism* (Cambridge: Cambridge University Press, 2006), 126.
44. Case C-65/98 *Eyüp* [2000] ECR I-4747.
45. See in this respect C. McGlynn, *Families and the European Union: law, politics and pluralism* (Cambridge: Cambridge University Press, 2006), 122-126.

**IV-69.** Nevertheless, the same deference to national law that lies at the heart of *Reed*[46] also permeates the treatment of relationships between third-country nationals, though the level of protection is even less. Article 4(3) of the Family Reunification Directive[47] only states that Member States 'may' authorize the entry and residence of the unmarried partner 'being a third country national, with whom the sponsor is in a duly attested stable long-term relationship, or of a third country national who is bound to the sponsor by a registered partnership' and they may decide 'that registered partners are to be treated equally as spouses with respect to family reunification'. As McGlynn notes, this means that even the reciprocity requirement underlying *Reed* has been abandoned in this context.[48] Remarkably, the definitions used in the context of asylum proceedings are somewhat broader. In Council Directive 2003/9,[49] the term 'family members' also includes an 'unmarried partner in a stable relationship, where the legislation or practice of the Member State concerned treats unmarried couples in a way comparable to married couples under its law relating to aliens' and the same definition reoccurs in other asylum legislation.[50]

**IV-70.** The foregoing overview of the legislative situation after *Reed*[51] serves a double purpose. First, it reveals the continued existence of some reluctance of the EU legislator to deal with alternative intimate relationships. *A fortiori* there is definitely no unambiguous embrace of same-sex relationships or same-sex marriages, although there is also no clear rebuke as is the case with for instance polygamy.[52] Also there is no legislation which somehow alters the definition of the term 'spouse'. It is clear that – given the limited alternative arrangements for registered partnerships that are created next to the regime for spouses – the term 'spouse' still does not refer to an unmarried partner. However, could it refer to a same-sex partner in a same-sex marriage? This brings us to my second point. The classic answer, under reference to *D and Sweden v. Council* would be that the 'term marriage means a union between two persons of the

46. Case 59/85 *Reed* [1986] ECR 1283.
47. Council Directive 2003/86/EC of 22 September 2003 on the right to family reunification (2003) OJ L 251/12.
48. C. McGlynn, *Families and the European Union: law, politics and pluralism* (Cambridge: Cambridge University Press, 2006), 133-134.
49. Article 2(d) of Council Directive 2003/9/EC of 27 January 2003 laying down minimum standards for the reception of asylum seekers ('Dublin II') (2003) OJ L 31/18.
50. See Article 15(1)(a) of Council Directive 2001/55/EC of 20 July 2001 on minimum standards for giving temporary protection in the event of a mass influx of displaced persons and on measures promoting a balance of efforts between Member States in receiving such persons and bearing the consequences thereof (2001) OJ L 212/12; Article 2(i) of Council Regulation (EC) No 343/2003 of 18 February 2003 establishing the criteria and mechanisms for determining the Member State responsible for examining an asylum application lodged in one of the Member States by a third-country national (2003) OJ L 50/1.
51. Case 59/85 *Reed* [1986] ECR 1283.
52. Article 4(4) of Council Directive 2003/86/EC of 22 September 2003 on the right to family reunification (2003) OJ L 251/12 for instance prohibits Member States from authorizing the family reunification of a further spouse if the sponsor already has a spouse living with him in the territory of a Member State. Critical of this outright prohibition, is C. McGlynn, *Families and the European Union: law, politics and pluralism* (Cambridge: Cambridge University Press, 2006), 135-136.

opposite sex'.[53] However both the outcome in *Reed*[54] and the outcome in *D and Sweden v. Council*[55] are conditioned on the absence of further developments in national law and EU law. The fact that since that judgment at least three Member States have introduced full-blown same-sex marriages, and that many others have registered partnerships that they are willing to treat as similar to marriage seem[56] to indicate that the 'general social development' goes in the direction of a broader understanding for modern forms of intimate relationships, which is inevitable if the law wants to keep in touch with social realities.[57] Moreover, whereas the development of EU legislation in this respect may be hesitant, the evolution is nonetheless apparent. Accordingly, maybe the conditions for a bolder approach may be about to be fulfilled. The simple solution, therefore, would be for the Court to accept that henceforth the term 'spouse' may encompass a partner in a same-sex marriage, even though the legislative history

53. Joined Cases C-122/99 P and C-125/99 P *D and Sweden v. Council* [2001] ECR I-4319, para. 34.
54. Case 59/85 *Reed* [1986] ECR 1283.
55. Joined Cases C-122/99 P and C-125/99 P *D and Sweden v. Council* [2001] ECR I-4319.
56. For case studies and overviews, see A. Weyembergh & S. Carstocea (eds), *The gays' and lesbians' rights in an enlarged European Union* (Brussels: Editions de l'Université de Bruxelles, 2006). On this 'trend', see also M. Bell, 'Holding Back the Tide? Cross-Border Recognition of Same-Sex Partnerships within the European Union', *European Review of Private Law* (2004): 631.
57. For an excellent account of the changing sociological patterns, and its consequences for the law, see C. McGlynn, *Families and the European Union: law, politics and pluralism* (Cambridge: Cambridge University Press, 2006), 23-41. The ECJ has an important role in ensuring that the law indeed is in sync with social reality, see in this respect the Opinion of AG Tesauro in Case C-13/94 *P* [1996] ECR I-2143 who describes the situation in respect of transsexuality as follows in para. 8: 'What I am concerned to emphasize is that the phenomenon of transsexuality, even though it is not of great significance in statistical terms, constitutes a reality today which has been discussed in various bodies, not only scientific but also legal, in particular from the point of view of fundamental personal rights. Consequently, *the law is faced with that reality – and is destined to come up against it to an increasing degree*. This is inevitable. In society as it is today, in which customs and morals are changing rapidly, citizens are guaranteed ever wider and deeper protection of their freedoms and social and legal studies are increasingly taking on present-day – and, for that very reason, real – values, on the principle that it is effective to do so, it would be unjustifiable to reject out of hand the problem of transsexuality – which certainly can still be assessed quite independently in moral terms – or simply to condemn it and consider it contrary to the law. *To my mind, the law cannot cut itself off from society as it actually is, and must not fail to adjust to it as quickly as possible. Otherwise it risks imposing outdated views and taking on a static role. In so far as the law seeks to regulate relations in society, it must on the contrary keep up with social change, and must therefore be capable of regulating new situations brought to light by social change and advances in science*' (emphasis added). Accordingly, at para. 24, he calls upon the Court to take a 'decision which is bold but fair and legally correct, inasmuch it is undeniably based on and consonant with the great value of equality'. The Court complied and decided that 'In view of the objective pursued by Council Directive 76/207/EEC of 9 February 1976 on the implementation of the principle of equal treatment for men and women as regards access to employment, vocational training and promotion, and working conditions, Article 5(1) of the directive precludes dismissal of a transsexual for a reason related to a gender reassignment'. For a further assessment of the legitimacy for the Court to take such a step, see N. Nic Suibhne, 'Free movement of persons and the wholly internal rule: time to move on?', *Common Market Law Review* (2002): 767-769 who contrasts Case C-13/94 *P* [1996] ECR I-2143 with Joined Cases C-122/99 P and C-125/99 P *D and Sweden v. Council* [2001] ECR I-4319 and Case C-249/96 *Grant* [1998] ECR I-621.

would not favour such reading.[58] It would require for the Court to overturn *Reed* and *D and Sweden v. Council* on this point, though to the extent that the Court would be dealing with an institution various Member States actually call 'marriage' that step may not be insurmountable. However, I submit that, even in the absence of such an interpretation, Member States, while not under an obligation whatsoever to create same-sex marriages in their internal legal order, may no longer refuse the recognition of same-sex marriages whenever that would be an obstacle to the free movement of persons.

**IV-71.** First, Directive 2004/38/EC extends certain rights to persons beyond the worker, self-employed person, or EU citizen who have made use of their own right to move to and reside in another Member State. Actually, the creation of EU citizenship may have – at least as far as residence is concerned – taken away some of the pressure to the extent that the partner may often also be an EU national with an autonomous right of residence, though the judgment of the *Verwaltungsgericht*[59] cited above shows that this will not always be the case. Accordingly, if the net result is that thus two persons of the same-sex may de facto live together in another Member State as if they were married as a matter of EU law, there may often not be much to gain for a Member State from withholding legal recognition of that relationship. However, Article 2(b) of the Directive focuses entirely on the existence and the extent of legislation of the host Member State which treats registered partnerships as equivalent to marriage and as argued above the effect of Article 3(2)(b) is uncertain. However, whereas the Directive may extend certain rights and clarify the extent of the public policy exceptions to the free movement of persons, it cannot restrict those rights, which flow directly from the Treaty, per se. Accordingly, to the extent that other restrictions to the free movement of persons, not provided for in the Directive, arise then those need to be treated directly on the basis of the Treaty. Therefore, if partners in a same-sex marriage are not covered – as the *Verwaltungsgericht* Karlsruhe[60] seems to imply – by Directive 2004/38/EC, then it still needs to be assessed whether their situation is nonetheless covered by the Treaties directly. I submit in that respect that the judgments in *Carpenter*[61], *Jia*[62] and *Metock*[63] demonstrate that the Court recognizes that the forced separation from one's family members may constitute a major obstacle to the free movement of persons. The Court in these cases, moreover, demonstrates a strong desire to protect family life, even when the likely impact on the free movement of persons is doubtful.[64] Admittedly, two of those cases concerned heterosexual marriages and one concerned ascendants, but there does not seem to be a valid reason why an intimate relationship that one of the

58. See in respect M. Bell, 'Holding Back the Tide? Cross-Border Recognition of Same-Sex Partnerships within the European Union', *European Review of Private Law* (2004): 620-621.
59. VG Karlsruhe, 9 September 2004, 2K 1420/03, *IPRax* (2006): 284-287.
60. VG Karlsruhe, 9 September 2004, 2K 1420/03, *IPRax* (2006): 284-287.
61. Case C-60/00 *Carpenter* [2002] ECR I-6279.
62. Case C-1/05 *Jia* [2007] ECR I-1.
63. Case C-127/08 *Metock* [2008] ECR I-6241.
64. See for instance the critical assessment in L. Jadoul & F. Vanneste, 'Case C-60/00. Mary Carpenter v. Secretary of State for the Home Department (E.C.J. July 11, 2002)', *Columbia Journal of European Law* (2003): 447-455.

Member States is willing to describe as 'marriage' should in any manner be less worthy of protection, solely because the partners are of the same-sex. Furthermore, even beyond the right to residence or the right to live together with a life companion there may be obstacles to the free movement flowing from the non-recognition of a same-sex marriage, as the reason why spouses are to a certain extent given particular benefits in the host State is precisely because also the denial of such advantages may discourage people from moving to another Member State.

**IV-72.** Moreover, it cannot be argued that the concept of marriage in EU law cannot encompass same-sex marriages. First, the flip side of the fact that Article 9 of the Charter of Fundamental Rights of the EU links the right to marry to 'the national laws governing the exercise of these rights', is that the Charter explicitly envisages that Member States may have divergent views as to what constitutes marriage. If all Member States unequivocally agreed that the 'term marriage means a union between two persons of the opposite sex'[65] there would have been no need to make a reference to national law. Accordingly, it cannot be that in the context of the free movement of persons a concept of marriage would be used that excludes a priori the recognition of same-sex marriages. I do not consider it inevitable that the Charter of Fundamental Rights, with all its mechanisms for ensuring a high and dynamic level of human rights protection, would somehow have frozen the meaning of the concept of marriage, or any other fundamental right, and 'entrench the status quo'.[66] Second, it can also not be the case that the EU concept of marriage would be linked to procreation, as the ECJ has already accepted that the female to male transsexual partner should be entitled to a survivors' pension as the legal spouse of the deceased wife.[67] Whereas formally such a relationship may look as a heterosexual relationship in that there legally is one man (albeit formerly a woman) and one woman, this hardly meets the picture of the traditional heterosexual marriage.

**IV-73.** The classic response in the absence of harmonization should moreover be mutual recognition. However, as argued above, mutual recognition only plays to the extent that the fundamental policy consideration has been seriously taken into account by the other Member State.[68] Moreover, as the EU has no competence in respect of family law in general and marriage in particular, it could be argued[69] that whereas this

65. Joined Cases C-122/99 P and C-125/99 P *D and Sweden v. Council* [2001] ECR I-4319, para. 34.
66. On this fear, see C. McGlynn, *Families and the European Union: law, politics and pluralism* (Cambridge: Cambridge University Press, 2006), 93, who refers in this respect indeed to Joined Cases C-122/99 P and C-125/99 P *D and Sweden v. Council* [2001] ECR I-4319 and the broader concern of Weiler about a Charter which 'sticks to the rusty and trusty formulae of yesteryear, around which constitutional consensus already exists and thus avoids innovation', see J. Weiler, 'Editorial: Does the European Union Truly Need a Charter of Rights?', *European Law Journal* (2000): 96.
67. Case C-117/01 *K.B.* [2004] ECR I-541. For more on that case, see I. Canor, 'Case C-117/01, *K.B. v. National Health Service Pensions Agency, Secretary for Health*, judgment of the full court of 7 January 2004', *Common Market Law Review* (2004): 1113-1125.
68. See, *supra*, at IV-48.
69. See in this sense, albeit in the context of the protection of public health, the Opinion of AG Bot in Joined Cases C-171/07 and C-172/07 *Apothekerkammer des Saarlandes* [2009] ECR I-4171, para. 33.

cannot preclude the requirement that the Member States exercise their competences in accordance with EU law, they may still decide on their own concept of marriage and their own level of protection of 'family life'. Accordingly, the question arises whether it is nonetheless possible for a Member State to justify its refusal to recognize a same-sex marriage that was validly concluded in another Member State. For the reasons set out above,[70] the way these fundamental considerations - which are likely to relate to the Member State's specific concept of the family - can be brought to the fore in the context of the free movement of persons is through the public policy exception, which the ECJ has also recognized in this respect in the context of the recognition of another aspect of the status of the person - the name - in a case relating to European citizenship.[71] Whereas this public policy exception is legally distinct from the public policy exceptions of the Member States' private international law, it is clear that it will often de facto coincide with it for all practical purposes, at least to the extent that the *ordre public international* of a particular Member State objects to same-sex marriages, which seems an issue that is often unsettled.[72]

**IV-74.** Above, I have put forward a cumulative four-prong test for assessing the admissibility of sensitive national constitutional values.[73] The Court needs, in my opinion, to assess first, the compatibility of the value put forward by the Member State with the EU legal order; second, the potential interference with other fundamental rights protected by the EU legal order; third, the consistency with which the national legal order protects this right and; fourth, a proportionality test. I submit that justifications for national measures denying certain rights to same-sex spouses who have made use of their free movement rights may run afoul of any of these prongs.

**IV-75.** First, the compatibility of the values put forward by the Member State with the EU legal order need not be problematic, though much depend on what argumentation the Member State puts forward. Positive defences, based on respect for family life and the sanctity of marriage, are admittedly not wholly incompatible with the EU legal order, if only because Article 9 of the Charter of Fundamental Rights of the EU explicitly refers back to the national legal orders. However, argumentation that would openly or impliedly be based on homophobia cannot be reconciled with the principle of non-discrimination on grounds of sexual orientation as laid down in Article 21 of the Charter. The judgment of the European Court of Human Rights in *Karner v. Austria*[74]

---

70. See, *supra*, at II-7 et seq.
71. Case C-353/06 *Grunkin and Paul* [2008] ECR I-7639, para. 38
72. On this issue, see M. Bell, 'Holding Back the Tide? Cross-Border Recognition of Same-Sex Partnerships within the European Union', *European Review of Private Law* (2004): 627. See also the opinion of the EU Network of Independent Experts on Fundamental Rights, 'Avis sur la possibilité de la par chaque Etat membre, du mariage homosexuel ouvert aux Pay-Bas et en Belgique et le rôle de l'exception d'*ordre public* international du droit international privé de chaque Etat membre', available at <http://ec.europa.eu/justice/fundamental-rights/files/cfr_cdf_avis2_2003_fr.pdf> (23 May 2012) from which it appears that the opinions of the Member State experts vary widely on the matter of the *ordre public international* of their respective states.
73. See, *supra*, at I-71 et seq.
74. ECtHR, 27 July 2003, *Karner v. Austria*.

serves to remind us that behind the protection of the 'traditional family unit' may all too easily lurk a non-justifiable discrimination of homosexuals.[75]

**IV-76.** Second, whenever Member States are putting strong emphasis on particular values, the Court must ensure – as it has, for instance, done spontaneously in *Promusicae*[76] – that other fundamental values are not be trampled upon. The non-recognition of same-sex marriages seems problematic for three reasons. First, Advocate General Jacobs has stressed in his Opinion in *Standesamt Stadt Niebüll* that 'a person's name is a fundamental part of his or her identity and private life, the protection of which is widely recognised in national constitutions and international instruments'.[77] I cannot see why the fact of being married would be any less fundamental for a person's identity and private life. Second, the protection of family life need not necessarily be limited to the traditional heterosexual couple with children. As argued above,[78] precisely because the Charter refers to the laws of the Member States in respect of marriage and family life, the EU legal order actually envisages the possibility of non-traditional marriages and alternative forms of family life. If the enthusiasm of the Court in protecting family life in cases like *Metock*[79] and *Carpenter*[80] extends to less traditional forms of family life, where the Court has already set its first steps in cases such as *K.B.*[81] and *Eyüp*[82] but is still somewhat hesitant, then a Member State's blunt non-recognition of same-sex marriages with direct consequences on the ability of the partners to live together as a family seems difficult to reconcile with the EU legal order. Third, whereas certain more traditional views on the family may explain, and even justify, why a Member State does not introduce a same-sex marriage and may even not consider other forms of registered partnerships, in cases of non-recognition of a foreign marriage in the context of the free movement of persons, there is a further problem. Upon balance, in case of non-recognition a Member State is taking away something, the marital status, which another Member State has granted – and was entitled to grant in light of Article 9 of the Charter of Fundamental Rights of the EU, which both need to respect while acting within the scope of EU law – on the basis of the sex and/or sexual orientation[83] of the persons concerned. This seems difficult to reconcile with the

75. See in this respect, and its link with Article 21 of the Charter of Fundamental rights of the Union, M. Bell, 'Holding Back the Tide? Cross-Border Recognition of Same-Sex Partnerships within the European Union', *European Review of Private Law* (2004): 622.
76. Case C-275/06 *Promusicae* [2008] ECR I-271.
77. Opinion of AG Jacobs in Case C-96/04 *Standesamt Stadt Niebüll* [2006] ECR I-3561, para. 55.
78. See, *supra*, at IV-72.
79. Case C-127/08 *Metock* [2008] ECR I-6241.
80. Case C-60/00 *Carpenter* [2002] ECR I-6279.
81. Case C-117/01 *K.B.* [2004] ECR I-541.
82. Case C-65/98 *Eyüp* [2000] ECR I-4747.
83. I deliberately use both in light of the difficulties that arise from the Court's judgment in Case C-249/96 *Grant* [1998] ECR I-621. Whereas the ECJ seems correct to hold that discrimination on the grounds of sexual orientation falls outside the scope of Article 157 TFEU which focuses on discrimination on ground of sex, the problem is that in some cases the distinction is difficult to make: if the recognition of the same-sex marriage is refused on the grounds that both partners have the same sex, which seems self-evident in light of their likely sexual orientation, the distinction between the two is subtle. For a critical appraisal of the Court's judgment in this respect, see J. McInnes, 'Case C-294/96, *Lisa Jacqueline Grant v. South West Trains Ltd,*

fundamental values reflected in Article 21 of the Charter of Fundamental Rights. In this respect I am somewhat inspired by *Romer v. Evans*[84] of the US Supreme Court, a case which will undoubtedly receive wide attention again in light of the adoption of Proposition 8 abolishing same-sex marriages briefly allowed by the California Supreme Court, in that in a sense 'a special disability' is imposed on the same-sex couple precisely because of the same-sex nature of their relationship: unlike the own nationals of the Member State[85] who could never marry in the first place, the validly acquired marital status from the same-sex couple is taken away and with it potentially also a whole series of social advantages that depend on that status.

**IV-77.** Third, the consistency test should assess how strongly the Member State actually feels about the subject. This may turn out to be a rather tricky question, depending on whether one uses a formal or functional test. In principle I would advocate a functional test, which assesses to what extent it is genuinely problematic for a Member State to grant the benefit invoked by the same-sex couple. After all, the question of whether a Member State must recognize a same-sex marriage arises only insofar as the denial of a particular benefit constitutes an obstacle to the free movement, which requires a case-by-case analysis. It may well be that a Member State has not adopted the concept of same-sex marriage, but is otherwise quite liberal in the way it treats same-sex partnerships. In those circumstances, a Member State should not be allowed to hide behind its non-adoption of same-sex marriages if that would result in treatment that is less than the treatment it would give as a matter of national law to other same-sex partnerships – this is almost an application of *Reed.*[86] The problem with this approach is evidenced, however, by the judgment of the *Verwaltungsgericht*

---

Judgment of the Full Court of 17 February 1998, [1998] ECR I-636', *Common Market Law Review* (1999): 1043-1058; see further C. McGlynn, *Families and the European Union: law, politics and pluralism* (Cambridge: Cambridge University Press, 2006), 139-142 and the very critical literature cited therein. For the underlying debate, see A. Koppelman, 'Why Discrimination Against Lesbians and Gay Men is Sex Discrimination', *New York University Law Review* (1994): 197-287. For my argumentation the point is largely moot, however, as both grounds of discrimination are prohibited by Article 21 of the Charter of Fundamental Rights of the Union.

84. *Romer v. Evans*, 517 U.S. 620, 116 S.Ct. 1620, 134 L.Ed.2d 855 (1996). The serendipity that also the strongest defence of equal treatment of same-sex partnerships in the EU so far was made in a similarly named case (Case C-147/08 *Römer* [2011] ECR I-0000), is too striking to leave unnoticed.
85. However, this raises the interesting question whether the outcome of the review should be different if one of the partners – or even both – has the nationality of the host State, most notably in a situation akin to Case C-370/90 *Singh* [1992] ECR I-4265 where a person who married while living in another Member State returns home. In my view the answer is no: the importance of stability of the civil status is such that the free movement of persons would be too much hampered if Member States could sequentially second-guess the validity of decisions as to that status validly taken in another Member State. Just like Germany could not second-guess the name of Leonard Mattias Grunkin-Paul upon his return to Germany, Member States should also not be allowed to call into question other decisions as to the civil status of the person. After the explicit overruling of Case C-109/01 *Akrich* [2003] ECR I-9607 by Case C-127/08 *Metock* [2008] ECR I-6241, I am inclined to make even no distinction in respect of a couple where both hold the nationality in the absence of proof of fraudulent circumvention of the national prohibition on same-sex marriages.
86. Case 59/85 *Reed* [1986] ECR 1283.

Karlsruhe.[87] Formally, Germany has introduced a *Lebenspartnerschaft* that extends an important number of rights of married couples to the partners of such a registered partnership, which stands open for both homosexual and heterosexual couples but is for the former category the sole option. However, because of the so-called Abstandsgebot there is a constitutional restriction on how far such a *Lebenspartnerschaft* may be assimilated with marriage.[88] The functional equivalence of marriage and *Lebenspartnerschaft* may thus be deceptive as to the underlying constitutional concerns that have precisely forced the legislator to create two distinct regimes, which it indeed must keep sufficiently apart.[89] The distinction weighs in any event so much that the *Verwaltungsgericht* Karlsruhe[90] is of the opinion that treating the Dutch same-sex marriage as akin to a *Lebenspartnerschaft* is of no avail when it comes to deciding on the right of residence of the same-sex spouse.

**IV-78.** Fourth, the proportionality test may give mixed results as well. In line with *Schindler*[91] the Member States are entitled to determine the level of protection of family life they want to achieve. However, this needs to be nuanced. First, the level of protection is not entirely set by the Member State, but should, in light of the other prongs of our test be the level set by the Member State *to the extent that the Court has not found the need to balance it with competing fundamental values*. Second, in light of the emancipating force of the free movement of persons extensively argued above,[92] even then it is still necessary to balance the refusal to recognize the marriage with the overall discouraging effect on the free movement of (homosexual) persons.[93] Accordingly, it may be very difficult to justify the denial of the right of residence to the same-sex spouse of a Union worker,[94] as the interference with the right to family life and its discouraging effect may be so much as to undermine the proportionality of any other national consideration, hence cases like *Carpenter*[95]. The answer may, however,

87. VG Karlsruhe, 9 September 2004, 2K 1420/03, *IPRax*, 2006, 284-287.
88. For more, see R. Koolhoven, 'Het Nederlandse opengestelde huwelijk in het Duitse IPR – de eerste rechterlijke uitspraal is daar!', *NIPR* (2005): 139-140.
89. See in this respect the judgment of the German Constitutional Court which seeks to keep the two as far distinct as possible, Bundesverfassungsgericht, 17 July 2002, *Neue Juristische Wochenzeitschrift* (2002): 2543.
90. VG Karlsruhe, 9 September 2004, 2K 1420/03, *IPRax* (2006): 284-287.
91. Case C-275/92 *Schindler* [1994] ECR I-1039.
92. See, *supra*, at III-60 and III-61.
93. One could argue that the Treaty is concerned with the free movement of persons, and the potential discriminations on ground of nationality and not with the free movement of homosexual persons and potential discriminations on ground of sexual orientation. However, it is clear that if an important group of persons may be discouraged from making use of their free movement rights because of certain other discriminatory policies that result in the non-recognition of foreign acts – which is a matter of discrimination on the grounds of nationality/origin – the issue becomes also one of free movement of persons.
94. To the extent that this right of residence would – contrary to what I have argued, *supra*, at IV-68 – not already flow from Article 3(2)(b) of Directive 2004/38/EC of the European Parliament and of the Council of 29 April 2004 on the right of citizens of the Union and their family members to move and reside freely within the territory of the Member States amending Regulation (EEC) No 1612/68 and repealing Directives 64/221/EEC, 68/360/EEC, 72/194/EEC, 73/148/EEC, 75/34/EEC, 75/35/EEC, 90/364/EEC, 90/365/EEC and 93/96/EEC (2004) OJ L 158/77.
95. Case C-60/00 *Carpenter* [2002] ECR I-6279.

be different in respect of some minor social advantages, such as a preference for young married couples in obtaining social housing or other benefits.[96]

**IV-79.** Upon balance, I submit that Member States should in principle not be allowed to refuse to recognize same-sex marriages validly concluded in another Member State. This may strike as far-reaching, but it remains to be seen how upsetting this is for Member States. On the one hand, there is a further perspective beyond the narrow issue of same-sex marriages. First, as *Grunkin and Paul*[97] demonstrates, the same problems extend to all issues relating to the civil status of the person. If we genuinely want to encourage free movement - if only for the emancipating reasons set out above - then we will have to ensure that the stability of the civil status of persons in free movement is sufficiently protected, even though I admit that precisely in respect of the name the ECJ has already made some inroads on public policy grounds.[98] Nevertheless, taking the civil status seriously may be done through the type of mutual recognition demonstrated above, but may also require in the long run better coordination - if not harmonization - of the rules of conflict[99] and perhaps even the family law of the Member States.[100] The drafters of the European Constitution have understood this need and have at least proposed a legal basis for 'measures concerning family law with cross-border implications' in Article III-269(3), which has been taken over - albeit with additional institutional guarantees - in the post-Lisbon codification in Article 81(3)

96. In this respect it may be noted that the Court in Joined Cases C-122/99 P and C-125/99 P *D and Sweden v. Council* [2001] ECR I-4319, paras 59-60 clearly draws a distinction between material benefits and the impact on private life and family life: 'refusal by the Community administration to grant a household allowance to one of its officials does not affect the situation of the official in question as regards his civil status and, since it only concerns the relationship between the official and his employer, does not of itself give rise to the transmission of any personal information to persons outside the Community administration. The contested decision is not therefore, on any view, capable of constituting interference in private and family life within the meaning of Article 8 of the European Convention for the Protection of Human Rights and Fundamental Freedoms.'
97. Case C-353/06 *Grunkin and Paul* [2008] ECR I-7639.
98. Case C-391/09 *Runevič-Vardyn* [2011] ECR I-0000; Case C-208/09 *Sayn-Wittgenstein* [2010] ECR I-0000.
99. See on this J. Meeusen, 'Instrumentalisation of Private International Law in the European Union: Towards a European Conflicts Revolution ?', *European Journal of Migration and Law* (2007): 287-305. For examples of solutions that States have already implemented through international agreements, see M. Bell, 'Holding Back the Tide? Cross-Border Recognition of Same-Sex Partnerships within the European Union', *European Review of Private Law* (2004): 628.
100. See in this respect S. Sánchez Lorenzo, 'What Do We Mean when We Say 'Folklore'? Cultural and Axiological Diversities as a Limit for a European Private Law', *European Review of Private Law* (2006): 201-205, who argues in respect of same-sex marriages at 204: 'This simple diagnosis reflects a difficult paradox: despite appearances, different national understandings on family law show a Europe lacking in common principles and values, multicultural and full of national idiosyncrasies. This clearly makes the unification of European law more difficult. Unification is, however, the only way in order to solve the problems arising from this diversity in international relationships. We need a consistent and common understanding of 'marriage' and 'spouse'. Here is the paradox'. On the difficulties ahead in this respect, see also M. Antokolskaia, 'The Harmonisation of Family Law: Old and New Dilemmas', *European Review of Private Law* (2003): 28-49.

TFEU.[101] Second, enhanced mutual recognition or more accommodating legislation – especially if also a solution is gradually adopted in respect of non-marital partnerships – does not only mean that a Member State must put up with new forms of intimate relationships it is not yet familiar with, but it also ensures that those relationships it does encourage are also protected abroad. For instance a deeply Roman-Catholic Member State may have some difficulties in accepting same-sex couples, but could perhaps find comfort in the fact that other forms of partnership, for instance, those accommodating the specific needs of the clergy, which it may promote, might also be recognized in turn abroad. On the other hand, the mutual recognition is primarily a functional recognition, not dissimilar to the recognition which the ECJ also requires of Member States in the context of company law. For instance, as a result of *Überseering*[102] the applicant company, which was duly incorporated in the Netherlands but had its real seat in Germany as far as German law was concerned after the shares had come into the hands of two Germans, does not become a fully fledged German company nor should it be treated as such – however, the German authorities must accept that it is still a fully fledged Dutch company whose legal personality should not be called into question and who should be allowed to carry out all possible legal transactions, unless there is a specific overriding public policy concern to the contrary. Similarly, in *Cartesio,*[103] the ECJ has accepted that the Member State of incorporation may even have to accept – albeit only for a transitional period – that a company which has lost all its connecting factors with that Member State still continues to exist if it is in the process of incorporating abroad. In both cases the very existence of the companies at issue may otherwise be in doubt as to national law. Yet, in order to allow the smooth operation of the internal market the Member States concerned must at least allow these companies to function, without, however, having to otherwise give up on its internal legislation. If such sacrifices can be made to ensure the free movement of companies, there can hardly be a reason to be less demanding when it comes to natural persons.[104]

## §14.03 CONCLUSION

**IV-80.** If the EU *ordre public* is truly distinct from the *ordre public* of its Member States, it is sheer inevitable that tensions between the two legal orders will arise. However, upon balance these tensions can be surprisingly well contained through a subtle interplay of techniques that help to assert the primacy of EU law and other techniques that work to ensure to that the concerns of the Member States are sufficiently taken into account. 'Unity in diversity' is not simple to attain, but it is not entirely out of reach, provided the Member States and the EU institutions – most notably the Court, but also

101. See on this also M. Bell, 'Holding Back the Tide? Cross-Border Recognition of Same-Sex Partnerships within the European Union', *European Review of Private Law* (2004): 631-632.
102. Case C-208/00 *Überseering* [2002] ECR I-9919.
103. Case C-210/06 *Cartesio* [2008] ECR I-9641.
104. The ECJ is, moreover, generally more generous in its protection of natural persons, compare for instance Case C-210/06 *Cartesio* [2008] ECR I-9641 with Case C-9/02 *de Lasteyrie du Saillant* [2004] ECR I-2409.

the legislator - work together in a loyal manner.[105] My criticism of the judgment in *Heemskerk and Schaap*[106] indicates that these tensions are not always addressed with sufficient clarity, but upon further analysis its solution is not a reason for pessimism. The recent judgment in *Michaniki*[107] could likewise be read by pessimists as the ECJ imposing EU law over the Greek Constitution - and they are probably right as to the immediate result - whereas I am far more optimistic in that the judgment could also be seen as an invitation to the Greek authorities, in a spirit of cooperation, to adapt the legislation to make it more in line with the exigencies of EU law, which are not per se incompatible with the Greek constitutional concerns about the plurality of the press and the integrity of the decision-making process. Moreover, as the judgment in *Promusicae*[108] demonstrates the Court is also well capable of balancing conflicting interests at the level of the Union. The outcome of both balancing acts is not set in stone, but depends on evolutions both at Member State and EU level. This is well-demonstrated by the short case study on the status of same-sex marriages, where I have argued that the societal and legislative evolutions of recent years should militate for a more progressive approach.

**IV-81.** With these insights, we have an important last piece of our puzzle. So far, I have demonstrated that there is a concept of EU *ordre public*, distinct from its Member States (Part I); I have identified the various forms in which it comes to the surface throughout EU law (Part II) and the various values that are protected by it (Part III); and finally, it has been argued that the ensuing tensions can be contained surprisingly well (Part IV). Accordingly, it is now time to bring these four themes together in Part V with some final considerations as to the constitutional importance of our insights in respect of the EU *ordre public*.

105. Compare also P. Mengozzi, 'Les principes fondamentaux du droit communautaire el le droit des États membres', *Revue du Droit de l'Union Européenne* (2002): 435-460.
106. Case C-455/06 *Heemskerk and Schaap* [2008] ECR I-8763.
107. Case C-213/07 *Michaniki* [2008] ECR I-9999.
108. Case C-275/06 *Promusicae* [2008] ECR I-271.

# PART V
# Constitutional Implications of a More Coherent Concept of EU *Ordre Public*

## INTRODUCTION

**V-1.** The preceding parts have taught us that there is a concept of EU *ordre public* distinct from, but in close interaction with, the legal orders of the Member States (Part I). The analysis in the second and third Part have revealed the enormous breadth of the values that could arguably be said to be covered by EU *ordre public* (Part III) and the very diverse forms in which EU *ordre public* becomes manifest (Part II). The relatively wide breadth the concept has been given throughout my analysis is of course somewhat of my own making. I started off from a definition of EU *ordre public* as the complex of norms at the very heart of a political entity (in this case the EU) expressing and protecting the basic options taken by that entity regarding its political, economic, social and even cultural order. At the end of this book, it appears appropriate to assess whether this encompassing approach has something to offer for those who seek to better understand the EU constitutional order, beyond the fact that this analysis has already resulted in an analysis of such diverse issues as fundamental rights, competence, free movement, citizenship, democracy, federalism or essential procedural requirements. The question that needs to be addressed now is whether my broad approach may result in a coherent system that takes into account the nuances discussed above, but may also offer some new outlooks for further development of the concept of EU *ordre public* in the future.

**V-2.** At the end of Part IV, it was argued that when it comes to coherence there is at least some room for cautious optimism in one aspect. It turns out that, despite the fact that the EU *ordre public* is distinct from the legal orders of the Member States, the constitutional system seems quite capable of channelling potential tensions in a manner that largely avoids direct confrontations between the EU legal order and the legal order of the Member States. This is so, despite the fact that the potential for conflict is prima facie enormous as often highly sensitive values are at issue and the range of issues where I defend a role for the EU *ordre public* is far from negligible. If coherence is possible at this level, perhaps it is not impossible to put things in an even broader perspective.

**V-3.** I started this research project because I grew intrigued by the Opinion of Advocate General Jacobs in *Salzgitter.*[1] As discussed above,[2] he takes issue with the classic doctrine of *Sytraval*[3] which requires the ECJ to raise of its own motion norms in respect of competence and essential procedural requirements, but not the other 'higher rules of Community law' even though they contain norms – such as the fundamental rights – which may arguably be as important, if not more important, for the constitutional order of the Union. The appeal of such an approach was almost immediately self-evident to me, as was, however, its major weakness. How does one determine what is important or not for being treated as a matter of *ordre public*? The Court had already held in *Eco Swiss*[4] that Member States should treat the EU rules on competition as a matter of *ordre public*. The importance of competition law for the EU legal order can hardly be denied, but allowing it to be raised *motu proprio* by the Court seemed incompatible with the judicial architecture of the Union as it would fundamentally upset the role of the General Court in competition cases. So, ever since I have wondered whether a better understanding of EU *ordre public* could also offer a way out of this conundrum. At the end of the discussion on the duty of the EU courts to raise issues of their own motion,[5] I have left the issue somewhat open as *Sytraval*,[6] and its progeny are still good law *de lege lata*. However, maybe a more principled approach towards EU *ordre public* may result in good reasons to nuance that case law *de lege ferenda*.

**V-4.** The final Part of this book, therefore, seeks to propose a way to structure a broad concept of EU *ordre public* in a manner that gives credit to the diversity of the ways in which the concept becomes apparent throughout the EU legal order and the multitude of values that have been discussed. Moreover, ideally the concept must be compatible with the complexities of the EU constitutional legal order which encompasses independent EU institutions, Member States, and natural and corporate citizens. Finally, like any critical reconstruction the concept should not only have sufficient connecting factors with the current realities of the case law, but also offer the prospect for some further adjustments *de lege ferenda*. In this way, I seek to counter the scepticism of Prechal and Shelkoplyas that:

> the proposed choice of 'components' of European public policy at best strikes one as random. It also reveals the complete absence of a standard which could be used

1. Opinion of Advocate General Jacobs in Case C-210/98 P *Salzgitter v. Commission* [2000] ECR I-5843, paras 125-150.
2. See, *supra*, at II-191.
3. Case C-367/95 P *Commission v. Sytraval and Brink's France* [1998] I-1719.
4. Case C-126/97 *Eco Swiss China Time* [1999] ECR I-3055. See also, *supra*, at II-164 et seq.
5. See, *supra*, at II-205.
6. Case C-367/95 P *Commission v. Sytraval and Brink's France* [1998] I-1719.

for expanding the tentative scope of such an eclectic phenomenon as public policy.[7]

**V-5.** Therefore, I first seek to draw the contours of a model that encompasses these various functions. I believe the model proposed at the end of Romain's analysis of the concept of *ordre public* offers a promising starting point, but his '*définition générale de l'ordre public*'[8] needs serious refinement for it to be applied to the complex realities of the EU legal order (Chapter 15). Upon the basis of these insights, a model of the EU *ordre public* is then put forward (Chapter 16). Finally, the descriptive and creative force of the model is tested in proposing certain potential adjustments *de lege ferenda* to the operability of the concept of EU *ordre* (Chapter 17).

7. S. Prechal & N. Shelkoplyas, 'National Procedures, Public Policy and EC Law. From Van Schijndel to Eco Swiss and Beyond', *European Review of Private Law* (2004): 602.
8. J.-F. Romain, 'L'*ordre public* (notion générale) et les droits de l'homme' in *L'ordre public: concept et applications*, ed. J.-F. Romain, M. Grégoire & V. Simonart (Bruxelles: Bruylant, 1995), 59-60.

# CHAPTER 15
# Building the Model

**V-6.** At the end of his excellent analysis of the concept of *ordre public*, Romain proposes a bold '*définition générale de l'ordre public*', which is worth reproducing in full:

> *L'ordre public général* est l'ensemble des principes de base qui gouvernent l'ordre juridique général d'un Etat démocratique, principes qui peuvent être classés en deux catégories :
>
> - les principes fondamentaux de cet Etat (*l'ordre public fondamental*), écrits et non écrits, qui tendent à la protection de droits et des libertés fondamentales des individus et à définir les garanties et les règles à l'origine de l'ordre politique et juridique des [*sic*] cet Etat, en ce compris les bonnes mœurs, principes auxquels il ne peut être dérogé ni par les particuliers, ni par l'Etat lui-même, sauf les restrictions et sous réserve des modifications légalement admissibles strictement organisées ;
> - et les autres principes essentiels à cet Etat (*l'ordre public essentiel*), qui tendent à protéger l'intérêt général réalisé dans l'*ordre public* juridique, économique et social de l'Etat auxquels il ne peut être porté atteinte par les particuliers[1].

**V-7.** His definition is of course primarily focused on the national context he concentrates upon in his analysis. However, I am tempted by his approach as a starting point for my analysis of the EU *ordre public*. First, the totality of his definition is wide enough to encompass the various concerns I have set out at the outset that the EU *ordre public* should be able to deal with (the complex of norms at the very heart of a political entity – in this case the EU – expressing and protecting the basic options taken by that entity regarding its political, economic, social and even cultural order), which has led us to examine a multitude of topics ranging from fundamental rights to consumer protection. Nevertheless, his distinction between *ordre public fondamental* and *ordre public essentiel* offers an elegant way to recognize that, on the one hand, to re-use just these

1. J.-F. Romain, 'L'*ordre public* (notion générale) et les droits de l'homme' in *L'ordre public: concept et applications*, ed. J.-F. Romain, M. Grégoire & V. Simonart (Bruxelles: Bruylant,1995), 59-60.

two examples, consumer protection and fundamental rights may indeed both carry sufficient weight as to deserve to be treated as a matter of EU *ordre public*, but that, on the other hand, a principled explanation may be given why their *ordre public* status may still result in very different consequences. The proposed model, moreover, seeks to offer in its definitions a role for both the State and its citizens, which seems appropriate for a 'legal order [...] the subjects of which comprise not only Member States but also their nationals'.[2] The model needs, however, to be refined for it to be made applicable to the EU legal order.

**V-8.** First, the concept of the State (l'*Etat*) requires further explanation when dealing with the EU. In the context of the EU legal order there are de facto two levels of governmental authority. It seems self-evident to connect the concept of EU *ordre public* with the EU and its institutions. However, at the same time there is a crucial role for the Member States. This role, moreover, plays out at three levels. First, the Member States form the *pouvoir constituant*[3] of the Union.[4] As Masters of the Treaties they have the *Kompetenz-Kompetenz*, it falls upon them to draw up the constitutional framework of the Union. Second, they are represented in the institutions of the Union, most notably in the Council,[5] and thus part of the governmental authority of the Union. Third, the Member States are also 'legal subjects'[6] of the Union who must carry out EU policies by translating them into their own legal order, at which level they are of course also 'the State' and, moreover, bound by their national *ordre public fondamental* which at times may be difficult to reconcile with the demands of the EU legal order.[7] The model will, therefore, have to take into account that the State in EU terms is not one monolith, but actually comprises of both the institutions and Member States whereby the latter are, however, both master of the rules and their subject.

**V-9.** Second, the key principle behind the *ordre public fondamental* is that neither the citizens nor the State may deviate from it, subject to admissible restrictions and duly enacted amendments. This enables me to explain why the rules on competence and the essential procedural requirements should be treated as a matter of EU *ordre public*,[8] as the institutions should not in their ordinary discharging of their duties deviate from

2. Case 26/62 *Van Gend & Loos* [1963] ECR 1.
3. On the concept, see C. Möllers, 'Pouvoir Constituant - Constitution - Constitutionalisation' in *Principles of European Constitutional Law*, ed. A. Von Bogdandy & J. Bast (Oxford/Portland: Hart, 2007), 183-226. While I definitely have some sympathy for the criticism by Baquero Cruz about clinging on to this concept, see J. Baquero Cruz, 'The Legacy of the Maastricht-Urteil and the Pluralist Movement', *European Law Journal* (2008): 408-410, it appears - as evidenced by the IGC drafting the Lisbon Treaty - that the Member States are not ready to fully make the switch to a model based on a federal constitutional pact whereby the Member States *collectively* hold the constituent power. That being said, even if this stage is reached, the *ordre public fondamental* would then still reflect the limitations that may exist on the Member States acting collectively - and these are likely not much different from the current restrictions.
4. Article 48 TEU.
5. Article 16(2) TEU.
6. Case 26/62 *Van Gend & Loos* [1963] ECR 1. An indirect, but quite telling, expression of this can be found in Article 4(2) TEU where the equality of the Member States before the Treaties is reaffirmed.
7. See, for instance, Case C-213/07 *Michaniki* [2008] ECR I-9999.
8. Case C-367/95 P *Commission v. Sytraval and Brink's France* [1998] I-1719.

them. Yet, this also offers a strong basis for arguing[9] that also fundamental rights need protection at the same level in line with the Opinion of Advocate General Jacobs in *Salzgitter.*[10] The institutions are indeed entitled to restrict fundamental rights and freedoms within the limits set out in the Charter of Fundamental Rights of the EU and the ECHR, but they cannot do away with them altogether. In turn, a basis seems to appear for the review by the ECJ of the acts of Member States acting within the scope of Union law, encompassing both instances in which they implement Union law and instances where they deviate from it.[11] Neither situation may result in deviating from the *ordre public fondamental.*

**V-10.** Third, one could object that precisely because the Member States are the *pouvoir constituant* they may escape the impact of the EU *ordre public*. This is, however, not true. First, the argument only makes sense to the extent that they are acting as the Masters of the Treaty. In the ordinary state of affairs they are bound as legislators by the rules that are binding on the institutions and in their executive capacity by the rules adopted by the institutions as a matter of primacy. Second, the Member States have of course the power to duly enact the necessary amendments to the Treaties. The rules on competence and institutional balance are fundamental, but not immutable. The *Barber*-protocol could arguably even be cited to demonstrate that the Member States may even deviate from rules such as the equality between men and women, which are arguably part of the fundamental rights the Union generally recognizes. One could even go further and point out that nothing prevents the Member States to abolish the Union altogether. This is true, but there may be limits nonetheless on the powers of the Member States. On the one hand, the Member States, as actors under international law, are bound by those rules of international law they cannot deviate from, i.e., *jus cogens*. On the other hand, the Member States, as parties to the ECHR are not precluded from transferring their competences to a supranational body, but must ensure that this body offers equivalent protection.[12] Whereas as *pouvoir constituant* they may thus amend or even abolish the EU legal order, the Member States must still ensure that the net result offers equivalent protection. The level of this protection may be subject to debate, however, as discussed above,[13] the ECtHR has in turn found at the heart of the ECHR an *ordre public européen*[14] which is modelled around 'the ideals and values of a democratic society',[15] the content of which need not be repeated at this point.[16] Accordingly, our model needs to be adjusted for these limitations. At the same time, these limitations seem to justify my approach which entails the explicit inclusion of *jus*

9. See, *infra*, at V-32.
10. Opinion of Advocate General Jacobs in Case C-210/98 P *Salzgitter v. Commission* [2000] ECR I-5843, paras 125-150.
11. Case 260/89 *Elliniki Radiophonia Tiléorassi* [1991] ECR I-2925.
12. ECtHR, 18 February 1999, *Matthews v. UK*; ECtHR, 30 June 2005, *Bosphorus Hava Yollari Turizm ve Ticaret Anonim Şirketi v. Ireland.*
13. See, *supra*, at I-37 et seq.
14. ECtHR, 23 February 1995, *Loizidou v. Turkey* (preliminary objections), para. 75.
15. ECtHR, 30 January 1998, *United Communist Party of Turkey and others v. Turkey*, par. 45; see also ECtHR, 7 December 1976, *Kjeldsen, Busk Madsen and Pedersen v. Denmark*, para. 53; ECtHR, 7 July 1989, *Soering v. UK*, para. 87.
16. For more, see, *supra*, at I-44 et seq.

*cogens* and these core values at the heart of the ECHR into the concept of EU *ordre public*.

**V-11.** Fourth, as indicated, the attractiveness of the *ordre public essentiel* is the potential for including a whole series of principles and norms that seek to protect the general interest. The key lies, therefore, in norms that strike a societal balance which private parties should not upset. This is, however, also its conceptual weakness, to the extent that the norms at issue are rather diverse. They encompass, first, a series of norms related to the economic order of the Union, in particular the key rules on competition law and the *lex moneta*. Above, I included in the discussion of the EU *ordre public économique* also the rules on free movement. It is submitted, however, that while these may be binding on private parties,[17] they are primarily imposing obligations on the Member States. Therefore, I am not retracting their status as part of the EU *ordre public*, but they must be fitted into the model in a manner that ensures that also Member States may not deviate from them, which means that they must rather be given a place at the level of the *ordre public fondamental* so that they may bind both the Member States and private parties. The same must *mutatis mutandis* apply to the rules regarding state aid, the customs union and citizenship of the Union. Conversely, to the extent that the rules on competition law are not exclusively applicable to enterprises[18] but may also bind the government, some adjustments in the other direction will have to be made as well. Second, increasingly, the Union is also competent to regulate non-economic issues. The strongest form for doing so is the adoption of EU criminal law. It seems hard to argue that individuals could validly choose not to comply with such rules.[19] Finally, the Union legislates - and authorizes its Member States to legislate, sometimes even at the expense of the free movement – in respect of a whole series of non-economic interests. This is the point where our model may reach its saturation point, as the line between *ordre public* and general interest becomes very thin indeed. For this reason, the model needs to be refined in two ways. First, the concerns to be included should primarily correspond to the concerns addressed by the public policy exceptions in the Treaties. Accordingly, the focus is on public health, public security, public morality and public order. Nevertheless, other concerns, such as consumer protection and social protection may be included, at least to the extent that they are the expression of underlying concerns of EU *ordre public*. Arguably, this is the case with some rules of EU consumer protection law, which are linked to the establishment of the *ordre public économique*[20] and some aspects of EU social law, such

17. Case C-341/05 *Laval un Partneri* [2007] ECR I-11767; Case C-438/05 *International Transport Workers' Federation* [2007] ECR I-10779.
18. See for instance Case 13/77 *GB-Inno-BM* [1977] ECR 2115. For more on the state action doctrine, see J. Baquero Cruz, *Between competition and free movement: the economic constitutional law of the European Community* (Oxford: Hart, 2002), 127-161.
19. At least to the extent that they have been implemented by the Member States, see Case C-105/03 *Pupino* [2005] ECR I-5285; Joined Cases C-387/02, C-391/02 and C-403/02 *Berlusconi* [2005] ECR I-3565. The need for implementation by the Member State does not, however, undermine the importance of the rules for the EU legal order.
20. See, for instance Case C-168/05 *Mostaza Claro* [2006] ECR I-10421.

as the *Working Time Directive*,[21] which seeks to ensure health and safety at work.[22] Second, there may be need for some further differentiation to take account of the fact that when dealing with these issues, the private interests of the parties may gradually overpower the general interest at issue.

**V-12.** The end result may therefore be more of a sliding scale than a bifurcated model as suggested by Romain.[23] Actually, this, too, corresponds to some of the functional approaches[24] defended in the literature.[25] This has, moreover, the advantage that also the consequences or the impact of the EU *ordre public* status of a norm may be better adjusted in function of their place in the ensuing hierarchy,[26] taking into account the finality of the rule and the context in which it needs to be applied. Prime example in this respect is the EU *ordre public* status of the essential competition rules, which must nonetheless be reconciled with different outcomes in cases such as *Eco Swiss*,[27] *Renault*,[28] *Manfredi*[29] or be explained against the different procedural background of preliminary reference proceedings, direct actions before the EU courts or various recognition procedures.

21. Council Directive 93/104/EC of 23 November 1993 concerning certain aspects of the organization of working time (1993) OJ L 307/18.
22. Case C-84/94 *United Kingdom v. Council* [1996] ECR I-5755.
23. J.-F. Romain, 'L'*ordre public* (notion générale) et les droits de l'homme' in *L'ordre public: concept et applications*, ed. J.-F. Romain, M. Grégoire & V. Simonart (Bruxelles: Bruylant, 1995), 59-60.
24. C. Picheral, 'L'*ordre public* écologique en droit communautaire' in *L'ordre public écologique – towards an ecological public order*, ed. M. Boutelet & J.-C. Fritz (Brussels, Bruylant: 2005), 112 et seq.; see also J.-F. Romain, 'L'*ordre public* (notion générale) et les droits de l'homme' in *L'ordre public: concept et applications*, ed. J.-F. Romain, M. Grégoire & V. Simonart (Bruxelles: Bruylant, 1995), 60.
25. E. Picard, 'Introduction générale: la fonction de l'*ordre public* dans l'ordre juridique' in *L'ordre public: ordre public ou ordres publics? Ordre public et droits fondamentaux*, ed. M.-J. Redor (Bruxelles: Bruylant, 2001), 21-22 and 54-55.
26. On the link between EU *ordre public* and hierarchy, see also R. De Lange, 'The European Public Order, Constitutional Principles and Fundamental Rights', *Erasmus Law Review* (2007): 6-7.
27. Case C-126/97 *Eco Swiss China Time* [1999] ECR I-3055.
28. Case C-38/98 *Régie nationale des usines Renault* [2000] ECR I-2973.
29. Joined Cases C-295/04 to C-298/04 *Manfredi* [2006] ECR I-6619.

# CHAPTER 16
# A More Coherent Model of EU *Ordre Public*

**V-13.** The model which I propose, while developed further in the following paragraphs, may be represented schematically in Table 16.1.

*Table 16.1 EU Ordre Public*

<table>
<tr><td rowspan="9">Ordre Public Fonda-mental</td><td rowspan="9">EU level</td><td rowspan="2">Pouvoir Constituant</td><td colspan="2">Jus cogens</td></tr>
<tr><td colspan="2">European Public Order (core ECHR)</td></tr>
<tr><td rowspan="7">Institutions (all of the above) +</td><td colspan="2">International law binding on the Union</td></tr>
<tr><td colspan="2">EU Fundamental Rights</td></tr>
<tr><td colspan="2">Competence</td></tr>
<tr><td colspan="2">Essential Procedural Requirements</td></tr>
<tr><td colspan="2">Financial Interests of the Union</td></tr>
<tr><td rowspan="2">Basic values</td><td>Constitutional (national procedural autonomy, federalism, unity in diversity, democracy, institutional balance, loyal cooperation, primacy)</td></tr>
<tr><td>Moral (human dignity)</td></tr>
<tr><td rowspan="5"></td><td rowspan="5">Member States</td><td rowspan="5">(all of the above) +</td><td colspan="2">Citizenship</td></tr>
<tr><td colspan="2">Free Movement Rules</td></tr>
<tr><td colspan="2">Customs Union</td></tr>
<tr><td colspan="2">State Aid (+ rules on competition law if exceptionally applicable to MS)</td></tr>
<tr><td colspan="2">Lex moneta</td></tr>
</table>

<table>
<tr><td rowspan="6">Ordre Public Essentiel</td><td rowspan="6">Private Parties</td><td rowspan="6">(all of the above – to the extent applicable) +</td><td>EU criminal law</td><td rowspan="3" colspan="3">Public interests<br>No deviation</td></tr>
<tr><td>EU external action</td></tr>
<tr><td>Competition law</td></tr>
<tr><td rowspan="3">Other protective rules</td><td rowspan="3">Sliding scale of public character</td><td>Strong</td><td>For example health, safety, morality</td></tr>
<tr><td>Medium</td><td>For example consumer protection</td></tr>
<tr><td>Low</td><td>For example culture</td></tr>
</table>

**V-14.** The model presented above has two major functions. On the one hand, it offers an overview of what may be comprised by a concept of EU *ordre public*. If there is such a thing as EU *ordre public*, it must have content that can be ascertained. Accordingly, this model serves as an inventory of that content, and in that it corresponds largely to the values discussed above in Part III. On the other hand, it also helps to create a hierarchy within this concept of EU *ordre public*. This hierarchy is crucial because it allows explaining the variety of manifestations of EU *ordre public* discussed in Part II, and offers a basis for suggesting some more rigour in determining the conditions for their application.

**V-15.** Moreover, the model also offers a basis for the interplay between the legitimizing and delegitimizing strand of the *ordre public* that is so prominent in the study of Picheral of the European *ordre public*[1] and which has also been stressed by Combacau.[2] The hierarchy explains, on the one hand, how the higher level takes measures targeting the lower level(s) to strengthen the values protected by the EU *ordre public*. Accordingly, the institutions act vis-à-vis both the Member States (for instance in the context of state aid) and private parties (e.g., EU criminal law or the enforcement of competition law) and the Member States vis-à-vis private parties (e.g., criminal measures taken to enforce EU rules, as in *Lindqvist*[3]). In a sense the EU *ordre public essentiel* is reflected in the competences of the Union to take protective measures, whether with the specific

1. C. Picheral, *L'ordre public européen: droit communautaire et droit européen des droits de l'homme* (Paris: CERIC – Documentation française, 2001).
2. J. Combacau, 'Conclusions générales' in *L'ordre public: ordre public ou ordres publics? Ordre public et droits fondamentaux*, ed. M.J. Redor (Bruxelles: Bruylant, 2001), 420 et seq.
3. Case C-101/01 *Lindqvist* [2003] ECR I-12971.

aim of protecting certain interests as for instance in the case of health and safety at work or even, as in Article 114(3) TFEU as part of a broader legislative programme of harmonization in the interest of the internal market, which itself is a matter of EU *ordre public*. It thus offers a basis for the police powers of the Union. On the other hand, the hierarchy also sets the conditions of the delegitimizing strand of the *ordre public* in that it sets the limits for the possibility of the lower levels to deviate from EU rules. Accordingly, the EU legislator may at times have to restrict fundamental rights, but is still bound by the unassailable core of the fundamental rights at issue.[4] Likewise, the Member States may for instance deviate from the free movement of goods, but must still respect fundamental rights.[5] Accordingly, in this respect the model both explains and curtails the police powers of the Member States.[6] The distinction between these two strands is, however, relative. As *Schmidberger*[7] demonstrates, the two levels often seamlessly flow into each other. In that case, the authorization by the Austrian authorities of a manifestation on the Brenner highway formed at the same time a limitation of the free movement of goods the limits of which needed to be assessed in the light of higher EU law and a form of governmental action aimed at strengthening the fundamental freedom of expression as part and partial of the national and Union constitutional order. Similarly, the judgment in *Krombach*[8] shows how the legitimizing and delegitimizing strands of the *ordre public* are often two sides of the same coin: *ordre public* legitimizes the decision of the German courts not to enforce the civil judgment at issue and conversely delegitimizes the original French court's decision that was taken in violation of Article 6 ECHR.

**V-16.** The model starts on the basis of the distinction between *ordre public fondamental* and *ordre public essentiel*. For the reasons set out above, a further distinction is made first in respect of the *ordre public fondamental* between the Union level and the Member State, in recognition of the fact that both have governmental functions, but are nonetheless in distinct roles in the EU constitutional order. The EU level is then distinguished further in a level for the Member States acting as Masters of the Treaty and the Union institutions in the day to day operations of the Union. The basic principle behind the model is that each level is bound by certain rules from which it may not deviate. The lower you get in the hierarchy, the more rules of EU *ordre public* are to be reckoned with, as each next level is also bound by the rules that are binding on the higher levels, at least to the extent that they are applicable to the lower-ranking actor.[9]

4. Joined Cases C-402/05 P and C-415/05 P *Kadi v. Council* [2008] ECR I-6351.
5. Case C-368/95 *Vereinigte Familiapress Zeitungsverlags- und vertriebs* [1997] ECR I-3689. See also, *supra*, at IV-30 on the scope of the field of application of the Charter of Fundamental Rights of the EU.
6. See in this respect also the question as to the scope of the duty to protect fundamental rights in the EU, see J. Suerbaum, 'Die Schutzpflichtdimension der Gemeinschaftsgrundrechte', *Europarecht* (2003): 390-416; L. Jaeckel, 'The duty to protect fundamental rights in the European Community', *European Law Review* (2003): 508-527.
7. Case C-112/00 *Schmidberger* [2003] ECR I-5659.
8. Case C-7/98 *Krombach* [2000] ECR I-1935.
9. I add this clause to stress the limits of the implications of this model. It does not flow from the hierarchical position of the core of fundamental rights protection that they would in any sense expand the competences of the Union to act in their protection beyond the competences

**V-17.** The top layer of the model corresponds to the level of the Member States acting as Masters of the Treaty. Their only limitations are the limitations public international law attaches to their acts. On the one hand, these are the rules of *jus cogens*, which will thus trickle down the entire pyramid.[10] On the other hand, as all Member States are a Party to the ECHR, they are in principle precluded from transferring their competences to a supranational body if that does not offer equivalent protection.[11] The absolute minimum in that respect must be the core rules of the ECHR, which the Strasbourg Court itself refers to as setting out the European Public Order.[12] Notably absent from the list, especially if one considers Article 3(5) TEU are any references to the principles of the UN Charter. This is a deliberate omission because of the appeals judgment in *Kadi*.[13] It cannot be excluded, however, that Member States may be inclined to argue that their obligations under Article 103 of the UN Charter should also be seen as framing their room for manoeuvre under international law, and that they should therefore be included. From an international law perspective, that appears a valid claim. It remains, however, to be seen whether the inclusion of Article 103 UN Charter into the top level of the model would result in a different outcome for the appeals in *Kadi*.[14] The pull from Article 103 of the UN Charter may still be mitigated by a counter-pull from the need for effective fundamental rights protection, though the original judgments of the General Court[15] suggest that the balance may then indeed be struck differently.

**V-18.** The second layer of the model concerns those principles from which the EU institutions may not deviate in the ordinary discharging of their function. The institutions are of course also bound by the preceding layer. Accordingly, as *Poulsen*

---

conferred upon the Union by the Treaties – compare in this respect Article 51(2) of the Charter of Fundamental Rights of the European Union and the Declaration 1 concerning the Charter of Fundamental Rights of the European Union (2007) OJ C 306/249. Likewise, the fact that the rules as to free movement and State aid are included as a matter of EU *ordre public fondamental* does not by itself imply that these norms have horizontal direct effect so as to be fully binding on private parties. Yet, to the extent that these rules are applicable to private parties, as for instance in Case C-415/93 *Bosman* [1995] ECR I-4921 they will have the same weight. Similarly, to the extent that private parties are affected by a State aid decision, the *ordre public* status of the rules on State aid and the exclusive competence of the Union will prevent private parties from circumventing these rules through the national civil courts, see Case C-119/05 *Lucchini Siderurgica* [2007] ECR I-6199. See also, *infra*, at V-27.

10. See, as to the validity of secondary law, Case T-306/01 *Yusuf and Al Barakaat International Foundation v. Council and Commission* [2005] ECR II-3533; Case T-315/01 *Kadi v. Council and Commission* [2005] ECR II-3649. But see also at the level of the interpretation of secondary law Case C-286/90 *Poulsen and Diva Navigation* [1992] ECR I-6019 or at the level of the implementation of the free movement, the prohibition to expel own nationals in Case 41/74 *van Duyn* [1974] ECR 1337.
11. ECtHR, 18 February 1999, *Wait and Kennedy v. Germany*; ECtHR, 18 February 1999, *Matthews v. UK*; ECtHR, 30 June 2005, *Bosphorus Hava Yolları Turizm ve Ticaret Anonim Şirketi v. Ireland*.
12. ECtHR, 23 February 1995, *Loizidou v. Turkey* (preliminary objections), para. 75.
13. Joined Cases C-402/05 P and C-415/05 P *Kadi v. Council* [2008] ECR I-6351.
14. Joined Cases C-402/05 P and C-415/05 P *Kadi v. Council* [2008] ECR I-6351.
15. Case T-306/01 *Yusuf and Al Barakaat International Foundation v. Council and Commission* [2005] ECR II-3533; Case T-315/01 *Kadi v. Council and Commission* [2005] ECR II-3649.

*and Diva Navigation*[16] demonstrates, the scope of secondary legislation is curtailed by *jus cogens* and as dramatically demonstrated by the appeals case in *Kadi*[17] the institutions may not escape core fundamental rights protection. At the same time, in light of Article 3(5) TEU it appears appropriate to also include the other norms of international law, at least to the extent that they are binding on the Union.[18] Actually, at this level, as we are dealing with secondary law-making and the judicial review thereof, the entire EU human rights catalogue, which is a matter of primary law formally laid down in the Charter of Fundamental Rights of the EU, presents itself as binding on the institutions when adopting secondary law. Undoubtedly, the EU institutions may at times validly restrict certain fundamental rights,[19] but they cannot escape their binding force.[20] Furthermore, the institutions may neither deviate from the rules on competence, nor from the rules laying down essential procedural requirements. These two categories are, as was extensively argued above,[21] indeed already explicitly treated as a matter of *ordre public* in the context of judicial review of the validity of acts of the institutions.[22] Moreover, as the financial means of the Union are essential for the realization of the policies of the Union and the Union has experienced first hand the devastating effect indications of fraud may have on its own credibility,[23] it seems appropriate to include also the protection of the financial interests of the Union at this level.

**V-19.** The second level encompasses, finally, also the basic values of the EU legal order. On the one hand, these concern the basic constitutional values of the EU legal order. These were discussed extensively in Part III. They concern those constitutional principles that shape the EU legal order by determining the relationship between the institutions and between the institutions and the Member States. At issue is first the principle of primacy,[24] which ensures at this level that the Member States can never plead their national law before the EU courts in order to escape obligations under EU law,[25] nor can they invoke national constitutional principles to limit the Court's

16. Case C-286/90 *Poulsen and Diva Navigation* [1992] ECR I-6019.
17. Joined Cases C-402/05 P and C-415/05 P *Kadi v. Council* [2008] ECR I-6351.
18. This nuance is important. The EU is committed to international law, and the validity of its acts may well be challenged on the basis of both international agreements and customary international law. However, it must first be ascertained that the Union is actually bound by the norms that are being invoked against it, which is not always self-evident, see Case C-366/10 *Air Transport Association of America* [2011] ECR I-0000. That case does not answer, however, what the consequences are of the fact that the Member States may nevertheless be bound by certain norms of international law the Union is not. For those instances, however, there is Article 351 TFEU, which may also be considered as an expression of the Union's principled respect for international law (and a solution for the conundrum that appears if Member States are – fully in line with my model – at the lower level bound both by the Union rules and their international obligations.
19. Case 44/79 *Hauer* [1979] ECR 3727.
20. Joined Cases C-402/05 P and C-415/05 P *Kadi v. Council* [2008] ECR I-6351.
21. See, *supra*, II-191 et seq.
22. Case C-367/95 P *Commission v. Sytraval and Brink's France* [1998] I-1719.
23. Case C-432/04 *Commission v. Cresson* [2006] ECR I-6387.
24. See, *supra*, III-26; see also, *supra*, II-155 et seq.
25. Case C-236/99 *Commission v. Belgium* [2000] ECR I-5657, para. 23; Case C-358/03 *Commission v. Austria* [2004] ECR I-12055, paras 12-13.

jurisdiction or the impact of its judgments.[26] Second, there is the principle of direct effect. Third, the principle of loyal cooperation must be included together with the related principle of institutional balance. Together their EU *ordre public fondamental* status helps justifying those instances where the Court had to craft new remedies to restore the overall constitutional balance, as in *Zwartveld,*[27] or *Chernobyl.*[28] Fourth, there are the principles relating to democracy and the rule of law, which may similarly justify exceptional adjustments by the ECJ to the impact of the Treaty rules, as in *Les Verts.*[29] Finally, the principles that ensure that sufficient weight is given to the Member States in the EU legal order must be included, the federalism concerns as expressed through the (background) principle of subsidiarity and national procedural autonomy.[30] The latter principles must indeed also be binding on the institutions, which may otherwise upset the constitutional balance between the EU legal order and the Member States. Combined, these constitutional values account, however, for both the basic rule of national procedural autonomy and its twin exceptions of equivalence and effectiveness.[31] Furthermore, including these federalism-related principles at this level, offers a basis for the principled balancing of the interests of the Union and the Member States, as argued in Part IV.[32] Taken together, these principles ensure a legal order based on 'unity in diversity' in line with Article 4(2) TEU.

**V-20.** On the other hand, there are also basic moral values that are binding on the Union institutions. In essence, they are all related to the principle of human dignity. As the biotechnology case[33] demonstrates, the principle is binding on the EU institutions. It inspires, moreover, several legislative initiatives aimed at protecting this value, as in the case of the fight against trafficking in human beings[34] and child pornography[35] or the public morality exceptions as in the case of, for instance, the rules relating to broadcasting.[36] Finally, as demonstrated by cases such as *Omega Spielhallen*[37] and

26. Case 9/65 *San Michele v. High Authority* [1965] ECR 27. See also Case 106/77 *Simmenthal* [1978] ECR 629.
27. Case C-2/88 Imm. *Zwartveld I* [1990] ECR I-3365; Case C-2/88 Imm. *Zwartveld II* [1990] ECR I-4405.
28. Case C-70/88 *European Parliament v. Council* [1990] ECR I-2041.
29. Case 294/83 *Parti Ecologiste 'Les Verts' v. European Parliament* [1986] ECR 1339.
30. For the need to strike a balance between the EU and its Member States, and its translation into competing constitutional principles, see, *supra*, III-46 et seq.
31. Case 45/76 *Comet* [1976] ECR 2043; Case 33/76 *Rewe* [1976] ECR 1989.
32. See, *supra*, at IV-6 et seq.
33. Case C-377/98 *Netherlands v. European Parliament and Council* [2001] ECR I-7079.
34. Directive 2011/36/EU of the European Parliament and of the Council of 5 April 2011 on preventing and combating trafficking in human beings and protecting its victims, and replacing Council Framework Decision 2002/629/JHA (2011) L 101/1.
35. Directive 2011/92/EU of the European Parliament and of the Council of 13 December 2011 on combating the sexual abuse and sexual exploitation of children and child pornography, and replacing Council Framework Decision 2004/68/JHA (2011) OJ L 335/1.
36. Directive 2010/13/EU of the European Parliament and of the Council of 10 March 2010 on the coordination of certain provisions laid down by law, regulation or administrative action in Member States concerning the provision of audiovisual media services (Audiovisual Media Services Directive) (2010) OJ L 95/1.
37. Case C-36/02 *Omega Spielhallen* [2004] ECR I-9609.

*Dynamic Medien,*[38] this principle, too, may give rise to the need to balance the full effect of EU law with certain national considerations flowing from this principle.

**V-21.** The third layer relates to the Member States, this time when acting within the scope of Union law. As argued above, Member States are governmental actors, a fact which suggests that they should only be bound by those rules that are part of the *ordre public fondamental.* However, in a sense they are also the first legal subjects of the Union, and in that sense it must be avoided that through their actions they may upset the basic policies of the Union.

**V-22.** Member States are of course also bound by the higher layers. Accordingly, their ability to expel their own citizens, for instance, is limited as a matter of *jus cogens.*[39] Similarly, it becomes obvious that when they are acting within the scope of EU law, their acts, too, are subject to the EU human rights standard,[40] which does of course not preclude that a stricter national standard may apply additionally.[41] In this respect one may recall that respect for fundamental rights, and the rule of law is a precondition for accession to the Union under Article 49 *jucto* Article 2 TEU,[42] which may, moreover, be enforced vis-à-vis recalcitrant Member Sates through the extraordinary procedure of Article 7 TEU. They may rely on the principle of national procedural autonomy,[43] but must conversely also ensure the effectiveness of EU law,[44] cooperate loyally with the Union[45] and respect the division of competence.[46] In particular, they are subject to the principle of primacy. While this cannot of itself result in the invalidity of national acts contrary to EU law,[47] which indeed would be incompatible with the federal balance struck as a matter of EU *ordre public fondamental,* the principle does have profound effects on the margins left to the Member States. National courts must set aside conflicting legislation, notwithstanding contrary national constitutional provisions.[48] Member States face dire consequences if they fail to fulfil their obligations under EU law, including the risk of fines under Article 260 TFEU and the duty to compensate

38. Case C-244/06 *Dynamic Medien* [2008] ECR I-505.
39. Case 41/74 *van Duyn* [1974] ECR 1337.
40. Case 260/89 *Elliniki Radiophonia Tiléorassi* [1991] ECR I-2925.
41. Article 53 Charter of Fundamental Rights of the Union; see also, *supra,* IV-30. Indeed, to avoid all doubts in this respect, we are still discussing aspects of the EU *ordre public.* Undoubtedly, Member States are additionally still also bound by their national *ordre public fondamental.*
42. On the pre-accession human rights conditionality, see A. Albi, 'Ironies in Human Rights Protection in the EU: Pre-Accession Conditionality and Post-Accession Conundrums', *European Law Journal* (2009): 48-51.
43. Joined Cases C-430/93 and C-431/93 *Van Schijndel and Van Veen* [1995] ECR I-4705.
44. Case C-432/05 *Unibet* [2007] ECR I-2271; Case C-286/06 *Impact* [2008] ECR I-8025.
45. Case 804/79 *Commission v. UK* [1981] ECR 1045, paras 30-31; Case 325/85 *Ireland v. Commission* [1987] ECR 5041, paras 15-16.
46. Case C-119/05 *Lucchini Siderurgica* [2007] ECR I-6199; Case 804/79 *Commission v. UK* [1981] ECR 1045.
47. See, *supra,* at IV-13 and IV-14.
48. Case 106/77 *Simmenthal* [1978] ECR 629, para. 24.

private parties for breaches of EU law by any governmental organ[49] including the national courts,[50] irrespective of national law.

**V-23.** However, the Treaties also impose additional obligations the Member State may not escape. In particular, the Member States are the primary guarantors of the free movement of goods, persons, services and capital, of which the EU *ordre public* status was defended above.[51] That status was *a fortiori* asserted in respect of European citizenship.[52] Admittedly, also the institutions may not unduly restrict the fundamental freedoms. However, whereas the institutions may shape the free movement through harmonizing measures, the free movement rules are unreservedly binding on the Member States. Of course, they may at times restrict those fundamental freedoms for reasons of general interest, which at times may even flow from respect of higher norms of EU *ordre public* as in *Schmidberger.*[53] However, the existence of legitimate exceptions does not take away the *ordre public fondamental* status of these norms vis-à-vis the Member States.[54] Similarly, the Member States are bound to guarantee the effective functioning of the customs union. Furthermore, as economic actors they must ensure that the basic rules regarding competition in the internal market are respected. This explains the *ordre public* status of the rules on state aid,[55] and it requires that the Member States respect the other competition rules, in particular Articles 101 and 102 TFEU the *ordre public* character of which was confirmed in *Eco Swiss*[56] and *Manfredi,*[57] in the exceptional cases that these rules govern their activities. Finally, fully in line with the monetary policy of the euro being an exclusive competence of the Union, at least for those Member States that have adopted the euro as their currency,[58] Member States are precluded from any action that might undermine monetary stability or undercut public confidence in the euro, such as abusing its introduction for rising fines.[59]

**V-24.** The second half of the scheme concerns the *ordre public essentiel.* These norms are the product of the institutions and the Member States acting within the scope of Union law. They are accordingly not binding on these actors in the sense that they may not deviate from them, as they determine the content of these norms and may thus at will – at least within the limits of the *ordre public fondamental* – alter them, but they

49. Joined Cases C-6/90 and C-9/90 *Francovich* [1991] ECR I-5357; Joined Cases C-46/93 and C-48/93 *Brasserie du Pêcheur* [1996] ECR I-1026.
50. Case C-224/01 *Köbler* [2003] ECR I-10239; Case C-173/03 *Traghetti del Mediterraneo* [2006] ECR I-5177.
51. See, *supra,* at III-80 et seq.
52. See, *supra,* at III-54 et seq.
53. Case C-112/00 *Schmidberger* [2003] ECR I-5659.
54. The *fundamental* freedoms are fundamental for a reason, see also T. Kingreen, 'Fundamental Freedoms' in *Principles of European Constitutional Law,* ed. A. Von Bogdandy & J. Bast (Oxford/Portland: Hart, 2007), 549-584.
55. Opinion of AG Geelhoed in Case C-119/05 *Lucchini Siderurgica* [2007] ECR I-6199, para. 62.
56. Case C-126/97 *Eco Swiss China Time* [1999] ECR I-3055, para. 36.
57. Joined Cases C-295/04 to C-298/04 *Manfredi* [2006] ECR I-6619, para. 81; see also Opinion of AG Geelhoed in Case C-119/05 *Lucchini Siderurgica* [2007] ECR I-6199, para. 62.
58. Article 3 TFEU.
59. Case C-359/05 *Estager* [2007] ECR I-581.

are mandatory for private parties. At issue are these norms that seek to regulate the general interest, in a manner that private parties cannot be allowed to undermine.

**V-25.** Perhaps the strongest manifestation of the *ordre public essentiel* is formed by the rules of EU criminal law. These encompass, first, the various instruments of EU law whereby the Union requires the Member States to criminalize certain behaviour[60] and, second, those norms whereby Member States of their own motion criminalize certain behaviour to ensure the effective enforcement of EU law.[61] It is beyond doubt that these rules seek to establish a social order which private parties may not disturb, on the risk of often severe punishment.

**V-26.** Within the framework of the EU external action, another rather aggressive set of rules of this nature has been developed by the Union, which are enforced with a severity that is usually akin to criminal sanctions, though often with far less procedural guarantees. The practice of the Union to impose trade sanctions on unwilling regimes, has expanded ever further into restrictions on every-day business transactions between private parties that may well sweep up the innocent,[62] the reformed[63] and the suspect[64] alike. The Court has in the past justified these often far-reaching restrictive measures by weighing them against the atrocities which the Union through its external action rightly[65] seeks to combat,[66] though both the ECJ[67] and the GC have in recent times – fully in line with the prominent status fundamental rights have in our model – insisted on far better procedural safeguards.[68]

**V-27.** Individuals are, moreover, as economic agents the primary targets of the EU rules on competition law. It is therefore not surprising that agreements which are contrary to Article 101 TFEU are deemed automatically void[69] or that the enforcement of contrary arbitral awards may be denied as a matter of public policy.[70] It is, moreover, no coincidence that EU competition law may also be enforced through the imposition of administrative sanctions. As the model implies that lower levels are also bound by the higher levels of the model, they, too, are bound by *inter alia* the state aid and the free

60. See for instance Directive 2011/92/EU of the European Parliament and of the Council of 13 December 2011 on combating the sexual abuse and sexual exploitation of children and child pornography, and replacing Council Framework Decision 2004/68/JHA (2011) OJ L 335/1; Directive 2011/36/EU of the European Parliament and of the Council of 5 April 2011 on preventing and combating trafficking in human beings and protecting its victims, and replacing Council Framework Decision 2002/629/JHA (2011) L 101/1.
61. See for instance Case C-101/01 *Lindqvist* [2003] ECR I-12971.
62. Most notable example so far is probably Case C-117/06 *Möllendorf* [2007] ECR I-8361.
63. Case T-284/08 *People's Mojahedin Organization of Iran v. Council* [2008] ECR II-3487.
64. Case T-327/03 *Stichting Al-Aqsa* [2007] ECR II-79*.
65. Often the acts committed correspond indeed to violations of the core rules of international law and the essence of the fundamental rights that form the top level of the EU *ordre public fondamental*, which the EU institutions thus rightly seek to protect.
66. Case C-84/95 *Bosphorus Hava Yollari Turizm ve Ticaret AS* [1996] ECR I-3956, paras 24-26.
67. Joined Cases C-402/05 P and C-415/05 P *Kadi v. Council* [2008] ECR I-6351.
68. Case T-284/08 *People's Mojahedin Organization of Iran v. Council* [2008] ECR II-3487; Case T-256/07 *People's Mojahedin Organization of Iran v. Council* [2008] ECR II-3019.
69. Article 101(2) TFEU.
70. Case C-126/97 *Eco Swiss China Time* [1999] ECR I-3055.

movement rules, at least to the extent that these rules are applicable to them. Accordingly, for the sake of clarity, I am not arguing that my model is in any way premised on or suggesting that these rules have full horizontal direct effect. However, to the extent that these rules are applicable, they are binding on private actors just like they are on Member States[71] – which in my view implies that those individuals may also enjoy the same exceptions as Member States.[72]

**V-28.** Finally, there are numerous acts of EU law which seek to regulate all kinds of aspects of the public good and even more instances where EU law – in the absence of harmonization – allows Member States to set their own standards in this respect. Whereas the latter category is a matter of the *ordre public essentiel* of each individual Member State, although the values protected are usually far from alien to the EU legal order, the former set of acts are part of the EU *ordre public essentiel.* Several of these acts focus squarely on the general interest, subjecting particular interests to the protection of the society as a while from dangers, diseases and other threats. However, the balance between public interests and general interests is often unclear. Above it was discussed how most Member States, for instance, treat consumer protection as a matter of *ordre public de protection*, imposing binding rules but primarily in the interest of weaker private parties, with the result that the powers of, for instance, national courts are rather limited.[73] By contrast, the outcome of cases such as *Rampion and Godard*[74] or *Mostaza Claro*[75] seems to suggest that the EU legal order sees also an important underlying public interest in consumer protection, as an instrument for attaining the societal objectives of the Treaty. Accordingly, there may be need for a more nuanced approach towards these aspects of the EU *ordre public essentiel*, taking into account the sliding scale along which public interests outweigh the private interests. While drawing up a hierarchy is far from self-evident in this respect, and will ultimately require the ECJ to carry out a case-by-case analysis of the relevant act of EU law at issue, there may be some pointers in the Treaties. First, the grounds for justifications laid down in Article 36 TFEU indicate the traditional concerns (public health, public security, public order, public morality) the drafters of the Treaties wanted to make sure would continue to be protected even in a context of free movement. EU measures that seek to protect these matters should therefore also be accorded sufficient weight. Second, the concerns listed in Article 114(3) TFEU that need to receive a high level of protection, again public health, but also environmental protection and consumer protection, indicate a clear intent to have these societal values emphasized in the EU legal order. Good examples are the decision in *Raverco*[76] to refuse an importer of contaminated food to re-export the goods to China where the product would not be illegal, or the acceptance in *Aher-Waggon*[77] that environmental

71. Case C-438/05 *International Transport Workers' Federation* [2007] ECR I-10779.
72. Case C-415/93 *Bosman* [1995] ECR I-4921, para. 86.
73. See, *supra*, at II-174.
74. Case C-429/05 *Rampion and Godard* [2007] ECR I-8017.
75. Case C-168/05 *Mostaza Claro* [2006] ECR I-10421.
76. Joined Cases C-129/05 and C-130 *Raverco* [2006] ECR I-9297.
77. Case C-389/96 *Aher-Waggon* [1998] ECR I-4473.

standards are minimum standards that do not guarantee the free movement of goods to Member States which seek even higher protection. Admittedly, the consumer protection cases are more a mixed bag, as there the private interest is more prominent, though some rules of consumer protection are also adopted because of their deeper ramifications for the credit system,[78] or because of safety concerns.[79]

**V-29.** Furthermore, the Lisbon Treaty has, in this respect, introduced a series of horizontal clauses that similarly emphasize a series of concerns of general interest, albeit at times linked to particular fields: equality between men and women;[80] a 'high level of employment, the guarantee of adequate social protection, the fight against social exclusion, and a high level of education, training and protection of human health';[81] no 'discrimination based on sex, racial or ethnic origin, religion or belief, disability, age or sexual orientation';[82] environmental protection and sustainable development;[83] consumer protection;[84] animal welfare;[85] religious rites, cultural traditions and regional heritage.[86] Most of these interests are not entirely novel to the EU legal order. The EU has for instance a strong record on ensuring equal protection between men and women[87] and is at times quite decisive in matters of animal welfare.[88] Such a long list, however, only seems to aggravate the problem as it does little to offer some kind of hierarchy. Yet, on a closer look there are a few elements that may help. First, some elements continue to return, such as public health and environmental protection. Second, some of these norms – in particular the non-discrimination standards – reflect the EU fundamental rights standard. Finally, others such as the religious rites, cultural traditions and regional heritage seem far less imposing and are basically formulated as a further consideration to qualify the far more fundamental principle of respect for animal welfare.[89] However, respect for the Union's 'rich cultural

78. Opinion of AG Mengozzi in Case C-429/05 *Rampion and Godard* [2007] ECR I-8017, para. 108 in respect of Council Directive 87/102/EEC of 22 December 1986 for the approximation of the laws, regulations and administrative provisions of the Member States concerning consumer credit OJ (1987) L 42/48.
79. Council Directive 85/374/EEC of 25 July 1985 on the approximation of the laws, regulations and administrative provisions of the Member States concerning liability for defective products (1985) OJ L 210/29, as since amended by Directive 1999/34/EC of the European Parliament and of the Council of 10 May 1999 amending Council Directive 85/374/EEC on the approximation of the laws, regulations and administrative provisions of the Member States concerning liability for defective products (1999) OJ L 141/20.
80. Article 8 TFEU.
81. Article 9 TFEU.
82. Article 10 TFEU.
83. Article 11 TFEU.
84. Article 12 TFEU.
85. Article 13 TFEU.
86. Article 13 TFEU.
87. Taken from a very long list of cases which seeks to ensure the equality of both men and women, see, *inter alia*, Case 43/75 *Defrenne* [1976] ECR 455; Case C-407/98 *Abrahamsson* [2000] ECR I-5539; Case C-227/04 P *Lindorfer v. Council* [2007] ECR I-6767.
88. Case C-96/06 *Viamex Agrar* [2008] ECR I-1413; Case C-207/06 *Schwaninger Martin* [2008] ECR I-5561. See also Case C-455/06 *Heemskerk and Schaap* [2008] ECR I-8763, with Opinion of AG Bot.
89. Article 13 TFEU.

and linguistic diversity' and 'Europe's cultural heritage', features prominently among the revised objectives of the Union.[90]

**V-30.** Upon balance, the ECJ will in the course of interpreting various acts of EU law have to decide on a case-by-case basis how weighty the public interest concern is and how consequential this is for private parties.[91] However, in general there seem to be very strong general interest provisions, such as public health – *sensu lato*, also encompassing environmental protection and animal welfare – public safety and public security, but also the specific expressions of the principle of non-discrimination, which the Court should generally seek to protect to the fullest. In light of the link, the ECJ sees between consumer protection and the objectives of the Treaties it appears that these concerns, too, may be taken by the Court as generally dominating the private interest, though maybe a distinction should be made between those aspects, such as product liability[92] which have a direct link with public safety and others that relate to the inequalities in the relationship between businesses and consumers[93] unless these can be linked to other elements of the EU *ordre public*.[94] Similarly, the EU social law

90. Article 3(3) TEU.
91. Case C-415/10 *Meister* [2012] ECR I-0000 seems a good example. The applicant, a 50-year-old woman of Russian descent, had been turned down numerous times by the respondent when she applied for a job, despite meeting all the requirements as to qualifications. She suspected that she was being discriminated against on the basis of age, sex or ethnic origin. To prove this, she wanted to compel the defendant company to provide her with the details of the candidate that was hired instead. The ECJ refused to read such a right into the equal protection directives, as they would conflict with the right to privacy of the successful applicant. However, the Court did accept that the blunt refusal to give any feedback, taken together with other elements, may very well be indicative of discrimination, thus reversing the burden of proof. As AG Mengozzi explains in para. 23 of his Opinion: 'Upsetting that balance between the person who claims to have suffered discrimination and the defendant would not be the only risk involved were a right to information for victims to be recognised. Indeed, such a case also raises the question of rights of any third parties referred to in the documents or information submitted'. Yet, at the same time the effective enforcement of Union law, effectively combating discrimination nevertheless partly pulls into the other direction. The end result is a balance struck between the equal protection of the applicant, the procedural rights of the defendant, the privacy of third parties and the effective enforcement of Union law, all of which are aspect of the EU *ordre public* affecting private parties.
92. Council Directive 85/374/EEC of 25 July 1985 on the approximation of the laws, regulations and administrative provisions of the Member States concerning liability for defective products (1985) OJ L 210/29, as since amended by Directive 1999/34/EC of the European Parliament and of the Council of 10 May 1999 amending Council Directive 85/374/EEC on the approximation of the laws, regulations and administrative provisions of the Member States concerning liability for defective products (1999) OJ L 141/20.
93. See in this respect *inter alia* Directive 2005/29/EC of the European Parliament and of the Council of 11 May 2005 concerning unfair business-to-consumer commercial practices in the internal market and amending Council Directive 84/450/EEC, Directives 97/7/EC, 98/27/EC and 2002/65/EC of the European Parliament and of the Council and Regulation (EC) No 2006/2004 of the European Parliament and of the Council ('Unfair Commercial Practices Directive') (2006) OJ L 149/22; Council Directive 87/102/EEC of 22 December 1986 for the approximation of the laws, regulations and administrative provisions of the Member States concerning consumer credit (1987) OJ L 42/48), as amended by Directive 98/7/EC of the European Parliament and of the Council of 16 February 1998 (1998) OJ L 101/17.
94. An attempt to do just this was done by the ECJ in Case C-168/05 *Mostaza Claro* [2006] ECR I-10421, para. 37, where the Court compared the provisions of Council Directive 93/13/EEC of 5 April 1993 on unfair terms in consumer contracts (1993) OJ L 95/29 to the role played by

contains provisions, such as the Working Time Directive[95] which seeks to protect health and safety[96] or the equal protection labour legislation which seeks to protect fundamental rights,[97] that may justify far-reaching intervention against private parties, whereas other legislation, such as the legislation on the transfer of undertakings[98] may be focused more on the private relationship between worker and employer. Finally, the impact of weaker interests, such as cultural traditions and regional heritage may by contrast often be rather limited.[99]

Article 101 TFEU, the EU *ordre public* status of which is also confirmed by this Model, in achieving the objectives of the Treaty.

95. Council Directive 93/104/EC of 23 November 1993 concerning certain aspects of the organization of working time (1993) OJ L 307/18.
96. Case C-84/94 *United Kingdom v. Council* [1996] ECR I-5755.
97. Both the classic legislation in respect of the equal treatment of men and women (in particular Directive 2006/54/EC of the European Parliament and of the Council of 5 July 2006 on the implementation of the principle of equal opportunities and equal treatment of men and women in matters of employment and occupation (recast) (2006) OJ L 204/23), and the legislation combating other forms of discrimination, see Council Directive 2000/78/EC of 27 November 2000 establishing a general framework for equal treatment in employment and occupation (2000) OJ L 303/16, as illustrated by cases such as Case C-54/07 *Feryn* [2008] ECR I-5187 and Case C-303/06 *Coleman* [2008] ECR I-5603.
98. Council Directive 2001/23/EC of 12 March 2001 on the approximation of the laws of the Member States relating to the safeguarding of employees' rights in the event of transfers of undertakings, businesses or parts of undertakings or businesses (2001) OJ L 82/16.
99. Yet, see, *infra*, at V-43.

# CHAPTER 17
# Perspectives Flowing from the Model

**V-31.** The model outlined above seeks to offer an encompassing overview of the EU *ordre public*, but at the same time structures the EU *ordre public* in a hierarchical manner, which invites for a differentiated approach as to the consequences that flow from the EU *ordre public* status of a norm or principle of EU law. The model allows for differentiation depending on both the level at which action is taken and the corresponding actors (EU, Member States, private parties) and the nature of the norms at issue. Accordingly, the sliding scale underlying the model should be reflected in the ensuing remedies. The variety in manifestations of the EU *ordre public* outlined in Part II suggests that this is already largely the case. The question is whether the model outlined in this Part may help to do this in a more coherent manner.

## §17.01 SALZGITTER REVISITED

**V-32.** In the first place, the model helps to explain why the ECJ should not of its own motion raise just any norm of higher EU law. However, it also reveals that the current practice restricted to the rules on competence and essential procedural requirements is too narrow. Advocate General Jacobs argued that:

> in the light of the Court's role as the guardian of the rule of law, it would be unacceptable if the Court were precluded from raising of its own motion a manifest and grave substantive illegality, for example an infringement of a fundamental right or of Article 85 of the EC Treaty (now Article [101 TFEU]), whilst being able to raise of its own motion infringements of certain procedural rules[1].

I submit he is half right. The model suggests that fundamental rights are indeed to be included among the rules of EU *ordre public* which the EU courts should raise of their own motion. However, that is not true for Article 101 TFEU. Apart from the practical

1. Opinion of AG Jacobs in Case C-210/98 P *Salzgitter v. Commission* [2000] ECR I-5843, para. 137.

difficulties of holding otherwise,[2] which would greatly upset the procedure before the General Court in competition cases, there is also a more fundamental reason. The rules on competition are undoubtedly crucial for the EU legal order, which is precisely why they are included in the model of EU *ordre public*. However, they seek primarily to steer private behaviour. I do not deny that these rules contain the margins within which the Commission operates, as do all grants of competence. Yet, not including these rules higher in the hierarchy recognizes that it nevertheless is the Commission, under control by the Court, who develops a competition policy that may vary over time, whereby certain practices which once were legal may no longer be so at a later point in time.[3] Yet, at the same the place of the competition rules in the model indicates that it is important, though, to ensure that private parties are not allowed to upset that balance unchecked.[4] Put differently, for the institutions competition law is a policy, albeit an important one, among many, even though it is to be acknowledged that the Treaties set unusually strong limits on the policy margin left in this domain; for private parties it sets the outer limits of their economic freedom, even when they are acting in domains, such as sport, which may not immediately be associated with economic competition.[5] Accordingly, I submit that *de lege ferenda* the Court should open up the category of norms and principles it may – or even must[6] – invoke *motu proprio* with the norms of *jus cogens* (as they flow from an even higher level in the model), the EU fundamental rights, the rules that seek to protect the financial interests of the Union and the other general principles of EU law that structure the EU constitutional order. However, it should not go as far as to include also Articles 101 and 102 TFEU.

## §17.02 AN INCREASED ROLE FOR NATIONAL COURTS

**V-33.** In the second place, for the model to operate well a lot of trust is to be placed in national courts, which are after all the ordinary courts of EU law, and a lot is expected from them. First, they, too, have a role to play in guaranteeing that the Union itself complies with the EU *ordre public fondamental*. Admittedly, national courts are in

---

2. The Union courts already struggle with ensuring respect for the rights of defence when they are raising pleas of their own motion, see Case C-89/08 P *Commission v. Ireland* [2009] ECR I-11245; Case C-197/09 RX-II *M/European Medicines Agency (EMEA)* [2009] ECR I-12033.
3. See for instance the rules laid down in Commission Regulation (EU) No 461/2010 of 27 May 2010 on the application of Article 101(3) of the Treaty on the Functioning of the European Union to categories of vertical agreements and concerted practices in the motor vehicle sector (2010) OJ L 129/52 which seek to be tighter than the rules laid down in Commission Regulation (EU) No 330/2010 of 20 April 2010 on the application of Article 101(3) of the Treaty on the Functioning of the European Union to categories of vertical agreements and concerted practices (2010) L 102/1. No one would argue that the Commission was somehow violating the EU *ordre public* in the intermediate period when it allowed the motor vehicle sector more margin; conversely, however, if that sector violates either regulation it is acting contrary to the EU *ordre public* at their level.
4. Case C-126/97 *Eco Swiss China Time* [1999] ECR I-3055.
5. Case C-519/04 P *Meca-Medina and Majcen v. Commission* [2006] ECR I-6991; Case C-49/07 *MOTOE* [2008] ECR I-4863.
6. See, *supra*, at II-197.

principle not in a position to strike down acts of the Union,[7] but that does not make them powerless. On the one hand, they have the power to refer preliminary questions as to the validity of EU acts to the ECJ, and it should be welcomed if national courts were to be sufficiently vigilant and critical when confronted with acts of the institutions. The potential increase in case-load for the ECJ would be largely off-set by the fact that problematic acts may be detected earlier, and the effect this may have on the EU legislator which may become more self-critical as well. On the other hand, the national court has a default role to play, whenever the ECJ is precluded on practical or jurisdictional grounds to offer relieve. The former situation occurs in situations of urgency and has already been recognized by the ECJ,[8] the latter situation arises - even after the Lisbon Treaty - in respect of CFSP acts, the validity of which is largely beyond the reach of the ECJ, so that national courts must step in.[9] Therefore, it is submitted that, fully in line with the principles of subsidiarity and loyal cooperation - also principles protected as a matter of EU *ordre public fondamental*, national courts should through their vigilance assist the ECJ in ensuring that the EU institutions do not violate the EU *ordre public fondamental*.

**V-34.** Second, the national courts will have to be far more critical vis-à-vis their own Member States in ensuring that they comply with those rules that are specifically targeted at them: citizenship, free movement, customs union, state aid and, for the countries that have adopted the euro, the *lex moneta*. Does this mean that national courts should henceforth raise these issues always of their own motion? The answer is somewhat more nuanced. It is clear that EU law would definitely not bar such an approach, and under *Simmenthal:*

> a national court which is called upon, within the limits of its jurisdiction, to apply provisions of Community law is under a duty to give full effect to those provisions, if necessary refusing of its own motion to apply any conflicting provision of national legislation, even if adopted subsequently, and it is not necessary for the court to request or await the prior setting aside of such provision by legislative or other constitutional means[10]

However, as outlined above in Part II, that approach is to be mitigated by the principle of national procedural autonomy, which not coincidentally is placed in the model together with primacy as one of the constitutional principles that are part of the concept of EU *ordre public fondamental*. Accordingly, the national court will only have to intervene *motu proprio* in case of a systemic failure, which would prevent the normal enforcement of EU law. Therefore, in the ordinary course of events national courts must of their own motion draw the consequences from any inconsistency between

7. Case 314/84 *Foto-Frost* [1987] ECR 4199.
8. Case C-465/93 *Atlanta Fruchthandelsgesellschaft* [1995] ECR I-3761. For more on this power of the national court, see G. Anagnostaras, 'The incomplete state of Community harmonisation in the provision of interim protection by the national courts', *European Law Review* (2008): 586-597.
9. This seems also required after the Lisbon Treaty as a result of the new Article 19(1), second sentence, TEU.
10. Case 106/77 *Simmenthal* [1978] ECR 629, para. 24.

national law and EU law as appears from the debate before it, but they must not raise EU norms that are not yet at issue in the debate. Yet, it is submitted that precisely in respect of the rules on state aid and free movement Member States may have an interest to bend the rules and create such systemic failures, as demonstrated by the state-aid case of *Lucchini*.[11] Accordingly, Member States courts should never a priori assume that certain national limitations on their ability to act *motu proprio* will always preclude them from raising issues of material EU law in these domains. In instances where there is a risk for collusion the national court must act, if necessary of its own motion, to safeguard EU *ordre public*. Moreover, it could be argued that, at least in some instances where the procedural inequality between a Member State and a private party who should otherwise benefit from these rules is important,[12] Member States should be precluded from pursuing their self-interest by violating rules of EU *ordre public* that specifically target that Member State. I think in this respect, for instance, of the situation in *Estager*,[13] where a criminal defendant may not even fully realize that his punishment is enhanced, not because of the nature of his crime, but purely because of the dubious exchange rate used by the Member State. Similarly, in immigration cases, where Member States have a tendency of shaping the rules in a manner that guarantees maximal rejection of residency applications, Member States should not be allowed to hide behind procedural rules to refuse to take into account that someone is a citizen of the Union.[14] Accordingly, while I do not suggest that national courts must henceforth raise all issues relating to EU citizenship, free movement, the customs union, state aid or the *lex moneta* of the euro, of their own motion, they should do so in cases where systemic failures or the inequality between the parties make it likely that those aspects of the EU *ordre public fondamental* that are targeted on the Member States, would otherwise be persistently under-enforced. In any event, I thus do not agree that 'national courts should, in principle, not be asked to apply certain – substantive – [Union] law provisions *ex officio* and as a matter of public policy, if the Luxembourg courts do not do so either',[15] as their roles are markedly different.

**V-35.** All this requires, however, that national courts are up to their tasks. In particular, Member States must continue to ensure that their judges are well-versed in EU law, and this long after the training programmes the Union tends to set up on the occasion of a pending enlargement phase have elapsed. The need to stay in touch with the evolution

11. Case C-119/05 *Lucchini Siderurgica* [2007] ECR I-6199.
12. Compare, in a similar vein, the argumentation put forward by the ECJ to justify that certain rules of EU consumer protection law must be raised by national courts of their own motion, namely because of their link with the essentials of the EU *ordre économique* (Case C-168/05 *Mostaza Claro* [2006] ECR I-10421, para. 37) and because of the risk that in situations of great inequality between the parties some may otherwise even not know of their rights (Case C-429/05 *Rampion and Godard* [2007] ECR I-8017, para. 65).
13. Case C-359/05 *Estager* [2007] ECR I-581.
14. See, however, *contra*, a Dutch judgment of the Afdeling bestuursrechtspraak Raad van State, Nr. 200308607/1, 2 March 2004. See in this respect also J. Jans *Doorgeschoten? Enkele opmerkingen over de gevolgen van de Europeanisering van het bestuursrecht voor de grondslagen van de bestuursrechtspraak* (Groningen: Europa Law Publishing, 2005), 8-17.
15. S. Prechal & N. Shelkoplyas, 'National Procedures, Public Policy and EC Law. From Van Schijndel to Eco Swiss and Beyond', *European Review of Private Law* (2004): 611.

of EU law is, moreover, not restricted to judges. For the model set out here to function, it is important that all actors in the legal process – lawyers, prosecutors, *référendaires* – develop an EU law reflex, which universities should kick-start but which takes a lifetime of maintenance.

## §17.03 A SLIDING SCALE OF PUBLIC AND PRIVATE INTERESTS

**V-36.** In the third place, there may be need for a more coherent approach towards the impact of EU law on private parties. There is little doubt as to the EU *ordre public* status of those rules that are enforced through criminal or administrative sanctions. Among them are also the rules of EU competition law. On the one hand, under Regulation 1/2003[16] the Articles 101 and 102 TFEU may also be enforced by national authorities, whereby appeals against the sanctions imposed will be brought before national courts. On the other hand, these rules may also be at issue in other procedures whereby private parties seek to enforce these rules vis-à-vis each other.[17] The effect of the EU *ordre public* status of the norms will, however, depend on the context. It is submitted that the national court should again only intervene *motu proprio* in the procedure to compensate for systemic failures. Accordingly, I submit that both the outcome in *Renault*,[18] where the national court was not allowed to refuse *exequatur* of a judgment that may have been contrary to Article 101 TFEU delivered in another Member State, and *Eco Swiss*,[19] whereby the ECJ argued that an arbitral award should be checked against the competition rules as a matter of national public policy before *exequatur* is granted, are both compatible with the model. Actually, the time limit in *Eco Swiss* ultimately prevented the national court from proceeding with that review, and this, too, is acceptable provided that time limit is not unduly short[20] given the role the principle of national procedural autonomy plays in the model presented.

**V-37.** The problem is, however, rather how national courts should deal with other instruments of secondary legislation. I have submitted above that a more nuanced approach seems necessary, depending on the strength of the private interests involved if compared to the public interest at stake. I would like to make this concrete with looking back at a few examples, which will not only demonstrate the proposed sliding scale, but also explain how the model may deal with some further complications.

16. Council Regulation (EC) No 1/2003 of 16 December 2002 on the implementation of the rules on competition laid down in Articles 81 and 82 of the Treaty (2003) OJ L 1/1.
17. See for instance Joined Cases C-295/04 to C-298/04 *Manfredi* [2006] ECR I-6619; Case C-453/99 *Courage* [2001] ECR I-6297. Undoubtedly, the private enforcement of EU competition law, as envisaged by the Commission for further development in its Commission Green Paper, *Damages actions for breach of the EC antitrust rules*, COM (2005) 672 final, offers another example of the legitimizing strand of the EU *ordre public*.
18. Case C-38/98 *Régie nationale des usines Renault* [2000] ECR I-2973.
19. Case C-126/97 *Eco Swiss China Time* [1999] ECR I-3055.
20. Case C-126/97 *Eco Swiss China Time* [1999] ECR I-3055.

**V-38.** In the light of the model, it appears that *Van der Weerd*[21] makes perfect sense. While the Directive at issue in that case[22] in the abstract did seek to protect public and animal health, the Directive was being invoked belatedly solely to protect the private interests of the farmer who tried to escape the protective measures. In the absence of any public interest or a systemic failure that would have made enforcement of EU law unduly difficult, there was no reason to require the national court to invoke the Directive of its own motion.

**V-39.** I have argued in Part III that EU social law should be treated as a matter of EU *ordre public.*[23] I argued in that respect that this would enhance the output legitimacy of the EU legal order in realizing a more social Europe and tried to link this to the absence of a pan-European social security as a fall-back position. While I believe that this may indeed play a role, I have no difficulty admitting that the weight of these arguments may be rather limited. Accordingly, in a more nuanced approach the rules on working time,[24] which clearly have a health and safety component,[25] may carry so much weight that they may at times be enforced even in the face of contrary agreements,[26] though even these judgments do not preclude that deviations are possible, though the burden of proof will lay with the employer.[27]*A fortiori* it seems defensible that employees may be in a position to sign away – at least once the transfer process has taken place, and in the absence of duress – certain rights under the Directive on transfers of undertakings[28] which primarily safeguards the private interests of the workers. Accordingly, while the rights of employees of a transferred company under the Directive 'must be considered to be mandatory, so that it is not possible to derogate from them in a manner unfavourable to employees',[29] the Court has nonetheless decided that:

> although in accordance with the objective of the Directive the interests of the employees concerned by the transfer must be protected, those of the transferee, who must be in a position to make the adjustments and changes necessary to carry on his operations, cannot be disregarded[30].

21. Joined Cases C-222/05, C-223/05, C-224/05 and C-225/05 *Van der Weerd* [2007] ECR I-4233.
22. Council Directive 85/511/EEC of 18 November 1985 introducing Community measures for the control of foot-and-mouth disease (1985) OJ L 315/11.
23. See, *supra*, at III-86 et seq.
24. Council Directive 93/104/EC of 23 November 1993 concerning certain aspects of the organization of working time (1993) OJ L 307/18.
25. Case C-84/94 *United Kingdom v. Council* [1996] ECR I-5755.
26. Joined Cases C-131/04 and C-257/04 *Robinson-Steele* [2006] ECR I-2531, para. 68; Case C-124/05 *Federatie Nederlandse Vakbeweging* [2006] ECR I-3423.
27. Joined Cases C-131/04 and C-257/04 *Robinson-Steele* [2006] ECR I-2531, para. 68. Interestingly, even though the health objective of paid annual leave may no longer be met in the case of a person who is on sick leave during the whole year (in the case of partial absence due to illness, the right to paid leave may be exercised at a different time of the year), the worker still is entitled to monetary compensation *in lieu,* see Joined Cases C-350/06 and C-520/06 *Schultz-Hoff* [2009] ECR I-179.
28. Council Directive 2001/23/EC of 12 March 2001 on the approximation of the laws of the Member States relating to the safeguarding of employees' rights in the event of transfers of undertakings, businesses or parts of undertakings or businesses (2001) OJ L 82/16.
29. Case C-499/04 *Werhof* [2006] ECR I-2397, para. 26.
30. Case C-499/04 *Werhof* [2006] ECR I-2397, para. 31.

**V-40.** Also the enforcement of EU consumer protection law may need a second look. The introduction of an intermediate level of mandatory law, which would be binding on the parties, but would only result in a relative nullity of the transaction if properly and timely requested by the protected party, may at times be preferred. The ECJ has, however, done its utmost best to circumvent national laws that seem to take such an intermediate approach.[31] It is submitted that this is only justified to the extent that a public interest can be made explicit. In this respect I am swayed by the Opinion of AG Mengozzi that 'Directive 87/102 does not pursue solely the objective of protecting consumers who obtain consumer credit but also and primarily that of ensuring the creation of a common market in consumer credit',[32] so it would have strengthened the judgment of the Court in *Rampion and Godard* if the Court had stressed this aspect, rather than the inequality of the relationship between the parties.[33] By contrast, the link between the idea, inspired by old Article 2 TEC, that strengthening consumer protection 'is essential to the accomplishment of the tasks entrusted to the [Union] and, in particular, to raising the standard of living and the quality of life in its territory' while not wrong per se may be too little of an explanation, as all acts of the Union are in one way or another adopted with a view of realizing the breathtakingly broad objectives of Article 3 TEU. Therefore, it may well be that the duty to invoke the Unfair Commercial Terms Directive[34] *motu proprio*[35] may have less to do with its status as a measure of EU *ordre public essentiel* but, as argued above,[36] more a matter of *effet utile* of the level of protection the ECJ assumes the EU legislator wished to offer in order to effectively combat inequalities in a particular context.[37] It would be preferable if the Court would therefore say so explicitly.

**V-41.** Also the cases discussed above[38] in respect of the Brussels Convention[39] or Brussels I Regulation[40] all seem to fit the pattern. First, the rules on jurisdiction are

31. Case C-429/05 *Rampion and Godard* [2007] ECR I-8017; Case C-473/00 *Cofidis* [2002] ECR I-10875; Case C-168/05 *Mostaza Claro* [2006] ECR I-10421.
32. Opinion of AG Mengozzi in Case C-429/05 *Rampion and Godard* [2007] ECR I-8017, para. 108.
33. The Court only mentions the 'dual aim of ensuring both the creation of a common consumer credit market (third to fifth recitals) and the protection of consumers who avail themselves of such credit (sixth, seventh and ninth recitals)' in passing, but then focuses more on the need to protect the weaker party, see Case C-429/05 *Rampion and Godard* [2007] ECR I-8017, paras 57-69.
34. Council Directive 93/13/EEC of 5 April 1993 on unfair terms in consumer contracts (1993) OJ L 95/29.
35. Case C-168/05 *Mostaza Claro* [2006] ECR I-10421; Joined Case C-240/98 to C-244/98 *Océano Grupo Editorial* [2000] ECR I-4941.
36. See, *supra*, at II-168.
37. Nevertheless, despite this insight, it has been argued that consumer protection inherently entails an element of the protection of the 'public interest', justifying an active role for the courts dealing with such cases, see G. Poissonnier, 'La C.J.C.E. donne au juge national le pouvoir d'appliquer d'office le droit communautaire de la consommation', *European Journal of Consumer Law/Revue européenne de droit de la consummation* (2007-2008): 137-142.
38. See, *supra*, at II-137 et seq.
39. Convention of 27 September 1968 on Jurisdiction and the Enforcement of Judgments in Civil and Commercial Matters (1978) OJ L 304/36.
40. Council Regulation (EC) No 44/2001 of 22 December 2000 on jurisdiction and the recognition and enforcement of judgments in civil and commercial matters (2001) OJ L 12/1.

mandatory, but they primarily protect the private interests of the parties in guaranteeing a particular forum, so that it seems correct that the ECJ in *Kapferer*[41] did not require the Austrian courts to raise the jurisdictional issue *motu proprio* given the fact that the defendant had missed two opportunities to raise the issue either before the lower court or in his appeals brief. Second, the enforcement cases offer a first example of how norms of the *ordre public fondamental* may affect the outcome of cases concerning the enforcement of civil or commercial judgments, which concern otherwise in essence private interests. It is submitted that also under the model presented the different results reached in *Krombach*[42] and *Renault*[43] are not contradictory. In the former case the enforcement of the judgment could rightly be rejected because the enforcement stage offered the first time in the procedure where the fundamental rights concern, a matter of EU *ordre public fondamental* could be taken into account. In the latter case, however, the concerns about the correct application of the rules of competition law – a matter of EU *ordre public essentiel* – could well have been dealt with earlier before the courts of the Member State the judgment originated from, so that in the absence of any systemic failure there was no reason to deny the enforcement of the judgment.

**V-42.** Finally, I submit that also the outcome of *Heemskerk and Schaap*[44] may be reconciled with the model, at least if one considers – in the face of the scant reasoning in the judgment –the more extensive argumentation I have proposed above.[45] The rules at issue in that case[46] strongly protect important public interests, in particular animal welfare and – even higher in the hierarchy – the financial interests of the Union. I therefore agree with Advocate General Bot that the appropriate action would have been to require the national court, despite national procedural autonomy, to raise the issue *motu proprio*, even at the risk of *reformatio in pejus*[47] as this is the only manner to enforce the level of protection the Union requires, especially taking into account the risk of collusion between the government and the applicants. However, as the EU fundamental rights standard – in a spirit of respect for the constitutional traditions of the Member State and in a spirit of mutual loyal cooperation, basically expressions of the federalism concerns that can be considered as part of the EU *ordre public fondamental* and thus higher in the hierarchy than the animal welfare concerns and on equal footing with the concern about the EU public finances[48] – takes account of more

41. Case C-234/04 *Kapferer* [2006] ECR I-2585.
42. Case C-7/98 *Krombach* [2000] ECR I-1935.
43. Case C-38/98 *Régie nationale des usines Renault* [2000] ECR I-2973.
44. Case C-455/06 *Heemskerk and Schaap* [2008] ECR I-8763.
45. See, *supra*, at IV-44.
46. Council Regulation (EC) No 1254/1999 of 17 May 1999 on the common organization of the market in beef and veal (1999) OJ L 160/21; Commission Regulation (EC) No 615/98 of 18 March 1998 laying down specific detailed rules of application for the export refund arrangements as regards the welfare of live bovine animals during transport (1998) OJ L 82/19. See also Commission Regulation (EC) No 639/2003 of 9 April 2003 laying down detailed rules pursuant to Council Regulation (EC) No 1254/1999 as regards requirements for the granting of export refunds related to the welfare of live bovine animals during transport (2003) OJ L 93/10.
47. Opinion of AG Bot in Case C-455/06 *Heemskerk and Schaap* [2008] ECR I-8763, paras 85-146.
48. If two values at the same level are pulling in different directions then balancing of interest is the natural consequence. In this case that balancing would heavily favour deference to the national fundamental rights norm, as this is a new element at this stage of the debate, and the financial

protective national constitutional rules it may nevertheless be explained why in this particular instance before a Dutch court the duty to raise the norms *motu proprio* may appropriately be waved.

## §17.04 WHATEVER HAPPENED TO THE CULTURAL ORDER?

**V-43.** From the start I have included in my definition a place for the protection of the cultural order. In particular, at several stages I have argued in this respect for far greater sensitivity of the EU legal order for linguistic issues.[49] Prima facie that dimension is underplayed in the model. The reason for this is that this cultural dimension is often hard to grasp. Moreover, there is no such thing as EU culture, which could inspire the EU *ordre public*, though there is undoubtedly a European cultural heritage which the post-Lisbon EU Treaty explicitly recognizes.[50] The primary concern is, however, to allow for sufficient diversity among the various cultural traditions of the Member States. That concern, however, is very much present in the model, as the net balance of the competing constitutional values that are at the heart of the EU *ordre public fondamental* basically boils down to ensuring 'unity in diversity'.[51] Seen from that perspective, the entire EU legal order breathes this sensitivity towards national cultural identities, diversity and pluralism. Against that background, my plea to give *de lege ferenda* more weight to the protection of the languages of Member States, taking into account that cultural, religious and linguistic diversity are also protected by Article 22 of the Charter of Fundamental Rights of the Union, seems well in line with the model presented in this Part, and it appears that since the Lisbon Treaty the Court is indeed increasingly willing to take local sensitivities[52] or linguistic diversity[53] into account.

## §17.05 CONCLUSION

**V-44.** The final Part has resulted in a model to describe and structure the EU *ordre public*. The model is undoubtedly not perfect. In essence, it focuses strongly on a functional approach[54] towards EU *ordre public*, which is based less on what it is (even though at least the contours of its content are defined), but rather on what can be done with it. Yet, therein also lies its strength, I hope. The model seeks to reconcile a

---

interest of the Union will only be marginally endangered to the extent that the Netherlands is – regardless of the outcome of whether recovery of the funds given to Heemskerk and Schaap is possible –under an obligation to compensate the EU budget.

49. See in particular, *supra*, at III-105 et seq.
50. Article 3(3) TEU.
51. See, *supra*, at V-19.
52. Case C-208/09 *Sayn-Wittgenstein* [2010] ECR I-0000; compare also Case T-232/10 *Couture Tech v. OHIM* [2011] ECR II-0000 where the local concern about the use of former communist symbols is integrated into a Union concept of public policy.
53. Case C-391/09 *Runevič-Vardyn* [2011] ECR I-0000.
54. A criticism also Romain, whose definition I used as a basis for my model, was well aware of, see J.-F. Romain, 'L'*ordre public* (notion générale) et les droits de l'homme' in *L'ordre public: concept et applications*, ed. J.-F. Romain, M. Grégoire & V. Simonart (Bruxelles: Bruylant, 1995), 60-61.

comprehensive approach towards the EU *ordre public*, which is given an important substantive, legal content, with a nuanced approach as to its consequences, taking into account both the finality of the rule, which explains its place in the hierarchy, and the context in which it needs to be applied. The model appears, moreover, to correspond largely with the state of affairs *de lege lata*. Yet, beyond its descriptive qualities, the model also offers the basis for some modest proposals for changes *de lege ferenda*: a somewhat broader concept of *ordre public* for the purpose of determining whether the EU courts should raise an issue of EU law *motu proprio*, a more central role for national courts, a more nuanced approach towards the impact of mandatory EU law on private parties and, finally, a greater sensitivity towards the diversity of national cultural identities.

# Conclusions

**1.** In the introduction to this book, I evoke the prospect of a journey throughout the wondrous world of EU law in search of a concept that has been described as a 'mystery'[1], the *ordre public.* I even warn that:

> attempts to define it have been likened to adventuring into quicksand, riding a wild horse on a journey into the unknown or walking along a path amidst thorny bushes[2]. So, if we are to survive this perilous adventure into the unknown, we had better expect the unexpected and prepare ourselves for winding roads leading into the far corners of the law[3]

At this point, we have come at the end of this voyage, so it is appropriate to pause and reflect. Did we reach our destination? What did we encounter along the way? What have we learned from undertaking this journey? Moreover, as travellers have to make choices at crossroads one has to wonder: what opportunities did we forego by taking the route I have plotted? Or put more positively, where are there still new challenges that await keen explorers? It is time to make a balance of our quest for the EU *ordre public.*

**2.** It is difficult to describe the final destination of an investigation into the EU *ordre public.* At the start, it was not even certain that this mysterious concept even truly exists. The first accomplishment, therefore, is undoubtedly the conclusion that there indeed is such a thing as an EU *ordre public.* What is more, I submit that it is related to, but independent from the concept of *ordre public* as it appears in the context of the legal orders of the various Member States or in the context of the ECHR. Moreover, mysterious as the concept may be, the EU *ordre public* can to a large extent be described. It has a content that can be ascertained, though the result is not so much a

1. E. Picard, 'Introduction générale: la fonction de l'*ordre public* dans l'ordre juridique' in *L'ordre public: ordre public ou ordres publics? Ordre public et droits fondamentaux*, ed. M.-J. Redor (Bruxelles: Bruylant, 2001), 17.
2. J.-F. Romain, 'L'*ordre public* (notion générale) et les droits de l'homme' in *L'ordre public: concept et applications*, ed. J.-F. Romain, M. Grégoire & V. Simonart (Bruxelles: Bruylant, 1995), 8.
3. See, *supra*, Introduction, at 2.

monolith but more akin to a set of Russian dolls. Nevertheless, layer after layer, the essence of the EU *ordre public* can be unveiled. Admittedly that content may be in constant evolution to the extent that the Union itself is evolving, but that does not preclude us from taking snapshots of how the EU *ordre public* looks like at the beginning of the second decade of the twenty-first century. If the *ordre public* is an 'unruly horse', then it has nonetheless proven possible in Part V of this book to cage the animal for study purposes with a model that seems fairly good at describing the content of the EU *ordre public* and that appears to account for the plethora of forms in which the concept appears in the EU legal order. Moreover, the model allows not only to describe the concept of the EU *ordre public*, but it also forms the basis for a few modest suggestions for the role the concept may play *de lege ferenda*: a somewhat broader concept of *ordre public* for the purpose of determining whether the EU courts should raise an issue *motu proprio*, a more central role for national courts, a more nuanced approach towards the impact of mandatory EU law on private parties and finally a greater sensitivity towards the diversity of national cultural identities.

**3.** With that the mountain of the EU *ordre public* has probably not been conquered, but mountains never are – at best they condone climbers on their slopes. So, at least as important as reaching the summit, if putting forward a model may be equated with that, is the winding road that has led there. The end result seems to indicate that the starting point, a broad definition of the EU *ordre public* as the complex of norms at the very heart of a political entity (in this case the EU) expressing and protecting the basic options taken by that entity regarding its political, economic, social and even cultural order, was a fortuitous one, even though it forced the exploration of these four vast dimensions. Along the way, I therefore got a chance to look more closely at several major doctrines and topics of EU law, albeit always through the lens of the EU *ordre public*.

**4.** First, an important part of the book deals with the free movement of goods, services, persons and capital. This is hardly surprising, as the Treaties even provide for a reference to public policy in this context. Accordingly, in Part II the breadth of that public policy exception was explored extensively and compared with related exceptions in the context of the recognition of judgments, competition law or even Article 347 TFEU. Particular emphasis was moreover laid on the free movement of persons in general and EU citizenship in particular. The study of the free movement did, moreover, not end with the discussion of the public policy exception. In Part III, it became clear that underlying the free movement are values that justify its inclusion into my model of EU *ordre public*. On the one hand, emphasis has been laid on its role for the realization of the internal market and thus for the *ordre public économique* of the Union. On the other hand, I have argued that underlying the free movement of persons – and ultimately also underlying the other freedoms – hides a deeper dimension. At the heart of the concept of free movement sits an important emancipating force, which justifies including the four freedoms in my model of EU *ordre public*. Given the additional political dimension that is included in the concept of EU citizenship, the link between the EU *ordre public* and EU citizenship should follow *a fortiori*.

**5.** Second, another area that receives broad attention across the book is more procedural in nature. It concerns the question when courts, both at the level of the EU and in the various Member States, must raise EU law of their own motion. This focus is also unsurprising, as here too, the concept of *ordre public* is very much at the forefront of the Court's case law. The analysis in respect of the EU level has revealed a rather consistent practice as to when the Court may or, at times, must raise issues of EU law *motu proprio*. Nevertheless, the final part has given the opportunity to put forward a suggestion for expanding the norms the Court should invoke of its own motion in a principled manner. In this way, it is in particular possible to include the fundamental rights catalogue in that body of norms, without upsetting the whole procedure in direct actions. In this way, I meet halfway between the current system and the criticism put forward by Advocate General Jacobs in *Salzgitter*.[4] At the level of the national courts, the picture is somewhat more blurred, as several principles seem to pull in various directions. The basic principle is national procedural autonomy, which should make the answer to this question primarily a matter of national law. Yet, its twin exceptions of equivalence and effectiveness at times pull the other way. I argue that whenever there is a risk of a systemic failure that would prevent that the norms of EU law would otherwise be brought into the debate properly, because of the effect of national procedural law or because of something atypical about the parties or the setting, that national courts must intervene by raising the relevant norms of EU law *motu proprio*, as is demonstrated forcefully by the case of *Lucchini*.[5] Moreover, it appears that the ECJ has also developed a wholly different theory that appears somewhat confusingly in parallel with the national procedural autonomy and its exceptions in cases concerning consumer protection. Even in the absence of systemic failures the ECJ has interpreted specific consumer protection directives as requiring that national courts raise some provisions aimed at protecting the weaker party of their own motion as a matter of *effet utile* on the apparent assumption that this is the only way to ensure the level of protection the legislator had in mind. Finally, I am somewhat critical of the case of *Heemskerk and Schaap*,[6] not so much for its result, but for giving the unfortunate impression that the Court may virtually abdicate when confronted with strongly held national constitutional norms, whereas in my view a more explicit principled reasoning may support the same result in a manner that better acknowledges the various interests at stake, both at the level of the Union and at the level of the Member States.

**6.** Third, the journey has taken us through the broader constitutional landscape of the Union. At various points, attention was paid to issues of decision-making, competence and judicial protection. Often the shadow of the Lisbon Treaty is hanging over the analysis, though virtually all points made held even true before its entry into force. Nevertheless, some of the changes the Lisbon Treaty brings, such as the more formal status of the Charter of Fundamental Rights of the EU,[7] the additional emphasis placed

4. Opinion of AG Jacobs in Case C-210/98 P *Salzgitter v. Commission* [2000] ECR I-5843.
5. Case C-119/05 *Lucchini Siderurgica* [2007] ECR I-6199.
6. Case C-455/06 *Heemskerk and Schaap* [2008] ECR I-8763.
7. Article 6(1) TEU.

on respect for the national identities[8] or the more explicit role of national courts in providing judicial protection[9] seem to underscore some of the arguments brought to the fore in this book. In particular, the focus was constantly placed on the interaction between the EU legal order and the national legal orders. Along the road, the principles of subsidiarity, direct effect and primacy have all been visited and re-visited, to stress how the effectiveness of Union law may be guaranteed, without, however, needlessly upsetting the national legal orders.

**7.** Perhaps one of the most important lessons flows from Part IV. There it is submitted that upon balance there is reason for cautious optimism, in that the Union is quite capable of defusing conflicts between the EU and the national legal orders. Admittedly, some of the instruments in the toolbox may at times appear a bit blunt, and for some the manual instructions about when and how they should be used may be unclear, but the net result is upon balance reassuring. That is not to say that there are no challenges ahead. First, the introduction by the Lisbon Treaty of the binding Charter of Fundamental Rights of the EU, with various references to the national legal orders makes clarity about the scope of and interaction between national and EU standards evermore pressing. Second, with societal evolution inevitably come new problems. The analysis of the position of same-sex marriages in the EU legal order (the recognition of which I defend at both the EU level and the level of the Member States) is just one example of what the future may hold in this respect. My analysis must primarily be read as a strong plea for a Union which is open and inclusive and enables as many persons as possible to fully experience the emancipating potential the Union has to offer, not merely – as has so far been the focus – regardless of their nationality, but also regardless of their moral convictions or any other ground for discrimination put forward by Article 21 of the Charter of Fundamental Rights of the EU. Third, in order to answer such challenges I propose a more stringent test for the acceptability of national constitutional values as a justification for not fully applying EU law. I accept that the EU *ordre public* may often – as for instance in the case of the free movement of services as demonstrated by *Omega Spielhallen*,[10] a case which has extensively been commented upon across this book – be an appropriate vessel for channelling these national values. However, as the ECJ determines the scope of the public policy exception, this requires an assessment of the compatibility of the promoted value with the EU legal order, an inquiry into the genuineness of the concern, a check whether in advancing the national value the Member State is not trampling on other values protected by the EU legal order, in particular through the Charter of Fundamental Rights of the Union and finally a proportionality test, which may then be as deferential as the current *Schindler*[11] proportionality test which takes into account the level of protection a Member State wishes to pursue.

8. Article 4(2) TEU.
9. Article 19(1), second sentence TEU.
10. Case C-36/02 *Omega Spielhallen* [2004] ECR I-9609.
11. Case C-275/92 *Schindler* [1994] ECR I-1039.

**8.** From the start, I have opted for a functional approach. I set out to see how the EU *ordre public* operates and how it could be made to operate better in the EU legal order. That choice has, however, also brought with it certain limitations. There are still numerous issues I was not able to research, either because they did not fit the pattern, or simply because of time and space constraints. At the same time, these limitations open up the possibilities for further research.

**9.** First, I wrote this book from an EU perspective. It would be interesting to see what the impact of my model would be on the various national legal orders. How does the concept of EU *ordre public* that is presented here interact with the national concepts of *ordre public*? Are all Member States as optimistic as I am about the potential for defusing potential conflicts? After all, a case such as *Michaniki*[12] has two sides: either it is read as an attempt by the EU legal order to override the Greek Constitution or it is read, as I do, as a reassurance that the EU legal order is open to the Greek constitutional concerns and an invitation to the Greek authorities to meet halfway. Are all Member States open to a greater role for their national courts in steering cases involving an EU law element? I did neither have the time nor the resources to carry out the extensive comparative study that is necessary to answer these questions for a Union of 27 members, but that does not mean that I underestimate their importance. Quite to the contrary, in the short discussion at the end of Part I about the manner in which the ECJ finds the law, I stress the importance of comparative law for finding the solution that will be most acceptable for the national legal orders.

**10.** Second, at various instances across this book some influence of my exposure to and interest for US constitutional law comes to the fore. I genuinely believe that there is still a lot that could be learned about the EU legal order by contrasting it with the United States who have after all the benefit of over two hundred years of experience in balancing state and federal interests, despite economic turmoil, civil war, racial tensions and two world wars. However, experience has taught me that to truly make such a comparison requires a very careful approach and a deep insight in both legal orders. Accordingly, I have restricted myself to these passing references, though I can see numerous avenues for further exploration, including the concept of 'ordered liberty',[13] federal common law, pre-emption, State sovereignty and State immunity or the creation of remedies.

**11.** Third, the nature of this venture required me to reduce major monuments of the EU legal order to mere building blocks for my theory about EU *ordre public*. Virtually none of the major constitutional principles and concepts received the grand treatment they truly deserve. Subsidiarity, democracy, legitimacy, transparency, direct effect, division of competence and harmonization all are the worthy subject of multiple separate books and have merely been touched upon across this book. But then again, I never set out to climb those mountains, too. I do not feel at the end that the place these principles and concepts have been given in my model would be much different if I had analysed

12. Case C-213/07 *Michaniki* [2008] ECR I-9999.
13. *Palko v. Connecticut*, 302 U.S. 319, 58 S.Ct. 149, 82 L.Ed. 288 (1937).

them deeper, but that does not brush away the potential for future research or the possibility of further refinement.

**12.** Finally, the functional approach towards EU *ordre public* has led me to leave much theory beneath the surface. The federalism concerns, the balancing of fundamental rights or the institutional balance, all raise deeper issues about legitimacy, decision-making, or even the nature and function of law. The many examples taken from sensitive domains as abortion or gambling have ethical, political, medical or economic dimensions I have not been able to do justice, but which I am well aware deserve to be analysed by those better versed in those disciplines. Nevertheless, perhaps precisely because the model tries to steer away from these issues and focuses strongly on a legal content for the EU *ordre public*, it may at least be a useful tool for lawyers who often are not trained in those fields, either.

**13.** The end of one voyage should open up the prospect of new travels to be undertaken. For now, however, it is important to take stock of what has been achieved: a journey across the landscape of the EU constitutional order has revealed an EU *ordre public*, related to, but distinct from, the legal orders of the Member States, the content of which can be ascertained and the practical impact of which can be tailored to the complexities of a 'legal order [...] the subjects of which comprise not only Member States but also their nationals'.[14] Accordingly, the EU *ordre public* is presented as a multi-faceted concept that protects an impressive list of core values at the heart of the EU legal order in a correspondingly wide variety of ways that conscientiously take into account the sensitivities of the various national legal orders without being dictated by them. In essence, the EU *ordre public* is a key tool for realizing the Union's unofficial but forceful motto: 'united in diversity'.

14. Case 26/62 *Van Gend & Loos* [1963] ECR 1.

# Table of Legislation

## EU legislation

Regulation No 1 of the Council of 15 April 1958 determining the languages to be used by the European Economic Community, *Official Journal, English Special Edition (I)* (1952-1958), 59, 334

Council Directive 64/221/EEC of 25 February 1964 on the co-ordination of special measures concerning the movement and residence of foreign nationals which are justified on grounds of public policy, public security or public health, *Official Journal, English special edition: Series I Chapter 1963-1964*, 117, 82, 85, 93, 94

First Council Directive 68/151/EEC of 9 March 1968 on coordination of safeguards which, for the protection of the interests of members and others, are required by Member States of companies within the meaning of the second paragraph of Article 58 of the Treaty, with a view to making such safeguards equivalent throughout the Community, *Official Journal, English Special Edition 1968 I*, 41, 350

Convention of 27 September 1968 on Jurisdiction and the Enforcement of Judgments in Civil and Commercial Matters (1978) OJ L 304/36, 173, 441

Regulation (EEC) No 1612/68 of the Council of 15 October 1968 on freedom of movement for workers within the Community, *Official Journal, English Special Edition 1968 II*, 475, 99, 109, 286, 297, 335, 365, 393

Directive 69/493/EEC of 15 December 1969 on crystal glass, OJ, *English Special Edition* 1969 (II) 599, 150

Regulation (EEC) No 2603/69 of 20 December 1969 establishing common rules for exports *Official Journal, English Special Edition* 1969 (II), 590, 141

Regulation (EEC) No 1408/71 of the Council of 14 June 1971 on the application of social security schemes to employed persons and their families moving within the (1971) OJ L 149/2, 320

Council Directive 75/35/EEC of 17 December 1974 extending the scope of Directive No 64/221/EEC on the coordination of special measures concerning the movement and residence of foreign nationals which are justified on grounds of public policy, public security or public health to include nationals of a Member State who exercise the right to remain in the territory of another Member State after having pursued therein an activity in a self-employed capacity (1975) OJ L 14/14, 94

Council Common Position 2005/329/CFSP of 25 April 2005 relating to the 2005 Review Conference of the Parties to the Treaty on the Non-Proliferation of Nuclear Weapons (2005) OJ L 106/32, 171, 276

Directive 2005/29/EC of the European Parliament and of the Council of 11 May 2005 concerning unfair business-to-consumer commercial practices in the internal market and amending Council Directive 84/450/EEC, Directives 97/7/EC, 98/27/EC and 2002/65/EC of the European Parliament and of the Council and Regulation (EC) No 2006/2004 of the European Parliament and of the Council ('Unfair Commercial Practices Directive') (2006) OJ L 149/22, 155, 247, 432

Council Decision 2005/511/JHA of 12 July 2005 on protecting the euro against counterfeiting, by designating Europol as the Central Office for combating euro counterfeiting (2005) OJ L 185/35, 46, 311

Council Framework Decision 2005/667/JHA of 12 July 2005 to strengthen the criminal-law framework for the enforcement of the law against ship-source pollution (2005) OJ L 255/164, 332

Directive 2006/24/EC of the European Parliament and of the Council of 15 March 2006 on the retention of data generated or processed in connection with the provision of publicly available electronic communications services or of public communications networks and amending Directive 2002/58/EC (2006) OJ L 54/1, 152–153

Council Regulation (EC) No 764/2006 of 22 May 2006 on the conclusion of the Fisheries Partnership Agreement between the European Community and the Kingdom of Morocco (2006) OJ L 141/1, 171

Directive 2006/54/EC of the European Parliament and of the Council of 5 July 2006 on the implementation of the principle of equal opportunities and equal treatment of men and women in matters of employment and occupation (recast) (2006) OJ L 204/23, 433

Council Framework Decision 2006/783/JHA of 6 October 2006 on the application of the principle of mutual recognition to confiscation orders (2006) OJ L 328/59, 48, 163, 332

Regulation (EC) No 1987/2006 of the European Parliament and of the Council of 20 December 2006 on the establishment, operation and use of the second generation Schengen Information System (SIS II) (2006) OJ L 381/4, 104

Council Regulation (EC) No 168/2007 of 15 February 2007 establishing a European Union Agency for Fundamental Rights (2007) OJ L 53/1, 386

Council Common Position 2007/140/CFSP of 27 February 2007 concerning restrictive measures against Iran (2007) OJ L 61/49, 260

Directive 2007/23/EC of the European Parliament and of the Council of 23 May 2007 on the placing on the market of pyrotechnics (2007) OJ L 154/1, 150

Regulation (EC) No 864/2007 of the European Parliament and of the Council of 11 July 2007 on the law applicable to non-contractual obligations (Rome II) (2007) OJ L 199/40, 172, 187

Council Decision 2007/551/CFSP/JHA of 23 July 2007 on the signing, on behalf of the European Union, of an Agreement between the European Union and the United States of America on the processing and transfer of Passenger Name Record (PNR) data by air carriers to the United States Department of Homeland Security

media services (Audiovisual Media Services Directive) (2010) OJ L 95/1, 426

Commission Regulation (EU) No 330/2010 of 20 April 2010 on the application of Article 101(3) of the Treaty on the Functioning of the European Union to categories of vertical agreements and concerted practices (2010) OJ L 102/1, 436

Commission Regulation (EU) No 461/2010 of 27 May 2010 on the application of Article 101(3) of the Treaty on the Functioning of the European Union to categories of vertical agreements and concerted practices in the motor vehicle sector (2010) OJ L 129/52, 436

Directive 2011/36/EU of the European Parliament and of the Council of 5 April 2011 on preventing and combating trafficking in human beings and protecting its victims, and replacing Council Framework Decision 2002/629/JHA (2011) L 101/1, 332, 426, 429

Regulation (EU) No 492/2011 of the European Parliament and of the Council of 5 April 2011 on freedom of movement for workers within the Union (2011) OJ L 141/1, 99, 297, 320, 335, 337, 365, 396

Directive 2011/92/EU of the European Parliament and of the Council of 13 December 2011 on combating the sexual abuse and sexual exploitation of children and child pornography, and replacing Council Framework Decision 2004/68/JHA (2011) OJ L 335/1, 162, 332, 426, 429

Regulation (EU) No 1173/2011 of the European Parliament and of the Council of 16 November 2011 on the effective enforcement of budgetary surveillance in the euro area (2011) OJ L 306/1, 311

Regulation (EU) No 1174/2011 of the European Parliament and of the Council of 16 November 2011 on enforcement measures to correct excessive macroeconomic imbalances in the euro area (2011) OJ L 306/8, 311

Regulation (EU) No 1175/2011 of the European Parliament and of the Council of 16 November 2011 amending Council Regulation (EC) No 1466/97 on the strengthening of the surveillance of budgetary positions and the surveillance and coordination of economic policies (2001) OJ L 306/12, 311–312

Regulation (EU) No 1176/2011 of the European Parliament and of the Council of 16 November 2011 on the prevention and correction of macroeconomic imbalances (2011) OJ L 306/25, 312

Council Regulation (EU) No 1177/2011 of 8 November 2011 amending Regulation (EC) No 1467/97 on speeding up and clarifying the implementation of the excessive deficit procedure (2011) OJ L 306/33, 312

Council Directive 2011/85/EU of 8 November 2011 on requirements for budgetary frameworks of the Member States (2011) OJ L 306/43, 312

# Table of Cases

## Civil Service Tribunal



## Court of First Instance/General Court

## European Court of Justice

## Board of Appeal of the OHIM



## EFTA Court

## European Court of Human Rights

## International Court of Justice



## National Courts

### Belgium



### Germany

## Netherlands



## Spain



## United States



## *Other Documents*

## EU documents

## Other documents

ILC Draft Articles on State Responsibility, *ILC's 1996 Report*, GAOR, 51st Sess., Supp. 10, 125, 27

ILA, *Interim Report on Public Policy as a Bar to Enforcement of International Arbitral Awards*, London Conference (2000). <http://www.google.be/url?sa=t&rct=j&q=&esrc=s&source=web&cd=1&ved=0CDwQFjAA&url=http%3A%2F%2Fwww.ila-hq.org%2Fdownload.cfm%2Fdocid%2FE723662E-053C-415A-A4C7822577AE6B4F&ei=phPFT868Kojs8gPr-MTZCg&usg=AFQjCNFHXadopA03NVuxeHqmmHH1eRNOzw&sig2=i1OZzNGI-5eW9A3rYLwDIA> 29 May 2012, 25

ILA, *Final Report on Public Policy as a Bar to Enforcement of International Arbitral Awards*, New Delhi Conference (2002). <http://www.google.be/url?sa=t&rct=j&q=&esrc=s&source=web&cd=1&ved=0CEAQFjAA&url=http%3A%2F%2Fwww.ila-hq.org%2Fdownload.cfm%2Fdocid%2FBD0F9192-2E98-4B17-8D56FFE03B80B3EA&ei=IRTFT9ezMoqj8QOqjJ3mCg&usg=AFQjCNHqz7oa7RvnBkyX8EKCOCrQ41N-Fw&sig2=W5JjTw3DmHXDRXjcNdl8hQ> 29 May 2012, 25

ILC Draft Articles on State Responsibility with Comments. <http://untreaty.un.org/ilc/texts/instruments/english/commentaries/9_6_2001.pdf> 29 May 2012, 27

AIPPI – Finnish Group, report Q186, *Punitive damages as a contentious issue of Intellectual Property Rights*. <https://www.aippi.org/download/commitees/186/GR186finland.pdf> 29 May 2012, 60

# INDEX

## B



## C

**D**

**F**

**J**



**K**



**L**

**R**

**W**

www.ingramcontent.com/pod-product-compliance
Lightning Source LLC
LaVergne TN
LVHW020647300926
849161LV00004B/845